Steve Shapin

Science Studies Unit
Univ of Edinburgh .

Portrait of Haldane
at Work on Education

Also by Eric Ashby

Challenge to Education
Scientist in Russia
Technology and the Academics
Community of Universities
African Universities and Western Tradition
Any Person, Any Study

Also by Eric Ashby and Mary Anderson

Universities: British, Indian, African

Adam Sedgwick's Discourse on the Studies of the University (edited, with introductory essay)

The Rise of the Student Estate

LORD HALDANE OF CLOAN
1856–1928
Lord Chancellor, Secretary for War,
philosopher

Drawing by Sir William Rothenstein, 1916

Portrait of Haldane
at Work on Education

ERIC ASHBY AND MARY ANDERSON

 Macmillan

First published 1974 by
THE MACMILLAN PRESS
London and Basingstoke
Associated companies in New York,
Dublin, Melbourne, Johannesburg and Madras

SBN 333 15075 9

Printed in Great Britain by
J. W. ARROWSMITH LTD.,
Bristol

Contents

List of Illustrations

Acknowledgements

For the material in this book it was necessary to draw upon collections of private papers. These are the Haldane papers (National Library of Scotland), the Asquith and Fisher papers (Bodleian Library), the Passfield papers (British Library of Political and Economic Science), the Lloyd George papers (Beaverbrook Library), the Gosse papers (Brotherton Library, University of Leeds), and the Balfour papers (British Museum). We are grateful for the help we have received from members of the staff of the libraries where they are housed, and also for permission, where it was needed, to quote from some of these papers.

Sir David Stephens, clerk of the parliaments, and Mr Maurice Bond, clerk of the records in the house of lords record office, kindly helped us to trace some records of parliamentary proceedings. Mr Keith Percy, of the University of Lancaster, who is working on the history of civic universities, generously gave us some transcripts of the Chamberlain papers at Birmingham University and extracts from an unpublished autobiography of M. W. Travers in the University Library at Bristol. Mr Norman Higham, librarian at Bristol University, gave us a copy of Haldane's address to the University College Colston Society in 1902.

We are indebted to the Scottish National Portrait Gallery for permission to reproduce the drawing of Haldane by Rothenstein, and to the National Portrait Gallery for permission to reproduce the cartoon by F. C. Gould.

The book has been greatly improved as a result of criticisms by Sir William Mansfield Cooper, who read the first draft, and we are very grateful to him for these criticisms. We have benefited also from conversations with other scholars, especially Professor Talmon of the Hebrew University of Jerusalem. Through the generosity of the Rockefeller Foundation, one of us (E. A.) was able to finish writing the book as a resident scholar under idyllic conditions at the Villa Serbelloni in Italy.

Finally we wish to record our thanks to Mrs Bridget Boehm who did much of the preliminary typing of the book, Mrs B. K. Knights, who typed the whole of the final draft, and to Mrs M. M. Anderson for reading the proofs and arresting many small errors.

E.A.

M.A.

In February 1974 one of us (E.A.) was privileged to give the Gregynog Lectures in University College, Aberystwyth, under the title *Haldane and the University of Wales*. The lecturer is asked to incorporate the content of the lectures in a book. Chapters 1, 6 and 8 contain the substance of the lectures.

The true analogy to the historian is the portrait painter. No two portraits are alike or have the same meaning. The individual in the picture cannot be exhausted. All the painter can do is to take certain features expressive of his meaning and put them on canvas. That is all the historian can do.

from a report in *The Times* of 15 December 1926, of the opening remarks by Lord Haldane when he presided at a lecture given by Professor C. W. Alvord, at Bedford College, London.

Introduction

The inscription on Lord Haldane's tombstone in the burial ground at Gleneagles records that he was secretary of state for war and lord high chancellor, and the specific achievement of his career selected to be carved in stone is: 'Through his work in fashioning her army he rendered invaluable aid to his country in her time of direst need.' It is not likely that Haldane composed his own epitaph. Thomas Jefferson, who did, preferred to omit the fact that he had been president of the United States, and to have instead on his tombstone the words: 'Father of the University of Virginia'.

The theme of this book is that Haldane's deepest and most enduring commitment was to the improvement of education and that, like Jefferson, he hoped to be remembered for his services to the cause of universities. '. . . I have lived', he told a meeting of former students eight years before his death, 'in the cause of education perhaps more than in any other of the several causes I have been engaged in for many years. . . .' And on another occasion, two weeks later: 'I have lived for universities. They have been to me more than anything else. . . .'

Yet at his death in 1928 scant recognition was given to his concern for education. Four and a half columns of obituary in *The Times* contained only one brief paragraph about his educational interests, and the long leading article in the same issue only one sentence. In the months afterwards some of his admirers redressed the balance: Mansbridge in a letter to *The Times* and Heath in a collection of commemorative articles in *Public Administration*. And Morgan, a fellow Scot familiar with Haldane's work, wrote: 'Great as were his merits in other fields, it may be that when the final estimate of his life-work is made, the first place will be given to his ungrudging services on behalf of education of every grade.'

Let us make it clear at the outset that we are not presenting a final estimate of Haldane's lifework. That is why we call this book a portrait. It is a portrait of Haldane's work for education, done in the interstices of a full life as lawyer, cabinet minister, lord chancellor.

It is surprising, over forty years after his death, that the story of Haldane's preoccupations with education has not been told already; though it is not surprising that when he died, barely ten years after the armistice, he should stand in public esteem as the man who reformed the British army in time – just in time – to meet the holocaust of 1914. His sister, Elizabeth Haldane, chose a soldier to write his official biography; and although the biographer, Maurice, guided by Haldane's autobiography, gave due attention to Haldane's educational work, it was as chronicler rather than as critic. Neither Maurice, nor any others who have written about Haldane's career, have assessed and interpreted his contribution to the organisation of education in Britain. Even around 1956, at the centenary of Haldane's birth, comparatively little was published about his concern with the cause which he himself said he had 'lived for'. There was a good general survey by Lockwood in a second series of essays about him in *Public Administration*, and in 1960 a lecture by Logan on Haldane and the University of London; and that was about all. Even those professional historians who have strayed into the field of university history do Haldane much less than justice; they leave an impression that they have not examined important sources and they have not resolved glaring inconsistencies. Assessments of Haldane's contribution range from unstinted admiration to sceptical disapproval. 'There is', wrote Hetherington in 1932, 'no University in these islands which is not in Lord Haldane's debt', and Duff wrote in 1961: 'No man in British history has done so much for so many university institutions.' To counter this encomium there is the innuendo propagated by two distinguished academics in Lancashire, Hopkinson and Muir, that Haldane in his autobiography exaggerated the influence he had on the rise of the civic universities, especially on the creation of the University of Liverpool. There are criticisms, too, by Hearnshaw and by Logan, of Haldane's proposals (or, rather, those of the commission under his chairmanship) for the University of London. And there is, in Sadler's correspondence, a clear hint that Haldane's scheming on behalf of educational reform was heartily disliked in some quarters. Even testimony about Haldane's style of working on royal commissions is conflicting. Thus Bellot, writing of his handling of witnesses at hearings of the royal commission on the University of London, said that Haldane pressed 'his view pertinaciously upon the medical witnesses'. But Henry Jones, writing of Haldane's handling of witnesses at hearings of the royal commission on the University of Wales, said: 'His treatment of the witnesses was perfect, for his questions brought out their views, and he never attempted to make them say what he would most like to hear.'

So anyone who decides to portray Haldane at work on education has a clear job to do. There is no shortage of material for the job. Among the rich sources are the verbatim records of the two university royal commissions over which Haldane presided, a form of literature which is unfamiliar because it requires unusual stamina to digest it. There are unpublished and largely untapped departmental records from the treasury, the privy council, and the board of education; important because Haldane exerted a great deal of his influence silently, behind the scenes. There are revealing passages in the memoirs of Fitzroy, Fisher, and the indefatigable Beatrice Webb, and in the private papers of the period. There are the many addresses which Haldane gave as apostle and propagandist to win public support for his schemes, and the many speeches he made in debates on educational issues in parliament. And there are reports of committees which have remained unexamined owing to the chronic apathy about education at the time and the neglect of educational history since. A remarkable instance is the record of the privy council 'trial' of 1902 which was summoned to determine whether the Victoria University should be divided into separate autonomous universities in Lancashire and Yorkshire (described on p. 6.4f) and which decided a vital issue of educational policy for Britain. It received perfunctory notice in the contemporary press and is now almost wholly forgotten.

One of Haldane's favourite maxims was written by his hero, Goethe: 'He who would accomplish anything must limit himself.' Our portrait of Haldane tries to catch the light from only one facet of his life. His prime educational interest was in the promotion of universities. But he wanted universities to be an integral part of a coherent system of education such as is only now, in the 1970s, beginning to develop in Britain. His vision was of a national system of education with universities at the pinnacle, permeating (as he used to say) the whole of education beneath them and, through adult education, beyond them. Even those who may be familiar with Haldane's work on universities are not likely to know about the part he played in paving the way for the Education act carried by Fisher in 1918, or about his preoccupation with the creation of educational provinces in Britain, or continuation schools, or the promotion of adult education. What we have tried to do is to assess – in the pattern of a portrait-biography – Haldane's contribution to the British system of education, illuminated by new material and matured by the passage of time. And we have tried to put on paper an impression of how he appeared to those of his contemporaries who talked with him about education.

1 Appointment with Mr Haldane

The visitor is ushered in. Haldane is standing to receive him; grave, friendly, almost deferential. He is heavily built, broad pale face, rotund body. (Violet Bonham Carter called him 'spheroid' and Beatrice Webb wrote that he was more like a French seventeenth-century abbé than an English politician.) He speaks gently, in a thin smooth voice, and puts the visitor at ease. With disarming geniality he creates an atmosphere in which any business can be settled amicably. He lights a cigar and listens to the visitor respectfully. When the time comes for him to talk he speaks without emphasis but with a quiet, confident logic and an apparently effortless mastery of facts which astonishes many who come to consult him; never arrogant, though at times ponderous, assembling more evidence than the argument needs; occasionally standing by the fire and reinforcing his point with what Austen Chamberlain (when Haldane spoke in parliament) called 'penguin-like gestures'.

The compelling impression Haldane created was one of reasonableness and, as one of his admirers put it: 'Thought itself made flesh'. His pride was to use his mind as an intellectual mill. The mill ground too fine for some listeners – 'no-one can invest a subject in a more lucid fog' – but for over a generation people sought his help or advice on legal topics, defence, political schemes and above all, on education. During Haldane's last illness at the end of his life, Beatrice Webb, often his severe critic, sought to cheer him by calling him the 'great consultant'. It was an apt compliment, for much of Haldane's achievement in public life, except as war minister and lord chancellor, was not due to the direct exercise of power on his part, but to the subtle way in which he could infect other people with his enthusiasm, persuade them to his views, equip them with his advice, and enlist their loyalty and affection. What were the qualities which gave him this high reputation?

First, an astonishing capacity for work. As a young lawyer and MP he could speak for a couple of hours in court; travel to Bradford and

address 3000 people; return the same night, reading briefs in the train;
arrive at his chambers at 3.30 a.m. to find another urgent brief to be
read; get up at 7.30 a.m. to read it, and appear in court again to speak
at 9.45 a.m. After which, as he wrote to his mother: 'Not a bit tired,
only hustled a little.' A second quality was to tackle decision-making
from principle, not expedience. As war minister, reorganising the army,
he spent the parliamentary recess in 1908 'studying the characters of
Generals, ancient and modern, with the end in view of learning to
choose my own young ones aright.' Working from principle can lead
to a sterile academicism; but Haldane, although he was steeped in
nineteenth-century German philosophy, remained solidly pragmatic
in politics. He had some utopian visions – one of them was an integrated and coherent educational system – but when he was engaged in
practical politics and not oratory he approached utopia by plodding
step by step on the ground, rarely by heroic global designs; each step
prepared by painstaking consultation and consolidated by fact. A
third quality which gave Haldane such influence over affairs was the
way he would mobilise his whole daily life – domestic and public – to
achieve his purpose. He would become infected with an idea, often
an idea got from someone else; for he was not an imaginative innovator.
He would decide that the idea ought to be turned into a decision.
He would then design a strategy to achieve this end. If the strategy
required public propaganda, he would address meeting after meeting
on the topic. If it required political backing, he would coax the key
politicians, one at a time, at dinner parties, in committees, at week-end
house parties. Hospitality to his friends was one of his relaxations.
He was said to have the best chef in town and the finest cellar in Scotland.
But the dinner parties and the after-dinner talk over cigars were not
mere relaxation; often they were deliberate moves toward the translation of ideas into reality. It was an essential element in Haldane's
technique that he should deliberately create for himself a central place
in the web of society; never – and this is what gave people such confidence in him – to further his own personal ends, always to further
ends with which he, quite objectively, identified himself. He was
'Public-spirit personified'.

Of course this technique invites criticism. Haldane did deliberately
orchestrate his friends and acquaintances, and to some of them this
looked like opportunism. And his pertinacity, when he had made up
his mind to identify himself with an issue, was inseparable from the
complete confidence he had in the issue itself and, as he rose from

success to success, in the impression he created that he (perhaps *only* he) could cause the issue to be resolved. There was a certain puzzling inconsistency between his modesty (it was only in his letters to his mother that he slipped, to please her, into pardonable exaggeration) and a faith in himself which A. G. Gardiner said 'amounts to inspiration.' To the fulfilment of his designs he brought patience, and imperturbability, a relentless tenacity, which wore down resistance. It would be gross misrepresentation to say that Haldane was prepared to concede on matters of principle in order to get results, but within the framework of his principles he was never obdurate; he was always ready to conciliate opposition by compromise; sometimes (as in the episode when he persuaded Irish MPs to co-operate over reform in the University of London, which we describe on p. 38f.) by doing an undisguised political deal with them. But his supreme weapon was the number and accuracy of his facts, his candour in deploying them, and an unquenchable optimism. '*Toujours bien, jamais mieux*' was the motto attached to him.* He never bullied his opponents nor humiliated them; indeed it was a criticism of his life as a politician that he set out to enlist the sympathy of both liberals and conservatives rather than play the party game.

Also among the qualities which supported his reputation was his generosity in entering into the interests of friends and strangers alike and the soundness of the disinterested advice which he gave them. In bitter adversity shortly after the outbreak of world war I, when he was in political exile, rejected by the people and hounded by the press, he was still willing to spend time and trouble on those who came to him for advice. Christopher Addison, who was then parliamentary secretary to the board of education, wrote: 'On many occasions . . . I went to Haldane for criticism and advice. He was ever ready to help, for he is too great a man to sulk, and did not scorn to assist a minor Minister in relatively small affairs.' It was his misfortune, John Buchan said some years before, that all men spoke well of him; though this of course was never in fact the case. Beatrice Webb was censorious about his addiction to good living, though by her standards most of

---

* Sometimes this attitude gave people the impression that he was complacent. It is related that he was present at a reception for those high-powered evangelists, Moody and Sankey. The evangelists asked the guests in turn: 'Are you saved?'. But to Haldane, 'standing with his back to the fire, calmly surveying the scene, Moody could only say in veneration: "I can see it is all right with you, brother".'

her friends must have appeared self-indulgent (Tawney, not himself exactly a sybarite, described the Webb's hospitality as 'exercises in asceticism described by Mrs Webb as dinners'). H. G. Wells peppered him with an envious irony (his 'urbane voice that carried his words as it were on a salver, so that they seemed good even when they were not so'). Among his contemporaries in parliament Lloyd George did not disguise his dislike of Haldane's scheming – but then Lloyd George was a virtuoso in a similar technique. Also Haldane frequently, and conspicuously over the Education act of 1902, irritated his fellow Liberals because he would not toe the party line. Even men with similar aspirations for education in Britain, like Sadler, regarded him as an ominous influence.

But Haldane's massive learning and composure and obvious dedication to the public good prevailed against such criticism. Even when he was no longer a powerful political figure people continued to seek his support or to ask his advice because of the sheer weight of his wisdom. In August 1928, two weeks before he died, Beatrice Webb wrote to Haldane's sister: ' . . . we still hope, as time goes on, the complete restfulness of life will bring Lord Haldane back as a leading Consultant for all young movements and their representatives.'

Haldane never held a portfolio in education. Indeed, when he was offered one in the first Labour government he turned it down. Nor did he ever hold either of two other ministerial offices where influence can be brought to bear on universities: the treasury or the privy council. Yet his work for education was sustained for a longer stretch of his life than was his work for the army or for the law; and his influence on education was as enduring as it was on the war office or on the lord chancellorship. His own writing repeatedly makes it clear that (like Jefferson) he set more value upon his contribution to universities than upon the glittering political prizes that he won. 'My whole soul', he wrote of the time he first took ministerial office, 'had been for years in the effort to bring about reform in higher education and in other departments of administration.' To understand how this concern arose, it is necessary to look back at Haldane's youth and upbringing.

Richard Burdon Haldane was born in the comfortable environment of Charlotte Square, Edinburgh, in 1856. His father was a prosperous lawyer, a writer to the signet. His mother came of Northumbrian stock with impressive legal connections, including a lord chancellor (Lord Eldon) and a distinguished judge (Lord Stowell). It is not possible to separate out nature, nurture, and the elements of chance which together determine a man's personality and his achievements. But we can discern how the combination of these three factors influenced Haldane's education; and it was his education which kindled the lifelong interest which we portray in this book.

Strict calvinism was the spiritual environment of Haldane's home. At their small country estate, at Cloan in Perthshire, Haldane's father would hold Sunday evangelical meetings alternately in a loft on the estate and in neighbouring villages; and Haldane's mother came from a home where the head of the family had become a convert to the Plymouth Brethren. So it was natural that Haldane should describe himself long afterwards as a 'grave and pious' youth. Had he been sent, as many upper class Scottish boys were in those days, to school and university in England (his cousin went to Eton and Balliol) his piety would doubtless have been somewhat alleviated by anglicanism. But Haldane's father chose to keep his son in the more puritan atmosphere of Edinburgh: he sent him to the Edinburgh Academy (which Haldane recollected as 'never an interesting period to me') and to Edinburgh University.

It was in this environment that Haldane had to release himself from the spiritual constraints of his upbringing; a release made all the more difficult because Haldane was deeply attached to his parents and they were wise and patient in the way they brought him up. But even at school, he tells us, he had religious doubts, and at sixteen, when he enrolled as an undergraduate, he had already the maturity and the courage to confront the assumptions under which he had been reared. At the university his personality unfolded rapidly. His fellow students, young like himself, were mostly serious and hardworking. He found himself sitting side by side in the lecture rooms with the sons of farm labourers. This democratic tradition of Scottish universities, and their emphasis on philosophy and logic, drew from Haldane a response which lasted throughout his life. He tramped the hills with his fellow students in search of 'spiritual ground', as he put it, 'on which we could firmly plant our feet.' He went through what would now be called an identity crisis. Law was to be his profession but it had no remedy for his perplexity. Theology at Edinburgh offered him no comfort. Only in philosophy was he able to see strands of thought which might resolve his doubts.

At this point in his career, only two years on his way to a degree, Haldane reached a cross-road of choice which influenced the whole of his subsequent career. Like all such crucial decisions, the choice was determined by a blend of nurture, nature and chance. He had to reconcile his own thought and conduct with his home environment. He had the innate integrity and intelligence not to compromise over this reconciliation, nor to patch over the cracks in his belief. And by chance one of his professors, Blackie, knew how to advise Haldane what to do.

The choice was either to stay in Edinburgh, where he could get professional training but (he believed) no prescription for the art of living; or to go on, as his cousin had, to Oxford; or to do something else. Blackie had trained in Germany and he advised Haldane to put himself under the great metaphysician, R. H. Lotze, in Göttingen. Haldane's parents – and this is a testimony to their liberality – allowed their son, still only seventeen years old, to make his choice. He chose Göttingen, and in April 1874 he set sail for Hamburg.

Under the unwritten code of *Lernfreiheit* German students led a very different life from those in Britain. They were two or three years older when they came to the university. Their social origins were more like those of undergraduates in the 1870s at Oxford and Cambridge than like those of Scottish students, but they were without the collegiate supervision imposed upon Oxford and Cambridge undergraduates or the constraints of regular examinations imposed upon Scottish students. There were student societies (the *Verbindungen*) notorious for riotous behaviour, drinking, and duelling, but co-existing with this brutal side of student life there was devotion to serious scholarship at a level which (according to one of Haldane's letters to his parents) put to ridicule '4 out of 5 of the working students who come from Oxford or Cambridge.'

Into this sophisticated and adult society Haldane came as a perplexed, serious boy, eight years younger (he wrote) than the average among his fellow students. His home still powerfully influenced his life in Göttingen. He wrote to his parents: 'I feel the want of Sunday very much, for the day does not exist here. . . . I should like to be in the loft at the fortnightly meetings and was thinking that you would be preaching as we came to Goslar on Sunday. Are Moody and Sankey gone to London or back to America? If there is an account of their last visit to Edinburgh in any paper I should like to see it very much and also should like a report of the great cricket match. . . . I am reading through the Romans and through John's Epistles with Candlish's sermons. . . . Everything is green and beautiful but it is not home and I long for Cloanden.'

But despite bouts of homesickness Haldane revelled in the intellectual life.

Only about twenty students attend each lecture, the lecture rooms being indeed very small and numerous and the number of professors being in the ratio of one to every ten students. The professors for the most part look as if they had seen more books than soap and tailors' shops, for most of them are men of about 60, wearing coloured spectacles, broad Tyrolean hats, with dirty, badly shaven faces, and their clothes almost tumbling off. They sometimes lecture in Latin, sometimes in German, it being much the same to them & to the students. . . . There are no such things as examinations in the classes, much less anything so contemptible in the German eye as prizes – a great improvement on us and which I think accounts for the fact that the Germans are so much better informed, since they do not cram things as with us, but really learn them. . . . The lectures are admirable, very clear & intelligible though on subjects difficult to explain.

Reading philosophy and Goethe, talking with students – he was made member of a *Verbindung* – listening to professors, walking in the hills round the town, Haldane dispelled his depression and came to terms with his doubts. Two people in particular were responsible for this enlightenment: Professor Lotze, to whom Blackie had introduced him, and Fräulein Schlote, who gave him language lessons and introduced him to the study of Goethe, a study which took him back to Germany year after year for a generation.

I spent a very pleasant afternoon [he wrote to his parents] with Professor Lotze on Monday. I had a long conversation with him on the relation of Philosophy to religion, on materialism, the immortality of the soul, and so on. He said that a lifetime's reflection on these subjects (he is 65 and about my father's build, and like him very active) had convinced him that no ascertained truth in philosophy clashed with religion. . . . He did not believe that philosophy and Christianity had much in common – they were not necessary to each other's existence, but the reason of this was that their spheres were different.

And a few weeks later he wrote:

I have just returned from a visit to Lotze who invited me to come and sit for a while with him. I had an exceedingly pleasant time and a long talk in which he expounded the nature of faith and pointed out the relationship between it and positive knowledge, at the bottom of which it lies. . . . I proposed to him some difficulties that had come up in an analysis that I have been making lately of Causation in Willing, whereupon he got quite excited in pointing out how by faith philosophy raised itself above such difficulties in the freedom of the will and yet took the most scientific course. . . . I told him that philosophy was my *Herz-studium* but that I felt it to be very insufficient unless it culminated in faith.

These quiet conversations with Lotze set Haldane's intellectual and spiritual course for a lifetime. Thirty-six years later, in 1910, when he addressed students in Aberystwyth, he paid a moving tribute to this.

. . . I was bidden [he said] to choose for myself whether I would go to Oxford or to a German university, and I chose Göttingen because Lotze was there. I was only seventeen, little more than a boy. I remember vividly how spiritually as well as intellectually anchorless I felt in the early days of my residence in the old University town . . . the figure that stood out above all the others was that of my old master, Hermann Lotze. I had the privilege, boy as I was, of seeing him often in his study as well as of listening in his lecture-room, and to the end of my life I shall hold the deep impression he made on me – of a combination of intellectual power and the highest moral stature. It seems to me but yesterday that he used quietly to enter the lecture-room where we students sat expectant, and, taking his seat, fix his eyes on space as though he were looking into another world remote from this one. The face was worn with thought, and the slight and fragile figure with the great head looked as though the mind that tenanted it had been dedicated to thought and to nothing else. . . . Our feeling towards him as we sat and listened was one of reverence mingled with affection.

A man can be judged from those he adopts as his heroes. It is not difficult to see why Haldane in maturity had an affection for Germany and a dedication to the cause of universities. A German university had led him out of the perplexity of youth into the assurance of manhood. A German professor had demonstrated to him how to combine intellectual rigour with moral principle. German *Gelehrter* – Kant, Hegel, Schopenhauer and, above all, Goethe – shone a light ahead for his career.

Haldane spent only about four months in Göttingen. He came back
to Edinburgh in time to re-enrol at the University for the new academic
year. How much Germany had done for him is evident from the
temporary surge of disappointment he had on returning home. 'Can
you believe it?', he wrote to a fellow student in Germany (Hugo
Conwentz) in October 1874, 'I actually dislike my own country now.
The people seem to think of nothing but how to make money and
never how to attain to a high culture.' But this impulse of disillusion-
ment soon passed. Haldane threw himself with enthusiasm into the
study of Hegel (one of the legends about him was that he would rise
and light his own fire between five and six on dark winter mornings
in order to read *Wissenschaft der Logik*). In 1876 he graduated with
first class honours in philosophy and carried off a medal and two
scholarships, one of which signified that he was the ablest student in
philosophy of his year in the whole of Scotland.

The moment had come to embark on a career. Haldane, with this
excellent academic record, could doubtless have pursued his *Herz-
studium* as a profession. He used to quote, nostalgically, the lines from
Lucretius:

But sweeter far to dwell remote, aloof
In some high mansion, built on Wisdom's hill:
Thence watch the errant crowd go to and fro,
Matching their wits, striving for precedence,
Toiling and moiling, hurrying night and day
To rise to fortune and possess the world.

Many successful men entertain a similar placid pipe-dream, but
currents of ambition or social responsibility sweep it away. Despite his
protestations in favour of the contemplative life, Haldane was in no
doubt that his place was with the 'errant crowd'. He did not forsake
his affection for philosophy, but these frequently quoted lines from
Lucretius were never his guide. From the outset his mind was set on
law and, through law, on politics. Even when still an undergraduate
at Edinburgh he had begun to read concurrently for a law degree as an
external student in the University of London; but he failed the first
examination. From graduation he went straight to read law in the
offices of two Edinburgh firms of writers to the signet, and, so that
he might qualify himself to become a barrister, to eat dinners in
Lincoln's Inn; for London, not Edinburgh, was to be his stage. He
moved there in the latter part of 1877 and was called to the bar in 1879.

Haldane was not a man of means. His father had recently died, and he had to make his living as a barrister. From almost the start of his career in London, however, he began to involve himself in politics and in what was in those days the essential concomitant of politics: society. In 1880 – he was still only twenty-four – he was electioneering for the Liberals. He became a member of Brooks's Club. He laid foundations for his political friendships, spending long evenings with his contemporary, Asquith, 'concentrated on ideas', and, during walks they took together at Cloan, talking over 'what could be made of the future.' It was at this very embryonic stage of his political life that Haldane made his first venture into organisation on behalf of the party. Eager to preserve the association of young Liberals which had been formed by Albert Grey to fight the 1880 election, he trudged through deep snow early in 1881 to rally support for what became the famous 'Eighty' Club, so named after the great Liberal victory of that year, and destined to play an active part in promoting the Liberal cause for another generation.

Haldane's Liberalism was, for those days, radical. He, along with other young progressive Liberals of his generation, became concerned with the future of the working classes. For him this was no remote, theoretical concern, for some of them had been his classmates in Edinburgh; though the farm labourer's son enrolled in a Scottish university was a world away from the masses of the poor, underpaid and ill-housed, in London slums. It had been commonly assumed that the shocking gulf between comfort and poverty was immutable and that – to resurrect the cliché – a man was expected to accept the state of life to which God had called him. But, perhaps as a backlash to the grim implications of Darwinism for the condition of man, there was in the 1880s a stirring of conscience. An economic recession in the late 70s and early 80s stirred up radical thoughts; some people recognised what Galsworthy called the 'grin on the face of Fate'. Complacency among the well-to-do was challenged by an introspective social conscience among some of their sons and daughters. It took material form in the establishment of 'settlements' in the East End of London, some of them sponsored by public schools or Oxbridge colleges. It took ideological form in socialist and anarchist propaganda, in the suffragette movement, and in all sorts of radical-eccentric societies such as the National Anti-vaccination League, the National Anti-vivisection Society, the Society for Psychical Research, the Theosophical Society. All these had one thing in common: they opposed conventional Victorian ideals. Edward Carpenter (who describes this transition vividly in his autobiography) called it 'a large social and intellectual restlessness that in turn made members of established society nervous. . . .' But not all became nervous. Others – Haldane among them – saw opportunity, not apprehension, in this social ferment. In 1890, five years after he had entered parliament, he wrote to Mrs Humphrey Ward: 'The thought has come strongly upon me for the last six months that there is near at hand the greatest opportunity for trying to make our public position one of real and noble influence that ever has been. These great social questions which have exercised the minds of men for so long are at last before us practically or presently will be so.'

Here was a convergence of Haldane's philosophical idealism (stimulated at that time by the writings of T. H. Green) with his desire for action. It was natural that he should see education as the panacea for the solution of class differences. He became a member of the Council of the Workers' Education League and he gave a course of philosophy lectures at the Working Mens' College. He lectured also at the St James's and Soho Radical Club (the centre of the 'International' in London) on the socialist theories of Lassalle and Marx. He was hotly criticised afterwards for his views, so he may already have been declaring his faith that it was neither Capital nor Labour which created wealth, but Mind.

But all these were part time interests. Haldane's main energies had to go into his work at the bar. It is a testimony to his industry and capacity that by 1885, only five years after embarking on his profession and still under the age of thirty, he was firmly enough established to stand for parliament. In June 1885 Gladstone resigned and a short-lived Tory administration followed under Lord Salisbury. In the general election at the end of the year, Haldane was returned to parliament for East Lothian, a seat which he captured from the Tories and held for twenty-five years. It was the first election under the new franchise act which raised the United Kingdom electorate from about three millions to about five millions. Haldane tramped his constituency to enlist support from the newly enfranchised householders. His electioneering among them reinforced his faith in education. 'When I went into those spotless and speckless cottages', he wrote, long afterwards, 'there I saw books, and there was an atmosphere of education there, and I used to feel that these men were not what was ordinarily understood by labourers but were people with mind and knowledge just

like what was possessed by their most highly educated neighbours. . . .
I learned a great deal there and I learned this: that no political creed is
worth anything that does not embrace the spiritual side as well as the
material side.'

It was with these earnest and noble sentiments that Haldane went into
politics: to uplift, to reform, and above all, to educate. He was never,
by his own admission, a good 'party man'; he believed for instance,
that the business of the Opposition was not to oppose, but to criticise;
but he did believe in the party system and his aim was to endow Liberalism with ideals for the moral and intellectual development of the nation.
These political ideals and this faith in education and progress must of
course be judged in the context of the 1880s, not the 1970s, otherwise
they would be condemned outright as intolerably priggish. But even to
Haldane's contemporaries there was a certain inconsistency between
the idealism of his principles and the pragmatism of his practice. On the
public platform Haldane was the austere visionary, unhurried by
emotion, propagating high ideals; in the lobbies of the house of
commons and over the dinner table in his own home he was the subtle
schemer, scheming indeed in the highest public interest – never for
himself – but ready to compromise, to seize the right moment, to
conspire in ways which sometimes generated mistrust, even from such
an arch-conspirator as Beatrice Webb.

So, in portraying Haldane at work on education, one has to interpret
his speeches with discernment. It is the duty of a speaker to select
themes appropriate to his audience. It follows, therefore, that when
Haldane speaks to students, he emphasises the high responsibilities of
being a student, when he speaks to the Workers' Educational Association, he emphasises the need for adult education; and so on. That these
professions of faith were not always consistent does not surprise anyone
who has to make public speeches. This is not to say that Haldane was
disingenuous; even less that he was deceitful: just that, like anyone in
public life, he had to be many-sided in opinions as well as in activities,
shifting his priorities to suit his hearers. Bernard Shaw put the inconsistency beautifully in a salty letter to Haldane, written in 1907 after
Haldane had delivered an address steeped in Hegelian sentiments, as
lord rector of Edinburgh University:

I read your address to those unfortunate students very carefully;
and I must say that it is like your right honourable cheek to talk
to them like that. Why will people not tell the truth? Here are

you, the most conspicuous living example in the kingdom of the realisation of all these students' ambitions – a Scotch philosopher who has beaten all the practical men and statesmen at their own game. This you have achieved by doing exactly what you liked; smoking a good deal too many cigars; eating in a manner that shocks Mrs Sidney Webb; and generally making the greatest possible success of the world, the flesh and the devil. And yet you go down and tell those unhappy young people, in lofty and inspiring periods, that you did it all by a life of contemplation, aloof from the world at Weimar.

This is comedy, but it illustrates the difficulty of portraying a public man from his own testimony. How, to turn to a serious question, is one to decide what Haldane's views were about the function of MPs as representatives of their constituents in a democracy? That Haldane regarded his membership of parliament as a high duty there is no doubt. But was it a duty to lead, or to reflect, opinion among the people? Addressing a meeting at Cambridge in 1891, he said:

> ... it is no function [of MPs] to mould ideas; that is to be done outside, that is your work at the University; that is the work of the thinkers, of the teachers, of the preachers, of the evangelists of the gospel of progress in every part of the country.... We MPs are the sons of our nation and our age. Behind that age we cannot remain, neither can we advance before it. The work has to be done outside before the House of Commons can take it up.

But among his political colleagues Haldane advocated a different emphasis. Writing to Ronald Ferguson in 1889 he said:

> What we have to do at home is to try to gain the confidence of the electors and to mould their opinions. To my dying day, I think, I shall maintain the proposition ... that a democracy has not got, as is assumed in practice, a body of definite opinion, for the expression of which in Parliament it seeks delegates, but that it is an assembly of human beings earnestly seeking guidance from those of whose sympathies it is sure.

And, in his maturity, a generation later, speaking in the house of lords: 'I have all my life believed in putting before the democracy, and pressing upon it, new conceptions, and in no department has that been more strikingly necessary than in the case of education.' And if the democracy did not respond to the conceptions, Haldane was prepared to go further. The nation, he told the house of lords in 1916, 'has been very unhappy with regard to ideas about education. This is reflected in the Cabinet, in Parliament and in the country. Therefore the only way is for the leaders to take a definite decision without waiting for any particular mandate. . . .'

Haldane's work on education was a sustained reconciliation of these two conflicting ideas: on one hand, that in a democracy it is the people, not their leaders, who decide; on the other hand, that in a democracy the minority who are educated have a responsibility toward the majority who are not, and must decide on behalf of the majority. The utopian solution was education for all.

'Chance', wrote Poincaré, 'comes to the prepared mind.' But the opposite is also true: a man may be fortunate enough to come into a scene as though it were prepared for him. This was certainly the case for a politician with strong interests in education beginning a career in 1885. For over two decades there had been a growing dissatisfaction with the schools and colleges and universities of Britain. The dissatisfaction had been voiced by three very articulate critics whom the public could not ignore: Lyon Playfair, Matthew Arnold, T. H. Huxley. Lyon Playfair returned from the International Exhibition in Paris deeply depressed about the backwardness of technical education in Britain; he wrote in 1867: '. . . the one cause upon which there was most unanimity of conviction is that France, Prussia, Austria, Belgium, and Switzerland possess good systems of industrial education for the masters and managers of factories and workshops, and that England possesses none.' Matthew Arnold's criticism covered a much wider field. His famous comparative study of schools and universities on the continent, published in 1866 and several times reprinted, led him to the indictment that Oxford and Cambridge were not universities in the continental and traditional sense at all, because the superior faculties (law, medicine, even theology) had atrophied there, but were 'places where the youth of the upper class prolong to a very great age, and under some very admirable influences, their school education. . . .' T. H. Huxley, concerned chiefly with what he called the 'state of barbarous ignorance of even the rudiments of scientific culture', used his brilliant eloquence in a string of addresses to awaken the public to the need for reform in education. Nor was the agitation confined to academic evangelism. Successive governments had responded by setting up commissions and committees of enquiry:

the commissions on Oxford and Cambridge which reported in 1852; a select committee on scientific instruction in 1868; the Devonshire commission, which worked from 1871 to 1875; the Samuelson commission in 1884; and, for Scottish higher education, a commission appointed in 1876 which included both Playfair and Huxley. During Haldane's novitiate in parliament this era of awakening led to some useful reforms. There was a growing consensus about need, but a sharpening controversy about means. The deeply divisive question – which nowadays seems quite unreal – was whether education should be a responsibility of the state or should be left as far as possible to private agencies encouraged by the state. Gradually legislation crept in the direction of state support. The Technical Instruction Act of 1889 empowered local authorities to levy a penny rate for this purpose; and the Local Taxation (Excise and Customs) Act of 1890 authorised the application of the so-called 'whisky money' for the same purpose. In 1889 the Welsh Intermediate Education Act transferred to local authorities the control of secondary education previously vested in the Charity commission; and in 1891, twenty-one years after the introduction of universal elementary education, it was made free. The most important step toward state patronage of education was taken in 1899 when, following a royal commission under the chairmanship of Bryce (which included Sadler, who appears later in this story), the government set up a central education authority under a minister (there had not been one before), and it was called the board of education.

Haldane took no part in these developments. Some of them were the achievement of A. H. D. Acland, whom Haldane watched at this time, obviously with some envy, for he confessed privately in 1894: 'I would rather be like Arthur Acland, with all his fanaticisms, than anyone else I know just now. . . .' It was another sign of his instinct, even in his early years in politics, to make education his platform.

But his first educational preoccupation was not with schools, but with universities. Here, too, there was a fresh breeze of reform, but it was very gentle and it did not disperse the infirmities about which men like Playfair and Huxley had been writing for years. Oxford and Cambridge had freed themselves from the constraint of religious tests and were rising toward the crest of a renaissance in teaching and research. The initiative, with periodic jolts from royal commissions, came from within. From Trinity College, Cambridge, Henry Sidgwick wrote that 'the long, long, canker of peace is over and done; the only thing soon will be to avoid radicalism.' It was he who opened the campaign – still not quite over – to admit women to Cambridge on equal terms with men. In Oxford, Jowett and others like him had created the image of the college as a nursery for leaders in politics and administration; and most of Haldane's close colleagues in the party were from Oxford. Oxford was not only a school for character-building; the ideas sown by Mark Pattison's famous tract, *Suggestions on academical organisation*, published in 1868, were already restoring the university as a great centre for scholarship. But this revival of intellectual energy at Oxford and Cambridge touched only a tiny fraction of the population in England, and even that fraction was not selected primarily on scholarly merit. In the late 1880s the combined student population in the two universities did not exceed 5000. Scotland offered its sons and daughters better opportunities: there were then some 6800 students in the four universities; but reforms in teaching and organisation at the Scottish universities were overdue. What was happening in Britain was a delayed response to the forebodings of men like Playfair: that Britain would fall behind the Continent if she did not recruit into industry, commerce and administration men with more than a secondary school education. The institutions which needed encouragement were those in the industrial cities (in 1885 even Owens College, Manchester, had only just over 400 students apart from those in the medical school). The blueprint which influenced Haldane most at this time was the one proposed by Arnold (Haldane, as a student, had met him in Edinburgh and remained his fervent disciple). Arnold envisaged a national system of state-aided education, integrated from school to university, under a minister of state assisted by an advisory council. He advocated a regional organisation for higher schools, under 'provisional boards', co-ordinated with the universities. He did not want a proliferation of degree-giving institutions in England, but rather some eight to ten centres monitored by examinations under the University of London.

Arnold died three years after Haldane entered parliament, but Haldane eagerly inherited Arnold's legacy of ideas, though he modified some of them in the light of his experience. The task ahead – and this is true of much of Haldane's work – was to transmute these ideas into the gritty details of legislation. This – it appears again and again in his portrait – was Haldane's contribution to education: to work on splendid aspirations until they could be fitted into a practical and acceptable administrative framework. Apart from certain lapses, due to over-optimism, which will appear in our portrait, he was a master craftsman in the art of the possible.

But in 1885, Haldane had to apply the art of the possible to his own career. In the Victorian age a man could not devote himself to politics unless he had some assured source of income. So Haldane's first objective was to establish himself at the bar. He had neither the temperament nor the sense of histrionics to excel at criminal law or before juries; he felt, besides, the want of the humanistic training of the older universities for this type of work. So he chose to specialise in the sort of civil cases where he could turn his Scottish philosophical training to account: cases of appeal before the house of lords and privy council which called for skill in applying the psychology of advocacy, and skill, above all, in establishing the first principles of law from a mass of intricate fact. He soon acquired prominence in this type of pleading, and a reputation for enjoying the sympathy of the supreme tribunals. In 1890, ten years after being called to the bar, he was appointed a queen's counsel at the early age of thirty-three. He worked immensely hard, and was more and more in demand in the courts. Briefs came pressing in on him from industrial magnates and colonial governments. His fees, already in the region of £2500 a year, mounted rapidly. A clear road lay ahead: the road to a distinguished and affluent practice as a barrister; beyond that a judgeship, leading perhaps, to appointment as one of the lords of appeal. But this was not the road Haldane chose. Writing in 1894, he said he had no intention of allowing his legal practice to 'swallow' him up. His goal was still political office 'not legal office, but one like the Local Government Board or the Scottish Office'.

The strategy needed for success in politics has to be every bit as arduous and deliberate as the strategy needed for success at the bar. But it is a very different kind. A politician has to be known, and what he stands for has to be known. Haldane set about deliberately to fulfil these two requirements. What he stood for needed no contriving; his background, his temperament, his intellectual interests, his sensitivity to the human condition: all these predisposed him to align himself with social reformers; not, of course, revolutionaries or extreme radicals – their programmes were utopian and impractical and therefore not politically viable – but with those reformers who believed in progress, gradualism, a steady evolutionary change from what is, to what is somewhat better. Several other young members of parliament had similar interests. They were led by Asquith, who with Haldane's help,

had been returned for a constituency adjacent to his own in 1886. One
of the group, somewhat older than the others, but newly elected like
them, was Arthur Acland, who as we have just mentioned shared with
Haldane a special interest in education and a faith in its efficacy in a
democratic society.

There were plenty of issues which needed an injection of liberalism
(both in its political and philosophical meanings) in the late 1880s. At
home there were the problems focused by the slump and the widening
of the electorate: questions of urban social welfare and labour relations,
votes for women and the payment of members, local government
reform, and above all – education. Abroad there was the perennial
problem of Ireland, and beyond, the problem of devising a bond of
empire that would withstand the divisive forces of developing nationalism. These overseas interests brought Asquith's group in touch with
two of the more senior politicians, Rosebery and Morley – Rosebery,
imaginative, personable, progressive, architect of the concept of liberal
imperialism, at that time the 'glittering hope' of the Liberal party;
Morley, deeply interesting to Haldane and his friends for his political
association with Gladstone and the wide range of his literary interests.
But over home affairs the radicalism of both men proved too tepid for
the younger group, and in 'thinking and working out an effective
programme' they soon felt obliged to become their own pacemakers.
In the sharing out of this work, Haldane took as his special subjects:
'the extension of university education, women's suffrage, and housing'.

His colleagues now knew what he stood for. They knew, too, that
he was no obedient and compliant backbencher, but a man of independent views, with a gift for propagating those views by what his
admirers called persuasion and his adversaries called intrigue. It was
perhaps as much due to this reputation for independence, as to
Haldane's shortcomings as a public speaker, that alone of his close
colleagues he was not given office when Gladstone formed his last
administration in 1892, or, indeed, when Rosebery succeeded to the
premiership in 1894. He is on record himself as saying that he did not
want office so soon. Whether or not this was so, we doubt whether he
would have refused a post if he had been offered one. But he still had
to consolidate his position at the bar, and anyway he was beginning to
experience what was to be the enduring satisfaction of his career: the
satisfaction of influencing events by remote control, often anonymously, through informal conversations, talks at weekend house
parties, acting as go-between to convey embryonic policies, modifying

them all the time so that consensus could be reached, narrowing gaps between opposing views, proposing names for appointments; in short, Haldane had become the confidant of a wide variety of people. He had become (in the words of Beatrice Webb) 'an influential man'.

The second requirement was to be known to the right people; and there is no doubt that between 1890 and the turn of the century Haldane did deliberately become a 'society figure'. It may be too cynical to suggest that Haldane acquired friends in order to make use of them, but his excursions into some sections of society were certainly not in search of soul-mates. That he was attracted in the early 1890s by the dazzling, though sometimes precious sophistication of the 'Souls' is not surprising. The mingling of birth and intellect, the new ideas, the brilliant talk: all these were likely to draw him. There was the added appeal of elegant and witty women, for women figured as prominently as men in these gatherings, and for Haldane, as for Goethe, women were among the best instructors in the ways of the world. It was through Lady Horner of Mells – the wife of a close friend – that Haldane was first introduced into this fashionable society, and though never a 'paid up' member, came to be invited to their dinners and house parties. He became a frequent guest of the Tennants at Grosvenor Square; often a visitor at Panshanger, Taplow and Stanway. In this way he developed contacts with those of different political persuasions – with Alfred Lyttelton, for instance, George Wyndham, and above all Balfour – and, as at the bar, made friends who were later to help him with his educational projects. That he mixed at other house parties with the racing set is surprising; though as Lady Desborough recalled later, the social sets of that period were by no means exclusive, and there was a good deal of intermingling between them. Through relaxed weekends with these varied people, Haldane had, by 1900, extended his circle of acquaintances, assimilated the opinions and conceits of some of the sharpest minds in British society, and gained an insight into convictions and prejudices other than his own.

It was, of course, not enough to frequent these coteries of the establishment. Haldane had to make himself the centre of a coterie. As early as 1886, he and Asquith started an annual dinner at 'The Blue Posts', a public house in Cork Street. Eight guests were invited: four distinguished in letters and four – irrespective of party – in politics. Throughout his career Haldane used the dinner party, lubricated by superb cooking, choice wines, and much admired cigars, as an instrument for discussing, refining and influencing political policies. That

Haldane was conscious of his new social status as a queen's counsel is evident from a letter to his mother, early in 1890: '. . . it is quite curious to see what social importance even people like Lady Rosebery and the Spencers attach to it.'

During the latter years of his apprenticeship to politics, the house parties, the dining clubs and the salons provided a colourful backcloth to Haldane's serious work at the bar and in parliament. But he had also to become as much an expert in social reform as he was already becoming in constitutional law. For this he drew upon the ideas of another coterie, utterly unlike the 'Souls' or the race parties or the assemblies of radical liberals. He was admitted to the circle of the Webbs, to the earnest and censorious company of Fabian socialists. It was an experience as significant in its way as his sojourn in Göttingen.

We do not know exactly when Haldane met Sidney Webb. They were born within three years of each other (Webb in 1859). In 1885, at the time Haldane entered parliament, Webb was introduced by Bernard Shaw to the recently formed Fabian Society. Webb was at that time a civil servant, but his ambition was to write and work for socialism. The Fabian creed – the politics of attrition, through fact piled on fact – exactly matched his temperament. By 1887, Haldane and Webb were acquainted and a year later they were exchanging ideas at a meeting of the Fabian Society. The friendship between these two men was to become a most fruitful partnership in the cause of higher education. About the same time, Haldane was also meeting another earnest and much more intimidating socialist, Beatrice Potter. There is even a legend that on one occasion, towards the end of 1890, Haldane, after discussing with her the possibility of creating a radical socialist alliance, turned to more personal matters and proposed marriage. But this rests only on a passage in Beatrice's diary which is susceptible of other interpretations and is in any case inherently improbable; and when Beatrice became secretly engaged to Sidney Webb in July of the following year, Haldane was warm in his congratulations. To Beatrice he wrote that this was 'no ordinary marriage' but 'a big event' from which 'great things' would result; and years later, when acknowledging a copy of her joint work with Sidney on *Industrial democracy*, he hailed it as 'a tribute to the real meaning of the marriage of you two'. To enlist human relationships in the cause of politics was something which Haldane found intelligible and fine. Reviewing the events of 1891, Beatrice wrote in her diary of Haldane and other political associates 'appearing on the horizon – comrades which a word or an act might transform into friends'. After her marriage in 1892, Haldane had a third coterie where he became a familiar figure; the socialist salon over which Beatrice Webb presided at her home in Grosvenor Road.

But we have to add one more line to our portrait of Haldane in 1890. We wrote above that it was 'inherently improbable' that Haldane ever sought to marry Beatrice. The ground for this is that in the year when this conversation is thought to have occurred Haldane had been shattered by an event which left a permanent scar on his inner life. He was engaged to be married and his fiancée (for reasons which are still obscure) broke the engagement. Haldane took this blow with Roman courage; but every now and again in his correspondence, especially when he wrote to console others in misfortune, he wrote words which showed that the wound had never quite healed. Soon after the break, in the summer of 1890, he wrote to Mrs Humphrey Ward: 'But when a soul has missed the goal towards which it was striving, and is still staggering, it naturally, in recovering its balance, seeks to restore the prop which it knows of old and has never found to fail.' His response to the shock was to drive himself into public work, activity, even into the social round; but certainly not to offer himself, in the same year, to another woman. Beatrice's own diary bears witness to the depth of his feeling. 'In spite of the successful professional life,' she wrote about him seven years later, '... he is a restless, lonely man – in his heart still worshipping the woman who jilted him seven years ago.' And when similar calamities befell other people, Haldane offered the remedy by which he had cured himself. Listen to his message to the young John Simon, written after Simon had lost his wife: 'There is only one solace for personal grief, and that is work for the country. Briefs at the Bar will not provide it. You must throw yourself into public service of some sort. Why not find a constituency?'

2 Apprenticeship

Haldane's first appearance on the educational stage was a modest one. In 1888, as a graduate of the University of Edinburgh rather than as a member of parliament, he took part in a deputation from the general councils of the Universities of Edinburgh and Glasgow which waited on the secretary for Scotland (the marquis of Lothian) to criticise and if possible influence the latest of a series of bills – all of them abortive – brought before parliament to achieve some of the reforms proposed by a royal commission which had reported as long ago as 1878. The graduates from these two universities were concerned to increase their own representation on the university courts, which were the small and powerful executive governing bodies of Scottish universities; but they also expressed sympathy with student pretensions to representation on these bodies. They did not recommend any increase in the existing representation – students were already represented by the rector whom they elected, and an assessor whom he nominated – but they did give support to the claims of the recently formed Students' Representative Councils to be associated in this representation. Haldane was particularly emphatic about this, urging the admirable way in which the student councils were working, and strongly pressing that students should be given indirect representation through the new machinery they provided. For he had a deep conviction in favour of the enlistment of students in the affairs of universities. Anyone from an Oxford or Cambridge college could be forgiven for regarding such a conviction as misconceived (indeed, Haldane's cousin, Lord Camperdown, thought it would be 'improper' even to give statutory recognition to the new Students' Representative Councils). But to anyone educated in a Scottish university and familiar with the tradition of *Lernfreiheit* in Germany, it was a perfectly natural attitude. '. . . I consider', Haldane said, when debating the issue of statutory recognition a year later, 'that a University should be regarded as a kind of democracy where there is citizenship and where all internal affairs should be under the control of the various classes interested.' He was,

22

as later pages of this portrait show, somewhat ambivalent about what he meant by 'a kind of democracy'; but the experience of his under-graduate days – the crofter's son beside him in the lecture room, the independent and relatively unsupervised style of life of Scottish and German students, the way they were treated, and responded, as adults – all this experience was distilled into his concept of the university as a community of senior and junior partners engaged in a common pursuit; an idealised concept, perhaps, but one which served him as a guide to practical policies.

In 1889, the last of the series of Universities (Scotland) bills – the bill that was ultimately to reach the statute book – came before the house of commons. On its second reading in June, Haldane made his debut as a speaker on higher education. The reform of Scottish univer-sities was a topic of minor interest to English members and Haldane spoke to a very thin House. This, as he told the empty benches opposite him, was one of the peculiar difficulties of the subject! But this did not detract from the vigour of his performance; nor had it deterred him from coming with a well prepared brief. The standpoint he adopted – which he made plain from the outset – was highly characteristic. He found much to criticise in the bill, and reserved full liberty of action in committee; but since on balance he judged the advantages 'enormously' preponderated, he felt unable to put the 'slightest obstacle' in the way of the second reading. As a Scottish member, he could not incur the responsibility of holding up reform on which so much of Scottish opinion had been agreed for so long.

The reforms most urgently sought were amendments to the con-stitution of the universities, and an extension of their teaching power. Haldane championed the cause of both and used them as a yardstick for judging the merits of the bill. On the constitution, he was largely satisfied. Responsibility for business and finance was to be transferred from the professors of the senatus to the court, for 'men cannot be made both judges and advocates in their own case without prejudice to the interests of justice.' He extended a special welcome for the pro-vision that the rector, in nominating his assessor, might take the opinion of the Students' Representative Council. But his major concern was to have the teaching improved, to secure for the students of Scotland the immensely more varied and effective education which he had experien-ced in Germany. This, he insisted, called for two practical reforms. One was to abandon the system whereby professors augmented their salaries, sometimes to the level of affluence, by collecting the fees of their students. Paid into a' common university chest, the fees could be used to support a far greater number of teachers, with the added advantage that professors would be rid of the temptation to enlarge the size of their classes. (In England, he pointed out, there were few professors who received more than £700–1100 p.a.; whereas in Edinburgh the professor of anatomy in 1886–7 received £2811, a sum which in Germany would maintain seven professors, and in Scotland ought to maintain three.) The other reform was to extend the system, already pursued in the medical faculty, whereby students were able to prepare for degree examinations by attending the courses of private teachers (similar to the coaches common in Oxford and Cambridge); men who were not on the staff of the university. The purpose was simply to enable the universities to increase their staff–student ratio without having to pay for it. This in turn called for a complete revision of the examination system. Under the existing system the private teacher was unable to compete with the university professor. The professor was assisted in degree examinations by an associate examiner, who in theory enjoyed equal responsibility with him; but since the associate was invariably a younger man, he was unable to assert his authority. The professorial monopoly in examinations had long been the object of controversy in the Scottish press, and was one of the scandals the new legislation would be expected to redress. On these issues Haldane was more anxious; for they were left for decision to the statutory commission that was to give effect to the bill. The failure of the bill to give guidance on such matters of principle was, indeed, one of his main criticisms, especially in view of reservations he had about the composition of the commission. But he put his mind at ease over this particular misgiving with a reflection which was significant in view of his later activities: 'Were it not that the Chairman [Lord Kinnear] is a judge of distinction and of most judicial mind who will approach the matter in a thoroughly fair spirit, I should despair of the Commission doing any good,' he declared; but 'as the Chairman is, after all, the most important person on the Commission,' he was ready to admit the character of the president 'got over' the disadvantage 'to some degree'.

What is also interesting to those watching him at work on higher education is what he omitted to say in this speech. The English civic university colleges had just received an unprecedented treasury grant which was to become an annual event, and was the forerunner of the massive subvention now administered to all universities by the University Grants Committee. But unlike other speakers, he did not call for an increase in the state aid proposed for the Scottish universities. An annual grant of £42,000 had been provided in the bill; and whilst he admitted he would have been glad of a further £10,000 from the government, it was in keeping with his realistic approach and liberal instincts that he preferred to rely on the redeployment of the considerable resources already at the disposal of the Scottish universities, rather than hold out for additional sums which he saw no likelihood of obtaining. Nor did he take the opportunity which this speech offered (since MPs then, as now, were not obliged to stick closely to the point) to put in some propaganda about the need to extend university education in England, though this was later to become one of his common themes. Playfair, in the same debate, did press, as he had been pressing ever since the 1860s, for more public support to 'make sufficient provision for higher teaching in all our great towns'. But Playfair was thirty-seven years his senior, and was moved (as Haldane was not, until later on) by the need to expand higher education in order to promote industry, not just to enrich culture. Haldane may well have been influenced by his instinct to confine himself to immediate and limited goals, and to matters he understood, for his acquaintance with universities was confined to his student experience and his membership of the Edinburgh general council. At first hand he knew little at that time about the machinery of government or the conduct of academic affairs.

This immaturity was evident in his attitude to the much debated issue of 'extra-mural'* teaching in Scotland. Despite the emphatic warning of the commissioners of 1876 about the danger that any extension of the system would present to the quality of the teaching in Scottish universities, Haldane was not deterred from ranging himself with the substantial body of opinion amongst Scottish graduates which pressed for it; what he failed to see was that this was a recipe for a university on the cheap. And three years later, when he took the initiative of raising a debate on the early draft ordinances of the commission, he still sponsored the general councils' view, dismissing the provision that had been made for assistants and lecturers who were to be on the university payroll as wholly inadequate for the extension

---

* This had in the context of Scottish universities an entirely different meaning from the one now attached to it in British universities. It denoted the private teacher, the coach, who taught for university examinations (particularly in medicine) but was not on the university staff.

of teaching power that was needed. On this later occasion, he was again outshone by more experienced educationalists. Professor Jebb, Conservative member for Cambridge University, and latterly a professor at Glasgow, contributed a persuasive defence of the commissioners' attempt to promote the expansion of Scottish universities from within, maintaining that 'those who knew the Scottish and English universities' would agree that it was of the greatest importance to the efficiency of a university that its teaching should not be cramped by habitual regard to the examinations. The extra-mural system 'would surround the universities with an indefinitely large fringe of teachers ... each following the impulse of individual enterprise, each selecting his subject at will, less with a view to the interest of the academic commonwealth than to the prospect of successful competition' – an assertion which Jebb might well have made about the university he represented in parliament. Sir Henry Roscoe, himself one of the statutory commissioners, and then at the height of his renown as pioneer of the civic university, dealt even more effectively with the attack Haldane had mounted, taking specific issue with him on the score of his analogy with conditions in Germany. 'The number of professors in German universities is, as my hon. Friend has stated, very large', he declared, but it was well known that the German universities were supported entirely by the state, and it was 'obvious that it was perfectly impossible for the Commission to attempt to apply the German system to Scotland.' Haldane's motion was decisively defeated; and on the specific issue of extra-mural teaching the statutory commission, reporting in 1900, unreservedly endorsed the earlier opinion of their predecessors. (To substitute 'a widely ramified system of preparation for examinations' for university education would be an infinitely greater evil than the mischief it was proposed to redress.) But it was a sign that Haldane was beginning to understand the subject that when in 1892, he had continued to press for a 'very large extension' of the teaching power of the Scottish universities (which, indeed, they needed) he had gone on to explain: 'It is not extra-mural teaching I am insisting upon, though that is a good thing. What is wanted is a reorganisation of professorships and the extension of lectureships on a substantial footing'; and that when he had reiterated the need for a reform in the examination system, he had acknowledged that 'teaching is a very important part of the question' and that what was wanted in Scotland was 'the addition of a stronger examining body not entirely independent, but standing in a sort of reciprocal connection.' Moreover, although the voting had gone against him, the careful statistical comparisons he provided between the teaching facilities in Scotland and Germany produced a disturbing picture which Roscoe's riposte could have done nothing to remove.

That Haldane, along with other members of parliament familiar with Scottish education, should have taken part in debates on the reform of Scottish universities was, of course, no evidence that he had a commitment to the cause of higher education. But there is evidence that such a commitment was germinating: as early as 1887, Haldane was getting himself involved in an issue which daunted all but enthusiasts in that cause, namely the organisation of the University of London. I have, he told his mother, 'been closeted for hours with Arthur Balfour' (a kindred spirit despite his very different educational background – Eton and Cambridge – and his conservative politics). They were conferring about the problems of the University of London, which 'are giving me a great deal of trouble at this moment but the trouble is well worth taking.' Just what sort of trouble Haldane was taking is not clear, though the problems were clear enough. London, the heart of an empire, had no proper university. There were colleges of higher education, already with distinguished men on the staff: at University College, Ramsay, Lankester, Karl Pearson, Croom Robertson, and (until 1882) Haldane's own uncle, Burdon Sanderson; at King's, Lister, Millar Thomson, Hopkinson and S. R. Gardiner; at South Kensington, Huxley, Armstrong and Ayrton. But the University itself was an examination machine.* The value of such a machine at that time was immense, for admission to examinations for the external degree was open to all comers, and by guarding jealously its standards, the University was able to establish a high standard for the currency of its degree, and so to put on the gold standard of learning the awards not only of the London colleges, but of those civic university colleges which were established in half a dozen English cities at that time, and even some colleges overseas. But to segregate the responsibilities for teaching and examining was to run into a serious danger: that examinations would become the master and not the servant of higher education; and this is what happened.

---

* Cf. Professor Hales in a letter to *The Times*: '. . . Now the London University imparts no learning; it teaches nothing; it gives neither lessons nor lectures; it provides no information; it only asks questions. It is a rigorous and many voiced catechist.' Quoted by the principal of King's, in evidence to the Selborne Commission, June 1888.

Lehrfreiheit was shackled by the syllabus. So, on grounds of prestige for the Empire's capital, on grounds of educational philosophy, and in response to a rising dissatisfaction among many graduates of the University of London themselves, there was a need to form the London colleges into a teaching university. But there were disputes and difficulties in the way. All sorts of propaganda for reform were being circulated. On one hand the dilatory response of the university senate prompted the formation of an *Association for Promoting a Teaching University for London* in 1884 (backed by names as formidable as Bryce, Huxley, Lister, Playfair, Kelvin and Tyndall), which from an early stage began to favour the establishment of a second university; on the other hand the body of graduates (convocation) – or at any rate some of them – wanted to convert the existing institutions into a kind of federal university. By 1887, there were four separate schemes under discussion, and the confusion was such that it could only be resolved from outside. The trigger for a parliamentary enquiry was a petition from the two illustrious colleges, University and King's, to be called Albert University. Nothing short of a royal commission could handle this situation, and one was set up in 1888, under Lord Selborne, to consider the proposal. The commission rejected it; but no agreement could be reached on its own recommendations, and four years later a further royal commission (the Gresham commission), this time under Lord Cowper, was appointed to make another attack on the problem.

Haldane took no part – no visible part, at any rate – in these discussions; and he had not yet perfected his technique of manipulating educational policies invisibly from the wings of the political stage. There were proceedings in parliament in connection with the renewed proposals for a separate teaching university in 1891 and 1892; but Haldane neither initiated them, nor contributed to them. He was, however, consolidating his understanding of educational problems. His signature appeared – along with many others including Bryce and Edward Grey – below a public protest, printed in the *Nineteenth Century* in 1888, against the stranglehold of examinations over education. This was nothing new. Although examinations for the civil service, introduced in 1870, had rid Whitehall of nepotism, and (through the payment-by-results system) had lifted the standards of teaching in schools, they had for many years been under attack. A more significant incident occurred in 1890, when Haldane was invited to serve on the council of University College, London. Here was definite evidence of his growing commitment to the cause of universities. We do not know how he came to be invited; it may have been a suggestion from his uncle, Burdon Sanderson (now in the Waynefleet chair of physiology at Oxford), or it may simply have been that he was a young member of parliament who obviously had a distinguished career ahead of him and who was known to his fellow MPs to be keen and very well informed on university affairs. At any rate the significant fact is that Haldane, a very busy barrister and a man still establishing himself in English society, regarded this invitation as one to accept. He served for eight years, until 1899, but made no forceful impact on the college. It was still, for him, a phase of incubation for his educational ideas.

After ten years in parliament, Haldane was known, and what he stood for was known. In February 1896 he figured in 'Spy's' series of famous lawyers, contributed to *Vanity Fair*, under a title which must have pleased him: 'A Hegelian politician'; for it was as a politician-philosopher that he wanted to be known. Despite his busy life at the bar and in parliament and his week-ends in society, he found time to publish a translation of Schopenhauer, a biography of Adam Smith, and numerous articles in the reviews on themes of politics and philosophy. In the house of commons he identified himself with liberal principles whether or not they were wholly acceptable to his senior colleagues in the Liberal party. One colleague described him as a man 'who is not prevented by the ties of Party from taking that independent view of questions which his own research and his own judgement enable and call upon him to take.' He was spoken of as 'one of the ablest exponents of what has been called the New Liberalism.'

On what evidence did Haldane acquire this reputation? In the house of commons he espoused measures of reform that marked him out as radical and progressive: leasehold enfranchisement (where he helped to bring in a bill to empower urban authorities to make compulsory purchases of land, and to exclude any element of 'unearned increment'); women's suffrage (where he himself introduced a bill for the removal of women's disabilities in 1892); and death duties (where he chaired the committee which worked out the details of the measure that formed the central feature of Harcourt's budget in 1894, assisted in its drafting, and played an important part in seeing it through its various stages in the House). But perhaps the clearest indication of his commitment to the New Liberalism was provided

by the public addresses he gave outside the House: for it was here
that he expounded the philosophy behind his action in the legislature.
His utterances on these occasions added up to a testament of patrician
socialism, innocent of any revolutionary fervour, an affair of the mind
rather than of the heart, pursuing the principles of liberalism to their
logical conclusion – which was a lot further than some liberals were
prepared to go. Listen to him addressing Cambridge dons and undergraduates at a meeting of the 'Eighty' Club in the Lion Hotel on
30 May 1891. First, a hand held out to socialism:

> I hope to see the Liberal party throw far more energy into its
> sympathies with the labour movement than it has done in the
> past. . . . We need for our development as a Party not only universal
> franchise, the franchise which shall enable the labourers, be they
> male or female [at this point his audience cheered] to make their
> voices heard in the councils of the nation, but also a measure which
> shall enable them to send, through the medium of payment of
> representatives out of public funds, those people to do their business
> in Parliament who are best fitted to do so. . . .

Then a little sally of flattery to his audience: the Liberal party ought
to go more rapidly on social questions, but it was fettered by its
mandate and could not go ahead of its constituents. The business of
the house of commons was 'not to elaborate new ideas and put them
before the country and press for their acceptance. The business of
the house of commons is to give a practical shape and legislative
form to ideas which are sent to it from outside. . . .' Then came
Haldane's commitment to collectivism to which he had been converted
in what Beatrice Webb called 'a sort of vague metaphysical way':
'we no longer concern ourselves with individuals, however numerous
or important, but we devote our attention much more to the community as distinguished from the individuals who make it up. There is a
sense of the corporate life of the nation, and of the claim which that
corporate life has upon us, which it seems to me was almost
unknown. . . .' And he went on to talk about the virtues of the
'collectivist idea': the desire to vindicate the claims of labour to a
larger share in the produce of industry, as against capital. It was a
speech which drew characteristic comment from Sidney Webb,
who lost no opportunity to encourage and prompt. Over Haldane's
efforts on the land question, he had written:

Last night was a great success for you – will you pardon my saying that you are unduly diffident about your own capabilities in the House? . . . I am . . . very thankful that I have always believed in you. If I were a woman it would seem natural that I should say something pretty & encouraging. I cannot do that: but this I know – the [? that] life brings with it its own encouragement. And I *know* which side is right.

Now, less lyrically, but more purposefully, he wrote: 'I read your Cambridge speech & liked much of it. May I commend to your holiday reading an article by me in the July number of the *Economic Journal* on "The Difficulties of Individualism"?'

Haldane was only thirty-four when he gave this address to the 'Eighty' Club at Cambridge. He had been called upon to deputise for a more senior member of his party, Robert Reid, whose claims to the woolsack were to thwart Haldane's plans in 1905. But it was a rising reputation as much as his foundation membership of the Club which earned him the invitation; and the custom of printing the speeches given on these occasions enabled him to set his ideas before a wider audience.

So at forty, Haldane was already a distinguished lawyer, an intellectual radical in politics, devoted to gradualism, but a gradualism constantly kept on the move; a man who was out to democratise society, smoothly and (so far as possible) imperceptibly, through legislation and education. His political philosophy had its roots in Edinburgh and Göttingen: the community of Scottish students where distinction depended on intellect, not birth; the strenuous pursuit of truth in discussions with Lotze; the light shed by Goethe on the whole art of living. 'A man of advanced ideas . . . an exceedingly profound thinker': this was *Vanity Fair's* verdict on him in his fortieth year.

It was, all the same, a surprising honour to be invited by the students of Edinburgh in 1896 to stand as a Liberal candidate for the coveted office of lord rector of the University; lord rectors were usually much higher up the ladder of fame. Its significance for our portrait of Haldane is that this invitation came from students; it was a vote of confidence from youth. Haldane's student sponsors set out his virtues and qualifications in the *Student* magazine for 5 November 1896. It is a generous testimonial, though slightly apologetic because the sponsors were themselves embarrassed about Haldane's youth:

the ablest student of philosophy in his year in the whole of Scotland . . .
the youngest Queen's Counsel in the last fifty years . . . conspicuous
as a political thinker . . . a man who regards politics 'not as a sphere
for the exercise of Machiavellian astuteness, but as a subject of high
seriousness' . . . 'the most distinguished ornament' of the school of
thought which had introduced Hegel to England. So (ends the testimonial) 'we do not enunciate any controversial proposition when we
say that Mr Haldane if elected to the Lord Rectorship would honour-
ably fill the high traditions of that office. He is still a young man, but
he has clearly shown himself possessed of abilities which argue well
for his future career . . . .'

Haldane was not elected, but this was, in part at any rate, a reflection
of the political scene. He was defeated by Lord Balfour of Burleigh,
seven years his senior, who was secretary for Scotland in the new
Conservative government which had driven out the Liberals in
1895. Haldane kept his seat in parliament, with an increased majority
in his constituency, but political office was now out of reach until
the Liberal party got back into power, and it was to be ten years
before that happened. But this was Haldane's opportunity to concentrate his interest in higher education. He seized the opportunity.
To be in opposition and not even to hold a shadow portfolio of education were not disqualifications: they were positive benefits for his techniques of persuasion. He was ready now to embark on the first major
educational campaign of his career. He entered upon it in close partnership (or, as some of his contemporaries would have put it, close
conspiracy) with Sidney Webb. Their objective was to make the University of London an institution worthy of the Empire's metropolis.

We have already (p. 27f.) introduced the reader to some of the
intricacies of the University of London. They form no part of a
portrait of Haldane, but the portrait must be given a background.
In 1894, when the Gresham commission reported on the University,
it was an institution without students or teachers: it comprised only
candidates and examiners. Graduates had a place on the governing
body, but not teachers from the institutions which prepared students
for London degrees. So those who taught had no control over syllabus
or examination.

The recommendations of the Gresham commission would have
gone some way toward remedying these grave defects if they had
been adopted. Three abortive attempts were made to give legislative

effect to them: one in 1895, which collapsed because Rosebery's Liberal government was defeated; another in 1896 and a third in 1897, when both bills were withdrawn owing to the opposition they generated largely from a militant section of the University's own graduates. 'The whole affair', T. H. Huxley had written about it, 'is a perfect muddle of competing crude projects and vested interests . . . anything but a patch-up is, I believe, outside practical politics at present.' It was in 1896 that Haldane began to exercise his growing skill in consensus politics on this thorny problem. He had no official standing over the issue. He worked backstage. Plans were hatched over austere dinners in the Webbs' house, in co-conspiracy with the indefatigable Sidney.

Sidney Webb had already become involved in higher education in the metropolis. He was chairman of the technical education board of the London County Council, and it fell to him to decide how to use the valuable endowment Hutchinson had given for socialist education. It was following Haldane's legal advice (and probably much more than legal advice) that it was used to found (or, as one observer put it, 'to conceive in sin') the London School of Economics.

Over the University of London, the political problem was to narrow the gap between the supporters and the opponents of the Gresham report until a bridge could be thrown across the gap. The supporters wanted to create a university empowered to teach as well as to examine, with its governing bodies (senate and academic council) controlled by teachers in the London colleges, and to relegate the direction of external examinations to an advisory committee of the senate. The opponents saw this as an eclipse of the University as an imperial examinations board with worldwide influence and its replacement by a predominantly local institution. 'All day long', wrote Haldane to his mother in the summer of 1896, 'I have been working at the London University Bill trying to get cantankerous people to agree. I think we are now in sight of a settlement but it has been a tough job.' And three days later: 'Alas the University Bill is dead. The Bishops have killed it.' But the bishops reckoned without the pertinacity of the reformers. In the following January Professor Ramsay (professor of chemistry at University College and shortly afterwards to be awarded a Nobel prize) had some good news for the advocates of a teaching university. This passage from a letter he wrote to William Allchin (another supporter of the Gresham report) testifies to Haldane's reputation: 'Things are taking a new devt wh it

is impt – most impt – you should know of. Mr. Haldane is negotiating
& I should be glad if you cd meet him if poss. & talk over the matter.'

The outcome of the negotiations was the University of London
Commission bill of 1897. It would have been impolitic to reject the
framework of the Gresham commission; so the negotiators' task
was to find a formula of reconciliation within this framework. By
July 1897 a formula had been found which was commended to convocation (i.e. the graduates) by their chairman and supported by
various dignitaries including the University's member of parliament,
Sir John Lubbock. In essence the formula gave equal status to both
proposed roles of the University, but put each role under a separate
governing body: a council for external students to preside over its
function as imperial examiner and an academic council to preside
over its function as a teaching university, both under the sovereignty
of a senate on which representatives of both these interests sat.

Educationally, this constitutional compromise was the least interesting feature of the bill; the novel idea was to create a category of
'recognised teachers', a status which the university could confer on
teachers of suitable distinction and seniority in any institution within a
thirty mile radius. Since these institutions included polytechnics,
teacher-training colleges, and the like, this was a device to incorporate
into one system the best of all tertiary education in the metropolis,
to create a new pattern of university which would cater for the traditional and the new studies, for external, evening, part-time and full-
time students; in a word, to put all higher education in London under
one immense umbrella.

It was Sidney Webb's novel idea, it seems, not Haldane's. The story
is told that Haldane asked Webb: 'What is your idea of a University?'
Webb smiled, 'I haven't any idea of a University. Let's sit down and
see what we can make of it . . .': the deductive method over again!
But what Haldane wanted was simple and clear; it was to provide in
London that personal encounter between master and disciple which
Lotze had given Haldane in Göttingen. Beatrice Webb, with her
terrible candour, makes this clear. 'Haldane', she wrote in *Our partnership*, 'to gain his higher aim, would willingly have scrapped the system
of external examinations by which alone London University awarded
its coveted degrees.' (This was true, but ironical, considering that
Haldane himself was once a candidate for one of these examinations!)
'But', she went on, 'he realised, under Sidney's influence, if not the
undesirability, at any rate the political impracticability, of over-

throwing what had already taken deep roots.' However, though Beatrice Webb might write thus condescendingly about Haldane's ideas, she had no hesitation in acknowledging his capacity to steer ideas through parliament. 'If [the bill] goes through', she acknowledged in her diary for 26 July 1897, 'it will be due to Haldane's insistence and his friendship with Balfour – but the form of the Bill – the alterations grafted on the Cowper Commission Report are largely Sidney's. . . .' We have a vivid insight into Haldane's strategy on this occasion for he wrote in detail about it to Fitzroy at the privy council:

> I still have hopes of the negotiations [he reported at the beginning of July]. A month ago I got the Convocation party to agree to accept the Bill if the enclosed amendments were inserted. I took them at once to Lord Herschell [chancellor of the University]*. He was favourably disposed towards them. The delay has been with the Senate party, but I understand that Ld Herschell has convened a meeting of their representatives for Monday. If they will agree to the substance of the amendments & the Lord President is disposed to adopt them in the H. of Lords, I think I can get the Bill accepted in the Commons with very little discussion. Mr Balfour tells me he can find time on this hypothesis. . . . The important thing is to proceed without delay. . . . Meanwhile I enclose – as a private document from myself – the amendments which embody what has been accepted by the Convocation opposition. . . .
>
> I ought to add that the composition of the Commission will be a very delicate point. Before the Ld President decides on this, I should like to come to talk with you. Ld Davey would be acceptable as Chairman, but if Ld Lister goes on I am inclined to believe that the best way of allaying the suspicions of the Convocation party is that – should the Duke approve – I should go myself. I have – I think – the confidence of the opposition party, & I am Vice President of University College. I need not say that I have no ambition to serve, but I have the feeling that it may avert difficulty.

The bill was due to be introduced into the house of lords on 20 July 1897. Up to the last moment Haldane and Sidney Webb were 'rushing about London trying to get all parties to agree', in a veritable offensive of conciliation. Herschell's consent had to be confirmed; Lubbock's vote had to be secured. But to no avail. The bill passed all

---

* And a brother-in-law of Haldane's uncle, Professor Burdon Sanderson!

stages in the house of lords, but the session was already too far advanced for any protracted debate in the house of commons: on 2 August it was withdrawn without a second reading.

The next incident in the story throws into relief Haldane's obsession with the issues of higher education. Three times, proposals to reform the University of London on the lines of the Gresham report had failed. A busy and successful lawyer, a politician whose career could well lead to the high office of lord chancellor, a reasonably affluent bachelor, welcome at the salons and house parties of Victorian society – Haldane might well, after the failure in August 1897, have dropped his interest in universities for the time being. But on 16 October he wrote privately to Balfour, seeking a fresh place for the bill in the government's legislative programme. This time, Haldane wrote, not much opposition was to be expected.

> From letters I have seen I gather that the Senate stands in its approval of the Bill as arranged, and that the majority of Convocation take the same view. . . . The real opposition comes from Dr Collins and Fletcher Moulton. I do not think they can get any substantial support in the House, for the Bill is strongly supported by Herschell, Bryce, Acland, Stuart, Cozens-Hardy, and all are leading people. . . . Lubbock is of course in two minds, and he will have to make some show of opposition but I believe he would be heartily glad to have the matter disposed of. . . . Dillon says his Irish will not oppose and I think I can do something with Healy – whom I saw before the House rose.

Balfour was responsive. 'I should very much like to get this London University question out of the way, and on the whole what you say seems satisfactory and reassuring. As soon as I get to London in November I will have a talk to Devonshire upon the subject.' Having cleared the way with Balfour, Haldane lost no time over the preparation of a fourth version of the bill. The interested parties were called to a conference in the senate room on 14 December 1897. A re-draft of the bill – almost identical with the 1897 version – was agreed upon. Early in 1898 it had an easy passage through the house of lords; and in June it came up for the critical debate at a second reading in the house of commons.

Haldane was no orator. His piping voice, his 'penguin-like' gestures, his sometimes tortuous and over-subtle logic, put him at a disadvantage where opposition had to be silenced by eloquence. But this was an occasion – one of the rare occasions of drama in his political career – when his deep commitment to a cause lifted him above these disqualifications.

It was not quite as dramatic as Haldane (and some of his biographers, who followed Haldane's own version of it) made out. Haldane wrote in his autobiography that after a succession of speeches fiercely attacking the bill he sprang to his feet 'for once like one inspired' and turned the tide of opinion. In fact he had not waited for a hostile tide to establish itself. After only two members had spoken in opposition, he immediately weighed in with a powerful defence. The context of his speech was predictable. It was a careful and reasoned argument for a teaching university in London: to bring distinguished professors into the metropolis; to extend to the 'working classes' opportunities for higher education already enjoyed by their European cousins; to improve technical education so that Britain could stand up better against foreign competition in trade; a bill essential for 'catching up' (as he put it) with other capital cities.

> These are the reasons upon which those of us who are interested in the Bill appeal to the House to pass it. We feel that it is a Bill which is required, and which is absolutely necessary, and a Bill without which university education in London can make no progress. . . . We feel that we have got here a measure which in itself embodies the best tradition of the past and which completes the work of Bentham and Austin, of Mill and Grote, of the men who were the pioneers of university education in London; and that it is a measure which, if it is allowed to bear fruition, will place us in a position at least as good as that of any metropolis in the world.

Lubbock then spoke in opposition as Haldane had foreseen (his attack thus coming after Haldane's defence – not before as Haldane recalled in his autobiography); and with only two of the remaining speakers venturing to challenge the bill, it received its second reading without a division. Haldane certainly exaggerated the drama of the occasion, but he did not exaggerate the effect of his intervention. Asquith, in a graceful note of congratulations, wrote of never before having known a case in which 'a single speech converted hostile and impressed indifferent opinion in the House'; and Chamberlain, from the other side of the House, generously offered similar compliments. Although built on inaccurate detail, Haldane's claim to have tipped the balance was well enough founded. And what is significant for a portrait of

Haldane is the importance he himself attached to the occasion, when, years later, he wrote his reminiscence of it. He *wanted* to be regarded by posterity as the man who secured reform in the University of London. His own emphasis showed where his heart lay.

The unopposed passage of the bill at its second reading was not, of course, the end of the affair. There was detailed criticism right up to the last, in which Haldane himself was not spared. ('He has got Scotch universities on the brain,' taunted an old opponent, 'and he does not understand at all what we want in London.') But it was in committee that the bill ran into real danger. Haldane had agreed to take charge of it at this stage, and at first all went well. Quite suddenly a threat developed from a quarter which Haldane had thought covered. Tim Healy appeared at the head of the Irish members of the committee, and in private parley with Haldane made it clear that the vital Irish vote would be withheld unless something was done to improve higher education in Ireland, Haldane, with evident relish, describes the sequel in his autobiography. Very well; if this was to be the price of the Irish vote, he would pay the price. He would himself go to Ireland privately and of course unofficially, to discuss and work out reforms in the Irish Universities acts, and he would steer them through parliament. The story of his visit as he himself remembered it is worth re-telling, for it shows what lengths he would go to in pursuit of his enthusiasm for higher education. He approached Balfour and secured his authority to try his hand at direct negotiations with the Irish. During the summer of 1898 he made himself familiar – as familiar as anyone can become without having lived in Ireland – with the problem; and early in October he slipped away to Dublin with a plan (described on p. 59f.) in his pocket. There followed a series of meetings which were bizarre even for Ireland. First, the provost of Trinity College had to be assured that an Irish Universities bill would not interfere with that proud and venerable institution. Then the archbishop and the Dublin hierarchy had to be persuaded that the plan would in fact create a *de facto*, if not *de jure*, Catholic university. In both these missions Haldane was successful. Then he went on to Belfast for similar consultations. Here, moves to provide higher education for catholics would not be likely to generate enthusiasm. So (he wrote) 'I talked . . . only as an inquirer but guided the conversation on to the main points of the scheme.' Again, Haldane's scheme won general consent. So far so good. But there was still the cardinal at Armagh to be reckoned with, and Haldane was advised to approach

him as inconspicuously as possible. He took this advice so literally
that when he reached Armagh by rail, he went on foot from the
station to the cardinal's residence, in the dark! And how he cleared
this last hurdle – 'with toes in the air' – he reported triumphantly to
his mother, as he waited for the Dublin mail to take him back to England:

> I left Dublin with the warning of the Archbishop that I should
> probably fail with Cardinal Logue the Primate. I descended on him
> at Armagh, & lo – in half an hour we had settled everything in
> accordance with my scheme, & were settling down – he in his
> red hat & I – over two dozen oysters (it is Friday) & a bottle of Cham-
> pagne. . . . Healy & Dillon are much moved over my mission, & I
> think I have a chance of a statue in the Phoenix Park.

This astonishing escapade propitiated the Irish members, and in
fact it did much more: it laid the foundation for a reform of Irish
higher education which was enacted ten years later. This was not the
only occasion on which Haldane engaged in political trading. Over
the previous bill he wrote to Wace, the principal of King's College,
on 26 July 1897: 'I undertake, if you leave the Bill as it stands, to
support a recommendation to the Commission . . . . I will use such
influence as I have. . . .' The act to set up a statutory commission for
the University of London received the royal assent on 12 August
1898. Immediately Haldane got down to the next task, which was
to influence the work of the commission. His proposals for its membership had already borne fruit. Lord Davey, for whom Haldane had
devilled as a junior, was chosen as chairman; and among the members
were two of Haldane's other suggestions: Creighton, already associated
with Haldane and Webb over the London School of Economics, and
Busk, the chairman of convocation. Haldane's offer to serve on the
commission himself was not taken up, possibly out of regard for his
professed reluctance; but in any case he could exercise his influence
just as effectively without being a member. Hewins (the first director
of the London School of Economics and closely involved with the
Webbs and the University) testified to Haldane's mole-like persistence:
Haldane (he wrote) is 'very much behind the scenes' and exercising
'great influence' on the reconstruction of the University.
Haldane had accepted the compromise, that implanting a teaching
function into the University should not be allowed to weaken its
examining function; and the Gresham concept – that the senate
should have authority to approve 'schools' of the University where

its teaching could go on – was of course consistent with his policy to enlarge opportunities for higher education. But he evidently had misgivings about a proliferation of recognised schools, for in the following year (1899) he was advising the clerk to the privy council (Fitzroy, through whom Haldane exerted a strong vicarious influence on the council's educational decisions) to resist the application from Royal Holloway College to be recognised as a school, because it was away in Surrey, twenty miles out of London. But Holloway's importunity prevailed, and in the end Haldane advised Fitzroy on the amending legislation which was necessary.

At the turn of the century Haldane was still absorbed in the part he was playing in remodelling the University of London. No detail was too trivial, no effort too tiresome, no setback too dispiriting. With a sort of persevering buoyancy he carried the negotiations forward and sustained the morale of those who had to take responsibility. A word in the right quarter at Westminster, a dinner party to reconcile views, a letter to Fitzroy at the privy council: day by day progress was made. (Had he not reminded Sidney Webb a few years before how difficult it was to 'drive rapidly without the co-operation of the great personalities'?) So at each step, it was Haldane who secured co-operation.

In retrospect Haldane was less than satisfied with the compromise act. It was, he wrote in his autobiography, far from ideal. He told the house of lords, when the University's affairs were again before parliament a generation later, that the bill of 1898 was 'thoroughly second rate'; and on another occasion explained that it was 'the utmost we were then able to do for getting the teaching side brought within the University'. But at the time he was enthusiastic; indeed when he turned his energies to higher education in the north of England four years later he commended the new type of federal university as a model for Liverpool, Manchester and Leeds.

Four years of negotiation over the Gresham report, drafting, seeking to compromise between conflicting views, and occasional log-rolling, had deepened Haldane's understanding of academic affairs; it had also whetted his appetite for more. He had demonstrated to himself and to his colleagues his flair for the strategy and tactics of policy-making, his rare ability to turn those earnest discussions in Beatrice Webb's drawing room and the talk among carefully chosen companions round his own dinner table into practical political decisions. His apprenticeship was now completed.

3 Co-conspirators

At the turn of this century some social reforms were so obviously necessary – in the eyes of the 'New Liberals' at any rate – that the only problem was how to achieve the reforms. With education it was otherwise. That every citizen should be able to read and write and do simple arithmetic was a necessity. That some citizens (but how many?) should have schooling up to the age of eighteen, to become proficient in literary studies and mathematics: this, too, was a necessity. That local authorities should make provision for technical and commercial education in night schools, or part time; this, too, was acknowledged and its goal was clear: it was to train technicians. But over university education there was a need to re-define goals. Their traditional functions remained as important as heretofore: to cherish learning, to educate recruits for certain professions, to ensure (in the words of the bidding prayer at Cambridge) 'that there may never be wanting a supply of persons duly qualified to serve God both in Church and State.' But for a generation before 1900 there had been warnings (we mention them on p. 14) that to be qualified to serve the state required training in new professions, especially the professions of science and technology applied to industry. Since the 1860s there were signs that Britain was losing her competitive advantage over foreign countries in trade because the British were not applying science to manufacture and because their facilities for higher education in technology were inferior to those in Europe and America. Even in pure scholarship – as Haldane himself had discovered – the universities of Germany had an attraction which even Oxford and Cambridge could not rival. To spend a year in Giessen or Göttingen, Berlin or Heidelberg, was the aspiration of scores of young American and British academics.

The warnings had not gone unheeded. The virtual monopoly of Oxford and Cambridge for English higher education was already over. Stimulated by developments in London and Manchester these ancient universities were themselves responding to the mood of the time, and were including technologists among their graduates. The royal commission on technical instruction published in 1884 encouraging evidence of the response of the new universities and colleges to the needs of industry: applied chemistry under Roscoe in Manchester, in no way inferior to that in the Zurich Polytechnic; courses on laundry chemistry under Jackson at King's College, London; courses on brewing, bread-making, glass and pottery under Graham at University College (who had also 'a large consulting practice for brewers'); metallurgy in Sheffield; textile technology in Leeds, shipping in Liverpool: all colleges supported by local industrialists who contributed funds and encouraged – indeed expected – curricula and research to be relevant to local interests. So there certainly was some progress toward the adaptation of higher education to national needs; but it was fragmentary, empirical, often fortuitous. There was no national plan, and no sign of an articulated purpose between schools and universities, universities and employers, employers and government. Much remained to be done in England and Wales; and the Scottish universities, once models for the rest of the kingdom, had responded even less to the times. There was a simple reason for this. To have modelled themselves on the newer style of curricula would have weakened their treasured tradition of broad general education, and put in its place the specialisation in science and mathematics essential for professionals. But the price of holding on to the Scottish tradition was high: Scottish graduates were having to come south after graduation in order to qualify themselves for posts requiring specialist training. So the Scottish universities, by the end of the nineteenth century, were under fire even from their most loyal friends. '. . . the four Scottish universities [said Haldane in 1901] . . . in the main owing to their sluggishness and want of ideas of their governors [are] of little use from the point of view of the application of science to industry. . . .'

This was the climate of opinion which convinced Haldane that he had to think not only about means, but about ends in higher education if he was to influence government policy. Like many others before him he turned first to Germany. It was shortly before the close of the century that he began a series of annual visits to Weimar and later to Ilmenau, to help his friend Hume Brown, who cherished the ambitious project of revealing the greatness of Goethe to the English speaking world. Their joint enterprise was to collect material for a full scale biography. One of the remarkable features of British academic life in the nineteenth century – indeed until world war I cast its shadow

over Europe – was our sustained enthusiasm for importing German
culture.* As long ago as 1844, over fifty years before Hume Brown's
Goethe pilgrimages, Jowett returned from a visit to Germany determined to bring the light of Hegel into Oxford. In Jowett's college,
Balliol, the use of German became 'almost a Balliol affectation'. In
1868 some of the reforms which Mark Pattison urged upon Oxford
in his *Suggestions on academical organisation* were inspired by Germany.
And in the same year Matthew Arnold published his report to the
Schools Enquiry commissioners, which included his impressions of
the universities of Prussia and his terse conclusion: 'our university
system is a routine, indeed, but it is our want of science, not our want
of liberty, which makes it a routine. It is in science that we have most
need to borrow from the German universities. The French university
has no liberty, and the English universities have no science; the German
universities have both.' In 1897, nearly thirty years after Arnold's
report, came the reports from the special inquiries branch of the board
of education under one of Haldane's near-contemporaries, Michael — *Morant ?*
Sadler. These, too, found in German education patterns for Britain
to copy. So there was nothing original about Haldane's tactic to
call the German university as witness in the indictment of British
universities; though he had the capacity, which Jowett and Pattison
and even Arnold and Sadler did not have, to carry his case beyond
advocacy into political action. He prepared his case as carefully as he
prepared cases at the bar; first mastering the historical background
as far back as Wilhelm von Humboldt; then extracting the basic
features of German universities which (in his view) gave them their
superiority; and then – the practical politician taking over – he worked
the themes which came out of these studies into speeches and addresses
and articles, to inoculate as it were, public opinion.

Haldane supplemented his first-hand experience of German higher
education with reading about higher education in France and the United
States. In France universities had barely recovered from their Pro-
crustean centralisation imposed in 1808 by Napoleon, administered
(as Playfair wrote) 'with the power of a military despot and with the

---

* Bryce, in an introduction to a book by J. Conrad (*The German universities
for the last fifty years*) translated in 1885, remarks how, in the 1840s, German
universities were regarded as parents of revolution; but that by the 1880s the
danger was that England would be too keen to imitate them, forgetting the
dissimilarity of conditions between the two countries, 'and ignoring in particular
the great difference caused by their dependence on the State.'

professional instincts of a drill sergeant' and not withdrawn until the partial decentralisation introduced in 1896–8. Haldane found them, as Arnold had found them, paralysed under excessive state control. In America, however, a genuine viable mutation of higher education was taking place. The Morrill Act in 1863 created conditions for founding the land grant universities. They were a response to the new society of the American frontier, with a twofold aim: to teach 'useful arts' like agriculture and engineering and to transmit a literary and humanistic culture less precious than that in the Eastern colleges. By the turn of the century they had established themselves and were challenging the supremacy of older elitist institutions, just as institutions in London and Manchester were challenging Oxford and Cambridge. Haldane's interest was captivated by the concept of the land grant university and he had evidently met people familiar with the University of Wisconsin (one of the more successful ventures) for in an address to Scottish teachers he singled it out as a place which cherished pure culture and the applications of science to industry and which carried its educational mission beyond the campus to anyone willing to listen, by summer schools, extension lectures, and the like. Here was a paradigm for Haldane's thinking: the democratic tradition of the Scottish university, with a curriculum more relevant than the Scottish curriculum, and a concept of extension work quite unknown in Scotland. It is not surprising that Haldane wrote to James Thursfield in 1902: 'from the United States we have at least as much to learn as from Germany.' Later he had reservations about the relevance of the Wisconsin pattern for Britain, on the ground that it was one which distracted the university from its prime function. When representatives of the Workers' Educational Association held it up as a model in their evidence before the royal commission on the University of Wales, Haldane cautioned them, and added that Wisconsin 'is not really one of the first American universities' (see p. 164).

And so, in these years around the turn of the century, Haldane was engaged in an exercise which would now be labelled 'comparative education', as a deliberate preparation for a political campaign to improve the British universities. The experience which, as it were, completed his brief, was a visit in April 1901 (during his annual Goethe-pilgrimage) to the *Technische Hochschule* at Charlottenburg. It was one of nine polytechnics in Germany (the others were at Hanover, Aachen, Brunswick, Dresden, Darmstadt, Karlsruhe, Stuttgart, and Munich) set up for higher education in technology. He was lyrical in his admiration: 'by far the most perfect University I have ever seen', he said in evidence to the privy council; manned by a great staff, crammed with students and apparatus, and making a close study of every new invention. It was a surprising and somewhat uncritical enthusiasm for a man so dedicated also to philosophy and Goethe. At the time – although he changed his mind later on – Haldane was not even disturbed by the way the Germans had excluded tech- nology from their universities and forced it to become segregated in polytechnics. This was an unexpected lapse in his judgement, for in fact the British universities, which brought students of technology and of the humanities together in the same institution, had chosen a pattern better than the German pattern. But Haldane's imagination was caught by the *relevance* of the Charlottenburg education and – com- pared with institutions trying to do similar work in Britain – with the lavish way the state had financed it. So the drawbacks of segregation were dwarfed by the exciting prospect (which we depict in the next chapter) of creating a 'London Charlottenburg'.*

After the impact of Charlottenburg in 1901 Haldane was ready to take his ideas to the public. He told teachers at Dumfries that educa- tion seemed to him 'the most important, without exception, of the great social reforms which await treatment at the beginning of the twentieth century', and proceeded to develop a blueprint for educa- tional policy which he had first sketched a few months before to businessmen at Liverpool. It was inspired by his experience in Germany, but Haldane was always very careful to warn his hearers against mere imitations of foreign models. Any lesson learnt from a foreign country must – he always stressed – be adapted to the style and genius of the British people. The outline of the blueprint was as follows: First, Britain should have a genuine educational *system*, not the haphazard assemblage of schools, univer- sities, and colleges which were so many unwoven threads of education, not a woven fabric. Second, it should be organised in regions, each with a university as 'the brain and the intelligence' of the whole, and

* It is interesting that Friedrich Paulsen, the great authority on German universities, took a different view. In his famous essay (translated in 1906, but Haldane is known to have been familiar with his writings before then) he says: 'It is to be regretted that the new professions requiring higher training were not articulated with the old "faculties" ... It was due to the ascendancy of philological-historical culture and the aversion of the new humanism to every- thing "realistic" and "utilitarian".'

with teacher-training as an important part of each university's function.
Third, control of the organisation should be decentralised, under
'local administration and control, fostered and assisted by the State'.
Fourth, the pattern of curricula should have the 'double aim' of pure
culture on one hand and application of scientific and other knowledge
to practical life on the other.

There was nothing dramatic about this; not even original, for it
contained little more than a development of ideas worked out by
Matthew Arnold thirty years before. Bryce, Morant, and Webb had
called for expansion of higher education. Playfair, Huxley, and Roscoe
had preached, with more eloquence than Haldane, the cause of science
in the service of industry. But the very fact that Haldane's blueprint
was undramatic is evidence of his political skill. Utopian schemes end
up in the waste paper basket, not as acts of parliament. This scheme
was, in the long view, politically practicable at every point and
(equally essential) it would not need to be carried out all at once.
It is likely, too, that Haldane deliberately fudged the issue of how
education in higher technology was to be organised: whether in
universities (most of which at that time were too poor to support
it on the scale of Charlottenburg), or in newly created polytechnics
on the German model. To have been doctrinaire about this would
have been to limit the options for action.

The value of Haldane's blueprint, then, was not in its originality,
but in its feasibility. This was his unique contribution to the reform
of education in Britain, that nearly all the schemes he submitted had
the credibility of an architect's design which is accompanied by a
quantity surveyor's estimate. Hence the response of his friends when a
little book containing his educational addresses was published in
1902. 'I am exceedingly glad', wrote Morant,

> to read your bold stirring of the dry bones – may it indeed make
> many of them live. You have said what needs saying over & over
> again, & you have said it pointedly and with illustrations which
> ought to make the Englishman listen if anything will. I cannot say
> how deeply I sympathise with your impatience at the smallness of
> vision which seems always to limit our education rulers and edu-
> cation speeches.

Two other letters from friends illustrate the emphasis in Haldane's
message which appealed to enlightened academics. Pringle Pattison
(a lifelong friend and then professor of philosophy in Edinburgh)

wrote: 'I always read about Education with a sinking heart . . . . But your appeal is largely conceived & strikingly put. . . . I think your insistence on what one might call the double-celled ideal of the University – the University of free culture and the technical high school – is full of guidance.' And – significant in view of Haldane's subsequent association with the problems of the University of London – Lord Davey, who had been chairman of the commission to make statutes for that university in 1898, wrote:

> The conception of the double aspect or objective of the higher education is most important. Whether the two objects – culture and professional training – can be carried on concurrently in one University I have some doubt. In the London University we are in a perpetual conflict between the two conceptions of the work of the University and seem at present in danger of falling between the two stools and doing neither efficiently . . . .

During the ten years of eclipse of the Liberal party, which did not end until 1905, Haldane rose to a position of influence and importance. He was, technically, simple a member of the Opposition; one who had never held office, in a party bitterly divided over home rule and the Boer war, and weakened by a vacillating leadership. But in 1902 (he was still only forty-six years old) he was made a privy councillor. He was described in a letter written by his contemporary Asquith (whose political career was already more successful than Haldane's) as the man who 'does all the brain-work of the Liberal Party, and, though never in the Cabinet, thinks for those who are.' He did not achieve this standing by ingratiating himself with the rank and file of the party; just the opposite: Haldane had made himself unpopular by carrying his educational mission across party lines and openly fraternising with Conservatives; even with Balfour, with whom he shared so many interests. He was 'the intermittent astral control of the Unionist Cabinet.' His blueprint for a national system of education was an offer to either party. As he told the guests at one after-dinner speech: 'I do not care what Government is in – (laughter) – if it will only take up science.'

Even to chronicle his activities over these years gives some impression of the endless machinating intelligence: combining with Asquith and Grey to restore the Liberal party, scheming with the Webbs to promote a new movement for national efficiency – whether within the Liberal party, or in a new political grouping; figuring in the membership

of bipartisan clubs as different as the 'Co-efficients' (dedicated to the
Webb's campaign for efficiency in politics) and 'that curiously English
coterie of men of all parties and callings recognised as distinguished
in public life' called, simply, the Club. His growing relish for the
ideas of the Webbs is evident from his eager response to Sidney's
famous article in the *Nineteenth Century* of September 1901, with its
challenge to the progressive Liberals to work out a programme of
national efficiency, not least in the sphere of education, where he had
called for a systematic scheme from infant school to university.
'We are delighted with the "Escape from Houndsditch" ', Haldane
wrote to Sidney on 5 September, after dining with Asquith and one
or two other colleagues. 'That is *your* speech for the new movement
& it is a very important one. . . . Well, no one can say that your
line is stale or that it is not suggestive. The difficulty will be to live
up to it. We begin our Campaign in the end of this month . . . I –
in my humble rôle – go to Glasgow, Dundee & Liverpool (where I
have to address them on Education) besides a go off in my own constituency.' '[I]f success does come', he added in a note to Beatrice
shortly afterwards, '. . . SW should at once come into the House &
take a leading part in directing his own part of the programme of
Efficiency. It is your word – a large part of the items are yours – you
have worked it out.' It was, indeed, as 'a link in our chain proposals',
and an 'item of "Efficiency in Tertiary Education" ', that Haldane
viewed his speech to the industrialists at Liverpool: his first major
pronouncement on educational objectives. All the time, too, he was
catching in the net of his acquaintanceship people whose position or
experience would promote his – Haldane's – labours in the national
interest: civil servants like Fitzroy at the privy council and Morant
at the board of education; philosophers through the Synthetic Society
(another dining club); members of the Fabian circle through the
salon now presided over by Beatrice Webb; and – at the other end of
the social spectrum – the prince of Wales, who had first expressed a
wish to meet him in 1894 as a potential lord chancellor of his reign,
and who in 1898 invoked his help in overcoming the financial difficulties of the Imperial Institute by getting the University of London
to establish its headquarters there. Haldane's social charm must have
been formidable, for after the prince's accession Haldane was frequently
amongst the guests invited to meet him at his special request.

Fortified by allies as diverse as the British throne and the Fabians,

Haldane was now ready for his next sally into the educational system. The initiative on this occasion came from Sidney Webb. In 1900 Webb became a senator of the University of London and he remained chairman of the London County Council's technical education board; so he was able to take an integrated view of London's educational needs. The new senate was engaged in remodelling the University on the lines laid down by the commissioners appointed by the 1898 act. It was Webb's aspiration to make the remodelled University a great centre for applied science. His first step – typical of him – was to draw up a memorandum; Beatrice records that he was doing this in March 1901. The next step was to test the temperature of public opinion. In June articles on the need to train scientists and engineers appeared from his pen, anonymously, in *The Times*. In September there followed the essay in the *Nineteenth Century*, signed this time, urging progressive Liberals to put their weight behind a comprehensive policy on education and particularly 'a large policy of Government aid to the highest technical colleges and the universities. The statesman who first summons up courage enough to cut himself loose from official pedantries on this point and demands a grant of half a million a year with which to establish in the United Kingdom a dozen perfectly equipped faculties of science, engineering, economics and modern languages would score a permanent success.'

Meanwhile, in the spring of 1901 Haldane made his seminal visit to the *Technische Hochschule* at Charlottenburg (p. 44), and in the following September he, too, was writing an article, to be given also as a lecture, on similar lines, inspired by Charlottenburg. The institution was only twenty-one years old. It had been created from the amalgamation of two technical institutes and lavishly financed by the Prussian government. By 1901 it was already famous throughout Europe. Again and again Haldane eulogised Charlottenburg in parliament, in addresses, and in reports and commissions. Here was an essential educational weapon to combat the growing international threat to Britain's industries. From different directions Haldane and Webb converged on the need to create a similar institution in London. Webb's next burst of propaganda is recorded in Beatrice Webb's diary; towards the end of April 1902, she wrote, Sidney was preparing an article on the University of London for the June issue of the *Nineteenth Century* 'in the hope of catching a millionaire', and here, in developing the theme of his *Times* articles, he made a specific plea for a 'British Charlottenburg'.

The stimulus to improve higher technological education in London came from Sidney Webb, and he continued to work with Haldane until the project was successfully launched. But from 1902 it was Haldane who took command. On 9 May he wrote to Webb (the letter is quoted in part below) about the opening moves to launch 'our big scheme'. Already it was 'our' scheme; before long it became 'my scheme': 'I have a big business on hand just now', Haldane wrote three months later to Pringle Pattison, 'which needs all the strength one has – the creation of a school for the Empire for the application of Science to Industry – which is to have its seat in the Metropolis.'

There was already a considerable development of applied science in London at University College and King's College (p. 42) but nothing on the scale of the German polytechnics. In South Kensington there were two institutions: the Royal College of Science, including the School of Mines (they were technically two divisions of one institution), both under the board of education, and the Central Technical College of the City and Guilds Institute of London (re-named in 1907 the City and Guilds College), managed by a board drawn from the city companies. Neither University College nor King's could be transformed into a Charlottenburg. But – and this was the leap of imagination which made the prospect exciting – there was a possibility that a great centre for science and technology might be created at South Kensington, if the institutions already there could be incorporated and if some of the land, which belonged to the 1851 Exhibition commissioners, could be made available for more buildings. This was the idea which germinated slowly in the minds of Haldane and Webb. To turn the idea into reality required money, government consent to surrender its colleges in South Kensington, co-operation from the City and Guilds, agreement on the part of the 1851 Exhibition commissioners to release land, and negotiations with the University of London so that any London Charlottenburg would not be separate from the University, as the German polytechnics were, but associated with the University, to comprise a focus for science and scholarship in the Empire's capital. A formidable set of obstacles; and the sort of challenge which Haldane welcomed. He designed his strategy and went into action.

First, finance. Rumours were going about that the firm of Wernher and Beit was contemplating making a gift to University College, London, to encourage applied science. On 9 May Haldane called on the London partners. The outcome of his call – and his remorseless persistence in pursuing a scheme once he had espoused it – is evident from the letter which he wrote to Sidney Webb the same day, the one about 'our' scheme:

I saw the four London partners of W. B. & Co this afternoon & had an hour with them. It was just in time. There had been no talk of a million – but they were pondering giving £100,000 to U. Coll. This I have *stopped*. They will give the £10,000 only. But I have undertaken to prepare a scheme for a Committee or body of Trustees to *begin* our big scheme. They will give us £100,000 to start it, & help us to get more. The partners are keen to do something. Could you come at 5.30 on Monday to the H of C – & you & I will talk over the scheme of such a Committee, to be independent of, but to work along with the University Authorities. If I can get Rosebery and Arthur Balfour to serve on it I think we may get a million. I believe W. B. & Co. will give much more than £100,000 really. Will you think out the outline of such a scheme.

Haldane was in his element. By the end of the month he had secured support from Rosebery, Balfour, and the duke of Devonshire, who was lord president of the council; and at some stage in the summer he had received gracious permission to be able to write: 'The King himself is keen. . . .'

Haldane knew better than most men that the scheme would fail unless there were, behind these august dignitaries, support troops comprising the men who really draft the decisions to be made. One of these he had already enlisted: Fitzroy, clerk to the privy council. 'It is a great scheme', Fitzroy wrote, 'and worthy of the fertile and daring brain of its organiser.' In June there was a conference under the *aegis*, now, of Rosebery. Haldane, Webb, and Messrs Wernher and Beit were there; and new recruits to the venture: Rucker, on behalf of the University of London, and the permanent head of the treasury, Mowatt, in his capacity as a member of the 1851 commissioners, trustees of the coveted site in South Kensington. At this meeting Haldane 'explained succinctly the scheme so far as it could be outlined, under the peculiar conditions of its inception. . . .' Some progress was made: there was optimism as to the site, from the 1851 commissioners, and there was the prospect of a maintenance grant from the LCC and further aid from the Rhodes Trustees, for Cecil Rhodes and Alfred Beit had been associates.

In the Christmas recess of 1902 Haldane resumed his campaign. The Webbs had now become his staff officers. He wrote from Cloan on 3 January to Beatrice, asking that Sidney (who, it has to be remembered, was a member of the LCC) should prepare a draft letter for Rosebery to send to the LCC, to secure a promise of a maintenance grant for the new institution. The letter, vetted by Haldane, must have had a familiar ring to Webb's colleagues on the LCC! After writing about the way the British had lagged behind other countries in provision for advanced instruction in scientific technology and facilities for research Rosebery's letter went on: 'Perhaps the most perfect instance of such provision is the great College of Applied Science at Charlottenburg, alongside of the University of Berlin, erected at an outlay exceeding £500,000 and costing £55,000 a year. From its portals there issue every year some 1200 young men of 22 or 23 years of age, equipped with the most perfect training that science can give. . . .'

The letter elicited an appropriate response: in July 1903 the LCC promised a maintenance grant of £20,000 a year. Of course it was not just the letter which persuaded the Council. The very choice of Rosebery as sponsor silenced some critics. And then Haldane never entrusted delicate negotiations solely to the written word; he appeared himself before the LCC's subcommittee to explain the scheme. The decisive factor was probably Sidney Webb's skilful presentation of the case to his colleagues. Ramsay MacDonald, also a member of the LCC, is reported to have said: 'Mr Haldane and Mr Sidney Webb had presented a pistol at the head of the Council.'

By July 1903 the first objective was secured: the promise of enough capital and recurrent funds to launch 'our big scheme'. But the scheme itself was still no more than a sketch-plan. It was part of Haldane's technique to begin with modest objectives, until enough people were committed, and then to enlarge the objectives as opportunity arose. That is what happened this time. If the specification for a 'London Charlottenburg' had been too precise, the blueprint too detailed, there would have been less room to compromise, less freedom for adaptation. Haldane was a man who hung on to his options as long as possible. 'Our big scheme' began simply as a new college in South Kensington in addition to those already there. But by the summer of 1903 another powerful mind – Morant's of the board of education – had got to work on the scheme with the question: Why not contemplate a massive consortium or merger or partnership (deliberately left undefined) between all the institutions of science and technology at South Kensington? The board of education *might* be persuaded to hand over the Royal College of Science and the School of Mines, to become part of the London Charlottenburg; and the City and Guilds *might* be persuaded to do the same with their institution. The whole complex (still growing in the imagination of its founders) *might* (in ways still undefined) be brought under the jurisdiction of the University of London, for the administrative headquarters of the University had recently been moved to South Kensington and the Royal College of Science and the City and Guilds College were already schools of the University. There were other prospects for change on the site, too, for the School of Mines had found itself unable to cope with the demand for experts for the gold mines in South Africa, and the Institute of Mining and Metallurgy had appointed a committee to enquire into the education of mining engineers.

Haldane's technique was to leave options open, but not beyond the point when it was clear that a choice among options would be politically feasible; then he was quick to force the pace. Some time between July and October 1903 he produced a document marked 'private', undated and unsigned, which lifted 'our big scheme' to a higher level.* His aim, clarified in this document, was to co-ordinate and extend existing institutions in South Kensington to provide a system of instruction in technology worthy of the metropolis. He envisaged a central institution (or a group of institutions; that option was still kept open) which would be closely related to, and largely controlled by, the University of London. But one step at a time: for the present, all that was needed was sufficient money to set the scheme in motion, sufficient co-operation between the institutions to assure their common interest, and a sufficiently close co-operation with the University of London to make it an effective partner. This objective could be achieved by bringing all the interested parties round the same committee table to discuss the terms of a partnership: the government, the University, the LCC, the City and Guilds, the trustees, and representatives of the technological institutions who would be the 'customers' for the products of these colleges. It was only a first step; but Haldane could not resist giving a glimpse of the distant horizon: a mobilisation, ultimately, of all the educational resources in South

* The private and unsigned memorandum was a device he used again, in 1916, when he wanted to involve himself in planning post-war educational reforms (p. 136).

Kensington into one great college; to be an integral part of the University; extending its influence beyond London and the provinces, even to centres of industry in the colonies.

Having drawn up this anonymous document, Haldane was able to entrust its administrative follow-up to the ruthless energy of Morant in the board of education. Morant persuaded the president to widen the terms of reference of the proposed committee to review the School of Mines; its remit should now be to consider the future of the whole complex of colleges in South Kensington. In November 1903 Mowatt (who had just retired from the treasury) was secured as chairman, and in April 1904 a strong committee was appointed. It did not include Haldane himself, but his eyes and ears (and voice) were present, for Sidney Webb was there as the LCC representative and Mowatt was a member of the University Colleges grants committee whose chairman was now Haldane.

In the following December the committee ran into trouble: Mowatt, its chairman, fell ill and on 29 December had to resign. This was a misfortune which could not be allowed to hold matters up. Haldane was at Cloan for the recess. On the last day of the year he wrote to Morant:

> The situation is serious as regards S. Kensington, & an effort must be made . . . . My own burden, as you know, is not a particularly light one, but I gathered that you would possibly suggest my name if I could do the work. Well – I was to some extent responsible at the beginning of this business, & I have kept myself informed of what was going on. I am willing to try my hand if you wish it. . . . I will *make* the time if it seems good to you.

Haldane's offer was eagerly accepted. The president of the board of education (Lord Londonderry) speaking of it afterwards, said: '. . . I was at my wits end to find a substitute. But my mind turned, and so did the minds of those associated with me, to one individual, and our only doubt was as to whether the gentleman in question could find leisure to devote his great mind and great ability to the discharge of the duties given up by Sir Francis Mowatt. . . .'

In January 1905 Haldane took control of the committee. On 20 February a preliminary report was agreed and signed. The final report came a year later. The first report was designed to probe resistances and to measure their strength; the second report was designed to overcome or to circumvent them. There were three difficulties to be overcome. One was to persuade the board of education to part with two 'imperial assets', namely the Royal College of Science and its associated School of Mines. Not only would this be tantamount to giving taxpayers' money to the consortium and ultimately to the University; it might also arouse jealousy among provincial universities. Another difficulty was to reach some concordat about the government of the cluster of colleges; Haldane suggested no more, at first, than a composite council in which each co-operating institution had an 'adequate share in the general control'. The third difficulty was to design a link with the University of London which would on the one hand avoid the German pattern: the separation of higher technology from the university (Sidney Webb felt strongly about this; he discussed it when he gave evidence to the royal commission on university education in Ireland, in 1901), and on the other hand would leave the maximum initiative to the new institution, an issue on which other people felt equally strongly. Thus when T. H. Huxley was at the Royal College of Science he fought hard to keep the college 'clear of any connection with a University of any kind'; and when he thought the Gresham commission might recommend a take-over of the College, he wrote 'I am ready to oppose any such project tooth and nail. I have not been striving these thirty years to get Science clear of their school-mastering sham-literary peddling to give up the game without a fight.'

Huxley was gone, but there were others still at South Kensington who shared his views; so Haldane had to proceed warily. He said as much to the somewhat over-eager representatives of the University when they pressed at a conference with the committee for the immediate incorporation of the new institution. The difficulty of the turnover at once, he told them, was 'a difficulty which I do not think anybody can appreciate who has not got the miserable misfortune to be an MP negotiating with the Government and a lot of other bodies', a difficulty which necessitated 'proceeding diplomatically step by step'. And, as an illustration of what he meant by 'diplomatically', what could be clearer than Haldane's rebuke to one professor at the meeting. In order to bring the proposed college within the purview of government grants for research, it was necessary to stress that its purpose would be to teach *advanced* science and technology. Professor Pearson strongly objected – and more than hinted that this proposal came from someone who knew nothing about teaching students! We can see Haldane's disarming smile and hear his gentle voice as he replied:

'It is quite true as Professor Pearson says that the amateur has been at work in this report but he must remember that we are a special kind of professor called into existence for the higher education of the Treasury and therefore we have our own methods and language.'

By 31 March 1905, only one month after the preliminary report was issued, Morant was able to tell Haldane privately that the government had agreed to hand over the Royal College of Science and the associated Royal School of Mines. Official confirmation followed on 3 April and in June the treasury agreed to give an annual grant of £17,000 (raised in November to £20,000) to the new institution.

Haldane, having first attained all the objectives in the first report of his committee, released the report to the press in June, after taking a lot of trouble to ensure that it would have a good reception. Thus it was arranged that one member of the committee, Sir W. White, should 'see *The Times*' beforehand. The press coverage was enthusiastic, not only about the scheme but about Haldane, who was now identified as its originator (Sidney Webb having faded, as usual, into the background). Haldane is, wrote the *Morning Post*, 'perhaps of all public men the most single minded in his appreciation of the nation's educational needs'. And *The Times* drew attention to Haldane's apostolic writings in *Education and empire*, published three years earlier, and the prospect of their realisation in an Imperial Charlottenburg in South Kensington. It was a personal triumph, though in fact the credit deserved to be more widely distributed: to Morant, whose energy drove the scheme forward from within the board of education, to Mowatt, whose goodwill helped to ensure treasury support, and to Webb, whose influence on the LCC and the senate was critically important.

Not that 'our great scheme' was accomplished yet; but Haldane had secured government approval for it. He now undertook personally to negotiate with the many bodies whose interests had to be satisfied. On 7 July 1905 his committee met representatives of the University of London. His gambit was:

Well, now, that brings me to what we are here today to do. Some of you, I have no doubt, have wondered until now that we did not take evidence in a formal fashion. I have had a great deal of experience of these Committees, and I always find that the formal taking of evidence after a certain point is much the least profitable way of doing things, and therefore it occurred to us that . . . what would be most useful would be that we should meet today and have a friendly talk about the whole matter. . . . We are very ready to learn here, but I am in hopes that it may turn out that our purpose is your purpose.

Toujours bien, jamais mieux! Haldane got an unequivocal promise of support from the University, though they still pressed for immediate incorporation of the London Charlottenburg into the University, and on this Haldane had to drag his committee's feet, for the City and Guilds were not inclined to perform *hara kiri*, and it would have been imprudent to hand over the other two colleges, which were regarded as 'imperial assets', without at least some minuet of disengagement. The next objective was concurrence from the City and Guilds. Again, Haldane's gift of cultivating friends came in handy; for the chairman of the City and Guilds Council was Haldane's old colleague at the bar, Lord Halsbury. A compact was reached: the City and Guilds College could become part of the scheme, provided it did not lose its identity.

The government were won over; the City and Guilds were amenable; the LCC had blessed (and promised to finance) the scheme. The committee were unanimous that as an interim arrangement there should be a governing body representing all the co-operating interests and that the whole complex of colleges should be recognised as a school of the University of London. But some members of the·committee wanted to go farther and faster than this and to pledge that the new institution would become fully incorporated into the University. To go as far as that would inevitably diminish the independence of the institution and might well arouse hostility from the parties whose co-operation was essential. An irreconcilable split developed in the committee itself. With a less experienced chairman than Haldane this might have been serious. But Haldane knew what to do; he persuaded the committee to sign a unanimous report with an open acknowledgement of their disagreement! And to quell any apprehension that this disagreement might hold things up, the committee suggested that the question of full incorporation into the University might be considered later, together with changes which might become necessary in the constitution of the University itself, by that ultimate placebo for constitutional ailments: a royal commission.

Haldane was by training and predilection a philosopher. He would employ expediency or accept compromise in order to get a decision, but his mind returned to principles, and it is possible to discern principles – though somewhat eroded by political realism – in much of his writing on education. An early draft of the final report of this committee (abandoned probably on Morant's advice because it was regarded as doctrinaire) is unmistakably in Haldane's devious and ponderous style:

> We are well aware that a love of logical organisation is not specially characteristic of the people of this country, and we naturally have no desire to make recommendations which the existence of deep-seated national characteristics is likely to render ineffective. The recent Education Act, however, and still more the manner in which the Act is being administered over considerable parts of the country by the most enlightened local authorities are compelling, to an extent previously unknown, the recognition of the fact that education must be regarded as an organic whole and that its development is successful in proportion as it is guided by a policy which regards it in all its bearings and aims at settled objects. It appears, therefore, well worth considering whether, before this country largely extends her provision for this type of education, as she will have to do, and no doubt will do, in the immediate future, an attempt ought not to be made to get at some general recognition of the principles which should, theoretically at least, underlie any such extension.

The final report of Haldane's committee on the future of the South Kensington college was launched with as much care for press publicity as was the first report. Though signed on 8 January 1906, it was not issued until 5 February, for fear (according to a note in Haldane's handwriting) it should 'fall flat' in the excitement of the January general election.

It was an election which returned the Liberal party to power and brought Haldane into the office for which he is remembered in history: as minister not for education but for war.

4 Above the Snow-line

For any man of normal physique, a career which comprised practice at the bar, a leading role in opposition politics, the re-organisation of the University of London and the creation of a London Charlottenburg would suffice. But during these ten years when the Liberal party was out of office Haldane's campaign for higher education spread far outside London to issues in Ireland (as we have already noted on p. 38) and in the north of England. Our portrait of Haldane must now take account of these activities.

Haldane's interest in Irish universities was partly a bargain to secure the support of Irish MPs for the University of London bill in 1898. But it would be unfair to suggest that he had no higher motive than this. Six months before the passage of the bill he had spoken eloquently in parliament in favour of easier access to higher education for Irishmen. In the debate on the address, in February 1898, he boldly supported Dillon's plea for denominational university education for Irish Roman Catholics, pledging himself to support any steps the Conservatives might take 'free from Party bias' to solve the problems of Ireland. 'The question before the House', he said:

> is, substantially, whether the Catholics of Ireland, four-fifths of the population of the island, are to go without University education. . . . It is no use saying they can go to the Universities, for experience has proved that they won't go . . . . When I think of the difference between my own country of Scotland and the condition of things that exist in Ireland in this matter I am ashamed. Honourable Members sometimes speak – I don't think that they really speak deliberately after having considered it – but they speak lightly of a University education as if it was a sort of luxury. Well, I can only say, speaking from my own knowledge, that it represents the life and backbone of the people of Scotland . . . .

The plan which he took on his cloak-and-dagger visit to Ireland was a replica of the London model. The Royal University of Ireland was an examining body; teaching was done in the Queen's colleges in Belfast, Cork and Galway. Haldane's proposal was to create two teaching universities, one in Belfast and one in Dublin; to give each of them an internal and an external (i.e. examining) function; to give each university *de jure* a non-sectarian constitution but to make sure that *de facto* the university in Dublin was governed by catholics and the university in Belfast by protestants.

Haldane returned from Ireland with sufficient backing for his plan to encourage the government to act. By the end of October – within two or three weeks of his visit to the cardinal at Armagh, Haldane had sent Balfour a confidential note of proposals for the cabinet, and before the end of December a draft of an Irish Universities bill was ready. But on Kings Cross station, where Balfour and Haldane met to travel together to Hatfield, Balfour had to confess that he could not get the support of his colleagues, and the proposals were dropped. Haldane's efforts were not in vain, for ten years later the proposals were exhumed (at Haldane's suggestion) by the Liberal government and they became the basis of the successful legislation in 1908 which established the Queen's University of Belfast and the National University of Ireland, with University College, Dublin, as a successor to Newman's Catholic University.

Our portrait now depicts an episode which – if Haldane had done nothing else for British universities – would have secured him a distinguished place in the history of higher education. A generation afterwards, in recollection of this episode, he wrote: 'My relations with Balfour [over the university question] had become rather close ever since the London and Irish problems had engaged our efforts. But with these results I could not rest, and I went to him again about what was new.'

'What was new' was nothing less than the whole pattern for university education in England and Wales. When the new century dawned in 1900 there were five universities in England (Oxford, Cambridge, London, Durham, and the Victoria University) and one in Wales. All, in a sense, were federations of colleges. Up to the middle of the nineteenth century even the universities of Oxford and Cambridge were primarily examining bodies for teaching done in the colleges, although by 1900 this was no longer true: university teaching had become important, especially in science. Durham's constituent colleges never had the independence of Oxford colleges, but there was a framework of federation, and Armstrong College in Newcastle taught for

Durham degrees. The universities of London, Wales and the Victoria University were all co-ordinating bodies, prescribing the curriculum but (except in London since 1898) not teaching it. Teaching for Victoria University degrees was done under the control of three constituent colleges: Owens College in Manchester, University College in Liverpool, and the Yorkshire College in Leeds. And teaching for degrees in the University of Wales was done in separate colleges in Aberystwyth, Bangor, and Cardiff.

In March 1900 a charter was granted for a new university, in Birmingham, to serve 'the Midland Districts of England'. Its champion was the MP for West Birmingham, Joseph Chamberlain. It was a symbol of civic pride and it stirred the imagination of civic leaders in other cities to contemplate having fully fledged universities in their own cities. In the autumn of 1901 the MP for one of the divisions of Liverpool, A. F. Warr, invited Haldane to address a group of business men in that city to support a movement to detach the University College from the Victoria University and to set it up as an independent University of Liverpool.

To create a new university to serve the Midlands was one thing; to start splitting up the Victoria University into separate independent universities was quite another. It raised a fundamental problem. Parliament was well disposed toward the creation of more centres of higher education; the bill for the University of Birmingham was passed without much opposition. But did this have to mean a proliferation of degree-giving bodies? Or could it be achieved by bringing all new colleges of higher education in England under the academic control of London, or of the Victoria University, or of Birmingham? In other words, should the English higher education system expand by maintaining only three massive universities, with many affiliated colleges teaching for one or other of their degrees? Or should the larger cities have their own autonomous civic universities?

Many eminent men ventilated their fears about an unrestrained multiplication of universities in England. Matthew Arnold wanted Oxford, Cambridge, and London to be the only bodies with authority to award degrees. The commissioners appointed by the treasury to inspect university colleges in 1896 (Warren of Oxford and Liveing of Cambridge) urged that universities should not 'needlessly' be multiplied; London colleges should all be brought under the University of London, and colleges elsewhere should be grouped, as the northern ones were under the Victoria University. In the debate on the University of London bill of 1898, Lubbock pointed out that if (as was proposed) colleges wanting to be affiliated with London had to lie within a thirty mile radius, then it would be almost impossible to resist demands for universities elsewhere, 'and whatever difference of opinion there might be in the House, all interested in the higher education of the country would agree that any considerable multiplication of universities would be very undesirable.' Mowatt, at the treasury, held similar views: any plea for a new university 'should be very closely scrutinized because the multiplication of degree-giving bodies in a State is the certain forerunner of a depreciation in the value of a degree.' These fears were crystallised into one epithet, attributed by Haldane to Bryce: the pejorative label of 'Lilliputian Universities'.

So Liverpool's campaign to hive off from the Victoria University, to have a university of its own, would obviously be strongly opposed. It raised an issue of great importance. The future of English universities would depend on how the issue was resolved. Haldane realised this and eagerly came to the support of Liverpool.

University College, Liverpool, had allies in its aspiration. Huxley had strongly supported the idea that a university 'should exist in every great centre of population' (his argument was quoted in the petition from Birmingham in 1899). Creighton, in one of the last utterances before his death in January 1901, and quoted in the Liverpool case for a university, wrote: 'There is an absolute need that the number of universities should be increased; that each locality that is of importance should have its own university adapted in many ways to suit local needs.'

Haldane defined his own attitude to the controversy when he addressed the Liverpool businessmen on 22 October 1901. We are proud, he said, of Oxford and Cambridge. We do not seek to disturb their splendid traditions.

But that does not make the educational reformer desire the less to see the expansion of another kind of teaching which they are not adapted to give. . . . The Victoria University and the University of Wales have taken the way we want. Let us assist still further the magnificent private efforts which made them what they are today. Why should not Liverpool and Manchester . . . possess, as in Germany they certainly would, their own Universities? How ridiculous it is to dread that such Universities would prove Lilliputians! Why should Leeds not be the headquarters of a Yorkshire

University? Why should not Birmingham, where the energy and influence of Mr Chamberlain have brought about a remarkable fresh development, be the centre for the Midlands; and why should not Bristol, where the soil so far has proved somewhat less fertile, be made by State cultivation the centre for the South-West of England?

It was beginning to be clear, now, what was emerging in Haldane's mind. It was a grand scenario of regionalism, with universities benignly presiding over the educational systems in each region, reminiscent, perhaps, of the way each German state had its presiding university, but, unlike German universities, a scheme to be financed by local civic spirit supplemented by aid from parliament. At a dinner in his honour after his Liverpool speech he went so far as to say that the days of federated universities were 'over'.* It was not to be so simple as that. In an episode of seminal importance, the claim of University College, Liverpool, to break away from the federal Victoria University and to award its own degrees was put on trial by the privy council.

Haldane's main objective was to multiply centres for higher education. Blocking the path to this objective was the unresolved controversy between the expansionists, who wanted each of these centres to be able to award its own degrees, and the restrictionists, who wanted the centres to be affiliated to one or other of the existing universities, and to confine degree-granting power to these existing universities. The restrictionists rested their case on the belief that a proliferation of degrees would debase the currency. The expansionists rested their case

* Haldane's frequent allusions to federalism in universities support the charge that 'no-one can invest a subject in a more lucid fog'. On occasion he commended the pattern of the University of London, which was at that time undoubtedly federal in structure. In his evidence to the privy council committee over Liverpool (p. 65ff.) he affirmed '. . . that the particular form of federal constitution which Victoria University has is cramping and restricting the development of the constituent Colleges, and ought to be abandoned.' It was not until he was concerned with the University of Wales that he distinguished clearly between federation and devolution in a collegiate university. By that time he had come to regard federation as a pattern in which the university neither finances the colleges nor has a hand in appointing their teachers, but which may exert a stranglehold on their teaching by controlling the curricula and the examinations. By contrast, devolution in a collegiate university was a pattern in which the university had overall control of the finances of the colleges and influence over the appointment of their senior academic staff, but which entrusted to the colleges a much greater degree of autonomy over curricula and examinations.

on the belief that each city would support (and finance) a university granting its own degrees with more enthusiasm that it would support a college affiliated to a university in some other city.

Haldane's next task, therefore, was to remove this obstacle in his path. The petition from Liverpool, submitted on 23 April 1902, was an opportunity to force a decision. But Haldane was laying his plans before then. Fitzroy, at the privy council, records (on 28 February 1902) that he had 'another talk with Haldane on the Northern University question. He is very keen for a hearing before the Privy Council and will take his coat off for the occasion, notwithstanding the amount of work with which he is occupied in other directions . . . .' Meanwhile Haldane had put the same idea into Balfour's ear. He advised Balfour to take advantage of the situation at Liverpool to appoint a 'very strong Committee of the Privy Council' to report on the issue.

The alternative was to have a royal commission. Haldane, backed by Fitzroy, opposed this; their objections emerge clearly from the wording of the confidential memorandum which the lord president put to the cabinet:

> It would, I think, be possible to appoint a fairly impartial Committee of the Council who would not have any strong preconceived opinions on the question, whereas if the Royal Commission were appointed in the ordinary way, it would probably be necessary to place upon it men with strong opinions one way or the other with the result of an inconclusive Report or of separate Reports.

The cabinet came down in favour of a privy council hearing, and by November the members of the committee had been chosen. It was composed of privy councillors who might have seemed to be innocent of preconceived opinions: the earl of Rosebery, Lord James of Hereford, Lord Balfour of Burleigh (secretary for Scotland), Sir Edward Fry (an ex-lord justice of appeal), with the lord president himself, the duke of Devonshire, in the chair. But was it entirely coincidence that two of the members (Balfour and Rosebery) were familiar with the non-federal pattern of the Scottish universities, another (Fry) had supported the recent reconstruction of the University of London, and none were publicly identified with what Haldane, in writing to Chamberlain at this time, referred to as 'Oxford notions of what a University ought to be'? And was it entirely coincidence that Rosebery, as Haldane recalled later, was 'not unnaturally much interested on my account', or that Fry, as a result of a long association with Haldane at the bar, was on terms of close friendship with him?

Haldane offered to lead the case on behalf of Liverpool himself, without a fee; but before the case came on he was made a privy councillor, which disqualified him from doing so. Instead, therefore, he appeared as leading witness and he advised on the choice of counsel: Lyttelton ('who knew little about higher education but was tactful and also well known to the members of the Committee'), Sidney Webb, and Kemp ('my old friend . . . who was one of my "devils" at Lincoln's Inn in those days'). The hearing lasted for three days, from 17 to 19 December 1902. It resolved itself into a fight between Liverpool (for its independence) and Leeds (to preserve the integrity of the federal Victoria University) conducted on occasion with unseemly venom. Ripon gave evidence against Liverpool like 'a wild animal at bay' and Acland (also opposing Liverpool) lost his temper when cornered by 'mere' lawyers. Haldane, who had characteristically mastered all the details, was in his element; courteous, unruffled, and with an inexhaustible supply of facts and figures. The case was about a proposed university in Lancashire, not Yorkshire. But when it was necessary to confound the witnesses from Yorkshire who came to oppose Liverpool, Haldane said: '. . . I am not a Yorkshireman, and my knowledge of Yorkshire has been derived from visits there and a close study of calendars and materials; but I have studied this, I venture to think, more closely than some of the Yorkshire witnesses have themselves.' And a few minutes later he said, sweetly: 'I have got a statement which I have prepared and copies of which I will hand to my friend.' He then produced a list of institutions for higher education in Yorkshire towns with more than 20,000 inhabitants, and a second table setting out their functions. He then ran through them: Leeds, Sheffield, Bradford, Halifax . . . serving a population of three or four millions, until he reached his point: that far from opposing a dissolution of the federal Victoria University, Yorkshire ought to support it. Leeds could be the seat of another great university, surrounded by 'schools of the University' in other Yorkshire towns, with an effect 'the same as the effect is in London at the present time – a great co-ordination of every kind of education and a great stimulus in the teaching of these institutions.'

It was another opportunity to preach the gospel of regionalism for universities. And when taxed with the question: what could these three separate universities do which could not be done by the present Victoria

University? – Haldane's answer was again the case for regionalism. 'The
Victoria University has an area of . . . 10,000 square miles. It ranges
over a territory 100 miles in length, and the University resolves itself
into nothing more than a degree-giving and examining board . . . .'
And he went on to say that this was an obstruction to local participation in the affairs of the college where teaching is done, for 'by no
amending of the charter can you give it that contact with the important
local people . . .which would make it the real, living, permeating force
that a body with co-ordinate functions, and within a convenient area
would be.' 'You attach', he was asked, 'the greatest weight to the
limitation of the sphere of influence of which you spoke yesterday?'
'The very greatest weight' was Haldane's reply.

In due course Haldane had to deal with the fear that to multiply
degree-giving bodies would be to lower standards; an early version of
the 'more means worse' argument. 'Can you suggest to us', asked Sir
Edward Fry, any way to prevent a cheapening of the degree, 'supposing
small Universities become prevalent in this country. You have thought
of the subject more than most people?' Haldane was ready for this.
External examiners would maintain the parity of degrees, and they
would have to be selected so that they could not be over-ruled by the
in situ professor.

Throughout Haldane's evidence there are glimpses of educational
horizons far beyond the limited enquiry of the privy council committee. In advocating university status for the colleges in Liverpool,
Manchester and Leeds, Haldane was looking as an ultimate objective
to a regional university which incorporated technical institutes and
polytechnics, some of them wealthier than the universities because they
were financed by local authorities. And at one point he hinted at a
still wider jurisdiction for universities: the colleges of the Victoria
University, he said, were 'too little autonomous in so far as they have
not got the powers necessary to enable them to organise education
from top to toe [our italics] in their district'.

Haldane's *Case* to the privy council committee is a veritable manifesto
for his beliefs about higher education, matured after a dozen years of
thought:

> I desire to see the extension of University education in England
> to a very large class of persons who cannot at present obtain it . . .
> all those who are about to follow any profession or occupation
> which requires knowledge, reflection and judgement. . . . The more

of these persons who get a University education the better.... I regard higher education as an end in itself.... The changing conditions of the world in the twentieth century make higher instruction more necessary than formerly. In many spheres of life where natural capacity and special qualities of character, such as energy and courage, may have sufficed in the past, the possession of special knowledge, the application of trained intelligence, is now absolutely necessary for success.

He then went on to describe the importance of universities for the nation's industrial life (putting in some propaganda, of course, for the Charlottenburg concept), 'and the encouragement of research because it appeals specially to the great commercial classes of this country....' But this, he wrote, 'is one aspect only of the effect of applying intelligence, knowledge and thoroughness to the whole conduct of life....'

The opponents struggled to prevent a verdict. To grant Liverpool's petition, said Acland, 'prejudging the settlement of the whole of this enormously important question of supplying a University education to this great country, and this great empire' after consideration of only 12–15 hours, would be disastrous. And Ripon: '... the whole of this discussion raises most forcibly the general question of University education in this country ... it is a question which ought not to be decided upon the individual application of any of the Colleges....' But the privy councillors were not impressed; indeed Rosebery – even if he had no preconceived opinions about the issue – certainly had preconceived opinions about two of the witnesses. His hostility toward Acland and Ripon was frankly a legacy of his unhappy relations with them in his cabinet of 1894–5. In reply to a jocular inquiry from Balfour of Burleigh over lunch, Rosebery made the enigmatic response that his association with Acland had been 'like that of the three colleges whose federal ties we are asked to dissolve'; and when Acland and Ripon concluded their evidence, he flung a piece of paper over to the chairman (the duke of Devonshire) with the comment: 'Ripon and Acland were the two most taciturn members of my Cabinet, so now you understand what I suffered.' Fitzroy, indeed, formed the impression that the 'violence of the line taken by Lord Ripon and Acland has had a very marked effect on Lord Rosebery's attitude towards the question; as the Duke says, "his principal object has been to make them look ridiculous".' And it was surely Acland who inspired Rosebery's comment about one of the experts who had replied to a single question of counsel in a lengthy speech: that he was 'like the rock smitten by Moses.'

These were the actors, and these their prejudices, in a scene which made educational history in England. The privy councillors granted Liverpool's petition. On 16 February 1903 the king in council approved a report which recommended that the colleges at Liverpool and Manchester should receive charters as separate universities; but that before these charters were granted Leeds should be given the opportunity to make proposals for a university in Yorkshire; and that in framing these or similar charters 'the effect of the multiplication of such Universities should not be lost sight of' and due consideration be given to the points on which joint action was desirable.

All the parties, even Leeds, were satisfied with the outcome. Haldane wrote a flattering letter to Fitzroy, whose reaction was: 'I can, at any rate, claim to have succeeded so far as the two main objects for which I have striven are concerned: first, to get the subject dealt with by a Committee of the Privy Council instead of a Royal Commission, and secondly, to obtain from that Committee a decision in favour of University development on modern lines, in compliance with the exigencies of commerce and industry.'

Haldane himself was very proud of this victory for his views. 'The date of this Order in Council', he said, when, nine years later, he was installed as chancellor of the University of Bristol, 'is, I think, a memorable one. It gave State recognition to a new policy, but for which we might not have been assembled here tonight. The principle was accepted that the number of the English Universities was to be increased and their headquarters were to be in cities.' The campaign for civic universities had been won, but it was not in Haldane's nature to leave it at that. The gains had to be consolidated. So we find him still concerned in the affairs of Liverpool, and still acting as consultant to Fitzroy, when it came to settling the details of the charters for the new universities. The immediate problem was to define the exact nature of the joint action required of them. Fitzroy had anticipated trouble about this when the ruling was being considered: 'No doubt the scope and scheme of joint action will give rise to much discussion on points of detail', he had written to the duke on 14 January. 'Haldane for one is, I know, anxious that as free a hand as possible should be given to the universities to make their own arrangements. . . .' Later, when it transpired that Manchester and Leeds wanted obligatory consultation to cover even degree courses and subjects of examination, Haldane again pressed his view. 'I own', he wrote to Fitzroy at the beginning of April,

> that I think the Manchester and Leeds proposal a mischievous one. If you would like to know how heavily the four Scotch Universities are suffering from an analogous provision, Struthers [of the Scottish education department] ... will give you the last information. The experience has been disastrous. The more progressive Scotch Universities have found themselves hampered. ... I am very keen, therefore, that, if you can, you should let Liverpool shape its own Courses of instruction without being vetoed by Universities which may have other views of their work.

Ultimately a reconciling formula from the principal of Edinburgh, Sir William Turner, enabled this course to be taken. But it was not until Fitzroy had sounded Haldane on the formula that he ventured to act on it: 'Haldane came to see me about a clause I had drafted for insertion in the Charters of Liverpool and Manchester Universities, providing against science degrees being given for purely technological attainments', he recorded on 4 May. 'The suggestion came from Sir W. Turner, and I was glad to hear Haldane accept it with eagerness.' And in the explanatory memorandum he prepared for circulation to the committee, he backed his recommendation with the argument Haldane had supplied earlier: 'The experience of Scotland where an analogous provision has been in force since the Act of 1889, is, it is understood, of one voice as to its effect in hampering initiative and arresting enterprise, and it would surely be a pity when Liverpool is prepared to concede so much to the principle of co-operation to impose a condition which strains unanimity and may retard progress.'

This conflict of views was resolved but now a new one appeared. Sheffield was not content to remain a federated college attached to Leeds. Why not two universities in Yorkshire? The privy council did not put up much resistance, and by March 1905 a charter for a separate university at Sheffield was being negotiated. The draft ran into difficulties over mandatory consultation. If Sheffield had to submit its statutes and ordinances to Manchester, Liverpool, and Leeds, then these three universities should be obliged to submit theirs to Sheffield! To placate Sheffield, Fitzroy had to persuade the privy council committee to find another compromise. This compromise had to take note of the jealousy between Leeds and Sheffield. One way out (favoured by Rosebery) would be to oblige Sheffield to consult only the Lancashire universities. But this would cause umbrage in Leeds. In the end, a classical solution was reached: the tutelage of Sheffield should be subject to a time limit. On 3 April 1905 Fitzroy wrote to Rosebery:

> . . . I had the opportunity of going into the matter with Haldane when he was here a few days ago. He quite agrees that a reciprocal arrangement, if practicable, would be best, but in the circumstances is content with what is proposed. Of course, as he says, if they had all started together, the case would have been different, but Sheffield comes in late and ought to be satisfied with obtaining its University on these terms: its objection to submit changes in its Statutes to Leeds ignores the position of the latter, as one of the constituents of the late Victoria University, and the rights that attach to it in consequence: rights which in his opinion it would be hard to ask it to surrender. He thinks a time limit, which you will observe has been introduced, ought to remove all Sheffield's objections as in seven, or, if they press for it, five years time we can say to the other Universities – either Sheffield shall go entirely free or be put on terms of complete reciprocity.

A draft charter for Sheffield was approved on 29 May 1905, 'thus bringing to an end a series of very responsible negotiations. . . . Few Committees of the Privy Council have been concerned with so large a task as bringing four Universities into being and prescribing all the conditions under which they should work in concert – a step which will have the most important consequences upon the development of university organisation.'

A drawback of the mole-technique is that the mole is rarely visible to the public. So it is not surprising that Haldane's claim to have played a large part in founding civic universities should have been challenged. That he did make this claim is not in doubt. When he was given an honorary degree at Liverpool he wrote to his mother: 'the degree . . . was conferred on me as the real founder of the University.' But this was no more than a pardonable indulgence in filial exaggeration, often to be found in Haldane's letters to his mother. In his autobiography he is more careful: 'one of the first of the new University movements on which I set to work was that in Liverpool, where my public-spirited friend, A. F. Warr, MP for one of the divisions . . . prepared the ground for me . . . . Liverpool presently made a splendid response.' Haldane did, nevertheless, expose himself to criticism from others who were instrumental in helping to create a university in Liverpool, and so to set a pattern for civic universities. Hopkinson, who as the first vice-chancellor of the newly-constituted University of Manchester, was in the middle of the negotiations, wrote that from the statement in Haldane's autobiography 'it appears that he had really not much knowledge of the subject . . . . On this question Haldane, in spite of his great ability and the interest he took in the subject is often quite mistaken.' And Muir, whose ideas played an important part in the early days of Liverpool, frankly instanced Haldane's account as an example of the readiness of people of importance to exaggerate their own achievement. According to Muir, Haldane's claim 'to be the real founder of the Liverpool University can certainly not be upheld', but except in the letter to his mother this is a claim he never made.

It is not difficult to reconcile these conflicting opinions. First, there was the mole-technique. It was Beatrice Webb who reflected that in the movement for new forms of universities at the beginning of the twentieth century 'Haldane will have played one of the principal *though unseen* parts' (our italics). Second, the whole style of Liverpool University owed much to the charismatic figure of Mackay, who was professor of history there; a Scot, steeped in the Scots tradition, with a passionate, almost mystical, vision of what a university should be, and a grim determination to create one in Liverpool. And Muir was Mackay's disciple. If vision alone were enough to create a university, Mackay could have done it. But before a university can be born, there has to be a midwife as well as a father. To be midwife was the essential part Haldane played; it was a part none of his critics could have played. The prospect of Mackay patiently negotiating with Fitzroy and the privy council would – from all accounts of Mackay's personality – have been ludicrous. On some details Haldane's recollections were at fault and in his enthusiasm for the new pattern of civic universities, Haldane did tend to overlook the fact that other people, too, were enthusiastic. These are fair targets for criticism. But his critics overlooked (or were ignorant of) the formidable difficulty of turning airy aspirations into the unexciting legalese of charters and statutes. No one can say that without Haldane it could not have been done. But it is pretty clear that without Haldane it would not have been done so quickly, so smoothly, and so wisely. Rhetoric may conceive an idea: it takes negotiation to deliver it.

On one detail Haldane's recollection was seriously at fault. In retrospect, proud of the part he had played in creating the civic universities, he wrote that after the Victoria University was reconstituted 'further new universities were set up with all possible speed. Besides Liverpool, Manchester, and Leeds, Birmingham, Bristol, and Sheffield received Charters.' In fact, the University of Birmingham received its charter three years before all this happened, in 1900, and its political midwife was Chamberlain.

Encounters between the two midwives led to some illuminating exchanges. In the summer of 1902 Haldane sent Chamberlain a copy of his essays, *Education and empire*. Chamberlain replied: 'I think that we agree in attaching chief importance now to the higher education.' Haldane, fresh from his success in launching the scheme for a London Charlottenburg now wanted Charlottenburgs to be attached to some of the regional universities.

> It seems to me [he wrote] that what would appeal most really to the public would be the proposition to add to the local Universities thoroughly equipped organisations for the development of the application of science to commerce and especially industry. This we might put forward as an entire policy. . . . We could point to a start made in London, & propose a second start for the Centre of England, to be localised in Birmingham University . . . . This once made a real & living institution the rest of the University would tend to grow, & it would be easier to get endowments for it. At least this is what I think as regards London & probably the same thing is true of Birmingham. The only effective way of getting the money is by private appeals to very rich men. I think that under your auspices I could manage something of this kind with regard to Birmingham, & I should be prepared most willingly to do my best . . . . Of course a thoroughly practical plan of the institution would have to be elaborated, with the special character of Midland industries in view. The Birmingham Charlottenburg should have its own special characteristics. So at least it strikes my mind.

This letter elicited a merited snub from Chamberlain: 'I think you can hardly be aware of any of the details of the Birmingham scheme which is much more advanced than you appear to suppose. We have laid out plans for a technical University, the buildings of which will cost a million when fully realised.' Later, when Chamberlain gave a speech at Leeds in 1903, he said: 'I heartily rejoice that Mr Haldane – by no means the first in the field, but still welcome, however

late – (laughter) – should lend his influence and advocacy to the formation of Charlottenburg schools all over the country.' But at this
stage Haldane and Chamberlain had fallen out over another matter,
namely Chamberlain's enthusiasm for empire preference to encourage
trade. Haldane regarded this policy as disastrous. His remedy for the
ever increasing competition from abroad was not the imposition of
imperial preference, but technological education in Britain, to improve
the efficiency of British industry. However, as we record later in this
chapter, Haldane was to become partner with Chamberlain's son a
couple of years later, in 1905, when they were pressing for systematic
grants to the new civic universities.

A committee of the privy council had set a pattern for higher
education to which even the most recent universities in Britain
conform. It is surprising how little publicity the episode received.
Sidney Webb described (in an article in the *Cornhill* in April 1903)
how in the middle of February 'a few of the London newspapers
reported, briefly and obscurely enough, an official decision of no small
moment to the future of English education. The other newspapers
did not notice it at all and public opinion is still unaware that a decisive
step in national policy has been taken. The decision was that of a
special committee of the Privy Council. . . .' Taken in conjunction
with the reorganisation of the University of London, the creation of
the University of Birmingham, and the foundation of university
colleges at Reading and Southampton, 'the simultaneous approval
of the creation of three new universities in the northern counties
may fairly be said to mark an epoch. We are actually engaged, on
no small scale, in the business of making universities. We are evidently
going, during the next few years, to endow each part of England with
its own local university.'

Haldane noted the same indifference.

'It has always seemed to me that this decision of the Government as
advised by the Privy Council in 1903 was a step of the first importance
in the history of higher education. Little notice was, however, taken of
it by the public or by writers about English education. The thick
printed volumes containing the documents and the evidence repose
undisturbed in the library of the Judicial Office in Downing
Street.'

And again, in an article years afterwards:

'this question was brought to trial by the State before a very high tribunal, and a firm decision was given in favour of the principle. It is remarkable, as showing how slight has been the public interest in education, that the newspapers hardly noticed and did not report the proceedings* which took place before the Special Committee of the Privy Council which conducted a semi-judicial inquiry into the subject in the end of 1902.'

Our portrait of Haldane at the turn of the century emerges from the causes he espoused: a teaching university in London, English Charlottenburgs, autonomous civic universities in four northern cities. But there was one cause which he declined to support, namely pressure for massive financial backing from the taxpayer. He was on record in Hansard (20 June 1889) as saying: 'nor do I think we are in great need of money in the Scotch Universities.' In 1898 he refused to support a plea that the University of London should be state-supported, as Strasbourg University was. In December 1895, December 1901 and February 1904, deputations waited on the chancellor of the exchequer to press for additional grants for higher education. Haldane did not take part in any of these deputations. And when Sir Norman Lockyer, addressing the British Association in 1903, declared that £24,000,000 was needed to bring British universities to the level of those in America and Germany, this sensational suggestion elicited no response whatever from Haldane.

It was not that Haldane disapproved of state aid to universities; indeed on appropriate occasions he advocated it. So we must seek other reasons for his lukewarmness. One reason is that he understood, as some of his naive contemporaries failed to understand, how a too willing generosity from the state can promote parsimony from private donors. Moreover his whole strategy for higher education rested on the belief that where your treasure is, there your heart is also: the local community which helped to finance its civic university would take pride in it and cherish it. '. . . I know of no better way', he said, 'of endowing and supporting a great seat of learning than through the munificence and liberality of the citizens of a great city. . . .' And on another occasion:

> That the State ought to do more than it does in the way of endowment, I agree . . . . But I am not sure that I wish to see the burden transferred to the State in the wholesale fashion that is sometimes

---

* The proceedings were in fact reported in *The Times*, but without comment.

suggested. . . . Probably nothing conduces more to national efficiency than frugality in the use of national resources. The private donor should be encouraged and not left to expend his generosity in regions which do not concern the State directly. In writing this, I do not mean that the Government ought not to spend public money generously upon the Universities. I mean that it should not be spent unless and until a case for the necessity of such expenditure has been clearly made out.

Even over state support for the University of London, after its re-organisation in 1898, Haldane was strangely cautious. Following a deputation from the University of London to the treasury on 13 December 1900, the permanent secretary drew up proposals for a grant-in-aid. The chancellor of the exchequer (Hicks Beach) commented on the proposals:

I put this before the Lord President, who confidentially consulted Mr Haldane. The latter considers that your figures as to the help now given to the University are substantially accurate – and thinks that any Government help now to be given should be doled out in the most guarded & measured way: he does not wish those who now direct the Senate to be entrusted with more than you have suggested, but deprecates any announcement that the amount can never be exceeded.

Another reason for this muting of the financial consequences of his great schemes for the expansion of universities may have been purely political, a deliberate ploy on Haldane's part, so that he could retain the confidence of those in authority. It is significant that the chancellor's comment went on to say: 'The Lord President attaches much import-ance to Mr Haldane's opinion, with which he generally concurs. . . .' Finally, we must not exclude an ideological reason: the disciple of Green and Adam Smith would naturally not wish to allow educational institutions to become parasitic upon a central government.

At any rate, Haldane's views about state support for universities began to change soon after the turn of the century. In 1902 while still busy over Liverpool, he wrote to Chamberlain suggesting: 'I should like also to see a lump sum grant to each University which would raise locally as much more – say of £50,000 to be applied in strengthening the scientific & economic sides.' And Haldane had no misgivings about tapping rich men to support higher education.

'As you know, we have made a good start in London – where I am glad to say I now see my way to £330,000 out of £600,000 which we want at once. London ought to be made the Educational Capital of the Empire.' Despite their disagreement over other matters, Haldane and Chamberlain were eager to act as partners over higher education. 'There is one subject', Chamberlain wrote to Haldane, 'on which I fancy that you and I are nearer together than other men are on anything – I mean *Highest* Education.' But co-operation was to be with the son rather than the father. It was Austen Chamberlain, as chancellor of the exchequer, who invited Haldane in March 1904 to undertake a challenging task: to become chairman of a treasury committee to look into the distribution of state grants to university colleges in England.

Parliament had made its first grant-in-aid to the English university colleges in 1889. The annual sum to be distributed between them was £15,000. By 1903 it had risen to £27,000. In February 1904 a deputation from the university colleges waited on Austen Chamberlain to press for an increase. His response was to propose a doubling of the grant in 1904–5, with a possible further increase to £100,000 in 1905–6. Up to 1904 allocations were made by an *ad hoc* committee on a simple principle: they were roughly proportional to the annual cash income from other sources to the colleges, for work in arts and science of university standard, subject to a report on efficiency; no grant (save the one to Manchester) could exceed £3000 or one quarter of the local income; and colleges whose income was less than £4000 per annum were not eligible for grant.

Chamberlain coupled his proposal for a larger grant with a decision to set up a small independent committee to advise him on its apportionment. 'I shall endeavour', he told the deputation from the university colleges, 'to get gentlemen whose competence is recognised by all of you.' Haldane was to be chairman. His colleagues were Mowatt, Woods (formerly president of Trinity College, Oxford), and Cripps (an MP, and hardly perhaps a welcome choice for Haldane, because he had been leading counsel for the Yorkshire college against Liverpool in the famous privy council hearing). The secretary was a treasury man, Higgs. Continuity with past practice was assured because Woods had served on the quinquennial inspection committee in 1901–2 and Higgs had been secretary of that committee. The committee's terms of reference were to report how state aid to university teaching could be most effectively organised and applied. Their discretion was subject to three conditions: that assistance be given only for instruction affording education of university standard in great centres of population; that assistance be given with the object of stimulating local benevolence; that existing requirements of a minimum local income to qualify for grants be maintained. There were obvious defects in the existing system. For one thing, there was no continuity. Since 1889 no fewer than five *ad hoc* committees had been appointed to distribute the grant; struggling and needy but promising institutions were excluded from grants; the subjects qualifying for grant were limited to arts and science; the system of giving grants was too mechanical, giving no consideration to special areas of weakness in the colleges.

In eleven months the committee produced three reports. Only the third of these, issued on 23 February 1905, raised points of substance. Beneath the surface of the committee's work Haldane took care to keep up a running informal exchange of notes with Chamberlain (preserved in treasury records) so that Chamberlain could be well informed about the committee's intentions (and be softened up about them) in advance of publication. Some softening up was evidently necessary, for in December 1904 Chamberlain was expressing disquiet about the committee's intentions. Their exchange of letters is a revealing example of an early dispute about *dirigisme* attached to state grants to universities.

I have been so busily engaged with my Constituents [wrote Chamberlain on 21 December 1904] since I saw you on the subject of Grants to University Colleges that I have had little time to reflect upon the suggestions which you made. I confess, however, that the more I think of them the more difficulties do they present to my mind.... I cannot help fearing that the line which the Committee contemplate taking will be met with very serious criticism from the Colleges interested.... Your idea, as I understand it, is, that, after making a small increase to the semi-permanent Grants now given, the balance of the £100,000 available should be preserved for distribution from year to year by a Committee to be appointed by the Treasury according to their views of the urgency of the cases presented to them by different Colleges. I think this would tend to an interference with the independence of the Colleges which would be regrettable....

Haldane replied on the very same day, with a masterly defence of his proposals:

> I have your letter, & were I not compelled to leave town tomorrow for some days I should much prefer to ask you to let me come to see you to writing. The questions you raise have been under the close consideration of some of us for years past. . . . I quite agree that if you are dealing with a modern & thoroughly enlightened University College you may leave it to work out its own destiny. This is open under our recommendations. What we demur to is a stereotyped scheme applicable to all Colleges without discrimination . . . to distribute without laying down lines such as we indicate is to perpetuate what already exists to far too great an extent. . . . I would not write confidently had I not realised from personal observation both in England & Scotland the mischief of stagnation which the existing system has left to grow up unchecked. . . . If the Governing bodies only realised how little we contemplate interfering with the liberty of those that are efficient they would not question what we propose. But alas, they are not all efficient.

Haldane offered to call on Chamberlain early in January 1905 to discuss all this before the report was drafted. There is no record of their meeting but clearly Haldane's views prevailed, because they survived to inspire the final report.

This report shows unmistakable signs of its chairman's pen. (One wonders whether Haldane, like some other energetic chairmen of committees, left the secretary with little else to do but to keep records and arrange meetings.) For Haldane, the operation was one more stage in his master plan for an integrated educational system. The committee (so ran the report) considered that they should aim 'at devising such a scheme for the application of the new annual grant as may form a step in a policy for the development of the educational efficiency of the University Colleges'.

The main recommendations of the committee were:

(i) The grants should be allocated partly according to the existing mechanical principle of 'payment by results' (i.e. in proportion to the colleges' incomes from other sources) and partly by a system of earmarked grants to remedy defects in three special areas: post-graduate research; books and equipment; salaries and superannuation.

(ii) Following the example of the Carnegie Trust for Scottish universities, the committee proposed that recipients of the grant should have direct access to an 'impartial authority', which they spelt out as a committee comprising representatives of the treasury and suitably qualified academics and 'possibly' the board of education. This committee, unlike its *ad hoc* forerunners, might also be the body which visited and inspected the colleges. Also, unlike its forerunners, the committee itself would receive the money hitherto sent direct to the colleges from the treasury and would distribute this and would submit an annual report to the treasury to be laid before parliament. Here was the genesis of the present University Grants Committee.

(iii) Consideration should be given (the wording is tentative: here was Haldane being careful not to fetter the discretion of the proposed committee) to enlarging the categories of work qualifying for grant, from the present restricted areas of arts and sciences, to include law, medicine, engineering and architecture.

These proposals, tame as they seem today, were considered to be too radical to be adopted by simple administrative action. Chamberlain presented them to his cabinet with the following comment:

This Committee [the Haldane committee] has now presented three Reports. . . . The third Report is a much more important document, since it proposes not only new conditions of distribution for the future but also the establishment of a permanent Committee to advise the Treasury on the subject. . . . The Report is a very valuable document, as was to be expected from the wide knowledge of the gentlemen who signed it and from the attention they have given to the subject for many years. I have directed that it shall be laid before both Houses and communicated to the Colleges concerned, so that we may have the benefit of the observations and criticisms of all those who are interested in University education before we finally decide on our course of action.

We do not know what the cabinet thought about the report. But the views of the colleges are well documented in the treasury records. On the whole the report was welcomed by academics. They liked the idea of a permanent committee to administer the grants, though there was a little nervousness as to whether this might not lead to 'irksome, and even injurious' government influence; and they commended the proposal that grants should be settled for five year periods and not annually. The reception was sufficiently encouraging for Murray of the treasury to suggest a course of action which was accepted without modification by Chamberlain, and after approval by Balfour, formed the basis for a treasury minute of 18 July 1905. By the terms of this minute the treasury readily accepted the proposal for a permanent committee which they undertook to 'endeavour . . . to constitute' in the following autumn; agreed to the double principle of allocation, although with some ninety per cent of the total grant being assigned on the existing basis for a period of not less than five years; and agreed that the balance of the grant should be reserved for books and equipment, post-graduate awards, and superannuation. But the treasury did not consider it prudent to put post-graduate students in direct relation with the proposed committee (this was a function of the department of scientific and industrial research twenty years later); also the treasury felt unable to sanction a special grant for supplementing teachers' salaries; and they insisted on strict adherence to a minimum local income before a college could qualify for treasury aid.

The treasury reason for turning down any supplementation of salaries was a frankly selfish one. Murray's memorandum on this point was: 'A very considerable rise in all these salaries is going on, as we find whenever anybody of the kind is wanted for a public Department; and I do not see any reason for making special efforts to raise the market against ourselves.' Against which Chamberlain commented: 'I entirely agree.'

Haldane's reaction to this emasculation of the committee's report is not known. It may well have contributed to the little bursts of criticism against the treasury which punctuated some of his speeches in the house of lords years later. The treasury, he said, speaking in 1915, 'looks at things in a penny wise and pound impotent fashion'. And again, in 1918: '. . . nothing is more likely to stultify and reduce to folly what we are endeavouring to do in the Bill than to introduce the Treasury as an expert in educational matters.' In the event, therefore, Haldane's committee made little immediate impact on the grant system, either by way of widening the discretion of the grant-giving committee (for the principle of earmarking had been reduced to a shadow of the original proposal mooted to Chamberlain toward the end of 1904) or by tack-

ling the major historical anomalies. But it did make an essential contribution in proposing a standing committee to deal with the grants in a
new way. Chamberlain did not in fact keep to the intention of appointing this committee in the autumn of 1905; it was left to the incoming
Liberal government, with assistance from Haldane himself in his ministerial capacity, to carry out the main proposal of the committee.

Intrigue, conspiracy, subterranean machinations: these were the
epithets which Haldane's enemies applied to his methods. If the words
are detached from their sinister implications they are fair comment.
Behind every tactical success in educational policy – for the University
of London, the consortium of colleges in South Kensington, the
northern universities, the apparatus for state support of higher education – lay not only Haldane's overt efforts, but also carefully contrived
dinner parties, confidential notes to ministers, a word in the ear of
The Times editorial staff, an evening hatching propaganda with the
Webbs, a critically important house guest at Cloan. If a portrait of
Haldane is to do justice to him, his motives for employing these
devious manoeuvres must be examined.

That personal ambition was not the motive is clear from an important episode which occurred in 1902. The days of the Conservative
government were numbered. The Opposition had hopes of a victory,
with cabinet office for their leading personalities. Some Liberals were
already dubious about Haldane's loyalty to the Liberal cause: on
educational issues he had worked closely with Conservative ministers
– Balfour, Devonshire, Hicks Beach, Chamberlain – and they trusted
him. The house of commons assumed that on issues of education
Haldane would be stubbornly bipartisan. After the episode in 1902
Haldane described himself as a 'pariah', a speech he had made in
parliament 'to which he entirely adhered' having 'excluded him from
the Tabernacle'. It came about in the following way.

In March 1902 the Conservative government introduced a bill
intended to lay the foundation of a national system of education. In
essence it was to abolish the school boards and to bring the board
schools, the voluntary schools, and further education, under the
authority of county or county borough councils. The bill roused
bitter hostility among dissenters, and largely on this account it was
opposed by a majority of Liberal MPs.

For Haldane the bill did not go far enough. He wanted education to
be reorganised under local control, but in localities much larger (and

more sophisticated) than county councils. His vision was of an England
divided into educational provinces, each presided over by a council
which would include experts on education, and under the 'permeating
influence' (an expression he was constantly using at that time) of the
local university. But the bill was a step in the right direction and
Haldane – always conscious that in politics half a loaf is better than no
bread – gave it strong, though critical, support at the first and second
reading, in defiance of Liberal opinion. His two speeches, coming
from a man so obviously disinterested in the party-political consequences
of what he was saying, created a great impression. Despite its imper-
fections, he said, the bill presented a measure by which 'a real and
substantial advance may be made in the only direction in which education could progress.' His ideal was that education should be treated
as an organic whole 'in which you would have primary, secondary
and tertiary education . . . linked together and permeated from the
top with the intention of the university and not the spirit of the church.'
Again, a glimpse of the grand regional plan: in Birmingham, he said,
the university authorities had entered into an arrangement with the
adjoining counties of Worcestershire and Staffordshire; in the same
way Liverpool might cover one half of Lancashire and Manchester
might cover the other half, 'and so on through the entire country.'

This idealistic vision threatened the denominational schools and
many other vested interests. Lloyd George, vehemently defending the
interests of the non-conformists, attacked Haldane: 'You cannot base
any good system of education on an injustice to a large section of the
community. . . . Politically speaking, my hon. friend seems always
to be above the snow-line . . . . Let him descend from the region of
eternal snow and come down to bare facts . . . .' (a reproach which, on
a later occasion, drew from Haldane the riposte that the snow-line
was 'a place from which a clear and wide prospect is sometimes
to be had . . .'). Even the gentle Grey demurred: 'I venture to say that
anyone who knows the penetrating zeal, the single-mindedness, the
great knowledge, the hard work spent on education by my hon. and
learned friend will differ from any course he takes on an educational
matter with the greatest regret. . . .'

On 8 May 1902 the bill passed its second reading with a substantial
government majority. But it was not yet safely on the statute book,
and Haldane was anxious about the opposition to it. He turned, as he
had on previous occasions, to the media – such as they were then –
which might influence public opinion. On the day before the passage

of the second reading, at Birmingham, he addressed the University on
'Our system of education' and subtly introduced *his* desired system:
provincial councils, and the provincial university closely linked with
the system administered by local authorities within its boundaries.
In July he was with the Webbs conspiring with Sidney to create a
literary 'demo': a symposium on the education bill to appear in the
next issue of the *Nineteenth Century*, to strengthen the hand of the
Conservatives. The symposium duly appeared in the October issue.
There were further speeches, well reported in the daily press. Of a
speech in North Berwick, *The Times* reported on 1 October: 'In
regard to the powers of the Bill, he favoured the creation of larger
areas and the policy of increasing the powers and responsibilities of
municipal bodies. The system of devolution proposed by the Bill
struck him as a step in the right direction.'

Two months later the bill cleared its final hurdles and reached the
statute book on 20 December 1902. But this was not the end of the
matter. The bill covered England and Wales but excluded London.
Soon after its first introduction to parliament it became an open secret
that a strong section of the cabinet wanted the education authority
for London to be a joint committee of borough councils (almost
certain to lack expertise in educational matters) instead of the London
County Council. This, for Sidney Webb, who had achieved so much
for London education through the technical education board, was a
threat to the ark of the covenant. Haldane was drawn in to avert what
seemed to Beatrice Webb 'a disaster of the first magnitude'. The partnership agreed upon an intense conspiracy. Even before the Education
(London) bill (1903) appeared, the campaign against it was launched.
On 20 July 1902 Haldane lunched with the Webbs; at the lunch
Sidney was deputed to write a memorandum on the educational issues
involved in London and Haldane undertook to convey it through
Hugh Cecil to Balfour. The memorandum, running to fifty-five
pages, was soon prepared. The copy preserved in the *Passfield papers*
bears this pencilled note in Sidney's hand: 'Comments on the Education
Bill for London projected by the Conservative Gov during 1902 – used
to convince Conservatives, Churchmen & Educationalists in the
autumn of 1902.'

The contents of this document belong to educational history and
are not germane to our portrait; except for one point made by Webb
which reveals how closely his ideas and Haldane's coincided. An
authority formed out of the borough councils, Webb wrote,

would have little sympathy with Higher Education, and would
certainly be disinclined to do anything for the development of a
Teaching University for the Metropolis . . . experience shows that
all inexperienced administrators of education tend to begin by
exaggerating the importance of the schooling given to the mass,
and by undervaluing the training of the small minority who possess
superior ability. . . . To supersede the experienced members of the
School Board and Technical Education Board . . . by raw recruits
from the Borough Councils . . . would be as regards all forms of
higher education, to put back the clock by many years.

Haldane duly conveyed the memorandum to Hugh Cecil who acknowledged it (from Lucerne) on 29 September, saying that on his
return to London he would have it copied. And he went on, 'I propose
to send it to Arthur Balfour, Walter Long, Anson, & Londonderry,
also to Whitmore & Freddy Smith. I shall say that it comes from you
but emanates ultimately from a Progressive source. . . . I have long
been in favour of the LCC having the control of London Education.'
Throughout the autumn and winter of 1902–3 the conspirators
continued to be busy. On 2 November Haldane arranged for the
Webbs to meet the prime minister (Balfour) at a small dinner party.
Two weeks later the dinner party was held, at which Beatrice 'seized
every opportunity to insinuate [into Balfour] sound doctrine and
information as to the position of London education.' At the beginning
of January Haldane wrote to Beatrice from Cloan to say that 'things
about London are still in the balance.' Balfour had been warned that
he would break up the Unionist party in London if he favoured the
LCC. 'I hope', added Haldane, 'Sidney has collared the Daily Mail.
This is important.' A few days later, in a 'strictly secret' letter to Sidney,
Haldane wrote, 'I felt so anxious about London that I went & saw
Arthur Balfour on the subject. I put the case as strongly as was compatible with the moderation that was necessary.' During January 1903
Haldane brought *The Times* 'down on our side'. Sidney visited the
Daily Mail offices nightly for a week to edit the educational material,
and had interviews with *The Times*, *Telegraph*, and *Morning Post*.
Haldane peppered Sidney with notes: on 16 February, that Mowatt
had had a 'very satisfactory talk about the Bill' with the chancellor
of the exchequer, and Haldane himself an equally satisfactory talk
with the secretary of state for India. Two days later: 'Don't relax
any effort. Great pressure is being put on the Government by the

London MPs or some of them. We will do all that can be done in the House. . . .' Again two days later: 'I hear that the London Members are coming round to the LCC idea. Hart Dyke, who is working for us, told me that Hayes Fisher had informed him that three quarters of the London Unionist members were *now* for the Bill on LCC lines. I am keeping our people quiet. . . .'

In March there was a set-back. On account of two by-elections the government had it in mind to postpone the bill altogether. This would not have suited the conspirators. Sidney, at Haldane's request, called on the prime minister's private secretary and on the Conservative Whip, to urge them to introduce the bill. In the event it was introduced by Anson on 3 April 1903. On the face of it, the bill was a defeat for Haldane and the Webbs: a compromise, with thirty-six LCC members, thirty-one borough council members, and twenty-five co-opted members. Haldane, writing from Ilmenau in Germany, was disappointed and declared he would vote against the bill unless it was remodelled. On 28 April, at the second reading of the bill, Haldane criticised it in a major speech, with (for him) unusual flights of rhetoric:

> London is the Metropolis of the Empire . . . the greatest city in the world . . . the place in this country to which we ought to be able to look for educational light and leading. . . . I, for one, shall never be satisfied until I see students from the distant parts of the Empire flocking to the universities in this country, and especially in London, for that higher education, that post-graduate training, in search of which they now go to the Continent or the United States. It is little short of a scandal that we should be able to provide so little education of that rank in the great Empire of which London is the Metropolis.

To entrust this high duty to borough councillors!

But there was room for compromise without loss of face. Provided the LCC could control co-option, there could be a majority (despite the borough councillors) on the side of the angels, and (more important) on the side of Haldane and the Webbs. So Haldane emphasised the necessity of getting really enlightened persons among the twenty-five to be co-opted. Haldane voted against the bill, but his 'brilliant suggestions' were noted by the bill's supporters. Following some amendments in committee the bill was passed in the early summer of 1903 in (Beatrice Webb reflected) 'almost exactly the shape Sidney would have given to it'. The conspirators had won.

5 At the Cabinet Table

In November 1905, nine years after Haldane had been invited by the students of Edinburgh to stand for the office of lord rector and had lost the election, he was invited again. For a second time the student magazine contained lyrical accounts of his eminence and virtues: 'On the question of education, Mr Haldane, as an expert, has no rival in the kingdom.' 'The best product of our Alma Mater . . . "Brain of the Empire".' This time he was elected (though not solely on his own reputation: he swept in also on the wave of the incoming tide of Liberalism). He certainly lived up to specification, for the student magazine of January 1907, commenting on his year of office, called him 'the most popular Lord Rector of modern times'. His speech at the dinner to commemorate the opening of the Union shows how cleverly he could match himself to his audience. In *his* day as a student, he told them, they were very much under the professors. When the students left the lecture rooms they went on thinking about the lectures and the professors until they came back to the lecture room. Now, he said, all that was changed (which drew laughter and applause). Students now, after giving an ungrudging but strictly limited meed of admiration to their professors, betook themselves to the other side of university life. The university was a state of which the student was a citizen. No wonder he was popular at Edinburgh and could always command a good student audience there.

A month after the rectorial election there came a far more important Liberal victory. In December, after nine years in opposition, the Liberal party was back in power. Haldane, of course, had anticipated the victory for some time. Already in 1901 he was urging Sidney Webb to seek a place in parliament. He wrote about it to Beatrice: 'What a lot of work he could do at the L[ocal] G[overnment] Board or in the Education Office! . . . Think over this seriously please.' For himself, even at that time, he contemplated the lord chancellorship.

The ensuing story of appointments to the new Liberal government is well known. Campbell-Bannerman became prime minister and refused to go to the house of lords to leave Asquith to lead in the commons. Haldane did not become lord chancellor. He was offered the attorney-generalship or the office of home secretary. He declined both. In his autobiography he explains why he did not want to be a law officer:

I had had the best that the Bar itself could give me. But that was not the main reason for rejecting anything short of office in the Cabinet. My whole soul had been for years in the effort to bring about reform in higher education and in other departments of administration. To accept the Attorney-Generalship was to abandon influence which I had possessed even under the outgoing Unionist Government.

He became secretary of state for war, and, according to Beatrice Webb, was 'in a state of exuberant delight over his new task'. This was the decade of Haldane's great political ascendancy, when he created his place in history as a war minister and lord chancellor. But if these achievements were set aside, and if his work over these years were to be measured by nothing more than his 'spare time' activities in education, his place in history would still be distinguished. He was now in the full tide of his career, only in his fiftieth year, affluent (he said himself that he had to give up £15,000 to £20,000 a year at the bar in order to take office), influential, famous. Contemporaries often recalled his heavy build and massive head, contrasting with a cat-like tread and a thin piping voice. They remembered his invariably gentle, almost suave manner. Amery (perhaps a hostile critic) said 'there was something about him of the old-fashioned family butler.' But there was no doubt that he had a presence; Osbert Sitwell saw him, some years later: 'How well I can see him now, in my mind's eye, with his head bent, tortoise-like, a little to one side, entering the room with the air of a whole procession.' His time was divided between his comfortable house in Queen Anne's Gate and his estate at Cloan: a life-style, as Beatrice Webb observed, very remote from his concern for democratic institutions! His official preoccupation was the war office; but if he were seen – as he often was – walking across St James's Park with Fitzroy of the privy council, it could be assumed pretty reliably that they were discussing the future of the University College in Bristol, or the problems of higher education in London, or the pattern of state endowment of universities in Britain. It is only toward the middle of this phase of his career, in 1909, that his astonishing energy began to be eroded by illness. Nature, as he wrote, 'pulled me up rather suddenly' as a result of all night sittings in parliament and his work at the war office. His eyesight gave him trouble and it was found that he had diabetes, a disease which in pre-insulin days could be controlled only by an austere and troublesome diet. But the catalogue of his activities over these years showed no sign of thinning out. He was for ever pushing some imaginative educational plan and he used every academic engagement he could as a platform for propaganda.

There was no shortage of such engagements. Beside discharging the duties of the rectorship of Edinburgh University Haldane opened university buildings in Liverpool and Sheffield, and he received honorary degrees from Oxford, Cambridge, Manchester, Birmingham, Sheffield and Durham. Whenever he got the opportunity he expounded his philosophy of education. Those who aspired to found new university colleges came to regard Haldane as having a sort of academic Midas touch in negotiation: had he not negotiated reform in the University of London, the establishment of the Imperial College, and the creation of the idea of civic universities out of the federal Victoria University? We get a glimpse of the regard in which he was held from a letter written in 1913, when Haldane had become lord chancellor, by the newly appointed principal of Hartley College, Southampton, to Selby-Bigge, permanent secretary of the board of education:

> When I had the pleasure of sitting next to you at the Clothworkers' Dinner . . . your description of Lord Haldane's zeal for the New University movement which he is championing raised in my mind the reflection that he might possibly like to be asked to lay the Foundation Stone of the New Buildings for this College. Southampton is the centre of a barren area. It is the proper place for the location of a University if Lord Haldane's scheme is to be complete. Will you kindly advise me as to whether my proposal to Lord Haldane would be likely to receive favourable consideration.

Haldane was duly approached by Selby-Bigge, and was obliged to return one of his rare refusals, characteristic in its courtesy:

> I am reluctantly forced to say that there is no chance of my being able to lay the foundations of Hartley College Buildings this summer. The preparation of the address I have to deliver on the

1st September, and of two other addresses, coming on top of much other work, has driven me to annex every possible evening.

Nevertheless, a year later, Haldane was writing to Selby-Bigge: 'On Saturday, 20th, I go to Southampton to open the new Hartley College buildings. Could you get someone to send me some pabulum.' This was served up as 'The value of University training to democracy', in which he developed the theme – a novel one at that time – of the social function of a university.

Haldane's development of this theme at Southampton was interrupted by the war, which soon brought disaster to his own political career. But – to go back to the beginning of his tenure of cabinet office – one of his concerns outside the war office remained the promotion of a regional organisation of education.

There were now four northern universities, co-operating, through the Northern Universities joint matriculation board, to set a common examination for schools in the region. The examination had two functions: it gave schools in the region a scale against which to measure their achievement, and it guaranteed a minimum uniform standard for admission to the participating universities. This was a prototype of what some people were calling 'Haldane's scheme'. His next objective was to create a similar educational alliance in the south-west of England. University colleges (taking external London degrees) had been started in Reading and Southampton in 1902 and there had been a university college at Bristol since 1876. Westward of that there was an academic vacuum. Already in 1901, speaking at Liverpool, Haldane was asking why Bristol should not become an academic centre for the south-west of England. And he took up the same theme in a stirring address at the annual dinner of the University College Colston Society in Bristol in 1902. He was at first inclined to throw out the suggestion that Bristol, Reading and Southampton might affiliate into some sort of federal university. Enthusiasts in Bristol naturally wanted something much more individual than that. We have a charming glimpse of how one of them, M. W. Travers, a young science professor there, made his contribution to the campaign. It is to be found in an unpublished fragment of his autobiography. The date is January 1905.

At about 3 pm I was at Mr Haldane's chambers in New Court, Lincoln's Inn. I had sent him an abstract of my report to the College Senate and Council. . . . He told me that, as his party was not in office, he would not be directly concerned in any negotiations between the College and the Government, but as no party matter was involved, his advice would certainly be asked before any decision was taken. However, he could speak authoritatively as to the conditions which must be fulfilled before a Charter would be granted.

Speaking of the address in which he had recommended Bristol to consider affiliation with Southampton and Reading to form a University of the three University Colleges he said, – 'The day of composite Universities has gone by'. . . . Then speaking of my criticism of the somewhat complex constitution of modern universities he insisted that the Court could perform a real function in keeping the University in touch with a wide public. . . . He suggested that I should see Mr Walter Long . . . Sir Michael Hicks-Beach . . . and the Duke of Beaufort, and get them to form a committee external to both bodies,* and consisting mainly of Conservatives (this was interesting as coming from a Liberal statesman), to approach the two bodies, and to ask them to accept the principle of co-operation in the formation of a University.

Haldane invited Travers to keep in touch to report progress, although Travers himself had misgivings that his action 'might meet with more than criticism from high authority' because he was not acting on behalf of the College council at all. However he did keep in touch with Haldane and at the Royal Society soirée in June he met Haldane who said he 'was pleased with what we were doing'.

By December 1905 Haldane was in a key position to influence aspirations like these, for on 11 December a new standing committee of the privy council was set up to deal with matters concerning higher education which fell outside the scope of the privy council committees provided for under the Oxford and Cambridge Act of 1877 and the Universities (Scotland) Act of 1889; and Haldane was made a member. This committee was very influential in advising the government until its functions were gradually taken over, first by the treasury committee appointed in 1911 to administer state grants, and ultimately by the University Grants Committee. It is interesting, therefore, to put on record the genesis of the committee and to note the specific mention of Haldane's name in the memorandum. It was a memorandum from Fitzroy to the lord president of the council:

---

* i.e. the governing bodies of both the University College and the Merchant Venturers' Technical College; Haldane was insistent the University must include both.

Petitions for supplementary Charters to University Bodies and in connection with other matters touching the interests of Higher Education are often received and referred by the King in Council to a Committee of the Privy Council: it would be convenient to call into existence a standing Committee to deal with such petitions, when necessary, which with your approval I would propose should be constituted, unless otherwise ordained for any special purpose, as follows – the Lord President, the President of the Board of Education, and Mr Haldane, who I understand would always be glad to give his assistance.

This was the body which in 1908 was asked to consider a petition from the college at Bristol for university status. It was an occasion when Haldane's enthusiasm trapped him into one of his rare misjudgements.

There was no difficulty about a pattern for a charter; the charters recently granted to the four northern universities were perfectly satisfactory models for Bristol. But Fitzroy shared Haldane's desire to organise education by regions, under the *aegis* of regional universities, and to promote this he suggested that the universities of Wales and Birmingham might be approached to see whether they would cooperate with a new university at Bristol to form a joint matriculation board, to do for the west-country what the Northern joint board was doing for Lancashire and Yorkshire. 'It is conceded on all hands', wrote Fitzroy, 'that one of the most important functions of the new type of University is the influence it may exercise on secondary education within the area from which it draws its students, and the cooperation of Universities whose influence is felt over the same area tends to maintain a uniform standard which is of great value.' On 20 November 1908, Fitzroy recorded Haldane's prompt agreement with this proposal; but they had both, surprisingly, left out of account the sentiments of Welshmen, who did not want their university, barely fifteen years old, to become an integral part of the English system.*
It was the president of the board of education, Runciman, briefed by his officials, who saw this point and declared himself 'strongly opposed to the idea of a Joint Matriculation Board such as you suggest'. Fitzroy, with the authority of the lord president, advised Haldane to drop the

---

* By the time he became chairman of the royal commission on the University of Wales, Haldane had come to understand the sentiments of Welshmen over this!

idea and Haldane – never a man to permit his prejudices to prevail over good evidence – wrote: 'I am impressed with what Mr Runciman says. I concur in thinking that we must, at all events for the present, drop the idea of a uniform matriculation test.'

Meanwhile Haldane was acting as *amicus curiae* on behalf of Bristol's petition for a university; never conspicuously, never officially (it was hardly the business of a secretary of state for war), putting in a timely word in Whitehall or over cigars at a carefully contrived dinner party in Queen Anne's Gate. We catch a moment of this in an exchange of letters between J. W. Arrowsmith (a member of the Bristol University College council) and Haldane, over the need to persuade the Bristol Corporation to guarantee an annual subvention to the University. 'Dear Mr Haldane', he wrote on 15 March 1909:

> . . . The question now arises as to the Corporation grant and we want Mr Fitzroy to write a strong letter . . . pointing out that the Charter will be granted when the Privy Council are assured as to the amount which the Corporation are prepared to grant to the University. If only I knew Mr Fitzroy well enough to write him a personal note I would not trouble you: perhaps this may be the last time I shall need to bother you but you have all through been so good to us amidst all your worry I am asking your help so far. . . .

A week later Haldane wrote to Fitzroy, 'Arrowsmith of Bristol writes to me; he is a very good fellow, & I think he is probably right in saying that a letter from you at this juncture would be of importance. Perhaps you would communicate with him appropriately.' Four days later a note went to the Bristol city council from the privy council. The city council granted the proceeds of a penny rate to the aspiring university college, and a charter was granted on 22 May 1909. Three years later Haldane was installed as chancellor; it was at his installation there that he made his moving confession of faith in the function and future of civic universities.

The penny rate from the city of Bristol was more than a material contribution to the University's income; it was a symbol of the civic responsibility which Haldane believed was essential to sustain his system of universities for the people. '. . . I appeal to all of you,' he said at his installation as chancellor of Bristol, 'to workmen and employers, to the man who can just manage to educate his children and to the wealthiest alike, to concern yourselves in a great civic cause . . . . What is requisite

... is that the city should be proud of its University and should feel that it is its own child. ...'

Haldane had chosen his words very deliberately: 'workmen';'the man who can just manage to educate his children'. He was speaking in the wake of grave industrial strife, and, looking to education as the nostrum for social ailments, saw in these new civic universities an insurance for democracy. They would open the doors of Whitehall to working class boys who were clever enough to graduate and to gain entry to the civil service. Labour leaders, he told his audience in Bristol, were quite right in complaining that the prizes of state were far too much reserved for the upper classes. He enlarged on this theme at length earlier in the year, in April, when he gave evidence to the royal commission on the civil service (on which his sister sat as a member). The whole of his evidence is an exalted declaration of faith in the efficacy of education for responsible leadership. (One is reminded of Rashdall's verdict: that the great contribution made by universities in the middle ages was that they put the administration of human affairs in the hands of educated men.) There was a revealing exchange between Haldane and Philip Snowden (also a member of the commission). Snowden asked him:

I take it, it is your view that we cannot devise a thoroughly democratic system of entering into the Civil Service until we have very much widened the education ladder?

To which Haldane replied:

That is exactly my view, and I should like to join hands with you, Mr Snowden, tomorrow in saying that the great mode of access to a democratic system in this country was to put other things aside and to deal with the education system from its foundation.

We have already noticed (p. 74) Haldane's cautious attitude toward parliamentary endowment for higher education. If universities were to flourish they must command the loyalty of the regional communities they served; they should be largely endowed, therefore, by local authorities and local industry. In Liverpool and Bristol, he exhorted the cities to finance their own institutions; this was at the root of the idea of a civic university. But in the decade in which we are now watching him at work it became evident to him that local support would need to be powerfully augmented by the state if his aspirations for a democratic society were to be sustained. One reason for his change of view was his experience as chairman of the royal commission on the University of London; for he saw that University as the centre of learning for an empire, not merely for the London region. So the man who was unenthusiastic in 1903 about Norman Lockyer's inflated appeal for state support to British universities was, by 1914, concerned to secure machinery that would extract maximum support from the treasury. For the disbursement of public money on such a scale as this, it was essential to have machinery in which both the universities and parliament had confidence. The story of the construction of this machinery (the forerunner of the present University Grants Committee) is a veritable Whitehall comedy. The characters on the stage were ministers and officials in the board of education and the treasury. But hovering in the wings, and at times directing the play, was none other than the secretary of state for war.

Before the Conservative government resigned in 1905, Austen Chamberlain as chancellor of the exchequer had undertaken to appoint a standing committee to distribute the treasury grant-in-aid to universities and university colleges, as recommended by Haldane's *ad hoc* committee in 1904–5 (p. 80). But he left office without doing so. No sooner was Haldane in the new government than he assisted Asquith, the new chancellor, to repair this omission. 'I am very glad you have decided as you have done about the Advisory Committee', he wrote from Cloan on 28 December 1905. 'We will make some suggestions as regards names next week.' About six weeks later on 5 February 1906, the treasury announced the appointment of the committee.★ The membership was unexceptionable, the terms of reference were clear; and at first everything ran smoothly. But, in its report published in July 1908, the advisory committee drew attention to the fact that university institutions were receiving parliamentary grants through three departments: the treasury, the board of education, and the board

★ Two of the members, Woods (the chairman) and Sir Francis Mowatt, had served under Haldane on the committee which advised the previous government (p. 76). The new members were W. J. Collins, an MP; H. Jackson, a fellow of Trinity College, Cambridge; and the man who fourteen years later was to become the first chairman of the University Grants Committee: W. S. McCormick. McCormick had worked with Haldane on the Carnegie Trust for Universities in Scotland, and H. Frank Heath, in his biographical note of McCormick in the DNB, confirms that it was Haldane who secured his appointment to the treasury committee in 1906. It was one of the most fruitful appointments Haldane influenced.

of agriculture. Some co-ordination was desirable between these three sources of funds. The committee recommended that all state aid for university education should be brought under the review of a single authority. They suggested that after a transitional arrangement there should be introduced 'a Scheme that would comprise in a single vote the whole aid granted by Parliament to Universities and University Colleges for education of University character and standard.'

This raised the curtain on the comedy. Which department in Whitehall should be responsible for administering this consolidated vote? The advisory committee reported to the treasury. The treasury, in some puzzlement, sought advice from the board of education. They got advice; in sixteen typed folio pages from the incisive pen of Robert Morant, perhaps the most formidable permanent secretary the board ever had. Morant's reply was composed after extensive discussion with his minister, Runciman (just appointed to succeed Birrell), and Runciman (wrote Morant in a covering letter) 'has had a talk with Haldane . . . and tells me that Haldane is in strong agreement'. In brief, Morant's proposal was that the treasury advisory committee (consisting largely of its existing members) should 'for a period of (say) five years' act as an advisory committee to the board of education, and should ultimately be handed over to the board of education. It was a take-over bid.

Morant's letter was despatched to the treasury on 17 December 1908. The minute it provoked from a senior official there (T. L. Heath) was unambiguous: on 14 January 1909 he wrote:

> This is an able letter from the B/Ed, but it is directed too exclusively and obviously to the one main object of getting the control over the £100,000 and its distribution under the B/Ed. . . . I think in fact that the B/Ed as at present administered is not qualified to take up the business without risk of friction . . . . I feel certain that the Board (as at present administered) would try to dictate to the Universities and University Colleges as they are now trying to do to Secondary Schools. . . .

There the matter rested until Sir P. Magnus, on 23 June 1910, asked a question in parliament about the consolidation of state grants to university institutions. Accordingly Runciman returned to the attack, supporting his case (that the board of education should take over responsibility for administering the grants) by saying that English universities, including the University of London, would welcome this arrangement. But the chancellor of the exchequer was Lloyd George, and he was not prepared to hand over the grants or the advisory committee; he played for time by saying he would await the outcome of a deputation from the University of London.

The next move was with Morant. By this time the royal commission on the University of London, under Haldane's chairmanship, had begun its sittings. So Morant proceeded to invoke Haldane's opinion: 'I think [he wrote in his brief for Runciman] that Haldane has quite reached the point of seeing the advisability of Unification of the Grants in this Board. He was much struck that the representative of Oxford University [in parliament] should have plumped for this board.' Armed with Morant's brief, Runciman sought the support of Asquith, who had become prime minister. There was a typically Asquithian response from No. 10 Downing Street: that the prime minister was disposed to think it well to let the question lie for a time 'as it seems to him to be full of diffties & not immediately urgent.'

The wrangle between the treasury and the board of education continued through 1910 and into 1911. Haldane did not appear on the stage at all, but it is clear that he was operating behind the scene. 'It is now being urged', wrote Morant in a warning message to his minister on 5 January 1911,

> by Mr McCormick and Sir Francis Mowatt [two members of the advisory committee] and is being apparently seriously considered by Sir George Murray and Mr Haldane, that the separate sets of Grants should be unified in the Treasury, removing from the Minister of Education responsibilities he at present holds in regard to University Colleges. . . . Is it not time something was done of a definite nature to indicate . . . that the problems they have been coolly discussing and the suggestions they have been working out are matters in the first place for the Minister of Education . . . .

And Morant went on to express his resentment that Mr Haldane should discuss these matters 'with two irresponsible outsiders whilst the Minister of Education is kept entirely in ignorance.' The fact is, concluded Morant, that 'the Treasury is in abysmal ignorance of the present state of affairs [in higher education] and has no conception of the close interrelation both of the work of individual University Colleges with that of Secondary Schools and Technical Institutions, and also of those Colleges with the various functions of this Board.'

Morant's tetchiness over Haldane's attitude was misconceived, for by now it was evident that Haldane's royal commission, and Haldane himself, had come round to the view that the minister of education *was* the proper person to administer state grants to university institutions. At this point Haldane himself briefly passed across the stage. We have the record in a memorandum from Frank Heath, who was in charge of the Universities branch at the board of education, written to Morant's successor a year later:

> . . . Haldane had an important part in [the negotiations] and saw the P.M. about it because he is strongly of opinion that the funds necessary for the support of the modern Universities . . . will never be forthcoming from the State until they form part of the Education budget placed before Parliament for Education. He has said this repeatedly and he strongly supported the transfer as the first step towards getting all the University money into a single pot in the control of the President of the Board.

Following Haldane's intervention with Asquith and a careful sounding of opinion in the university colleges, came the capitulation. 'The Prime Minister', Heath recalled, 'declared that any objections he feared as arising from the Universities were removed, and he informed Mr Runciman that if Mr Lloyd George would consent to the transference, he, the Prime Minister, would agree.' It was left to Runciman to negotiate the transfer direct with Lloyd George, but he was given an unambiguous clearance from Asquith. '. . . speak to him & don't write', ran the message from Murray at the treasury, '. . . and tell him that the Prime Minister is entirely in favour of the Scheme & that the Treasury will be very glad to get rid of the job.'

So Lloyd George was consulted by Runciman, and shown the proposed list of a new advisory committee, in a memorandum entitled 'Unification of University Grants under the Universities Branch of the Board of Education'. Runciman has left a precise record of this consultation (this is significant in view of what followed). Lloyd George imposed various conditions for consenting to the transfer, including an insistence that 'whoever is on the Committee . . . Sir John Rhys *must* be a member of it'. (Rhys was principal of Jesus College, Oxford; a distinguished celtic scholar and a protagonist for education in Wales.)

Runciman agreed and on 17 June 1911 he issued a formal minute appointing a fresh standing committee, this time responsible to the

board of education.* It seemed as though the inter-departmental tussle
was now at an end, and the board of education, with the ready concurrence of the universities and colleges, had won the game. But
Runciman had reckoned without the unpredictability of the celtic
temperament. At a cabinet meeting on 11 August 1911 Lloyd George
pushed a note across the table to Runciman, reading:

> I observe you stated in the Hse the other day that the control of U.
> Grants had passed from the Try to the Board of Education. What
> on earth made you say this? I never even discussed the question with
> you. I must put this right in the Hse on Appropriation Bill. The
> Colleges are furious and Austen [Chamberlain] attacks it. D.Ll-G.

Runciman replied to this note reminding Lloyd George that he had
agreed to the transfer, that the treasury had agreed, and that far from
the colleges being furious, their heads had passed amiable resolutions.
Back came a second note from Lloyd George:

> I never even heard of it. Who did you correspond with? You never
> submitted the proposal to me. Why did you not do so? Austen was
> the first man to mention it to me. I cannot acquiesce in your state-
> ment. The Cabinet never even considered the matter. Was it men-
> tioned at all to the PM? D.Ll-G.

Runciman reminded him of his conversation concerning the committee and Sir John Rhys, to which he assented but said across the
table that that was the committee only. And then Runciman wrote to
him to say that the prime minister had twice fully discussed it, and that
the transfer of the committee was on the record in published official
documents. Lloyd George, wrote Runciman afterwards, 'had nothing
to add to this'.

What provoked this outburst? Simply that Austen Chamberlain had embarrassed Lloyd George on the issue, and there was uneasi-
ness among the Welsh. During September 1911 a formula of compromise was reached between the two ministers: the committee remained
attached to the board of education but the treasury was given a kind of
veto over its decisions and its membership. Morant protested to his

---

* It was, for the first time, exclusively composed of academics: McCormick
as chairman, Professor J. A. Ewing, Dr William Osler, Miss E. Penrose, Professor
Walter Raleigh, Sir John Rhys, and Sir Arthur Rucker; to advise the board of
education as to the distribution of exchequer grants available from the board for
university education in England and Wales.

chief over this compromise but Runciman silenced him, stating that the committee remained a board of education committee, and he anticipated no trouble over reappointments. But there was to be other trouble. Lloyd George would not consent to the vote for the University of Wales being transferred from the treasury. It now looked as though the grant system might be fragmented; the board of education aiding the University of London, the treasury aiding the University of Wales; and one or the other left to aid the remaining university institutions.

Meanwhile there had been changes in the cast on the stage. The querulous Morant had been replaced by the more urbane Selby-Bigge and Runciman had been replaced by J. A. Pease, a Quaker. In January 1912 (three years after the first exchange of correspondence between Morant and the treasury) Pease was being briefed to continue the wrangle and to secure a clean take-over. 'If the treasury', wrote Pease, 'raise any objection the matter will be one for cabinet decision & Haldane's help will then be valuable....' Once more Haldane's virtuosity as negotiator was invoked, not formally at cabinet but in Haldane's preferred milieu: the unrecorded private conversation. Haldane, we are told, 'addressed Lloyd George forcibly on the subject'. We do not know what he said, but at 'the end of the talk Lloyd George said to Haldane that their conversation had completely altered his (George's) attitude on the matter and that he agreed with Haldane that the Grants should be on the Board of Education Votes.' But even Haldane could not predict Lloyd George's wiliness. For despite this change of heart the treasury still wanted to *appear* not to have capitulated. In a frankly disingenuous way (as Selby-Bigge reported in a very confidential note to his minister) the permanent secretary to the treasury (Chalmers) wanted the chancellor of the exchequer to be able to say to Austen Chamberlain that no change whatever had been made in the position, and that he and the treasury retained just as much control over university grants as formerly. But he also wanted the universities and the advisory committee to go on believing that the position of the treasury had changed, and the board of education, on the advice of its own committee, would decide how the sum was distributed.

Following a meeting on 2 February with Lloyd George. Pease recorded a fresh compromise: 'I have agreed to the vote remaining on Treasury & I have arranged with the Chancellor today that my department will be the only one for the Univ. Comtee to deal with.' And

a second face-saver from the treasury embodied the final arrangement, on 21 February 1912:

> ... I am directed by the Lords Commissioners of H.M. Treasury to
> state that, as a result of the further consideration which has been
> given to the question of the Grants for Universities and Colleges,
> Great Britain, My Lords have come to the conclusion that it will be
> better that the actual provision for such grants should continue to
> be made upon that Vote (Class IV, vote 7). It would not be regular
> to make so considerable a change in the form of the estimates
> without consulting the Public Accounts Committee.

By the earlier compromise the 'substance' lay with the treasury and the
'letter' lay with the board of education. Now the compromise was
reversed: the treasury would have formal control of the vote; the
board of education actual control. This is substantially what Haldane
wanted, but a diary entry which Austen Chamberlain made a few days
later reveals Haldane's irrepressible tenacity. He still wanted to secure
the letter as well as the substance. Whilst at Grillion's, Chamberlain
wrote, Haldane had:

> sought me out to talk about the administration of the University
> Grants. He is trying to get them put under the Board of Education
> which he says has now been reorganized and has an admirable
> University branch, through which he urges they would obtain much
> larger grants than they do from the Treasury. Against him, he said,
> Lloyd George quoted me as being strongly opposed to the transfer
> of these grants from the Treasury to the Board of Education. This is
> quite true, for I have always feared that the Board of Education
> would seek to impose their views of what ought to be taught upon
> the Universities and would stereotype the University courses:
> whereas the Treasury, not being in this matter a department of
> specialists, was content merely to ascertain that the work carried on
> was of a University standard and that certain other necessary
> financial conditions were observed.

This passage from Chamberlain's diary is often taken to be the
explanation for the decision taken in 1919 (when he was chancellor of
the exchequer) to put the University Grants Committee under the
treasury and not under the board of education. But in fact Chamberlain
changed his mind and became reconciled to Haldane's view (p. 151).
Safeguarding the autonomy of universities was an ancillary reason,

but not the main one why the UGC was placed under the treasury.

The cares of the war office, the propagation of regional universities, the design of machinery for state aid to higher education: even all these were not enough to fill Haldane's diary. His heaviest educational commitment during this phase of his career was undoubtedly to the University of London. We have already seen him at work there, as far back as 1887, when he was conferring with Balfour over its problems, and we have depicted his vigorous co-conspiracy with Sidney Webb over the University of London Act 1898 and the creation of a London Charlottenburg.

It was in January 1906 that the departmental committee under Haldane had recommended the creation of a great institution for science and technology at South Kensington. But nineteen months passed before the College was created. No one questioned the need for higher technological education in London; the delicate negotiations to secure a site were well in hand; the sources for finance were assured. The delay was due solely to disputes about control. The tidy solution was to integrate the new College completely into the University of London. But this would have meant concessions from the other interested parties: the government (which owned the Royal College of Science), the LCC (with its responsibility for further education in the metropolis), the City and Guilds Institute (which owned part of the property and had pioneered technical education), the 1851 commissioners (who controlled the site), and the several rich men who had promised endowments to the new college. There were strong reasons against integration. The University had only just emerged from the most drastic reform it had ever undergone. There was still dissent within the University between those dedicated to its old function as an external examining board for the Empire, and those striving to re-create it as a teaching university. The University itself was ambivalent about accepting a new and unusual addition which might turn out to be a formidable cuckoo in its academic nest; but which, if refused, might become a rival university. And enthusiasts for the institution were apprehensive that its freedom would be constrained if it were not autonomous. 'Success in the work before the Institution', wrote Ogilvie of the board of education, who had served on the departmental committee, 'may demand action and relations of a kind quite foreign not only to existing University traditions but to any conception of the elasticity permissible within a University. . . .'

There is no doubt that Haldane's departmental committee, in recommending initial autonomy for the College, leading to possible ultimate integration with the University, had papered over the cracks which were bound to appear as soon as anyone began to draft a precise constitution. For months there were meetings and exchanges of memoranda between the board of education and the University. At times it seemed as though the University might modify its constitution in ways which (as Morant put it) would render it more fit to be 'suzerain' of the new Institution. At times it was feared that Haldane (invisible in these negotiations but still actively engaged in them) might 'hand the whole thing over straight to the University'. In fact although Haldane still favoured incorporation, and was determined in the end to get it, he was prepared to compromise for a quick solution. Over all the arguments lay the shadow (or, as some would put it, the hope) of a royal commission to enquire into the constitution of the University of London; and this was used as a justification for delaying any decision at all about the new College. Delay was the one thing Haldane did not want. Once more, he appeared at the critical moment to influence events. We know that in May 1906 a meeting was held in his room at the war office to try to get the various parties to agree. Haldane 'doesn't bark', wrote a civil servant (Sykes) who attended this meeting and reported it to Morant, 'He purrs. . . . But I hope & trust his scratch is being nipped in the bud so to speak.' For nearly nine months negotiations dragged on. But on 13 February 1907, the same civil servant was able to report to Morant that he had met Haldane at dinner; Haldane had said, 'Well, the new President [McKenna had just succeeded Birrell at the Board of Education] has a very simple course open to him . . . to get that Charter, which has been circulated, through as soon as possible.' The very same day McKenna wrote to Haldane as follows: 'On the lines of the Final Report of the Departmental Committee. . . . I can settle the matter at once and the Charter already circulated could be put through promptly. . . . On the merits I think the Report of the Departmental Committee is right, including as it does, a proposal for a Royal Commission to be subsequently appointed. . . .' McKenna straight-way conveyed this decision to the University, adding that the senate should be informed that he would be prepared, 'say 12 months' after the institution at South Kensington had been established, to advise the appointment of a royal commission to consider its amalgamation with the University. 'I am glad', wrote Haldane to Morant, 'of the progress you have made in getting this troublesome matter settled. It is very satisfactory.' Indeed it was; it had all worked out as Haldane wished. In July 1907 a charter was granted to create the Imperial College. In December 1908 the University itself asked for a royal commission to secure the incorporation of the College. The commission was appointed on 24 February 1909, just as Haldane was approaching another turning point in his career. He was within sight of achieving what he wanted as secretary of state for war. Early in May 1908 the Webbs had found him confident of finishing his work at the war office in eighteen months. He was – despite the responsibilities of office – anxious to involve himself in educational problems again. He offered himself as chairman of the royal commission (the evidence for this is in a private and personal note from Morant to Buckle of *The Times* on 16 February 1909). His offer was accepted and he embarked on four years of intensive enquiry which in its concluding stages, somehow, he combined with the supreme office of lord high chancellor.

It was characteristic of Haldane that he took great pains to pick his team, though he did not get all his own way. Sidney Webb, who had worked for years to create a comprehensive system of higher education in London, plied Haldane with suggestions. But the days when the Webbs were Haldane's most trusted co-conspirators were over, and it seems likely that Morant had more influence than Webb on the choice of names. At any rate only one of Webb's suggestions (Lord Milner) was adopted.*

There was an entertaining exchange of notes about the inclusion of a woman on the commission. Webb, not surprisingly, suggested one: Mrs Bryant, and later, after consultation with Beatrice, came up with a list of six, with a preference for the formidable Jane Harrison of Newnham who 'smokes furiously & will not object to the Chairman's cigars, or to any masculine unconventionality in the way of ease & comfort'. Haldane, notwithstanding his predilection for women's rights, was lukewarm about having a woman at all on his commission; and Morant believed that the only point of having a woman on the

---

* Among Webb's other suggestions were Lord Avebury, Herbert Fisher, Bertrand Russell, and Gilbert Murray. It is difficult to imagine them working as a team. The final choice was: Lord Milner, Sir Robert Romer, Lawrence Currie, E. B. Sargant, Mrs L. Creighton, W. S. McCormick, and Morant himself, whose inclusion Haldane made a condition of his accepting the chairmanship.

commission was to deal 'with the details of Women's Education.'
Gregory Foster had advised Morant: 'I cannot think of any woman
who will be the slightest use on the Commission.' In the end Mrs
Creighton (about whom Haldane had expressed 'some personal
disinclination') was appointed; but Haldane had his way over one
essential appointment: John Kemp, who had helped him over the
Liverpool case and, more recently, in drafting legislation for the army,
was appointed as one of the secretaries.

In hindsight the composition of this commission was criticised.
There was, for instance, no medical man, and the commission made
far-reaching recommendations about medical education, though it
was not Haldane's intention to include this in his terms of reference.
It was added as an afterthought, on the prompting of the American
Abraham Flexner. The members were almost entirely graduates of
universities other than London; this, too, provoked some resentment.
But it was, by and large, the sort of body Haldane liked to work with:
'small and impartial, not representing interests, but rather of a judicial
and decisive nature.'

The terms of reference, to the annoyance of some members of the
senate, went far beyond the question of the incorporation of the
Imperial College of Science and Technology. 'Our task', asserted the
report, 'may, therefore, be shortly stated as follows: To examine the
existing provision for university education in London in the light of
what we think ought to exist, and to make practical recommendations
towards the realisation of the ideal.' Besides sittings to hear evidence,
the commission met seventy-two times to discuss its impressions and to
classify its opinions. It commissioned a historical report from Sir W.
Allchin. It devoured books, previous reports, and parliamentary papers.
And it sought evidence not only from witnesses in Britain, but from
Germany, France, Canada, and the United States. Its massive report
was published just over four years later.

A line by line analysis of the report would be a fruitful topic for the
historian of education, but it does not directly concern us here. In later
years Haldane protested that the report was a consensus of the whole
commission (as indeed it was) and ideas in it should not be attributed
to him alone. But his personality dominated the hearings. His educational philosophy permeated the theoretical passages in the report.
His capacity to design institutions consistent with his philosophy is
evident in many of the report's recommendations. And so the report
illuminates at many points our portrait of Haldane.

It illuminates, for instance, his courtesy with witnesses. Some of them must have been nervous at the prospect of submitting themselves to cross-examination by a famous barrister. But Haldane's manner was relaxed, urbane, disarming. He would never browbeat a witness; still less try to trap a witness into supporting opinions dear to his own heart. Repeatedly he told witnesses not to assume, from the slant of a question, that it disclosed the commission's views. 'I am not pronouncing on it,' he told one witness over the level of entry into the University, 'but I have a doubt in my mind.' When he was chairman of the commission on the University of Wales, a similar courtesy characterised his questions: 'Sometimes when we put suggestions I am afraid that people run off with the idea that we are putting preconceived views. We are of course only testing opinion and trying to bring out points which people have overlooked.' 'You must never assume that anything is in the mind of the Commission because we cross-examine witnesses severely on their proposals: our business is to elicit their views by questions or putting counterproposals?' Only occasionally do his convictions colour his comment. Thus on the London commission, speaking to Lord Justice Fletcher Moulton over external examinations, he allowed himself to say: 'As you know, the whole tendency of University education abroad is against you. . . .' (Haldane's colleagues on the commission were not always so cordial. Thus Morant questioned Sir A. Keogh: 'I want to get it clear. I keep putting it more crudely than you do in order to get your exact meaning.' To which Keogh replied: 'You certainly put it crudely.')

The report illuminates, too, Haldane's deductive approach to educational issues. He could have guided his colleagues into a pragmatic solution of the problem which had precipitated the commission – the future of the Imperial College – and then led them to propose some consequential readjustments in the organisation of the University. But he set to work quite differently: the commission first decided what were 'the essentials of a university in a great centre of population', and then discussed 'the application of the foregoing principles' to the specific problems of the University of London.

The specific problems arose from two notorious defects. First, as we describe on p. 27, for most of its history the University had comprised not students and teachers, but candidates and examiners. The external degree had won a worldwide reputation and brought benefits to thousands of graduates. So the graduates of the University, organised in convocation, were a powerful lobby defending the external degree and suspicious of any increase in power among the teaching staff. Second, the teaching institutions attached to the University as 'schools' were financially and educationally independent of it. They varied in quality and level of teaching from the excellent to the mediocre; and the University was unable to influence them through the power of the purse or the power to make appointments; its only effective influence was to prescribe a rigid syllabus and to pass or fail the candidates who sat the examinations. And this sole influence, as an examining board, had a paralysing effect upon the teacher, for he put his students at risk if he introduced any innovation into the curriculum. A consequence of both these defects was a persistent weakness in the government of the University. It was powerless to co-ordinate the institutions which taught for its degrees; and the teachers in these institutions were, for the most part, powerless to influence the examinations for which they prepared candidates.

Before prescribing the remedy for these defects, the commission set itself to describe the paradigm of a city university in the twentieth century; and it is this section of the report which is imbued with ideas upon which Haldane had reflected for years. In one passage after another we are back in Göttingen among the pupils of Lotze, but not in nostalgic retrospect. The commission discusses how to adapt the *spirit* of the German university, not its structure or its constitution, to the English civic university in a community which wants its graduates to work in commerce, industry, and government. 'Speaking generally', says the report, 'it may be said that in nearly every case the development of the modern English universities is the gradual evolution of a complete group of Faculties in institutions originally founded for the pursuit of science and technology.' And it goes on to make the point that this utilitarian bias is no obstacle to the achievement of a true academic attitude. (One recollects Samuel Alexander's famous epigram: 'Liberality in education is a spirit of pursuit, not a choice of subject.')

Over the spirit of pursuit, the commission is emphatic and clear. It is essential that students 'should be able to work in intimate and constant association with their fellow students ... and also in close contact with their teachers. The University should be organised on this basis ... students and teachers should be brought together in living intercourse in the daily work of the University. ... The main business of a university is the training of its undergraduates ....' But the training of undergraduates must not be separated from post-graduate work and research: '... it is in the best interests of the University that the most distinguished of its professors should take part in the teaching of the undergraduates from the beginning of their university career ... it is the personal influence of the man doing original work in his subject which inspires belief in it ....' And the commissioners quote Helmholtz: 'Anyone who has once come into contact with one or more men of the first rank must have had his whole mental standard altered for the rest of his life.' This is what a reformed University of London must offer to its students.

It was, of course, a frontal attack on the external degree. To abolish external degrees at that stage was, the commissioners knew, impracticable. But the report emphasises that they are a poor substitute for internal degrees, and that they cannot be taken as evidence that the graduate has been educated; only that he has acquired a certain level of knowledge. And the trend of policy in the University should be to make full-time education accessible to all who are qualified for it and who want it, so that external degrees become redundant. The one concession which the commissioners make to the obvious fact that such a trend as this will take a long time is to advocate the provision of university education for evening students, by teachers exempt from any teaching in the day time, appointed by the University, with qualifications as high, and salaries at the same level, as teachers in colleges catering for full-time students. And that was the stimulus for Birkbeck College, of which Haldane later became president.

The practical consequences of these convictions were obvious. A reformed University of London must have considerable control over the colleges which teach. The colleges must look to the University as both their paymaster and as the 'employer' of their professors. The control of finance and property and general policy would rest in a small executive composed of laymen and a few academics. But the academic power, over curricula, examinations, and the like, should be delegated to university-wide faculties, and boards of studies, cutting across the entrenched interests of individual colleges. Complementary to this concentration of influence from the periphery towards the centre, there should be a dispersal of influence from the centre to the periphery. If the University appoints the right professors, then it can devolve upon them responsibility for what they teach and how they examine, and the inexorable control of curricula and examinations from the centre can be relaxed, even to the extent that the degree would bear the title of the college where it was earned.

The identification of examinations with education was – indeed still is – a tenacious misconception in English education. It had troubled Haldane for years. Students at Scottish universities in the early nineteenth century commonly did not take degree examinations. They came to the university to 'get' education; they returned to farm and village with class certificates certifying that they had attended, but without a degree – which in any case they did not need. In English universities (except among affluent undergraduates at Oxford or Cambridge) the compulsion to take examinations and to get degrees was ineradicable. Not that Haldane objected to healthy competition, hard work, and the lustre of academic honours. What he objected to were examinations which distorted, and did not stimulate, education. In his opinion – and the commissioners shared it – the examinations organised by the University of London were a positive hindrance to good education. The commissioners were crystal clear on this issue, and there is no doubt whatever that their verdict embodied one of Haldane's most powerful convictions. The following passage from the report sums it up (though the style strikes us as more eloquent than Haldane's own drafting):

> We are convinced that both a detailed syllabus and an external examination are inconsistent with the true interests of university education, injurious to the students, degrading to the teachers, and ineffective for the attainment of the ends they are supposed to promote.... Even the so-called Internal examinations of the University of London are practically external, because of the large number of institutions involved, and the demands of the common syllabus.... The effect upon the students and the teachers is disastrous.... They cannot pursue knowledge both for its own sake and also for the sake of passing the test of an examination.... We shall make recommendations which will dispense with the necessity of the syllabus, by ensuring the appointment of teachers who can be trusted with the charge of university education.

And the report goes on to advocate what is now called 'continuous assessment':

> It appears to us only fair that due weight should be given to the whole record of the students' work in the University. If the academic freedom of the professors and the students is to be maintained ... it is absolutely necessary that, subject to proper safeguards, the

degrees of the University should practically be the certificates given by the professors themselves, and that the students should have entire confidence that they may trust their academic fate to honest work under their instruction and direction.

The commissioners went on to apply these principles to the University of London in great detail, and – almost incidentally – proposed a solution for the specific problem of Imperial College, namely that it should be incorporated into the University and supervised by a special committee for technology, separate from the structure of the faculties. But the report covered much more than this, and Haldane's influence pervades many other passages. There is, for example, an interesting section on the status of students, where *Lernfreiheit* – the reverse face of the coin of *Lehrfreiheit* – is mentioned. (It is a noteworthy feature of the influence of Germany upon British higher education, that *Lehrfreiheit* luxuriated in British universities, but *Lernfreiheit* never took root.) So it is interesting to read the suggestion that students should be relieved of the 'rather onerous obligation' placed on internal students to attend a given amount of instruction as a condition of admission to its examinations. In its 'schools' the University, says the report, should confine itself to approving the curriculum, and not compel any student to take more than he desired. The excellence of the teaching should be relied upon to commend it to candidates for degrees. The only exceptions to this discretion should be in medicine and technology, where attendance has to be compulsory.

There are other suggestions to encourage *Lernfreiheit*. For example a medical student should be able to arrest his course in order to pursue further than is required of him 'any subject which fascinates his attention and appeals to his mind'. The commission considered, too, whether students should be free to migrate from one university to another during their undergraduate career, as they did in Germany; but this was rejected because not all British universities were organised in the same way.

The commissioners considered another question of great interest to Haldane, namely the contribution which the University could make to higher education in the colonies. They prescribed that external degree examination for colonial territories should be discontinued, and replaced by examinations planned in conjunction with the colonial office, adapted to local needs. Then, say the commissioners, the University 'would have abandoned once for all the pernicious theory underlying its present practice that the kind of education it thinks best for its own students must be the best for all peoples who own allegiance to the British flag'. A whole generation passed, until the Asquith report on higher education in the colonies (1945), before this warning was heeded.

Finally, we pick from the report one other interest to which Haldane returned toward the end of his life: its passages about adult education. The Workers' Educational Association (WEA) was flourishing at that time and it had acquired, through the work of Tawney and others, a reputation for the pursuit of knowledge (though predominantly knowledge about economics and political science) at a high standard and without distortion by examinations. To support the WEA tutorial classes was, the report said, a new and hopeful field 'for the spread of a pure love of learning – the main function of a University.' 'We think', concluded the commissioners, 'the University should consider the work it is doing for these men and women one of the most serious and important of its services to the metropolis. . . .'

To what extent was Haldane himself responsible for the great report on the University of London? His fellow members on the commission were themselves men of strong views and broad experience. But Haldane had been reflecting on the problems longer than any of his colleagues, and he certainly would not have put his signature to recommendations inconsistent with his principles. It is pretty clear from his correspondence (and from the style of parts of the report) that he gave a lot of attention to the drafting. And one only has to look back at Hansards as early as 1889 and to read some of his speeches, to find in embryo some of the considered recommendations of the commission. Bellot criticises Haldane's chairmanship as tendentious ('committed . . . to particular solutions of his own'). This, we think, is a misconceived criticism. Occasionally, as he questioned witnesses, Haldane's personal views did come to the surface. It would be undesirable, he suggested (in discussing Imperial College) to have more than one university in London. His preference for internal examinations and his dissatisfaction with external examinations were undisguised. He wanted polytechnics to remain places for sub-university work, not to ape Charlottenburg and so become unsuitable for workers; but as to higher technological education: 'we are rather anxious' to avoid a sharp line of demarcation, as in Germany, between universities and technological institutions. He reiterated his view that the quality of the university can be no better than the quality and personality of its teachers. He revealed his own conviction in his question: 'Is not the tendency of our time in all educational spheres and notably in the Universities to look to the record [of students' work] more and more' in assessing candidates for degrees? He responded in a lively way to any witness who favoured teaching by seminars: the romantic picture of the *Gelehrter* surrounded by his disciples. And – consistent with his sentiments since he supported the student petition from Edinburgh in 1888 – he made sure that the report gave due attention to student representation (on the court), student organisations, and amenities for student life. But to call this 'committed . . . to particular solutions of his own' is surely to exaggerate.

The report was signed at the end of March 1913 and published in April. Its publication (Haldane told his mother) caused a 'great stir'. It was welcomed by the press. The *Times Educational Supplement* called it a 'frankly revolutionary document'. Indeed for London it was, for if it had been adopted the University would have become faculty-controlled, the external degree would have been phased out, member colleges of the University would have been free to diversify their curricula and their procedures for awarding degrees, and student *Lernfreiheit* would have secured a foothold in English higher education. And there were other sweeping recommendations, e.g. to reorganise medical and legal education and to bring hospitals and inns of court into the sphere of influence of the University. But it was obviously going to be controversial, and editorials appealed to individual institutions in the University to sink their interests for the good of the whole. 'Let us have criticism and plenty of it', wrote *The Times*, but '. . . let there be also the larger view, the wider outlook of its authors.' For anyone familiar with the University's history this was expecting too much. By May the council of the University of London Graduates' Association had lodged an emphatic protest against recommendations for the external work. Convocation, more judicially, appointed six subcommittees to examine the commission's recommendations on six fields of study. Asquith wisely staved off a request in parliament for a discussion of the report, but response at the official level was prompt and favourable. On 14 August the board of education appointed a departmental committee under Sir George Murray (now retired from the treasury) to recommend 'specific arrangements and provisions' required to give effect to the scheme of the report. The committee included in its membership Selby-Bigge, McCormick, and Kemp, with Heath as secretary. It met on 14 October and thereafter regularly until the third week in July 1914. It entered into what must have been tedious negotiations with all the parties concerned: convocation, the medical schools, Imperial College, Bedford College, and of course the militant 'externals'. In April 1914 the committee was able to produce an interim and confidential report. It endorsed the recommendation to concentrate the headquarters of the University and (as far as possible) its main teaching units in Bloomsbury. This was conditional upon King's College moving from the Strand to the Bloomsbury site and it is noteworthy, in view of later criticism (p. 160), that King's was represented as 'quite willing' to consider this. Even the 'externals' indicated a willingness to compromise on a formula proposed by Sidney Webb in a private letter to Haldane which is preserved in the records of the board of education. By July 1914 Fletcher Moulton was hopeful that he could secure the approval of the 'externals' to the compromise. Meanwhile negotiations with the medical schools were going quite well. The only implacably intransigent institution was the Imperial College, which had precipitated the whole enquiry.

So by July 1914 Haldane had little reason to be disappointed at the outcome of the mammoth task to which he had given so much time. It was indeed remarkable that a 'frankly revolutionary document' should have been flexible enough to have promoted the first moves, at any rate, in what might have been a sustained and profound evolutionary change in the University.

Although the affairs of universities took up most of the time and energy Haldane could put aside for work on education, he returned repeatedly in his speeches to the concept of a unified, articulated state system of education, a ladder from primary school to university, and beyond to adult education, with no rungs missing. The prospect at the turn of the century that the Liberals might return to power was the opportunity to refurbish and present to the public this grand scheme. Haldane made this the theme of many of his speeches. He knew that politicians could remain in office only so long as they responded to what the public demanded; and over education Haldane made it his business to create demand through public speaking, and then to devise response through private conspiracy. And so we watch him in 1901, addressing his audience in Dumfries: '. . . what I feel to be the great problem today is the welding of the educational system of this country into one complete whole, in which elementary education, secondary education, and the university shall all be indissoluble parts of one system. . . . The universities must be not merely detachable super-structures, but the brain and intelligence which permeate the whole system.' Again, at the Colston Society in Bristol in 1902: 'For my part I do not believe any system of education will ever be satisfactory which does not link together the primary, the secondary, and tertiary system, and make the tertiary the head, with a University dominating the whole edifice with what the Germans call *Geist* – a spirit of intelligence.' And in 1903, at St Andrews, he was saying that education must be put under popular control. As an election drew closer, he reminded his audience, at Ealing in 1904, that the Liberal party's programme for social reform, including national education, would have to depend on the 'voice of the country'. (But in fact the Liberals did not wait for the voice of the country before laying their plans for a national system of education; even before the general election of January 1906 had confirmed the new government in power, with an unexpectedly large majority, a cabinet committee including Lord Crewe and Haldane was already at work, and Haldane was grasping the nettle of sectarian education by giving Crewe the quite ruthless advice that voluntary schools should be controlled by a popularly elected majority of managers: 'no popular control, no rate aid, would thus be the principle.') He realised where the opposition lay, though he under-estimated its virulence: 'To confine the functions of the State to purely secular teaching would avert many difficulties and is what I should personally prefer. But public opinion has not yet been driven to acceptance of this. . . .' Soon after the Liberals took office Birrell did in 1906 introduce a mild bill to amend the Education acts of 1902–3 by prescribing full public control of rate-aided schools and appointment of teachers without reference to religious belief. The bill passed the commons but was thrown out by the lords. Haldane, then busy at the war office, realised that he couldn't stir his colleagues to 'a large policy' about education. Public interest in educational reform was too small; the vested interests of the churches were too great. He is not on record as having pursued the idea of a comprehensive educational system again until 1913. By the winter of 1912 the end was in sight of his labours on the London royal commission. The office of lord chancellor – although on his own admission it was an excessively onerous one – did not fill his life. He began another campaign for reform of the infra-structure of education. 'When I was at the War Office', he told the 'Eighty' Club

in April 1913, 'I was appalled to find that of the recruits we took
something like 13 per cent could not read or write. . . . Surely that
shows something wrong with our national system? . . . The State will
never be in a sound position until you have redressed the situation of
today.' And in Manchester, in the same year: 'I have been for four
years chairman of a Royal Commission on university education,
which has been a great education to me because I have learned how
utterly chaotic and backward is the state of education – elementary,
secondary, and higher – in this country.'

These were strong words from a man so little given to exaggeration
and rhetoric. This time he did stimulate support from his colleagues.
Early in December 1912 it was agreed that Haldane should become
chairman of a hybrid committee of ministers, officials, and educational
experts, to work out a comprehensive scheme of reform. Once more
it brought him into conflict with Lloyd George, though their association began amicably enough; for Lloyd George was a member of his
committee* and – as chancellor of the exchequer – a key member.
Moreover Lloyd George was thinking on what were (for Haldane)
the 'right' lines. For he told Haldane that he would be reluctant to
find any large sum except for a scheme which would strike the
imagination and could fairly be represented as a stage towards the
establishment of a national system of education regardless of denominational squabbles. This, from Lloyd George who was under perpetual
pressure from the nonconformists, was an encouraging start. But
nonconformists were not the only ones who would have to be appeased
if Haldane's concept was to be approved; for it was on too big a scale
to be entrusted to the existing machinery of local government.
Local authorities would have to surrender some of their present
powers to larger areas; and this would certainly raise great opposition.
Furthermore, any coherent educational system would require universities to submit themselves to surveillance by the board of education.
Haldane was vague about this last consequence. It was 'somehow or
other connected with the idea that the status of the Board of Education
should be improved and that it should be in some way extended or
glorified so as to really fit it to deal with University Education.'

* The other members included Pease, president of the board of education;
Runciman, formerly president of the board, and now translated to agriculture;
Selby-Bigge and Struthers, permanent secretaries respectively of the board of
education and the Scottish education department, and A. H. D. Acland, a member
of the board's consultative committee.

So wrote the board's secretary, Selby-Bigge to his president, Pease.

The climax came early in 1913. On 10 January Haldane wrote to his mother: 'I am off to Manchester to speak there tonight & to make an important pronouncement on Education by desire of the P.M. and Ll.G. I have worked out our new Education plans & have been given charge of the business.'

It was indeed an important pronouncement. Haldane announced to the Manchester Reform Club that the government had decided that education was 'the next and most urgent of the great social problems to be taken up'; that: 'Until we have given democracy that equality of educational opportunity, the democracy will always be restless.' He told them that a national and unified education system was needed, working from the top downwards, through the agency of the new university machinery; and that to secure this end, administrative areas larger than counties would be needed – possibly counties could be grouped in areas in which the university interest might provide a centre for secondary schools and the training of teachers.

Haldane left no doubt that he was making an official pronouncement: 'what I am now going to say to you, I say not casually or with any light sense of responsibility, but after consultation with the Prime Minister and with the Chancellor of the Exchequer.' But this was not the view of the chancellor of the exchequer! Just as Lloyd George had repudiated Runciman's announcement about the source of university finance eighteen months earlier (p. 98), so he now repudiated what he called Haldane's 'magniloquent speech' in Manchester. No, said Lloyd George: land, not education, was to be the next great subject to be taken up by the government. And as for Haldane's consultations with Asquith, Pease, and himself, Lloyd George admitted that they had occurred, but Haldane 'had spoken quite vaguely to each, representing to each in turn that he had fully consulted the other two and had their sanction for his proposals. . . .' (This indictment has the ring of truth; it was Haldane's style.) The cabinet, said Lloyd George, had not been consulted at all. Lloyd George in any case took a poor view of the speech. 'Interminable verbiage' was his description of it to the editor of the *Manchester Guardian:* 'and he added something more scathing about "a barrel of tallow" – a picturesque description of Haldane's physical peculiarities – which, when set fire to could indeed produce "any amount of smoke but no flame". . . .'

Haldane, however, got his own way. The king's speech at the

opening of parliament on 10 March 1913 announced: 'Proposals will be submitted to you for the development of a national system of education'; and, as lord chancellor, Haldane had the satisfaction of reading the speech to the lords himself! He wrote to his mother: 'The King's Speech has got the Education policy in, & that will count for more than Crowns and Swords of State, and robes. . . .'

Thereafter the hybrid committee continued to meet and make progress. Asquith on 17 March confirmed that the bill would be introduced in that session. And Haldane, intent on making audible 'the voice of the country', threw himself again into a circuit of speeches: to the National Union of Teachers on 25 March, to secondary and technical school teachers on 29 March, to the 'Eighty' Club on 4 April. It was no set speech. He cleverly adapted himself to each audience. To the elementary school teachers he is said to have spoken for ninety minutes (after the ejection of half a dozen heckling women at the beginning). He assured the teachers that he did not have in mind a central bureaucracy; there would be local devolution to take advantage of local enthusiasm, and he emphasised the importance and status of the teacher and hinted at the need to introduce a four-year training course, bringing them into the university atmosphere. To the secondary school teachers he stressed the need to relieve universities of the burden of secondary school work (and so to raise the level of sixth forms) and the need to do away with the 'old fashioned' system of degrees by examinations in favour of the student's record. The *Times Educational Supplement* commented on both speeches under a headline: 'The promised land'; but made the pertinent point that most of what Haldane had said was not new. The important point was that 'no less a personage than the Lord High Chancellor of England' was saying it.

During the early months of 1913 the bill took shape. By April a first draft had been prepared. It contained twenty-six clauses which included provision for a comprehensive system of schooling, for continuation schools, and for provincial associations composed from local authorities: all objectives for which Haldane had been campaigning. At the beginning of May Selby-Bigge sent a copy of the bill to Haldane with a long covering letter, apologising for its length and adding: '. . . but I know your patience is inexhaustible.' Haldane replied with a characteristic note of encouragement:

Coming up from Durham in the train today I got time to dig into your Education Bill. I think it an excellent start off. . . . But the essence of it all is that the money must be promised with it. . . . As to this I will see my colleagues. The Bill if it passes with the money grant will lay the foundations of a great system, and will I think sustain the first and most difficult stones of the edifice.

There was a preliminary discussion at cabinet which (Haldane wrote) 'might have been worse', and, he added, '. . . I have had a good private talk with Lloyd George.' As an earnest that the bill was being taken seriously, the government issued a communiqué on 14 July – when it was clear that such an ambitious measure could not be dealt with before the session ended – announcing their intention to proceed instead with a one-clause bill which would form a not inappropriate peg (as they put it) on which to hang a statement of policy for a national system of education. On 22 July Pease, as president of the board of education, introduced this one-clause bill. The commons received the accompanying statement of policy with guarded approval; 'a very large overcoat on a very small peg', as one MP put it. And it did not go unnoticed that Lord Haldane had had a hand in the matter.

After the summer recess, work on the bill was resumed. By December 1913 a fresh draft was circulated to the cabinet. The king's speech at the opening of the new session again included the bill in the government's programme. Haldane concentrated on securing the money, which meant persuading Lloyd George to include it in the finance bill, and, of course, getting cabinet approval. He adopted his familiar strategy. 'Late tonight', he wrote to Selby-Bigge on 20 April 1914,

> I drove the PM to Downing Street after dinner & had a talk . . . . My talk was an excellent one. I think he will agree to £500,000 for 14–15, £3,500,000 (with a carry over) for 15–16 & £4,250,000 for 16–17. This last figure is a little over what you mentioned to me. But an inspiration came to me & I proposed to offer £20,000 a year apiece to Oxford and Cambridge for *Science*. This turned the scale . . . . I hope I have made a good start for you.

There is an undated fragment of another note from Haldane to Selby-Bigge, written shortly afterwards: 'It was satisfactory that the Cabinet passed our plans tonight so far as money goes. We have now to deal with Parliament.'

Haldane had, of course, to carry the chancellor of the exchequer with him, as well as the prime minister. This called for a different

technique, including a barrage of blandishment. So, in briefing
Lloyd George on what to say about educational reform in the house of
commons, Haldane was not above recourse to flattery; he expressed
the hope that Lloyd George would 'take the fullest credit for a great
reform which the country will owe to your courage and imagination.'
Lloyd George responded well. On 25 June the finance bill passed the
house of commons.

The next evening there was a celebration at the National Liberal
Club. Haldane described the budget as 'the greatest budget that my
rt. hon. friend has yet introduced, and its inner purpose deserves well
to be understood. . . . The inwardness of the present Budget is the
purpose which is latent in it of a great reform which will put the
chances of the coming generation on a footing such as we have not
yet seen.' Lloyd George, not to be outdone in flattery, thanked the
lord chancellor

> for his superb exposition . . . . I have never regretted more than I
> do tonight that the Lord Chancellor has left the House of
> Commons. . . . It was a great speech and it displayed not merely
> the great intellectual qualities of the Lord Chancellor but . . . his
> thoroughly kind heart. What he did not reveal to you was that he
> had a great part not merely in the construction of this Budget,
> but in its initiation and in its inspiration.

Once again it was too late in the session to put the education bill
through parliament. On 7 July Asquith announced that it would be
postponed again. This time it was swept out of sight by the tide of
the German armies.

On the brink of fulfilment Haldane's hopes for education had been
dashed. Only one item – and that an unexpected one – was salvaged.
In the ministerial changes brought about by resignations at the outbreak
of war, Christopher Addison became parliamentary secretary to Pease
at the board of education. Addison already knew Haldane and fortunately he was a lively diarist. He records on 12 June, on the eve of the
war: 'Pleasant hour with Haldane. Miss Haldane happily absent.'
So his relationship with Haldane was evidently cordial, and it was
natural that he should consult Haldane. He records (on 2 December
1914) 'Selby-Bigge seems inclined to fold his hands, resign himself
to fate, and surrender without a struggle all the advances promised
by the Budget.' Addison was determined that despite the war – or
indeed because of it – the government should do something straight

away about technical training. His chief, Pease, was inclined to limit proposals to trade schools, but authorised Addison to prepare something more ambitious. By 10 December he was already consulting Haldane about it. He got hearty encouragement, Haldane adding that 'we must link our application on to the war somehow or other.' With the help of officials Addison produced a plan. It was despatched from the board to the treasury in January and on 29 January Addison was summoned by Haldane for what was to become a historic interview. Haldane's greeting was: 'Addison, this document has compromise written all over it. Just tell me frankly what you would like to do if you had a free hand?' Addison expanded into a much more comprehensive scheme for assistance to science and technology for the benefit of industry. To his delight, Haldane's reaction was to say that he and Lloyd George, with Pease's full consent, wanted Addison to undertake the 'chairmanship of a small committee to work out a scheme whereby national assistance could be given to scientific and industrial research.' He suggested that Heath (of the Universities branch) should be one of the members and warned Addison to 'avoid axe grinders like poison.'

By 20 March Addison had a much fuller scheme ready. The draft was discussed at a lunch arranged by Pease 'in the little room off the main Dining Room' at the Carlton, with Haldane there, together with Lloyd George, McCormick and Addison. All went promisingly. 'Haldane charged me at the end to keep the ball rolling and placed on me the responsibility for carrying on the campaign.' The scheme envisaged the formation of a central committee of research, nation-wide in its scope. At first it was thought that this could be set up under the minister for education, even though the jurisdiction of the board was confined to England and Wales. Later, however, it was found necessary to resort to a constitutional device that was to inspire one of Haldane's most ambitious projects when he came to plan for post-war educational development: a two-tier structure under the auspices of the privy council, with an executive committee, served by an advisory council of experts.

The scheme was approved in May 1915. This month saw also the shattering climacteric of Haldane's career. He had already resigned himself to the inevitable postponement of his long-laid plans for the University of London, just as the Murray committee was about to recommend action upon them. He had secured the funds to launch a peaceful educational revolution, only to see the bill shelved until parliament could think about such things again. But in his political career he was, up to 1914, on the top of the wave; only fifty-nine years old and at the height of his influence. When he left the war office in 1912 to become lord chancellor, *The Times* showered encomium upon him: 'Everything, or almost everything, that Lord Haldane set out to do when he took office he has accomplished . . . by sheer force of character, by invincible good humour, and by an imperturbability which has seldom been equalled by any public man. . . .'

The wave was to dash him on a cruel shore. He now had to eat the bitter fruit of his long and profound affection for German culture. As hostility toward Germany became more feverish, criticism of his pro-German proclivities began to spread. Then came twisted rumours about his notorious secret mission to Germany, shortly before the war. News of his visit had of course leaked (though he tried to throw reporters off the scent by pretending he was there on educational matters) and it was interpreted as an attempt to parley with the enemy. Frequently Haldane pleaded with the government to clear his name by releasing a statement about the mission, but his pleas were refused.★ The mystery about this visit, coupled with Haldane's frequent, and sometimes too fulsome, allusions to the superiority of German education, industry, and culture, prompted a mean and virulent press campaign against him. In September 1914 he felt obliged to offer his resignation from the office of lord chancellor. It was refused and in January 1915 he was given a place in the war council. But Asquith could not, or would not, withstand the storm of censure. On 26 May 1915 he jettisoned Haldane. It was a bitter shock, second only to the far off catastrophe of his broken engagement, twenty-five years away. Some of his parliamentary colleagues (but not all) turned their backs on him. He was actually assaulted in the streets, his life was threatened and, even a couple of years later, he was still having to be shadowed, for his safety, by detectives.

★ Beneath his composure there was a deep resentment about this. In 1915 he did unburden himself about it to Lord Mersey, saying: 'my life is uncertain and I should like to feel that I had told the story to someone who could in case of need repeat it.'

6 On the Periphery of Power

When Haldane attended the palace to surrender his seals of office the king invested him with the order of merit, but that was cold comfort. Just what loss of office meant to him is vividly caught by Fitzroy, in a rare glimpse of Haldane with his defences down, on a farewell visit to the privy council immediately after his surrender of the great seal:

> May 26 [1915] ... Haldane, who had just left the King and been invested with the Order of Merit, came in. He had all the air of the fallen Minister, and I could not help recalling the fate which had overtaken another philosophic Chancellor [Francis Bacon] three hundred years ago .... He seemed thoroughly broken, and said goodbye to us with undisguised emotion. 'There has been', he said 'a lot of mud flung, and I must try to give myself a coat of whitewash'.

Haldane's love affair with German philosophy, inspired by that far-away student sojourn in Göttingen, was, in a way, the cause of this disaster to his political career. But at the same time it equipped him to meet adversity. Over his broken engagement he had told Webb that he was never so much himself 'as when hope goes & black misfortune crowds round.' He endured this mutilation of his influence with a noble stoicism and without a trace of self pity. C.P. Scott records having had lunch with him on 27 January 1917, when 'Haldane spoke quite dispassionately of the extraordinary persecution to which he had been subjected.' And Marie Belloc Lowndes, a close neighbour of Haldane, recollects:

> I saw him constantly ... when it can truly be said hundreds of thousands of English men and women believed him to be very little better than a traitor. He took his astounding fall ... not only with great dignity but with a kind of magnanimity which I thought moving .... He always walked from his house in Queen Anne's Gate to the House of Lords and he was such a singular-looking

being that he was often accosted by people who knew him from pictures which appeared in the press. Sometimes these passers by would fling violent abuse at him. Occasionally strangers would tell him they were sorry his work for his country . . . seemed to be forgotten.

In this second purgatory Haldane again found consolation from the Webbs. Beatrice had written to him on 4 June: 'Sidney & I have been very much perturbed by the events of the last weeks – more especially by the scandalous attack on you. We admire – more than we can express – your splendid & silent self-sacrifice. . . .' He dined with the Webbs on 14 June; it was the beginning of a new chapter in benign co-conspiracy, to help reconstruct the post-war society of England.

For Haldane's response to adversity was to work for the future, not to brood over the past. As ex-lord chancellor there was judicial work for him to do in the appeal courts. Two weeks after he relinquished office he wrote to Rosebery: 'I am now full of judicial work. . . . I have also educational work on hand that much wants pushing on.' Two months later he had set his compass for the future. He wrote on 29 August to Beatrice Webb (paraphrasing his mentor, Goethe): 'I have decided that he who would accomplish anything at all must limit himself & that I must concentrate on National Education.' It is a sign of his magnanimity that he accepted two invitations from Asquith: one to visit France to investigate the débacle of the battle of Loos; another, to join the privy council committee on scientific and industrial research. (Asquith, too, was being as generous as he could politically afford to be. In a note from the secretary of the board of education to Fitzroy at the privy council it is on record: 'As regards the composition of the Committee of Council, I understand that the Prime Minister was particularly anxious to associate Lord Haldane with the scheme . . . .') By the end of 1915 he was sitting regularly in the house of lords, making education his platform; and by April 1916 even the wounds which Lloyd George had inflicted on him less than a year before were healed: after dining together on 4 April 1916, their somewhat uneasy alliance was resumed.

Let us stand back from this portrait of Haldane for a moment. We see a man with astonishing resilience and unquenchable faith in the future. He could, in his sixtieth year, have lived on his lord chancellor's pension and discharged his obligation by sitting in the appeal courts. There was little encouragement to think about post-war England, for 1916 was the year of the Somme when (as A. J. P. Taylor put it) 'Kitchener's army found its graveyard.... Not only men perished. There perished also the zest and idealism with which nearly three million Englishmen had marched forth to war.' This defeat, even more than his private adversity, must have been a terrible burden for the man who had been responsible for the army. Yet in 1916 Haldane added to his legal work and his privy council committee at least four other tasks: the chairmanship of committees on air power and coal conservation, membership of the education subcommittee of Asquith's Reconstruction committee, and the chairmanship of another royal commission, to examine university education in Wales.

In December 1916 Asquith's government fell and Lloyd George, with a small war cabinet, assumed personal control: 'the nearest thing England has known to a Napoleon....' Haldane wrote to Asquith: 'The old machine, by means of which I used to try to work, is now destroyed, and I do not see any prospect of another coming into existence, which would either take me on or which I could take on.' Lloyd George did in fact flirt with him: on 17 April 1917 Haldane told his mother that Lloyd George wanted him to come back ('all difficulties must be put aside for the nation wants your brains badly'). Nothing came of this, though Haldane did accept the chairmanship of another – and as it turned out very important – enquiry into the machinery of government. But educational reform remained the focus for his enthusiasm. Once the war was over, he told C. P. Scott, he would be able to devote himself entirely to education. Meanwhile he had committed himself, in April 1916, before Asquith's downfall, to a project after his own heart: chairmanship of the royal commission on university education in Wales.

Haldane was not the government's first choice as chairman. The original membership, proposed after discussion with Lloyd George and McKenna, is to be found in a letter from the board of education to the treasury on 25 February 1916. Viscount Bryce was to be chairman. We do not know why or how the switch was made. Bryce, who was in his seventy-eighth year, may have declined the task. Haldane's name was an obvious alternative, and it is likely that Sir Henry Jones, whose name also appeared on the proposed list of members and who was a close friend of Haldane and of Lloyd George, had a hand in the decision to invite Haldane. In these circumstances it can be assumed that Haldane had no part in drawing up the terms of reference or in picking the team he was to work with. It was an interesting team. In contrast to the membership of the London commission, there were no Olympian figures such as Milner or Romer. The commissioners were scholars or administrators in fields of special interest to Wales: literature, philosophy, music, science, medicine, agriculture.* Two of the members (Jones and Edwards) were Welsh by birth and up-bringing and prominent in the Welsh renaissance at the end of the nineteenth century, and Bruce was the son of Lord Aberdare, whose report on Welsh education in 1881 was regarded as the educational charter of modern Wales. The commissioners were charged to make a full scale examination of the organisation of university education in Wales, although the circumstances which precipitated their appoint-ment were interestingly similar to those which precipitated the royal commission on the University of London. In London the problem was how to associate the Imperial College with the University; in Wales it was how to associate the proposed medical school at Cardiff with the University. But in Wales, as in London, the explicit reason for the commission was a side issue. The Welsh colleges wanted (and needed) more money from the treasury. The advisory committee for university grants, after visiting the colleges in 1913, recommended an increase in grant but coupled their recommendation with misgivings about the lack of an adequate co-ordinating authority which could be entrusted with the allocation of grants among the three colleges, at Bangor, Aberystwyth, and Cardiff. Meanwhile a committee of enquiry set up by the board of education to examine proposals for a national medical school in Wales also recommended financial support but with similar misgivings. So, in February 1915, the treasury issued a minute declining to sanction grants recommended by either committee unless the University and the colleges could agree on reforms in their constitution. They failed to agree, whereupon the treasury announced a decision that grants would be increased on condition that the University and its colleges asked for the immediate appointment of a royal commission. To this *dirigiste* demand the University capitulated, perhaps more willingly than might have been expected, for there was – as the commission subsequently discovered – a growing sense of 'discomfort, dissatisfaction and disappointment'

* The members were: Viscount Haldane (chairman), W. N. Bruce, Sir William Osler, Sir H. Jones, Sir Owen Morgan Edwards, Professor W. H. Bragg (who did not attend any of the meetings at which evidence was taken), W. H. Hadow, A. D. Hall, and Miss Emily Penrose.

in the federal structure of a university which had no physical presence except through its three independent colleges.

The commission was announced on 12 April 1916, with Haldane as chairman. His appointment was well received. For one thing he was not an Englishman – the Scots could be expected to approach Welsh problems with more sympathy. Also he had frequently spoken with enthusiasm about educational progress in Wales (even saying in parliament in 1899 that Scotland had everything to learn from Wales in higher education!). In Aberystwyth he was remembered as having made a memorable address to students in 1910, telling them that the Welsh, like the Scots, were idealists but – unlike the Scots – imaginative rather than reflective and therefore capable of important innovations in education and religion. So when the *Times Educational Supplement* commented on the commissioners, it must have gratified Haldane to read in the correspondence columns afterwards a letter from a Welsh MP, E. T. John: '. . . the assistance of a statesman of genius so outstanding, of such conspicuous erudition so entirely sympathetic and appreciative as Lord Haldane is warmly welcomed. The catholicity of his temperament, with all its Continental implications arouses no prejudice in the Principality, while his intimate knowledge of Scottish conditions and his study of the problems of university administration peculiarly commend his appointment to the people of Wales.'

Haldane plunged into the work of the commission with energy and enthusiasm. Here again was the familiar technique. He led the commissioners through a meticulous study of the state of the University and its history, followed by thirty-one sessions at which witnesses were examined (there were only four occasions which he did not attend at all). Then came another thirty-six deliberative sessions before the report was signed on 6 February 1918. The meetings were held in London but of course Haldane realised how important it was, if the report was to be credible, to appear on the spot. So in June 1916 the commissioners took the road and visited Cardiff Swansea, Aberystwyth, and Bangor. 'The Welsh Expedition', he wrote to his friend Gosse, 'was a success', and afterwards he often spoke warmly of his visit. 'We became very much moved', he told the house of lords in a debate on the Education bill two years later, 'by what we found there. We found that part of the country – the Principality – moved and permeated by the spirit of education. . . . It has the advantage of a democracy permeated by ideas.' The visit evidently made a good impression. William George wrote to his brother, Lloyd George: 'I had the pleasure of meeting your friend Lord Haldane today. He was very suave & cordial and appears to be very keen on making a good job of it.'

Haldane examined witnesses with the familiar disarming approach. On 15 December 1916 (for instance) three students appeared before the commission. Included in their case was a request that students should be represented on the senate (the body which would have responsibility for academic affairs) rather than the council (the executive body) or the court (a very large and ineffective body). This request, in the context of English and Scottish universities, was an innovation. Haldane listened patiently. 'The Senate particularly?', he asked. 'Yes' was the reply. 'I see', he said, 'you have fixed your mind upon the Senate. But, no doubt, you are not averse to our considering the other bodies in addition or alternatively, as the case may be. We have spoken of representation upon some of the governing bodies of the University, it may be the Senate or the Court or both, but can you point out in any concrete fashion the utility of that? Do not imagine that in putting the question I am doubting it, but I just want to get your reasons?' Haldane exercised, too, a firm control over his fellow commissioners. When Osler ventured to assure the town clerk of Swansea, on the question of the technical college there, that there would be no difficulty about a technical college of the first rank becoming a constituent college, Haldane interposed: 'This is really a matter for the Commission to debate. I think that we had better keep this for our own discussion?'

The detailed recommendations of the Welsh royal commission, as of the London one, are relevant to our portrait of Haldane only in so far as they illuminate his character and his ideas. But this is just what some of the recommendations do, for they are (to use Haldane's favourite word at that time) permeated with his philosophical concepts about universities, and are couched in language which reveals his deepening conviction that democracy would not survive without an educated citizenry. Above all, the report on Wales, like the report on London, has a powerful theme running through it to which all minor issues were harmonised. For London, the theme was a university fit for the metropolis of the Empire. For Wales, the theme was a university as a national expression of the spirit of the Welsh people. It was a theme consistent with many of Haldane's cherished beliefs. His dedication to *Lehrfreiheit* was easily translated into the need to cultivate a university in Wales free to develop its own peculiarly

Welsh identity, uninhibited by the proximity of England.* His insistence on the importance of introducing technical education took on a new meaning in Wales, for the colleges there began as liberal arts colleges to which technology had to be added, whereas in England many of the civic universities began as technical colleges which had to be humanised. His popular theme, that higher education should permeate the whole society, was peculiarly relevant to Wales, where the university colleges had been endowed – as it was commonly said – 'from the pence of the people'. Many passages in the commission's report and, more significantly, many references in Haldane's speeches afterwards, indicate that he was really excited by the potentialities for higher education in Wales; it lifted his speeches to unaccustomed levels of eloquence. 'You have an opportunity', he told the court of the University at its first meeting after it was reconstituted, 'which no other university in the kingdom has. Will you use it? Will you make the most of it? If you do, then I venture to say that you will not only have profited yourselves, but you will have set an example to the rest of the United Kingdom. . . .'

We can suppose that Haldane left recommendations on some issues to his colleagues: Osler for medicine, Hadow for music, Hall for agriculture. But three issues discussed in the report deserve special mention because they were certainly greatly influenced by Haldane himself and he often referred to them in his speeches afterwards. The first is a beautifully lucid exposition of the differences between a university which is a federation of colleges and a university in which there is a devolution of authority and responsibility to colleges. In Wales there was the weakness of London over again: a university which stifled initiative in its constituent colleges by controlling examinations and curricula but which was powerless to control the quality of teaching or the allocation of public finance. It was an arrangement which produced 'unprogressive uniformity' but which was unable to prevent wasteful duplication among the colleges. The remedy was similar to that proposed for London: give the University control over the treasury grant by making the grant to the University for distribution among the colleges, and give the University control over the appointment of professors and heads of departments in the colleges; but leave to the colleges a maximum of autonomy in the design of

[handwritten margin note: But his own experience at London imp.]

---

* 'You are a very quick people although you have been terribly downtrodden by English examiners', he told the University College at Swansea.

courses and the setting and marking of examinations. 'The principle is not federalism but devolution. . . .'

The second issue which clearly caught Haldane's imagination was a proposal from Caernarvon county council to involve a cross section of the public in the policies of the University. According to the constitution of the English civic universities and the University of Wales, *de facto* government was by a small body called the council (which delegated academic affairs to the senate); but the council was the executive for a very large body called the court, which might contain between 100 and 200 members, representing local authorities, graduates, learned societies, educational bodies, and so on. If those who drafted this pattern ever expected much from the courts, they were disappointed; in most universities their meetings were little more than annual parties which listen to an address, transact a little formal business, and have tea. The Caernarvon county council proposed to put life into the court of the University of Wales. Their submission ran:

> The University Court should be peripatetic and should sit for a number of days at the visited centre when conferences with members of the local education authorities and teachers would be held, public lectures on educational questions given, and public meetings held at which awards and honours gained by local students would be announced – following the precedent of the Eisteddfod and its conferences and sectional meetings.

The commission fixed on this imaginative idea with enthusiasm. Listen to Haldane pursuing it in an exchange with Lloyd George's brother during one of the hearings: it would, said Mr W. George, make a meeting of the university court an 'Eisteddfod' of its own, a 'real high festival for education . . . something really fine'.

'A great occasion?' asked Haldane. 'Yes.'

'And possibly it might sit in public so that the people might hear?' And George supplied the crescendo: 'And men of outstanding eminence coming there to lecture, and everything of that sort giving pomp and circumstance to the gathering.'

'A couple of days' meeting?' 'At least a couple of days . . . .'

'Which should focus the attention of Wales?' 'Yes and guide the policy of Wales in educational matters for the coming year and be an inspiration and guidance for the people. . . .'

When the commission framed their recommendations they gave prominence to this idea. 'Our conception of the University Court', they wrote, 'is that of a Parliament of higher education. . . .' They enlarged the court to 200 or more and greatly increased the representation of local authorities (though not to give them at least fifty per cent, which was what Denbigh and Caernarvon wanted).★ And the commissioners' euphoric proposal was that the court 'should not hurry through its formal agenda in one day with its attention divided between the business and the clock or railway-guide, but should set out deliberately to spend four or five or six days on the discussion of both the practical affairs and the broader aims of higher education. . . . Great projects of reform and development might be discussed. . . .' That Haldane himself was captivated by the idea is evident from his address to the court when it held its first meeting under the new constitution: '. . . the scheme was that the Parliament of the University . . . should discuss these great matters. We did not contemplate that it should discuss after the easy-going fashion of such University Courts as exist in more strictly Saxon countries.' Great principles, he went on to say, would be discussed at the court on behalf of the people of Wales. The purpose 'is to recognise the very highest education – education of the university type – as part of the national life . . . . That is the new principle, a principle which has not been applied to any other University in the United Kingdom. . . .'

The third issue to which Haldane was personally committed, and which filled his interests for the last phase of his life, was the obligation of the University to undertake extra-mural work. The Welsh people did not need any prompting about this. Their adult education movement was already vigorous. Indeed at one point in the hearings Haldane had to caution the representatives of the Workers' Education Association (WEA) against making too great a call upon the resources of the University: 'Do not pour out your treasure over too wide an area, otherwise it will be lost. The content of a university is like a precious liquid – there is not too much of it.' The significance of Haldane's interest in adult education at this time is that he was beginning to see in this the solution to a dilemma: the dilemma (as he put it to students in London a few years later) of how to bring what is

★ Other new elements in the court included representatives of the students, MPs for Wales and Monmouthshire, tutorial classes, the National Library of Wales, the National Museum of Wales, the Welsh Agricultural Society, and the Hon. Society of Cymmrodorion.

really higher education to bear upon the democracy. On one hand he stood uncompromisingly for quality in higher education. In this sense he was an elitist and said so, though he wanted everyone capable of joining the elite to have the opportunity to do so. On the other hand he wanted the whole of British society to be permeated by the influence of the universities. 'Until you get an enlightened democracy', he told the people of Swansea, 'you will not get an inspired democracy.' The solution was not to bring the people indiscriminately into the universities (he would have opposed mass higher education as it is talked about today); it was to take the universities to the people. Hence, for Haldane, the great political importance of the extra-mural departments of universities and his pleasure at the enthusiasm for this activity in Wales.

The report met with general and spontaneous acclaim.

> The people of Wales have every reason to congratulate themselves and to be grateful for the findings and recommendations of the Royal Commission, for the proposals of the Commission are at once sane and imaginative ... the final adoption, rejection, elucidation or development of the more important proposals [submitted to the commission] has been almost invariably influenced by an appreciation of the spirit which animates the Welsh renascence of today. ... Throughout the report there run, as golden threads, notes of intimacy and sincerity. ...

The University welcomed it and the Colleges too, though perhaps with some apprehension that devolution might give them less freedom than federation. What mattered most was the response of the government. Lloyd George was by this time prime minister.* He and Fisher (now president of the board of education) received a deputation from the University on 14 August 1918, and Lloyd George made a most welcome statement. Provided the recommendations of the royal commission were in the main adopted, he said, the government would give financial backing:

> The Report is one of the most important documents, I think, in the history not merely of education in Wales, but of Wales itself; it is a very able document and its conclusions seem to be, in the

---

* His opinion of the Welsh colleges had not been flattering. He is on record as saying that 'in order to get a proper reorganisation of the Welsh University, the first thing would be to hire somebody to anaesthetise the three Principals.'

main, very practical and very sensible. . . . What I propose is this:
We should give £1 for £1. If you raise a penny rate, we will
give the equivalent of it.

This was just what the commissioners hoped for, because the idea
of a rating levy throughout Wales was the brain-child of Sir H. Jones,
which initially had run the gauntlet of Haldane's scepticism (he had
turned it down when he first heard about it, in the garden of a hotel
on the Menai Straits) but which was ultimately included as one of the
recommendations.

Not everything went according to plan. The medical school, in
particular, remained a problem until it received a special charter in
1931. But by May 1919 the University had prepared its submissions
for reform. A petition and draft charter were lodged with the privy
council on 17 June 1920 and on 13 August 1920 the supplementary
charter was approved by the king in council. Haldane had little to
do with these negotiations, but he gave an impressive welcome to
the reorganised University in the two memorable addresses from which
we have already quoted. It was typical of him not to reminisce about
the past but to turn the attention of his audience to the future: 'The
business of the Royal Commission', he told the academics of Cardiff,
'has been to dig. It is the business of Wales to plant and water.'

Another task in the cause of higher education was completed. Not
all the commission's hopes were realised. In particular the court never
measured up to the ambitious role offered to it. It was hard to believe
(wrote the historian of the University thirty-five years afterwards) that
the proposal, 'attractive though Lord Haldane had found it, was ever
more than a pleasing fantasy'. But the other recommendations were
so sound and practicable that it was not until 1960 that another commission was needed to re-examine the University of Wales. The
indecisiveness of its report (published in 1964) is in striking contrast
to the solidity of the structure Haldane and his colleagues built in
1916.

Haldane was now ready for the next task. There could be no more
telling postscript to the task he had completed in Wales than his
laconic note to Gosse, written on 25 November 1920: 'I leave for
Wales this morning – to open the University. I return by sleeping
car through the night. Tomorrow night I start again for Cloan. . . .'

We must now take the reader back to 1916, for Haldane, in the

years after his downfall, had other educational interests beside the
University of Wales. It was true, as he frequently said, that he had
lived for universities. But he came more and more to regard the
successive stages of education as indivisible. It was only the outbreak
of war which held up the first wave of legislation to reform the school
system which Haldane and Lloyd George (neither of them with any
formal responsibility for education) had inspired. As secretary of
state for war Haldane had been shocked at the amount of illiteracy
among recruits. To reconcile his lofty views about universities and
his liberal ideals of democracy, he had to accept a logic which made
it plain that even in a perfect society not every boy or girl could
aspire to become a bachelor of arts. There must be honourable and
satisfying alternatives to higher education. So, having witnessed
(as he told the house of lords) the establishment of ten new universities
in the country* and having acted as midwife to some of them, Haldane
turned his attention more and more to other levels of education.

So, back to 7 April 1916, when Beatrice Webb wrote in her diary:

> We dined with Haldane last night – for one of our periodical talks.
> He was looking very well & is in good form in spite of his political
> retreat. He has been seeing something of his former colleagues – even
> Lloyd George & has been trying to persuade him to take up a great
> scheme of technical ½-time education 14–18 after the War. 'Tho' I
> have not been heard of' he said somewhat pathetically, 'I have been
> very busy – I have a room in the Ed. department'.

His mind, wrote Beatrice, was 'running much more on raising the
standard of education of the whole population than in [the] old days.'
A fortnight before this dinner party Haldane had given the foundation
oration at University College, London. His conversation with the
Webbs doubtless ran on the same theme. For Haldane got preoccupations – it would be exaggerating to call them obsessions – and his
preoccupation was now with vocational training. 'But you, after all',
he told his audience of students, 'can never be more than a nucleus.
The vast majority of our working countrymen are wage earners,
belonging to the industrial classes. Do the interests of the nation

* Haldane was exaggerating a little! His list included London (which was not
formerly a teaching university), Birmingham, Liverpool, Manchester (*pace* the
Victoria University), Leeds, Sheffield, Bristol, Armstrong College attached to
Durham, and two universities in Ireland.

require that they too should be infused with the reflective habit which is born of knowledge? My answer is an emphatic yes.' He did not shirk the issue by devious speech: 'You cannot in practice give complete equality in educational opportunity to all classes.' Few children of the working class can really get on to the educational ladder. But the problem is not insoluble: 'the greatest educational discovery of the most recent years appears to me to be that of the latent possibilities of what is called vocational training.' Haldane's formula was modest enough on modern standards: compulsory education to fourteen; then a bifurcation at which the middle and upper class and those of the working class so exceptional as to be able to tread the narrow ladder would go to secondary schools; and the great mass of elementary pupils would go into jobs. But for these there should be compulsory continuation classes such as Germany (Haldane had the courage to mention this) had so successfully developed. The day-release classes (as we now call them) were to be no mere craft-training: they were to have intellectual content and (he did not specify what he meant) 'physical and spiritual content' as well. The old faith in the efficacy of education was as strong as ever. For a quarter of a century, he told his audience, he had represented a Scottish constituency where farm labourers were of the very highest quality. And why? They 'had been educated in Scottish schools as hardly an English farm labourer in the Southern Counties is ever educated.'

How were these aspirations to be turned into legislation? Already part of Haldane's message had got across to the public. People were realising that Britain's unpreparedness to fight Germany was as much educational as military; that the defeat of Germany would buy time to equip Britain's educational system to compete with the post-war world. Buy time, but no more: so that even with guns blazing across the Channel and train-loads of wounded arriving at Charing Cross and Victoria, plans had to be laid to improve education. The *Times Educational Supplement* carried, from October 1915 to May 1916 a string of articles pressing for a royal commission on education. Haldane, recollecting that dust was accumulating on his royal commission report on London, opposed this pressure. A royal commission, he told the house of lords, 'simply means an opiate to send restless people to sleep, the putting of things off and nothing being done for four or five years. We cannot wait for four or five years.' The best way to push things forward would be to have an inconspicuous and discreet committee to review sketch plans already on the drawing board and to advise parliament how to proceed next session. With his astonishing pertinacity, Haldane now saw an opportunity to revive the draft bill of 1914. The thinking had already been put into it; the political atmosphere then had been brought to the right temperature. The operation abandoned in July 1914 (when Asquith announced that the bill could not be introduced in that session of parliament) could simply be resumed.

Haldane's campaign in the ensuing months of 1916 to reach this objective makes breathless reading. Some circumstances were in his favour. He was installed, unofficially, in the board of education. He had Asquith's somewhat remorseful support. He had no public office to fill his days with routine. But the smear still stuck. Even in 1917 Mr Pemberton Billing, in the house of commons, questioned the government on Haldane's membership of various committees and added: 'Is the right hon. Gentleman aware that Lord Haldane is universally distrusted by the people and that the action of the Government is looked upon as an affront to them?' There were cries of 'no'; but it was a sharp reminder that Haldane was an embarrassment to any government.

On 4 April Lloyd George came to dine at Queen Anne's Gate. At the dinner were McCormick, Blair (chief education officer of the LCC), Struthers and Heath. Haldane wrote to his sister afterwards that they had made out a plan which Lloyd George had undertaken to try to put through. 'He and I have made an alliance on Edn once more', he added. He also sent a note to Lloyd George: 'After you left I found this in today's Times published in the Educational Supplement. It shows how people are moving towards the ideas we were speaking of & I send it to you. Tonight's talk was a very useful one. You may accomplish more than you can easily realise.' The enclosure was a cutting calling on the government to respond promptly to the demand for investigation and action in the cause of educational reform, without a prolonged enquiry. Haldane was keen to restore the educational alliance with Lloyd George, and on 10 May wrote to him to say that he had spoken to the prime minister about 'our plan for a small private Committee of Educational experts to consider principles & policy' and that Asquith had been quite agreeable. 'The Committee', he went on, 'need not be announced, & should be as private & informal as possible. I saw Vaughan Nash [secretary of the Reconstruction committee set up by Asquith in March 1916] who agrees that it will not interfere with the Reconstruction Committee.'

This Reconstruction committee had been set up to prepare what Haldane, when speaking in the house of lords in December 1915, had called a Peace Book; and by the beginning of May, Vaughan Nash was already in touch with Selby-Bigge about the planning that was needed for post-war development in education. At the end of the month, Selby-Bigge submitted a case for appointing a reviewing committee on the lines of the earlier one presided over by Haldane in 1913, and on 23 June, the Reconstruction committee endorsed this proposal, resolving, however, that the decision should be kept secret, and that 'if any question arises concerning the necessity of reviewing the education system of the country as a whole, it should be stated that the Reconstruction Committee has taken up the matter.' This disposed of the call for a royal commission, and on 30 June Crewe took the opportunity to announce that the government had decided not to have one.

Haldane, meanwhile, had been working away on his own: on one hand pursuing his notion of a private committee of experts, and on the other preparing to launch a public campaign with a major speech in the house of lords. Towards the end of May he wrote to his mother that he was ready 'with full material' for the opening of the campaign; but in view of the controversy surrounding him, he was more than ever sensitive to the need for careful timing, and it was not till July that he judged it safe to put his motion in the lords.

The house of lords speech, delivered on 12 July, was a masterpiece of close argument, perhaps the greatest education speech of his career. The notice was: 'To call attention to the training of the nation and to the necessity of preparing for the future.' Haldane began with some striking facts. Ninety per cent of young persons got no further education after the age of fourteen. 'I have often wondered how many Watts's, Kelvins, and Darwins have been lost in the vast mass of untrained talent which the children of the working classes afford.' Then came a plea for continuation schools. Of 5·85 million young persons between the ages of sixteen and twenty-five in England and Wales, 5·35 million got no education at all. He reminded their lordships that plans to remedy this deplorable state of things were worked out long ago and in 1913 and 1914 were included in the king's speech; all that was needed now was to revive these plans. Education was, to the British public, a 'tiresome' word, and Haldane (he was inconsistent on this principle) concluded that 'the only way is for the leaders to take a definite decision without waiting for any particular mandate . . . .'

Somewhat unwisely perhaps, and certainly gratuitously, for it was not an integral part of his argument, Haldane criticised the education given by Oxford and Cambridge, not on its quality (which he admitted was excellent) but on its lack of relevance to the art and science of administration in public affairs. Perhaps he did this in order to provoke debate and to draw their lordships' fire away from the issue he really cared for. If this was his purpose he succeeded. Some of the lords plunged into a spirited defence of the classics (employing the common fallacious argument – which Haldane did not fail to notice – that because some classicists are superb administrators, the classics are a good educational training for administration). Curzon, in particular, castigated Haldane on this part of his speech. All this ensured good press coverage, and the debate went on for three days.

The most searching criticism of Haldane's speech came from outside the House, from Sadler, writing to *The Times*. ' . . .the fear haunts one', wrote Sadler, 'that the fundamental issues of the business have not yet been thought out . . .' and he instanced five 'cardinal points upon which, so far as I know, no agreement has yet been reached throughout English inquiries into our educational needs'. These included the career prospects for teachers, the attitude of employers to continuation classes, the financing of private schools, and the very perplexing question: 'What spiritual authority shall decide the content of the religious training given in schools under public management . . .?'

It was a letter from a man who knew as much about the education system as Haldane did, and they were real (if scarcely 'cardinal') points that he raised. But the letter was coloured by dislike and (probably) jealousy of Haldane. For Sadler had set his heart on becoming president of the board of education (in which he was disappointed) and he suspected Haldane of working behind the scenes in ways which (among other things) might deprive him of this opportunity. Two days after this correspondence, Sadler wrote in a private letter: 'Lord Haldane has written me an angry letter. I have replied quietly at length. He is really plotting, & resents being found out & hindered.'

Haldane was indeed plotting. Shortly afterwards – or so it seems, for it is not possible to determine the exact date – he ventured to bring a plan of his own to official notice by means of a memorandum which has been preserved amongst the records of the Reconstruction committee. The first surviving version of this memorandum is type-

— his 'penguin-like gesture' —

written, and not only unsigned and unaddressed, but undated and unheaded. But a slightly amended copy bears the pencilled heading: 'Mem: by Lord Haldane. Reviewing Sub Comm:' and both style and content strongly confirm this provenance. The purpose of the memorandum was to draw attention to the need for new administrative machinery to meet the growing demand for an expansion in the national system of education: a need represented as all the more pressing in view of the recent establishment, on a nation-wide basis, of the privy council committee to deal with the application of science to industry. 'What is wanted is a Body which, while not unduly meddlesome in details, should work out great principles, and on this Body the representatives of both England and Scotland would have to sit.' It was proposed that 'the Lord President of the Council, Lord Crewe, should preside – just as he does already in the case of the application of Science to Industry – over a special Committee of the Privy Council containing Cabinet and ex Cabinet Ministers, and that under this Committee should work a Committee of experts responsible to it, whose business it would be to prepare and work out plans and keep the machinery moving.' The memorandum then went on to discuss membership. For the main committee, the names which 'occur[red]' were Crewe, Balfour, and Chamberlain, together with Tennant for Scotland and the president of the English board of education. '*To these might be added* [our italics] the name of Lord Haldane.' For the subcommittee, Selby-Bigge, Struthers, McCormick and Blair were mentioned. There remained the question of the presidency of this body, and this was easily solved: 'The suggestion made by the expert members is that they would welcome Lord Haldane as Chairman of this Committee, and there is reason to think that Lord Haldane has no objection to serving on both, and indeed would prefer to serve on the Sub Committee and would be able to find the time for the purpose.'

Then came the disclosure of Haldane's long-term goal (not of course for himself, but for the country). 'It would be quite sufficient to set up the new Committees by a minute, without saying whether or not they were to be permanent, but it is to be hoped that they would grow into a permanent organization for the supervision of National Education.' It is interesting to reflect on the different course which our educational system might have taken if this permanent organisation had materialised. It might have been a parallel development to the department of scientific and industrial research (which did materialise from the other committee to which Haldane referred in his memorandum). It would presumably have had surveillance over all education, from the nursery school to the university and beyond. But matters did not end that way. Haldane's proposal for a committee of the privy council served by an expert subcommittee was dovetailed into the government's own plan for a reviewing subcommittee of the Reconstruction committee. The decision to appoint a reviewing committee, reached by the Reconstruction committee in June, had been announced in the house of commons on 18 July; a formal memorandum, with proposed terms of reference and composition, was submitted to Asquith on 25 July; and on the 26th, the last day of the debate in the house of lords, Crewe reiterated the government's pledge to proceed with the appointment of the committee, a pledge which drew from Haldane renewed protest against the needless delay of a further general enquiry. Since the second day's debate on the 19th, he had been up to Cloan. Before leaving for Scotland on the 20th, he had written to Gosse of his fear that Crewe would prove 'dilatory' on the final day of the debate. 'Immediate & vigorous action is what is wanted.' A period of repose at Cloan was apt to clear his mind, and it seems likely that he drafted the memorandum during his stay there and launched it on his return – shortly before, or immediately after, the conclusion of the debate. However this may have been, the original reference to a committee of the privy council, made in the first surviving draft of the memorandum was amended in pencil to read 'Reviewing Committee', and formal invitations to serve on such a body were duly despatched from the Reconstruction committee on 8 August. Haldane was amongst those invited, and it was explained that the chairmanship would be taken by Crewe who proposed 'to delegate a considerable amount of work to a Sub Committee of experts'. It was also announced that a preliminary meeting of the committee would be held at the privy council office on 11 August. This was its one and only meeting; but it made the decision Haldane wanted. He was asked 'to prepare in association with a group of English and Scottish educational experts a memorandum outlining the questions which required consideration'. That same day he wrote to Gosse: 'We met today – the Cabinet Committee – & I was unanimously placed in a position of great responsibility for plans & power to mould them. All were most cordial. We resolved on secrecy, so it will be difficult for the "Times" to hear anything definite. And as my plan has been adopted & put through it can hardly now be upset.' The experts he gathered round him were Selby-Bigge, Blair, Heath, McCormick and Struthers: all tried collaborators, four out of six of them Scottish. It was the membership he had in mind when discussing the proposal with Lloyd George.

Haldane lost no time in complying with the Reviewing committee's request. By 17 August he had drafted a memorandum for his colleagues to consider. It began with the characteristic deductive approach: 'Agreement in general principles is the foundation of progress in agreement on details' – and he set out eleven propositions which appeared 'to emerge from discussion'. Continuation schools and educational provinces subsuming local authorities were of course included, and one of his older motifs was there: the award of certificates at secondary schools, which should be the normal passport to the university, based more on the school record than on a mere examination. He put as his priorities the reorganisation of the final year at elementary schools, raising the leaving age to fourteen, a system of continuation schools, and more secondary education.

In August 1916 the president of the board of education, Henderson, became paymaster general. He was succeeded by Crewe, who adopted an attitude which evidently upset Haldane's plans. He wrote to Gosse on 27 August:

As to Education what I am going to write is very private. After I left Crewe seemed to me to have yielded to the importunities of the old set. As a result of what I looked on as a breach of the spirit of our understanding, a breach the significance of which I don't think he realised, I sent him an ultimatum. I will not go on but will conduct an independent campaign unless I am given a sufficiently free hand. I await his reply, which may mean a breach. But this is a secret between you & me. It accounts for his reticence to you.

But the storm blew over. On 15 September he wrote again to Gosse: 'I had an excellent final interview with Crewe & Asquith this morning, & arranged my Education organisation. I only hope it will not be meddled with again.'

There was some complaint in parliament (on 8 August) and in *The Times* (on 11 August) about the secrecy surrounding the enquiries into education, but protest was stilled by an announcement made in the house of commons on 10 October. The government was evidently still on the defensive, for it had prepared an answer in anticipation of a supplementary question which was not in fact asked: 'The Committee is a Sub Committee of the Reconstruction Committee and is composed entirely of Ministers and ex-Ministers. I cannot undertake at the moment to give the names but I will consider the matter.'

During the autumn Haldane pressed on with his two-pronged attack: on some days, speeches to stimulate interest; on other days, meetings at his home in Queen Anne's Gate. At home his subcommittee met regularly. It is fascinating to watch how, during these years out of office, Haldane operated on the periphery of power by making his own home, as it were, a field headquarters. On one day the education subcommittee would meet in his upper smoking room. On another day the committee on the machinery of government (set up in 1917) would meet two floors below. 'We sit twice a week', wrote Beatrice Webb, 'over tea and muffins in Haldane's comfortable dining room discussing the theory and practice of government.'

The education subcommittee met almost weekly from 10 October to 27 November. On 15 November the first version of a report for the reviewing committee was drafted. It was headed 'Memorandum. Strictly confidential' and was signed by Heath, though it was written in the first person as from Haldane. It may be that this style was simply to conform with the wording of the resolution that Haldane should prepare the paper 'in association' with the experts. Or it may be that the paper went further than the experts were prepared to go; certainly one of them, Selby-Bigge, severely criticised it afterwards.

It was a tough document, in some ways (e.g. over continuation schools and the need for larger local education authority areas) going beyond the draft bill of 1914. It emphasised the time lag in educational reform: 'A nation gathers the full fruit of the education it has given some 20 years after the child is born, and the national plans for education like those for the navy must be drawn accordingly.' It condemned the existing fabric of education as being 'weak from bottom to top'. It pressed for compulsory continuation schools and an adequate supply of teachers: 'If we can lay these two girders well and truly we shall find the rest of our programme relatively easy and simple.' Then came advocacy for larger education authorities, 'to maintain a great service of teachers', to administer scholarships, and 'to facilitate other important reforms in higher education'. This is far from the neo-Hegelian *étatism* which some of Haldane's critics attributed to him. On the contrary (as Haldane pointed out) while there is much to be said for state action in matters of urgency and for limited periods, an undue extension of state action is likely to weaken local initiative; so his recommendation was devolution, but devolution to institutions strong enough to accept the responsibility.

Officials of the board of education did not care much for Haldane's report, and on 20 November one of the experts, Selby-Bigge, wrote to Nash that he was labouring on a separate memorandum from the board to the reviewing committee. Criticism in the office focussed mainly on the pivotal recommendation of larger areas and Selby-Bigge, in a departmental minute on a second draft of Haldane's document, put his finger on the essential weakness of the proposal. For once Haldane, the superb tactician, wanted to go too far too fast. For years he had been preaching Matthew Arnold's doctrine – that British education should be organised in provinces – but Haldane had never really faced up to the fiscal consequences of this policy. The provincial councils, he often said, should *control* the educational system, maintain the teaching service, administer the scholarships. To discharge these functions the councils would need the backing of financial authority. Without money they would be powerless. If they were to have money it would be at the cost of local government sovereignty. One civil servant in the board of education returned a minute to Selby-Bigge dismissing the proposal as 'quite out of touch with realities . . .' and went on: 'I therefore refrain from offering any comment on it'. Was this a sign that on the periphery of power Haldane had overlooked the necessity to carry civil servants with him when it came to propose political action?

Haldane's report was never considered by the reviewing committee, for in December the government fell and the committee and its sub-committee were among the casualties. It was an eclipse for Haldane too. He lost his privileged (if anomalous) position in the board of education. Lloyd George appointed Fisher to be the board's president and he set up a new Reconstruction committee. At Fisher's request the old reviewing committee was dissolved and replaced by a panel for education under the chairmanship of W. G. S. Adams. Haldane's name was not on the panel; nor was he needed as consultant at the board of education: for not only was Fisher himself a scholar and an ex-vice-chancellor; to replace Heath (who had been appointed secretary to the new D.S.I.R.) he brought in Gilbert Murray from Oxford. This permeation of the board by distinguished academics was exactly what Haldane (himself an academic manqué) had wanted. The success of Haldane's own policies made him superfluous. This happens to success-ful men, and it is a mortifying victory.

But there was a bright edge to the cloud. Fisher liked and respected Haldane (Fisher had been one of the first to write a note of sympathy when Haldane lost office in 1915). Although he did not bring Haldane officially into his machine, the two men had many talks about education. Fisher (Haldane wrote to his sister) 'is very sympathetic to my programme. . . . There seems to be a real prospect of getting something done. He is putting nursery schools, continuation schools, improved secondary education and physical training in his programme.' And Fisher, in his autobiography, acknowledges Haldane's influence in both speeches and 'private consultations with the officers to the Board of Education'.

From January 1917 until Fisher's Education bill was passed in August 1918, Haldane campaigned and conspired unsparingly to support Fisher's reforms. He addressed meetings up and down the country. He spoke in the house of lords. He lobbied colleagues. He conferred with civil servants. Wherever he could make a move on the chessboard of politics toward winning the game – which was to put his 1914 reforms, brought up to date, on the statute book – he made the move. He was content, apart from occasional nostalgic references to his own earlier endeavours, to give all the credit to Fisher. His eyes were never off the game, and Fisher was generous in allowing Haldane to watch it from close by. We get a glimpse of this generosity on 20 February, when a preliminary memorandum for a comprehensive scheme of reform was agreed in principle by the war cabinet after half an hour's discussion. Fisher must have told Haldane of the good news straight away, for on 22 February Haldane was already writing to Lloyd George: 'It was with very great pleasure that I learned confidentially from Fisher that you had given your approval to his plans for educational reform. They are admirable plans & this is a great step on. It has never before been taken & I hope to be of all the little use I can in furthering the new departure in education which your Government has taken.'

But Haldane's current preoccupation was to press for provincial councils, although he must have known by now that his views were opposed by board of education officials, other experts like Sadler, and local authorities themselves. Here he went much further than Fisher was prepared to go. In practically every speech Haldane 'plugged' provincial councils as he had long ago conceived them, with a university at the head permeating the schools and other educational institutions beneath. Thus at Perth on 6 January 1917: 'it was inevitable that we should have larger areas and more powerful authorities.' And at Huddersfield, a few days later, he was reported as saying: 'Why should they not take the West Riding, London, and Lancashire, and make them into educational provinces . . .?'

Criticism of these views continued but they seemed to make no impression on Haldane. Fisher himself was sufficiently moved to try the idea out in a deliberately vague way, when he made his first major speech in the house of commons on 19 April. There was a need, he said, 'that the county authorities, either separately or combined together in provincial committees, should make complete and progressive schemes for education in their respective areas. . . .'

Haldane's speeches, now laced with compliments on Fisher's 'brilliant performance', continued to press for provincial councils – authorities which would 'control their university, continuation schools, scholarships, and the supply of teachers'. On 9 May he launched a spring offensive in the house of lords, which led to a full debate on the issue. All the arguments were redeployed: provincial regions in which things could be worked out according to the *genius loci;* the analogy of the successful devolution of education to one province already: Scotland; the idea extended to the rest of the kingdom with seven or eight provinces for England and Wales.

(It is interesting to reflect that this concept of devolution to large provinces is in fact about to happen in England and Wales over the management of rivers. There are to be ten great regional water authorities, with powers to raise money by precepts on the rates and to control water resources in their regions.)

But their lordships were not prepared to welcome the idea of educational provinces. Crewe must have expressed the view of many even of Haldane's friends when he suggested in the debate that Haldane had under-estimated the difficulty of grouping local authority areas and that he seemed to be approaching 'extremist' views on the subject; and there were murmurings that the French educational system might provide a better model for England than the German system.

When Fisher moved the first reading of the Education bill on 10 August 1917, he used Haldane's proposals as a backcloth for his own. There *could*, he said, be eight or nine provincial councils, with wide powers, including the power to levy a rate.

That, I understand, is the scheme advocated by Lord Haldane, who, of course, speaks on all educational questions with great authority. Or the Board might be empowered by Statute to provide for the establishment of provincial associations after consultation with the authorities concerned, the local education authorities being empowered to delegate administrative and educational functions to these associations . . . . The Bill follows the second of these paths.

But Fisher had misunderstood Haldane.* The bill provided just the sort of 'start off' he wanted; it also provided, as firmly as he could have wished, for continuation schools. After reading Fisher's speech, Haldane sent him a generous note of congratulation.

It was only a first reading of the bill and much remained to be done. The house of commons rose on 21 August without the bill having been given a second reading. 'My chief concern', wrote Haldane to Gosse, 'is to help to stir up a current which will carry Fisher's Bill into law. For the Philistines will obstruct him presently if we do not work. . . .' So, after his summer holiday at Cloan, Haldane took the road again to campaign for Fisher's bill: Edinburgh on 28 September, then Dundee, then Glasgow, then Chelmsford (where he vigorously protested at the government's suggestion that they might not be able to include the bill in the coming session). But some of Haldane's speeches at that time may have been what is now called 'counter-productive'; for whilst he was hammering away at the need for provincial councils, Fisher and officials at the board of education were preparing to bow to the storm of opposition from local education authorities directed against the administrative provisions of the bill, and especially the clause about provincial associations.

Instead of pressing forward with the existing bill during the remainder of the session, the government decided to introduce an amended bill to take account of the local opposition at an early stage

* Haldane repudiated the assumption that his scheme for provincial authorities or councils included power to levy a rate. In his congratulatory note to Fisher, written on 13 August, he protested: '. . . I have never wished to do more than develope (sic) these much as you propose, & in particular I have always repudiated the idea of giving to Provincial Authorities rating powers independent of those of the L.E.A.s. The control of State Grants through properly devised and approved schemes by the Provincial Authorities is another matter.' That Haldane was misunderstood over this, was partly his own fault, for although he pointed to the Scottish Education Fund as an example of the way provincial councils might be financed, he was deliberately reticent about the details of such an arrangement, claiming indeed, that the government would be far better at devising a viable scheme than he would!

in the following session. This was presented for a first reading in the house of commons on 14 January 1918, and although as Fisher explained the new bill was substantially the same as the previous one, certain changes had been made in the administrative provisions. Thus the earlier clause, proposing no more than voluntary provincial associations, was withdrawn; and all that was left of Haldane's 'preoccupation' was a weak substitute (clause 6) facilitating the federation of local education authorities for certain purposes. The bill went its way smoothly, and on completion of the committee stage Haldane wrote to Fisher: 'A line of warm congratulation. You have taken a great Bill through Committee, & you have also established a very high & valuable parliamentary reputation. It was a great thing for the country when [you] accepted office as Minister of Education.' In the house of lords Haldane warmly (and selflessly) acclaimed Fisher's achievement, and even mildly rebuked Lord Gainford (who was Pease, a former president of the board of education, who had been responsible for drafting the bill of 1914) when Gainford could not resist a 'friendly charge ... of plagiarism', and quoted clauses from the 1914 bill to show that Fisher's bill was not original. 'It is', said Haldane magnanimously, 'the largeness of spirit of the Bill and the way in which it is welded into an organic whole with a new spirit that distinguishes it from previous attempts in education.' But Haldane himself could not resist striking one more blow for provincial councils: '... when I look at Clause 6 I find that it is not in as good a form as the original clause in the original Bill .... I want to see these local education authorities federating and taking into counsel the teachers of the universities in their localities for much larger educational purposes.'* (Was this an early symptom of the futile obstinacy of an ageing man?) On 8 August the bill received the royal assent. For Haldane another campaign was over – one which had been conducted by remote control, as it were, from the dining room table and the smoking room of 28 Queen Anne's Gate.

All credit for the new reforms went to Fisher. Even Lloyd George (who was in a position to know better) makes no mention of Haldane's part when he praises Fisher's work in the *War memoirs*. But there were people who realised that the successful passing of the Education act was only the last move in a long and sometimes frustrating political

---

* Although – and this is significant in view of a speech he made nine years later (p. 166t.) – Haldane went on to say: 'I certainly shall not move any Amendment in committee on this subject but shall be thankful for what I have got.'

negotiation in which Haldane had made the opening moves and which he had loyally supported after he had been deprived of the final laurels. One of these people was Selby-Bigge. After the first reading of the bill in 1917, Haldane had written to congratulate him, as the permanent secretary of the board of education. Here is Bigge's reply. It is a fitting verdict on the whole campaign:

Dear Lord Haldane,

Many thanks for your letter of the 17th. I am glad you like our Bill. Much of it is of course familiar to you, and if not its actual parent you certainly are a blood relation, and you are entitled at all events to a share in the congratulations on its birth. You have also done yeoman service in preparing the way for it in the Country . . . . If we can get the Bill on the Statute Book and get on the Estimates a pair of millions which will by a natural process breed other millions, we shall have done something for a better England.

7 Ebb-tide

Beatrice Webb's assessment of Haldane, if one makes allowance for her monstrous egotism, is more penetrating than that of any of his contemporaries. But she was deplorably sanctimonious about some of Haldane's indulgences and this, we believe, led her to misjudge his attitude to success. The food he ate, the cigars he smoked, and the company he kept, all came in for her censorious and feline comment. Haldane, she wrote in her diary, had 'a childish liking, mingled with personal vanity, in being "in the know" with, I will not say a finger, but a whole hand in the pie'. 'His foible has been to be in with all those who were wielding world power and to let the other side know it. He has always delighted in power and the appearance of power. . . .' And again: 'He is, in short, a *power* worshipper.'

People who accept great responsibility and do so willingly (even eagerly, as Haldane did) are commonly thought to worship power. Some do. But many do not; they regard it as an inevitable component of responsibility, to be valued only because access to power makes it possible to discharge responsibility well. In our portrait of Haldane we do not discern a relish of power for its own sake. What we do discern is a sweeping gusto for the techniques of politics: to be in possession of all the necessary facts, to know all the right people, to have fore-warning for trends of opinion and intuition for timing – not to enhance power, but to persuade a whole nation to take another step toward what Haldane believed to be the good society. This is not a worship of power; it is a pride in responsibility.

Beatrice Webb misjudged also Haldane's vanity. Satisfaction over his achievements he undoubtedly enjoyed, though he did not boast about them except to his mother. But did he really enjoy flattery? Beatrice Webb wrote that 'self seekers and promoters of causes . . . habitually and often grossly kowtow to him – for it is only too obvious that he likes it.' Doubtless people did flatter him, for he had great influence, but it is a false conclusion to assume that he liked flattery. He probably decided, as other influential men have, that it saved time not to expostulate; better to put up with it in silence. One suspects that Beatrice Webb, when she wrote about Haldane, was sometimes holding a mirror to herself. On 28 March 1926, for instance, Haldane reviewed, in the *Observer*, Beatrice's *My apprentice-ship*. The review was judicious, restrained, and in places gently critical ('Her rejection of the contributions made by politicians', Haldane wrote, 'seems excessive in its emphasis'). Beatrice, in her diary, bridled at this criticism. Haldane was hurt, she concluded, because she had not written enough, or appreciatively enough, about him in her book! She excuses herself: the omission was due to absent-mindedness. She rationalises the omission: '. . . Haldane is exactly one of the person-ages who will come off unduly badly in memoirs. . . .' And she ends with the condescending comment: 'All of which makes me more regretful that I did not give him his due; he shall get it in the following volume.' And then Beatrice's essential compassion breaks through: 'But alas! he is not likely to be there to read it.'

It is surely obvious that Beatrice Webb's assessment of Haldane is tangled up with Beatrice Webb's assessment of herself. '. . . now and again', she wrote, 'our diverse scales of values have obviously clashed and then we have become for a time antagonistic or indifferent to each other. There has even been not a little mutual contempt.'

So, when it comes to putting into our portrait Haldane's attitude to power, we prefer to observe Haldane rather than to listen to Beatrice. The test of whether a successful man has succumbed to the temptations of power comes in his old age. Retirement from office affects successful men in diverse ways. Some feel envy and hostility toward those who supplant them and although they may try to conceal it, it shows in pathetic gestures to prolong influence and to deplore change. Others give a benevolent welcome to their successors and may even be inclined to praise their efforts uncritically. Haldane was generous toward those who supplanted him. Of course, after retire-ment, it is natural for a man who has made history to want to remain close to where history is being made. A cynic might label his kindness and approval of his juniors as ingratiation, so that he may remain admired by them. Whether Haldane used his charm consciously or unconsciously to keep the confidence of Fisher and Selby-Bigge, Fitzroy and McCormick, we do not know; but throughout this ebbing tide of his influence Haldane never repined. Of course he liked to be consulted, and often he was not. Of course his vanity was stirred (e.g. by his reception when he went to Bristol as chancellor

– the University 'looks on me as its father' – and when he laid the foundation stone for the University College of Nottingham – 'The reception was wonderful'), but a little vanity is a harmless indulgence to which an old man is entitled, provided he does not use it to bore his friends. Above all, he never sulked when he saw great things happening to education without his help, he was never bitter, he never obstructed. And when he was once more invited into office to help the first Labour government, he was firm about the conditions under which he would do it but he accepted without condescension.

At the end of world war I Haldane was already a sick man. For nearly ten years he had suffered from diabetes and there was some permanent damage from the eye trouble he had in 1909. It was diabetes which again laid him low in 1918. Dean Inge visited him in September and recorded: 'Then we went to Cloan. . . . I had some prayers with old Mrs Haldane, who seems quite unchanged, but Lord Haldane is now an old man. . . .' And a similar report was made to Mrs Inge in the previous summer: '. . . Lord Haldane is not the man he was; he is ageing in every way.' But there was no self-pity and no surrender to bodily ailments. Haldane drove himself relentlessly to continue his educational evangelisation. He still spun his web across Whitehall. Thus, in May 1919, when there were rumours that Fisher might be leaving the board of education, Haldane wrote to T. Jones in the war cabinet offices: 'I am concerned about the persistent rumours that Fisher may be moved from the Board of Education. Probably these rumours are quite premature, but I am certain that to move him from his present office would be a profound mistake. He has magnificent work in front of him, which he alone can do . . . . I think the P.M. knows this, but it is very desirable that it should be present to his mind.' Through his contacts in the house of lords and through Fisher and Selby-Bigge, Fitzroy and McCormick, Haldane was able to watch closely the changes in the educational scene during the post-war years. Three changes particularly interested him: the financing of universities, the re-organisation of Oxford and Cambridge, and the creation of new civic universities. Let us turn from Haldane's portrait for a few pages to sketch this scene.

First, the financing of universities. On pp. 99–101 we describe the petty wrangle between the treasury and the board of education in 1912 over which of these departments should distribute parliamentary grants among the universities and university colleges. The final outcome was that the grants were largely controlled by the board of education, but were divided between the treasury and the board's votes as follows (the figures are for 1918–19): treasury votes of £22,000 for English universities as degree-giving bodies, and £149,000 for arts and science work in English universities and colleges; and board of education votes of £65,000 for work in technology and medicine, and £32,000 for the Imperial College of Science and Technology. The £149,000 from the treasury was transferred in quarterly instalments to a deposit account of the board of education and paid out on the recommendation of an advisory committee (presided over by McCormick) appointed by and responsible to the board of education. But – it is an echo from the time of Lloyd George at the treasury – the treasury retained control of the grant for higher education in Wales (£36,500), and there were separate arrangements for the universities of Scotland and Ireland. It was an anomalous and untidy arrangement. On 19 December 1918 Fisher broached the matter with the chancellor of the exchequer (Bonar Law): 'The existing division of University Grants between the Votes of the Treasury and the Board of Education is inconvenient, and difficult to justify on any principle. The distinction indeed is only a formal one as regards England, because the main part of the Treasury grant (the £149,000) is transferred in quarterly instalments . . . and actually paid out by the Board.' And he went on to cite (slightly inaccurately) the recommendation of the royal commission on the University of Wales, which was that payments to the Welsh colleges should in future be entrusted to the board of education. The treasury was disposed to acquiesce. An official minuted: 'Mr Fisher's . . . proposal that the State grants in aid of University work should be borne on the Vote for the Board of Education can be agreed to . . . .' And on 18 January the chancellor of the exchequer (now Austen Chamberlain) wrote: '(i) I agree as to the transfer of votes from Try to M/E.'

It seemed that the principle for which Haldane had been contending – that education, and therefore finance for education, should be regarded as one organic whole – was on the eve of acceptance. But four days later Austen Chamberlain countermanded the decision, directing 'that in view of the conversation with Mr Fisher yesterday the decision on point (i) must be held up for the time being.' For six months the two departments exchanged notes and negotiated. The outcome was the exact opposite of the solution for which Haldane had been working. Virtually all grants in aid of university education in the United Kingdom were put on the treasury vote, and their distribution was to be by the treasury on the advice of a committee appointed by them, to be known as the University Grants Committee.

It is commonly supposed that the deciding factor in this turnabout was an argument suggested by Austen Chamberlain seven years earlier, and subsequently attributed to Fisher, namely that 'the Board of Education would seek to impose their views' upon the universities and that the autonomy of universities would be better safeguarded if grants came from the treasury. This supposition is wrong. The deciding factor is clear in a letter from T. L. Heath at the treasury to Fisher, on 3 May 1919. Since the committee to administer the grants was to be one for the whole United Kingdom, it had to be appointed by one authority with jurisdiction for the three kingdoms. The writ of the board of education ran only in England and Wales. Therefore, it had to be the treasury which appointed the committee, after consultation with the board of education, the secretary for Scotland and the chief secretary of Ireland. In his autobiography Fisher refers to the safeguarding of autonomy as a *consequential* advantage, but makes it clear that the prime reason for the decision was that the jurisdiction of the board of education did not extend over Scotland.

Throughout these negotiations Haldane was only an observer. There is no evidence that he was consulted by ministers or officials. Nor – and this is consistent with our portrait of him – is there any evidence that he attempted to influence the outcome although it went against one of his strongly held principles. On the contrary: in a speech in the house of lords a year later (on 21 July 1920) he complimented the government on setting up the UGC and said that the whole system had been 'put on a better footing'. In the 1930s another attempt to transfer the grant to the board of education was contemplated. The president of the board drafted a letter: 'I should like you to consider whether the UGC should not become responsible to the Board of Education rather than the Treasury. I do not imagine that there is another European country where the universities are considered to be outside the province of the Ministry of Education.' But the letter was not sent. Only in the 1960s – amid querulous misgivings among some academics – was Haldane's wish fulfilled.

The second change in the educational scene was the incorporation of Oxford and Cambridge into the system of treasury grants. This had to be preceded by a royal commission on these two universities. Asquith was chosen as chairman. It was, even Asquith's sympathetic biographer admits, 'a bad appointment'. The report was dull and unadventurous. Sir Charles Firth had written to Haldane: 'Several people here have expressed a wish that you were its chairman instead of Asquith. My impression is that Asquith's views on higher education are those prevalent at Balliol in 1870, and that he has learnt nothing about it since.' Nevertheless when the Oxford and Cambridge bill was introduced into the house of lords on 19 April 1923, Haldane praised the report, and the nearest he came to criticism was to say: 'It did its work in a conservative fashion, and in University matters that is sometimes not undesirable.'

The third change in the educational scene was in an area much closer to Haldane's affections: in the civic universities. Since 1905 he had been on the standing committee of the privy council for the modern universities of England and Wales, and we have already described its important activities in the early years of the century and the part which Haldane played in them. The committee was still in existence but it was consulted less and less as time went on. The treasury grants committee, under McCormick, had since 1911 given advice on the sort of problems which had previously been referred to the privy council committee. After the committee was metamorphosed into the UGC, under the same chairman, in 1919, this privy council committee was replaced in 1923 by a fresh privy council committee for all universities in England and Wales. Haldane was not appointed to this, though he continued to serve occasionally on the corresponding committee for Scottish universities and assisted at a hearing in 1923 about the entry requirements for the universities of Scotland.

For good economic reasons the board of education and the UGC did not share Haldane's enthusiasm for additions to a network of regional universities in England. But the pressure to add universities was kept up. Haldane's interest was, for instance, enlisted in 1918 by the proponents for a federal university of the south-west, to embrace the college at Exeter and three other colleges in Devon and Cornwall. He was quoted as having been 'rather impressed'. But Fisher and McCormick firmly turned the proposal down. It was as well; it would have been federalism in its most enervating form. Two years later, in 1920, there was a petition for a charter to raise the college at Reading to university status. That, too, was turned down for the time being. Fifteen years earlier a decision of this kind would have rested, virtually, with Haldane and Fitzroy at the privy council. But this petition was dealt with as petitions still are today. Fitzroy, as clerk to the privy council, sent it to McCormick, as chairman of the UGC. There is no

evidence that Fitzroy turned to Haldane at any stage for advice. They
were in touch over university affairs in Scotland, and in 1923 there was
one last flicker of their long partnership. As Fitzroy was about to retire,
he noted in his diary:

> In compliance with Haldane's wishes, I wrote two letters on matters
> he wanted taken up before I retired: (1) [here came a request to have
> something done about the inferior food supplied by the contractor
> to the judges in the privy council!]; (2) the present position of the
> movement to establish a University at Reading, which in 1921 was
> held up for the collection of sufficient funds.

It was as gently as this that the ebb-tide of Haldane's influence in
Whitehall ran out in the years immediately after the war; and for a
reason which was – though he never put it this way himself – a great
compliment to his work. What he had done, since the turn of the century, was to help establish a machinery for the planning and financing
of education which superseded his personal influence, or that of any
other single official.

It is a further testimony to the way Haldane confronted old age that
this eclipse cast no shadow over his enthusiasm, nor did his poor health
deter him from taking on exhausting work in the cause of education.
He had proselytised for Fisher. He was now proselytising for adult
education. In 1920–1 he addressed fifty or sixty meetings up and down
the country. Hardly a year went by, up to 1927, without a major
speech from him in the house of lords. He wrote letters to the press.
In 1921, and again in 1922, he went to Germany and (an example of his
dogged integrity) he had the courage to tell an English audience, in a
speech at Wigan, 'I went to find out things for myself. . . . They are
seeking to educate their democracy . . . unless we make the advance of
our education as great as theirs, we shall presently be in a position of
peril. . . .' His home in Queen Anne's Gate remained a centre for
educational dialogue. He happily accepted ornamental offices, such as
the presidency of Birkbeck. And, as we describe later, he threw the
whole of his remaining energy into the last preoccupation of his life:
adult education.

But in 1922 there was a more urgent, short term, preoccupation.
The post-war boom had burst. Lloyd George's government had to
make drastic economies. They appointed, under Sir Eric Geddes, a
committee to recommend cuts in government expenditure. The
report (the Geddes axe) came out in February 1922. It threatened to

emasculate the Education act of 1918 and it put the universities, bulging with post-war students, on starvation rations. On 8 February 1922, just before the Geddes report was released, Haldane spoke eloquently in the house of lords, to try to dispel the apathy of their lordships over education. It was a plea for discrimination in the use of the axe – for everyone knew that savage cuts were inevitable. 'Germany', he said, 'is spending more liberally by a great deal than we are here on education, although her people are very poor.' We shall lose our competitive position with America and Germany, he warned them, unless we spend money on the education of our people. His warning was prophetic, but it made little impression on his colleagues on either side of the House. Then (in a surprising flash which disclosed his astonishing powers of political adaptation) he went on to warn their lordships that interest in education was becoming a 'monopoly of the Labour Party. I do not rejoice over that. I am not a member of the Labour Party, although I have great sympathy with it as being the only Party that is really keen about education. I have spoken for it and supported it on that ground, and on that ground alone.' The government, he told the coalition, 'has not been a reflective government'. It was the debate on the king's speech, and Haldane moved an amendment to underline his warning. It was simply to ask ministers to lay down principles (the deductive method again) for discrimination over the economies to be made. The response was depressing. Viscount Peel (a member of the government) declared: 'I would frankly say to the noble Viscount that if he and those who are interested in these subjects are going to constitute little zarebas of their own and to establish certain areas of administration within which profane people must not venture, then the chances of any economy must be very much reduced.' One feels that the old man was no longer getting from the lords the respect due to him after a lifetime of service. The amendment was negatived. The axe fell, and Haldane's most cherished clause in the 1918 act – the provision for continuation schools – was assassinated. The decision to raise the leaving age to fourteen was not cancelled but the extra supply of teachers needed for this measure was not forthcoming; it is on record that in 1922 a quarter of the classes had more than sixty pupils.

There were, however, moments of sunshine for Haldane in this cold economic climate. In 1920 he had a tumultuous welcome in Bristol, as chancellor of the University. His car broke down and students hauled him through the streets in a cab chanting: 'Who saved

England? . . . Haldane.' And in June 1922, when he laid the foundation
stone for another regional university, in Nottingham, he was drawn
into the hall by students on an improvised throne. He spoke for an
hour, back on his old theme: the Nottingham University as a centre
for the East Midlands. Then, in 1924, came the brief Indian summer of
his political life. We have quoted how, two years earlier, he had
declared in the house of lords his sympathies with Labour. There were
signs of his inclination even before that. Speaking to the students in
Swansea in 1921 he had said: 'I know what I would do if I were leader
of the Labour movement. I would put every ordinary item of the
programme in the second place, and I would say, whatever the merits
of all these items, the first way to accomplish them is to educate your
people.' In January 1922 he disclosed publicly to Asquith his disenchant-
ment with the Liberals, by declining to attend a meeting of Asquith
Liberals in the Central Hall, Westminster. Explaining, at some length,
to Asquith: 'My public life has for long been bound up with the cause
of Education, more than anything else', he reaffirmed his sympathy
'with the great spirit and tradition of Liberalism' and then set out the
conclusion which must have been a very painful one for him to reach:

> It was for this reason that three years ago I decided for the future
> to work with whatever party was most in earnest with Education
> in the widest sense. . . .
>
> I observed then, as I observe now, the almost complete lack of
> harmony between my strong conviction on this subject and the
> programme of official Liberalism. . . . In the official programme,
> and even in your own speeches, I can find no response about the
> thing I care for before any other at this moment, and regard as
> the key to reform generally.

The election of December 1923 foreshadowed the defeat of the
Conservative government, and at the end of the month, Ramsay
MacDonald went to Cloan to discuss what part Haldane would be
prepared to play in the formation of a Labour administration. Haldane
declined the presidency of the board of education, explaining that
what education now needed was money, not reform. 'I said', he
told Beatrice Webb later, 'I would willingly join & help in any way I
could, subject to certain conditions. I must lead in the Lords as
Lord Chancellor. . . . To this he [MacDonald] agreed after a night's
sleep at Cloan.' It was no surprise that he turned down the portfolio
of education. No more legislation was needed at that time, and he saw

that he would be in a more influential position to determine the flow of public money as lord chancellor with a seat in the cabinet than in a lesser office.

Parliament resumed on 12 February 1924, after the change of government. Haldane's first speech on that day plunged straight into the need for more education in science. In this he was on firm ground. The concept of science-based industry was beginning to take root; the use of scientists in war had proved how profitable their work might be in peace. On other educational themes, however, Haldane was by now becoming quite unrealistic. Strikes and industrial disputes had bedevilled three previous governments. Haldane still nursed the illusion that education of the masses would 'tranquillise' them; once they understood both sides of the tensions between capital and labour they would go back to their mines and railways and factories content. It was a quixotic notion, which could have been dispelled by conversation with any Marxist. Hence the irony of Haldane's last preoccupation. Adult education was – it still is – a great and worthy cause, but not for one of the major reasons which Haldane supposed.

This last preoccupation we come back to later. But before that we turn aside again from our protrait of Haldane to examine the background. For there was an undischarged invoice in Haldane's educational transactions; the great report of the royal commission on the University of London. We have described (p. 111f.) how a departmental committee worked on the report up to the outbreak of war. Haldane took no part in this, nor did he defend the report against the criticisms it received when discussion of it was revived after the war. But some (though by no means all) of the criticism was misconceived and we believe that our portrait should include discussion of the fate (and vicarious influence) of the report.

Even before the end of the war Fisher initiated a move. In a confidential print to the cabinet on 5 February 1917, containing an outline of changes necessary for a complete and satisfactory scheme of educational reform, Fisher included 'provision of a sum to enable the recommendations of the Royal Commission on the London University to be carried into effect'. On 24 November, at Fisher's request, Sir George Murray submitted a report on the progress his committee had made up to the outbreak of war. Consideration of the matter was suspended in the early part of 1918, presumably while the Education bill was being put through parliament, but on 31 July a memorandum was completed and circulated on 1 August to the cabinet

committee for home affairs. The purpose of the memorandum was to
seek cabinet approval for a resumption of work by the Murray committee with a view to legislation, as an agreed measure, on the basis
of the Haldane report. In enumerating arguments for this approval
it is significant (in view of later criticism) that Fisher put first: 'The
present constitution of the London University is admittedly bad and
cumbrous.* The Report of the Royal Commission suggests a form of
constitution *more effective, more respectable, and more conducive to the
educational autonomy and development of the constituent colleges'* (the italics
are ours). Austen Chamberlain challenged the proposed expenditure
on the University of London on the ground that it would be disproportionate to that on other universities. This elicited from Fisher a
further note (this time a secret one for the war cabinet) defending his
proposals, and asking again for a 'general concurrence to the scheme
for a reformed and invigorated University for London, which is set
out in the [royal commission's] report'.

By January 1919 arrangements had been made for Fisher to meet the
'externals', and later in the year draft legislation was actually drawn
up in the board of education. There is no evidence that Haldane took
part in any of these negotiations (though he and Fisher were seeing
something of one another, and Haldane was known to be involved
in the acquisition of the Bloomsbury site). In May 1920 it was publicly
announced that the site was on offer to the University, but a condition was that King's College should transfer to the site; and this
King's refused to do. So at the end of 1920 there was stalemate again.

The next attempt to break the stalemate was made by Charles
Trevelyan, who was president of the board of education in the short-
lived Labour government of 1924. On 30 July he submitted the
following memorandum to the cabinet:

Proposed Departmental Committee on London University.

I am anxious to be in a position to introduce legislation to put the
government of the University of London upon a satisfactory
footing.... A strong Royal Commission, appointed in 1909 and
presided over by the present Lord Chancellor, reported in 1913....

---

* In Fisher's earlier draft of this memorandum (23 July 1918) this sentence had
continued:
'and the meetings of the Senate present a scene of Polish anarchy which
involves the whole University in discredit.'

I have reviewed the present position and have consulted with a selection of the most important academic authorities. There is a strong desire for reform in many quarters, but there is also a general feeling that some of the findings of the Haldane Commission require reconsideration in view of the long period that has elapsed. I therefore wish for the approval of the Cabinet to the appointment of a Departmental Committee.... I should propose that the Reference should be as follows: 'To consider the Final Report of the Royal Commission on University Education in London ... and ... to indicate what are the principal changes now most needed in the existing constitution of the University of London. ...'

On 5 August the cabinet (with Haldane present) agreed to appoint the committee. The chairman was to be Lord Ernle; but he had to resign on grounds of health after the first few meetings and an MP, E. Hilton Young, was appointed in his place. The committee reported in March 1926. A bill based on the report was introduced in June and received the royal assent in December.

Over the fundamental need – that the University should exercise an effective central control through the power of the purse – the new act achieved Haldane's main objective. But in other measures the committee, and the act based on its report, diverged from the pattern of organisation devised by the royal commission. The commission wanted a university organised as departments of study; the committee wanted to preserve a university of semi-independent institutions. The commission wanted *de facto* academic sovereignty to be devolved upon the faculties; the committee wanted to retain a strong academic council. The commission wanted to subordinate the external side of the University; the committee rejected this and recommended that for reasons of policy as well as of history, the external side should remain. But behind the facade of contrasting detail, the implicit philosophy in the two reports was similar; so much so, in fact, that when the bill was debated in the house of commons (at the second reading in November) the main opponent of the bill (Dr Graham Little, MP for the University and representative of the 'externals') rested his opposition on the assertion that the departmental committee's report was the 'lineal descendant of the Haldane Commission Report', whereas the main champion of the bill (Hilton Young himself) rested his advocacy for the bill on the assertion that it was 'almost directly contrary' to the recommendations of the commission.

These exchanges illustrate the difficulty of giving the report of the commission its rightful place in history; and the difficulty is compounded by the inflamed rhetoric which was aimed at it by some of its critics. Perhaps the most hysterical verdict is Hearnshaw's:

> The Haldane Commission was dominated and controlled by a small group of able and resolute men who were filled with that admiration and envy of Germany (mingled with fear of her) which prevailed in high places in the days before the war. They believed in bureaucracy; they worshipped organisation; they loved system and consistency; they longed for centralisation and co-ordination . . . they were inspired by the confidence that comes from philosophic doubtlessness and they were prepared for the ruthlessness which the enforcement of rigid principle requires.

The outburst ends: 'In particular· they lacked sympathy with King's and were ready to sacrifice her on the altar of organisation.' The author was the historian of King's, so his excesses may have been due to a surfeit of loyalty; but they carry one revealing message. The crude smear on Haldane and his Germanophil tendencies prompts one to ask whether some of the condemnation of the royal commission report may not have been mixed up – as Haldane himself believed – with prejudice against Haldane himself: a residue of the antipathies of 1914–16. More moderate, but hardly more judicious, was the verdict of Bellot: that the schemes of both Haldane and Webb for the University of London were highly doctrinaire and neither paid much heed to history.

Whether the commission's plan for a super-civic university in London, with devolution rather than federalism among the colleges, would have been a failure is arguable. Logan thinks it would have failed. But what, in justice to Haldane, has to be remembered is that in 1909–13 the key witnesses who came before the commission did not think so. The commission's provisions for incorporation were backed by Hill (the vice-chancellor), Miers and Rucker (the principal and past principal of the University) and a majority of the academic council. The proposals for faculty organisation were backed by Hill (though with reservations), Miers, Rucker, the whole of the academic council, and the professorial board of University College, not to mention such men as Foster and Ramsay. Over the 'civic' type of government there was some division on the academic council but a majority in favour, with support from Roscoe. The small non-representative senate was supported by Roscoe, Hill, and Foster.

Of course since 1909–13 circumstances had changed and this doubtless accounted for the volte-face which some of the witnesses to the Haldane commission (including Miers) deftly performed when as members of the Hilton Young committee they put their signatures to its report. The UGC had appeared on the scene; the colleges had become stronger and more prosperous; the jealousy between the external and internal sides of the University had abated; experience of incorporation had been disappointing. But there must still have been a lot of misunderstanding or merely ignorance about the commission's report. For instance the commission, far from proposing the suppression of college autonomy, specifically reserved for the colleges what matters most: devolution over courses and examinations. That Haldane himself was committed to academic autonomy in the colleges is clear from an address he gave to the Old Students' Association of the Royal College of Science in 1920. He asserted then that the colleges of the University 'should teach for their own degrees and examine for degrees which they should control ... with only such supervision as was required on the part of the University to see that they did not lower the level of what was entrusted to them'; a principle, he went on to say, of 'devolution and complete autonomy'. We confess that we do not find these sentiments consistent with Hearnshaw's charge that the commission 'longed for centralisation and co-ordination'; nor with the suggestion that Logan makes, that Haldane thought the schools of the University 'had to be destroyed so that the new University could rise, phoenix-like, from their ashes'.

It has been remarked that Haldane was surprisingly reticent in his autobiography about the London royal commission, considering that it was, in some ways, the most massive assignment he had undertaken in educational work. It has been suggested that this reticence was due to Haldane's perplexity at the ultimate rejection of his report. We doubt whether this is the explanation, for he made frank and revealing comments about it in the debate on the second reading of the University of London bill in the house of lords in June 1926. He gave no impression then that the solution to the problems of the University had eluded him. A more likely explanation is that he was writing his autobiography in 1926 at a time when the whole question of the future of the University was still *sub judice*. To have indulged in polemics about the issues at such a time would have been totally out

of keeping with Haldane's character; and to have introduced controversy into the book would have been inconsistent with its reflective
theme – he was writing with 'all passion spent'.

Haldane's lifelong commitment to education was dominated by three
major preoccupations: first, a network of regional universities;
second, educational provinces, permeated by the provincial university,
to provide improved primary and secondary education and continuation classes for the masses; third, adult education. Of course this was
not the working out of a deliberate life-programme. But it is not
imposing too rigid a logic on his career to suggest that there was an
inner coherence about it; each preoccupation fell in place naturally
from what Haldane had learnt from the previous preoccupation. It
was the young Scottish graduate who saw the need for a more
democratic higher education in England. It was the 'midwife' of civic
universities who realised that if their quality was to be maintained there
would have to be alternatives for the 'masses', and who campaigned
for continuation schools and for the permeation of all schooling in a
region by its local university. It was the chairman of royal commissions
on London and Wales, and the missionary for the 1918 Education act,
who heard the call to carry the evangel of knowledge through adult
education to those who had been born too early to benefit from these
reforms, in the mines and factories and farms. It was the successful
war minister who saw that 'General Staff Work' was as urgently
needed for the whole educational system as it was for the armed forces.

On the whole his preoccupations were reinforced by a shrewd and
pragmatic judgement. His advocacy could not be faulted when he
asserted that education at school and university was not only good for
its own sake: it was demonstrably important for the British economy
in peace and war. But Haldane's faith in the social efficacy of education
rested on less secure foundations. 'Educate your people', he told the
Scottish teachers at Dumfries, way back in 1901, 'and you have
reduced to comparatively insignificant dimensions the problems of
temperance, of housing, and of raising the condition of your masses.'
A lifetime in the ruthless game of politics did nothing to dispel this
cloudy illusion. Twenty-one years later he was telling the (surely
sceptical) house of lords:

> ... I will venture to say to your Lordships that if that larger frame
> of mind [expanded by education] had been more diffused among the
> working classes to-day you would have avoided a great many

strikes and contests . . . . I can only say again . . . that the effect of any movement of that kind [he was speaking about adult education] is more tranquillising, more calculated to avoid violent unrest, more calculated to allay jealousies than anything else that I see.

As far back as 1881 Haldane had lectured at the Working Mens' College and he must have been familiar with the university extension classes organised by Oxford and Cambridge since the 1870s. These were too dilettante to be regarded seriously as education, but the tutorial classes organised under the Workers' Educational Association (WEA) with the cooperation of the universities were otherwise. They were the first effective revival of sustained adult education for workers since the days of the Mechanics' Institutes. At their best (they often fell short of it) they took the form of year-long seminars,· at which the students were expected to submit written· work, and this, under the inspiration of men like Tawney, reached 'university standard'. Albert Mansbridge, one of the pioneers in this movement, recalls how Haldane became interested when he helped to organise a series of lectures in 1907–9, in Westminster Abbey and the royal gallery of the house of lords. (In 1909 Haldane took the chair at one of these lectures, given by Masterman, on democracy, and was pestered by suffragettes.) So adult education was a lifelong interest for Haldane, but it did not begin to become one of his preoccupations until he had listened to witnesses before the royal commissions on London and on Wales. What he heard there so appealed to his philosophical proclivities that he began to invest the WEA tutorial class (which was commonly a down-to-earth study of economics and political science) with an almost sacramental significance; an affair (as he called it) 'of the spirit'. Listen to extracts from his questions to representatives of the WEA at the Welsh commission: 'I want to get from you first a conception of the WEA' – and Haldane went on to outline it himself: not technical education, not school education, 'but the higher forms of education . . .?' The witness agreed. '. . . to suggest the great ideas connected with the search after truth which is the peculiar province of the University?' The witness agreed again. '. . . for that purpose', Haldane went on, 'it is one of your objects to bring in contact with the worker the man who is full of the university spirit and comes straight to the worker from its atmosphere, and communicates the flavour of the university teaching in its distinctive form?' This, replied the witness, was one of the justifications for the title *University* tutorial classes.

'Just as the well-to-do man who has been through the University takes up his book of poetry, philosophy or science in the evening, so you want your workers trained and encouraged to do that?' The witness, perhaps a little perplexed at the drift of the questioning, suggested that the practical worker might have something to contribute to the knowledge of the teacher too! The witness expressed a desire that some tutorial classes should be taken by professors. 'You are, I think', replied Haldane, 'right in your desire for that . . . the personality of a distinguished professor counts for a good deal.' Then Haldane went a stage farther: 'When you do discover first rate students you would like the scholarship system [to enter the university] made available to them?' And it was only when the WEA representatives wanted to reproduce in Wales the pattern of a land grant university (Wisconsin) in the United States that they got beyond the bounds of Haldane's enthusiasm and he had to warn them (as we quoted on p. 129) not to put too great a strain upon the University's resources.

The fruits of this experience on both royal commissions were strong recommendations to support extra-mural education, and Haldane's addresses and speeches in the house of lords afterwards show how deeply he identified himself with these recommendations. (Unlike Asquith, the chairman of the commission on Oxford and Cambridge, for whom – so his daughter said – the term extra-mural education was one which 'made my father wince'.)

Haldane was not included in the subcommittee on adult education set up by Lloyd George's Reconstruction committee in 1917 under the chairmanship of the master of Balliol, A. L. Smith, but he enthusiastically endorsed the committee's excellent report. By 1920 the cause of adult education had risen high enough among Haldane's priorities to be included in a house of lords speech. In 1870, he told the House, the government provided for the education of youth; now it was their duty to provide for the education of adults deprived of intra-mural university education. He commended the work of Mansbridge and the WEA and emphasised (as a political point) the tranquillising value of WEA classes for those who did not have the good fortune to be among the elite admitted to universities. The speech does disclose how Haldane was (as Beatrice Webb often accused him of being) a very patrician sort of radical. 'I am not suggesting', he said,

that you should contemplate the time when the working man will enter the walls of the university. He will do so, I hope, but he cannot do so in more than small numbers. I am contemplating the time when if Mahomet does not come to the mountain, the mountain will go to Mahomet. I am looking forward to the universities, through extra-mural work, reaching every district that requires it, training a new class of university tutor and, armed with that organisation, extending their beneficent work to the colliery district, the pottery districts, and the factory districts all over the country. Until you do that you will not have completed your system of giving educational opportunities, nor will you have laid the foundations of that tranquillity which you can only attain when you have got rid of class consciousness.

The speech made some impression. Crewe slipped in a brief reference to the 'very interesting suggestions' which Haldane had made 'on the possibility of universities stretching out tentacles, so to speak, all over the country'.

By the autumn of 1920 adult education had become Haldane's chief preoccupation. He was again busy at his familiar technique: a double-pronged campaign; at one time round the fireside at Queen Anne's Gate, plotting with Mansbridge, Tawney, Laski and others; at other times evangelising at public meetings to create a climate of opinion conducive to the raising of public money to support the movement. It was his last major service to education and it fell into the pattern of so much else which he had done. He did not create a new idea, others had done that a long time ago. He did not (though he tried to do this) succeed in lifting the idea to a higher philosophical (in his old age he would have called it 'spiritual') level. What he did do with the idea was to help to encase it in an institution. Haldane, drawing on his past experience with the army, saw the value of an organisation 'on something like a General Staff principle'. To institutionalise adult education would be to protect it, to confer status upon it, to give a sense of coherence to its practitioners. And so, in Queen Anne's Gate, the British Institute of Adult Education was founded in 1921. Haldane became its first president, and every year until 1927, even in the year when he was lord chancellor, he attended the annual conference and delivered an address. His value to the adult education movement was immense, not because of what he said (the addresses contain little that was both new and practicable) but because of the publicity given to his speeches. At that time he and Archbishop Temple were the two great public figures whose espousal of the movement kept it in the public eye. This publicity was essential, for Haldane's romantic vision of working class people 'who preferred to read Plato and Wordsworth to amusing themselves on the football field' while true of a tiny minority was, of course, a mirage as an aspiration for British society. The adult education movement remained a minority one, albeit a very significant minority, and minority movements need sponsors in high places. It was too much, perhaps, to hope that in the transient tenure of the Labour government much could be done for adult education. Under Trevelyan at the board of education the first complete code of regulations for the administration of grants for adult education was drawn up; but Haldane was disappointed: 'Trevelyan made vigorous efforts,' he wrote, 'but the importance of adult education was not fully taken in, although the principle was accepted.'

In 1925 Haldane was once again out of office, in his seventieth year, and far from well. But he threw his energy into the work of adult education. We know that he held a private conference with some university vice-chancellors, presumably to encourage them to cherish extra-mural work; and in the house of lords he appealed again to the government (in March 1925) to give a lead to the nation in promoting adult education in the 'University spirit', supporting his plea by assuring the House that he had 'gone about amongst' the working classes a good deal and he knew they would respond.

In this twilight of his life Haldane's faith in the efficacy of education never failed and he never missed an opportunity to reaffirm it. Thus, in what was his last address to students, when he opened the premises of the National Union of Students in 1925, he told the audience: 'the higher you go in education the more you find men and women . . . think in the main alike . . . .' But the twilight was growing deeper. Sometimes Haldane had to sit while giving an address. He was becoming a little deaf. On 19 November 1925 Beatrice Webb wrote:

Lunched today with Haldane (I wonder whether it is the last time?) The hand of death seemed to be moulding his features. To me it was inexpressibly sad watching him eating, drinking, and smoking away his life, though he looks so far gone that what he does matters little . . . there is a look of *vacancy* on his face which is new. . . . 'A death's head' said Sidney as we left the house.

A couple of years later his memory was playing tricks on him. On 9 March 1927 he said in the house of lords:

When the Education Bill of 1918 was before this House, I well remember moving a clause, which the Government accepted, enabling them to divide England for educational purposes into provinces which should be somewhat the size of Scotland. Wales would be one, Yorkshire would be one and Lancashire would be one, and it would be left to the provinces to work out their educational salvation in their own way. To me it is certain that half the questions we have been discussing today would have been solved long ago in these regions if that course had been taken . . . .

But our examination of the records shows that he never moved such a clause. He may have realised himself that his race was nearly run, for he wrote to Beatrice Webb from Cloan on 1 January 1927:

I reply on New Year's Day to your Christmas day letter. Not that the beginning of the year interests me much. Death may come during that year, & this may cause suffering to others. But for those who have to meet it, it comes to seem no more than an event implied by life. . . . I shall be here till just after the middle of January. Then I have appeals to hear. . . .

The race he had run was dedicated to the application of rational thought to the solution of political and social problems, and it was only in the last decade of his life that the rational regions of his mind succumbed to utopias. From adult education he expected far more than was good for the movement's own future. At first he welcomed WEA classes for the dubious reason that they offered – so he thought – the solution to his dilemma: how to preserve universities for the intellectual elite and yet to diffuse the university spirit through the masses. He assumed that intelligent manual workers would be content to study at night in tutorial classes and go back, still content, to their mines, dock, and looms. 'The idea of leisure', he said in a book of essays prepared by members of the British Institute of Adult Education, 'must change'. Leisure must be spent not in self-indulgence or mechanical amusement 'but in the liberation and development of the soul'. 'Spirit'; 'soul': gradually Hegelian terms, invested now with ecclesiastical connotations, drifted into his addresses. 'The work of diffusing higher education among the working classes is indeed a new missionary work,' he wrote in the same essay, and he suggested that in 'days when it is becoming more and more difficult for the Churches to attract students to the ministry, there is here thrown open a new missionary career, from which a spiritual side which may be very real is not excluded.' And in an article in the *Hibbert Journal* on 'The churches and higher education' he went further: whereas idealists, he explained, might be deterred from the profession of parish clergy by the existing route to the pulpit, they might be attracted to it if it were approached by a training designed in the first place for those wishing to undertake extra-mural teaching for universities. The prospect of teaching as well as preaching from the pulpit might provide a positive appeal. Thus might universities come to the aid of the church, and adult education acquire an added dimension.

This suggestion raises the whole question of whether the church should confuse what is Caesar's and what is God's. (Had not Lotze told him, over fifty years ago, that philosophy and Christianity belong to different spheres?) Fortunately Haldane was not drawn into controversy on this point. The speculations of his old age are really irrelevant to his contribution to adult education in the last decade of his life. Although most people engaged in adult education today have a much more modest conception of its role in society, they are deeply in Haldane's debt. He was the first major statesman to act as spokesman for the movement in parliament. He inspired the founders at a time when they were beset with frustrations. He helped to make adult education in England and Wales what it is today: incomparably the best of its kind in Europe.

8 Epilogue

Our portrait of Haldane must speak for itself. But having lived in his company, so to speak, for a couple of years, we find ourselves asking questions about the portrait we have drawn, and hazarding answers.

For us the most interesting question is this: to what extent did his education and his predisposition for philosophy affect what he said and did in politics? When *Vanity Fair* published a 'Spy' cartoon of Haldane in 1896, and labelled it 'A Hegelian politician', we may guess that Haldane was pleased with the title. But did the ideas of Hegel (or of English Hegelians like Green and Bosanquet) permeate (to use Haldane's word) his political platform?

We can put the question into a wider context. Intellectuals who enter public life can no longer practise the expertise they acquired as students. They have to be generalists, although if they have graduated from an English university, they are likely to have been trained as specialists, in classics, say, or law, or science. As public men, they are obliged to make speeches. In composing these they tend to go back to the indelible impressions of the one subject they mastered, and to take these as texts: the classicist, to Aristotle and Plato; the biologist, to Darwin and Mendel; the economist, to Mill and Keynes. Haldane's training was in philosophy and law. He had called philosophy his *Herz-studium*. Did his familiarity with Hegel and Schopenhauer and Goethe colour his public addresses and his political strategies?

His public addresses, yes. When Haldane was preparing some of these, especially if they were to be given to students, he drew heavily on his pre-political past; so much so that to understand these addresses it is essential to have some inkling of what Hegel meant by certain expressions which Haldane used. Rarely did academic audiences hear from him pragmatic advice from the practical statesman; what they heard was usually a distillate of philosophical ends rather than of political means. (It was this which elicited the witty rebuke from Bernard Shaw which we quote on p. 12f.) Hence the inscrutable phrases which obfuscate some of Haldane's most carefully composed speeches, phrases like 'the ethical life', 'the University spirit', the 'soul of a people'. He talked all round these terms but he did not define them. They were drawn from his rich store of nineteenth-century *Weltanschauung* and they undoubtedly meant much more to him than they did to his audiences.

The addresses include some strikingly Hegelian themes. 'The University', he told students at Edinburgh, 'is the handmaid of the State, of which it is the microcosm – a community in which also there are rulers and ruled, and in which the corporate life is a moulding influence.' And, a few minutes later in the same address: 'Such a University cannot be dependent in its spirit. It cannot live and thrive under the domination either of the Government or the Church . . . . It can recognise no authority except that which rests on the right of the Truth to command obedience.' A handmaid of the state independent of the state? The riddle is solved by Hegel. The state and all institutions within it – universities, associations, families – must live and have their being in rational thought. To be ethical is to accept the doctrine that the ultimate standard of truth and reality rests on an institutional rationality, an inner coherence of the state and all its parts (of which the university is one). The 'spirit' of a nation or of a university is measured by the degree to which it possesses this self-consistency. Morality (it is social morality which is meant) is living according to this faith in the rational, being obedient to it, doing one's duty (*Pflicht*) by it. It follows then that there should be no conflict between the state and its universities. The condition for *Freiheit* (freedom) is *Einheit* (unity, oneness). The framework of freedom within which the university operates is consensus about this doctrine. So Haldane is never heard to say (as we hear today) that universities must be independent of the state in order to be free to criticise the state. That, to Hegel, would have made no sense; the organs of the body do not criticise the body in which they function.

We have already described the problem which confronted Haldane when he preached on one hand democratic access to universities, and on the other, the need to preserve at all costs the university as the place where the 'highest' knowledge is pursued with an uncompromising passion for excellence. Many times he warned his audiences that the gates must be open for the working classes to enter but that in fact very few may expect to get in. Hegel had reflected on a somewhat similar problem. For him the prescription for *Einheit* in the state was

an honoured bureaucracy of leaders in whom the masses, sufficiently
enlightened to understand the purpose of the state, were prepared to
put their trust. To oblige the masses to do this would not be compulsion. What may look like compulsion is only the process of persuading
the masses to choose what they really want (which is what the state
knows is best for them) instead of what they think they want. Haldane,
of course, would not put it as crudely as this, but there is an echo of
Hegel in his Edinburgh lecture: having told the students that 'the
highest is also the most real' he went on to say that the highest should
be made manifest by dispelling the mists of ignorance, and if that is
done 'what is highest will in the main assert its authority with the
majority.' And the purveyors of the highest: they are the leaders to
be turned out by the universities. This Hegelian legacy is surely
behind Haldane's ambivalent statements about the duty of politicians,
to which we referred on pp. 13–14. When he addressed the
'Eighty' Club in Cambridge (an audience of potential leaders) he told
them that politicians can only respond to public demand: they – the
audience – must provide the ideas. But to his fellow parliamentarians,
on more than one occasion, he took the opposite view: that governments
must not wait for popular demand before acting for the public good;
they must lead. And Haldane's frequent and exhausting circuits of
public addresses: were these not consistent with Hegel's dictum,
that to achieve *Einheit* it is essential to persuade the masses that what
the state wants for them is for their own good?

When Haldane talked about the 'soul of a people', as he did to an
enthusiastically receptive audience in Aberystwyth, he was again
influenced by Hegel and perhaps Herder. Every nation has a *Volksgeist*,
a soul of its own. Its language is the expression of its soul. All its
institutions (including again the university) have to be in tune with the
spirit of the nation; indeed, since the university is the nursery for
leaders, it is the nation's prime channel for the expression of its soul,
together with its literature and its art and music. So when Haldane
came to preside over the royal commission on the University of
Wales, his encouragement to the University to be distinctive, even
un-English, was not just to curry favour for his recommendations for
reform; it was consistent with all he had learnt in the Germany
(euphoric from the triumph of 1870) of his younger days, about the
philosophy of nationhood.

Haldane must often have been told how perplexing some of these
concepts were to British audiences, and Webb took him gently to task

for some of his views on democracy. The nearest he came to clarifying what he meant by such words as morality was also reminiscent of Hegel. He adjured his audience to cultivate hero-worship. 'Nothing is more stimulating to him who is striving to learn ... so much as reverence ... for the personality of a great intellectual and moral hero.' In other words the specification for a high morality and a noble soul is better not put into words, but seen in people. To understand what is meant by the 'soul' of ancient Greece, look with reverence at Socrates. Haldane drew his ethical principles not from the church but from the morality inherent in science and scholarship: a passionate dedication to accuracy as the approximation to truth; a consensus about truth which was truly cosmopolitan (he noticed this vividly after his mission to Germany in 1912); humility, earnestness in seeking knowledge. (He quoted with approval the words of Lessing: that if God were to offer him Truth in one hand and the Search for Truth in the other, he would choose the Search.)

And how do these noble sentiments correspond to Haldane's daily business in Westminster or at Queen Anne's Gate, conspiring, compromising where necessary, identifying himself (though not always very zealously) with party politics? Or at one of Lady Horner's week-end parties, in the high society which Beatrice Webb so heartily despised? Here Hegelian thought had to be reconciled with expediency; here Haldane's social conscience and compassion compelled him to search for the pragmatic, the opportune, solution. But this was not an attitude of hypocrisy. Indeed it was a neo-Hegelian, Green, who taught that self-realisation cannot be attained except by serving society rather than self. The way to serve society, if one has the gifts, is to enter public life and, as Haldane had to explain to Beatrice Webb, this entailed familiarity with the whole spectrum of society, from country houses to crofters' cottages. Haldane's decision to go into politics was made in a spirit of altruism, not ambition. Having got into politics he had to discover how the philosopher-statesman can work within the system. It is a system hedged about with numerous constraints: the powerful drag of precedent, the massive stability of parliamentary procedure, the prejudices, the conventions. Even if he had wanted revolution, he had the sense to know that revolutions do not benefit society as much as progress through adaptation. So, like a poet who decides to write sonnets in classical form, Haldane set to work to master the techniques for effective political action within the constraints. This he did superbly, and in ways which would not have brought disapproval from his German mentors. For it was Hegel himself who, deeply preoccupied with the fallibility of political systems, saw the need to combine reason with passion in order to achieve political ends. And the ends Haldane sought would certainly have appealed to Hegel. That Haldane himself realised the necessity for compromise is evident from a passage in his appreciation of his old friend Fry. 'He had', Haldane wrote about Fry,

> an intense sense of the necessity of uprightness, and strong conviction that no result could be just in which morality and law appeared to become divorced. So strong was this sense in him that I think it would have actually stood in his way had he sought to exercise his powers in the arena of political life. In that field a certain giving is as essential to success as the most justifiable taking.

What did Haldane achieve? Our portrait, we hope, answers this question. But how much of his achievement is still visible? Our answer to that is that it lies in the foundations of our whole system of education. Without Haldane the University of London would undoubtedly have been reformed; civic universities (though possibly on a different and less flexible pattern) would have multiplied; the Charlottenburg idea or some variant of it would have been adopted; higher education would have been endowed by the state through some sort of University Grants Committee; adult education would have flourished; education by day-release would have appeared; the 1918 Education act would have been put on the statute book. But without Haldane, the style and tenor of all these would, we believe, have been the poorer; and – equally important – all of them would have been delayed. It was Haldane who, patiently over decades, created in the public mind and among politicians a consciousness of the need for quality and balance in education. With the monotonous persistence of the advertising patter on a commercial TV he propagated his beliefs until they became other peoples' beliefs; for example, the quintessence of the German concept of a university, so succinctly put by von Humboldt: that the teacher is not there for the sake of the student – both are there for the sake of knowledge ('beide sind für die Wissenschaft da'); that personal contact between teacher and student is the essence of a university; that students should study in order to *know*, not in order to pass examinations; that it was the duty of a democracy to offer equality of opportunity to learn, but not to appease the masses by any dilution of the criteria for excellence; that a democracy which is not permeated by education will be in danger. The very fact that we take these ideas for granted is evidence of the debt we owe to Haldane, for eighty years ago they were not taken for granted. He did not originate them, but through him they were institutionalised. And another testimony to the endurance of his achievement is that the institutions he helped to create, in order to preserve and promote educational ideals, now do what he, in the beginning, had to do single-handed. They have supplanted the dedicated individual.

And, last, we ask what was it in the man himself which enabled him to achieve so much? Haldane is, wrote Runciman to Churchill, our 'most industrious orator . . . if one may fairly call his formless and endless speeches oratory.' 'The smooth, persuasive voice inundates the House with a flood of words', wrote another observer. Even his ardent admirers, such as the students in Edinburgh, had to confess: 'Unfortunately he has a thin voice. He is no orator. His speeches are more enjoyable in the reading than in the hearing of them.' And as for his writing: 'I know I am a bad writer', he told his friend Gosse; and he told Asquith: 'beastly bad'. Beatrice Webb, always on the look-out for a penetrating generalisation, wrote: 'By common consent Haldane's writings are amateurish and undistinguished in substance and form; if they had not been the writings of a great public personage they would not be read.'

But Haldane was a great public personage, without the charismatic gifts of eloquence or an elegant style. Nor did he capture the imagination of the public through ostentation, like Disraeli, or through asceticism, like Ghandi. He lived well and comfortably as thousands of his contemporaries did. He was genial, generous, humorous, charming; but so were scores of other notables in British society whose names have been forgotten. He had a good mind and a first class memory; but so had many other Victorians who have faded out of the history books. He succumbed to harmless and amiable vanities. He struck some people (including Beatrice Webb when she was still Miss Potter) as pompous. His habit of looking on the bright side of things (*toujours bien, jamais mieux*) was mistaken by some people as complacency. His manner of working in politics – a word slipped in here, another there; an unsigned memorandum delivered on to a minister's desk at just the right moment; a dinner party at which the conversation was directed as inexorably as the moves in a game of chess: in the eyes of some people this was intrigue, all too devious to be trusted.

But Haldane was trusted. This was one ingredient of his success. Over a petition from a university college or an appeal to support adult education (and doubtless over hundreds of private and personal matters) the news that 'Mr Haldane is taking an interest in this' raised hopes and boosted morale. For if Haldane undertook to try to do something, his single-mindedness, his pertinacity, his capacity to mobilise all manner of resources, flattened out obstacles like a steam roller and, very often, left a smooth path which ordinary people could use to reach their goal. Once Haldane had seized upon one of his preoccupations, no mole could be more persistent; anyone obstructing him knew he was in for a campaign not for a matter of weeks or months, but, if Haldane thought it necessary, for years.

His indefatigable resolution when he pursued a cause would not have been effective, of course, unless he had been a superb administrator. Administration is the art of winning the willing co-operation of hundreds (sometimes thousands) of people to get something done which no individual could do alone. First, the administrator has to be clear in his own mind what he wants to get done. Second, he has to persuade other people that it is worth doing and that they want to help him do it (for successful adminstration depends on consent). Third, since great purposes cannot be achieved except through thousands of small steps, the administrator has to devise a strategy, to make sure that some steps are not taken prematurely (or the project will trip up), that some steps circumvent obstacles rather than try to climb over them, that progress is orderly and consolidated, and – very important – that those who are obliged to concentrate their energies on means never lose sight of the ends. Fourth, there is the supreme importance of timing. To take the right step at the wrong time can be fatal to the enterprise, and only a lively intuition can discern what is the right time. Finally, since the administrator is, as it were, conducting an orchestra in the performance of one of his own works, he must point to the players when he is applauded by the public; for without him they could play but without them he could not conduct. In other words the successful administrator must be self-effacing.

These were the elusive qualities which Haldane possessed in abundance. His sister recognised this; his mind, she wrote, was essentially an administrative one. And this brings us, full circle, to the early days when his personality was shaped by Goethe and Lotze and Hegel; for it has been truly said that administration is not a great strain on the intellect, but it is a very great strain on the character. The secret of

Haldane's achievement was that he understood himself, knew where his capacities lay, believed in everything he undertook to do and was unruffled by delays, serene in setbacks, steadfast in intention. His portrait speaks to us of a lifelong consistency of purpose; a compass set over books of philosophy and followed over forty years in politics. And the one thing that people knew about Haldane's purpose was that it never led him into conflict between personal ambition and the public good. For to work for the public good was his ambition. Elizabeth Haldane, writing to Beatrice Webb after her brother's death, told how so many of the people who had written to her 'speak of his character almost more than of his work as having influenced them'.

The Webbs had a profound influence on Haldane's opinions, for they were disinterested and frank critics, who criticised with genuine affection for him; and access to such criticism is very precious for public men. Their last letter to him is a touching epitaph. By the summer of 1928 his health was breaking up. On 14 August Beatrice wrote:

> ... Sidney & I frequently talk and think about you and our long years of common effort (some would call it common intrigue!) for the public good. Your sister tells us that you are ordered to give up all sustained public work alike in the judicial & political sphere. That will be a great loss for those particular worlds, but from the point of view of advanced movements I think you are very much more needed as the 'great consultant'. . . .

On 18 August Elizabeth Haldane replied: 'I read a bit of your letter and summarized the rest. He said "Very good sense" & was pleased. But he is terribly weak and I really have no hope of recovery.' On 19 August 1928, Haldane died.

References

Abbreviations

Autobiography	R. B. Haldane, *An autobiography* (1929).
CAB	Cabinet records, public record office, London.
ED	Board of education records, public record office.
H.Pp.	Haldane papers, National Library of Scotland.
Maurice	Frederick Maurice, *Haldane*, 2 vols (1937, 1939).
PC	Privy council records, public record office.
P.Pp.	Passfield papers, British Library of Political and Economic Science.
RECO	Ministry of reconstruction records, public record office.
T	Treasury records, public record office.

The bold figures preceding each source denote the pages, the light figures denote the lines of the text to which they refer.

Introduction

xiii, 16. *The nationalisation of universities* (1921) [Address to Old Students' Association, Royal College of Science, 9 Nov 1920].

17. *The ideal of the university* (1920) [Address to first meeting of the reconstructed court of the University of Wales, 25 Nov 1920].

21. *The Times*, 20 Aug 1928.

23. Albert Mansbridge, ibid, 21 Aug 1928.

24. H. Frank Heath, 'Lord Haldane: his influence on higher education and on administration', *Public Administration*, VI (1928) 350–60.

28. Alexander Morgan, 'Lord Haldane' in *Makers of Scottish education* (1929) 242–59.

xiv, 9. Frederick Maurice, *Haldane ... the life of Viscount Haldane of Cloan*, 2 vols (1937, 1939).

15. J. F. Lockwood, 'Haldane and education', *Public Administration*, XXXV (1957) 232–44.

16. Douglas Logan, *Haldane and the University of London* (Haldane Memorial Lecture, 1960).

23. H. J. W. Hetherington, *Theory and practice* (Haldane Memorial Lecture, 1932).

25. J. Duff, *The scale and scope of British universities* (Haldane Memorial Lecture, 1961).

29. Alfred Hopkinson, *Penultima* (1930); J. R. B. Muir, *Ramsay Muir: an autobiography and some essays*, ed. S. Hodgson (1943).

30. F. J. C. Hearnshaw, *The centenary history of King's College, London, 1828–1928* (1929).

32. Ref. **xiv**, 16.
34. Michael Sadleir, *Michael Ernest Sadler* (1949).
38. H. Hale Bellot, *The University of London: a history* (1969).

xv,   2. H. J. W. Hetherington, *The life and letters of Sir Henry Jones* (1924).

12. Almeric Fitzroy, *Memoirs* (1925); H. A. L. Fisher, *An unfinished auto-biography* (1940).

Chapter 1: Appointment with Mr Haldane

1,   5. Violet Bonham Carter, 'Haldane of Cloan', *The Times*, 30 Jul 1956;
B. Webb, *Beatrice Webb's diaries, 1924–1932*, ed. M. Cole (1956) 31.

15. Austen Chamberlain, *Politics from inside* (1936) 325.

17. Edmund Gosse, quoted Dudley Sommer, *Haldane of Cloan* (1960) 154.

20. A. G. Gardiner, 'Robert [sic] Burdon Haldane' in *Prophets, priests and kings* (1908) 204–12.

24. B. Webb to E. S. Haldane, 14 Aug 1928, H.Pp., 5917; copy, P.Pp., II, 5.

2,   5. *Maurice*, I, 57.

9. Ref. **1**, 17; p. 218.

35. B. Webb, diary, 6 Jan 1927; P.Pp., I, 2, vol. 41.

3,   5. Ref. **1**, 20.

17. Ibid.

31. Christopher Addison, *Politics from within* (1924) I, 60.

33. John Buchan, 'Lord Haldane' in *Comments and characters*, ed. W. Forbes Gray (1940) 315–19.

n. Albert Mansbridge, *The trodden road* (1940) 149.

4,   6. H. G. Wells, *Experiment in autobiography* (1934) 766.

20. 4 Aug 1928; H.Pp., 6032; copy, P.Pp., II, 5.

33. *Autobiography*, p. 170.

5, 12. An aside, whilst taking evidence during a session of the royal commission on the University of London in March 1912: *Univ. educ. in London, R. com., appx. to final rept.*, q.15746; 1913 [Cd 6718] XL.

18. *Autobiography*, p. 5.

34. 'The conduct of life' in *The conduct of life and other addresses* (1914) 3–27 [Address to the associated societies of the University of Edinburgh on 14 Nov 1913].

6, 27. 27 Apr 1874, H.Pp., 5027; quoted *Maurice*, I, 18.

40. *Maurice*, I, 20.

7, 15. Ref. **6**, 27.

17. 30 Apr 1874; H.Pp., 5927.

35. *Maurice*, I, 18.

8,   9. Ibid., I, 20–1.

30. 'The soul of a people' in *Universities and national life* (1911) 1–32.

9,   8. *Maurice*, I, 23.

12. A. Seth Pringle-Pattison, 'Richard Burdon Haldane', *Proceedings of the British Academy*, XIV (1928) 410.

25. *Autobiography*, p. 8.

10, 10, Haldane to Asquith, 22 Jan 1923, 18 Oct 1926; Asquith Pp., 18.

31. Quoted Samuel Hynes, *The Edwardian turn of mind* (1968).

11, 4. Ibid.

12. *Maurice*, I, 55.

23. Ibid., I, 33; *Daily Herald*, 5 Feb 1920.

12, 4. *The future of democracy* (1918) [Address to WEA, Coventry branch, 13 Apr 1918].

7. Cf. address to 'Eighty' Club at Cambridge in May 1904: *Constructive liberalism* (1904).

8. Cf. speech in house of lords: *H. L. Debs*, 9 Dec 1924, col. 21.

9. Cf. Haldane to Balfour, 16 Apr 1905: 'Thank God we are not all of one Party in the State – otherwise I should despair of the power to resist slumbrousness'; Balfour Pp., Add. MS. 49724.

10. Cf. 'The dedicated life' in *Universities and national life* (1911) 65–110 [Rectorial address to University of Edinburgh, 10 Jan 1907].

13, 10. Quoted, R. F. W. Heuston, 'Lord Haldane' in *Lives of the lord chancellors, 1885–1940* (Oxford, 1964) 200.

24. Address to 'Eighty' Club, May 1891: *Social problems* (1891).

33. *Maurice*, I, 49–50.

37. *H. L. Debs*, 24 Jul 1918, col. 1136.

14, 6. Ibid., 12 Jul 1916, col. 681.

15, 29. *Autobiography*, p. 115.

16, 32. Matthew Arnold, *Higher schools and universities in Germany* (1882).

17, 27. Ref. **15,** 29.

18, 17. Robert R. James, *Rosebery* (1963) 203.

24. *Maurice*, I, 49–50.

34. *Autobiography*, p. 107.

19, 4. B. Webb, *Our Partnership* (1948) 32.

28. Kenneth Young, *Arthur James Balfour* (1963) 143.

20, 4. *Maurice*, I, 50.

28. Kitty Muggeridge and Ruth Adams, *Beatrice Webb: a life, 1858–1943* (1967) 124.

36. 25 Jul 1891, P.Pp., II, I (II) 218; 16 Jan 1898, II, 4a, 76.

21, 1. 27 Dec 1891, diary; P.Pp., I, 2, vol. 14.

18. *Maurice*, I, 55.

24. *Our partnership*, p. 98.

30. John Simon, *Retrospect: the memoirs of the Rt Hon. Viscount Simon* (1952) 46.

Chapter 2: Apprenticeship

22, 8. J. I. Macpherson, *Twenty-one years of corporate life at Edinburgh University* (Edinburgh, 1905) 88; see also Eric Ashby and Mary Anderson, *The rise of the student estate in Britain* (1970) 32ff.

32. *H. C. Debs*, 20 Jun 1889, col. 352.

23, 13. Ibid., cols 348–53.

26, 1. Ibid., 9 May 1892, cols 449–54.

27, 17. Janet Beveridge, *An epic of Clare Market* (1960) 11.

29, 26. Sir Charles Russell, at a meeting of the 'Eighty' Club in Cambridge in 1891; *Social problems* (1891).

28. *The Student*, XI no. 3 (5 Nov 1896) 33–4.

30, 25. Ref. **29,** 26.
  27. *Our partnership,* p. 98.
31, 7. 30 Apr 1891; H.Pp., 5903; P.Pp., II, 5.
  11. 25 Jul 1891; ibid.
33, 33. *Maurice,* I, 78.
  34. Ibid.
34, 2. 15 Jan 1897, Allchin Pp.; quoted, Douglas Logan, *Haldane and the University of London* (1960).
  30. M. A. Hamilton, *Sidney and Beatrice Webb: a study in contemporary biography* (1932) 130.
35, 1. *Our partnership,* pp. 99–100.
  7. Ibid., p. 102.
  32. 3 Jul 1897; ED 24/5.
  35. Ref. **35,** 7.
36, 12. Balfour Pp., Add. MS. 49724, quoted (without date) *Maurice,* I, 79.
  29. H.Pp., 5904.
37, 8. *Autobiography,* p. 126.
  27. *H. C. Debs,* 14 Jun 1898, cols 257–67.
  37. *Autobiography,* p. 127.
38, 9. Henry Labouchere; *H. C. Debs,* 25 Jul 1898, col.1192.
  38. Confidential print of memorandum by Haldane: 'The Irish question', 20 Oct 1898; Balfour Pp., Add. MS. 49724.
39, 12. 15 Oct 1898; H.Pp., 5960.
  20. ED 24/5.
  30. Haldane to Fitzroy, 9 Jul 1897, ED 24/5.
  35. W. A. S. Hewins, *The apologia of an imperialist* (1929) I, 24.
40, 10. PC 8/510.
  20. Haldane to Webb, 2 Nov 1903; P.Pp., II, 4a, 18.
  25. *H. L. Debs,* 29 Jun 1926, col. 636.
  28. *The nationalisation of universities* (1921).

Chapter 3: Co-conspirators
42, 30. 'Great Britain and Germany: a study in education' in *Education and empire* (1902) 1–38 [Address at Liverpool, Oct 1901].
43, 15. Matthew Arnold, *Higher schools and universities in Germany* (1882) 152.
  25. *Autobiography,* p. 87.
  32. Cf. his addresses at Liverpool and Dumfries in 1901, published in *Education and empire* (1902).
44, 25. 30 Dec 1902; H.Pp., 5905.
45, 4. Transcript of proceedings before the committee of council, 18 Dec 1902, q.238; PC 8/605/89731.
  24. 'Universities and the schools in Scotland' in *Education and empire* (1902) 39–87; cf. ref. **42,** 30.
  n. Friedrich Paulsen, *The German universities and university study,* Eng. ed. (1906) 113ff.
46, 36. 5 May 1902; H.Pp., 5905.
47, 5. 21 Jul 1902; ibid.
  15. 1 Jun 1902; ibid.

25. *Maurice*, I, 112.
31. W. T. Stead, *The Right Hon. R. B. Haldane, K.C., M.P.* (Coming men on coming questions, VII, (1905)).
34. 10 May 1905; *Mining Journal*, 13 May 1905, ED 24/530.

48, 4. *Maurice*, I, 129.
18. P.Pp., II, 4b, 25.
22. Ibid., II, 4b, 28.
23. Haldane to Thursfield, 26 Sep 1901; H.Pp., 5905.

49, 22. 'Lord Rosebery's escape from Houndsditch', *Nineteenth Century*, L (1901) 366–86.
26. Cf. Haldane to B. Webb, 15 Sep 1901; P.Pp., II, 4b, 27.
40. 25 Apr 1902; *Our partnership*, p. 233.

50, 10. *Maurice*, I, 120.

51, 17. 9 May 1902; P.Pp., II, 4b, 36.
22. Ref. **50**, 10.
28. Diary, 28 May 1902; *Memoirs* (1925).
35. Fitzroy, diary, 25 June 1902; ibid.

52, 6. P.Pp., II, 4b, 63.
16. Lord Rosebery to Lord Monkswell, 27 Jun 1903, pubd in T. L. Humberstone, *University reform in London* (1926) appx I, pp. 167–71.
22. Minutes of LCC, 15 Jul 1903; ED 24/531.
26. B. Webb, *Our partnership*, p. 271.

53, 21. 'Memorandum on the proposed College of Technology'; ED 24/529. The printed copy preserved in the board of education bears a pencilled heading 'Mr Haldane's'.

54, 9. Morant to Mowatt, 25 Oct 1903, and to the president, 23 Jan 1904; ibid.
27. Ibid.
34. Lord Londonderry, at the annual dinner of the Institution of Mining and Metallurgy, 10 May 1905; ref. **47**, 34.
36. R. Coll, Sci., Dept cttee prelim. rept; 1905 [Cd 2610] LXI.
37. R. Coll. Sci., Dept cttee final rept; 1906 [Cd 2872] XXXI.

55, 14. *Univ. educ. in Ireland, appx to 2nd rept*, pp. 107–15 *passim*; 1902 [Cd 1900] XXXI.

56, 4. Uncorrected proof of minutes of conference between the departmental committee and representatives of the University of London, University College, and King's College, on 7 Jul 1905; ED 24/555.
8. ED 24/530.
10. Ibid.
15. Haldane to Morant, 26 Jun 1905; ED 24/530.
20. *Morning Post*, 3 Jul 1905; ED 24/530.
22. *The Times*, 3 Jul 1905.

57, 3. Ref. **56**, 4.
35. Ref. **54**, 37; paras 90–4.

58, 21. ED 24/530.
26. ED 24/529.

Chapter 4: Above the snow-line
59, 29. *H. C. Debs*, 16 Feb 1898, col.791.

60, 12. 20 Oct, 23 Dec 1898; Balfour Pp., Add. MS. 49724

15. *Autobiography*, pp. 132–3.

21. Ibid., pp. 133–4.

29. Ibid., p. 139.

61, 35. Matthew Arnold, *Higher schools and universities in Germany* (1882) 220.

40. *U.Cs Grants, Try cttee, rept by inspectors*, 31 Dec 1896; 1897 [245] LXX.

62, 7. H. C. Debs, 25 Jul 1898, col.1229.

10. 'Birmingham University', 23 Mar 1900; enclosure in memo to chancellor, 5 Dec 1900; T 1/9653B/3328/1901.

12. *Autobiography*, p. 139.

21. Petition of lord mayor of Birmingham and others, lodged with privy council, 24 Jun 1899; PC 8/516/82963.

26. Liverpool case, part 5; PC 8/605/89344.

63, 6. 'Great Britain and Germany' in *Education and empire* (1902) 32.

14. *The Times*, 23 Oct 1901.

n. Liverpool case, p. 77; ref. **62,** 26.

64, 14. *Maurice*, I, 140.

24. Confidential print, 12 Jul 1902; PC 8/605/88704.

37. Haldane to Chamberlain, 14 Aug 1902; Joseph Chamberlain Pp., JC 11/15/2.

65, 1. *Autobiography*, p. 141.

10. Ibid., p. 145.

16. Fitzroy, diary, 19 Dec 1902; *Memoirs*.

37. Transcript of shorthand notes of evidence, 17 Dec 1902, q.196; PC 8/605/89719.

66, 12. Ibid., 18 Dec 1902, qs 201, 202; PC 8/605/89731.

21. Ibid., q.208.

32. Ibid., q.216.

67, 8. Liverpool case, p. 75ff.; ref. **62,** 26.

19. Evidence, 19 Dec 1902, q.639.

22. Ibid., q.481.

30. Fitzroy, diary, 19 Dec 1902; *Memoirs*.

34. Ibid., 6 Feb 1903.

38. Ibid.

68, 2. Agnes Fry, *A memoir of the Rt hon. Sir Edward Fry* (1929) 137.

12. Order in Council, 16 Feb 1903.

20. Diary, 18 Feb 1903; *Memoirs*.

27. 'The civic university' in *The conduct of life and other addresses* (1914) 63–95 [Address delivered in Oct 1912].

39. Fitzroy to the duke of Devonshire, 14 Jan 1903; Harold Cohen Library, Univ. of Liverpool, MS. 2.96(13).

69, 11. Haldane to Fitzroy, 3 Apr 1903; ibid., MS. 2.96 (28).

19. *Memoirs*.

27. Enclosure to memo on Liverpool and Manchester draft charters, of 7 May 1903; PC 8/605/90602.

70, 19. PC 8/605/94286.

26. Fitzroy, diary, 29 May 1905; *Memoirs*.

33. *Maurice*, I, 144.

39. P. 90.

71, 8. Alfred Hopkinson, *Penultima* (1930) 122.

13. J. R. B. Muir, *Ramsay Muir: an autobiography and some essays*, ed. S. Hodgson (1943) 48.

19. *Our partnership*, p. 247.

72, 5. P. 146.

11. 11 Aug 1902; H.Pp., 5905.

32. Haldane to Joseph Chamberlain, 18 Sep 1902; Joseph Chamberlain Pp., JC 11/15/3.

37. 18 Sep 1902; H.Pp., 5905.

73, 2. J. L. Garvin and J. Amery, *The life of Joseph Chamberlain*, VI, (1969) 516.

8. Cf. Haldane in his address to the 'Eighty' Club at Cambridge in May 1904; *Constructive liberalism* (1904).

29. 'The making of a university', *Cornhill*, XIV (Jan – Jun 1903) 530–40.

37. *Autobiography*, p. 146.

74, 7. 'National education' in *After-war problems*, ed. W. H. Dawson (1917) 81.

16. *H. C. Debs*, 14 Jun 1898, col.233f.

34. Ref. **67,** 8.

75, 8. Introduction to Norman Lockyer, *Education and national progress: essays and addresses, 1870–1905* (1906).

22. 3 Feb 1901; T 1/9653B/3328/1901.

76, 4. 14 Aug 1902; Joseph Chamberlain Pp., JC 11/15/2.

8. 12 Mar 1905; ibid., JC 11/15/4.

31. Transcript of notes of reply by the chancellor, 17 Feb 1904; T 1/10215B/3211/1904.

77, 38. T 1/10370/22413/1905.

78, 18. Ibid.

31. *U.Cs Grants, Try cttee, 3rd rept;* 1905 [Cd 2422] LX.

79, 33. Confidential print, 17 Mar 1905; CAB 37/75.

80, 4. 'Observations by Mr Higgs', 31 May 1905; analysis of replies from university colleges by R. G. Hawtrey, 27 May 1905; T 1/10370/22413/1905.

7. Memo by Murray, 27 Jun 1905, ibid.; Try minute, 1905 [Cd 2621] LX.

33. *H. L. Debs*, 6 July 1915, col. 275.

36. Ibid., 31 Jul 1918, col. 218.

81, 30. Fitzroy, diary, 28 May 1902; *Memoirs*.

82, 8. *H. C. Debs*, 24 Mar 1902, col. 900; 5 May 1902, col. 703.

28. Ibid., 8 May 1908.

31. 'The education bill: a symposium', *Nineteenth Century*, LII (Jul – Dec 1902) 602–24.

35. *H. C. Debs*, 6 May 1902.

83, 4. *The Times*, 9 May 1902.

8. B. Webb, diary, 21 Jul 1902; *Our partnership*, p. 245; cf. ref. **82,** 31.

25. Ibid., 25 Apr 1902; p. 233.

31. Ibid., pp. 244–5.

36. P.Pp., IV.

84, 17. Enclosure in Haldane to B. Webb, 2 Oct 1902; P.Pp., II, 4b, 44.

20. Haldane to B. Webb, 2 Nov 1902; ibid., II, 4b, 47.

23. *Our partnership*, pp. 248–9.
28. Dated '30 Jan 1903' but seemingly in error for 3 Jan; P.Pp., II, 4b, 63.
31. 7 Jan 1903; ibid., II, 4b, 56.
32. *Our partnership*, p. 257.
34. Ibid., pp. 257–8.
38. P.Pp., II, 4b, 72.

85, 2. Ibid., II, 4b, 74.
    6. Ibid., II, 4b, 76.
    8. *Our partnership*, p. 263.
  17. 18 Apr 1903; P.Pp., II, 4b, 93.
  28. H. C. *Debs*, 28 Apr 1903, col. 703.
  35. Yoxall, ibid.
  39. *Our partnership*, p. 265.

Chapter 5: At the cabinet table
86, 6. *The Student*, no. 378 (2 Nov 1905) 26.
    7. Ibid., NS, XI (1913–14) 84.
  11. Ibid., NS, IV (1906–7) 371.
  22. Ibid., NS, IV special Union no. (2 Nov 1906) 41.
  29. 15 Sep 1901; P.Pp., II, 4b.
87, 12. *Autobiography*, p. 170.
  14. *Our partnership*, pp. 325–6.
  27. L. S. Amery, *My political life* (1953) 227.
  30. Osbert Sitwell, *Laughter in the next room* (1949) 98.
88, 3. *Autobiography*, p. 262.
  32. Alex Hill to Selby-Bigge, private, 6 May 1913; ED 24/1941.
89, 2. Haldane to Selby-Bigge, 9 May 1913; ibid.
    5. 13 Jun 1914; ibid.
  27. See above p. 63.
  29. 5 Feb 1902; *University for the West of England* (Bristol, 1902).
90, 17. Morris W. Travers, *Autobiography* (unpubd typescript): Bristol Univ.
      Library, DM 389.
91, 10. PC 8/618/95729. The memorandum was minuted by Crewe: 'I agree';
      and copies were transmitted to Birrell, at the board of education, and
      to Haldane. Cf. ED 24/511; ED 24/514.
  28. Fitzroy to the lord president, 13 Nov 1908; PC 8/672/101390.
  30. Appended note, ibid.
  35. Runciman to Fitzroy, 15 Dec 1908; PC 8/172/101635.
92, 4. Minute by Fitzroy, 16 Dec 1908, and by Haldane, 21 Dec 1908; ibid.
  21. Ibid.
  25. 22 Mar 1909; ibid.
93, 2. 'The civic university' in *The conduct of life and other addresses* (1914)
      63–95.
  20. *Civil Service, R. com.*, appx to first rept, q.1761; 1912–13 [Cd 6210] xv.
94, 25. Asquith Pp., 10.
95, 7. *U.Cs Grants, Try cttee, rept*, p. 7; 1909 [182] LXIX. ℧/
  14. Secretary, board of education, to treasury, 17 Dec 1908; T 1/10942A/
      22002/1908.

17. Morant to Murray, 17 Dec 1908; ibid.

33. T. L. Heath to Murray, 14 Jan 1909; ibid.

96, 4. Cf. H. F. Heath, 'Outline of the history of the transfer of the Treasury Grants to the Board of Education', 24 Jan 1912; ED 24/1938.

11. ED 24/567.

16. V. Nash to Runciman, 30 Jul 1910; ED 24/519.

38. Ibid.

97, 16. 9 Jan 1912; ED 24/519.

22. Ref. **96,** 4.

27. Murray to Runciman, 21 Apr 1911; ED 24/568.

35. Runciman to Murray, 23 May 1911; T 1/11525/4849/1913.

98, 1. ED 24/519.

27. Ibid.

33. Ibid.

99, 3. Ibid.

17. Minute by Pease; 11 Jan 1912; ED 24/1938.

24. Selby-Bigge to Pease, 25 Jan 1912; ibid.

36. 1 Feb 1912; ibid.

40. 2 Feb 1912; ibid.

100, 10. T. L. Heath to the secretary, board of education, 21 Feb 1912; T 1/11525/4849/1913.

32. Diary, 27 Feb 1912; Austen Chamberlain, *Politics from inside* (1936) 429.

101, 39. F. G. Ogilvie to Morant, 1 Sep 1906; ED 24/532.

102, 9. Morant to Sir William White, 1 Nov 1906; ED 24/531.

11. J. Sykes to Morant, strictly confidential, 13 Feb 1907; ibid.

23. Private, 15 May 1906; ibid.

29. Ref. **102,** 11.

35. 13 Feb 1907; ED 24/531.

40. McKenna to Sir Francis Mowatt, 19 Feb 1907; ibid.

103, 2. 21 Feb 1907; ibid.

10. B. Webb, diary, 19 May 1908; *Our partnership*, p. 411.

14. Morant to G. E. Buckle, 16 Feb 1909; ED 24/174.

25. Webb to Haldane, 3 Feb 1909; ibid.

32. Webb to Morant, 5 Feb 1909; ibid.

104, 1. Morant to Haldane, 4 Feb 1909; ibid.

3. Ibid.

5. Morant to Webb, 5 Feb 1909; ibid.

14. Abraham Flexner, *I remember* (New York, 1940) 140ff.

18. Ref. **103,** 14.

25. *Univ. educ. in London, R. com., final rept,* p. 26; 1913 [Cd 6717] XL.

36. Cf. *H. L. Debs,* 29 Jun 1926; col. 637.

105, 9. *Univ. educ. in London, R. com., final rept,* q.15809; 1913 [Cd 6718] XL.

14. *Univ. educ. in Wales, R. com., appx to 2nd rept,* q.8898; 1917–18 [Cd 8699] XII.

17. Ibid., *appx to final rept,* q.13973; 1918 [Cd 8993] XIV.

21. *Univ. educ. in London, R. com., appx to 3rd rept,* q.10130; 1911 [Cd 5911] XX.

25. Ibid., q.7807.

107, 9. Ref. **105,** 9; paras 64, 65, 69.

109, 4. Ibid., para. 85.

24. Ibid., para. 395.

28. Ibid., para. 291.

110, 3. Ibid., para. 403.

17. Ibid., para. 410.

25. Cf. letters to his mother, e.g. 20 Nov 1912; H.Pp., 5988; also *Maurice*, I, 325.

29. H. H. Bellot, *The University of London: a history* (1969) 21.

39. Q.4639; 1911 [Cd 5528] xx.

111, 4. Q.4291; ibid.

13. 17 Apr 1913; H. Pp., 5989.

15. *T.E.S.*, 6 May 1913.

28. *The Times*, 21 Apr 1913.

35. *H. C. Debs*, 17 Jul 1913, col. 1420.

40. Minute by J. A. Pease, president of the board of education, 14 Aug 1913; ED 24/1171.

112, 5. First report, 20 Apr 1914; ibid.

13. Webb to Haldane, 19 May 1914; ED 24/2019.

15. Ibid.

113, 4. 'Universities and schools in Scotland' in *Education and empire* (1902) 39–87.

9. *University for the West of England* (1920).

10. *The Times*, 12 Sep 1903.

13. Ibid., 12 Nov 1904.

26. Confidential print, 'Education Bill: Cabinet Committee', 12 Jan 1906; CAB 37/82.

32. *Autobiography*, p. 219; cf. Fitzroy, diary, 25 Apr 1906; *Memoirs*.

114, 5. *National education: speeches ... delivered at the 'Eighty' Club Dinner, April 4 1913* (1913).

9. *Lord Haldane's education proposals: from Lord Haldane's speech before the Manchester Reform Club ... 10th January 1913* (1913).

14. Cf. Pease to Selby-Bigge, confidential, 5 Dec 1912; ED 24/628. The first meeting was held in Haldane's room at the house of lords on 19 December; ibid. The appointment of the committee was disclosed in *The Times* on 24 January 1913, and attracted further comment in the 'Political Notes' of that paper on 25 April.

23. Selby-Bigge to Pease, confidential, 6 Dec 1912; ED 24/628.

115, 1. Ibid.

6. 9 [sic for 10] Jan 1913; H.Pp., 5989.

22. Ref. **114,** 9.

39. C. P. Scott, diary, 16 Jan 1913; *Political diaries* (1970) 68–9.

116, 6. 10 Mar 1913; H.Pp., 5989

9. *H. C. Debs*, 17 Mar 1913.

28. *The Times*, 31 Mar 1913; *T. E. S.*, 1 Apr 1913; ref. **114,** 5.

34. Draft bill, 26 Apr 1913; ED 24/638.

36. 1 May 1913; ED 24/628.

117, 4. 4 May 1913; ibid.

7. Haldane to Selby-Bigge, 9 May 1913; ibid.

14. *H. C. Debs*, 22 Jul 1913, col. 1907.

16. Sir James Yoxall; ibid., col. 1944.

19. ED 24/638.

32. ED 24/628.

36. Ibid.

118, 5. Haldane to Lloyd George, 26 Apr 1914; Lloyd George Pp., C 4/17/6.

22. *The inwardness of the budget; speeches delivered by the Rt Hon. Viscount Haldane . . . and the Rt Hon. D. Lloyd George at the National Liberal Club on June 26, 1914* (1914).

33. C. Addison, *Four and a half years* (1934).

119, 3. Ibid.

5. Diary, 11 Dec 1914; ibid.

18. C. Addison, *Politics from within* (1924) 48.

19. Addison to Pease, 20 Mar 1915; ED 24/1581.

24. Diary, 30 Mar 1915; ref. 118, 33.

28. Cf. J. A. Pease 'Proposals for a national scheme of instruction and research in science, technology and commerce', 6 Apr 1915; confidential print, ED 24/1581 (also pubd, with minor changes, refs 118, 33; 119, 18.)

33. Cf. Selby-Bigge to Addison, 18 Jun 1915; ED 24/1576.

120, 8. *The Times*, 11 Jun 1912.

17. Quoted Koss, *Lord Haldane*, p. 90.

Chapter 6: On the periphery of power

121, 13. Fitzroy, *Memoirs*.

19. Haldane to Webb, 27 Jul 1891; P.Pp., II, 2, 33.

23. C. P. Scott, *Political diaries*.

122, 5. M. Belloc Lowndes, *A passing world* (1948) 130.

10. H.Pp., 5912; copy, P.Pp., II, 5.

17. Quoted Heuston, 'Lord Haldane' in *Lives of the lord chancellors*, pp. 183–240.

21. P.Pp., II, 4g, 14.

30. Selby-Bigge to Fitzroy, 16 Jul 1915; PC 8/1129.

34. Haldane to Lloyd George, 4 Apr 1916; Lloyd George Pp., B 17/1/1.

123, 14. A. J. P. Taylor, *English history 1914–1945* (Oxford, 1965) 73.

18. *Maurice*, II, 45.

21. H.Pp., 5997.

25. 15/16 Mar 1917; *Political diaries*.

32. ED 119/82.

125, 2. *Univ. educ. in Wales, R. com., final rept*, p. 24; 1918 [Cd 8991] XIV.

9. *H. C. Debs*, 16 Jun 1899, col. 1388.

13. 'The soul of a people' in *Universities and national life* (1911) 1–32.

22. *T.E.S.*, 6 Jun 1916.

34. Haldane to Gosse, 2 Jul 1916; Gosse Pp.

39. *H. L. Debs*, 24 Jul 1918, col 1136.

126, 3. 28 Jun 1916; Lloyd George Pp., I 2/2/46.

19. Qs 6817, 6818: *Univ. educ. in Wales, R. com., appx to 2nd rept;* 1917–18 [Cd 8699] XII.

25. Q.5191; ibid.

127, 18. *The ideal of the university* (1920).

32. Ref. **125,** 2; para. 176.

128, 2. Ref. **127,** 18.

24. Ref. **125,** 2; para. 105.

38. Qs 14003ff., *appx to final rept;* 1918 [Cd 8993] XIV.

129, 13. Ref. **125,** 2; para. 190.

18. Ref. **127,** 18.

33. Q.12222; *appx to final rept.*

130, 7. *The University and the Welsh democracy* (1922) [Address delivered at the Central Hall, Swansea on 25 Nov 1921].

23. *T.E.S.,* 22 Aug 1918.

17. C. Addison, diary, 19 Mar 1915; *Four and a half years* (1934) I, 70.

131, 3. *T.E.S.,* 22 Aug 1918.

9. H. J. W. Hetherington, *The life and letters of Sir Henry Jones* (1924).

13. ED 24/2026.

15. PC 8/890.

21. *T.E.S.,* 24 Oct 1918.

27. D. Emrys Evans, *The University of Wales: a historical sketch* (Cardiff, 1953) 84.

37. Gosse Pp.

132, 15. *H. L. Debs,* 12 Jul 1916, col. 668.

26. MS diary, 7 Apr 1916; P.Pp., I, I, vol. 33.

133, 23 *The student and the nation* (1916).

38. Ref. **135,** 27; col. 679.

134, 17. *H. C. Debs,* 9 Aug 1917, cols 561–2.

25. 5 Apr 1916; H.Pp., 6012.

29. 4 Apr 1916; Lloyd George Pp., D 17/1/1.

40. Ibid., D 17/1/2.

135, 5. Memo by V. Nash, 8 May 1916; RECO 1/14/27.

8. 'Notes on the proposal for a Royal Commission on Education', 29 May 1916; enclosed in Selby-Bigge to V. Nash, 31 May 1916: ED 24/1173; RECO 1/14/56.

12. Extract from conclusions of meeting of 23 Jun, transmitted to the board of education on 11 Jul; RECO 1/14/73.

24. 22 May 1916; quoted Koss, *Lord Haldane,* p. 229.

27. *H. L. Debs,* 12 Jul 1916, cols 655–705.

136, 13. Adjourned debate; ibid., 26 Jul 1916.

25. 13 Jul 1916; *The Times,* 14 Jul 1916.

35. 15 Jul 1916; Michael Sadleir, *Michael Ernest Sadler* (1949) 273.

40. RECO 1/14/168.

139, 9. Arthur Henderson; *H. C. Debs,* 18 Jul 1916, col. 975.

11. Ref. **136,** 40.

19. Gosse Pp.

20. Cf. Haldane to Gosse, 5 Sep 1916; ibid.

27. Ref. **136,** 40.

35. Undated memo by V. Nash, ibid.
140, 1. Haldane to Gosse, 11 Aug 1916; Gosse Pp.
    7. 'Confidential. The reform of our system of education', 17 Aug 1916; ED 24/1461. Cf. Haldane to Gosse, 18 Aug 1916; Gosse Pp.
  29. Gosse Pp.
  33. Ibid.
  37. *H. C. Debs*, 10 Oct 1916, col. 15.
141, 3. Ref. **136,** 40.
  14. *Diaries, 1912–1924* (1952) 98.
  16. Cf. minutes of meetings; ED 24/1461, ED 24/1473.
  19. RECO 1/14/534; second draft [6 Dec 1916] ED 24/1473.
142, 6. ED 24/1473. Cf. RP No. 6, Confidential, Board of Education, 'Development of the National System of Education', initialled L.A.S.B., Dec 1916; ED 24/1461.
  9. 'Comments on Memorandum of 6 Dec', initialled L.A.S.B., 7 Dec 1916; ED 24/1473.
  22. H. W. Orange. 'Remarks on a Memo. unsigned and undated, recd on Dec 12 1916'; ibid.
  30. Extract from minutes of meeting of war cabinet, 15 Feb 1917; RECO 1/40.
  36. *T.E.S.*, 1 Feb 1917.
143, 3. Cf. Haldane's acknowledgement, 28 May 1915; Fisher Pp.
  8. *Maurice*, II, 45–6.
  11. H. A. L. Fisher, *An unfinished autobiography* (1940) 95.
  32. Lloyd George Pp., F 22/5/1.
144, 1. *T.E.S.*, 11 Jan 1917.
  4. Ibid., 18 Jan 1917.
  11. *H. C. Debs*, 19 Apr 1917, col. 1910.
  15. Address to representative managers of LCC schools on 23 Apr 1917; *T.E.S.*, 26 Apr 1917.
  17. *H. L. Debs*, 9 May 1917, col. 2.
145, 6. *H. C. Debs*, 10 Aug 1917, col. 795.
  10. 13 Aug 1917; Fisher Pp.
  16. 23 Aug 1917; Gosse Pp.
  20. *T.E.S.*, 4, 18, 25 Oct 1917.
  26. Ibid., 15 Nov 1917.
  n. Ref. 145, 10; ref. 144, 17.
146, 8. *H. C. Debs*, 14 Jan 1918, col. 55.
  13. 4 Jul 1918, Fisher Pp.
  22. *H. L. Debs*, 24 Jul 1918, col. 1131.
  28. Ibid., col. 1140.
147, 15. Selby-Bigge to Haldane, personal, 21 Aug 1917: enclosure in Haldane to Gosse, 23 Aug 1917; Gosse Pp.

Chapter 7: Ebb-tide
148, 9. 15 Nov 1925; P.Pp., I, 2, vol. 39.
  11. 6 Jan 1927; ibid., I, 2, vol. 41.
  12. 30 Mar 1926; *Diaries, 1924–32* (1956) 87.

30. 12 Aug 1926; P.Pp., 1, 2, vol. 40.

149, 5. 'The portrait of a lady', *Observer*, 28 Mar 1926.

9. 30 Mar 1926, *Diaries, 1924–1932*, p. 86; and further reflections, ref. **148,** 30.

21. Ref. **148,** 12.

150, 1. *Maurice*, II, 77.

3. Ibid., p. 114.

16. 30 Sep 1918; W. R. Inge, *Diary of a dean* (1949) 47.

18. 9 Jul 1918; ibid.

29. 13 May 1919, enclosed in T. Jones to M. Hankey, 14 May 1919; Lloyd George Pp., F 23/4/62.

151, 24. Fisher to Bonar Law, 19 Dec 1918; T 1/12324/20290/1919.

30. Ibid.

36. Ibid.

152, 8. See above, p. 100; cf. R. O. Berdahl, *British universities and the state* (1959) 57–8.

10. ED 24/1968.

19. H. A. L. Fisher, *An unfinished autobiography* (1940) 116.

27. *H. L. Debs*, 21 Jul 1920, col. 399.

34. Draft to Snowden, undated and marked 'Not sent'; ED 24/1977.

40. Roy Jenkins, *Asquith* (1964) 483.

153, 5. Quoted Koss, *Lord Haldane*, p. 237.

9. *H. L. Debs*, 19 Apr 1923, cols 741–8.

25. PC 8/1001.

32. Memo by A. H. Kidd, 26 Jul 1918, on the request from the 'Committee for the furtherance of University Education in the South-West' to send a deputation to the president of the board of education; ED 24/1946.

33. Minutes of proceedings of the deputation, 12 Nov 1918; ibid.

40. Fitzroy to McCormick, 10 Jan, 11 Apr 1921; PC 8/1075.

154, 10. 14 May 1923, *Memoirs*.

23. *H. L. Debs*, 8 Feb 1922, cols 66–77.

156, 1. *Maurice*, II, 77.

5. Ibid., pp. 114–15; *The Times*, 15 Jun 1922.

13. 26 Nov 1921; *The University and the Welsh democracy* (1922).

28. 16 Jan 1922, Asquith Pp.; quoted *Maurice*, II, 108–9.

38. Haldane to B. Webb, 23 Jan 1925; P.Pp., II, 4h, 26.

157, 35. 'Educational reform: general proposals'; Lloyd George Pp., F. 77.

37. Enclosure to confidential print on 'London University' drawn up by Fisher and circulated to the cabinet on 1 Aug 1918; ED 24/2007.

158, 10. Ibid.

12. Ibid.

16. 'London University: memorandum by Mr H. A. L. Fisher' 1 Nov 1918; ibid.

18. E. C. Perry, vice-chancellor, University of London, to Kidd, board of education, 18 Jan 1919; ED 24/2019.

19. ED 24/1196.

n. ED 24/2007.

159, 11. Ref. **158,** 19.

13. Ibid.

15. Eustace Percy to Hilton Young, 6 Feb 1925; minute of appointment, 16 Feb 1925; ED 24/1196.

39. *H. C. Debs*, 19 Nov 1926, col. 2113ff.

160, 15. F. J. C. Hearnshaw, *The centenary history of King's College* (1929) 453.

25. H. H. Bellot, *The University of London: a history* (1969) 33.

28. Douglas Logan, *Haldane and the University of London* (1960).

161, 22. *The nationalisation of universities* (1921).

27. Ref. **160,** 28.

31. Ibid.

35. *H. L. Debs*, 29 Jun 1926, col. 635ff.

162, 33. 'Universities and the schools in Scotland' in *Education and empire* (1902) 39.

163, 4. *H. L. Debs*, 8 Feb 1922, col. 66ff.

19. Albert Mansbridge, *The dedication of life* (Haldane Memorial Lecture, 1930).

21. E. C. F. Collier, ed., *A Victorian diarist: later extracts from the journals of Mary, Lady Monkswell, 1895–1909* (1946) 208.

164, 16. *Univ. educ. in Wales, R. com., appx to final rept*, q.12016ff.; 1918 [Cd 8993] XIV.

23. Violet Bonham Carter, 'Haldane of Cloan: Scottish lawyer who shaped the British army', *The Times*, 30 Jul 1956.

27. Cf. ref. **161,** 22.

165, 11. *H. L. Debs*, 21 Jul 1920, col. 229ff.

29. *Autobiography*, p. 296.

166, 5. Presidential address to British Institute of Adult Education, 20 Sep 1924; *The Times*, 22 Sep 1924.

13. *Autobiography*, p. 330.

18. Ibid., p. 300.

22. *H. L. Debs*, 18 Mar 1925, col. 589ff.

28. *The Times*, 27 Jun 1925.

29. Haldane to B. Webb, 18 Oct 1925; P.Pp., II, 4h, 40.

30. B. Webb, diary, 8 Nov 1926; P.Pp., I, 2, vol. 41.

36. Ibid., 19 Nov 1925; I, 2, vol. 39.

167, 9. *H. L. Debs*, 9 Mar 1927, col. 419ff.

18. P.Pp., II, 4h, 41a.

33. 'A vision of the future' in *The way out*, ed. Oliver Stanley (1923).

168, 2. 'The higher education of the people', *Journal of Adult Education*, I, i (Sep 1926) 10.

10. *Hibbert Journal*, XXVI (1928) 193–207.

Chapter 8: Epilogue

170, 15. 'The dedicated life' in *Universities and national life* (1911) 65–110 [Rectorial address, 10 Jan 1907].

171, 27. 'The soul of a people', ibid., pp. 1–32 [University College of Wales, Aberystwyth, 14 Oct 1910].

172, 1. Cf. Webb to Haldane, 13 Jun 1921; H.Pp., 5915; copy, P.Pp., II, 5.

5. Ref. **171,** 27.

13. Cf. his speech at the annual dinner of the court of the University of Leeds on 17 Feb 1912; *The Times*, 19 Feb 1912.

16. Ref. **170**, 15.

173, 13. Agnes Fry, *A memoir of the Rt hon. Sir Edward Fry, G.C.B.* (1921) 238.

174, 12. 8 Dec 1905; R. S. Churchill, *Winston S. Churchill*, II companion vol. (1969) 720.

13. A. G. Gardiner, *Prophets, priests and kings* (1908) 205.

16. *The Student*, XI, no. 5 (19 Nov 1913) 83.

17. Haldane to Gosse, 23 Aug 1917; Gosse Pp.

18. *Maurice*, II, 71.

22. B. Webb, *Diaries, 1924–1932*, p. 88.

175, 37. *D.N.B.*

176, 11. 9 Sep 1928; P.Pp., II, 4i, 31.

23. B. Webb to Haldane, 14 Aug 1928, H.Pp., 5917; copy, P.Pp., II, 5.

26. P.Pp., II, 4i, 30a.

Index

Aberystwyth, *see* Wales, University College of

Acland, A. H. D., 15, 18, 36, 65, 67, 114 n.

Adams, W. G. S., 142

Addison, Christopher, 3, 118–19

Allchin, Sir William H., 33, 104

Amery, L. S., 87

Anson, Sir William, 84

Arnold, Matthew, 14, 16, 43, 46, 61, 142

Arrowsmith, J. W., 92

Asquith, H. H., 1st earl of Oxford and Asquith: early political association with Haldane, 10, 17, 47; congratulates him on speech on U of London (1898) 37; praises his work for Liberal party (1902) 47; aided by Haldane over univ. grants committee (1905–6) 94; invoked over administration of grants (1910–11) 96–8 *passim*; staves off discussion of Haldane report on U of London (1913) 111; and development of national education (1913–14) 115, 117, 118; jettisons Haldane (1915) 120; compensatory offers to him, 122; remorseful support of him, 134; approached by Haldane over committee of educational experts (1916) 134; final interview about it, 140; Haldane's note to, on fall of Asquith coalition (Dec 1916) 123; preferred to Haldane, as chairman of commission on Us of Oxford and Cambridge (1919) 152; Haldane's praise of its work (1923) 153; Haldane's political dissociation from, over

education (1922) 156; his views on extra-mural work of univs contrasted with Haldane's, 164; mentioned, 174

Balfour, Arthur James, 1st earl of: social contacts with Haldane, 19, friendship with him, 35, and political fraternising, 47; negotiates with him over U of London (1887) 27, (1897–8) 35–6, 38, and Irish univ. question (1898) 38, 60; his support enlisted by Haldane over London Charlottenburg scheme, 51, univ. question in England (1902) 60, 64, and Education bill for London (1903) 84, 85; approves Haldane's proposal for permanent grants committee for univ. institutions (1905) 80; envisaged by Haldane as member of proposed committee of P. C. for education (1916) 138

Balfour of Burleigh (A. H. Bruce) 6th baron, 32, 64, 67

Beach, Sir Michael Hicks, 75, 90

Bellot, H. H., xiv, 110–11, 160

Birkbeck College: and Haldane commission, 107; appointment of Haldane to presidency of (1919) 154

Birmingham, University of: founding of (1900) 61, inaccurately recalled by Haldane, 72; his concept of its role, 63; his proposals for it, snubbed by Chamberlain, 72; his commendation of its regional activity, 82; mentioned, 83, 88

Birrell, Augustine, 113

Blackie, J. S., 6

U of London Commission, 103 →

Addison ~ early plans for DSIR, 118-20.

U of Wales Commission 127 → . Profs ē med school. (What

British involvt in alt of civis — c. 68 f

Regional schools — 81-84

Steve Sturdy

Wellcome Unit for the
History of Medicine
Manchester University
Aug 1990.

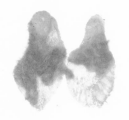

The Gift Relationship

by the same author

Commitment to Welfare
Income Distribution and Social Change
Essays on the 'Welfare State'
(*Allen & Unwin*)

Poverty and Population
Birth, Poverty and Wealth
Problems of Social Policy
The Social Division of Welfare

Richard M. Titmuss

THE GIFT
RELATIONSHIP

From Human Blood to
Social Policy

London . George Allen & Unwin Ltd

RUSKIN HOUSE   MUSEUM STREET

First published in 1970

© George Allen & Unwin Ltd 1970

ISBN 0 04 301026 1 cased
     0 04 301027 x paper

For Kay

Printed in Great Britain
in 10 pt Times Roman type
By Alden & Mowbray Ltd, Oxford

Preface

In the making of this book I have incurred many social debts. Gifts, solicited and unsolicited, in the form of advice, information and criticism have been received from a large number of people and organizations in many countries. A list of those who have helped with technical and statistical data is included in Appendix 7. I am grateful to them all for giving so freely of their time and knowledge.

In particular, I wish to record my special thanks to the following for much helpful comment and encouragement sustained over a period of years. Dr W. d'A. Maycock of the Lister Institute; the staff at the Department of Health and Social Security; the Director and staff of the Regional Transfusion Centres at Sutton, Birmingham and Manchester; Professor J. N. Morris of the Medical Research Council Social Medicine Unit, London School of Hygiene and Tropical Medicine; Mr Michael J. Reddin, Miss Sarah West, and Mr John Beddington (who also acted for periods as my research assistants); Dr B. Gullbring of the Karolinska Hospital, Stockholm; Dr Z. S. Hantchef, International Red Cross, Geneva; Dr A. Kellner, New York Blood Center; Dr R. Czajkowski, late of King County Central Blood Bank, Seattle; Dr J. M. Stengle, National Blood Resource Program, National Institutes of Health, Bethesda; Professor J. N. P. Davies, Albany Medical College, New York; Professor and Dr R. Stevens, Yale University; Professor Brian Abel-Smith, London School of Economics; Mr Charles Furth of George Allen & Unwin Ltd., London, and Dr Ida Merriam, Social Security Administration, Department of Health, Education, and Welfare, Washington.

To all those who completed questionnaires—and especially 3821 unknown blood donors in England—I also wish to express my gratitude. From their contributions I have learnt much.

Grants from the Nuffield Foundation Small Grant Program, the Department of Health and Social Security, the Social Research Division of the London School of Economics and the Joseph Rowntree Memorial Trust assisted me at various stages to undertake certain studies of blood donors and to analyse a mass of statistical and documentary materials. Without such financial help, in all a total of £3250, there would have been gaps in this book.

I alone am responsible for errors of fact and interpretation. All those who have helped me (not least my indefatigable secretary, Mrs Angela Vivian) are hereby absolved from any consequences of their acts of giving and friendship.

Richard M. Titmuss
Acton, London, W.3
February 1970

Contents

Tables

Chapter 1

Introduction: Human Blood and Social Policy

The starting-point of this book is human blood: the scientific, social, economic and ethical issues involved in its procurement, processing, distribution, use and benefit in Britain, the United States, the U.S.S.R., South Africa and other countries. The study thus examines beliefs, attitudes and values concerning blood and its possession, inheritance, use and loss in diverse societies, past and present, and draws on historical, religious and sociological materials. It investigates by a variety of research methods the characteristics of those who give, supply or sell blood, and analyses in comparative terms blood transfusion and donor systems and national statistics of supply, demand and distribution particularly in Britain and the United States. Criteria of social value, cost efficiency, biological efficacy, safety and purity are applied to public and private markets in blood and to voluntary and commercial systems of meeting steeply rising world demands from medicine for blood and blood products.

The study originated, and grew over many years of introspection, from a series of value questions formulated within the context of attempts to distinguish the 'social' from the 'economic' in public policies and in those institutions and services with declared 'welfare' goals.[1] Could, however, such distinctions be drawn and the territory of social policy at least broadly defined without raising issues about the morality of society and of man's regard or disregard for the needs of others? Why should men not contract out of the 'social' and act to their own immediate advantage? Why give to strangers? —a question provoking an even more fundamental moral issue; who is my stranger in the relatively affluent, acquisitive and divisive societies of the twentieth century? What are the connections then, if obligations are extended, between the reciprocals of giving and receiving and modern welfare systems?

[1] For an earlier attempt to define the territory of social policy and the roles and functions of the social services, see the writer's *Commitment to Welfare* (1968) and particularly Chapter 1.

11

To speculate in such ways from the standpoint of the individual about gift relationships led us inevitably into the area of economic theory. In particular, we were forced to ask 'economic man' questions about those institutions which are (or may be) redistributive in some form or other, and which during this century have come to be known as 'social services' or 'social welfare'. Examining, as a case study, one such manifestation of social policy, we came to ask: is medical care analysed in its many component parts—such as blood transfusion services—a consumption good indistinguishable from other goods and services in the private economic market? What are the consequences, national and international, of treating human blood as a commercial commodity? If blood is morally sanctioned as something to be bought and sold what ultimately is the justification for not promoting individualistic private markets in other component areas of medical care, and in education, social security, welfare services, child foster care, social work skills, the use of patients and clients for professional training, and other 'social service' institutions and processes?

Where are the lines to be drawn—can indeed any lines at all be pragmatically drawn—if human blood be legitimated as a consumption good? To search for an identity and sphere of concern for social policy would thus be to search for the non-existent. All policy would become in the end economic policy and the only values that would count are those that can be measured in terms of money and pursued in the dialectic of hedonism. Each individual would act egoistically for the good of all by selling his blood for what the market would pay. To abolish the moral choice of giving to strangers could lead to an ideology to end all ideologies.

As the questions grow so does the book. It moves from the particular and microscopic—human blood—to the general and fundamental issues posed by philosophers for centuries. Essentially then, the study is about the role of altruism in modern society— hence its title. It attempts to fuse the politics of welfare and the morality of individual wills.

Men are not born to give; as newcomers they face none of the dilemmas of altruism and self-love. How can they and how do they learn to give—and to give to unnamed strangers irrespective of race, religion or colour—not in circumstances of shared misery but in societies continually multiplying new desires and syndicalist private wants concerned with property, status and power?

We do not answer these great questions. Step by step, however, we found we were compelled to raise them in examining the extent to which specific instruments of public policy encourage or discourage, foster or destroy the individual expression of altruism and regard for the needs of others. Put in another way, we wanted to know whether these instruments or institutions positively created areas of moral conflict for society by providing and extending opportunities for altruism in opposition to the possessive egoism of the marketplace. If the opportunity to behave altruistically— to exercise a moral choice to give in non-monetary forms to strangers —is an essential human right then this book is also about the definition of freedom. Should men be free to sell their blood? Or should this freedom be curtailed to allow them to give or not to give blood? And if this freedom is to be paramount do we not then have to regard social policy institutions as agents of altruistic opportunities and, thus, as generators of moral conflict and not simply as utilitarian instruments of welfare?

In the course of inquiring and trespassing, by amateurish paths, into the territory of the political philosopher, the economist and the medical scientist we came to study systems of medical care and to address somewhat metaphysical questions to its constituent parts. For obvious reasons we could not examine all these parts in depth, sector by sector, and on a comparative cross-national basis; we therefore chose to investigate blood donor and transfusion services. We believe this sector to be one of the most sensitive universal social indicators which, within limits, is measureable, and one which tells us something about the quality of relationships and of human values prevailing in a society. It also happens to be a crucial medical resource factor; the future of surgical care and many forms of curative and preventive medicine are dependent on the supply of uncontaminated human blood and blood products. Yet over large parts of the world today blood for transfusion is scarcer than many other medical care facilities.

Though, in this book, we abstract for a time this particular sector from its medical care setting for intensive study we need to remember that we cannot understand the part unless we also understand the whole. 'Society has to be studied in the individual, and the individual in society; those who wish to separate politics from morals will never understand either.' Rousseau's thought may be applied to the individual as a potential blood donor and to the 'society' of medical care. We cannot understand in Britain the National Blood Transfusion Service without also understanding the National Health Service, its origins, development and values. Similarly, we cannot understand the blood donor or blood seller in the United States without understanding that country's systems of medical care.

There are some who argue from theories of political and economic convergence that we are today approaching the end of the ideological debate; within Britain and other Western societies and considered also in comparative national terms. These propositions are, we believe, dominated by economic and material maximizing values just as Marx offered, as an alternative to the capitalist market, a crude utilitarianism. This study, in one small sector of human affairs, disputes both the death of ideology and the philistine resurrection of economic man in social policy. It is thus concerned with the values we accord to people for what they give to strangers; not what they get out of society.

Chapter 2

The Transfusion of Blood

I

There is a bond that links all men and women in the world so closely and intimately that every difference of colour, religious belief and cultural heritage is insignificant beside it. Never varying in temperature more than five or six degrees, composed of 55 per cent water, the life stream of blood that runs in the veins of every member of the human race proves that the family of man is a reality.

Thousands of years ago man discovered that this fluid was vital to him and precious beyond price. The history of every people assigns to blood a unique importance. Folklore, religion and the history of dreams of perpetual youthfulness—of rejuvenation through 'new blood'—are filled with examples.

The 'blood is the life' says Deuteronomy (xii, 23). 'For this is my blood of the New Testament which is shed for you' (Matthew xxvi, 28). Ancient Egyptians were said to bath in blood to refresh their powers, and to anoint heads with oil and blood to treat greying and baldness. Ovid describes how Aeson recovered his youthfulness after drinking the blood of his son, Jason. The Romans were said to have drunk the blood of dying gladiators to imbue them with courage. In more recent time, it is reported that certain tribes of Central Australia give to sick old men the blood of young men to drink. Kublai Khan, expressing a widespread belief that the soul is in the blood, refused to allow the spilling of royal blood. Throughout South America the most popular method of driving out a bad spirit was by venesection in the belief that the demons escaped with the blood. Blood brother ceremonies in various countries of the world still fulfil functions of reconciliation and other social purposes while blood feuds—blood being repaid with blood—represented a powerful institution in medieval Europe and form part of conventions in some societies today.

For centuries then in all cultures and societies, blood has been regarded as a vital, and often magical, life-sustaining fluid, marking all important events in life, marriage, birth, initiation and death, and its loss has been associated with disgrace, disgust, impotence, sickness and tragedy. Symbolically and functionally, blood is deeply embedded in religious doctrine; in the psychology of human relationships; and in theories and concepts of race, kinship, ancestor worship and the family. From time immemorial it has symbolized qualities of fortitude, vigour, nobility, purity and fertility. Men have been terrified by the sight of blood; they have killed each other for it; believed it could work miracles; and have preferred death rather than receive it from a member of a different ethnic group.

The very thought of blood, individual blood, touches the deepest feelings in man about life and death. Attitudes to it and the values associated with its possession, inheritance, use and loss among men and women have been studied by anthropologists as one of the distinctive features of different cultures. Even in modern times, mystical and irrational group attitudes to blood have sharply distinguished certain Western societies—as in Hitler's Germany with its myths of 'Aryan' and 'Jewish' blood. Nor can we pursue such thoughts far without being reminded of the contemporary world-wide phenomenon of racial prejudice and its association with concepts of blood impurities, 'good' blood and 'bad' blood, untouchability and contamination.

Beliefs and attitudes concerning blood affect in varying degrees throughout the world the work of transfusion services in appealing for and recruiting blood donors. A deeply rooted and widely held superstition is that the blood contained in the body is an inviolable property and to take it away is sacrilege. In parts of Africa, for example, and particularly among the Bantu in South Africa, it is believed also that blood taken away cannot be reconstituted and that the individual will therefore be weakened, be made impotent, or be blinded for life; that the white man takes blood to ensure his domination over the black man; and that the needle piercing the skin is an act of aggression which results in the propagation of disease and sickness. We shall have more to say about such beliefs in later chapters when we discuss some of the problems of donor motivation and recruitment.[1]

[1] Further references to the historical literature concerning attitudes to blood are contained in: Wolstenholme, G. E. W., and O'Connor, M., *Ethics in Medical Progress*, A CIBA Foundation Symposium, Churchill, London, 1966; *World Health*, World Health Organization, Geneva, June 1968; League of Red Cross Societies, *Third Red Cross International Seminar on Blood Transfusion*, Medico-Social Documentation No. 27, Geneva, 1966; and Wood, C. S., 'A Short History of Blood Transfusion', *Transfusion*, No. 4, Vol. 7, July–August 1967, p. 299.

II

The growth of scientific knowledge about the circulation of the blood, the composition and preservation of blood, and the distribution of blood group genes throughout the human race has provided us with a more rational framework. But it is only in the last thirty years or so that scientific advances have made a blood transfusion service an indispensable and increasingly vital part of modern medicine.

Blood, in one form or another, appears in the earliest pharmacopeias. It was a favourite remedy centuries ago for lunacy and palsy and was prescribed for the rejuvenation of the old. The direct transfusion of blood into the circulation had, however, to await the discovery in 1616 that there was a circulation. As news of Harvey's work spread in Europe, there followed a wave of transfusion experiments. The first recorded attempt to transfuse blood from one body to another was made in 1665 at the suggestion of 'the busiest of men', Sir Christopher Wren.[1] Dr Richard Lower, the British anatomist, successfully transferred blood from one dog to another. Speculation naturally ensued, much of it centring around the commonly held view at that time that blood carried in it the secrets of individuality. Boyle, in writing to Lower, wondered 'whether the blood of a mastiff, being frequently transferred into a bloodhound, or a spaniel, will not prejudice them in point of scent'.[2] Samuel Pepys was even more imaginative. 'This did give occasion to many pretty wishes, as of the blood of a Quaker to be let into an Archbishop, and such like'.[3]

Two years after Lower's experiments, a French doctor, philosopher and astronomist, Jean Baptiste Denis, performed the first recorded blood transfusion on a human, the patient being a boy of 15 and the blood used being taken from a lamb. This experiment ended in disaster and charges of murder were preferred against the doctor. The practice of transfusing human beings with the blood of

[1] Some historians believe that the first transfusion was performed in 1490 in Rome on Pope Innocent VIII who lay dying of old age. It was proposed to rejuvenate him by injecting the blood from three young, healthy boys in his veins. There appears to be some question as to whether this blood was given intravenously or as a drink, but there is no doubt about the result. The boys died, the Pope died, and the doctor fled the country. (Clendening, Logan, *The Romance of Medicine*, Garden City Publishing Co., New York, 1933.)

[2] Cited in Mollison, P. L., *Blood Transfusion in Clinical Medicine*, Blackwell, 2nd edn, 1956, p. xxiii.

[3] Cited in Palmer, W. L., 'Serum Hepatitis Consequent to Transfusion of Blood', *J.A.M.A.*, Vol. 180, No. 13, 1962, p. 1123.

animals was, however, taken up in many countries but so many deaths were caused that it was made illegal in France, England and Italy, and in 1678 the Pope forbade it.[1]

Galen, the doctor of Marcus Aurelius, who was the first man to prove that arteries contained blood and not air, propagated the mistaken idea that blood passed from one side of the heart to the other by 'sweating'. This mistake lasted for centuries as did his enthusiasm for blood-letting. The trickles of purged blood in ancient Rome had become rivers by the eighteenth century when many surgeons, and even psychiatrists, reduced their therapy to the maxim 'purge and bleed'. This practice was only abandoned in the twentieth century.

As so often happens with scientific discoveries, little or no progress in the applied field of blood transfusion was made for a long time. One hundred and fifty years after Lower's experiments, Dr James Blundell, working at St Thomas's and Guy's Hospitals in London, invented an apparatus for directly transfusing blood and suggested that only human blood should be used for human beings. In 1818 he gave the first human-to-human transfusion. But the general use of transfusion apparatus had to await the brilliant work of a young Viennese scientist, Karl Landsteiner, who discovered in 1901 that there were different kinds of human blood and that the clumping together (agglutination) of red cells and their consequent destruction occurred if the wrong kinds of blood were mixed. It was finally determined that there were four main human blood groups, now called A, B, AB, and O, according to the presence or absence on the red cells of two chemical substances known as 'A' and 'B'. Safe transfusion, with the intermixing of the blood of two persons without the occurrence of clumping, was discovered to be possible if the patient received blood from a donor of the same blood group.

III

Once the major problems of blood grouping and Rh typing (see Appendix 1) were clarified and appropriate methods developed, blood transfusion became a common practice. This was made possible by the work of scientists in many countries (and notably in Britain) who contributed to great advances in knowledge and practice concerning the prevention of blood clotting after removal

[1] The work of Denis in France and Lower in England, occurring about the same time, is described in detail in Keynes, G., 'Tercentenary of Blood Transfusion', *Brit. Med. J.*, **ii**, 410, November 18, 1967.

from the body; the storage of blood under special conditions at very low temperatures; techniques of blood grouping and testing and cross-matching; methods and techniques of transfusion therapy; the development of special products and derivatives prepared from blood; the production of plasma substitutes which have some of the properties of plasma and can be used as temporary blood-volume expanders to make good loss of blood; an immense expansion of knowledge about the world distribution of blood group genes and blood diseases, and in many other fields of scientific study too complex even to enumerate from the literature.[1]

It must, however, be said that despite all these great advances in knowledge much still remains to be learnt. This was emphasized recently in discussions of the scientific, technical and ethical considerations in heart transplantation; '. . . It is significant' wrote three authorities at the Royal Postgraduate Hospital at Hammersmith, 'that analysis of antigenic composition of the red cell has still to be completed despite the lapse of over half a century since Landsteiner discovered the ABO antigens.'[2]

All these scientific and technical developments in the field of blood transfusion have not only produced new and, as yet, unsolved problems for the biological and medical sciences but they have set in train social, economic and ethical consequences which present society with issues of profound importance. It is part of the purpose of this book to explore these consequences. To help the general reader to understand their significance it will be necessary to provide in certain chapters and appendices a limited amount of scientific and technical information. This has been kept to a minimum. For those readers who want to know more we have added references to the relevant scientific literature.

In Appendix 1 an attempt has therefore been made to summarize a few of the more important facts about the composition of blood and blood transfusion therapy. Appendix 3 includes some information on the organization of the National Blood Transfusion Service.[3] In Chapter 8 we discuss in more detail the problem of infective

---

[1] Scientific developments in transfusion therapy from Landsteiner's discovery in 1901 to the 1960s are described in Hurn, B. A. L., *Storage of Blood*, Academic Press, London and New York, 1968.

[2] Dempster, W. J., Melrose, D. G. and Bentall, H. H., *Brit. Med. J.*, i, 177, January 20, 1968.

[3] Non-American readers interested in analogous developments in the United States are referred to Chapters 4 and 6. A short 'History of Blood Banking in the United States', by Dr L. K. Diamond was published in *J.A.M.A.*, Vol. 193, No. 1, July 5, 1965.

hepatitis (jaundice) the major hazard in blood transfusion. We also provide in various chapters some explanation of developments in transfusion techniques; in particular, of plasmapheresis.

At this point, however, and as a background to the next few chapters, we set out as briefly as possible a number of fundamental considerations which require to be borne in mind in understanding the problems of demand for and the supply of blood and blood products.

The Composition of Blood

Blood is composed of a vast number of minute cells (which give blood its colour) suspended in the pale yellow fluid known as plasma (containing, *inter alia*, immunoglobulin). The plasma transports these cells to all parts of the body as well as carrying foodstuffs and waste products. The red cells carry oxygen from the lungs to every part of the body so that the tissues may breathe. The life of a red cell in the human body is about four months. Every day a little less than 1 per cent of these red cells die and break up, and an equal number are formed. This ageing and death of red cells continues at about the same rate when blood is stored in the most favourable conditions, and also when they are transfused into another person. It follows that freshly taken blood will be richer in young and active red cells than blood that has been stored for a month: but even after this time three-quarters of the cells are still viable and active. In practice, stored blood is normally used within three weeks of being taken from a donor.

In the case of blood not used within three weeks the plasma is separated (in England this process is carried out in the Regional Transfusion Centres) and sent to plasma drying laboratories where it is processed to make dry powdered plasma that can be stored for years without deterioration. This powder can be reconstituted with distilled water when required, and it can be life-saving for people suffering from, for example, extensive burns and scalds—just as life-saving blood is for those who have lost blood.[1]

Further information on the composition and functions of blood and the uses of blood and blood products is contained in Appendix 1.

The Uniqueness of Blood

Despite the development of plasma substitutes and other products,

[1] Extracted from *Blood Plasma and Burns Treatment*, Jackson, D. MacG., Medical Research Council Burns Unit (a pamphlet produced by the National Blood Transfusion Service for blood donors, H.M.S.O., London, 1965).

advances in the freezing and preservation of blood to permit longer-term stockpiling, and the use of specific blood components, there is no substitute for the vast majority of patients for the direct use of fresh whole human blood. No alternative to whole blood and its main component elements has yet been developed in the research laboratory. The human body remains the only source. This study is, therefore, chiefly concerned with the collection, distribution and transfusion of whole blood.

Human Blood Soon Perishes

After 21 days of storage under refrigeration, blood has lost some of its usefulness because many red cells have been altered and chemical changes have occurred, making it undesirable and harmful to be used for transfusion. Administration of large amounts of blood that is near the 21-day expiration date causes potassium toxicity. This produces cardiac arrest and is more common in patients whose ability to excrete potassium is impaired, as in kidney disease.[1]

In some countries where there are serious shortages of whole blood the 'shelf-life' (as it is called) may be extended to 28 days. But in most countries it is accepted that the risks of blood transfusion are increased if the 21-day limit is exceeded.

This particular characteristic of '21-day perishability' presents great administrative and technical problems in the operation of transfusion services; in the estimation and prediction of demand from hospitals all over the country for blood of different groups; in the organization, forward planning and execution of blood donor programs; in the technical organization of compatibility tests and cross-matching; and in the distribution of supplies of whole blood in the right quantities and categories, at the right times, daily and even hourly, and to the right hospitals, operating theatres, wards and patients.

If the needs of patients at any hour of the day or night for anything from one to forty units of blood of a common or rare group are to be met without delay a high degree of statistical vision and administrative efficiency is demanded. These attributes are even more in demand if the wastage (by 'out-dating') of blood is to be kept to a minimum.

Two of the crucial tests to be applied to any blood transfusion system are thus the extent of delays or shortages and the amount of wastage in a specified period. We examine these criteria of medical

[1] Mathieson, D. R., 'Blood Transfusion: Services and Complications', *The Medical Clinics of North America*, Vol. 46, No. 4, 1962, p. 927.

and administrative efficiency in relation to the British and American systems in later chapters.

The efficiency or effectiveness of the system in handling '21-day perishability' ultimately depends, however, on the suppliers; on blood donors. The attributes required of donors if the needs of patients are to be properly met and if wastage is to be avoided are consistency, regularity, responsibility and honesty. Dramatic, emotional and episodic responses to appeals for blood are not the answer. No modern hospital and casualty service handling both 'normal' and 'abnormal' or emergency needs (e.g. as a result of multiple road accidents, plane disasters or sudden abortion demands) can be sustained in its blood requirements in a climate of crises demand and response. Again, these criteria of donor 'efficiency' are examined in later chapters.

All these human, technical and administrative problems allied to the characteristic of perishability, have led—particularly in the United States—to an intense research quest for alternatives and substitutes and for methods to prolong the life of blood by deep-freezing processes and other techniques. Much of this work has been further stimulated—again in the United States—by the knowledge of what one writer described as 'the enormous waste from outdating in the United States';[1] by the growing shortages of blood in that country; by the demands of the Vietnam War and, early in 1968, by the warnings issued by the National Research Council on the use of plasma preparations drawn from large numbers (or pools) of donors. As is explained in Chapter 8, the larger the pool the greater is the risk of infecting patients with hepatitis particularly if the blood is drawn from paid donors.

For over twenty years in Britain only 'small pool' plasma has been supplied by the National Blood Transfusion Service.[2] In the United States, however, large pools (often made up of blood from more than a hundred donors) are common in an estimated annual usage of over 300,000 units obtained, in the main, from commercial sources. Plasma obtained from large pools is commercially cheaper and, compared with whole blood, is easier to transport and can be stored indefinitely. The warnings issued by the National Research Council about the serious risks of hepatitis and the effects of any substantial fall in supplies on the general problems of blood short-ages and wastage constituted yet another stimulus to the research

[1] Huggins, C. E., 'Frozen Blood: Theory and Practice', *Proc. A.M.A. Conference on Blood and Blood Banking*, 1964.
[2] See Chapter 8.

22

quest for alternatives and substitutes. The American medical profession is (to quote from the National Research Council Statement) 'confronted with an impasse'.[1]

Extensive research programs, involving very large resources in dollars, laboratory equipment and research manpower, are being undertaken in the search for answers to these problems in the United States. Some of these programs are being undertaken in the hope that technology (in the shape of computers and automated inventory control systems) will reduce the 'enormous waste and expense' caused by the loss of blood through expiration;[2] some are looking to the development of plasmapheresis techniques by the pharmaceutical industry to increase the supply of blood from paid donors;[3] some are exploring the use of cadaver (or human corpse) blood;[4] some are studying the possibilities of extending the life of blood by a further week or two by the addition of certain substances (such as adenine), while others are concerned with improving techniques of freezing and storing blood at very low temperatures.

In blood transfusion systems where there are no shortages of voluntary blood donors and no significant problems of waste a great deal of this research and development is largely irrelevant. Even where the findings may be relevant (and much less disputable scientifically than they now are) it seems unlikely that their contribution will significantly reduce—or even stabilize—current needs for blood donors. Moreover, methods of prolonging the shelf-life of blood through low-temperature freezing and storage are very expensive and would greatly increase the cost per unit of blood, and there would still be a loss through processing of about 20 per cent of the red cells.[5]

Despite, therefore, all the scientific advances and technical accomplishments of the last twenty years and the gains that may be possible from further advances in the future it still remains true,

---

[1] Statement issued by the Committee on Plasma and Plasma Substitutes of the Division of Medical Sciences, National Research Council (published in *Transfusion*, Vol. 8, No. 2, March–April 1968). For further discussion see Chapter 8.

[2] See Chapter 4.

[3] See Chapters 4 and 8.

[4] As far as is known, developments in the use of human corpse blood have occurred only in the U.S. and the U.S.S.R. (see Kevorkian, J. and Marra, J. J., Transfusion of Human Corpse Blood Without Additives', *Transfusion*, Vol. 4, 1964, p. 112, Wood, C. S., *ibid.*, p. 302, and Yudin, S. S., *Sov. Med.*, 1938, *14*, 14).

[5] For a comprehensive review of the problems involved in the storage of blood and as a guide to the scientific literature see Hurn, B. A. L., *op. cit.*

throughout the world, that there is no substitute for the blood donor, and no alternative for the vast majority of patients to the use of fresh whole human blood. The prospect of 'biological eternity' for blood, even at −196°C, does not exist.

'All the research, official precautions, and new facilities would be of no avail without donors' said Dr T. J. Greenwalt, Medical Director of the American Red Cross, in May 1969.[1] In his view, donors are the key to the whole American situation. In that country, as in the rest of the world, the individual blood donor is as uniquely important as he ever was and, indeed, even more so than in the past because of the growing demand for blood. 'In fact, the collection of blood or more precisely the blood DONOR himself, is the fundamental question and remains the essential problem of transfusion through the world'.[2]

IV

The Selection of Blood Donors

For medical reasons, and in the interests of both donors and recipients, blood should not be drawn too frequently from donors. If a donor is bled too frequently, iron deficiency anaemia develops due to the loss of red-cell iron.[3] In Britain, the standard set and followed is two donations (or units) a year with five to six months elapsing between donations. In the United States, both the standards adopted and the actual practices appear to vary considerably.[4] In some of the community blood banks which are recognized to have strict standards (such as the New York Blood Bank and the King County Central Blood Bank of Seattle) the practice is 5 donations a year with appropriate intervals between donations.

Men and women between the ages of 18 and 65 are in most countries accepted as donors; these are the age limits set in Britain. In some countries the upper age limit is higher: in Switzerland, for example, it is 70. In others it is lower: for example, in France it is

[1] Reported in *Medical World News*, Vol. 10, No. 21, May 23, 1969, p. 33.

[2] Hantchef, Z. S., 'The Gift of Blood and some International Aspects of Blood Transfusion', *International Review of the Red Cross*, Geneva, October 1961, p. 3.

[3] Kliman, A. and Lesses, M. F., 'Plasmapheresis as a Form of Blood Donation', *Transfusion*, Vol. 4, 1964, p. 469.

[4] Standards for the medical selection, screening and care of donors have been set by the National Institutes of Health and the American Association of Blood Banks. See also 'General Principles of Blood Transfusion', *Transfusion*, Vol. 59, July–August 1963.

60. The usual donation at one time is around 400 ml.[1] In Britain, the usual donation is 420 ml. or about three-quarters of a pint. A healthy donor can spare 400–500 ml. of blood with no more ill effect than at the most a transient dizziness, and can make good this loss in about six weeks.

It is of the utmost importance, however, that all blood donors should be carefully screened on each occasion. The transfusion of blood can be a highly dangerous act. Quite apart from the problems of compatibility and cross-matching, and the need for the highest standards in the preparation of apparatus, and in the collection, storage, recording, labelling, transporting and transfusion of blood, there are serious risks of disease transmission and other hazards.

The health criteria set for donors to the National Blood Transfusion Service in Britain and the instructions for the medical examination and care of donors are printed at the end of Appendix 1. In addition to the importance of careful medical examination and supervision, what is also crucial is the truthfulness of the donor in answering questions about his present health and past medical history. This applies particularly in the case of serum hepatitis, malaria and syphilis which constitute the most serious risks in Britain and the United States of infecting patients with disease. The issue of donor truthfulness, and the conditions under which it may be encouraged or discouraged, is discussed in later chapters and especially in Chapter 8. Meanwhile, we append some notes on these diseases taken from an article by Dr J. Grant in *The Practitioner* in 1965 surveying the problem from the British standpoint.[2]

Homologous Serum Hepatitis

'The development of homologous serum hepatitis is a hazard which besets rather less than 1 per cent of recipients of whole blood or small-pool plasma. It is caused by the transmission of a virus from a carrier donor to a susceptible patient. The donor is probably not aware that he is a carrier, he gives no history of ever having had infective hepatitis himself (otherwise he would have been excluded from the donor panel) and no single test or battery of liver function tests has yet been devised which will reliably distinguish carriers of the virus from normal subjects.

[1] *World Health*, 'The Uses of Blood', World Health Organization, June 1968, p. 16.

[2] Director of the Regional Blood Transfusion Centre, Oxford (*The Practitioner*, Vol. 195, No. 1166, August 1965, pp. 184–5).

Recipients vary in their susceptibility. It has been found that a minute fraction of a millilitre of virus-laden blood was enough to cause hepatitis and it was for this reason that the production of large-pool plasma, made from the contributions of more than 300 donors, was abandoned in favour of limited pools derived from not more than ten donors.

Some patients suffer no upset from the transmitted virus, some may have only a transient liver dysfunction with or without jaundice and yet others may develop a rapidly fatal hepatic necrosis. The incubation period of infective hepatitis is about 20 to 40 days whereas that of homologous serum hepatitis is 40 to 160 days. Attempts have been made to find a means of killing the virus in the blood without damaging the plasma proteins, such as exposure to ultra-violet light, addition of chemicals or the storage of liquid plasma at room temperature for six months before use, but none of these methods has proved wholly satisfactory.

Malaria

People who have had malaria, particularly of the malignant tertian variety due to *P. falciparum*, or who have lived in a country where malaria is endemic, may harbour the parasites in their blood for many years. The parasites are carried in the red cells and they can survive blood-bank temperatures for at least two weeks. When such people offer their services as blood donors in countries where malarial infection is not endemic the red cells of the donations are discarded and only the plasma is used. In spite of these precautions malaria has occasionally been accidentally transmitted by transfusion even when the parasites were so few in number that only after a prolonged search of the donor's blood film was one found. If the clinician is alive to the possibility that a spiky pyrexia following transfusion may be due to malaria he can curtail the development of the infection by prompt treatment with antimalarial drugs.

Syphilis

In order to prevent the spread of syphilis by transfusion it is standard practice to test blood from every donation by one or other of the serological techniques generally acknowledged to be reliable, such as the Kahn, Wassermann or Meinicke tests. Although serological tests will pick up the one true positive in, say, 20,000 donations they are not a complete safeguard against infection by blood from a donor in the early stages of primary syphilis before the serological reactions become positive. Spirochaetes, however, cannot survive at the blood bank temperatures of 2° to 6°C for more than three or four days and since most of the blood used in hospitals has been stored for longer than this before use the risk is negligible. When ordering fresh blood for transfusion the clinician should bear in mind that one of his shields which prevents the transmission of infection is absent. In the rare event that blood containing spiro-chaetes has been given, the first sign in the recipient is likely to be a typical secondary stage rash developing about ten weeks after the transfusion.'

Considering only the transmission of disease from donor to patient, these are the chief hazards. The problem of hepatitis, in prevalence and severity, is in most countries of the world by far the most serious threat to the health and lives of those receiving blood and many of the products of blood.[1] It is discussed in a broader social and ethical context in Chapter 8 which also surveys the issues raised for blood transfusion services in the United States, Japan, Britain and other countries.

The objective in stressing the importance of the most rigorous standards in the selection of donors is that those who give blood should be normal and healthy people; the patient who uses a donor's blood has the right to expect the application of such standards. Few products of blood or whole blood itself can be considered to be entirely free of the risk of producing hepatitis. The subsequent condition of those who are recipients remains the ultimate test of whether the virus was present in the donation; in effect, therefore, the patient is the laboratory for testing the quality of 'the gift'.

v

The Uses of Blood and Blood Derivatives

The transfer of blood and blood derivatives from one human being to another represents one of the greatest therapeutic instruments in the hands of modern medicine. It has made possible the saving of life on a scale undreamt of several decades ago and for

---

[1] Readers who wish to pursue further these problems of disease transmission should refer to Professor Mollison's standard work *Blood Transfusion in Clinical Medicine* (4th edn, 1967); to Chapter XXII 'Infectious and Serum Hepatitis' in Dr J. R. Paul's *Clinical Epidemiology* (revised edn, 1966, University of Chicago Press), and to the articles in *The Practitioner* (August 1965). American readers may also wish to refer to the regulations of the Public Health Service, *Biological Products: Regulations*, Title 42, Part 73, U.S. Department of Health, Education, and Welfare, 1965-8.

conditions which would have been considered hopeless. As we shall see presently, the demand for blood increases yearly in every Western country as new uses are developed; as more radical surgical techniques are adopted which are associated with the loss of massive amounts of blood; with the increasingly widespread use of artificial heart-lung machines in open heart surgery (first developed in England in 1950), and for numerous other reasons both for the saving of life and the prevention of disease and disability.

The conditions which may necessitate a blood transfusion are many. Here we give only a broad idea of some of the more common uses today.

There are three main ways in which transfusion can save life:[1]

(a) *By supplying whole blood.* Blood loss, arising from haemorrhage caused by a wound, or in childbirth, results in a deficiency of both plasma and red cells. Replacement is achieved by the transfusion of whole blood.

(b) *By supplying red blood cells.* Anaemia may result from lack of red cells, for example, when the body produces red cells in insufficient numbers or when red cells are being rapidly destroyed. When blood is stored, the red corpuscles settle into the lower half of the bottle leaving the layer of plasma above. The plasma can then be removed and the concentrated red cells transfused. In this way the deficiency of red cells is repaired without giving plasma of which the anaemic patient has no need.

(c) *By supplying plasma.* Plasma alone may be lost when the small blood vessels or capillaries are damaged by crush injuries, by burning or by some types of intestinal disease. When plasma is lost the blood becomes thicker and the circulation slower, which means that the tissues are starved of the oxygen transported by the red blood cells. The transfusion of plasma dilutes the blood and, by restoring the volume of liquid, gets it flowing at the normal speed again.

Plasma is also of great value in cases of haemorrhage as an emergency transfusion fluid until supplies of blood of a suitable group can be obtained. The factors which determine the main blood groups are limited to the red corpuscles and are removed when preparing plasma: thus plasma, if suitably prepared, may be transfused to patients in any blood group. However, since plasma

[1] This statement is taken from *Blood Transfusion and the National Blood Transfusion Service*, H.M.S.O., 1968, pp. 10–11. See also *Notes on Transfusion*, H.M.S.O., 1963, and references to textbooks cited in this chapter.

is devoid of blood corpuscles, a patient suffering from a serious haemorrhage needs at least one pint of whole blood for about every pint of plasma given if the plasma transfusion itself is not to cause anaemia (it should be noted that the average person has about 12 to 13 pints of blood in his system).

Transfusions may be necessary in the following major groups of cases:

(i) Accidents, injuries, wound shock, burns and scalds (some serious accidents may require the transfusion of 20 pints or more of blood).

(ii) Gynaecological and obstetrical cases (for example, blood loss after childbirth—a few maternity patients may need 20 pints or more).

(iii) Operative surgery—particularly for cancer, abdominal surgery, cardiovascular surgery, chest surgery, neurosurgery, orthopaedic surgery, plastic surgery and so forth. During operative surgery the purpose of blood transfusion is to replace blood which is lost, and therefore the ideal transfusion medium is whole blood. In open-heart surgery, approximately 12 to 15 pints of fresh blood are needed to prime the heart-lung machine each time it is used. Including the blood required by the patient, as many as 60 donations may be needed for a single open-heart operation.[1] The first adult heart transplant patient in the United States required 288 units of blood.[2]

(iv) Anaemia, acute or chronic, including correction of the damage done to red cells by penicillin and other drugs,[3] coagulation disorders such as haemophilia, haemorrhages in ulcer and gastrointestinal cases, and many other medical conditions, exchange transfusions to save the life of the child when there is incompatibility of blood between mother and child,[4] and so forth. (It is estimated in the United States that complications due to the Rh factor will result from approximately 1 out of 15 marriages.)[5]

(v) The preparation of blood products; pooled plasma (prepared from the blood of a small number of donors to minimize the risk of disease transmission) and plasma fractions including fibrinogen, albumin, fibrin foam, thrombin and immunoglobulin (see Appendix 1). The latter, extracted from plasma, has proved of value in the

[1] Wolstenholme, G. E. W. and O'Connor, M., *op. cit.*, 1966, p. 34.
[2] Shively, J. A., *Medical World News*, Vol. 10, No. 21, May 23, 1969.
[3] *Brit. Med. J.*, 1966, **ii**, 658.   [4] See Appendix 1.
[5] American Association of Blood Banks, *Facts about Blood Banking*, Chicago, 1964, p. 7.

prevention and attenuation of measles, in the prevention of rubella, of poliomyelitis in certain defined circumstances, and possibly of infectious hepatitis.[1] Anti-D immunoglobulin, prepared from small donor pools, appears to be successful in preventing Rh-haemolytic disease.[2]

Few statistics are available which show the characteristics of blood users and the distribution of transfusions by categories of patients, blood groups or conditions. One reason for this lack of data is no doubt the fact that whole blood and blood derivatives are now used for such a great variety of medical and surgical treatments. It has, in fact, become in the short space of a few decades, an integral part of the work of the modern hospital. In later chapters concerned with the characteristics of those who give blood we return to the question of who receives blood.

This brief survey was intended to do no more than to indicate the remarkable 'elixir of life', human-saving properties of blood transfusions. As a substance, blood is a highly complex fluid; dramatically effective in many of its uses especially among the young and those suddenly struck down by accident or injury; a precious commodity yet in Britain without price; and if carelessly or wrongly used more lethal than many drugs. Yet it can be misused, wasted and prescribed as a placebo; these matters we shall consider later when we have to ask the questions: under what system of organized medical care is there less waste of human blood and less danger to recipients through the transmission of disease?

[1] *Annual Report of the Ministry of Health for 1957*, Part II, H.M.S.O., 1958, p. 99; *Monthly Bulletin of the Ministry of Health and the Public Health Laboratory Service*, 'Supply of human immunoglobulin in England and Wales for the prophylaxis of certain infectious disease', Vol. 26, September 1967; 'Report of Public Health Laboratory Service Working Party on Rubella', *Brit. Med. J.*, iii, 203, 1968; *W.H.O. Expert Committee on Hepatitis*, Second Report, W.H.O. Tech. Rep. Ser. No. 285, 1964, and 'Immune Serum Globulin for Prevention of Viral Hepatitis', Communicable Diseases Center, *Surveillance Report*, No. 29, Public Health Service, Washington, September 1968.

[2] See Chapter 3 and Appendix 1.

Chapter 3

The Demand for Blood in England and Wales and the United States

The demand for blood and blood derivatives is increasing all over the world. In high income countries, in particular, the rate of growth in demand has been rising so rapidly that shortages have begun to appear in a number of countries. In all Western countries, demand is growing much faster than rates of growth in populations aged 18–65 from whom donors are drawn. And despite a massive research effort in the United States to find alternatives it remains true that: 'In medicine there is no substitute for human blood.'[1]

In later chapters some evidence and illustrations are given of shortages of supply in the United States, Japan and other countries and of attempts that have been made on a commercial basis to import blood to meet rising demands. It is not possible, however, to estimate in any precise way national trends in demand for blood and blood derivatives. Statistical indicators are few and generally inadequate as they rarely take account of the unmet needs in a population for medical and surgical treatment (partly because of deficiencies in a country's medical services). Similarly, little is known on a national basis in many countries about the potential demand, if supplies were adequate, for blood and blood derivatives to be used for preventive and therapeutic purposes. Some examples are given later of shortages and unmet needs of these kinds among particular groups in national populations.

In the absence of estimates of demand, we have to turn to examine trends in recent years in the statistics relating to the collection and use of blood, and to such evidence as is available concerning hospital shortages, the postponement of surgical operations and other indices. Much of this evidence is included in Chapter 4. Meanwhile, however, to provide a general picture of the growth in demand we give certain overall figures for England and Wales, the United States and Sweden. They are taken from a variety of sources cited in Chapter 4.

Between 1948 (when the National Health Service was established)

[1] *World Health, op. cit.*, p. 16.

31

and 1967 the annual number of donations of blood rose by 269 per cent or from 9 per 1000 total population to 29 per 1000. During the same period the total population of the country rose by 12 per cent. Between 1956 (when the first attempt was made in the United States to survey the national supply position) and 1967 the respective increases in England and Wales were 77 per cent and 8 per cent. Whatever the real growth in demand has been since 1948 and 1956 these figures indicate that supply in England and Wales has been rising by about 6–7 per cent per year or at a much faster rate than the donor population aged 18–65 or the proportion of the population who experience annually a spell in hospital. Some part of this increase in supply has met the increase in the amount of blood actually demanded and used per 100 patients treated in hospitals; in 1958 the figure was 19·4 pints per 100 patients; in 1967 it was 24·4 pints—an increase of 26 per cent in eight years.[1]

Estimates have been made that 5,100,000 pints of blood were collected in the United States in 1956 and around 6,000,000 pints in 1966–7. These, as Chapters 4 and 6 demonstrate, are only very rough estimates. They exclude collections by the Armed Forces for their own needs in Vietnam and elsewhere and also collections by the pharmaceutical industry under plasmapheresis programs. They are further complicated by the problems of estimating blood waste through out-dating. However, if these totals are anyway near the truth, they suggest a rise in collections of 17 per cent in the eleven years (1956–67). During the same period the total population of the country increased by about the same percentage, namely 16 per cent. For reasons explained later, however, these estimates of collections are much less valid as indicators of demand than the statistics of donations for England and Wales.

Sweden is one other country which has a certain amount of data covering the last twenty years and which also shows a great increase in demand. Between 1949 and 1968 the yearly consumption of blood increased by 438 per cent while the total population of the country rose by only 13 per cent.[2] The increase of 438 per cent probably overstates the rise in actual demand because the blood transfusion services in Sweden were less well established in 1949 than they were in the same year in England and Wales. Nevertheless, the figures for Sweden of collections and use do provide further

[1] N.H.S. Note No. 13, Hospital and Specialist Services, Department of Health and Social Security, December 1968.
[2] Gullbring, B., 'Motiv för Blodgivning', *Läkartidningen*, Vol. 66, No. 4, 1969, pp. 359–63.

evidence on a national scale of the great increase in recent years in the demand for blood and blood derivatives.

There are many factors responsible for this world trend. Some of them relate to the major life-saving role of blood. Others are adding yearly to the relatively new role for human blood of acting as a vital preventive and therapeutic agent. In both these roles there are growth factors at work which suggest that there may be no predictable limits to future requirements for blood in high income countries. In the poorer countries of the world the potential demands are as great or greater; demands which at present are contained and limited by the gross deficiences in medical services both curative and preventive.

Surgery in its many branches has, for example, been given a new lease of life—and a life without foreseeable end—during the past twenty-five years by increases in the volume of blood available and the advent of effective blood transfusion services. The number of specific operations which today call for massive transfusions of blood is rising rapidly as a result of advances in knowledge and medical technologies.

Open-heart surgery, to cite one illustration of developments in major surgical procedures, and one in which the heart is temporarily by-passed with the blood being pumped through a heart-lung machine, is possible only because of the availability of donated blood. As many as 60 donations may be needed for a single open-heart operation.[1] A study of 200 patients who underwent open-heart operations at the National Heart Institute in the United States during 1962–3 showed that they required a total of 4093 pints of blood.[2]

The number of these operations has been rising rapidly. One report from California recording special collections of blood for open-heart surgery provides some indication of the growth in demand; the total number of pints used rose from 48 in 1957 to 13,016 in 1961.[3] A later study (1963–4) of hospitals in Massachusetts showed that of all the blood used $12\frac{1}{2}$ per cent was attributed to open-heart surgery.[4] Another American report warned that the

[1] Wolstenholme, G. E. W., *op. cit.*, p. 34.

[2] Rubinson, R. M. *et al.*, *J. of Thoracic and Cardiovascular Surg.*, Vol. 50, No. 4, October 1965, p. 575.

[3] Adashek, E. P. and W. H., *Arch. of Surg.*, Vol. 87, No. 5, November 1963, p. 793.

[4] Lund, C. C., 'Medical Sponsorship and Supervision: The Massachusetts Regional Blood Program of the American Red Cross' (*Proc. of the Conference on Blood and Blood Banking*, A.M.A., 1966).

'large amounts of blood required for open-heart surgery are placing a strain upon the procurement facilities of even the largest blood banks'.[1]

The number of open-heart operations has greatly increased in Britain in recent years under the National Health Service. At one London Hospital alone, over a hundred of these operations were carried out in 1965 whereas a decade earlier there had been none.[2] As more and more patients with heart defects and heart diseases can have the possibility of surgical relief offered to them, the need for blood continues to increase steeply.

Cardiovascular surgery is by no means the only major surgical procedure now calling for massive amounts of fresh blood. The use of the 'artificial kidney' requires a substantial number of pints. There are said to be some 23,000 potential candidates up to age 54 in Britain who might be treated on intermittent dialysis if the necessary resources were available.[3] In the United States, it is estimated that there exist about 10,000 potential recipients of renal transplants per year.[4] Developments in organ transplants in the next ten years could, indeed, create immense additional demands for blood. Already there are over 30 'spare parts'—in addition to hearts, lung, kidneys and cornea—which can be added or exchanged. In one American heart transplant case over 300 pints of blood were needed. The National Heart Hospital in the United States reporting, in 1966, on its 'artificial heart feasibility study' concluded that 'if artificial hearts become therapeutic' an additional 600,000 pints of blood would be needed[5]—a demand which, in the present state of blood donor programs in that country, could not be met.

Already at the local level in a number of countries, transplant operations are creating critical shortages of blood with serious

[1] Perkins, H. A. *et al.*, 'Low Molecular Weight Dextran in Open Heart Surgery', *Transfusion*, Vol. 4, No. 1, January–February 1964, p. 10.

[2] Until 1953 no means had been devised of keeping the patient alive long enough for the operation to be undertaken. The development of the heart-lung machine made it possible to operate on almost all cases of ventricular septal defect (popularly known as 'hole-in-the-heart'). It has been estimated that two babies are born every day in England and Wales with this defect. After operation, they can live active, normal lives. (*Blood Donors and Open-Heart Surgery*, Ministry of Health, H.M.S.O., 1966.)

[3] Kerr, D. N. S., 'Regular Haemodialysis', *The Cost of Life*, Symposium No. 9, *Proc. Royal Society of Medicine*, Vol. 60, No. 11, Pt 2, November 1967, p. 1199.

[4] Murray, J. E., 'Organ Transplantation: The Practical Possibilities', *Ethics in Medical Progress*, op. cit., p. 61.

[5] *Washington Report on the Medical Sciences*, No. 986, May 23, 1966.

effects on the condition of patients in need of less dramatic and more 'ordinary' surgical procedures. Transplant operations can thus mean 'surgical rationing' quite apart from their other disruptive effects on the work of a hospital.

Major cancer surgery, which also relies heavily on blood transfusions, is another demand category of greatly increasing importance. Advances in surgical techniques, the growing dominance of lung cancer and other malignant diseases in acute hospital work, and the rise in the proportion of the population aged over 55 in Britain and the United States all combine to inflate the demand for blood and blood products. For the United States it can be estimated that in 1966-7 about one-fifth to one-sixth of all the blood collected was used by under 10 per cent of the total population—those aged 65 and over who were Medicare inpatients.[1] Of all these patients discharged from short-stay hospitals, one in three required some surgical procedure.[2]

All these developments in surgical procedures and techniques represent a formidable challenge to blood donor programs—quite apart from their implications in terms of costs, resources, medical priorities and other aspects. But these are only the more dramatic growth-in-demand factors. Another, and numerically more important category, is the increasing recourse in modern medicine to surgery in all its forms, and for a larger proportion of the population. The more general surgical procedures, often involving the use of substantial quantities of blood, include such common operations as gastrectomy, mastectomy, hysterectomy, Caesarean section and other obstetrical and gynaecological procedures. Moreover, for many of these commoner operations, older people, children and 'poor-risk' patients of all ages are today accepted for surgical treatment and for an expanding variety of conditions. Quantitatively, general surgical and maternity patients account for a far greater proportion of blood use than the more publicized and dramatic operations.

The United States Public Health Service reported in 1966 that the total annual count of operations had risen by nearly $3\frac{1}{2}$ million to approximately 13·6 million in the six years ending June 1964

---

[1] *Health Insurance Statistics*, HI-2, November 30, 1967, and data supplied to the author by the Division of Policy and Standards, Bureau of Health Insurance, Social Security Administration, Baltimore, October 1968.

[2] Hellman, I. L., 'Medicare Discharged Patients July–December 1966', *Social Security Bulletin*, U.S. Dept. of Health, Education and Welfare, Vol. 32, No. 5, May 1969, p. 16.

or by 6 per cent a year.[1] This rate of growth probably exceeded that for medical consultations in general and admissions to all acute hospitals in the United States. In England and Wales, the number of surgical operations carried out on in-patients in all hospitals rose by 26 per cent to 1,817,365 between 1961 and 1966 or by just over 5 per cent a year. During the same five-year period the total population rose by 4 per cent.[2]

Some of the important factors which lead to the increasing use of surgical procedures and blood transfusion services are social and economic. Changes in population structures and particularly the rising proportion of the population surviving into the 60s and 70s represent one major factor. Both in the United States and Britain, surgical operation rates are substantially higher for people aged over 65. Other population groups with significantly above average rates are male children and women aged 15–64. High birth rates (past and present) and rising demands for abortions (notably in Britain since 1968) are contributory elements.

Allied to these factors are the greater availability of modern surgery to the poorer sections of the population—particularly in Britain—and, proportionately most significant of all, more and more road accidents, industrial accidents, burns and scalds (domestic and industrial) and 'accidents' in general ranging causally from race riots to ski-ing and other sporting activities. The massive increase over the past twenty years in road casualties does, however, dominate the statistical scene of violence. In Britain in 1965 there were nearly 400,000 road casualties, one-quarter of them classified as 'serious' and demanding prolonged hospital care.[3] Over 100,000 patients with head injuries are now being admitted annually to hospitals in England and Wales most of them caused by road traffic

[1] Public Health Service, National Center for Health Statistics, Series 10, No. 31, September 1966, and Series B–7, December 1958. See also Metropolitan Life Assurance Co., *Statistical Bulletin*, Vol. 47, July 1966.

[2] More precisely the statistics relate to numbers of in-patient discharges and deaths with surgical operations. They exclude operations performed in maternity units (*Report on Hospital In-patient Enquiry 1961* and *1966*, Part 1, Tables, Ministry of Health and General Register Office, H.M.S.O., 1963 and 1968). A substantial amount of surgery is also performed on an out-patient basis. Between 1961 and 1966 the total number of attendances at all surgical, accident and emergency departments increased from 27,258,000 to 29,102,000 or by 7 per cent (*Annual Report of the Ministry of Health 1961* and *1966*, Cmnd. 1754 and Cmnd. 3326, H.M.S.O., 1962 and 1967).

[3] Dawson, R. F. F., *Cost of Road Accidents in Great Britain*, Road Research Laboratory, Ministry of Transport, Report LR79, Road Research Laboratory, 1967.

accidents.[1] This represented an increase of more than 50 per cent on the number in 1955.[2] The Vietnam war involved, in 1968, the shipping of over 300,000 units of blood (about 6 per cent of total American blood use) from the United States and other countries.[3] In short, a more violent and accident-prone world makes proportionately greater demands for human blood.

In a quite different category is the growth in demand for surgery to be carried out in Britain from the richer sections of the populations of the developing countries. In recent years there has been an increase in foreign patients admitted to hospitals (and private institutions) in the London hospital regions, many of them from the Middle and Far East where the proportion of blood group B is much greater than in Britain. To meet this demand, especially as the operations concerned are usually those requiring large quantities of blood, can, it is said, 'cause an inbalance in the collecting routine of a transfusion centre and may even call for selective recruitment' of blood donors.[4] The rise in demand for abortions by women from abroad is another factor.

Surgery in its life-saving role is not the only branch of medicine which is increasing its demands on blood donors. A broad analysis of the use of blood in 1964, reported by the Ministry of Health, showed what happened to 5000 donations:[5]

Accident cases	522
Gynaecological and obstetrical cases	984
Medical patients	1611
Surgical patients	1883
	5000

The distribution of demand has probably changed since 1964 and it will, for a variety of reasons, differ in different parts of the country, for different blood groups and at different times in the year. Unfortunately, no comprehensive studies have been made of the uses of blood and blood products by categories of conditions or the characteristics of patients.

In addition to the use of blood for surgical, accident and maternity

[1] Lewin, W., 'Severe Head Injuries', *The Cost of Life, op. cit.*, p. 1208.

[2] *Brit. Med. J.*, **i**, 637, June 15, 1968.

[3] Shively, J. A., *Medical World News*, Vol. 10, No. 21, May 23, 1969, p. 28.

[4] James, J. D., 'Donors and the Collection of Blood', *The Practitioner*, Vol. 195, No. 1166, August 1965, p. 153.

[5] *Blood Transfusion and the National Blood Transfusion Service, op. cit.*, p. 9.

cases, there is also a greatly expanding medical area of use for whole blood, blood fractions and products. As indicated in Chapter 2 and Appendix 1, new methods of blood fractionation have resulted in recent years in the appearance of a multiplicity of blood products for transfusion.[1] While some of these have only a limited use— in comparison with the immense demands for whole blood for transfusions—their employment, in appropriate cases, may be life-saving. In individual cases, the demand for blood donations can be very great. 'One of my haemophilic patients had, for one bleeding episode, blood products from 750 donors and £1500 worth of anti-haemophilic factor obtained commercially from animal sources. Instead of being dead he is very actively working and living an almost normal life'.[2] Estimates have been made in the United States that if all the needs of haemophilic patients in that country were fully met they would require about one-sixth of all the blood collected annually—or about 1,000,000 pints.[3]

The use of blood products for other conditions is of growing importance as an instrument of prevention. Their increasing employment is raising formidable problems of blood donor supply throughout the world. This is particularly true—to take one example —of immunoglobulin, a plasma fraction, usually given by intramuscular injection and not by transfusion. This product is being widely used in Britain and other countries to prevent and attenuate measles in children, rubella and, in certain circumstances, poliomyelitis, tetanus, smallpox and other diseases.[4] In clinical trials reported from Liverpool and Baltimore in 1966–7, a specific immunoglobulin containing antigen against the Rhesus Factor has been successfully used as a method of preventing RH immunization of RH-negative mothers by their RH-positive babies.[5] British immunoglobulin also has been shown to be effective in preventing infectious hepatitis in schools and other institutions and among persons travelling to and working in low-income countries.[6] These

[1] See also Salsbury, A. J., 'Transfusion of Blood Products', *The Practitioner op. cit.*, p. 193.

[2] Girdwood, R. H., *Medical World*, Vol. 105, No. 11, November 1967, p. 23.

[3] See Chapter 12.   [4] See Chapter 2 and Appendix 1.

[5] Woodrow, J. C. and Donohoe, W. T. A., 'Rh-immunization by Pregnancy', *Brit. Med. J.*, ii, 139, October 19, 1968, and Masouredis, S. P., 'Report on the Clinical Use of Human Anti-D IgG in the Prevention of Haemolytic Disease of the Newborn', *World Health Organization* (stencilled) IMM/Inf/RH/66, 2, 1967.

[6] Report to the Director of the Public Health Laboratory Service, 'Assessment of British Gamma-globulin in Preventing Infectious Hepatitis', *Brit. Med. J.*, ii, 451, August 24, 1968, and Pollock, T. M. and Reid, D., *Lancet*, i, 281, February 8, 1969.

developments in preventive medicine, like many others, mean more demand for blood and more specially selected blood donors.

The use of immunoglobulin has, moreover, been advocated in the United States to prevent or modify serum hepatitis resulting from blood transfusions, especially for patients over the age of 40 where the mortality rate in that country among those developing hepatitis has been estimated to be as high as 23 per cent.[1] An editorial in the *Journal of the American Medical Association* concluded in 1962: '... the routine administration of gamma-globulin after blood transfusion should be given serious consideration'.[2]

If this advice were followed in the United States—which is confronted with a serious problem of serum hepatitis—for all blood recipients over the age of 40, it would mean that for every bottle of blood transfused, an additional $1\frac{1}{2}$ bottles would have to be collected to protect the recipient against the risks in the first bottle.[3] Translated into practical terms, such a preventive program would involve (a) at least a doubling of blood collections in the United States from around 6,000,000 to 12,000,000 pints[4] and (b) a substantial rise in the costs of medical care because immuno-globulin is a highly expensive product.

As yet, however, the evidence for its routine administration to recipients of blood transfusions is not conclusive.[5] Nevertheless, the expanding use of immunoglobulin and other products (such as albumin) for a variety of preventive purposes has had to be drastic-ally curtailed in a number of countries because of a world shortage—a situation which appeared to be worsening in 1969 in relation to the growth of demand.

Shortages in the United States have led to the commercial develop-ment of plasmapheresis programs and the marketing of plasma products, nationally and internationally, by the pharmaceutical industry.[6] Plasmapheresis, as a new method of drawing several

[1] Allen, J. G. and Sayman, W. A., *J.A.M.A.*, 180, 1079, 1962 and Mirick, G. S. *et al.*, *New Eng. J. Med.*, Vol. 273, No. 2, July 8, 1965. See also Chapter 8 which discusses in more detail the problems of serum hepatitis.

[2] Technically now known as immunoglobulin (*J.A.M.A.*, 185, 1037, 1963).

[3] Gibson, S. T., American National Red Cross, *J.A.M.A.*, 186, 272, 1963.

[4] The production of immunoglobulin in the United States increased by less than 10 per cent between 1963 and 1965 (personal communication, Dr H. Bruce Dull, National Communicable Disease Center, Public Health Service, Atlanta, U.S.A., January 16, 1967).

[5] Recommendation of the U.S. Public Health Service Advisory Committee on Immunization Practices (*Morbidity and Mortality Weekly Reports*, Vol. 17, No. 31, August 3, 1968, Washington, U.S.A.).

[6] See references in Chapters 4 and 8.

pints of blood a week from a donor, is described in Chapter 4 where some reference is also made to the problems involved in the import and export of blood and blood products.

In surveying briefly the many factors of demand for blood and blood products, scientific, technical, social and economic, it is clear that the need for blood donations will continue to mount at a rapid rate. In the foreseeable future, there appears to be no predictable limit to demand in countries like the United States and Britain, more especially if account is taken of unmet needs for surgical and medical treatment and the great potentialities of demand in many areas of preventive medicine.

Given the restrictions imposed, first, by the 21-day perishability of blood and, second, by the fact that donors should not give blood more than 2 to 5 times a year, at least two conclusions follow. One is that the most effective and efficient use should be made of existing supplies. The other is the need for more donors; in other words, for programs to increase the proportion of the adult population who donate blood.

We turn now to consider some of the facts about supply.

Chapter 4

The Supply of Blood in England and Wales and the United States

Virtually no comparable data relating to aggregate demand and supply are available on an international scale.[1] Blood transfusion statistics, even for high income countries, are deficient in most respects. Only a limited series of national statistics have been published for England and Wales. In the United States, despite the volume of documentation on individual blood banking programs, it is hard to establish—let alone reconcile—even national figures for donations, transfusions and usage in general.

What follows, therefore, is only a rough attempt to compare certain data for England and Wales[2] and the United States. Some of the administrative and institutional problems in organizing the supply of blood are, for England and Wales, described in Appendix 3. Because, in the United States, the problems of organization are so inextricably bound up with the difficulties of establishing any statistics on supply they are considered in this chapter. Questions relating to the financial costs of different blood collecting and distributing agencies and the problems of wasted blood are in general dealt with in later chapters. Separate chapters are also devoted to an analysis of the characteristics of blood donors. To avoid confusion, the term 'donor' is generally used throughout the study despite its inappropriateness in the case of those who are paid to supply blood.

I. ENGLAND AND WALES

In Table 1 we set out the main national statistics for the years 1946–68.

[1] Demonstrated, for example, by the inadequacies of the data and the lack of comparability shown in the results of international surveys by the League of Red Cross Societies (see *Enquiry and Questionnaire on Blood Transfusion*, Geneva, 1961, and *International Seminar on Blood Transfusion*, Medico-Social Documentation, No. 27, Geneva, 1966).

[2] The data for Scotland are similar. Rather than combine them (which would have added to the labours of this study) it was decided to use only the data for England and Wales.

41

Between the introduction of the National Health Service in 1948 and 1968 the following increases took place:

	%
Number of effective civilian blood donors	243
Number of blood donations	277
Number of bottles of blood issued	243

Increases of this magnitude cannot be attributed to population changes, to increases in the provision of beds and the number of patients treated under the National Health Service, nor to the choice of the base-line year. Whereas in some countries at the end of the 1940s blood transfusion services were in an early stage of development in England and Wales they had been expanded earlier. The effects of the Second World War, and particularly the large quantities of blood required to deal adequately with the expected and actual civilian air raid casualties, greatly stimulated the growth of a blood transfusion service on a national scale.[1]

TABLE 1

National Blood Transfusion Service: England and Wales.
Blood Donors, Donations and Issues, 1946-68[2]

1 Year	2 No. of effective civilian blood donors (at December 31)	3 No. of blood donations	4 Bottles of blood issued[3]	5 Bottles of blood issued per hospital bed[4]	6 Bottles of blood and dried plasma issued per 100 patients discharged or dying	7 No. of blood donations per 100 of 50 per cent of the population[5]
1946	267,057[6]	*	237,903	*	*	—
7	353,670	294,556	299,699	*	*	1·4
8	373,778	384,010	371,259	*	*	1·8
9	369,167	456,973	416,181	2·08	14·14	2·1

[1] See Chapter 11 (The Civilian Blood Transfusion Service) in *The Emergency Medical Services*, Dunn, C. L., History of the Second World War UK Medical Series, Vol. 1, H.M.S.O., 1952, p. 334.

[2] Source: Ministry of Health *Annual Reports*.

[3] Including Rh-negative blood and packed red cells and bottles of dried plasma. Each bottle of whole blood contains about ¾ of a pint and is the gift of one donor.

TABLE 1 *contd.*

1950	428,394	523,387	486,323	2·40	16·08	2·4
1	465,137	593,818	535,939	2·68	16·65	2·7
2	487,660	647,009	587,603	2·93	17·17	2·9
3	515,632	659,674	610,528	3·32	17·21	3·0
4	540,389	700,202	645,251	3·39	17·70	3·2
5	591,204	759,571	697,352	3·36	19·18	3·4
6	639,319	803,522	739,911	3·56	19·80	3·6
7	674,117	846,202	780,152	3·77	20·58	3·8
8	715,911	895,575	828,507	3·98	21·25	4·0
9	784,311	957,780	888,156	4·28	22·19	4·2
1960	853,763	1,024,141	964,246	4·67	22·29	4·5
1	927,362	1,077,659	1,019,206	4·91	23·87	4·7
2	975,175	1,119,353	1,057,914	5·11	24·08	4·8
3	1,027,737	1,165,530	1,097,534	5·34	23·93	5·0
4	1,059,059	1,240,602	1,163,801	5·67	24·63	5·2
5	1,090,809	1,299,541	1,209,890	5·92	25·11	5·4
6	1,178,111	1,374,884	1,187,789	6·15	25·75	5·7
7	1,243,957	1,418,549	1,224,791	6·67	25·95	5·9
8	1,280,901	1,446,551	1,273,829	6·58	26·25	6·0

*Not available.

⁴ For the years 1950–3 based upon total staffed beds in England and Wales omitting staffed beds classified as chronic sick, tuberculosis, fever, mental, and mental deficiency. For subsequent years based upon total staffed beds in England and Wales but somewhat different classifications were used at different periods; beds omitted were:

1954, long-stay, chronic, pre-convalescent, convalescent, rehabilitation, infectious diseases, mental, mental deficiency, tuberculosis and chest, tuberculosis chest and isolation, eyes and others.

1955, infectious diseases, chronic sick, mental deficiency and mental illness, pre-convalescent, convalescent.

1959–62, infectious diseases, geriatric, chronic sick, subnormality and severe subnormality, mental illness, pre-convalescent and convalescent.

1963–8, infectious diseases, chronic sick, geriatric, psychiatric, pre-convalescent and convalescent.

⁵ The proportion of the population who may be considered to be potential blood donors has been variously estimated at 29 to 50 per cent. Age, medical criteria, social criteria and blood group are some of the factors to be taken into account. Estimated national populations (June 30 each year) are taken from *Annual Abstract of Statistics.* For 1946–50 the estimates include all British Forces stationed overseas. For subsequent years they are estimates of the *de facto* home population.

⁶ This figure includes the Armed Forces; for all other years they are excluded.

43

As regards population changes we have used, simply for purposes of illustration, the estimate made by a number of authorities on the subject that, very roughly, 50 per cent of the population are medically eligible to donate blood. The main excluded groups are the young and the old, expectant and nursing mothers, the sick and other medically ineligible groups. On this basis the number of blood donations per 100 potential donors rose steadily from 1·8 in 1948 to 6·0 in 1968. This probably understates the rise because the combined proportion of the young and the old in the total population was higher at the end of the period than at the beginning.

On the demand side we may note from Table 1 that between 1949 and 1968 the number of bottles of blood issued per hospital bed rose by 216 per cent reflecting the increased use of whole blood for surgical and therapeutic purposes. If, instead of beds, we relate the use of blood to patients treated, we see that between 1949 and 1968 there was an increase of 86 per cent in the number of bottles of blood and dried plasma issued per 100 patients discharged or dying. What we cannot do because the statistics are not available is to relate the use of blood to those categories of hospital patients who actually need blood for surgical and therapeutic purposes. Had this been possible it is likely, for reasons given in Chapter 3, that the percentage increase would have been higher.

What is particularly striking about this table is the orderly, progressive and sustained rate of growth in the number of blood donors, blood donations and supplies to hospitals. It suggests that, in general, the Service has been responsive to changes and developments in medicine and surgery over the last twenty years. The application of new knowledge, invariably leading to the development of new techniques and procedures, rarely in the field of medicine makes its total impact in a relatively short period of time. In actual fact, the effects—when they can be measured—tend to take the form of a succession of waves spreading out over a long period of time from the centres of innovation and applied development. This, at any rate, is one interpretation of these statistics considered against the background of the remarkable advances made since the end of the Second World War in the use of human blood for surgical and therapeutic purposes.

This interpretation would need to be modified or even abandoned had there been any evidence since 1948 of serious shortages in supply. But, apart from the special case of immunoglobulin discussed in Chapter 3 (and even here the primary limiting factors affecting utilization in England and Wales have not included the supply of non-infected blood) there have not been any significant or prolonged shortages of whole blood for transfusion purposes.[1] Had there been such shortages one obvious answer would have been to have bled donors more frequently than twice a year. The Service preferred, however, to call upon larger panels of donors than to increase the standard of two a year. This is probably the lowest and most rigorous standard in the world from the viewpoint of the safety of both donors and recipients. In the United States, the standard is generally five a year; a minimum figure sometimes exceeded by some paid donors and some commercial blood-banking agencies.

To examine further these questions of adequacy of supply and the responsiveness of the Service to medical demands a special analysis was made of the regional monthly returns reported by each Regional Transfusion Centre to the headquarters of the National Blood Transfusion Service. The years selected were 1951, 1956, 1961 and 1965, and the results are set down in Appendix 3.

The main conclusions are broadly summarized below:

1. *Size of effective civilian donor panels* 1951–65

All the 14 regions increased the size of their panels. Most of them more than doubled or nearly doubled in size. The general trend was highly consistent and showed that all parts of the country contributed to meeting the rise in demand.

---

[1] Short-term local shortages at particular hospitals (and small nursing homes) and in particular areas have occurred from time to time, generally caused by sudden emergencies, local catastrophies (e.g. aeroplane and train crashes in rural areas, flooding, prolonged snowstorms, etc.). Multiple road accidents in remote areas during holiday periods (when fewer registered blood donors are at home) and other unpredictable calls may also result in temporary local shortages. In what is called a postal 'survey of consultants' opinions on supply' in 1967, conducted by two economists and published by the Institute of Economic Affairs, some allegations of shortages were reported. The authors have themselves referred to this enquiry as being 'subjective and impressionistic', and it is impossible to calculate sampling errors for their questionnaire since: (1) no attempt is made to define 'adequate', 'postponed' and 'delay', (2) the problems of sampling and defining consultant surgeons and consultant physicians are not discussed, (3) the response to the 'sample' of 640 was only 25 per cent (158 surgeons replied but although percentages are given for physicians we are not told how many there were in the 'sample' of 640, in the questionnaire group of 319, nor how many actually responded), (4) no explanation is given as to why only 319 questionnaires were sent out and how these were selected, (5) no information is given concerning the numbers or method of classification of surgeons in general hospitals, teaching hospitals and in private hospitals (Cooper, M. H. and Culyer, A. J., *The Price of Blood*, Hobart Paper 41, The Institute of Economic Affairs, 1968).

2. Number and proportion of donors newly enrolled and first donations from new donors 1951–65

Nationally, the number of donors newly enrolled per 1000 of the population and the percentage of new donors giving their first contribution virtually doubled during the fourteen years. Again, all regions contributed, the differences between them in respect of both categories being somewhat less in 1965 than in 1951. In other words, in all parts of the country a substantially higher proportion of the eligible population were contributing to the Service in 1965 than in 1951.

3. Proportion of General Public donors called who reported 1951–65

With the exception of two regions (Manchester and Liverpool) all regions with records for 1951 showed increases during the 14 years. In general, the chief impression given by these statistics is the high degree of consistency in reporting rates over the period. For the country as a whole, the percentage reporting rose with some fluctuations, from 45 per cent in 1948 to 52 per cent in 1968.

These findings do not support a widely held belief in the United States that a more affluent society is less willing to donate blood voluntarily for strangers. On the contrary they suggest, for England and Wales, that a society with higher living standards, more geographical mobility, fewer local ties and higher rates of employment among married women is more rather than less likely to give blood for the community.

4. The contribution of General Public donors and Institutional donors 1951–65

Despite substantial regional differences in the calls made on institutional donors (factories, offices, etc.) there was little change nationally over the 14 years in the proportionate contribution (about two-thirds from the general public).

These statistics, national and regional, interesting as they are about numbers of donors and donor responses, tell us nothing about the characteristics of donors by sex, age, marital status, income group and so forth. Hence it was decided to undertake a sample survey of some 3800 donors. Because of the wealth of material obtained the results are analysed and discussed in a separate chapter.

We now turn to consider some of the problems of supply in the United States.

II UNITED STATES

Unfortunately, it is not possible to present any series of statistics similar to those provided for England and Wales. For reasons which will become apparent later it is not even possible to estimate with any degree of precision the total annual volume of blood collections, transfusions and wastage (we discuss later the problems of outdated and wasted blood).

We have to rely, therefore, on (a) a number of incomplete attempts in recent years to survey the national position (b) some statistics for certain areas and cities—particularly New York and other cities—(c) statements by medical experts and administrators in the blood banking field and (d) data elicited by correspondence with blood banks, pharmaceutical firms and other organizations.

More information will be given in later chapters about various aspects of blood transfusion facilities and services in the United States.[1] We must, however, preface this review with some descriptive data which may help to explain the statistical inadequacies, confusion in terms, definitions and estimates, and the general lack of reliable facts relating to supply, demand and use.

In size and physical resources, the United States is an immense country with a great variety of social institutions, practices and customs; a fundamental reality of size and pluralism which must constantly be borne in mind in any attempt to generalize and draw comparisons with countries of the size and homogeneity of England and Wales.

A second major fact is that, unlike England and Wales and other countries, the United States has no national or even state blood program, and no single responsible authority at federal or state level. While there is legal provision for the formation of a policy in times of 'national emergency', through the co-ordination of the activities of all civilian blood banking facilities with those of the Department of Defense and the Federal Civil Defense Administration, under the direction of the Office of Defense Mobilization, this provision is normally inoperative.[2] In 1967 the Public Health

---

[1] For an historical account up to 1955 of the American blood banking systems see Brown, D. E., Appendix, *Hearings Before the Subcommittee on Antitrust and Monopoly of the Committee on the Judiciary*, United States Senate, 90th Congress, S.1945, U.S. Government Printing Office, Washington, August 1, 1967, pp. 106–13.

[2] United States, Executive Office of the President, Office of Defense Mobilization, *National Blood Program: Statement of Basic Principles* (see *Bulletin of the American Association of Blood Banks*, 10 (ii): 427, November 1957).

Service established, under its National Heart Institute, a National Blood Resource Program. This Government agency is not a blood banking program; it has no responsibility for collecting, processing or distributing blood but is 'a research and development program aimed at effecting economies and increasing the productivity of the national blood resource'.[1]

The principal reasons for the creation of this program were:

1. The lack of accurate, up-to-date records of the units of blood and blood products present in local blood banks, and the absence of any data on the blood supply of areas or regions. In these circumstances (which obtain all over the United States) and a general failure of co-ordination between hospitals and supplying blood banks, there are surpluses in some banks and areas, shortages in others and blood expiring in one hospital while operations are postponed in another.

2. The total national loss of donated blood through outdating, wasteful cross-matching practices, over-ordering of blood by physicians which is not used, maldistribution in the supply of both common and rare bloods, and other factors. It was estimated by the National Blood Resource Program in 1968 that over a million units of blood are lost annually in the United States through outdating. This loss, representing about 17 to 20 per cent of all blood collected, was further said to involve 'a multi-million-dollar annual loss'.[2]

3. In the absence of reliable and comprehensive data on blood supplies, and a virtual lack of donor panels or registration systems (and thus no systematic collected information about donors and their characteristics) it was not possible to estimate the immediate or long-term demand for and supply of blood and blood components either locally, regionally or nationally.

4. The belief that critical shortages of blood were increasing, particularly at weekends, during the summer months and over the Christmas period, caused partly by the foregoing factors and also by a failure of recruitment and replacement campaigns to obtain sufficient donors to meet demands.

5. The rising and heavy demands for blood and blood products in Vietnam. In 1968 war demands were running at an annual rate of

[1] Personal communication, Dr J. M. Stengle, Chief, National Blood Resource Program, March 28, 1967.

[2] This quotation and most of the information in these paragraphs is taken from *Studies Relating to the Feasibility of Development and Utilization of an Automated Donor Blood Inventory and Donor-Recipient Information System*, RFP. NHI–68–15, National Blood Resource Program, March 8, 1968.

over 300,000 units; before August 1966 blood had been obtained at donating centres in Japan, the Philippines and other foreign countries.[1]

For these reasons the Program was established to foster research and development aiming (a) 'to improve the efficiency of utilization by decreasing or eliminating the waste and expense caused by the loss of blood through expiration; (b) to decrease or eliminate the hardships imposed by shortages of blood and blood products; (c) to gather adequate data on the collection, processing and distribution of blood and blood products in the United States; and (d) to promote co-ordination and co-operation between facilities which handle blood'.[2]

With these long-term aims in mind, the major interest of the program is financially to support research studies which will explore the advantages, disadvantages and general applicability of an automated inventory and information system for the management of whole blood and blood products.

There is some hope, therefore, that in five to ten years' time there may be an improvement in the statistical information relating to the supply, use and demand for blood and blood products. But this is unlikely to take place for many years because of the numerous agencies involved and the financial and other interests opposed to changes in the present situation.

Currently, therefore, it is difficult to assemble information about the total activities of all blood banking systems. It has been estimated that there were in 1966–8 some 9000 central, regional and local blood banks in the United States concerned with the collection of blood from donors.[3] Some (for example, hospital blood banks) will also be concerned with processing, cross-matching and transfusion; some have the function of producing and preparing blood components; some operate solely as collectors, distributors and sup-

---

[1] *Wall Street Journal*, August 7, 1967 and personal communication C. J. Stetler, President, Pharmaceutical Manufacturers Association, Washington, October 6, 1966. See also Shively, J. A., *op. cit.* The writer has not found it possible to obtain information from the Defense Forces about the demand and supply position. It was reported in 1968 that most of the blood used by the Armed Services was obtained within the military establishment and at donating centres in foreign countries (for reference see preceding footnote).

[2] *National Blood Resource Program: Statement of Basic Principles, op. cit.*, p. 1.

[3] Jennings, J. B., *An Introduction to Blood Banking Systems*, Technical Report No. 21, Operations Research Institute, Massachusetts Institute of Technology, July 1966, and American Medical Association, *Directory of Blood Banking and Transfusion Facilities and Services*, 1969.

D

pliers of whole blood, and some provide a comprehensive community service.

This diversity of single and multipurpose agencies may be classified in terms of five distinct types of blood banks:

1. Fifty-five independent but co-operating American Red Cross Regional Blood Centers based on 1700 participating local chapters and accounting, according to rough estimates in 1967, for about 40 per cent of total blood supplies in the United States.

2. Some 6000 individual hospital blood banks, exhibiting great variations in function, and estimated to be responsible for about 20–30 per cent of total blood supplies.

3. About 100 individual, non-profit organizations, known as community blood banks, generally aiming to ensure an adequate blood supply for the communities in which they are situated. These agencies also exhibit substantial variations in function; some simply acting as collectors and distributors to hospitals, others performing a wide range of services. These community banks were thought in 1966 to account for about 15–20 per cent of total blood supplies.

4. An unknown number of individual, profit-making, commercial blood banks who generally obtain their blood supplies from paid donors, process it, and sell it to hospitals at a profit. These banks were believed in the early 1960s to account for some 10–15 per cent of total blood supplies; more recent estimates arrive at substantially higher figures. There seems to be no doubt that in recent years the percentage of blood supplied by these commercial agencies has been increasing partly at the expense of voluntary programs.[1] It is, however, difficult to arrive at precise figures of supply and use because commercial blood banks 'refuse to accept the return of outdated blood, and thereby, it is argued, increase the waste of blood.[2] Some estimates of the growth of commercialization up to 1967 are given later in this chapter and in Chapter 6.

[1] In 1964 it was reported that 'commercialism was growing' and that there had been 'an increase in commercial blood banks and the use of paid donors' (*Hearings Before the Subcommittee on Antitrust and Monopoly of the Committee of the Judiciary, United States Senate*, 88th Congress, on S. 2560, U.S. Govt. Printing Office, 1964, pp. 7, 17, 33, 42, and 161). By 1967 further increases had been reported—to 20 per cent and above (*Hearings on S. 1945, op. cit.*, 1967, pp. 10, 79 and 84. See also statement by Rouse, M. O., President, American Medical Asscn., on the increase in commercialism and the 'steady decline in blood procurement under the voluntary program', *Transfusion*, March–April 1968, pp. 104–8).

[2] *Hearings on S. 1945, op. cit.*, 1967, p. 21.

5. An unknown number of commercial blood banks directly operated by pharmaceutical firms who rely heavily on a newly developed method of drawing blood, called plasmapheresis. In non-technical terms, this means that after the donor has given a pint of blood, the red cells are separated from the plasma (the liquid part of blood as distinguished from the suspended elements) and injected back into the donor.[1] For the donor, the process takes less than an hour. Providing the strictest medical standards are observed, and that the donor is in excellent health and eats a nutritious, high-protein diet, it is claimed by some authorities that several donations a week can be given. Other authorities believe, however, that it is too soon to be certain that plasmapheresis may not involve serious long-term hazards for donors. The subject is further discussed in Chapter 6.

Plasmapheresis of donors is used by these blood banks to obtain plasma, plasma protein components, and platelets. Developments in this field of blood banking have grown immensely in recent years in the United States (due largely to the greatly increased demand for blood products for a variety of life-saving and preventive purposes). Various estimates in 1968 suggested that pharmaceutical firms were paying for 1–1½ million donations a year yielding, with 'double bleed' sessions, approximately 2 million units. A number of firms operate their own plasmapheresis centres; others obtain their supplies from 'independent blood contractors.' Some regular donors are, in effect, 'semi-salaried' and paid $150–200 a month for a specified number of donations; some are long-term prisoners. The high 'fees' paid by certain plasmapheresis centres is a contentious matter for voluntary and community blood banks who find their donors being 'lured away'. The consequences of this development are discussed in a later chapter.[2]

[1] In platelet-pheresis, donors may give two pints of blood at a single session which may last about 1 hour. After the first pint has been drawn the donor waits in a 'donor chair' while a high speed centrifuge separates the plasma and the platelets from the whole blood. When this is done, the red cells, white cells and some plasma are returned to the donor's veins. Then another pint is withdrawn, and returned in the same session.

[2] The evidence for this section on plasmapheresis is based on: Kliman, A. and Lesses, M. F., op. cit., 1964; Jones, A. L., 'Continuous-flow Blood Cell Separation', Transfusion, March–April 1968, p. 94; Lawson, N. S. et al., 'Therapeutic Plasmapheresis', Transfusion, May–June 1968, p. 174; Tullis, J. L. et al., 'Platelet-Pheresis', Transfusion, May–June 1968, p. 154; Wall Street Journal, March 1, 1967; St Petersburg Times, Miami (showing appeal for donors to earn up to $200 a month), February 23, 1967; personal communications, Dr T. J. Greenwalt,

51

National estimates of the quantities of blood collected by these different types of blood banks generally exclude the commercial plasmapheresis centers because no comprehensive figures exist as to the scale of their operations. Excluding such supplies, however, national estimates of collections in the early 1960s range from 5 to 6 million units a year; estimates of the proportion provided by donors paid in cash varied from 17 to 20 per cent and more. Much depends, however, on the definition of a 'voluntary blood donor' in the United States; this problem is analysed later.

What complicates any attempt to assess the national position are the great variations from city to city, state to state and community to community in the organizational structure, roles and functions of the five main blood banking systems, as well as the hospitals, the cross-matching, processing and research laboratories, the pharmaceutical firms involved in the manufacture and sale of blood components, and the many different agencies concerned with the recruitment of donors. The problem is further muddled by a considerable volume of inter-state and inter-community shipment (in refrigerated containers, by taxi, delivery van, truck, bus and plane) of blood supplies for transfusions, processing, 'credit repayments' and the manufacture of blood products; by the separate and large programs organized by the Defense Forces;[1] by the official closure of commercial blood banks for mislabelling blood and other misdemeanours;[2] by the sale of outdated and mislabelled blood to Puerto Rico, Cuba and other countries,[3] and generally, by the lack of data on the import and export of blood and blood products.

In the absence of state and national blood programs, a number of organizations have attempted to co-ordinate the activities and services of some of the agencies involved, to disseminate information, to facilitate the borrowing, exchange and lending of blood, to further the geographical transferability of individual and family 'blood replacement rights', to organize registers of rare blood donors, to develop codes of blood banking standards, and to collect blood banking statistics. The role of the newly established National

American Red Cross, October 16, 1968, and Dr J. M. Stengle, National Blood Resource Program, October 16, 1968. See also further references to plasmapheresis programs in Chapter 6.

[1] See, for example, Kiel, F., 'Development of a Blood Program in Vietnam', *Military Medicine*, Vol. 131, No. 12, December 1966.

[2] See, for example, *Hearings on S. 1945, op. cit.*, 1967, p. 89.

[3] See, for example, *Hearings on S. 2560, op. cit.*, 1964, p. 158, and Sugrue, F., *A Slight Case of Life or Death* (to be published), United Community Funds and Councils of America, Inc., New York, p. 10.

Blood Resource Program in some of these fields has already been described. Other active organizations are the Public Health Service, the American National Red Cross, the New York Blood Center, the American Association of Blood Banks (with a membership in 1967 of 1148 blood banks accounting for more than half of the blood transfused nationally and responsible for a National Clearinghouse Program for blood and credit exchanges between blood banks) the Committee on Blood of the American Medical Association, and numerous state and local medical and blood banking associations.

While this variety and abundance of individual and often competing agencies in the field of blood transfusion services and facilities makes difficult the provision of national statistics it does deliver, according to some of the interests concerned, a larger supply of blood than might become available under a less pluralistic and more centrally organized system. Other commentators view the present situation, however, as one of fragmentation and chaos. Senator Edward V. Long (Chairman of the Subcommittee on Antitrust and Monopoly set up to consider the antitrust laws in relation to blood supplies) said in 1967 that the nation's blood banking system is 'in utter chaos'.[1] To these issues we return in a later chapter. Meanwhile, we review the results of several attempts to collect national data on the supply and transfusion of blood.

The first attempt to survey the field on a national scale was made in 1956-7 by a body called the Joint Blood Council (now defunct). Its first report was produced in 1960.[2] Information of varying quality was assembled covering, it was estimated, about 80 per cent of all blood collected and 60 per cent of all blood transfused. Allowing for non-response and various gaps and discrepancies it was further guessed and estimated that in 1956 over 5,100,000 units of blood were collected and over 4,500,000 units were transfused.[3]

[1] *Hearing on S. 1945, op. cit.*, 1967, press release from Office of Chairman, August 1, 1967. S. 1945 and an earlier bill, S. 2560, were bills 'to amend the antitrust laws to provide that the refusal of nonprofit blood banks and of hospitals and physicians to obtain blood and blood plasma from other blood banks shall not be deemed to be acts in restraints of trade, and for other purposes'. The Subcommittee was appointed by the Committee on the Judiciary, United States Senate.

[2] Joint Blood Council, *The Nation's Blood Transfusion Facilities and Services*, Washington, 1960.

[3] There were (and probably still are) wide variations in the definition of a 'unit' of blood. The Joint Blood Council and the American Association of Blood Banks recommended the use of a standard unit of 450 ml. of blood with the addition of anti-coagulant or other preservative not to exceed 120 ml. The American Red Cross standard was 440 ml. Other blood bank agencies adopted

53

Calculated on the basis of 50 per cent of the population this gives a collection rate of 6·0 units per 100 population.

The Joint Blood Council, after producing a second report,[1] was dissolved in 1962 and subsequently the American Medical Association assumed responsibility for the publication of a Directory of Blood Banking and Transfusion Facilities and Services. The first directory was published in 1965 based on the results of a national survey of services and facilities in 1964. Of 8789 effective agencies to whom questionnaires were sent 63 per cent returned completed forms. These agencies (hospitals and blood banks of all types) reported the collection of 6,324,590 units and the transfusion of 4,262,333 units.[2]

If comparisons are made with the 1956 data it would follow that (ignoring for the moment differences in estimates and non-response) blood collections rose by 1,225,000 units or by 24 per cent (averaged over 1956–64 by 3 per cent a year). On the other hand, the number of units transfused fell by 238,000 or 5 per cent. Thus, the gap between collections and units transfused widened from 600,000 units to over 2,000,000 units. This could not be explained by a greater use of blood (fresh and outdated) for blood products which, at any period, account for only a small proportion of blood supplies.[3]

There are a number of possible explanations concerning the gap in both years and the difference between them:

1. That much of the non-response in both years can be attributed to small hospitals and similar institutions, voluntary long-term hospitals and mental hospitals (there was some evidence of this in the Joint Blood Council 1956 Report).

2. This pattern of non-response could account for a number of unreported transfusions particularly as the J.B.C. 1956 Report showed that the smaller hospitals (under 100 beds and between 100–299 beds) had a higher consumption of blood per bed than larger hospitals.

units in excess of 450 ml. The American Medical Association *Directory of Blood Banking and Transfusion Facilities and Services* (1965) used, for reporting purposes, whole blood units with a unit volume of 430 ml. or more. An American pint equals 500 c.c., a British pint 568·26 c.c.

[1] This provided data for 1961 on 6,231,602 collections and 4,216,861 transfusions (Joint Blood Council, 1962).

[2] No attempt was made to analyse the data provided on blood products and outdated, wasted blood.

[3] The Joint Blood Council 1956 report concluded that less than 1 per cent of fresh blood (not outdated) was converted to plasma (p. 30).

3. Under-reporting by these hospitals and the smaller community facilities could result in (a) some understatement of units transfused (b) a somewhat smaller understatement of units collected and (c) some understatement of units collected from paid donors (in 1956 all community blood banks reporting drew 49 per cent of their blood from paid donors. In the case of all hospitals reporting the proportion was 20 per cent. Voluntary hospitals made more use of paid donors in 1956 than governmental hospitals, and the non-response rate was much higher among the former).

4. Lack of data as to the number and categories of patients who received blood. The 1965 A.M.A. Directory, discussing the difference between collections and transfusions, said '. . . there is apparently often a lack of data as to the numbers and categories of patients who receive blood' (p. ix). Blood donor records are also deficient (the J.B.C. 1956 Report drew attention to the fact that 'Even names are frequently omitted from donor records', p. 37). It is hard to believe, however, that record-keeping in responding hospitals and blood-banking facilities actually worsened between 1956 and 1964.

5. Double-counting and duplication of reporting could account for some substantial over-statement of blood collections. Such overstatement may well have increased between 1956 and 1964 due in part to the growing complexity of the organization of blood-banking services in the United States and, consequently, more and more divisions of accountability at all levels.

6. The 1956 Report, which obtained detailed information on 2,517,000 transfusions, may have seriously over-estimated non-reporting in raising the national total of transfusions to 4,500,000.

7. By far the most important factor in comparing these estimates is 'wasted' blood. This may take three forms: (a) the medically unjustified use of blood by physicians and surgeons (discussed in another context in later chapters); (b) technical waste, i.e. contaminated, haemolysed, 'short' bottles; (c) outdated (time expired) blood not used for conversion into plasma and other blood products.

Obviously, no estimates are available or could be made available on a national scale of the medically unjustified use of blood. As regards 'technical waste', all the evidence suggests that this accounts for only a relatively insignificant fraction of blood collections.[1] It may have increased in the United States between 1956 and 1964; a report published by the American Medical Association in 1963 said that 'Litigation involving blood transfusions seems to be

[1] See Appendix 2.

55

increasing with geometrical progression'.[1] Even so, this form of waste could still only account for a very small proportion of the 'missing' 2,000,000 units of blood in 1964.

To a substantial extent then, the explanation has to be found in the third form of waste—which we shall call 'administrative waste'. It is the result of defects and inadequacies in planning, administration and organization; of failures to estimate and match demand and supply; of the over-ordering of blood; the 'hoarding and consequent waste of blood by hospitals and blood banks'; incorrect estimates of demand for blood of different groups; delays in transportation and many other factors in the system itself not connected with the quality of the blood or its actual use by physicians in hospitals. These and other causes of wasted blood, described in more detail earlier, constituted the main argument for the establishment of the National Blood Resource Program in 1967. It was this agency which estimated, partly on the basis of a study of the 1964 national survey, that between 15 and 30 per cent of all fresh blood collected annually was administratively wasted through out-dating.[2] Much the same estimate was made by Dr C. E. Huggins of the Harvard Medical School and Massachusetts General Hospital Blood Bank in 1969 in reporting: 'Blood may be thrown away one week, with critical shortage the next.'[3] If total collections for 1964 are put at 6,000,000 units (to allow roughly for double-counting and duplication) it would follow that the number of units wasted lies between 900,000 and 1,800,000 units.

To explore the matter further we bring together, in Appendix 2, some estimates on the use of blood in the United States and England and Wales. We show for England and Wales that in the years 1956, 1961 and 1965 about 9–11 per cent of blood issued was converted into plasma and other products; about 2 per cent was used for research purposes, and that wasted blood in total (technical and administrative) accounted for 1 per cent in 1956 and 2 per cent in 1961.

We then applied certain of these proportions to the United States data as reported in the 1956 J.B.C. Survey. We thus assumed similar proportions of whole blood collected being converted into plasma

---

[1] Randall, C. H., *Medicolegal Problems in Blood Transfusions*, Committee on Blood, American Medical Association, 1963, p. 1. See also Chapter 9.

[2] National Blood Resource Program, RFP. NHI–68–15, *op. cit.*, March 8, 1968, p. 3. See also statement reported in *The New York Times*, August 7, 1967.

[3] Addressing the Society of Cyrosurgery (reported in *Medical News, J.A.M.A.*, February 3, 1969, 207:5, p. 847).

and other products and used for research. We further assumed a similar proportion of total wasted blood in 1956, namely 1 per cent. The result of this exercise left unaccounted a total of 1,327,000 units of blood or 30 per cent of all blood collections actually reported in the J.B.C. Survey.

What proportion of this 30 per cent represented administrative waste of blood? What proportion was due to the under-reporting of transfusions and other discrepancies in the Survey?

The report itself came to no final conclusion beyond stating that the overall proportion of outdated and wasted blood 'may well be 10 per cent or more' (p. 34); that is, ten times higher than the proportion for England and Wales in 1956.

The 1964 Survey by the American Medical Association, which reported a gap of over 2,000,000 units between collections and transfusions, made no attempt to analyse use or estimate wastage.

Mr J. B. Jennings of the Massachusetts Institute of Technology who completed in 1966 a report on the state of blood banking in the United States was puzzled by these overall figures for 1956 and 1964.[1] Commenting on the figures for 1964 of 6,300,000 units collected and 4,300,000 units transfused he said '. . . a 33 per cent national wastage seems unreasonably high' (p. 59).

He therefore suggested, though without giving any evidence in support, that transfusions in 1964 had been under-reported by 700,000 to 1,200,000 units. It will be recalled that the 1956 Survey had estimated a transfusion total of 2,000,000 units under-reported.

We can only conclude that if the 1956 Report was approximately correct in its estimate that 10 per cent or more of blood was administratively wasted then such wastage must have increased by 1964 by anything from 50 to 300 per cent if the National Blood Resource Program's estimate was anywhere near the truth. Even if the 1956 surveyors did err on the optimistic side about the national rate of wastage it would still seem that a substantial increase occurred between 1956 and 1964.[2]

Later in his study Mr Jennings cited 'state-wide out-dating averages of about 16 per cent' (p. 68). Such averages have been

---

[1] Jennings, J. B., *An Introduction to Blood Banking Systems, op. cit.*

[2] The difference in wastage estimates for 1956 and 1964 cannot be explained by changes in the total of units of outdated blood converted into plasma. The estimate of such units for 1956 was put at 264,000. In 1968 the National Research Council (Committee on Plasma and Plasma Substitutes) estimated that some 300,000 units were currently used in the United States (*Transfusion*, March–April 1968).

reported for California[1] and Michigan.[2] He also undertook a financial study of outdated blood in the State of Massachusetts in 1964. It appeared that of all outdated blood between 31 and 57 per cent was unsalvaged—or wasted. Mr Jennings concluded that blood banks in Massachusetts wasted at least $300,000 in 1964, and possibly as much as $1,000,000, on outdated blood (p. 72).[3] Blood collections in Massachusetts in 1964 (202,000 units) represented approximately 3 per cent of total collections in the United States. If the waste of blood elsewhere was on the same scale, then the total financial costs in the United States of this element of waste alone must have amounted to between $10,000,000 and $33,000,000 a year.[4]

After Mr Jennings and other students of the problem of blood supply had completed their reports the American Medical Association published, in the middle of 1969, another directory of blood banking which brought together information relating to the year 1967.[5] Questionnaires were sent to 10,443 facilities which it was thought might have blood banking or transfusion services; 1435 reported no such operations or services. For the remainder the response rate was marginally lower (62 per cent) than in 1964.

In an effort to obtain a maximum response the survey was much reduced in scope and fewer questions were asked. Also, the statistics in the Directory were chiefly confined to blood collections and transfusions. Like the 1964 report, no attempt was made to estimate or analyse wastage. The Foreword merely cautioned that it 'would be erroneous to conclude that the difference between "units transfused" and "units bled from donors" represents wastage'.

For the nation as a whole, the 1967 totals were 6,610,166 units of whole blood collected and 4,348,003 units transfused. Compared with 1964, collections rose by 286,000 units and transfusions by

[1] Singman, D. et al., J.A.M.A., 194(6): 583:113, November 8, 1965.

[2] Anderson, H. D., Proc. 9th Congress Int. Society of Blood Transfusion, Mexico, 1962, p. 669, 1964.

[3] On costs of blood per unit in the United States and England and Wales, see Chapter 12.

[4] In a later study, published in 1967, Mr Jennings stated 'Approximately 50 per cent of all bloods demanded, crossmatched, and held for a particular patient are eventually found not to be required for that patient and are returned to the unassigned inventory' (Jennings, J. B., Hospital Blood Bank Whole Blood Inventory Control, Technical Report No. 27, Operations Research Center, Massachusetts Institute of Technology, December 1967, and Transfusion, November–December 1968, Vol. 8, No. 6, p. 335).

[5] American Medical Association, Committee on Blood, Directory of Blood Banking and Transfusion Facilities and Services, Chicago, 1969.

86,000. Thus, the gap widened to 2,262,000 units—or nearly one-third of all collections. The number of units transfused, though a little higher than in 1964, was below the estimated national total for 1956.

An analysis of the 1961, 1964 and 1967 data on collections was made by the writer in order to explore the trend in supplies contributed by different blood banking systems. Data were extracted from the three reports for (a) all American Red Cross Centers reporting a collection total in 1967 of 10,000 or more whole blood units (b) all non-profit community and hospital blood banks reporting a similar collection total in 1967 who had a percentage of 50 or more of paid donors in 1964 (questions on payment were not included in the 1967 survey) and (c) all commercial blood banks (classified as such in 1961 and 1964) reporting a similar collection total in 1967.

The analysis, therefore, was confined to the larger blood banks in these three categories in the United States. The results showed:

TABLE 2
Trends in Collections of Whole Blood Units 1961–7
by Selected Blood Banks, U.S.A.

	Percentage increase in collections 1964–7	*Percentage increase in collections 1961–7*	*Additional number of units collected in 1967 compared with 1964*
American Red Cross	9	18	247,911
Community and hospital banks	28	45	88,240
Commercial banks	119	242	365,300
All other banks	Decrease 8	Decrease 21	Decrease 415,875

One reasonable deduction to be drawn from this table is that the trend is towards larger blood banks—particularly the commercial banks and other banks who pay their suppliers. It would seem to follow, therefore, that in terms of the aggregate number of units collected there was less under-reporting of collections in 1967 than in 1964 and 1961. Other comments on this table are included in Chapter 6 where we discuss the characteristics of donors in the United States.

However, while under-reporting may have declined (recalling too that the response rate was only marginally lower in 1967 than in 1964) the problem of estimating national trends was, by 1969, much more complicated because of the phenomenally rapid growth of plasmapheresis programs undertaken by commercial and pharmaceutical banks and other facilities.

Reference has already been made to estimates that by 1968 some 1–1½ million donations a year were being acquired by pharmaceutical companies and other commercial organizations. As each plasmapheresis 'two-bag' supply yields about 700–800 ml. this total represents something like 2 million units of plasma for production scale fractionation. The critical question is thus raised: how many of these 2 million units were in fact included in the reported 6,610,166 collections for 1967?

The 1967 questionnaire, which dropped questions about payment for blood, types of blood banks, outdated blood and other issues, did include one new question: 'Does your facility engage in plasmapheresis?' The answers were not analysed or even added up in the report. However, a count by the writer showed that 460 facilities answered 'yes'. But no data were provided which would allow an estimate to be made in each case of the proportion of the units collected which were obtained through plasmapheresis programs.

A few pharmaceutical firms did respond to the questionnaire but many did not. Some run their own programs and recruit and pay blood suppliers but many buy their blood from 'middle-men'— commercial blood banks and other facilities. In order to obtain data on plasmapheresis programs the writer sent letters in 1968 with a series of questions to all pharmaceutical establishments in the United States and other countries (notably Japan) which had been officially licensed by the United States Public Health Service to manufacture blood products for sale, barter and exchange.[1]

The response was disappointing. A large number did not reply. Some did so but refused to provide information. Others supplied statistics which do not appear in the 1967 A.M.A. survey or which differ from the entries in the 1967 report. A few firms did, however, provide valuable estimates of national trends in plasmapheresis programs. It was this information which yielded the national estimate for 1968 of 2 million plasmapheresis units.[2]

[1] Establishments listed in *Biological Products* (revised January 1, 1968), Division of Biologics Standards, National Institutes of Health, Public Health Service Publication No. 50, U.S. Dept. of Health, Education and Welfare.

[2] For further reference to this inquiry, see Chapter 6.

Despite this help, however, it was still impossible to say how many of these 2 million units were included in the national collection total of 6,610,166 units. But if only half (say) were included it would mean that in 1967 5,610,166 units were collected for transfusion purposes—a total substantially lower than the figures for 1964 and 1961 and only a little higher than the national total for 1956. The number of 'missing' or 'wasted' units would thus be reduced to around 1,250,000.

The national statistical picture is so confused and unsatisfactory it can only be concluded that *either* the total number of units of whole blood collected for transfusion purposes has fallen both in terms of absolute numbers and even more so in relation to population growth *or* that the number of 'missing' or 'out-dated' units has risen both absolutely and relatively. The true answer, if all

TABLE 3

Trends in Collections of Whole Blood Units 1961–7 in Selected Cities, U.S.A.[1]

	1961		1964		1967	
	(a)	(b)	(a)	(b)	(a)	(b)
Boston	182,922	21	174,848	16	198,606	18
Chicago	154,433	29	181,630	37	170,406	33
Dallas	35,977	6	48,250	6	49,015	8
Denver	44,328	8	44,290	7	48,917	5
Detroit	167,784	20	154,099	20	163,105	20
Jersey City	6,200	2	19,589	5	40	1
Kansas City	40	1	1,166	1	Nil	Nil[2]
Los Angeles	230,549	15	221,045	15	263,531	14
Memphis	66,804	8	61,715	8	82,962	9
New York	358,762	62	232,201	62	261,012	46
Philadelphia	206,116	35	195,565	33	188,515	39
Pittsburgh	60,320	13	55,911	13	51,577	8
	1,514,235	220	1,390,309	223	1,477,686	201

Notes: (a) number of units of whole blood bled from donors.
      (b) number of facilities reporting.

[1] Abstracted from survey reports for 1961, 1964 and 1967.
[2] One commercial blood bank, licensed on January 1, 1968, reported by correspondence collecting 31,736 units in 1967.

the facts were known, probably contains elements of both trends—
a somewhat smaller decline in collections and a somewhat smaller
increase in 'missing' or 'wasted' units. Other possible factors relating
to under-reporting, over-reporting, duplication and double-counting
which also complicate attempts to compare one year with another
were referred to earlier.

As a final comment on the unsatisfactory nature of these national
blood supply statistics we present certain data for the 12 cities
listed in Chapter 6 and for which estimates have been made concerning the proportions of paid donations (see table 3, p. 61).

A study of these three reports for large cities does not suggest
that non-response was markedly higher in 1967 than in 1961. The
questionnaire was much shorter and simpler. Moreover, when
account is taken of the general trend—particularly in large cities—
towards larger blood banks and fewer facilities—the response rate
may have been higher in 1967 when measured in terms of the total
number of units of whole blood bled from donors.

It really is impossible to offer any explanation of the trends in
these 12 cities. In some of them (Chicago, Detroit, Kansas City,
Los Angeles, Memphis, and New York) there were very marked
increases reported by blood banks which were either run for profit
or which paid a large proportion of their donors (classified as such
in 1961 and 1964). For other blood banks there were marked
declines. In total, however, there is no evidence of any increase in
the number of units bled from donors even though the 1967 data
must have included some tens of thousands of units collected under
plasmapheresis programs.

We conclude this review of studies on the supply of blood in the
United States by citing various other inquiries for certain cities
and areas. In particular, we look at the situation in New York
City where the problem of blood supplies has probably received
more attention in recent years than in any other city or area of
comparable size in the United States.

The first comprehensive survey was undertaken by the New York
Academy of Medicine in 1956.[1]. This showed that 57 collecting
organizations collected 348,571 units of blood, 71 per cent in the
borough of Manhattan—a fact which is relevant to questions
concerning the characteristics of blood donors. For the city as a
whole, the Report showed also that the proportion of donors who

[1] Committee on Public Health, New York Academy of Medicine, *Human
Blood in New York City: A Study of its Procurement, Distribution and Utilization*,
New York (privately printed), 1958.

were paid was 42 per cent—a proportion that had, however, increased still further to 55 per cent by 1966. These questions of donor characteristics are pursued in Chapter 6.

In addition to blood collections in New York, thousands of units of fresh blood were shipped in from Southern and Midwestern States.[1] The total of units transfused was estimated for 1956 at 250,000; also, eight distributing organizations obtained, by their own production or by purchase, and distributed 23,708 units of blood derivatives. But this information was only partial because 'Few organizations maintained complete records . . .' (p. 40).

If we assume, on the basis of a collection total of 348,571 units, a pattern of use for blood derivatives and research on the English scale in 1956 (13 per cent) we are left with a wastage balance of 54,000 units—or 15 per cent. There are no estimates of waste since 1956 while the statistics of collections for 1961, 1964 and 1967 (see Table 3), inadequate and unsatisfactory as they are, suggest strongly that the decline is downwards. Reported collections in 1967 were nearly 100,000 units lower than in 1961 and amounted to only 261,012 units. On the other hand, estimates of the number of units transfused, published by the New York Blood Center, show a rise from 250,000 in 1956 to 330,000 in 1965.[2] It can only be concluded that either the under-reporting of collections had very substantially increased or that New York City was depending to a much greater extent on blood imported from other areas in the United States.

It is possible, of course, that the amount of blood wasted may have declined since 1956. But one report from the Center in 1966 had this to say: 'Although surgery postponed for lack of blood is a daily occurrence in New York City, a vast amount of blood is wasted because there is no central administration or over-all inventory. Increasingly, hospitals tend to hoard their own blood supplies because blood loaned is gone forever. Yet hoarded blood is often wasted blood. There are no records available on the amount of blood wasted, but estimates of experts vary from 10,000 to

[1] This was also the situation in 1963 (see *Hearings on S. 2560, op. cit.*, 1964, pp. 160–1).
[2] The New York Blood Center, *Report*, 1966. The Center, established in 1963, is operated by the Community Blood Council of Greater New York, a non-profit organization formed in 1959 by the City's medical, hospital and community health organizations to co-ordinate, expand and improve blood services in the metropolitan area and to engage in research on the problems of blood transfusion. The Center has developed a rare blood-donor registry, is organizing new volunteer donor programs and is conducting research on a large scale.

30,000 units a year'.[1] The Report went on to cite case histories from 'three of the largest and best hospitals in the city' to illustrate what was described as a 'chronically worsening situation of near-anarchy' in a 'city-wide anemia' involving some 8,000,000 people.[2]

Despite developments in the program of the New York Blood Center there was little improvement in the general situation by 1967–8. There were still acute and chronic shortages of blood particularly at Christmas and during the months of July, August and September when the problem of supply was becoming even more serious; elective operations were still being delayed and 'the number and scheduling of open-heart procedures at some major hospitals are governed to a considerable degree by the availability of blood'.[3] In the first six months of 1968, voluntary donations to the Center recorded a fall of 10 per cent compared with the previous year. The reasons were not known but the decline caused much concern. Racial unrest, it was thought, may have been a factor leading to a decline in voluntary motivation; the psychological effects of the Vietnam War—particularly among young people—may have also contributed. By the end of 1968 it was reported that 'many hospitals in the metropolitan area had drastically reduced the number of elective surgical operations because of the critical shortage of blood bank inventories'.[4]

Another relatively new factor in the New York situation—though by no means unique to New York—may have been the intrusion on a larger scale into the 'blood supply market' of international drug firms operating their own commercial blood banks, paying donors, and thus drawing on—or 'luring away'[5]—a limited number of donors in New York.[6] Some of these blood banks, and others operating as 'independent commercial contractors', had by 1969 developed extensive plasmapheresis programs. The effect of these in general has been to raise the price of blood; suppliers demand more money—especially for Rh-negative blood of which New York is chronically short.[7] No statistical information is

[1] New York Blood Center, *Report*, 1966, p. 9.

[2] These descriptions were in part taken from reports in 1962, 1964 and 1965 of investigations into the City's system of blood supply and distribution by *The New York Times* (see editorial April 3, 1962, the *Times Magazine*, March 29, 1964, and article by Dr Howard A. Rusk, February 28, 1965).

[3] Personal communication, Dr A. Kellner, Medical Director, New York Blood Center, March 6, 1967.   [4] *New York Times*, December 12, 1968.

[5] *Hearings on S. 1945, op. cit.*, 1967, p. 91.

[6] *Hearings on S. 1945, op. cit.*, 1967, pp. 114–15.

[7] New York Blood Center, *News Release*, March 24, 1966.

available, however, about how these commercial programs have affected the voluntary donor in New York—apart from the fact that the proportion of paid donations continues to rise.

In this discussion of supply and demand, it must not be assumed, as was emphasized earlier, that what obtains in New York is applicable generally. There are considerable differences in the situation from city to city, state to state. Some of these differences are illustrated in more detail in Chapter 6. Moreover, the vast majority of plasmapheresis programs, involving 2 million units, draw on suppliers in areas other than New York City.

In contrast with New York, however, Seattle, which had one of the best organized and effective blood banking and cross-matching agencies in the country under the leadership of Dr Richard Czajkowski (who retired in 1968), and which collected 35,000 units annually, reported in recent years an outdating proportion of less than 2 per cent.[1] The New York Blood Center and the Milwaukee Blood Center are other effective non-profit community blood banks recording low rates of wasted blood.

But these are recognized in the United States as exceptional institutions. Among the large urban and metropolitan areas only a minority of places—like Seattle—appear to have no chronic shortages of fresh blood. Generally, throughout the United States, there are widespread reports from many areas and by numerous experts of actual and potential demand exceeding the available supply of blood.

Despite all their statistical deficiencies, the survey reports for 1961, 1964 and 1967, when analysed in microscopic fashion, blood bank by blood bank, area by area, city by city and state by state, show a generally worsening situation in relative terms; actual declines in collection rates in some parts of the country when related to population structures; rates of collection from non-paid donors which have not responded to increases in population and particularly the older age groups; and striking percentage increases in many areas of the country in collections by commercial blood banks and the pharmaceutical industry.[2] It seems most unlikely, however, especially when account is taken of the problem of wasted blood

---

[1] Jennings, J. B., *op. cit.*, p. 130.

[2] Some of the largest increases in the number of units of whole blood collected by these commercial agencies between 1961–7 occurred in Alabama, California, Chicago, Cleveland, Indianapolis, Kansas City, Los Angeles, Memphis, Miami, New Jersey, New Orleans, New York State, Philadelphia, St Louis and Tennessee.

and plasma, whether these increases have compensated, since 1961, for the relatively lower rates of increase among other sectors of the blood banking system (see, for example, Tables 2 and 3).

We end this chapter, first, by citing a few comments by various authorities who have studied the issues of supply, demand and waste and, second, with some reference to an emerging international problem; the import and export of blood and blood products.

'It is well known,' wrote Mr Jennings in his 1966 survey, 'that surgery is not infrequently postponed or cancelled for lack of blood'.[1] He also reported that '. . . many hospitals are chronically short of blood'.[2] Dr R. F. Norris, Director, Pepper Laboratory of Clinical Medicine at the University of Pennsylvania, said, in a paper to the American Medical Association's 1964 Conference on Blood and Blood Banking: 'In recent years the need for professional (paid) donors has actually increased in the large blood centers because of the advances in so-called open-heart operations and other surgical procedures of such a magnitude as to require multiple transfusions. This need has been accentuated by the requirement that blood for such operations be freshly drawn from the donors.'[3] Dr I. Malootian of the Boston University Medical Center, discussing in 1964 the role of voluntary blood donors in relation to reported increases in the percentage of paid donors, said 'Hematologic and immunologic research has led to practices and advances in technique in our blood banks which were undreamed of even five years ago, yet despite the wider and wider application of blood and blood products we have fallen increasingly behind in the one area essential to making these advances available to the patient who needs blood procurement'.[4]

From Kansas City, Dr C. B. Wheeler of the Research Hospital and Medical Center discussing at the American Medical Association's 1964 Conference 'the dramatic increase of malpractice suits in blood tranfusion cases' emphasized that the 'blood supply problem in certain parts of this nation is acute'.[5]

At a meeting in Los Angeles in October 1966 of the American

[1] Jennings, J. B., *op. cit.*, p. 60.
[2] Jennings, J. B., *op. cit.*, p. 15 (citing conversations with Dr A. Kliman, Medical Director, Massachusetts Red Cross Blood Center, 1965–6).
[3] Norris, R. F., 'Hospital Programs', *Proc. A.M.A. Conference on Blood and Blood Banking*, 1964.
[4] Malootian, I., 'A Plan to Attract Voluntary Blood Donors', *Proc. 10th Congr. Int. Soc. Blood Transf.*, Stockholm, 1964, p. 1002.
[5] Wheeler, C. B., 'State Laws and Regulations', *Proc. A.M.A. Conference on Blood and Blood Banking*, 1964.

Association of Blood Banks much concern was expressed about the problems of demand and supply. One paper estimated that blood usage was increasing at the rate of 12 per cent a year (no precise figures were provided); others spoke of surgery being delayed, often for months; of hospitals demanding that patients pay for their transfusions in blood rather than in cash, and of the growth of commercialism in blood banking.

Emphasizing the shortages of blood, the President of the Association, Dr E. A. Dreskin, said: 'Although nobody wants to admit it publicly, nationally there has been a significant increase in delays of persons waiting for elective surgery because of imbalances of blood supplies.' He also reported that in some parts of the United States the situation was so acute that blood banks were offering trading stamps and tickets to movies or baseball games as inducements to donors, and that in South Carolina and Mississippi discounts on prison sentences were offered if prisoners donated blood.[1]

In other areas and states, Alabama, Arkansas, Georgia and Oklahoma, for example, the shortage of donors appears to have been so acute by 1967 that drug companies were increasingly seeking through the agency of intermediaries to use prisoners for clinical trials and to establish blood processing facilities at prisons to obtain plasma.[2]

The American Association of Blood Banks, in a statement in 1967 on behalf of Senate Bill, 1945, reported '. . . the need for blood has increased at a faster pace than the number of voluntary donors. As a result, there has been an increase in proprietory or commercial banks and the use of paid donors'. 'The demand for blood', concluded the statement, 'nearly exceeds all present resources'.[3] In November 1968 one pharmaceutical company estimated the national proportion of paid donors at 33 per cent.[4] Finally, we may note that towards the end of 1967 both the President of the American Medical Association and the Journal of the Association (in an editorial) warned the medical profession that the supply of blood from voluntary donors was not keeping pace with the increasing need for blood for patient care.[5]

In Chapter 6 we analyse in more detail the material relating to

[1] Dreskin, E. A. and others, *Proc. Couf. of the Amer. Assocn. of Blood Banks*, Los Angeles, October 1966, and *Hearings on S. 1945, op. cit.*, 1967, p. 91.

[2] *Hearings on S. 1945, op. cit.*, 1967, p. 91. For further references to the use of prisoners as blood donors, see Chapter 6.

[3] *Hearings on S. 1945, op. cit.*, 1967, pp. 84–5.

[4] Personal communication, Travenol Laboratories International, November 5, 1968.   [5] *J.A.M.A.*, 202:4, October 23, 1967.

the respective contributions to supply of the American Red Cross, hospital and community blood banks, commercial blood banks and other institutions and the part played in supply by different types of donors.

Meanwhile, and to conclude this chapter, we refer to the international market in blood and blood products. This appears to be growing in scale although precise evidence is hard to come by. There seems to be two major inter-related reasons for this trend. First, because of the increasing shortage of blood and certain blood products in a number of materially rich societies where demand is rising substantially. Second, new methods of blood fractionation have resulted in recent years in the appearance of a multiplicity of blood products. In some countries, for example, the United States, Japan and Sweden, production is principally in the hands of the pharmaceutical industry. In Britain it is the responsibility of the National Blood Transfusion Service.

Some pharmaceutical firms are developing extensive international markets in blood products. One American firm, for example, informed the writer that it was hoping to sell abroad in 1969 $1,000,000 worth of plasma products (immunoglobulin, albumin, fibrinogen and many other preparations). Some commercial blood banks in the United States sell plasma for fractionation to a Swedish pharmaceutical firm who also import retroplacental blood and out-dated blood from a number of European countries. The export of human blood and blood products from Japan was severely restricted by the Government in 1966 due to the shortage of blood supplies in that country. Latin American and Far Eastern countries are said to be exporting plasma and placenta for fractionation on an increasing scale to the United States. Possibly several millions of placenta are imported annually.

For reasons which we need not dwell on here it is not possible to explore all the ramifications of these commercial markets. In March 1966 the Commonwealth Government of Australia was forced, because of threatened commercial competition and a fear that voluntary donor systems would be destroyed, to prohibit the export of human blood, substances derived from human blood, and human organs or tissues including the placenta.[1, 2]

[1] Personal communication, His Excellency Senator K. Anderson, Minister of State for Customs and Excise, Sydney, N.S.W., July 19, 1966 (Amendments to the Customs, Prohibited Exports, Regulations, Sixth Schedule, March 24, 1966).

[2] This section is based on information derived from a large number of sources including the following: Dr R. Naito, the Green Cross Corporation, Osaka,

There are profits to be made in blood on an international as well
as a national scale. Can the voluntary community system only
survive then 'in an emergency such as war'?[1]

In the next chapter we consider the nature of the gift of blood.

Japan; Travenol Laboratories Inc., Illinois, U.S.A.; Cutter Laboratories,
Berkeley, California; Foreign Trade Division, U.S. Dept. of Commerce, Bureau
of the Census and Bureau of International Commerce, Washington, D.C.;
Division of Biologics Standards, National Institutes of Health, Bethesda, U.S.A.;
Merck Sharpe and Dohme, New York; Division of Industry Advice, Food and
Drug Administration, Washington, D.C.; Pharmaceutical Manufacturers'
Association, Washington, D.C.; and AB Kabi, Stockholm, Sweden.

[1] This was the view expressed by the Blood Bank Committee of the Chicago
Medical Society who opposed the entry of the American Red Cross into the
Chicago blood banking business (*Transfusion*, Vol. 4, 1964, p. 404).

Chapter 5
The Gift

I

In Chapter 2 we described the health criteria set for blood donors, and explained the need for high standards in donor selection in the interests of recipients because of the potentially lethal quality of human blood and the dangers of transmitting disease. We saw also that in the interests of the donors' health strict limits had to be placed on these acts of giving. The young, the old, the sick and the disabled, expectant and nursing mothers, and other clinically ineligible groups are medically forbidden to donate; thus, something like one-half or more of the population are dependent in terms of their therapeutic and prophylactic needs for blood and blood derivatives on the remaining half or less of the population—healthy, able-bodied men and women. Some with blood of a rare group will depend for their lives on the willingness to donate of a very few unseen people with identical blood. Others, like haemophiliacs, may have to rely, year after year, on the gifts of fifty strangers every year for their continued survival.[1]

For those who are eligible to give to the unknown few or the unknown many there are also limits to giving both in relation to the quantity of blood that may be donated at any one moment in time and to the intervals of time between donations.

The doctor, informed by science, decides which biological groups in society should be allowed to take part in the act of anonymously giving blood and the endeavour to save life. He determines the circulation of givers.

The doctor also decides which individuals should receive blood—and blood of a particular group—though he does not know the giver; nor does he know, and in the present state of medical knowledge he cannot know, whether the gift is a good one. In thus determining the circulation of gifts, he depends in large part on and has to presume the honesty and truthfulness of the giver. No society in the modern

[1] See Chapter 12.

70

world has established laws and penalties to enforce the giving of
blood and of truthful information by the giver concerning his state
of health. But it is only in the last twenty years or so that every
country's need for blood on a large and rapidly increasing scale has
raised in a new and impersonal guise these fundamental questions
of social relations; of giving, receiving, and repaying. Who, among
those eligible to take part in the act, should give blood; on what
principles, to whom, and why?

II

To 'donate' is to give implying an altruistic motive; strictly, and
perhaps more neutrally speaking, 'suppliers' should replace 'donors'
in the vocabulary of this study. Though in a sense misleading, we
shall, however, conform to the common usage. In a later chapter,
specifically concerned with those who donate blood, we attempt
to analyse and classify the motives of people who voluntarily and
spontaneously perform the act of giving.

To obtain sufficient quantities of blood, in the required blood
group proportions, at the required times, and in the required places,
are not processes which can be determined and controlled by the
medical profession despite its power to decide who may and who
may not give and the destination of the gifts. To give or not to give,
to lend, repay or even to buy and sell blood leads us, if we are to
understand these transactions in the context of a particular society,
into the fundamentals of social and economic life.

The forms and functions of giving embody moral, social, psychological, religious, legal and aesthetic ideas. They may reflect, sustain,
strengthen or loosen the cultural bonds of the group, large or small.
They may inspire the worst excesses of war and tribal nationalism
or the tolerances of community. They may contribute to integrative
processes in a society (binding together different ethnic, religious
and generational groups) or they may spread, through separatist
and segregationist acts, the reality and sense of alienation—as in
South Africa and the Southern States of the United States.[1]

Customs and practices of non-economic giving—unilateral and
multilateral social transfers—thus may tell us much, as Marcel
Mauss so sensitively demonstrated in his book *The Gift*,[2] about the

[1] The segregation of donated blood on 'racial' lines in South Africa and
Arkansas and Louisiana (two states with laws requiring the labelling of blood to
show 'racial' origin) are referred to in Chapter 11.

[2] Mauss, M., *The Gift*, translated by Cunnison, I., with an Introduction by
Evans-Pritchard, E. E., London, 1954.

texture of personal and group relationships in different cultures, past and present. We are reminded, whenever we think about the meaning of customs in historical civilizations, of how much we have lost, whatever we may have otherwise gained, by the substitution of large-scale economic systems for systems in which exchange of goods and services was not an impersonal but a moral transaction, bringing about and maintaining personal relationships between individuals and groups.

In some societies, past and present, gifts to men aim to buy peace; to express affection, regard or loyalty; to unify the group; to bind the generations; to fulfil a contractual set of obligations and rights; to function as acts of penitence, shame or degradation, and to symbolize many other human sentiments. When one reads the work of anthropologists and sociologists—like Mauss and Lévi-Strauss—who have studied the social functions of giving in different cultures, a number of themes—relevant to any attempt to delineate a typology of blood donors—may be discerned.

Acts of giving are, in many societies, a group affair, woven into the fabric of being, and take place in personal face-to-face situations —as in the *potlach* of the North American Indians and the *kula* of the Melanesians. Moreover, '. . . when gifts circulate in Melanesia and Polynesia the return is assured by the virtue of the things passed on, which are their own guarantees. In any society', observed Mauss, 'it is in the nature of the gift in the end to being its own reward'.[1] But time may have to pass before a counter-gift can be made; thus, the notion of time in relation to acts of giving and receiving is significant and implies the further notion of credit. More significant is the reality of the obligation or compulsion to give. In all that Mauss, Lévi-Strauss, Homans, Schwartz and others have written on gift-exchange there emerges a vivid sense of the immense pervasiveness of the social obligation—the group compulsions—to give and to repay, and the strength of the supporting sanctions; dishonour, shame and guilt.

Every gift-exchange dyad in such societies—and, maybe, in some senses in our own societies—is thus characterized by elements of moral enforcement. Whatever may be said about the initiatory gift (Simmel argued that the first gift is given in full spontaneity; 'it has a freedom without any duty, even without the duty of gratitude'[2]) the counter-gift or repayment becomes a compulsory act.

[1] Mauss, M., *op. cit.*, p. 34.
[2] Simmel, G., 'Faithfulness and Gratitude', in Wolff, K. (ed.), *The Sociology of Georg Simmel*, New York, Free Press, 1950, p. 392.

Malinowski, in his studies of the Trobriand Islanders, showed that gifts and counter-gifts comprise 'one of the main instruments of social organization, of the power of the chief, of the bonds of kinship, and of relationship in law'.[1] The social relations set up by gift-exchange are among the most powerful forces which bind a social group together.

These observations about the act of giving are mostly drawn from studies of non-industrialized societies where social life has often the texture of a constant give-and-take; a process also serving as a means of distributing goods in a non-monetary economy. At the end of his book Mauss makes an attempt, though sketchily, to apply some of these notions to complex, Western societies. He wrote, it should be noted, before the advent of blood transfusion services, and took his examples of modern gift relationships from the rise of systems of social security in France and Britain. 'The theme of the gift', he commented, 'of freedom and obligation in the gift, of generosity and self-interest in giving, reappear in our own society like the resurrection of a dominant motif long forgotten'.[2]

To what extent are these observations about gift-exchange in other cultural contexts relevant to the role of the blood donor in Britain, the United States, the U.S.S.R., South Africa and other countries? There are similarities in form and function; there are mixtures of elements of generosity and self-interest, spontaneity and compulsion, but there are also distinctive differences. These, to a considerable degree, are influenced by the particular characteristics of blood donor systems and the relationships set up, social and economic, between the system and the donor. As we shall see, collectively these relationships are strongly determined by the values and cultural orientations permeating the donor system and the society in general. There are, in fact, fundamental differences in systems of recruiting and rewarding donors of blood within certain industrialized societies and between such societies; between, for example, Britain and the United States and between the U.S.S.R. and Japan. But, before we pursue these thoughts further—which we attempt to do in a later chapter—we have to construct a typology of blood donors applicable, we would hope, to all societies with modern blood transfusion services.

First, however, it is necessary to point out that the gift of blood has certain unique attributes which distinguish it from other forms

[1] Malinowski, B., *Argonauts of the Western Pacific*, London, Routledge, 1922, p. 167.
[2] Mauss, M., *op. cit.*, p. 66.

of gift. We enumerate some of these but only briefly as we shall have occasion to return to the subject later in discussing the question whether blood transfusion constitutes a service or a market transaction. The following attributes assume that the gift is a voluntary, altruistic act:

1. The gift of blood takes place in impersonal situations, sometimes with physically hurtful consequences to the donor.

2. The recipient is in almost all cases not personally known to the donor; there can, therefore, be no personal expressions of gratitude or of other sentiments.

3. Only certain groups in the population are allowed to give; the selection of those who can is determined on rational and not cultural rules by external arbiters.

4. There are no personal, predictable penalties for not giving; no socially enforced sanctions of remorse, shame or guilt.

5. For the giver there is no certainty of a corresponding gift in return, present or future.

6. No givers require or wish for corresponding gifts in return. They do not expect and would not wish to have a blood transfusion.

7. In most systems, there is no obligation imposed on the recipient himself to make a corresponding gift in return.

8. Whether the gift itself is beneficial or harmful to an unknown recipient will depend to some extent on the truthfulness and honesty of the giver (information by the donor about himself which is deliberately withheld or misrepresented may be lethal to a stranger). Moreover, the intermediaries—those who collect and process the gift—may determine in certain systems whether it is potentially beneficial or harmful.

9. Both givers and recipients might, if they were known to each other, refuse to participate in the process on religious, ethnic, political or other grounds.

10. Blood as a gift is highly perishable (its value rapidly diminishes) but neither the giver nor the recipient wields any power in determining whether it is used or is wasted.

11. To the giver, the gift is quickly replaced by the body. There is no permanent loss. To the receiver, the gift may be everything: life itself.

The uniqueness of the blood gift, endorsed in different ways by each of these eleven propositions, becomes even clearer when comparisons are made with the attributes of other types of gift in modern societies. Professor Schwartz, in a paper on 'The Social

Psychology of the Gift', analyses (chiefly from the standpoint of American society) some of the roles that gifts play. He discusses in turn the gift as a generator of identity ('Gifts are one of the ways in which the pictures that others have of us in their minds are transmitted'); the gift as a personal tool in the aspiration for and protection of status and control (for example, gifts as 'conspicuous waste' to shame recipients); the gift as a 'gratitude imperative' in compelling reciprocity or controlling the behaviour of the recipient; and gift-exchange as a technique for the regulation of shared guilt.[1]

One common factor in all these roles is the absence of anonymity; givers and receivers have personally to know each other. This relationship does not exist in the case of blood in the vast majority of instances. If the principle of anonymity were generally abandoned (administratively, an immensely difficult task particularly in the case of pooled plasma and blood components) the consequences could be disastrous for givers and receivers as well as for all blood transfusion services.

It is, indeed, the particular and unique attributes of the blood gift which are responsible for provoking some fundamental issues, especially in those countries confronted with a shortage of voluntary donors prepared to give blood for strangers. These issues are discussed in later chapters.

III. A TYPOLOGY OF DONORS

In the following section, the main identifiable characteristics of different types of blood donors are classified under eight headings, partly to illustrate some of the problems involved in defining the 'voluntary donor'. In constructing this typology use has chiefly been made of information relating to systems and methods in the United States and England and Wales.[2] No attempt is made in this section to estimate the quantitative contributions made to the total supply of blood by each type of donor.

Type A: The Paid Donor

The donor who sells his blood for what the market will bear. He regards the selling of blood as in part or in whole a substitute for alternative ways of obtaining money. In no sense is it perceived by the seller or the buyer as a gift. It is a mechanical, impersonal

[1] Schwartz, B., 'The Social Psychology of the Gift', *Amer. J. Sociology*, Vol. 73, No. 1, July 1967, p. 1.

[2] Data relating to other countries are included in Chapters 10 and 11.

transaction conducted on a private market basis. The price will vary according to what are thought to be demand and supply situations (but accurate information about local 'markets' for different blood groups is not generally available to sellers), and according to categories of blood, their distribution and destruction through out-dating, and the effects of advertising.[1]

The treatment of blood as a market good thus sanctions the making of profits by blood bank buyers and distributors technically advised by members of the medical profession (in charging hospitals and patients); by the pharmaceutical industry in the sale, import and export of plasma and blood products, and by hospitals (in over-charging patients).[2]

As a market transaction, information that might have a bearing on the quality of the blood is withheld if possible from the buyer; such information could be detrimental to the price or the sale. Thus, in the United States blood group identification cards are loaned at a price to other sellers; blood is illegally mislabelled and updated; and other devices are adopted which make it very difficult to screen and exclude as donors drug addicts, alcoholics, and carriers of hepatitis, malaria and other diseases.[3] 'Many addicts', wrote Dr Norris and his colleagues, 'successfully conceal their addiction when examined for blood donation. Even granting that three-quarters of them will have one or more abnormal hepatic function tests, it is not feasible to use a group of these tests as a screening procedure for all blood donors.'[4] Another writer on the subject of truth concealment among paid donors concluded '. . . anyone who might need money to buy food and other necessities of life is a person who cannot be trusted'.[5]

The deliberate concealment of personal information—what one

[1] For example, 'Earn up to $200 per month in your spare time', 'A Bargain-Basement-Type Appeal in Miami Firm's Window' (Exhibit B, *Hearings on S. 1945, op. cit.,* 1967, p. 88). See also telephone directory advertisements for blood in New York and other cities.

[2] One case of a hospital in the United States making a $300,000 profit on blood in a year is reported in Sugrue, F., *A Slight Case of Life or Death, op. cit.*

[3] *Hearings on S. 2560, op. cit.,* 1964, pp. 44 and 184; *Hearings on S. 1945, op. cit.,* 1967, pp. 85–9; Sugrue, F., *op. cit.,* 1968, p. 13, and *Hepatitis Surveillance,* National Communicable Disease Center, Report 27, September 30, 1967, U.S. Public Health Service.

[4] Norris, R. F. *et al.,* 'Present Status of Hepatic Function Tests in Detection of Carriers of Viral Hepatitis', *Transfusion,* Vol. 3, 1963, p. 208. See also Chapter 8.

[5] Del Prete, F., *A Study of the IP Factor in Blood Donors* (presented to the Sixth Annual Meeting of the South Central Association of Blood Banks, Oklahoma City, March 1964), p. 5.

commentator described as the 'Avid Donor' in writing about the 'Integrity Factor'—is thus a particular characteristic of the paid blood donor and of the private market in blood generally, and one which is peculiarly not susceptible to control by public health departments or other authorities.[1] The question of control of standards raises the much broader issues of blood as an article of commerce; the legal, economic and ethical aspects of such issues are discussed in Chapter 9.

The paid donor has also been categorized by some writers as the 'mercenary donor'; one who is 'primarily motivated to donate by the prospect of a cash payment'.[2] He may attend regularly or irregularly; generally he is described in the United States as a 'walk-in donor'. In Latin America, Japan and other countries (as well as the United States) he may be described, for reasons that are obscure to the present writer and are likely to remain obscure, as a 'professional donor'.

Type B. The Professional Donor

With little justification we reserve the term 'professional donor' for those who yield blood on a regular, registered, semi-permanent or semi-salaried basis to distinguish them from the irregular, occasional, less frequent, 'walk-in donors'. They may be paid on a unit-fee basis but the actual payments are generally made weekly or monthly. In effect, some are part-time salaried and may receive, in addition, daily supplements of iron and medical supervision to ensure, if possible, high protein diets.

The great majority of these donors are suppliers once or twice a week to plasmapheresis programs (a process described in an earlier chapter) run by pharmaceutical firms and commercial blood banks in the United States.[3] They are not, of course, in any technical sense 'professionals'; they are not organized, there is no

---

[1] Some groups of blood buyers, organizing on conventional market lines, attempt to establish protective measures. Thus, in certain cities in the United States, in efforts to prevent paid donors from 'trying to give blood too frequently, each bank places a phosphorescent dye under the cuticle of a given finger after blood donation. This dye lasts approximately eight weeks and is visible under an ultraviolet light. At any bank, the presence of the dye on the finger of a prospective donor is a cause for rejection' (Dice, R. E., 'Paid Donor Programs', *Proc. A.M.A. Conference on Blood and Blood Banking*, Chicago, 1964).

[2] See, for example, Jennings, J. B., *op. cit.*, p. 94.

[3] See Chapter 6. Some plasmapheresis donors, double bled twice a week received $6240 per month in fees in 1968 (personal communication, Travenol Laboratories International, Morton Grove, Ill., November 19, 1968).

professional code of conduct,[1] and some are long-term prison 'volunteers' who 'usually need extensive supplementation of their diet'.[2]

Type C: The Paid-Induced Voluntary Donor

The donor who receives a cash payment but who claims that he is not primarily motivated by the payment. He acknowledges the community's need for blood but, unlike suppliers in Types A and B, he may have been induced to donate by group pressures at his place of work or in the community. Some unions in the United States, for example, offer $10 to $15 'to entice donors to give blood'.[3] These payments may form part of a process of stimulating 'competitive giving'; union groups compete with each other to reach monthly or yearly blood targets and employ money as a tool to induce giving. The groups that fail to reach their targets are presumed to experience guilt or shame.

Donors of this type expect to be paid for volunteering—paid for the trouble to which they have been put—and thus come to regard the payment either as a 'profit' or as a form of 'disturbance money'.

Although the distinction between Type C and Types A and B donors is a narrow one the main dividing line seems to be that the former are subject to personal group pressures whereas the latter are not. Individual spontaneity is not a dominant characteristic of Type C.

Type D: The Responsibility Fee Donor

Under a large variety of blood programs in the United States and other countries patients who have received blood are charged a fee variously called a 'responsibility' or 'replacement' or 'deposit' fee. The reason for the charge for the blood itself (quite apart from charges for processing and other technical procedures) is that if patients have not donated blood to the hospital (or associated institution like the Red Cross) then the hospital will 'lend' them the blood on condition that the loan is repaid in blood or money.

Having paid the fee which, for a serious operation, could involve

---

[1] Blood donor trade unions have, however, been organized in India and other countries (see Chapter 10). In Colombia, 'blood-selling rings' have been active. In 1964 it was reported in the American press that homeless young people had been killed by 'rings' who sold their blood to hospitals. In 1964 the price in Cali, Colombia, was said to be approximately $25 a quart (*Transfusion*, Vol. 4, 1964, p. 199).

[2] Kliman, A. and Lesses, F., 'Plasmapheresis as a Form of Blood Donation', *Transfusion*, Vol. 4, 1964, p. 470.

[3] Sugrue, F., *op. cit.*, 1968, p. 18.

25 units or more costing up to $1250 in 1968, patients can either (i) accept the situation (ii) replace the blood themselves and have the fee refunded (iii) find and persuade someone to replace the blood 'voluntarily' or for a cash payment and then have the fee refunded. The 'someone' could be a member of the family, a friend, a 'walk-in donor' or member of a blood plan group to which the patient belongs.

Such groups exist in large numbers in most areas of the United States. They make agreements with the American Red Cross (or other blood-collecting agency) on the number of units of blood the group will give each year. The quota is set to provide for the anticipated blood requirements of the members of the group and their families. The definition of the family presents difficulties; other problems encountered include geographical mobility (most groups are based on the workplace or membership of a local union, church, or community organization); the inability of some adults to donate on grounds of health, old age and many other factors, and the exclusion from coverage of 'high risk' cases, e.g. haemophiliacs, ulcer cases, those requiring open heart surgery, etc.[1]

The blood charge on patients—or 'responsibility fee deposit'—is, it is argued, a means of enforcing, through sickness, a moral obligation to donate blood.[2] Some hospitals carry the principle further by not offering the choice of blood or money and demand that patients pay for their transfusions in blood.[3]

Replacement charges are deliberately fixed at a high level irrespective of whether the patient can pay—generally above 'true' market costs as measured by what the hospital pays a 'walk-in donor' or commercial blood bank—so as to discipline the patient and his relations and to provide a strong financial incentive to repay the loan in blood.[4]

[1] On coverage, membership terms, exclusions, etc., see literature issued by, for example, the Co-operative Blood Replacement Plan, Chicago; the New York Blood Center; the Jewish War Veterans, New York; The Presbytery of New York City, and Segura, F., *op. cit.*, pp. 64–77.

[2] Patients, it is reported, 'often prefer to pay because they do not wish to ask other individuals to assist them by donating blood' (Southwest Blood Banks Inc. brochure, now known as Blood Services, Arizona, 1965).

[3] Leger, R. R., *Wall Street Journal*, March 1, 1967.

[4] A survey in 1961 of 311 members of the American Association of Blood Banks with a total usage of 1,539,045 units of blood showed a range of blood replacement fees from $7 to $50 with a weighted mean of $22.46. Processing fees of up to $30 represented additional charges per unit. Since 1961 all fees have risen substantially (*Transfusion*, Vol. 4, No. 3, May–June 1964).

Replacement-in-blood policies vary considerably; many hospitals and banks apply a two-for-one ratio, i.e. for every unit of blood used the patient is required to replace two units. Some impose a three-for-one rule. The patient is therefore charged for these units plus processing fees. Even the Defense Department has to arrange for two servicemen (giving a unit of blood each) to attend local blood banks in order to obtain one unit for its own medical needs.[1]

The basis for these policies is that losses—or waste—vaguely described by many hospital authorities as 'attrition', occurring in the whole blood banking system should be borne by the patient. The assumption is that waste in the system (over which the sick have no control) should be paid for by the sick. To encourage, therefore, replacement-in-blood donors the price for the units is fixed at a high level (in 1961 some hospitals were charging as much as $100 a pint[2]).

The additional units are required to cover: (a) administrative and technical waste in blood usage (including outdated blood); the profit practices of commercial blood banks in refusing to accept the return of outdated blood; research needs; the policies of some hospitals to make profits in particular departments of hospital administration in order to meet deficits in other departments; the preferences of rich patients to pay for their blood by cheque thus increasing the need for others to supply blood; and the need to provide blood for 'indigents' who have neither money nor kin and for reasons of age or disability cannot themselves repay the loan in kind.[3]

It has been found, however, that: 'It is most difficult to explain to a patient that in any of these instances, the second replacement is a *privilege* (original italics) extended by the hospital to assist the patient in paying for a laboratory service and not a form of usury'. It is also very hard to justify to patients, within the context of systems which heavily underline individual responsibility for blood replacement, a higher than a one-for-one ratio on the grounds that the hospital is attempting to meet the needs of 'blood indigents'. Some hospitals, therefore, adopt the method of deliberately outdating a

---

[1] *Hearings on S. 1945, op. cit.*, 1967, p. 95.

[2] *Hearings on S. 2560, op. cit.*, 1964, p. 159.

[3] *Hearings on S. 2560, op. cit.*, 1964, pp. 21, 53, 92 and 97; *Hearings on S. 1945, op. cit.*, 1967, pp. 10, 43, 80–1, 162 and 182–3; Mainwaring, R. L., 'Blood Banking Economics', *Proc. A.M.A. Conference on Blood and Blood Banking, Chicago*, 1964, and Wolf, R., *Seattle Magazine*, Vol. 5, No. 46, January 1968.

specified percentage of blood credits (advance donations) each year—a dubious commercial procedure.[1]

The relations of a patient undergoing open-heart surgery (or many other operations requiring substantial transfusions) may thus, as 'Responsibility Fee Donors', have to provide up to 60 pints of blood (equivalent to a 30-year blood debt for one donor at two donations a year) or pay the fee which, for the blood alone, could be in the region of $1500 to $6000.[2] The relatives of haemophiliac patients cannot even begin to find replacements; the treatment given free under the National Health Service in England to 41 haemophiliac patients requiring dental extractions needed a total of 3321 units of blood.[3]

In the following chapter we discuss whether 'Responsibility Fee Donors' can be classified as 'voluntary' donors. This question arose when the Medicare Hospital Insurance Program was being determined in Washington. As a result of strong pressure from blood bank representatives a 'blood deductible' was included in the provisions of the legislation. They argued that aged patients would not have any incentive to replace the blood or components they received if they did not have to pay for blood they failed to persuade others to replace. Without a financial penalty, it was said, blood supplies in the United States could be seriously endangered.[4]

Under the present law (1968), therefore, aged patients must replace or pay for each of the first three pints of blood (or packed red cells) they receive during each spell of illness (or benefit period) on a pint-for-pint basis. This blood deductible also applies to the supplementary medical insurance program and there is in addition

---

[1] Mason, C. C. and Kyler, W. S., 'Cost Analysis in Blood Banking', Chicago Blood Donor Services, Inc., Chicago, 1964, pp. 2–3.

[2] Normal practice in the United States is for the hospital or blood bank to send a letter to the 'patient's nearest-of-kin informing them of their replacement responsibility' (Hemphill, B. M., 'Blood for Open Heart Surgery', *Transfusion*, Vol. 2, No. 2, March–April 1962). Anthropologists undertaking field work have fewer difficulties in the collection o. data than students of social policy attempting to unravel the complexities of blood indebtedness in circumstances of death, divorce, marriage and remarriage—particularly in areas where blood is segregated on racial lines.

[3] Biggs, R. and Macfarlane, R. G. (eds), *Treatment of Haemophilia and other Coagulation Disorders*, Blackwell, Oxford, 1966, p. 159. See also Chapter 12.

[4] See, for example, *Executive Hearings Before the Committee on Ways and Means;* House of Representatives, on H.R.I. andOther Proposals for Medical Care of the Aged, 89th Congress, 1st Session, Part 2, 1965, pp. 767–70. For similar reasons, the average Blue Cross patient does not have blood coverage from the Blue Cross (*Hearings on S. 2560, op. cit.*, 1964, p. 80).

a $50 deductible per year for all covered expenses and 20 per cent co-insurance.[1]

In the first year of medicare operations (to September 1967) about one million units of blood were transfused for about one-third of a million aged medicare hospital admissions. About 2 per cent of all the medicare patients used well over half of all the blood transfused to medicare patients. Only about 25 per cent of the blood was replaced.[2] The financial incentive to enforce the giving of blood does not, therefore, appear to be very effective among the relatives and friends of elderly patients.

Type E: The Family Credit Donor
The eligible donor who makes a predeposit donation of one pint of blood each year in return for which he and his family (dependent and unmarried children up to age 19) are 'insured' for their blood needs for one year. Some of these credit plans provide extended coverage for an additional pint to include parents and grandparents on both sides of the family. Again, in some plans, those who are medically ineligible may pay either $10 or more a year or find an eligible donor who will donate in their name. But most plans exclude blood benefits from those having, on the date of enrolment, specified diseases and 'ailments'.[3]

These plans, it is said, relieve people of 'the worry of finding replacement donors'.[4] They are organized on an individual or group basis through the American Red Cross, the Blue Cross Community Blood Program, and other blood-collecting agencies on the same lines as for Responsibility Fee Donors.

Built into these programs is the model of the 'good husband-father'; the 'good' provider of blood; middle-class, puritan, thrifty, family-centred and insurance-minded.[5] The sanctions applied are a

[1] See *Your Medicare Handbook* (p. 31), Social Security Administration, Dept. of Health, Education, and Welfare, May 1968.

[2] Analysis supplied to the author by the Division of Policy and Standards, Bureau of Health Insurance, Social Security Administration, Baltimore, U.S.A., October 1968.

[3] Or, alternatively, they impose long waiting periods. There is usually a lengthy list of excluded 'bad risks', e.g. malignancies, haemophilia, blood diseases, cardiovascular diseases requiring surgery, congenital defects, active tuberculosis, aplastic anaemia, any disease or ailment for which a blood transfusion was required within the previous year, etc.

[4] For example, Cooperative Blood Replacement Plan, Inc., Chicago, brochure, 1966.

[5] 'Once upon a time there was an expectant father. He started off like any normal expectant father, but turned out to be quite a hero.' This was because

mixture of financial penalties (in the form of higher replacement donations or charges fixed in excess of 'true' economic costs) and shame in not fulfilling a familial function. In some parts of the United States it is, however, said that 'no stigma is attached' to the replacement of blood by money.[1] There are also many group blood assurance systems modelled on the same predeposit or credit bases. They are generally organized by employers.[2]

A more impersonal variant of these systems of obtaining blood and meeting blood charges is represented by the specialized blood insurance company. Blood policies indemnify policy holders against processing, cross-matching and administrative fees (up to a limit per transfusion) and cover blood transfusions for certain specified conditions.[3] Insurance premiums may in some plans be paid in blood (but not in certain states, e.g. Georgia).

Donors of the family credit type are sometimes described as 'lenders of blood'. These 'loans', or deposits or credits expire, however, at the end of one year. Normally, they carry no interest. The reason for this particular period of time is that a longer time-span of credit would bankrupt the system; human blood declines in value faster than money; in other words, there would not be enough blood forthcoming to maintain the surgical and medical services of the United States.[4]

The growth of blood insurance policy programs under which the premiums are paid in money has been heavily attacked on the

'our daddy-to-be had the foresight to establish blood credit for mother and baby' (the Maternity Care Plan of The New York Blood Center, brochure, 1966).

[1] Southwest Blood Banks, Inc., *op. cit.*

[2] Under many plans the basic required blood donation approximates to an annual donation of the number of units of blood equal to 20 per cent of the total number of employees, retired employees or members (see, for example, sales literature issued by the Blood Services Plan Insurance Company, Scottsdale, Arizona, 1966).

[3] Transfusions resulting from pre-existing leukemia, ulcers, cancer, aplastic anaemia, haemophilia and congenital cardiovascular disease requiring surgery are excluded. There may also be a 90-day wait on other transfusions excluding accidents (see, for example, sales literature issued by the Blood Service Plan Insurance Company, Scottsdale, Arizona, 1966).

[4] There is also the problem of inter-community, inter-employer and inter-state transferability of blood rights, deposits and credits. Given a situation in which there are thousands of individual, different and constantly changing plans, the difficulties of arranging transferability are clearly immense. Even where transferability is possible many hospitals will not accept 'paper credits' and insist on the direct shipment of blood. For these reasons there is a considerable volume of inter-state shipments by plane, truck, bus, taxi and other forms of transportation.

grounds that they undermine individual and family responsibility; that they are destructive of the spirit of voluntary giving; that they encourage the use of paid and professional suppliers of blood, and that eventually they could lead to an alarming shortage of blood in the United States. In 1967 it was reported that 'in many places hospitals are ignoring the policies and asking for blood to replace blood used, often on a two-for-one basis, instead of accepting the cash payment provided by the policies'.[1] Hospitals, it was pointed out, are not bound by any agreement between an insurance company and a policyholder.

Considering all the pressures, sanctions and penalties involved, donors of the Family Credit Type cannot be classified as spontaneous, altruistic donors.

Type F: The Captive Voluntary Donor

Donors in positions of restraint and subordinate authority who are called upon, required or expected to donate. If they do not they may be exposed to disapproval or shame, or they may be led to believe that refusal would adversely affect their future in some form or another. The moral pressures applied, by institutional authority and/or by the relevant social group, are often a complex mixture of penalties and rewards. The latter may take the form of money, non-monetary benefits or both and sometimes (as with prison donors) a remission of sentence.

Such donors as a category cannot be described, relatively speaking, as 'free agents', though there may well be men and women in these positions of subordinate authority who are (or would be) genuine volunteers in the sense that if they were released from authority (e.g. the Defense Forces or prison) and then donated without reward they would be described as Voluntary Community Donors (Type H).

The main groups of Captive Voluntary Donors are found in the Defense Forces, prisons and similar institutions.

In both the United States and England, prisoners donate blood though the numbers and proportions differ considerably as do the penalties and rewards and circumstances in which blood is given (in Chapters 6 and 7 we attempt to estimate the number of Captive Voluntary Donors in both countries).

In England the policy is to treat prisoners (and prison staff)

---

[1] *Hearings on S. 1945, op. cit.*, 1967, pp. 91–2. See also statement by the American Medical Association, *Hearings on S. 2560, op. cit.*, 1964, pp. 82–7, and Adashek, E. P., 'Blood Assurance Plans', *Proc. A.M.A. Conference on Blood and Blood Banking*, Chicago, 1964, p. 5.

like other members of the community and give them the opportunity to volunteer if they wish to do so. It is made clear, according to official policy, that whether they do or do not will not affect their prison sentences or grading; there are no tangible rewards, monetary or non-monetary. What is not known, and could not be ascertained without research, is how prisoners themselves view these arrangements.

In the United States, policy varies considerably from state to state and institution to institution, though judging by the numbers involved it seems that the use of prisoners as donors is widespread and may possibly be increasing.[1] Some donors are paid $5 or more a unit, on the understanding that no remission of sentence would be considered by Parole Boards. 'However', wrote Professor J. Garrott Allen, 'inevitably this sort of thing did weigh favorably on their records and the prisoners were well aware of it, despite the Parole Board's disclaimers and denials'.[2]

In California, Professor J. P. Conrad reports that there are 'three classes of incentives operating. Some donors receive $4 a pint (at the current rate) and donate as often as they are allowed to. Some donors contribute to blood banks, thereby accruing credit for their institution on the blood bank account. Undoubtedly there may be some effect accruing to a donor as a public-spirited person if he contributes under the second category, which may be taken into consideration in setting his term. There is no direct provision for remitting any part of the sentence on account of blood donation. Further, there have been a number of cases where patients, with unusual medical conditions requiring large amounts of blood, have been beneficiaries of drives at one institution or another to provide the abnormal amount of blood necessary. In such cases blood is donated gratis and the patient is "adopted" as a sort of ward of the institution'.[3]

In other states provision is made for remission of sentences. In the Commonwealth of Massachusetts, for example, an Act was

[1] See, for example, the studies of Professor J. Garrott Allen at the University of Chicago Clinics (involving a total of over 70,000 blood units) showing that the proportion of 'prison bloods to all bloods given' rose from nil in 1946-8 and 5 per cent in 1949-50 to approximately 75 per cent in 1959 (later figures are not available). Allen, J. Garrott, 'Post-Transfusion Hepatitis: A Serious Clinical Problem', *Calif. Med.*, 104: 293-9, April 1966, and 'The Advantages of the Single Transfusion', *Ann. of Surg.*, Vol. 164, No. 3, 1966).

[2] Personal communication, December 20, 1966.

[3] Personal communication, Professor J. P. Conrad, Chief, Research Division, Department of Corrections, California, January 26, 1967.

passed in 1965 whereby a prisoner 'of any correctional institution or jail or house of correction whose term of imprisonment is thirty days or more may have his sentence reduced by five days for each pint of blood donated by him . . .'.[1] Prisoners are limited to one donation every three months and any reduction of sentence so earned 'shall not be subject to forfeiture'. The Act forbids blood so donated being used commercially or for a profit.

In many states, however, blood obtained from prisons is used for commercial purposes.[2] The first plasmapheresis program started by Cutter Laboratories, a pharmaceutical firm of Berkeley, California, began in a prison setting.[3] In Georgia, in 1966–7, a local hospital seeking blood and a pharmaceutical firm were 'clashing head-on' for the rights to obtain blood from prisoners in the Reidsville State Prison.[4] By 1968 'bids' or tenders were being made in various areas by pharmaceutical firms operating plasmapheresis methods and other commercial interests for monopoly rights over prison blood.[5]

In terms of ethical principles, therefore, there is a fundamental difference in the official policies adopted in regard to prison donors in the United States and England.

There are also marked differences in the policies operating in relation to donors who are members of the Defense Forces.[6] In England, organized opportunities are provided from time to time for members of the Forces to donate blood like everyone else

[1] The Commonwealth of Massachusetts, Ch. 317, Section 129A, April 1965. According to Dr E. A. Dreskin, President in 1966 of the American Association of Blood Banks, 'South Carolina and Mississippi offer a five-day discount on prison sentences if the prisoner donates blood' (*New York Times*, October 29, 1966).

[2] The question of liability of the civil authorities having custody of prisoners for reactions or accidents sustained as a result of donating blood is discussed in *Transfusion*, Vol. 6, No. 6, November–December 1966, p. 614.

[3] *Conference on Plasmapheresis*, *op. cit.*, 1966, p. 48.

[4] Leger, R. R., *Wall Street Journal*, March 1, 1967.

[5] Personal communication, Mr K. W. Forbes, Marketing Staff Assistant, Travenol Laboratories International, Morton Grove, Illinois, December 2, 1968. Clinical trials and experimental studies in the plasmapheresis field have also been carried out in the United States on 'male volunteer prisoners' and 'paid male volunteers' involving the injection of Rh-positive cells followed by IgG anti-D (World Health Organization, 'Report on the Clinical Use of Human Anti-D IgG in the Prevention of Haemolytic Disease of the Newborn', stencilled, IMM/Inf/Rh/66/1, 1966).

[6] Considerable use is made of 'volunteers' from the Defense Forces in certain countries in Europe and the Soviet bloc (see Chapter 10).

without reward, monetary or non-monetary. It may well be, of course, that had they not been in the Forces they would not have volunteered. This is but one aspect of the problem of defining a completely voluntary act in society.

In the United States, however, many members of the Defense Forces appear to be rewarded in a number of ways: some are asked to volunteer at local blood banks where they are paid as 'walk-in donors' or where they receive credits;[1] some receive additional leave, and others receive additional food (steak is reported to figure prominently in such inducement meals).

Captive donors of this type undergoing various degrees of pressure and constraint, though some may be strongly moved by a sense of giving, particularly when blood is needed by hospitals treating members of the Defense Forces and their dependants, cannot in general be said to be performing a free, spontaneous act.[2] The ethical issues involved in the use of donors under conditions of constraint (particularly kidney donors in American prisons) are discussed in detail in *Ethics in Medical Progress*.[3] We return to these issues in a later chapter.

A further element in the concept of the Captive Voluntary Donor which is linked to the question of authority and subordination is represented by the problem of 'race relations'. This may be seen in the operations of the blood transfusion services in South Africa. A field study at the University of Natal *Blood Donation: The Attitudes and Motivation of Urban Bantu in Durban* showed many of the cultural and political limitations to the concept of the volunteer in such societies. In the eyes of the Bantu (who were not paid donors in Durban) the white man was taking his blood. 'It is remarkable that again and again the observers noted that many donors did not seem to understand fully why they were donating.' Ignorance was one factor, fear another; fear of the needle, fear of losing blood, fear of losing their job. 'They informed me that they did not like the idea of being forced to give away their blood. They have always refused to donate in the past, but this year for reasons unknown to them they were forced to come. "Why did you come if you were not

[1] Some communities face critical problems of blood supply when defense bases are moved or are phased-out (Dreskin, E. A., 'Blood Deposit Plans', *Proc. Annual Meeting of the AABB*, Los Angeles, October 1966).

[2] Butterfield, B., 'Operation "Open Heart": A Military Volunteer Donor Recruitment Program', *Proc. 8th Congr. Int. Soc. Blood Tranf.*, Tokyo, 1960, pp. 526–30, 1962; Allen, J. G., *op. cit.*, and Jennings, J. B., *op. cit.*, p. 125.

[3] Wolstenholme, G. E. W. and O'Connor, M., *op. cit.*

prepared to donate, despite being forced?" I asked. They were afraid of losing their jobs, so they had to come.'[1]

Type G: The Fringe Benefit Voluntary Donor

Donors who volunteer who are attracted or induced by the prospect of tangible rewards (other than medals and 'thank you' certificates) in non-monetary forms. The most general ones are: days off work on full pay; longer holidays; free holidays in 'rest homes' and other holiday centres; free meals after donating (for which there is no medical justification); iron, vitamin supplements and free medical care (for plasmapheresis donors in the United States); priority cards for medical consultations and hospital care (particularly in the U.S.S.R. and other East European countries); free baseball and football tickets (in the United States) and other forms of prizes and benefits.

Many of these fringe benefits are common in the U.S.S.R. where it is reported that about one-half of all blood donations are drawn from donors of this type and one-half from paid donors (in 1965 the pay for an average donation was 15 to 25 roubles or $17 to $28).[2] Fringe Benefit Donors are also to be found in substantial numbers in Eastern Europe, some Western European countries, the United States and some Latin American and African countries.[3]

When translated into money terms, some of these benefits for 'volunteers' are worth more than the prevailing rates of cash pay in the United States and the U.S.S.R. Further information and illustrations of the value of fringe benefits are provided in Chapter 10.

Type H: The Voluntary Community Donor

This type is the closest approximation in social reality to the abstract concept of a 'free human gift'. The primary characteristics of such donations are: the absence of tangible immediate rewards in monetary or non-monetary forms; the absence of penalties, financial or otherwise; and the knowledge among donors that their donations

---

[1] Watts, H. L. and Shearing, D. C., *Blood Donation: The Attitudes and Motivation of Urban Bantu in Durban*, Institute of Social Research, University of Natal, 1966, pp. 46–9. These matters are further discussed in Chapter 11.

[2] Vaughn, J., 'Blood Transfusion in the U.S.S.R.: Notes on a Short Visit'. *Transfusion*, No. 3, May–June 1967, pp. 212–29 and Wolstenholme, G. E. W., *op. cit.*, pp. 31–2.

[3] League of Red Cross Societies, IIIrd Red Cross International Seminar on Blood Transfusion, Medico-Social Documentation No. 27, Geneva, 1966, and Miller, G. W., 'International Aspects of Blood Banking', *Proc. A.M.A. Conference on Blood and Blood Banking*, Chicago, 1964.

are for unnamed strangers without distinction of age, sex, medical condition, income, class, religion or ethnic group.

No donor type can, of course, be said to be characterized by complete, disinterested, spontaneous altruism. There must be some sense of obligation, approval and interest; some awareness of need and of the purposes of the blood gift; perhaps some organized group rivalry in generosity; some knowledge that fellow-members of the community who are young or old or sick cannot donate, and some expectation and assurance that a return gift may be needed and received at some future time (as with Mauss's examples of gift-exchange in other societies). Nevertheless, in terms of the free gift of blood to unnamed strangers there is no formal contract, no legal bond, no situation of power, domination, constraint or compulsion, no sense of shame or guilt, no gratitude imperative, no need for penitence, no money and no explicit guarantee of or wish for a reward or a return gift. They are acts of free will; of the exercise of choice; of conscience without shame.

Virtually all donors in Britain and donors in some systems in a number of other European countries fall into this category.[1]

From this attempt to set out a typology of blood donors we can see that there are variations in the concept of the volunteer and many gradations of motives and behaviour from extremes of Types A–B to Type H. Moreover, in any comparative study of gift-exchange in modern societies, especially in such a deeply emotive field as human blood, the pattern of social responses is also seen to be inextricably moulded by cultural and moral values.

What do we know about the expressed motives for giving or not giving blood in different societies in differently organized structures of blood transfusion institutions? The simple answer is that we know very little for there have been few studies of any depth and scholarship. The two or three attempts which have been made to explore such questions are discussed in a later chapter where we also analyse the results of a field study of blood donors and their characteristics and motives in England in 1967.

First, however, we must set out what information is available concerning the social characteristics of blood donors in the United States and England and Wales.

[1] With the exception of a small minority of donors in prison and the Armed Forces. Tangible rewards in Britain may be said to be either minimal or negative: a cup of tea provided by other volunteers (often those who are too old to donate), and the reimbursement of travel expenses but only if such reimbursement is requested by donors.

Chapter 6

The Characteristics of Blood Donors in the United States

I

In the previous chapter we constructed a typology of blood donors. This attempt to classify the attributes of donors or suppliers of blood also took account of the pattern of values underlying different motivation and recruitment systems, monetary and contractual, non-monetary and non-contractual.

We now consider how the actual distribution and characteristics of donors in the United States and England and Wales relate to this typology. To what extent can donors in the two countries be allocated to one of the eight types A to H? We set out first what is known about the characteristics of donors in the United States, and begin with some estimates of the numbers falling within certain types.

II. THE UNITED STATES: THE NATIONAL PICTURE

Taking cognisance of double-counting, under- and over-reporting, the inter-state shipment of blood and other factors discussed in Chapter 4, we shall build our estimates of type distributions on the basis of a national annual collection total for the years 1965-6-7 of 6,000,000 units. We exclude from this figure collections by the Defense Services for their own needs in Vietnam and elsewhere, and we also exclude at this stage collections by commercial blood banks and the pharmaceutical industry for plasmapheresis programs (analysed separately later in this chapter).

It seems probable on the basis of the evidence provided in Chapter 4 that after excluding the plasmapheresis programs there was some decline in the national total of units collected between 1961-4 and 1967. When account is taken of changes in the size, age and sex structure of the population it can be concluded with more assurance that there was a decline between 1961 and 1967 per 1000 population (weighted) of the United States. For the purposes of this analysis of characteristics, we begin with the estimate of 6,000,000 units bled from donors and suppliers.

Of this total, the American Red Cross accounted for 2,932,700 units in the year ended June 30, 1967.[1] Collections from members of the Defense Forces represented 7·6 per cent and from prisons 2·2 per cent of the Red Cross total. For reasons given in Chapter 5, these units (in all 287,400) are allocated to type F (the Captive Voluntary Donor).

Of the remaining units (2,645,300) the Red Cross report that 'most of the blood collected by the Red Cross is the result of some kind of an assurance plan'[2] in the community or at plants and firms. In other words, these are 'tied' voluntary donors under a variety of local plans involving some form of replacement (in blood at the rate of 1 for 1 or more or in money), responsibility or family credit deposit arrangement.[3] If we interpret 'most' as 80 per cent—although there is evidence pointing to a higher figure—then we have to allocate 2,116,200 units to Types D (the Responsibility Fee Donor) and E (the Family Credit Donor). For some of these donations 'inducement' cash will have been paid but as no statistics exist we subtract only 1 per cent (211,600 units) and allot them to Type C (the Paid-Induced Voluntary Donor). We are then left with a balance of 529,100 units of which we allocate 95 per cent or 502,600 to Type H (the Voluntary Community Donor) and 5 per cent or 26,500 to Type G (the Fringe Benefit Voluntary Donor).[4]

It was made clear in Chapter 4 that detailed information about the operations of commercial blood banks is inadequate. A large number of such banks, officially licensed by the public health authorities, did not report their collections in the 1961, 1964 and 1967 surveys. Before the results of the last survey had been analysed the American Medical Association, in evidence to a Senate Com-

[1] Collected for civilian use (*Annual Report*, American National Red Cross, 1967).

[2] Personal communication, Dr A. S. Chrisman, Deputy Medical Director, Blood Program, American Red Cross, January 19, 1967.

[3] No payment is made by the Red Cross to donors but hospitals are charged a collection and delivery fee (called a 'participation fee') of $9 a unit on average in 1968.

[4] This is most probably a conservative estimate. It is known that many donors receive days off work, free meals, etc., from organized groups and employers but no precise statistics are available. In 1967 25·6 per cent of all donations were collected at workplaces (*Blood Center Operations 1967*, American National Red Cross).

91

mittee in 1967, estimated that commercial banks supplied 'approximately 20 per cent of the blood that is used in this country'.[1] Related to collections, the percentage might be lower or higher depending on differences in wastage rates in different sectors of the blood banking system.[2]

In Chapter 4, in analysing the 1967 survey, we showed that between 1964 and 1967 there had been an increase of 119 per cent in collections by the larger commercial blood banks throughout the United States. An unknown proportion of this increase was probably attributable to increased sales to the pharmaceutical industry. On balance, therefore, there would seem to have been some substantial expansion in the operations of commercial blood banks in recent years. However, although the estimate of 20 per cent is most certainly on the low side for collections we accept it at this stage for purposes of this analysis. We thus have to allocate 1,200,000 units to Types A and B.[3] All commercial bank donors (including an unknown proportion in prison) are paid.

After deducting from the 6,000,000 units the Red Cross and commercial bank collections we are thus left with a balance of 1,867,300 units. These are provided by two sources, hospital blood banks and community blood banks. Because of overlapping functions and conflicting interpretations of what constitutes a 'hospital bank' (which, as a hospital, may serve a community) and what constitutes a 'community bank' (which may serve a hospital) it is difficult to determine the respective contributions of these two sectors. Accepting first, however, the figures for the Red Cross and commercial banks we have to apply certain estimated proportions to the balance to arrive at the number of units contributed by hospital and community banks. Mr J. B. Jennings, in his analysis of blood banking systems, used percentages of 31 per cent (hospital) and 19 per cent (community).[4] We apply these proportions in allocating the balance of 1,867,300 units.

Hospital blood banks are thus allocated an annual collection of 1,157,700 units. In 1957 (the latest national data available) 20 per cent of hospital units were obtained from paid donors (Types A and B). It seems that this proportion increased significantly

---

[1] *Hearings on S. 1945, op. cit.*, p. 10.

[2] In the context in which the evidence was given it can be assumed that this estimate excluded plasma collections in plasmapheresis programs.

[3] Approximately 100,000 units were collected in New York City alone in 1966 by commercial blood banks (see p. 113).

[4] Jennings, J. B., *op. cit.*, pp. 39 and 42.

between 1957 and 1965–7; hospitals in many cities and areas were reporting in the 1960s considerably higher proportions, and were also drawing on paid donors in prisons.[1] Also, the average replacement fee per unit charged in hospitals to patients rose substantially, suggesting that more of the blood procured by hospitals had to be paid for.[2] Allowing, therefore, for some increase we assume a paid donor proportion of 25 per cent in 1965–7 (289,400 units a year).

The balance is very largely accounted for by responsibility, replacement and family credit donors (Types D and E).[3] Perhaps 2 per cent of hospital donors (23,200) in 1965–7 should be allocated to Type H (the Voluntary Community Donor). A similar proportion has been allocated to Type F (the Captive Voluntary Donor) for donations from members of the Defense Forces and prisoners.

The remaining units (709,600)[4] were collected by community blood banks of many different kinds using a combination of donor sources; paid and professional, paid-induced voluntary, captive voluntary, replacement and family credit and voluntary community donors.[5]

A statistical analysis by the writer of the American Medical Association's 1964 Directory showed that 35 per cent of all donations to community blood banks were bought in 1964 (questions about

[1] It was shown in Table 2 (Chapter 4) that the larger hospital and community blood banks who reported in 1964 that 50 per cent or more of their donors were paid registered an increase of 45 per cent in collections between 1961–7. This percentage increase was substantially higher than that registered by the Red Cross (18 per cent); the smaller hospital and community blood banks registered a decrease of 21 per cent.

[2] See American Association of Blood Banks, *Survey on Blood Bank Fees 1960*, *Transfusion*, Vol. 4, No. 3, May–June 1964 and American Medical Association, *Guide for Medical Society Committees on Blood* (brochure), 1966.

[3] In 1957 81 per cent of all hospitals surveyed operated replacement policies (*Joint Blood Council Report, op. cit.*, pp. 28 and 44). In 1960 practically all hospitals reporting to the A.A.B.B. had such policies (for reference see preceding footnote).

[4] This figure is lower than the total reporting in the A.A.B.B. survey and other estimates. The probable explanation of the difference is that a substantial number of units classified in this analysis under hospital banks might have been included here under community banks. The main effect, however, is to allocate a smaller proportion of donations to donor Types A and B.

[5] Some so-called non-profit community blood banks are controlled by local physicians who require patients to replace two or even three pints for every pint used and some also refuse to accept Red Cross credits. This is but one example of the problem of classifying banks and types of donors (see *Hearings on S. 2560, op. cit.*, pp. 182–3).

payment were excluded from the 1967 survey). We thus allocate 248,400 units to Types A and B. No further classifications as to donor types are given in the Directories for 1964 and 1967.

All the available evidence suggests that most of the balance (461,200 units) was collected under a variety of replacement, family credit and assurance plans (unlike the Red Cross a much smaller proportion was obtained from the Defense Forces). Mr Jennings, in his survey, concluded that community blood banks ' . . . are generally unable to motivate many purely voluntary donations and

TABLE 4

Estimates of Source of Blood Collected by Type,
United States, 1965–7

(annual figures)

Type	Number of units	%
A. The Paid Donor ⎫		
B. The Professional Donor ⎬	1,737,800	29
C. The Paid-Induced Voluntary Donor	211,600	4
D. The Responsibility Fee Donor[1] ⎫		
E. The Family Credit Donor[1] ⎬	3,138,000	52
F. The Captive Voluntary Donor	324,800	5
G. The Fringe Benefit Voluntary Donor	26,500	1
H. The Voluntary Community Donor[2]	561,300	9
	6,000,000	100

[1] A high proportion of these donors participate in blood assurance or insurance programs.

[2] If the facts were known some proportion of these units would probably have to be transferred to Type G.

therefore depend on the incentive provided by a blood insurance or assurance plan'.[1] Accordingly, and in the light of other information derived from many of the sources quoted in this chapter and in chapters 4 and 5, we allocate 5 per cent to Type H (The Voluntary Community Donor), 2 per cent to Type F (the Captive Voluntary Donor)[2] and 58 per cent to Types D and E (Responsibility Fee and Family Credit Donors).

There are so many inadequacies, gaps and errors in the statistical data that at various points we have been forced to employ what

[1] Jennings, J. B., *op. cit.*, p. 40.
[2] Some of these donors from the Defense Forces were also paid (see p. 104 in this chapter).

one can only call 'informed guesswork' based on months of work tabulating, checking and comparing the statistics in all the survey reports since 1956. In general, we believe we have erred on the conservative side in our estimates of the proportions of paid supplies. However, with these cautions in mind, we now sum up these approximate figures (see Table 4).

This table shows that about one-third of all donations were bought and sold.[1] Approximately 52 per cent were 'tied' by contracts of various kinds; they represented the contracted repayment in blood of blood debts, encouraged or enforced by monetary penalties; some of these donors will have themselves benefited financially, and some will have paid other donors to provide the blood. About 5 per cent were captive voluntary donors—members of the Defense Forces and prisoners. About 9 per cent approximated to the concept of the voluntary community donor who sees his donation as a free gift to strangers in society.

There are many myths in all societies and America is no exception. One of the most deeply held myths in that country today—as preceding chapters have illustrated—is that the voluntary donor is the norm; that most blood donations are contributed by volunteers.

The growth in recent years of plasmapheresis programs operated by commercial banks and pharmaceutical firms has had the effect of making the contribution of the voluntary donor an even less significant one in the United States. Later in this chapter we bring together the results of an inquiry in 1968 addressed to pharmaceutical companies and other commercial organizations operating such programs. Broadly, this shows an annual total of over 1,000,000 donations representing a yield of something like 2,000,000 units of plasma for fractionation to commercial blood products (i.e. albumin, gamma globulin, fibrinogen, Factor VIII, IX and fibrinolysin). All these supplies were bought; some from registered, quasi-salaried donors, some from 'walk-in', irregular and occasional donors. In all, perhaps 400,000 or so different individuals are paid for this yield of 2,000,000 units a year.

We now have to add these estimates to the totals in Table 4. The effect is to raise the annual national collection total to 8,000,000 units and the combined figure for Types A and B to 3,737,800 units. The adjusted percentages are:

[1] After this analysis had been completed one large pharmaceutical firm estimated, in correspondence, that on the basis of 6,000,000 collections a year 'one-third are paid donors' (Travenol Laboratories International, November 5, 1968).

TABLE 5

Estimates of Source of Blood (including Plasmapheresis Programs) Collected by Type, United States, 1965-7

Type	%
A. The Paid Donor	
B. The Professional Donor	47
C. The Paid-Induced Voluntary Donor	3
D. The Responsibility Fee Donor	
E. The Family Credit Donor	39
F. The Captive Voluntary Donor	4
G. The Fringe Benefit Voluntary Donor	0
H. The Voluntary Community Donor	7
	100

On the basis of 8,000,000 units a year, approximately one-half are bought and sold. The contribution of the voluntary community donor is only 7 per cent.

Apart from the great increase in paid plasma donations, all the evidence we have brought together suggests that the proportion of paid donations in the country as a whole has increased in recent years. Some of this evidence in the form of opinions and generalizations by leaders in the blood banking field has already been cited in earlier chapters. Much of it was summed up in 1967 in statements to a Senate Committee.[1]

Ten years earlier the Joint Blood Council survey had estimated the proportion of paid donations for the country as a whole at about 14–17 per cent.[2] It would seem, therefore, from Table 4 that the proportion has doubled and, if the 2,000,000 plasma donations are included, trebled.

The only other trend figures that have been published relate to New York City. The proportions of paid donations were: 1952 15 per cent; 1956 42 per cent; 1966 55 per cent.[3] The proportion of voluntary community donations fell from 20 per cent in 1956 to about 1 per cent in 1966.

An analysis of blood collections in certain Southern States which

[1] *Hearings on S. 1945, op. cit.,* pp. 10, 79, 81–3 and 84–5.

[2] *Joint Blood Council Report, op. cit.,* Table 16.

[3] Mason, C., *Transfusion,* Vol. 4, 1964, p. 404; New York Academy of Medicine, 1958, *op. cit.,* p. 20; and Kellner, A., New York Blood Center (personal communication, June 8, 1966).

appeared to have had in 1961 substantial surpluses of blood (presumably transferred elsewhere) shows considerable variations in the proportions paid:[1]

	Total units collected, 1961	% paid	Units transfused
Alabama	168,375	25	60,593
Arkansas	39,579	51	30,398
Georgia	160,338	8	98,803
Kentucky	75,781	10	50,190
Louisiana	91,275	27	79,989
Mississippi	35,227	30	33,379
South Carolina	52,964	8	41,518
Tennessee	203,992	48[2]	86,528

[2] In Knoxville, Tennessee, in 1963 approximately one-half of all blood units transfused had been bought, and one-half obtained through 'tied' assurance plans (Burkhart, J. H., 'The Knoxville Program', *Proc. A.M.A. Conference on Blood and Blood Banking*, Chicago, 1964, p. 1).

For a number of the largest cities estimates have been reported of the proportion of paid donations (excluding plasmapheresis collections by commercial banks and pharmaceutical firms):

	%	
Boston (5 teaching hospitals)	28	(1964)[3]
Chicago	60	(1964)[4]
Dallas	65	(1964)[4]
Denver	42	(1964)[4]
Detroit	39	(1964)[4]
Jersey City	92	(1964)[4]
Kansas City	41	(1964)[4]
Los Angeles	29	(1964)[4]
Memphis	68	(1964)[4]
New York	55	(1966)[5]
Philadelphia	24	(1964)[4]
Pittsburgh	39	(1964)[4]

[3] Lund, C. C., 'Medical Sponsorship and Supervision', *Proc. A.M.A. Conference on Blood and Blood Banking*, Chicago, 1964, p. 6.

[4] A.M.A. *Directory, op. cit.*, 1965. These are probably all under-statements because of non-reporting of some commercial blood banks.

[5] See previous footnote for New York. In 1963 four of the leading medical centers in New York obtained 50–70 per cent of all their blood from paid donors and commercial sources (*Hearings on S. 2560, op. cit.*, p. 100).

[1] Extracted from Joint Blood Council, *op. cit.*, 1962.

Blood Services (a community blood
  banking system operating in
  Arizona, Arkansas, California,
  Louisiana, Mississippi, Montana,
  Nevada, New Mexico, North Dakota,
  Texas and Wyoming)   70   (1964)[1]

[1] Jennings, J. B., *op. cit.*, p. 134.

An examination of individual entries in the survey reports for
1961, 1964 and 1967 showed that the larger commercial banks in
many of these cities recorded substantial increases in total collections
between 1964 and 1967 despite the general trend depicted in Table 3
(Chapter 4). This was also shown, though somewhat less markedly,
for hospital and community banks who were paying in 1964 50
per cent or more of their donors. It seems probable, therefore, that the
proportions of paid donations were higher in 1967 in these 12 cities.

These statistics for certain states and cities, while showing
considerable variations in the proportion of paid donations, also
indicate that Chicago and New York are not unrepresentative or
atypical in the general pattern of their sources of blood.

III. THE UNITED STATES: SOCIAL CHARACTERISTICS OF DONORS

We now turn from these broad estimates by types of donors to ask
more detailed questions about the demographic and social characteristics of donors. What are needed are statistics showing the age, sex,
marital status, social class, income group, religion and ethnic group
in relation to donor type. Despite the acute and chronic shortages
of blood in many areas and the growing concern about recruitment
of unpaid donors there is, nevertheless, a remarkable lack of information on these questions. Only a few limited studies have been
undertaken; these are summarized below:

1. *American Red Cross Survey, May 1964*[1]

Total number of individuals completing donor information card
—13,553.

[1] Information supplied by Acting Medical Director, Blood Program, A.R.C.,
September 1966.

%

Sex: Male   78 (of which 14 per cent were members of the Defense Forces)

      Female   22

      No answer   1

                 100

Age: (no sex classification provided):

	%
18–21	18
22–29	22
30–39	25
40–49	22
50–59	12
No answer	1
	100

First-time donors	25
Repeat donors	74
No answer	1
	100

2. *Irwin Memorial Blood Bank of the San Francisco Medical Society, 1964*[1]

Total number of individuals included in questionnaire survey—5581 (approximating to one month's collection rate of the bank). Of these donors, 8 per cent were paid (Types A and B); 31 per cent were replacement donors and 61 per cent were individual or group credit donors (Types D and E). In response to incentive questions, 46 per cent said—of current and prior donations—they were replacement donors for friends, and 12 per cent said they 'needed the money'.

The policy of this community blood bank is to limit, as far as possible, the use of paid donors. It will be seen that, in this study, 92 per cent were 'tied', credit donors. The use of replacement donors in cases of open-heart surgery (approximately 780 a year in 1962

	%
Sex: Male	80
Female	20

[1] London, P. and Hemphill, B. M., 'The Motivations of Blood Donors', *Transfusion*, Vol. 5, No. 6, November–December 1965.

Age: (no sex or status classifications published)

	%
Under 25	28
25–35	29
35–45	25
Over 45	17
	99

Marital status:

Single	33
Married	57
Divorced, separated and widowed	9
	99

Ethnic group:

White	90
Negro	6
American Indian, Oriental, etc.	4
	100

Family income:

$	
1,000	14
3,000	13
5,000	20
7,000	19
9,000	13
11,000	7
13,000	3
15,000 up	5
Not reported	6
	100

Religion:

Catholics	32
Protestants	51
Jews	3 ⎫

100

Others	2
No religious preference	10
No answer	2
	100

Employment:

Employed	82
Unemployed and not gainfully occupied	18
	100

First-time donors	19
Repeat donors	81
	100

for which the bank supplied blood) has presented serious difficulties.[1] It placed on the patient a responsibility to recruit a large number of donors (up to 20 and more) in order to obtain the required quantity of blood of the correct blood group. These and other problems compelled the bank to take over this responsibility. In doing so, it has been forced to have recourse to a much higher proportion of paid donors—despite the risks of serum hepatitis. Of 17,160 donors recruited for cardiovascular cases during the period 1956 to June 1961 27·1 per cent were paid donors.

Apart from this particular problem of open-heart surgery, it would seem that the Irwin Memorial Blood Bank is not typical of community blood banks as a whole in the United States in using such a low proportion as 8 per cent of paid donors. It was shown earlier that such banks paid for approximately 35 per cent of their donations in 1964.

The authors of this sample survey in 1964 came to the following conclusions: compared with United States census data for 1960 its donors were younger; the percentage of whites was 'reasonably representative of San Francisco'; and that, as a whole, they were of somewhat higher socio-economic status than the population as a whole. Bearing in mind that the old and the young, the sick and other

[1] Hemphill, B. M., 'Blood for Open-Heart Surgery', *Transfusion*, Vol. 2, No. 2, March–April 1962. Two years later, Professor Hackel of the Department of Natural Science, Michigan State University, expressed the opinion that 'if it were not for paid donors, I doubt that any but a very small fraction of these important operations could be performed' (*Hearings on S. 2560, op. cit.*, p. 28).

ineligible groups cannot donate, this is not surprising, particularly when it is remembered that most 'tied' programs cater for the middle classes and those in secure employment.

3. *Blood Services, Arizona (known prior to June 1966 as Southwest Blood Banks)*

This non-profit making community blood bank operates in 12 States, caters largely for small hospitals in small towns in the southwest, and collected about 200,000 units of blood in 1966. It claims to serve communities and people in one-fifth of the land area of the United States and take responsibility for the blood needs of 14,000,000 people.[1]

Study 1 in 1958

A survey of all donors during 5 one-week periods in 12 cities[2] representing a 10·3 per cent sample. The total number of individuals included was 12,759. Of this number, 76 per cent were paid and 24 per cent were replacement donors.

Data for age, marital status, ethnic group, income and religion were not collected. One of the main purposes of the survey was to ascertain employment status. On this question the results are shown in Table 6.

A number of important conclusions emerged from this survey. A disproportionately high proportion of blood donors were drawn from the lower occupation-income groups; 66 per cent of all donors were skilled workers, operatives, service workers and laborers; a further 14 per cent came from the Armed Forces. These were predominantly paid. Unlike the San Francisco study, the middle classes (ranks 1, 2, 3, 5) provided only 14 per cent of the donors though they represented 33 per cent of the employed population.

The survey also found that at the time of the inquiry 51 per cent of paid donors were unemployed; the proportion among replacement donors was 11 per cent. Unemployment in both groups was heavily concentrated among laborers, craftsmen, operatives and service workers.

[1] *Hearings on S. 1945, op. cit.*, pp. 2–3.

[2] February, April, June, August and November 1958. The cities were: Phoenix, Arizona; Albuquerque, New Mexico; El Paso, Houston, San Antonio, Lubbock, and Harlingen, Texas; Meridian, Mississippi; Little Rock, Arkansas; Cheyenne, Wyoming; Reno, Nevada; and Alexandria, Louisiana (Korzekwa, M. T., Jordan, W. Q. and Alsever, J. B., 'The Blood Donor: 1. Who are our Blood Donors?', *Am. J. Med. Sci.*, 240, 36, 1960). For a criticism of this survey's conclusions see London, P., *Hearings on S. 2560, op. cit.*, pp. 222–4.

TABLE 6

Survey Results 1958, Blood Services, Arizona

Occupation and income rank	Occupation group: employed persons in the 8 States U.S. 1950 Census[1]	Occupation group: total donors	Distribution of paid donors
	%	%	%
1. Professional-technical	7·8	5	4
2. Managers, officials, proprietors	9·0	2	1
3. Sales	6·6	4	3
4. Craftsmen, foremen	12·0	21	21
5. Clerical	9·4	3	2
6. Operatives	14·2	14	15
7. Service workers	11·2	10	11
8. Laborers	6·8	19	22
9. Farmers	13·3	2	1
10. Farm laborers	5·2	2	2
11. Armed Forces[2]	—	14	14
12. Students	—	2	2
13. Housewives	—	2	2
14. Not reported	4·5	—	—
	100·0	100	100

[1] Ranks 1–10 listed in order of approximate average annual income (Bureau of the Census, U.S. Dept. of Commerce, *Statistical Abstract of the United States*, 1958 edition, tables 279 and 410).

[2] In 1957 the Armed Forces represented approximately 4 per cent of the total labor force.

The proportion of donors of both sexes from the Armed Forces was higher (14 per cent) than that found in the Red Cross survey in 1964 (11 per cent) and in the reported national Red Cross figure for 1967 (7·6 per cent). Contrary to general opinion, they were all paid.

The survey also provided data on first time and repeat donors. Approximately 12 per cent of all donors were 'first-timers'; 88 per cent were repeat donors. Among the latter, a strikingly high proportion of blood was supplied by 'long-time' donors—mostly paid donors who had already donated on more than 9 occasions. 'This finding' said the report, 'lends support to our belief that the "willing" blood donor comprises a rather small percentage of the population . . .' It was also observed 'that a significant number of "new" replacement donors almost never return. These are truly the "unwilling" donors who have been "forced" into giving blood by social pressures'. The report also analysed certain questions on motivation; these will be referred to later.

Study 2 in 1965

This community bank undertook in 1965 a similar but more extensive donor survey.[1] It covered 30,396 donors in 16 cities in 9 States:

	%
Replacement donors	19·5
Insurance donors	2·0
Paid donors	78·5
	100

		%
Sex:	Male	94
	Female	6
		100

Age (both sexes):

18–20	9·2
21–25	17·8
26–30	16·4
31–35	15·1
36–40	14·7
41–45	12·1
46–50	8·1
51–55	4·8
56–60	1·8
	100·0

Marital Status (both sexes):

Single	37
Married	56
Divorced	6
Widowed	1
	100

[1] The data, unpublished at the time of writing, were kindly provided by Dr J. B. Alsever, Medical Director, Blood Services, Arizona, August 1966.

Education Status (partially or fully completing the following education levels—both sexes):

Elementary school	19
High school	57
College	24
	100

Ethnic group (both sexes):

White	78
Negro	8
Spanish-American	12
American Indian	1·6
Oriental and other	0·4
	100·0

Donor income (not family):

below $3,000	39
$3,000–5,000	32
$5,000–10,000	23
$10,000–15,000	3
Over $15,000	1
No information	2
	100

First-time donors	36
Repeat donors	64
	100

The only information about occupation supplied to the writer (as the data were still being analysed) was that 44 per cent of all donors were craftsmen and laborers. The proportion of all donors who were unemployed was 36 per cent.

Taking account of the improvements in economic conditions between 1958 and 1965 it would seem that the results for 1965 broadly confirm the findings of the earlier survey. The majority of donors came from the lower income and occupation groups; a slightly higher proportion were paid (nearly 80 per cent) and a somewhat lower proportion were unemployed. The finding in 1965 that only 6 per cent of donors were women is significant in relation to the proportion unemployed. It points to the fact that a strikingly high proportion of blood donors (particularly paid donors) were

105

drawn from the ranks of the unemployed. Whether these donors were in receipt of any form of insurance benefit or public assistance is not known.

As regards ethnic group, it is difficult to draw any conclusions about the proportion of donors (22 per cent) classified separately from 'White' in the absence of an ethnic group analysis of the populations of the 16 cities. A further complication is that in two of the States concerned (Arkansas and Louisiana) there are state laws concerning the racial segregation of blood. Blood has to be labelled as to racial origin and, in Louisiana, it is a misdemeanor for a physician to give the blood of one race to a patient of another race without the recipient's permission.

We defer further comment on these two surveys until we have presented some data concerning Chicago; a similar inquiry in 1965 to the Blood Services study was conducted by the Chicago Blood Donor Service.

Chicago Blood Donor Service Survey

This study covered a sample of 1689 donors.[1] We set out below the findings in the same order as for the 1965 Blood Services study. Alongside these findings we insert, where appropriate and where the data are available, statistics for the total population of Chicago City derived from the census reports for 1960.[2]

	%
Replacement donors	8·5
Insurance (inc. group)	
donors	1·1
Paid donors	90·3
	99·9

		1960 Census
	%	%
Sex: Male	93·7	48·6
Female	6·3	51·4
	100·0	100·0

[1] Unpublished information kindly provided by Dr Coye C. Mason, Medical Director, Chicago Blood Donor Service, Inc., Chicago, August 1966.

[2] *U.S. Censuses of Population and Housing, 1960, Final Report PHC(1)–26* (Chicago, Illinois, Standard Metropolitan Statistical Area) and *Statistical Abstract of the U.S.A., 1965.*

Age (both sexes):

18–20	9·2	6·3
21–25	17·8	11·4
26–30	16·4	11·5
31–35	15·1	12·1
36–40	14·7	12·6
41–45	12·1	12·4
46–50	8·1	12·3
51–55	4·8	11·1
56–60	1·8	10·3
	100·0	100·0

Marital Status (both sexes 18–60):	%	*1960 Census: Age 14+* %
Single	43·4	24·0
Married	49·2	63·1 (including 'separated')
Divorced	6·0	3·4
Widowed	1·2	9·5
	99·8	100·0

Education Status (partially or fully completing the following education levels—both sexes):

Elementary school	5·5
High school	75·8
College	18·8
	100·1

Ethnic Group (both sexes):		*1960 Census: all males*[1]
White	67·8	76·7
Negro	30·2	22·5
Spanish American	0·5 ⎫	
American Indian	1·1 ⎬	0·8
Oriental and other	0·4 ⎭	
	100·0	100·0

[1] The proportion coloured in the age group 20–59 in 1960 was approximately 21·9 per cent (*U.S. Census of Population and Housing 1960, Chicago, Illinois, S.M.S.A.*).

Donor Income (not family):		*1960 Census: males 20–64*
below $3,000	30·7	14·4[1]
$3,000–5,000	45·8	22·2
$5,000–10,000	21·1	52·0
$10,000–15,000	2·2⎫	11·4
Over $15,000	0·4⎭	
	100·2	100·0

Occupation (both sexes)		*1960 Census: male civilian employed*[2]
Professional, technical and kindred	4·4	8·8
Managers, officials and proprietors	1·2	7·8
Clerical and kindred	5·9	10·5
Sales workers	3·9	6·4
Service workers	13·8	8·7
Armed Forces	5·3	0·2
Craftsmen, foremen and kindred	16·2	19·3
Operatives and kindred	17·0	22·0
Laborers	29·1	6·9
Housewives	1·3	—
Students	2·1	Others and not reported 9·4
	100·2	100·0

Employment: (both sexes)		*1960 Census: total male civilian labor force*[3]
Employed	59·4	94·8
Unemployed	40·6	5·2
	100·0	100·0

---

[1] In 1965 15 per cent of all families and of all residents of the Chicago Metropolitan Area had incomes below $3000. For Whites it was 12 per cent; Non-Whites 29 per cent (Table 1, Current Population Reports, Series P–60, No. 53, December 1967, *Consumer Income*, U.S. Dept. of Commerce, Bureau of the Census).

[2] Including Armed Forces but excluding unemployed, students and retired.

[3] Including Armed Forces but excluding students and retired.

First-time donors	88·0
Repeat donors	12·0
	100·0

These five surveys represent, so far as the writer has been able to ascertain, the only studies undertaken in the United States of the characteristics of blood donors. Looking at the results as a whole, and comparing the data with relevant census statistics for the cities and States in question and nationally, the following broad conclusions emerge:

Sex

The great majority of blood donors are men, the proportion ranging from 78 per cent for the American Red Cross to 94 per cent in the Chicago study.

Age

Something like 40–45 per cent of all donors are aged under 30. Donors are, therefore, younger than the total adult population. One reason for this is the age limit imposed on blood donors; another the disproportionate number of donors from the Defense Forces and the coloured population.

Marital Status

Single donors are very markedly over-represented; married donors are similarly under-represented. This is to some extent consistent with the findings on age and the proportion of donors from the Defense Forces. There are other factors, however, which seem to be relevant; they are discussed later. The divorced appear to be more represented than in the population as a whole.

Donor Type

Apart from the American Red Cross, the proportion of paid donors (Types A and B) ranged from 8 per cent in San Francisco to 90 per cent in Chicago. All other donors included in the four studies were Responsibility Fee and Credit Donors (Types D and E). Voluntary Community Donors were represented only in the Red Cross study.

Occupation

The Blood Services studies and the Chicago study show that the professional and middle classes are substantially under-represented. The San Francisco finding that the majority of donors were of a

109

somewhat higher socio-economic status than the population of the city is explained by the fact that 92 per cent of donors were 'tied' or credit donors in programs appealing most to the middle classes and those in secure employment. The San Francisco community blood bank does not seem to be typical in this respect (and in respect of the low proportion of paid donors) of community blood banks as a whole or of the donor pattern in many large American cities.

The Blood Services and Chicago studies show that the majority of donors are manual workers (employed and unemployed); particularly laborers, casual workers and semi-skilled operatives. These classes are much more heavily represented than in the occupational labor force for the United States as a whole.

Unemployment

Unemployed men (and particularly the young unemployed) were very heavily represented in four of the studies (data on employment were not collected in the Red Cross study). The percentages were: San Francisco 18; Blood Services 1958 study 51 (paid) 11 (replacement); Blood Services 1965 study 36 (all donors); Chicago 41. The unemployment rate among males aged over 14 in non-agricultural industries in the United States varied between 5·4 and 7·1 per cent during 1958–63.[1]

Income

The proportion of donors with personal or family incomes falling below prevailing definitions of 'poverty base-lines' was substantially higher in the Blood Services and Chicago studies than for the United States as a whole. Donors in these studies were on average living at income standards considerably below average industrial earnings, and a large proportion were living in poverty.

First-time Donors

The proportions of donors who were new or first-time donors were: Red Cross 25 per cent; San Francisco 19 per cent; Blood Services 12 per cent (1958) and 36 per cent (1965); Chicago 12 per cent. These proportions are low compared with the data for England and Wales. One explanation (though no doubt there are many others) may be that many blood banks of all types in the United States (apart from the Red Cross) report that paid donors are more 'reliable' than other classes of donors. They therefore tend to

[1] *Manpower Report to the President*, U.S. Dept. of Labor, Washington, 1964, Tables A–8 to A–11.

be called on heavily in cases of open-heart surgery and other operations requiring massive transfusions of blood which the patient's family is unable or unwilling to provide on a prepayment or replacement basis.[1] The increased risk of serum hepatitis consequent on the use of blood from such 'call-in' paid donors is discussed in Chapter 8.

Ethnic Group

In the Chicago study Negroes and other coloured groups were more heavily represented than in the population of the city. This may also have been the case in the 1965 Blood Services study but it is difficult to draw any conclusion here owing to the problem of defining the population at risk catered for by the community blood bank in question. The authors of the San Franciso study reported that the percentage of whites in the donor population was 'reasonably representative of San Francisco'.

To what extent are these conclusions applicable to the United States as a whole? It is hard to generalize from such a few and scattered studies; nevertheless, their findings in respect to sex, income class, employment status and ethnic group are consistent with—or more heavily emphasized by—other facts presented in this and earlier chapters. In particular, it has been shown that only about 7 per cent of all donations in the United States are derived from voluntary donors who regard their donation as a free gift to strangers. 'It is a rare community' said Dr R. L. Mainwaring, Immediate Past President of the American Association of Blood Banks in 1964, 'which can run its blood program on strictly volunteer donors.'[2]

Donors in blood assurance type programs ('tied' donors) who contribute about 39 per cent of all donations seem to be donors, predominantly men, in secure employment. Such programs appear to draw heavily on skilled workers who are union members. Studies carried out by the Department of Community Services of A.F.L. and C.I.O. suggest that at least 35 per cent of all blood collected by the Red Cross comes from union members, chiefly as a result of organized programs at large factories and industrial plants.[3] If the facts were known, some of these donors would probably be classified as Fringe Benefit Voluntary Donors (Type G) and some as Paid-Induced Voluntary Donors (Type C).

[1] Adashek, E. P. and W. H., 'The Incidence of Hepatitis in Open Heart Surgery where Massive Blood Transfusions are Used', *Proc. 9th Congr. int. Soc. Blood Transf., Mexico, 1962*, 1964, pp. 631–7.

[2] Mainwaring, R. L., *op. cit.*, 1964, p. 3.

[3] Personal communication, Mr L. Perlis, Director of the Department, November 30, 1966.

It has also been shown that paid donors contribute about one half of all blood and plasma donations—something like 3¾ million donations a year. As to their characteristics, the general impression gained from a study of all that has been written about them is that the great majority are men, unskilled or semi-skilled workers and migrants on low earnings or unemployed. In the large cities in particular and in the Southern States Negroes seem to predominate. A typical report from a commercial blood bank in New York to the writer in 1968 ran as follows:

'We have approximately 4000 listed donors who annually contribute approximately 18,000 whole blood units. The average payment to each donor is six dollars with the RH negative donors receiving a higher payment.

95–96 per cent of the donors are men with about 75 per cent negro.'

A commercial bank in Miami, collecting some 22,000 units annually, reported to the writer that two-thirds of its donors were male and that 75 per cent were in the low income group. Another such bank in Newark, New Jersey, collecting 12,860 donations in 1968, said that 85 per cent of its donors were male, Negro, average age 28, and were drawn from the lower income group, part-time workers and many from the construction industry.

In all, the writer received statistics for 1968 from a large number of commercial banks (some operated by pharmaceutical firms) accounting for some 366,000 units of blood. While very few appear to maintain detailed statistics in respect of age, sex, marital status and other characteristics many provided summary accounts on similar lines to those quoted above.

It would seem that most paid donors (apart from those in prisons, in the Defense Forces or university students) fall into three categories:

1. Registered donors who contribute regularly and who are paid on a fee basis or are semi-salaried—'Professional donors' (this category figures largely in the plasmapheresis programs).

2. 'Call-in' donors; individuals (perhaps with less common blood groups) who are on a register of some kind and who respond to a call for blood on payment of a fee of $5–15 or more.

3. 'Walk-in' donors, who may be attracted by advertisements, who are paid $5 or more a pint depending on local circumstances, such as the extent of the shortage of blood and other market considerations.

Many commercial blood banks, often opening (at least in New York) from 7.30 in the morning to midnight, are better placed to attract 'Walk-in donors' because their 'store fronts' are located in Negro and Ghetto areas. In 1966 voluntary and private hospitals bought 100,000 pints of 'Skid Row blood from New York City's 31 pay-for-blood stores'.[1] They paid $35 a pint or more. The 1964 survey by the American Medical Association recorded a total collection from all sources in New York of 232,201 units.[2]

A typical journalistic account which appeared in 1963 described the scene:

'A bleary-eyed, vacant-faced man shuffles up to a building in an industrial part of town, checks the address with a scrap of paper in his shaking hand, and walks inside. In a bleak third-floor office, he joins a number of other men, many derelicts like himself. One by one they are summoned to a desk where an attendant asks a few quick questions and directs them to an inner room.

'This is not a flophouse. It is not an employment agency or a social service bureau for weary, homeless men. This is a blood donor center'.[3]

Similar accounts have appeared since 1963 of conditions in commercial blood banks in Chicago, Seattle, Georgia, Cleveland, Boston, Miami, Detroit, Cincinnati, Los Angeles, San Francisco, Washington, Baltimore, Philadelphia, New Jersey, Kansas City and many other cities in addition to New York.

Most of these accounts, however, are not the products of keen-eyed journalists but of physicians concerned about the problem of serum hepatitis (in Chapter 8 we discuss this problem in more detail). We may single out here one of the more distinguished of these authorities, Professor J. Garrott Allen of the Stanford University School of Medicine, and quote from a paper of his presented to a meeting of the American Surgical Association in 1966:

'Blood from some groups among donor populations produces more cases of icteric hepatitis than blood from other groups. The incidence of icteric serum hepatitis in patients receiving single transfusions when the donors are of the prison-Skid Row variety, is ten times that of volunteer donors, family or friends. This alarming

---

[1] Report by the New York Council for Civic Affairs quoted in the *Daily News*, August 1, 1967.

[2] *A.M.A. Directory*, 1965, *op. cit.*

[3] David, L., *Science and Mechanics*, November 1963. Exhibit presented to Senate Committee, *Hearings on S. 2560*, *op. cit.*, p. 165.

H

difference also obtains for multiple transfusions from prison donors, and this has been confirmed by others'[1]

'The paid donor', wrote Professor Allen in another paper, 'is often a cloistered resident of Skid Row where he and his colleagues are alleged to enjoy frequently the practice of the communal use of unsterile needles and syringes for the self-administration of drugs . . . There are also other unsanitary practices that prevail among this kind of population which favor repeated exposures to infectious hepatitis as well. Still another contributing factor, allegedly higher in this group than in the general population, is that of alcoholism, which appears to make such individuals more susceptible to an initial attack of either infectious or serum hepatitis'.[2] Other authorities have drawn attention to the fact that the purchase of blood attracts many alcoholics and other unfortunates who return frequently to blood banks and 'who know they will be deprived of money if they answer yes to questions about jaundice, malaria, other infectious diseases and hypersensitivity'.[3] Narcotic takers are known to be frequent blood donors.[4]

These paid donors have been variously described in many other papers (some of which are listed below[5]) as narcotics, dope addicts, liars, degenerates, unemployed derelicts, prison narcotic users,

[1] Allen, J. G., 'The Advantages of the Single Transfusion', *Annals of Surgery*, Vol. 164, No. 3, September 1966, p. 476.

[2] Allen, J. G., 'Immunization Against Serum Hepatitis from Blood Transfusion', *Annals of Surgery*, Vol. 164, No. 4, October 1966, p. 752.

[3] Hoxworth, P. I. and Haesler, W. E., 'Serum Hepatitis in Transfusion', *Proc. 8th Congr. int. Soc. Blood Transfr.*, Tokyo, 1960, p. 498, 1962.

[4] *Hepatitis Surveillance*, National Communicable Disease Center, *op. cit.*, September 30, 1967, pp. 28–35.

[5] Adashek, E. P. and W. H., *Arch. of Surgery*, Vol. 87, No. 5, p. 792, 1963; Allen, J. G., and Sayman, W. A., *J.A.M.A.*, 108: 1079, 1962; Carroll, R. T., *Transfusion*, Vol. 3, p. 191, 1963; Dougherty, W. J., *Weekly Report, U.S. Dept. of Health, Education and Welfare*, 1967, No. 16, p. 170; Dull, H. B., *J.A.M.A.*, 176: 413, 1961; Fitch, D. R., *et al.*, *Am. J. Clin. Path.*, 25: 158, 1955; Hemphill, B. M., 'The National Clearinghouse Program of the Amercian Association of Blood Banks', *Proc. A.M.A. Conference on Blood and Blood Banking*, Chicago, 1964, p. 2; Hoxworth, P. I., *et al.*, *Surg. Gynec. Obstet.*, 109: 38, 1959; Kellner, A., New York Blood Center (personal communication), March 6, 1967; Kunin, C. M., *Am. J. Med. Sci.*, 237: 293, 1959; Leger, R. R., *op. cit.*, 1967; Malootian, I., *op. cit.*, 1964, p. 1002; Mayes, B., Sausalito, California (personal communication), January 1967; *Medical World News*, March 15, 1963; Mirick, G. S., Ward, R. and McCollum, R. W., *New Eng. J. Med.*, 273: 59, 1965; Norris, R. F., Potter, H. P. and Reinhold, J. G., *op. cit.*, 1963, p. 202; Potter, H. P., *et al.*, *J.A.M.A.*, 174: 2049, 1960; Rubinson, R. M., *et al.*, *Journal of Thoracic and Cardiovascular Surgery*, Vol. 50, No. 4, 1965, p. 575; Wheeler, C. B., *op. cit.*, 1964, pp. 3–5.

bums, the faceless, the undernourished and unwashed, junkies, hustlers and ooze-for-booze donors. Many are said to give fictitious names and addresses (which makes it difficult to trace cases of hepatitis, malaria and venereal disease); to sell their blood to different blood banks, and to traffic in black markets of social security cards, 'rented' for 25 cents or so to serve as identity cards at blood banks. In Chapter 8 we examine the effects on recipients of blood supplies from these populations.

V

With the great expansion in plasmapheresis programs in recent years the problem of the effects on the donor's health of frequent and repeated donations has emerged as an important public health issue. At a conference of authorities on plasmapheresis in 1966 these health risks were discussed; the danger of iron deficiency anemia developing; local venous thrombosis at the site of repeated venipunctures; donors receiving back the wrong red cells, inadequate techniques for assessing haemoglobin levels, bacterial proliferation and contamination and other hazards to health particularly in the long run.

All authorities agree that donors should enjoy a diet rich in protein and amply nutritious to help the body manufacture plasma proteins quickly (perhaps supplemented with minerals and iron); that fluid intake should be above normal; that attention should be paid to sleep and exercise; that blood protein and other tests should be carried out frequently, and that poor 'Skid Row' types of donors should not be used.[1]

In the present state of knowledge it seems to be difficult and dangerous to reach firm conclusions about the long-term effects on the health of donors. One spokesman from the Division of Biologic Standards, National Institutes of Health, said in 1966: 'We are accumulating a tremendous amount of data about the donors that have been processed, beginning with Dr Sturgeon and his donor of 1954. We can seem now to get some pattern as to what happens to donors but it is obvious that we need a great deal more data before we can sit back and feel safe about what is being done to them'.[2]

[1] *Conference on Plasmapheresis, op. cit.;* Kliman, A. and Lesses, M. F., *op. cit.; A New Frontier in Medicine*, Fenwal Laboratories Brochure, Morton Grove, Ill., 1968.
[2] Crouch, M., *Conference on Plasmapheresis, op. cit.*, p. 106.

Dr J. N. Ashworth (also from the Division of Biologic Standards) while drawing attention at the same conference to the importance of determining protein levels and of avoiding the spread of hepatitis among donors was led to discuss the ethical issues:

'No one has yet mentioned the matter of obtaining the consent of the donor. It is not enough to just ask "Do you agree that you would like to do this?" but you should get his informed consent. Tell him exactly what is involved; how he might possibly be killed by some wrong cells and what is involved in the long run for him on this program. You should talk these matters over very carefully with your legal counsel because he is the man who must defend you in court. Determine if you should get a signed consent every time the donor comes in to give, not just the first time, so that he is continually aware of the exposure to danger to which you are subjecting him. What about the adequacy of your determination of his suitability before he gives—before he starts on the program? What about the adequacy of your identification of the cells? What of your identification of the donor as he comes in each time to make sure that he is the person that you identify on the bag of blood or on the records? . . . You are hiring this donor to perform something on him; you are not curing any of his ills'.[1]

Clearly, there are serious hazards from plasmapheresis and, consequently, equally clearly serious ethical implications (to these implications we return in a later chapter). 'One of the most important', said Dr T. J. Greenwalt, 'is exploiting for its proteins a population which is least able to donate them—the poorly nourished Skid Row population'.[2]

Earlier in this chapter it was estimated that in 1967 the national yield of human plasma from plasmapheresis programs (mostly run by commercial banks) was some 2,000,000 units. To conclude this chapter we bring together the data we were able to collect by correspondence and questionnaire from some of these organizations. They are national estimates and guesses (though in some cases precise statistics were given for specific programs) contributed chiefly by the medical directors of procurement.[3] No attempt was

[1] Ashworth, J. N., *Conference on Plasmapheresis, op. cit.,* p. 83.

[2] Greenwalt, T. J. (in 1966 Director of the Milwaukee Blood Center, subsequently Medical Director, Blood Program, American National Red Cross), *Conference on Plasmapheresis, op. cit.,* p. 2.

[3] The main sources of information, general and specific, were: American Blood Bank Service, Inc., Miami, Florida; Cutter Laboratories, Berkeley, California; Dade Reagents Inc., Miami, Florida; Pfizer Diagnostics, New York;

116

made to investigate technical standards and procedures, consent arrangements, frequency of bleeding and testing of protein levels and other matters. The inquiry was limited to ascertaining the number of donations and donors and their characteristics.

'Donors are aged between 18 and 60. About 75–80 per cent are male. The great majority are unskilled workers. Negroes and other minority groups (including prisoners) contribute disproportionately to their numbers in the national population. The average payment to the donor per donation is estimated to be $5·50'.

Among the answers which related to a commercial blood bank's own program the following description was fairly typical:

'Ninety per cent of our donors are male; 90 per cent are unemployed; 75 per cent are Caucasian and 25 per cent Negroid'.

And another, which also could not provide specific data:
'I have a distinct impression that males would predominate in the donor population on a ratio of approximately three to one. I would also be able to state that with respect to paid professional donors, there is a proportionately higher number of negro donors. These are generally of the laboring class'.

Statistically, it should be noted that for the whole of the United States during 1961–3 the proportions of the employed population aged 17+ who were classified as 'Laborers (except farm and mine)' were White 3·8 per cent; Nonwhite 11·9 per cent.[1]

The few reports that have appeared in the medical press which provide some information on the characteristics of plasmapheresis donors give the same general picture. One or two describe 'Skid Row characteristics', for example: 'Thanks to the advance of

Lilly Research Laboratories and Community Blood Bank of Marion County, Inc., Indianapolis, Indiana; Courtland Laboratories, Los Angeles, California and El Paso, Texas; Travenol Laboratories International, Morton Grove, Illinois (including Baxter Laboratories, Hyland Laboratories and Fenwal Laboratories); Community Blood Bank and Serum Service, Hoboken, New Jersey; Milwaukee Blood Center, Inc., Milwaukee; Blood Research Institute, Inc., Massachusetts; Children's Hospital Medical Center, Boston; United Biologics, Seattle (reported in *Seattle Magazine*, Vol. 5, No. 46, January 1968); Applied Immunology, Inc., Chicago, G. D. Searle & Co., and Blood Derivatives, Inc., Chicago (reported in *Hearings on S. 2560, op. cit.*, pp. 187–8) and Department of Pathology, University of Michigan, Ann Arbor, Michigan.

[1] *Selected Health Characteristics by Occupation*, National Center for Health Statistics, Public Health Service, Dept. of Health, Education, and Welfare, Series 10, No. 21, Table 38, August 1965.

science, the blood donors of Skid Row, who at one time exchanged their blood for the price of a drink or two, can now sell it two or more times a week—at $25 a pint . . . this is threatening to turn the Bowery boys into the Bourgeoisie.'[1] 'As the blood flows out of Chicago', ran another report, 'an unaccustomed golden tide washes into Skid Row'.[2]

Since these reports appeared in 1963 the payments made to donors appear to have become more discriminating. 'All of the donors in our program are paid for their blood at a rate which is determined by its commercial value to this company. Donors whose blood is used for the preparation of chemistry or coagulation controls are at the lower end of the scale and donors who have been immunized to produce specific blood-typing antibodies at the higher end. Probably very few of our donors rely on these payments as their sole source of income'.[3]

It has not been possible to obtain systematic statistical data on the number of prison donors who are involved in plasmapheresis programs.[4] It is estimated, however, that the number is substantial and that it is growing. Some prisons invite drug companies 'to bid on a bleeding program. The bids would involve a fund for those prisoners who volunteer and the prison itself'.[5]

VI

The findings of this survey of the characteristics of blood donors in the United States are discussed more generally in later chapters

[1] *Medical World News*, March 15, 1963, quoted in *Transfusion*, Vol. 3, 1963, p. 302.

[2] From the *Chicago's American*, March 14, 1963, cited in *Hearings on S. 2560, op. cit.*, p. 187.

[3] Personal communication, Dr A. Richardson Jones, Director of Research and Development, Dade Reagents Inc., Miami, December 17, 1968.

[4] As regards whole blood collections, it was shown in Chapter 5 that prisons contributed 2·2 per cent of total donations to the American National Red Cross in 1967, the proportion varying in regional centers from nil in some centers to 13·1 per cent in a South Carolina Center (*Blood Center Operations 1967, op. cit.*, p. 2). For commercial and other types of blood banks no national data exist but trend figures published for a number of specific programs (cited elsewhere) suggest that more use is being made of the 'Captive Voluntary Donor'.

[5] Personal communication, Mr K. W. Forbes, Marketing Staff Assistant, Travenol Laboratories International, Morton Grove, Illinois, December 2, 1968. See also the report of a dispute between a hospital in Augusta, Georgia (which relied on prison blood for open-heart operations) and Cutter Laboratories, Inc., a drug company, wishing to build a blood processing plasma facility at the prison, in the *Wall Street Journal*, March 1, 1967, p. 21.

where we consider their implications in relation to ethical issues, to questions of quality and safety, to questions of law and the professional freedom of the doctor, and to questions of cost and redistribution among different groups in American society.

Meanwhile, we conclude that, despite all the statistical inadequacies in the data presented, the trend appears to be markedly in the direction of the increasing commercialization of blood and donor relationships. Concomitantly, we find that proportionately more blood is being supplied by the poor, the unskilled, the unemployed, Negroes and other low income groups and, with the rise of plasmapheresis, a new class is emerging of an exploited human population of high blood yielders. Redistribution in terms of 'the gift of blood and blood products' from the poor to the rich appears to be one of the dominant effects of the American blood banking systems.

We turn now to an analysis of the characteristics of blood donors in England and Wales.

Chapter 7

The Characteristics of Blood Donors in England and Wales

I

In Chapter 4 and Appendix 3 we provided statistics of blood donors for the country as a whole and on a regional basis since the establishment of the National Blood Transfusion Service in 1948. They told us nothing, however, about the characteristics of the donor population by age, sex, marital status, income group and other attributes.

At the local donor session and at the regional level the staff of the Service have acquired, during these twenty years, much knowledge and experience concerning the recruitment of donors of different ages and social groups. But apart from one or two *ad hoc* and unpublished inquiries[1] no attempt has been made to fund this information in statistical form. Only impressionistic answers can be given in response to the question 'who gives blood?'

It is suggested in Appendix 3 that one of the reasons for this lack of inquiry is that the Service, as the national administrative agency responsible for the supply of blood and blood products, has never consciously been aware of a shortage or an impending shortage of potential donors. There have, therefore, been no internal or external pressures for more systematic information about the characteristics of those who give and those who do not give blood. Yet the Service has been in a unique position as the sole national agency to collect and analyse data on a national scale compared with the variety and multiplicity of agencies in the United States and many other countries. But why collect such information? In the opinion of the writer, no public service should be required as a matter of routine administrative processes to pile up, Kafka-like, vast masses of statistics just to satisfy computers and those who feed computers.

There must be then some reason or reasons; someone must be asking questions; scientific, technical, historical, policy or administrative questions. In the present instance, as earlier chapters have indicated, a variety of questions have been thrown up about the

[1] Birmingham Region, for example, made a study by sex and age of 10,000 donors in 1964. This is referred to later.

characteristics of blood donors; questions concerning the gift relationship, about attitudes, motives and values, about human blood as a service-bond or as a commercial commodity, and questions that need answers if blood transfusion services are viewed as systems of social redistribution.

With the assistance of the Ministry of Health and the National Blood Transfusion Service a pilot study was made in the summer and autumn of 1967 of some 3800 donors.[1] The questionnaire (see Appendix 5) was designed in co-operation with consultant staff and officials at the Ministry. The field work was carried out by the writer's research assistants, Mr Michael J. Reddin and Miss Sarah West, s.r.n., and the project, at different stages, was financed by grants from the Nuffield Foundation Small Grant Program (£750), the Ministry of Health (£600) and the Social Research Division of the London School of Economics (£600).

After an examination of regional trends (see Appendix 3) and statistics relating to donor populations and donor reporting rates for the general public, institutions (factories, offices, universities, etc.) and the Defence Services (described hereafter as G.P., I. and D.S. donors) it was decided to aim at a response sample of 3750–4000. Of this total, 65 per cent were to be drawn from the general public, 32 per cent from institutions and 3 per cent from the Defence Services to accord broadly with national proportions. On grounds of cost, organization, and administrative convenience, three hospital regions were selected, Birmingham, Manchester and South East Metropolitan. Regional blood transfusion staff organized the despatch of questionnaires. They also assisted in the selection and arrangement of donor sessions of specified types to provide this proportionate 'mix' of donors and to provide a representative 'mix' of urban, rural, institutional and social group donor populations.[2]

In the event, a total of 3813 completed questionnaires were received for computer analysis.[3] This total was made up of:

[1] It was originally described as a 'pilot study'. It was hoped that it might provide some useful guides if a larger survey were undertaken in the future by the Ministry.

[2] Donors in the sample donated at the following places: Billingshurst, Caterham, Littlehampton, Sutton, Sutton institutions and Wallington (Surrey), Hammersmith, Bermondsey and Bermondsey institutions (London), Coventry, Stoke-on-Trent, Walsall, Shrewsbury, Wolverhampton, Wall Heath and Waterloo St. (Birmingham) and Birmingham institutions, Altringham, Glossop, Oldham, Sale, Wigan, Roby St. (Manchester) and Manchester institutions and H.M.S. *Collingwood*.

[3] A further 8 G.P. questionnaires were subsequently received by post; these are included in some of the tables.

TABLE 7

Numbers of Donors by Region and Type of Donor Session

	General Public		Institutions		Defence Services	
Birmingham	902		237		—	
Manchester	679		246		—	
S.E. Metropolitan	1069		546		134	
Total	2650	69%	1029	27%	134	4%

In Appendix 3, Table 23, it is shown that for England and Wales as a whole in 1965 the reporting rates were 64, 33 and 3 per cent, and for the 8 regions with statistical records covering the years 1951–65 they were 71, 27 and 2 per cent in 1965.

Some 8000 questionnaires were despatched with routine call-up cards to panel donors who had approximately two weeks' notice (generally two dates were offered).[1] They were accompanied by a letter from the Regional Director asking for co-operation in the survey which, it was explained, was being conducted by the University of London to find out more about the characteristics of people 'who perform such a vital humanitarian service by giving blood voluntarily to the National Blood Transfusion Service'. Donors were asked to complete the questionnaires and to bring them to one of the sessions offered where Miss West would be available to help them if need be. They were assured of complete confidentiality.

Officials of the Service were a little concerned, and rightly, that the survey might injure relationships with donois particularly as questions were being asked which to some people might appear to have no connection with the act of donating blood. A careful watch was therefore kept on reporting rates. It was necessary here to distinguish between (a) session reporting rates and (b) the proportion of donors refusing to complete questionnaires.

As regards the former, the reporting rate overall for general public sessions was somewhat higher than normal; the corresponding rate for England and Wales as a whole was 53 per cent in 1967 (see Appendix 3). In the Birmingham region, which had proportionately

---

[1] Only registered donors (those who had given at least one previous donation) received call-up appointment cards and questionnaires. Thus, the survey of general public donors excluded 'first-time' donors unless a request was made for a questionnaire at a session included in the sample. Some first-time donors were included in I. and D.S. sessions.

more refusals than the other two regions,[1] the survey reporting rate was 61·4 per cent.

So far as the general public were concerned, there is no evidence then that the intervention of the survey significantly affected the willingness of registered donors to respond to the call to donate.

It is impossible to say, however, what effect the survey had on Institutional and Defence Services donors because of the different procedures adopted. Questionnaires were handed to volunteers as they came to the session at arranged intervals. This meant that donors had little time to reflect on the questions, particularly as the sessions were 'streamlined' so as not to keep donors waiting. The general effect was not to encourage the full completion of an admittedly complicated questionnaire—notably those questions relating to motives. This was recognized by the surveyors who had, however, undertaken to be as unobtrusive as possible. Moreover, these volunteers included a number of first-time donors to whom parts of the questionnaire were not applicable.

After excluding the first-time donors the response was considered in the circumstances to be reasonably satisfactory. In the Birmingham region, for instance, 55·6 per cent of all Institutional donors who were handed questionnaires completed them.

Not all the questions were answered by those who filled in the questionnaires, particularly Question 5 relating to motives. In Appendix 6 ('Analysis of Blood Donor Motives') by Mr John Beddington who also assisted the writer with the statistical, coding and computer processes, an examination is made of this problem and it is shown that 17·2 per cent of Institutional donors failed to answer Question 5 compared with 9·7 per cent of General Public donors. What also emerges is that the answers to the motive questions by Institutional donors tended to be general and rather perfunctory.

In the first drafts of the questionnaire these particular questions on motives (and also the question on publicity) were not included. It was thought that the whole area of motivation was too complex to explore, particularly by the techniques of a check-list of general reasons and open questions. There was also the further drawback that this survey (planned as a *pilot* study and not as a random national inquiry) excluded any study of non-blood donors, i.e. those who had never donated. The Ministry considered, however,

---

[1] In all three regions (G.P. sessions) there were 83 definite refusals to complete questionnaires (50 male, 33 female). In relation to the number of donors reporting, this represented a 2 per cent refusal rate. In the Birmingham region it was 3 per cent.

that in this pilot an attempt should be made to elicit responses to questions about motives; the experience gained might be useful in the event of a later and more comprehensive study of blood donor characteristics and motives.

Though the results must be interpreted with caution, Appendix 6 analysing this part of the questionnaire does suggest that the inclusion of the questions was worth while, and that donors—especially G.P. donors—welcomed the opportunity to comment and express their views. What was indeed remarkable was the amount of writing—and the number of words—which a large number of donors managed to squeeze on a relatively small form. One obvious lesson for future surveyors is the need to provide more space for donors to express their opinions and to offer advice and suggestions to the National Blood Transfusion Service. Another lesson is the need to make different arrangements and to allow more time to elicit information from Institutional donors.

Because of the special difficulties affecting Institutional donors (influencing mainly the response rate and the answers to the non-factual questions) somewhat more reliance can be placed on the results of the study of general public donors. Hence, in certain of the following tables we have separated the data for G.P. and I. donors.

Before the survey was embarked on the questionnaire was pre-piloted in the spring of 1967 in two areas, Westerham (Kent) and Bermondsey (London). Both were G.P. sessions. The call-up reporting rate was 57 per cent (about average), and of those attending approximately 98 per cent completed the questionnaire giving us 406 completed forms. These responses were regarded as satisfactory and, as a result of this test, some useful lessons were learnt and the questionnaire was accordingly revised.

II

We now present the main results of the pilot survey (more detailed tables will be found in Appendices 4 and 6). Comparisons are made from time to time with the population of England and Wales in respect of age, sex, marital status, social class and income group.[1] We also examine the distribution of number of children of married donors.

[1] For comparative purposes use was made of the Registrar General's reports for England and Wales of the census in 1961 and the sample census in 1966. The social class classification and coding of occupation and industry followed the definitions and rules adopted by the General Register Office.

In interpreting the comparisons we make of the donor sample and the general population one important point should be borne in mind. Apart from the factor of blood donor self-selection, the sample aged 18–64 was further selected to exclude the sick, the seriously disabled, expectant and nursing mothers, and others who had been rejected or deterred on medical criteria (see Chapter 2) from registering as blood donors or, if registered, from donating blood at a particular session.[1]

In this important respect, therefore, we are not comparing like with like. We are making comparisons between a self-selected and medically selected group and the total population of the country aged 18–64. It is not possible to exclude from this universe the non-healthy and non-eligible sections of the population. Two groups in particular are likely to be significantly affected: (i) women in the reproductive ages and (ii) older men and women among whom one would expect to find higher proportions of the 'non-healthy'.

Of the total donor sample of 3813:[2]

TABLE 8

All Donors by Sex and Session Type

	G.P.	I.	D.S.	Total	England and Wales, 1966 (ages 20–64 only)
	%	%	%	%	%
Men	53	74	100	60	45
Women	47	26	0	40	55

The sex distribution of G.P. donors is closest to that of the national population; part if not most of the difference could well be accounted for by the exclusion from the sample of expectant and nursing mothers.

The next table (in which we combine the I. and D.S. donors) shows the distribution by sex and age:

[1] But not all donors in the sample can be categorized as 'healthy and non-disabled'. There were blind and seriously disabled donors, ex-mental hospital donors, and some who were later found (after checks with donor records) to have mis-stated their age (they were over 65) in order to continue to donate.

[2] It will be noted that in many of the tables the numbers vary slightly. This is because a few donors omitted to fill in either their age, or their marital status, occupation and industry, etc.

TABLE 9

All Donors by Sex, Age and Session Type

| Age | Male | | | | Female | | | |
	G.P.	I. and D.S.	Total	E.W.	G.P.	I. and D.S.	Total	E.W.
	%	%	%	%	%	%	%	%
18–24	17	29	22	17	20	38	23	16
25–29	13	16	14	10	12	13	12	10
30–34	12	13	13	10	10	6	9	10
35–39	14	12	13	11	12	7	11	10
40–44	13	11	12	11	11	9	11	11
45–49	12	8	10	10	12	11	12	11
50–54	9	6	8	11	9	11	9	11
55–59	7	4	6	11	9	4	8	11
60–64	3	1	2[1]	9	5	1	5[2]	10
	100	100	100	100	100	100	100	100
No.	1412	886	2298		1245	270	1515	

[1] Including 1 donor 65+.   [2] Including 3 donors 65+.

For both sexes donors are somewhat younger than the general population. But this distribution is chiefly brought about by the decline in the number of donors aged 55+. A higher number of young donors of both sexes in the first ten years of donating balance the withdrawal of older donors of both sexes in the last ten years. The young come in to balance the effects of age as sickness and disability makes it more difficult for older people to take part in the act of giving.

If account is taken, however, not simply of the number of donors but of the life record of total donations by each individual then the pattern changes. As we shall see later when we take a 'generational' view of 43,391 donations, the older populations have made their contributions and merit their increasing dependence on the young and the healthy. Even so, as Table 9 shows, their current contributions are still significant—about 10 per cent of all blood donated comes from men and women aged over 55—the widowed, divorced and separated, far from being 'alienated' from society, contributing their due proportions (see Table 24, Appendix 4) along with the married and the single.

We may conclude from Tables 8 and 9, if some allowance is made for those who are unable to donate on medical and repro-

126

ductive grounds, that the donor sample closely resembles in terms of age and sex the structure of the general population. It is in fact more representative than the (unpublished) study of 10,000 donors from institutions by the Birmingham Regional Transfusion Centre in 1964. This analysis recorded only age, sex and session type. It showed, in comparison with the general population and the present study, a higher proportion of men and a lower proportion of women and, in terms of age-sex structure, the percentage distributions were less representative of the general population.[1]

We now consider marital status in relation to sex, age and session type. Details of this analysis, to avoid cluttering up the chapter with too many tables, are relegated to Appendix 4 (Table 24).

The main conclusions drawn from this breakdown as to the broad representativeness of the donor sample in relation to the general population are:

Ages 18–24: Males reasonably representative; females substantially less so presumably because of childbearing.

Ages 25–29: Males reasonably representative but, in contrast to ages 18–24, showing a somewhat higher proportion of married donors. The female proportions again show the effects of childbearing.

Ages 30–39: The distributions for males are very close to those of the general population. Among females the proportions approximate more closely (especially general public donors at ages 35–39) than at earlier ages.

Ages 40–49: The distributions for males are again very close. This pattern is now also apparent for females; clearly the 'reproductive effect' has now disappeared.

Ages 50–64: For both males and females the distributions resemble to an even more precise extent those for the general population. These similarities hold for ages 60–64 despite the small number of donors involved.

The general conclusion which emerges from these tables is that the donor sample broadly resembles the population in respect of age, sex and marital status when account is taken of the possible effects of the age-incapacity and reproductive factors. These factors cannot be statistically estimated. We do not have—and no one has—an accurate population 'universe' of potentially eligible donors against which we might compare the results of the pilot survey. Nor do we have any facts about the total number of donors in the

[1] Copies of the tables may be obtained from the writer.

country who gave blood in 1967. The most that we can do, therefore, is to observe the similarities and dissimilarities between the sample data and the data for the general population.

Two other points may be noted about Table 24. For most age groups, the general public donor is more representative of the national population than the institutional donor or the total of all donors. The institutional and Defence Services donor tends on the whole to be younger.

The second point—and a socially unexpected one,—is the consistency of the relative contributions of donors who are widowed, divorced and separated. Of the eight age groups from age 25, men donors in these categories record identical proportions as in the general population in three age groups, a higher proportion in one, and lower proportions in four. Among women, there is one identical proportion and seven higher ones.

It is hard to believe that these results are the product of chance. Of course, to be widowed, divorced or separated are different social and psychological states for men and women; it is regrettable that the relative smallness of the total sample did not permit a further breakdown. Whatever their motives, which may well be complex, it must be recorded, however, that judged by this survey the widowed, divorced and separated make, in total, a somewhat larger contribution to the National Blood Transfusion Service than their numbers in the general population would have indicated.

In Appendices 4 and 6 we examine the donor sample from a variety of viewpoints in relation to social class and gross income per week. There is in the sample some over-representation of social classes I and II and donors (or chief earners) earning more than £30 per week and, conversely, some under-representation of classes IV and V and donors (or chief earners) earning less than £15 per week. We discuss a number of factors which could account for this difference: the tendency to upgrade status (e.g. owners of shops and small-scale dealers reporting low earnings and describing themselves as 'directors'); the fact that 75 per cent of the donors came from the relatively more prosperous Birmingham and South East Metropolitan areas; administrative practices of blood donor teams which tend, for understandable reasons, to limit the opportunities to donate blood of semi-skilled and unskilled workers in, for example, the building, contracting and agricultural industries and those employed in small or scattered work units, on night-shifts or at times when it is difficult to attend a general public donor session near their homes.

In addition, three further factors are relevant to this question of representativeness. First, a higher proportion of the 'non-healthy' population of both sexes who are ineligible to donate are to be found in social classes IV and V and among low earners; second, in our donor statistics we took the occupation and earnings of chief earners and thus ignored the occupations of wives who were working and of some unmarried donors; third, the precise nature of the arrangements made in and by some institutions (factories, offices and stores, etc.) to provide a specific number of donors per session appears to have played an important role. For example, compared with General Public donors, there were proportionately fewer Institutional donors earning less than £15 per week although on average they tended to be substantially younger in age. It may be that opportunities of volunteering to donate are first given to executive and white-collar workers. If, as is often the case, there is no lack of volunteers from these classes the opportunities, at a single session, for manual workers—and especially those at the bottom of the Institution's hierarchy—will clearly be more limited.

Taking cognisance of all these factors and considering the way in which the 'sample' was picked and responded it is perhaps remarkable that the similarities with national data on social class and income are as good as they are. We conclude, therefore, that in terms of these attributes our blood donor population is broadly representative of the general 'eligible' population.

Lastly, in this consideration of representativeness we checked our material on the distribution of numbers of children, childlessness and mean family sizes with national data. Again we found that our distributions, means and percentages were in general accord with what is known on the national plane about family size and social class. Despite the relative smallness of the donor sample we discerned, for example, a tendency for the proportions of male donors with 4+ children to be inversely related to social class; this is, in fact, just what one would have expected to find in a much larger and more randomly selected sample of the population aged 18–64.

So far we have been considering the characteristics of donors in the survey from the viewpoint of 'representativeness'. As we have explained, the major difficulty here is that we have no true population universe. We cannot estimate one for the general population of eligible donors aged 18–64, nor do we have any relevant information for the total of actual donors in England in 1967. We have, therefore, had to use a variety of indirect methods and draw attention to similarities and dissimilarities in comparing the characteristics of our donors with data for the general population. On this basis, and after taking cognisance of a number of limiting and qualifying factors, we have reached the broad conclusion that the donors in the survey (and particularly General Public donors) closely resemble at many points the general population of the country. In relative terms, they are far more typical of the general population in respect of sex, age, civil status, social class and income group than blood donors in the United States.

But how typical are our donors of all donors in England? To this question we can give no clear answer. Nevertheless, despite the handicaps of a pilot study of this kind, we believe that we obtained a reasonably typical 'mix' of 3800 donors in our so-called 'sample'.[1]

One further minor qualification must also be mentioned. Our sample did not include any prisoners (Captive Donors as categorized under Type F in Chapter 5). For many years it has been the policy of the National Blood Transfusion Service to offer opportunities to donate voluntarily to all groups in the population including men and women in prison and other penal establishments. The accepted principle is that the Service should not discriminate against potential donors in Institutions who cannot present themselves at general public sessions. They are treated alike; that is to say, there are officially no material rewards for prisoners, remission of sentences or good conduct marks.

In 1967, for the country as a whole (including Scotland), 14,903 prisoners and 1175 staff members volunteered to give blood.[2] For the prisoners this represented a little under 1 per cent of the national total of blood donations in the same year.

Despite the fact that prisoners receive no benefit from donating there is, nevertheless, or may be thought to be, some element of compulsion or external pressure to donate. It would follow, therefore, if this 1 per cent is deducted (and we may include in this

[1] A special analysis was made for each of the three regions of the characteristics of the donor sample populations and these were compared with 1966 census data for the corresponding regional hospital board areas. The results showed that there were no significant differences for any of the classifications concerned (sex, age and marital status) between the three regional donor sample populations. Tests of statistical significance were also carried out for the main tables in this chapter and Appendix 4. The results (which can be obtained from the writer) have been taken into account in broadly interpreting the tables. To print them all here in detail might, it was thought, give a spurious impression of accurate representativeness. This would not be justified because of the difficulties already referred to of comparing the donor sample with the general population and the lack of basic data about all registered donors in England and Wales in 1967.

[2] *Report on the Work of the Prison Department*, 1967, Cmnd. 3774, p. 29.

proportion a small number of Defence Service donors) that the remaining 99 per cent of donors can be classified as Voluntary Community Donors (Type H).

III

Having discussed as far as we can the problems of assessing representativeness, the next section of this chapter is devoted to a summary of the main facts about the characteristics of donors as shown in Appendix 4.

For the convenience of those readers who may not wish to study the appendices in detail we, therefore, bring together here, in itemized form, some of the main facts:

1. Approximately 60 per cent of the donors were men; 40 per cent women. The sex difference would seem to be largely brought about by the withdrawal of younger married women as donors because of child-bearing. If the results of this survey are at all typical then women donors in Britain may be said to make a proportionately higher contribution to the national total of blood donations than in any other country in the world for which comparative data are available.

2. For both sexes donors are somewhat younger than the general population aged 18–64. This distribution is chiefly brought about by a decline in the number of donors aged over 55. A higher number of young donors of both sexes in the first ten eligible years for donating balances the gradual withdrawal of older donors of both sexes in the last ten eligible years. The young come in to compensate, theoretically speaking, for the effects of ageing as sickness and disability make it more difficult for older people to take part in the act of giving.

3. Even so, about 10 per cent of all blood donated came from men and women over the age of 55.

4. When account is taken of age-incapacity, health and reproductive factors, the donor population in terms of sex, age and marital status appears closely to resemble in most respects the structure of the general population.

5. Women over the age of 40 who are widowed, divorced or separated (considered as a single category) appear somewhat more frequently as blood donors than their numbers in the general population would indicate. More of them than men in the same category are long-service donors (having given more than 30 blood donations).

6. Men and women in social classes I and II and earning higher gross incomes per week represent somewhat higher proportions as donors than in the general population. The reverse obtains for both sexes in social classes IV and V and among those earning less than £15 per week. A number of reasons for these differences have already been given; others are mentioned in Appendix 4.

7. Between one-half and two-thirds of all blood donors of both sexes were in social class III and earned £15–30 per week.

8. Proportionately more high income/class donors and low income/class donors voluntarily gave blood at general public sessions than at workplace sessions. In other words, on average the community donor appears to be more representative of society than the employee donor.

9. Approximately 13 per cent of all chief earners in donor households had weekly incomes which, if all the facts were known, might have put them at a standard of living at or below Supplementary Benefits standards in 1967. About 70 per cent of all widow donors earned less than £15 per week, and about 24 per cent of the total were in social classes IV and V.

10. Young single men (aged 20–29) figured prominently in the contribution made by social classes I and II. Conversely, it was the older married men (aged 50–64) who figured prominently in the contribution made by social classes IV and V.

11. Married women in full-time employment (the majority aged over 30) appeared more frequently as donors than their numbers in the general population would indicate. This is true of all social classes but particularly of classes III–V. Combining the role of housewife with a full-time paid occupation did not apparently deter these women from voluntarily giving blood. The great majority did so in the community.

12. Donors in all social classes and income groups with large families of four or more children (or whose larger families had grown up) made their contribution to the National Blood Transfusion Service along with the childless and those with one to three children. Of all married donors of both sexes in all social classes aged 30–44 9 per cent had four or more children. In classes IV–V the proportion was 12 per cent. The thought may have been present among these donors that their children might need blood transfusions in the future.[1]

---

[1] About 150 donors in all gave this as their reason for donating (see Appendix 6).

13. Married women with children (or who had had children) were more likely to be blood donors than childless married women.

14. There were 3616 donors in our sample who had all given at least one previous donation. In all, they had contributed 43,391 pints of blood to the National Blood Transfusion Service. The range was from 2 to over 60 pints; the average being 12. Considered in terms of each sex separately, about 7 to 8 per cent of the total had been contributed by relatively new donors (1 to 4 pints); 25 per cent by long-service donors (over 30 pints).

15. These and other facts in Appendix 4 show that donors are not transient or sporadic givers motivated by sudden crises or urgent television appeals for blood. Many are 'attached' donors, giving regularly and consistently (the contribution of long-service donors had been spread over more than 15 years of giving).

16. When the computer had analysed all the data in terms of total blood donated (as compared with numbers of donors) in relation to sex, age, marital status, social class and other factors no markedly different major conclusions emerged. Women were shown, for example, to have contributed 38 per cent of all blood donations; men 62 per cent.

17. Some additional facts disclosed by this analysis included: relatively more men and women in social classes I, II and III aged 30–64 had given more than 15 pints as compared with classes IV and V; relatively new donors at ages 45–64 were making a sizeable contribution particularly among both sexes in classes IV and V; married men were more likely to be long-service donors than single men (partly because the state of being single is not usually a permanent state).

These findings which relate to numbers of donations must be treated more cautiously than others, principally because we did not obtain from donors any account of their circumstances and characteristics *at the time previous donations were made.* One cannot assume, therefore, for example, that donors who were married when the survey was undertaken had made all their blood donations during the period of the marriage. Errors of memory in relation to the number of previous donations were ruled out as the data were checked with official records.

The broad social implications of this first survey of the characteristics of donors in England are discussed in later chapters when we also consider the motivation material (Appendix 6) and make comparisons with the situation in the United States and other countries.

To end this chapter we provide a short analysis of the survey data on 'Giving and Receiving'.

IV

Blood donors in the survey were asked some questions about giving and receiving blood. We now analyse the main results, first in terms of the donors themselves, second in relation to the donor's immediate family.[1]

Excluding the Defence Services donors and a small number of other donors who could not be classified because of the omission of (or inadequate information about) age or marital status, there were 159 donors who had themselves received a blood transfusion. For a population of 3465 (M. 2062, F. 1403) this represented a rate of 4·6 per cent.

As Table 11 shows, the rate for women was higher than for men, namely:

M. 3·5 per cent
F. 5·9 per cent

A breakdown by three broad age groups gave the following percentages:

TABLE 10

Percentage of Donors by Sex in each Age Group who had Received a Blood Transfusion

Age	Males %	Females %
18–29	2·3	3·6
30–44	3·1	8·3
45–64	5·6	8·5

In each group the rates are higher for women, and for both sexes they increase with age. This age effect was to be expected (and incidentally provides some evidence that blood transfusions were remembered) if only because the number of years of exposure to the chances of a transfusion also increases.

The next table combines an analysis of marital status and social class (numbers were too small to allow a further breakdown by age):

[1] Future surveys of blood donors are advised not to include questions concerning 'other relative or friend'. The response to this part of the question in our survey was unsatisfactory; it is clear that donors had insufficient knowledge and that the definition of 'relative or friend' varied greatly. We do not, therefore, present an analysis of the replies to this part of Question 3.

TABLE 11

Percentage of Donors in each Sex, Marital Status and Social Class Group who had Received a Blood Transfusion
(number of donors in parentheses)

Social class	Males					Females				
	Percentage distribution of social classes	Proportion who had received a transfusion				Percentage distribution of social classes	Proportion who had received a transfusion			
		Married	Single	W/D/S	Total		Married	Single	W/D/S	Total
	%	%	%	%	%	%	%	%	%	%
I	11	4·8 (189)	8·8 (34)	0·0 (1)	5·4 (224)	11	8·2 (122)	0·0 (22)	0·0 (2)	6·8 (146)
II	20	3·8 (318)	4·3 (94)	0·0 (4)	3·8 (416)	26	7·2 (236)	4·0 (100)	9·1 (11)	6·3 (347)
III	56	3·3 (901)	2·9 (209)	4·3 (23)	3·3 (1133)	48	7·2 (389)	1·5 (200)	13·0 (46)	5·8 (635)
IV	11	1·2 (163)	0·0 (51)	0·0 (6)	0·9 (220)	13	8·7 (115)	0·0 (46)	0·0 (16)	5·6 (177)
V	2	5·6 (18)	12·5 (16)	0·0 (0)	8·8 (34)	2	0·0 (20)	0·0 (8)	0·0 (3)	0·0 (31)
IV/V combined	13	1·7 (181)	3·0 (67)	0·0 (6)	2·0 (254)	15	7·4 (135)	0·0 (54)	0·0 (19)	4·8 (208)
All	100	3·4 (1589)	3·7 (404)	2·9 (34)	3·5 (2027)[1]	100	7·4 (882)	1·9 (376)	9·0 (78)	5·9 (1336)[1]

[1] The total number of donors in this table (3363) is somewhat less because of the omission of (or inadequate information about) occupation. It also excludes the economically inactive and retired. It relates to 149 donors in all who had received a blood transfusion.

Although the number of donors in this table is somewhat smaller than in other tables in Appendix 4 (because of classification, etc., problems) nevertheless, the percentage social class distributions are virtually the same (see Table 26 in Appendix 4).

What is statistically significant about this table is that the receipt of blood increases with social class. The higher social class donors have had more blood transfusions than the lower ones—particularly men. Among men, the percentage excess of S.C. 1–11 over IV–V is 120 per cent. Among women, it is 35 per cent.

These differences cannot be accounted for by differences in age structure (donors of both sexes in S.C. IV–V tended to be older—see Appendix 4); by differences in marital status (see Table 11) or by differences—affecting women—in size of family (see Table 30). Nor is it reasonable to suppose that blood donors in the higher social classes are more likely to recall blood transfusions (and surgical operations) than donors in the lower social classes.

We conclude, therefore, that these differences are real ones and that in this group of donors the higher social classes received more blood transfusions (and surgical operations or other medical treatments necessitating blood). This is an unexpected finding. The whole weight of evidence on the social class incidence of mortality and morbidity, of industrial accidents and to a large extent of road accidents, and of the risks of childbearing among mothers with large families from poor homes would have indicated contrary results. In short, we would have expected—particularly under a free National Health Service—to find that, taking account of these factors, blood transfusions would be relatively more numerous among S.C. IV–V.

The data were rearranged to see whether any explanation could be found in the distribution of donors by session type and particularly in the selection of Institutional donors. The results are shown in Table 12.

The class relationships emerge in three of the four columns and more strongly among donors from Institutions.

Lastly, in this consideration of the proportion of donors who had themselves received a blood transfusion we related the data to the number of donations given (see Table 13, p. 138).

In many of the cells the number of blood recipients is very small; hence, any interpretations of the table can only be tentative. In general, however, it may be suggested:

(i) the percentage of women donors who have received blood is higher than that for men

136

(ii) unlike men, this increases as the number of donations given increases. Or put in another way, women in the sample who had received blood were more likely than men in the sample to be more generous givers of blood. This seems to apply to all social classes among women and among long-service donor men (30+) to social classes III–V

(iii) looking at the social class percentages, it appears that men and women donors in social classes I–II receive more blood; they also, as Appendix 4 suggests, give more blood.

TABLE 12

Percentage of Donors in each Sex, Social Class of Chief Earner and Session type who had received a Blood Transfusion

(number of donors in parentheses)

Social class	General Public		Institutions	
	Male	Female	Male	Female
I–II	4·8 (418)	6·4 (469)	4·2 (192)	7·0 (57)
III	3·2 (758)	6·2 (534)	3·5 (431)	4·5 (155)
IV–V	3·2 (154)	6·2 (145)	2·8 (109)	2·3 (43)
All	3·7 (1330)	6·3 (1148)	3·6 (732)	4·7 (255)

Whatever the tentative nature of these conclusions, it is a remarkable fact that men and women who have received blood transfusions should themselves voluntarily give blood and continue to give it on a generous scale. One of the most striking facts is that among all the women who had given 15 to 50 or so blood donations over 8 per cent had themselves received blood.

What we do not know in attempting to interpret all the percentages in this chapter and in Appendix 4 is the experience of those who have not given blood. It may be that those who have received blood between the ages of 18–64 are less likely to give than those who have not been recipients. It may be that the giving-receiving percentages vary by social class, age and other characteristics simply because the reasons for surgical or medical blood transfusions were more serious in one group than in another, thus debarring on medical grounds some recipients from becoming or continuing to be blood donors (in addition to having no data on non-blood donors it should also be remembered that we know nothing about the characteristics of donors who have ceased to

TABLE 13

Percentage of Donors in each Sex, Social Class and Number of Donations Group who had Received a Blood Transfusion

(number of donors in parentheses)

	Male				Female			
	Number of donations[1]				Number of donations[1]			
Social class	1–4	5–14	15–29	30+	1–4	5–14	15–29	30+
	%	%	%	%	%	%	%	%
I–II	4·3 (164)	3·9 (279)	7·0 (144)	0·0 (57)	3·4 (175)	7·5 (212)	8·1 (86)	9·4 (32)
III	4·7 (359)	2·6 (466)	1·3 (234)	6·8 (74)	4·6 (262)	5·5 (275)	7·8 (90)	6·1 (33)
IV–V	2·2 (91)	1·0 (97)	1·9 (52)	6·7 (15)	3·9 (76)	6·2 (65)	4·5 (22)	20·0 (10)
All	4·2 (614)	2·9 (842)	3·3 (430)	4·1 (146)	4·1 (513)	6·3 (552)	7·6 (198)	9·2 (75)

[1] Excluding the current one.

donate regularly, i.e. they are no longer registered on a panel). More important still, as we have indicated elsewhere, very little is known, medically and sociologically, about who receives blood and why.

Finally, we include some statistics in Table 14 on the second part of the question relating to blood transfusions received by the donor's immediate family (defined here as parent, husband/wife, children).

TABLE 14

*Percentage of Married Donors by Sex in whose
Immediate Family at least One Member or they
Themselves have Received blood*

	At least one receipt of blood	No receipt of blood	Total	Number of donors
	%	%	%	
Male	28·3	71·7	100	1708
Female	28·7	71·3	100	984

The percentages by sex are virtually identical. All we can say about this table is that over a quarter of the families of both men and women donors had received blood; three-quarters had not. But if this sample is at all representative of the total population of the country (Table 14 includes children and old people) then it seems a remarkably high figure; it is hard to believe that over one-quarter of all 'immediate' families have received blood at some time during the last twenty-five years or so. An alternative explanation is that the free receipt of blood by oneself or by a member of one's family at some point in the past is a motive for voluntarily giving.

The last two tables exclude transfusions received by the donor.

TABLE 15

*Percentage of all Donors by Social Class in whose
Immediate Family at least One Member has Received blood*

	Social class					
	I	II	III	IV	V	Total
	%	%	%	%	%	
At least one receipt of blood	24·4	25·5	23·0	19·0	22·6	
No receipt	75·6	74·5	77·0	81·0	77·4	
	100	100	100	100	100	
Total of donors	393	793	1879	389	62	3516

139

TABLE 16

Percentage of all Donors by Gross Weekly Income of Chief Earner in Donor's Family in whose Immediate Family at Least One Member has Received blood

	Not answered %	Less than £10 %	£10–15 %	£15–20 %	£20–30 %	£30–50 %	£50 + %	Total
					Income group			
At least one receipt of blood	16·7	19·6	20·9	20·1	24·3	26·7	25·7	
No receipt	83·3	80·4	79·1	79·9	75·7	73·3	74·3	
	100	100	100	100	100	100	100	
Total of donors	156	107	407	957	1387	603	206	3823

These two tables point in the same direction. They show that the families of higher income/social class groups received proportionately more blood than the families of lower income/social class groups. It was not only the better-off higher status donors who themselves received more blood but their families did so as well. This, again, is an unexpected finding bearing in mind what has previously been said about morbidity, mortality and accidents, and the fact that donors in social classes IV–V and earning less than £20 per week are on average older (and therefore are likely to have older families exposed to risk for longer periods) and also on average have larger immediate families. But although in a strict medical sense this finding may be unexpected in another sense it is not. What it could mean is that those individuals and families who receive more blood (and for conditions which do not as a consequence debar potential donors from subsequently donating) are more likely to give more blood. This, perhaps, within the context of an entirely voluntary system would not be an unexpected finding.

We explore further these issues in a later chapter where we discuss donor motivations.

Chapter 8
Is the Gift a Good One?

I

In Chapter 2 it was explained that to the recipient the use of human blood for medical purposes could be more lethal than many drugs. The transfusion and use of whole blood and certain blood products carries with it the risk of transmitting disease, particularly serum hepatitis, malaria, syphilis and brucellosis. Not only are there risks in infected blood and plasma but there are also risks in the use of contaminated needles and apparatus in the collection and transfusion processes. A brief summary of these risks was provided in Chapter 2.

In the United States, Britain and other modern societies the most dangerous of these hazards is serum hepatitis. It is becoming a major public health problem throughout the world. No scientific means have yet been found to detect in the laboratory the causative agent or agents of hepatitis in the blood before it is used for a transfusion or for conversion into various blood products. The quantity of infected blood that can transmit hepatitis may be as little as one-millionth of a millilitre.[1] The absence of a scientific check on quality and safety means that the subsequent biological condition of those

---

[1] Murray, R., *Bull. N.Y. Acad. Med.*, **31**, 341, 1955. Preliminary findings of studies carried out in the United States and Britain, published in 1969, report the identification of a specific factor in the serum of patients with acute viral hepatitis. This factor has been shown to behave as an antigen and has been called Australia antigen because it was first found in the serum of an Australian aborigine. The *British Medical Journal*, discussing these reports in an editorial, concluded: 'There have been many false trails to the elusive hepatitis virus and to the development of an effective vaccine. This may yet be another, but meanwhile results of attempts to grow this agent in tissue culture are awaited with great interest, and the use of tests for the antigen in screening potential blood donors certainly merits further evaluation' (*Brit. Med. J.*, **i**, 645, June 14, 1969. See also *Lancet*, **ii**, 143, July 19, 1969 and **ii**, 577, September 13, 1969; Cossant, Y., *et al.*, *Brit. Med. J.*, **ii**, 755, September 27, 1969 and *Brit. Med. J.*, **i**, 403, February 14, 1970; Zuckerman, A. J., *et al.*, *Brit. Med. J.*, **i**, 262, January 31, 1970, and *Transfusion*, Vol. 10, No. 1, January-February 1970, p. 1).

who receive blood constitutes the ultimate test of whether the virus was present in the donation; in effect, therefore, the patient is the laboratory for testing the quality of 'the gift'.

But few—if any—patients know that their bodies perform this role. They do not ask and in most cases are in no condition to ask: will this blood cause hepatitis? Who supplied it, in what circumstances, and precisely what safeguards were employed to ensure as far as humanly possible that this blood is not going to harm or kill me? Even if such questions were asked it has to be recognized that they could not be satisfactorily answered by those administering transfusions or blood products.

In these situations of consumer ignorance and uncertainty, as in many others in the whole field of medical care, the patient has to trust the medical profession and the organized system of medical care. He has no alternative but to trust. If, subsequently, he develops hepatitis and it is clinically diagnosed as such (which in many instances it is difficult to do) it is still virtually impossible in most cases to establish a causal relationship, and to connect the infection or the ill-health to the blood transfusion or the blood product. Many complex factors are involved in these difficulties of diagnosing, identifying and naming the causal agent(s); one being the long incubation period in serum hepatitis—possibly up to six months.[1]

Not only, therefore, has the patient no alternative to trust when receiving blood but, subsequently, and apart from a very small proportion of obvious cases of infection where causal attribution can be established, he can have no redress. He is not only unknowingly the laboratory test of 'goodness'; he and his family must bear the biological, social and economic costs of infected blood and misplaced trust in terms of physical incapacity, loss of earnings and career prospects, the effects on family life and other unquantifiable factors. These costs may be mitigated (as, for example, by subsequent free treatment under the National Health Service in England) but they may never be entirely eliminated. In many cases, the costs are irreversible.

For these and many other reasons those responsible for blood

[1] Serum hepatitis is a form of viral hepatitis indistinguishable clinically and by laboratory tests from infectious hepatitis, but differing from it in the following ways: a longer incubation period, usually stated to be 'between 40 and 180 days, occasionally 200 days', or 'between 50 and 160 days'; possibly a greater incidence in adults; no seasonal variation; transmission only by the parenteral route. Although infectious hepatitis usually spreads by the orofaecal route, it can be transmitted parenterally (W.H.O. *Expert Committee on Hepatitis*, Second Report, W.H.O. Technical Report Series No. 285, Geneva, 1964).

transfusion services have stressed the great importance of maintaining the most rigorous standards in the selection of donors. The state of health, the health history and the social habits of the donor become crucial because the laboratory cannot identify the virus. Again, however, there are definite limits to the clinical assessment of 'health'; no single test or battery of liver function tests has yet been devised which will reliably distinguish carriers of the virus from 'normal' subjects.

A great deal depends, therefore, on the truthfulness of the donor in the processes of medical examination, history-taking and selection.[1] Just as the recipient of blood has to trust the doctor so the doctor has, within limits, to trust the giver. Those responsible for making medical decisions and administering blood have to act in certain circumstances on the assumption that donors have been truthful.[2] In situations of total ignorance and total helplessness this is one social right the patient has; the right to truthfulness. Essentially, this is because he can exercise no preferences, and because one man's untruthfulness can reduce another man's welfare.

In different blood donation systems, therefore, we are led to ask: what particular set of conditions and arrangements permits and encourages maximum truthfulness on the part of donors? To what extent can honesty be maximized? Can this objective be pursued regardless of the donor's motives for giving blood? What principles should the medical profession, in the interests of patients and of the profession, consider as fundamental in the organization and operation of blood donor programs? These are the questions with which this chapter is chiefly concerned.

II

In discussing the problems of quality and safety we shall concentrate on the major hazard—serum hepatitis.[3] We shall not, therefore,

[1] Some account of the questions to be asked of prospective donors and the procedures to be adopted was provided in Chapter 2 and in Appendix 1 extracts are printed relating to the official instructions on the medical examination and selections of donors in England and Wales.

[2] 'Unfortunately there is no indication on the label of the blood container informing the physician whether the blood comes from a high-risk donor population or from a low-risk volunteer group. Until it is required that such information be added to the label, the patient's physician cannot properly assess the risk the transfusion may carry.' (Allen, J. Garrott, 'Post-Transfusion Hepatitis', *Calif. Med.*, 104: 4, April 1966, p. 297.)

[3] The risk of malaria has also grown very considerably in recent years in the United States, Britain and other western countries due to the immense increase

be concerned with other risks in blood transfusion and in the clinical use of blood products.[1]

What follows constitutes, in the main, first, a review of the evidence on the serum hepatitis risk in relation to donor character-istics and donor selection in different systems and, second, a sum-mary of what is known about the incidence of serum hepatitis in a number of countries.

As regards the former, most of the evidence comes from studies conducted in the United States and Japan. In 1966 some of the American literature was briefly summarized by Professor M. L. Gross:

'Hepatitis is the most widespread transfusion danger for the hospital patient, the result of contaminated blood. Its exact toll is elusive, but the *Journal of the American Medical Association* has editorially indicated that the hepatitis transfusion problem is significant and considerably more prevalent than previously thought. "It has been reliably shown", (ran the editorial), "that an essential therapeutic measure, blood transfusion, causes death in approxi-mately one of every 150 transfusions in persons over 40 years of age as a result of serum hepatitis. Since this is the age group to which most blood transfusions are given, and since many hundreds are given daily, such a high fatality rate becomes a problem."

'Key area studies—in Chicago, New Jersey, Philadelphia, Los Angeles and Baltimore—which have carefully followed up trans-fused patients are discouraging. The hepatitis scourge, they show, strikes about one in twenty-five to fifty patients, with sizeable death rates of up to 20 per cent in those stricken. "It appears that the incidence of hepatitis after blood transfusion is greater than prior estimates have indicated", states Dr John R. Senior, a Philadelphia researcher. Dr Garrott Allen of Chicago has reported hepatitis

---

in air travel. Malaria can be transmitted with whole blood and certain blood products. Only one case of *P. falciparum* malaria has occurred in Britain in the last ten years after a blood transfusion, however, and this was when an African student, a carrier without clinical symptoms, was accepted as a blood donor. The infrequency of malaria cases resulting from blood transfusions in Britain compared with the experience of other Western countries is said to be attributable to the effectiveness of the safeguards adopted (Shute, P. G. and Maryon, M., 'Imported Malaria in the United Kingdom', *Brit. Med. J.*, **i**, 781, June 28, 1969).

[1] These include: human and computer errors in blood grouping, cross-match-ing, labelling, patient identification and many procedures at all stages in the transmission of blood and blood products from the donor to the recipient; clinical misjudgments and 'medication error' in the actual use of blood and blood products (such as the risks inherent in single unit transfusions), and other factors.

K   145

danger so extensive that it surprised the most inured of the profession: 3·6 per cent of all transfused hospital patients later contracted the disease (the risk rises with the number of units transfused). Judging from these samples, there may be 75,000 cases of hepatitis yearly, with almost 10,000 deaths.

'More optimistic statistics have been garnered in Boston by Tufts University School of Medicine researchers with a hopeful transfusion rationale for the future. A twelve-year study of the nine Boston teaching hospitals has produced only 171 patients rehospitalized for post-transfusion hepatitis, 12 per cent of whom died. Since their total study represents about 5 per cent of the nation's one-year blood use, we might thus expect 3500 cases nationally. The actual toll of blood transfusion hepatitis is possibly between the extremes of the Boston and Chicago studies.

'One of the main keys to preventing hepatitis after transfusion, the Boston physicians found, was in the careful checking of the source of the blood. The epidemic-like hepatitis in other cities, they believe, is a direct result of pre-bottled blood supplied by commercial sources: 40 per cent of the blood in the Chicago sample was bought and more than 75 per cent of the blood in the Baltimore group was commercial. In the teaching hospitals of Boston, conversely, none of the blood was purchased from commercial blood firms.

' "No matter what method of case finding was used, the lowest incidence of post-transfusion hepatitis was seen when commercially supplied blood was avoided", state Drs Grady and Chalmers of Tufts University'.[1]

Professor Garrott Allen, referred to in the foregoing summary from Professor Gross's book and one of the foremost authorities in the United States, has shown in a series of studies that the risk of serum hepatitis from transfusions derived from prison and Skid Row populations is at least 10 times that from the use of voluntary donors. 'This greater risk rate is attributed to the fact that the paid donor is often a cloistered resident of Skid Row where he and his colleagues are alleged to enjoy frequently the practice of the communal use of unsterile needles and syringes for the self-administration of drugs. These rates increase with the numbers of transfusions, but they do not continue as a linear relationship after the first 5 or 6 units are given. There are also other unsanitary practices that

[1] Gross, Martin L., *The Doctors*, New York, 1966, pp. 173-4. For references to the U.S.A. literature see Professor Gross's book and Mirick, G. S. *et al.*, *op. cit.*, 1965.

prevail among this kind of population which favor repeated exposures to infectious hepatitis as well. Still another contributing factor, allegedly higher in this group than in the general population, is that of alcoholism, which appears to make such individuals more susceptible to an initial attack of either infectious or serum hepatitis'.[1]

A later study (in New Jersey) showed that the risk of hepatitis 'developing in recipients of blood known to have been donated by convicted or suspected narcotics addicts was 70 times that in the controls'.[2]

These and other American studies have also shown that the mortality rate from hepatitis in late middle age can be as high as 40 per cent, and in patients over 60 about 50 per cent.[3] Attack rates as alarming as 8·7 per cent—or nearly three times higher than the averages cited above—have also been reported. 'Post-transfusion hepatitis', concluded one such study, 'has been found to be much more common in our study than has generally been accepted in this country. Patients so affected may represent a continuing source of further infection and may themselves progress to chronic liver disease'.[4] Chronic hepatitis, post-hepatitic cirrhosis, portal hypertension and bleeding esophageal varices are frequent sequelae.[5]

What does emerge from these investigations is that in the United States the virus carrier rate is anything from six to ten times higher in the blood of some groups in the population than in others. These higher carrier rates have been identified among other categories of paid and professional donors and not just among the smaller population of Skid Row and prison donors. Over the past decade many studies in different parts of the United States have incriminated

[1] Allen J. Garrott, 'Immunization Against Serum Hepatitis from Blood Transfusion', *Ann. Surg., op. cit.*, 1966. At least 7 studies in the United States have shown an extraordinarily high incidence of hepatitis among narcotic and other drug users. Because they 'are frequently known to sell blood for money to buy more drugs' they represent 'a considerable public health hazard' (for references see *Hepatitis Surveillance*, National Communicable Disease Center, *op. cit.*, 1967). Due to a widespread sharing of syringes and needles outbreaks of hepatitis among heroin addicts have been reported in London. They were not, however, blood donors (Bewley, T. H. *et al., Brit. Med. J.*, i, 730, March 23, 1968).

[2] Cohen, S. N. and Dougherty, W. J., 'Transfusion Hepatitis Arising From Addict Blood Donors', *J.A.M.A.*, 203: 427, 1968.

[3] Allen, J. Garrott and Sayman, W. A., *J.A.M.A.*, 108: 1079, 1962 and Hoxworth, P., *Ann. Surg.*, 160: 763, October 1964.

[4] Hampers, C. L. *et al.*, 'Post-Transfusion Anicteric Hepatitis', *New Eng. J. Med.*, 271: 15, 753, October 8, 1964.

[5] Hoxworth, P. I. and Haesler, W. E., *op. cit.*, 1960, p. 496. See also Zuckerman, A. J., *Viral Diseases of the Liver*, London, 1970.

the paid donor (and blood obtained from commercial blood banks) as the major source of infection. The most recently reported of these studies was conducted by Dr Paul Schmidt and his colleagues at the National Institutes of Health, Bethesda.

This was a controlled prospective study (unlike many previous retrospective ones) of two groups of patients aged over 21 undergoing cardiac surgery at the N.I.H. hospital. There were no significant differences between the groups in respect of age, sex, type of heart disease, type of operation and severity of preoperative symptoms. One group received 94 per cent of their blood obtained from one or both of two commercial blood sources employing paid donors (in the Mississippi Valley area and an east coast port city). The second group received 97 per cent of their blood from voluntary donors in the Washington area. The average number of units of blood transfused per patient was 18·5 in the commercial group and slightly more (19·6) in the voluntary group.

In the commercial group, the total hepatitis attack rate was 53 per cent; in the voluntary group nil. This study suggests not only an extremely high attack rate among cardiac surgery cases (average age 47) transfused with paid blood in the United States but that an immense number of cases of infection are at present undetected. Because the number of patients involved was small (a total of 68) surveillance of the hepatitis risk is being continued and expanded on a nationwide basis. Further studies are also under way to eliminate the possibility of a geographic factor (because some of the paid blood was obtained from the Mississippi Valley area).[1]

Quite apart from all other 'costs' falling on the patient the financial costs of hospital care for hepatitis cases are high. Dr Zuckerman has reported that the 'average' patient suffering from post-trans-

---

[1] A report of this study (a copy of which was given to the writer by Dr Schmidt) was presented to the annual meeting of the American Association of Blood Banks in October 1968. It is to be published in the proceedings; an abstract has appeared in *Transfusion*, Vol. 8, No. 5, September–October 1968, p. 318 ('Icteric and Anicteric Hepatitis Following Open-Heart Surgery: A Direct Comparison of Paid and Voluntary Blood Donors', by Walsh, J. H., Schmidt, P. J. *et al.*). The results of an earlier retrospective study from the N.I.H. (covering 200 patients undergoing open-heart operations) was published in 1965. The 12 per cent hepatitis incidence shown was much higher than in previous open-heart studies and 'greatly exceeds the incidence commonly observed in this country after multiple transfusions'. A large proportion of the blood was obtained from paid donors (Rubinson, R. M., *et al.*, *J. Thoracic & Cardiovas. Surg.*, 50: 575–81, 1965). Further confirmation of the very high risk of hepatitis involved from commercial sources was reported by the National Institutes of Health as this book was in the press—see Walsh, J. H., *et al.*, *J.A.M.A.*, 211: 2, January 12, 1970, p. 261.

fusion hepatitis requires hospital treatment for 35 days.[1] In 1967 the average cost of a week in hospital (all charges) in the United States for Medicare patients was of the order of $1400.[2]

Nor is the problem of serum hepatitis confined to the use of whole blood. There is a serious risk in the use of whole pooled plasma and certain blood products. 'When plasma from relatively large pools' (of donors) 'is used' reported the *British Medical Journal*, 'the incidence can reach the alarming figure of 11·9 per cent, but if the plasma pool is prepared from less than 10 bottles the figure falls to 1·3 per cent. After a massive blood transfusion— and between 10 and 20 bottles is commonplace in modern heart surgery—the risk is once again increased'.[3]

For over twenty years in Britain only 'small pool' plasma has been supplied by the National Blood Transfusion Service.[4] In the United States, however, large pools (often made up of blood from several hundred donors) are common in an estimated annual usage of over 300,000 units. Moreover, a substantial proportion of the blood is obtained from paid donors.

Early in 1968 the issue of safety—already raised by the mounting evidence of contamination—was brought to a head in the United States with the publication of the plasma study by Dr Redeker and his colleagues.[5] Briefly, this showed that the combined treatment of pooled plasma with ultraviolet irradiation and storage at 30–32°C for six months by the pharmaceutical industry does not eliminate (as had been claimed) the risk of hepatitis. Hence, the Division of Medical Sciences of the National Research Council issued its warning in 1968: '... serious doubt is cast on the safety of all pooled human plasma preparations'. It recommended that 'the use of whole, pooled human plasma be discouraged and even discontinued unless a clear-cut case can be made for its unique requirements'.[6]

Plasma obtained from large pools is commercially cheaper and, compared with whole blood, is easier to transport and can be stored indefinitely. These facts explain a passage in the Council's

[1] Zuckerman, A. J., *Brit. Med. J.*, **i**, 174, April 20, 1968.

[2] *Health Insurance Statistics*, Social Security Administration, U.S. Dept. of Health, Education and Welfare, HI–1, November 20, 1967.

[3] *Brit. Med. J.*, **ii**, 426, August 20, 1966.

[4] Following a study by the Medical Research Council which showed a substantial risk from the use of large pool plasma (*Lancet*, **i**, 1328, June 26, 1954).

[5] Redeker, A. G. *et al.*, *op. cit.*, 1968.

[6] National Research Council, *op. cit.*, pp. 58–9. The Federal Government subsequently asked producers to stop shipping plasma interstate. (*New York Times*, November 3, 1968 and *J.A.M.A.*, 205: 5, July 29, 1968.)

report: 'the medical profession is confronted with an impasse'.[1] So, in a different sense, is the pharmaceutical industry in the United States. Although the findings on which this recommendation is based are being challenged it was reported in May 1969 that plasma pooled from many donors was likely to be banned in the future.[2]

The commercial development of plasmapheresis programs on a large scale to obtain supplies of plasma and to produce commercial products such as fibrinogen and others could theoretically constitute even greater risks of hepatitis because practically all these programs— and some 2,000,000 units—depend on paid donors. As Chapter 6 has shown, the great majority of these suppliers of plasma are poor, unskilled workers with a high preponderance of Negroes and various 'minority' groups such as prisoners. It has been claimed that as most of these suppliers are on a register they are more carefully screened and are under regular medical surveillance. At the same time, it is widely recognized that 'over zealous attempts' to screen suspected and actual carriers of hepatitis 'could seriously decrease the number of donors'.[3] The need for elaborate and expensive health, laboratory and identification checks—even to the extent of marking the foreheads of prison suppliers and checking fingerprints—was explained at the Conference on Plasmapheresis in 1966.[4] These are necessary—as well as persistent attention to the health and diet of donors—not only to reduce the risks of hepatitis but also because of the hazards to the donor's health. 'It is not certain that we know yet what to look for to show that a donor may continue indefinitely on plasmapheresis', said a representative at this Conference from one of the leading pharmaceutical firms engaged in such programs.[5]

Compared with the hepatitis risks involved in the use of 'walk-in', irregular, Skid Row donor types there may well be substance in the claim that more regular, selected, longer-term plasmapheresis donors have a lower carrier rate. But a great deal depends here— as it does with all donors—on two factors: the precise nature of external quality and safety controls exercised by some scientific supervisory agency (even though there are limits to effective screen-

[1] National Research Council, op. cit., p. 58.
[2] Medical World News, A.M.A., Vol. 10, No. 21, May 23, 1969, p. 32.
[3] Stengle, J. M., National Blood Resource Program, op. cit., 1968, p. 10.
[4] Report of Conference on Plasmapheresis, op. cit., pp. 37–53.
[5] Report of Conference on Plasmapheresis, op. cit., p. 47. Other speakers described long-term donors; one, for example, was a woman of 40, poor, with six children, who had to work part-time but who 'did not have time to fuss with her diet'. She was on iron medication and giving 3–4 units a week. In 10 years she had supplied about 250 units (pp. 76–7).

ing) and, second, the degree of *continued* truthfulness among paid donors.

As to the first, it has been repeatedly shown in the United States that the official public health standards designed to insure the continued safety, purity, and potency of biological products are only minimal standards and in many cases are either inapplicable, inadequate or ineffective (partly because of the inherent difficulties of continually inspecting and checking all procedures at blood banks).[1] 'Under the standards set by the National Institutes of Health, an ancient physician, a nurse and a former bartender can theoretically combine their resources to form a blood bank. They can draw most of their blood from Skid Row donors at the minimum fee and sell their blood to hospitals that seek the lowest bidder and are not concerned with the scientific aspects of blood banking'.[2] The great expansion during 1968–9 in chains of profit-making hospitals (newly built hospitals as well as voluntary hospitals bought by some 33 nationwide investor-owned companies) is likely to increase the risks as more blood is purchased from commercial banks.[3] Altruistic donors can hardly be expected to give their blood to profit-making hospitals.

With regard to the issue of truthfulness, again it has been repeatedly shown that paid donors—and especially poor donors badly in need of money—are, on average and compared with voluntary donors, relatives and friends, more reluctant and less likely to reveal a full medical history and to provide information about recent contacts with infectious disease, recent inoculations, and about their diets, drinking and drug habits that would disqualify them as donors.[4] There is also the additional problem of examining and questioning coloured donors. These medical procedures applied to well-educated white donors (including questions about yellow jaundice) may produce reasonably accurate answers, but a coloured

[1] See, for example, Chapter 6 and all the evidence submitted on *Hearings on S. 2560*, *op. cit.*, 1964 and *Hearings on S. 1945*, *op. cit.*, 1967 (especially pp. 186–8 referring to donors in New Jersey and Chicago).

[2] Wheeler, C. B., Associate Pathologist, Research Hospital and Medical Center, Kansas City, 'State Laws and Regulations', *op. cit.*, 1964, p. 5. Moreover, there are many blood banks not subject to the law; for instance, those that do not engage in interstate trade. See also Ashworth, J. N., 'Standards, Inspection, Accreditation Program of National Institutes of Health, Federal Control and Blood Banking', *Proc. A.M.A. Conference on Blood and Blood Banking*, Chicago, 1964.

[3] *Wall Street Journal*, October 13, 1969.

[4] See references in Chapter 6 and *Hearings on S. 2560*, *op. cit.*, 1964 and *Hearings on S. 1945*, *op. cit.*, 1967.

person, especially from a poor and unsophisticated background with inadequate medical knowledge and inadequate health services, could not be expected to know, for instance, whether or not he had had 'yellow jaundice', especially in his youth.

The fact, therefore, that the whole of the United States blood donor program—and particularly the plasmapheresis program operated commercially with paid donors—relies to a substantial extent on supplies of blood from Negroes suggests that the risks of transmitted disease may be increased.

All these issues of paid donors and voluntary donors in relation to the risks of hepatitis, discussed extensively in the United States, Japan and certain other countries, were summed up by Dr Wheeler of Kansas City in 1964: 'I take the position that blood obtained from commercial blood banks *is*, all things considered, more dangerous than blood obtained from non-profit banks . . . *it is my honest conviction that, all of the above things being true, there are more deaths caused by the use of blood from paid donors than from the use of blood from volunteer donors*' (original italics).[1] The only answer, according to other authorities, is to 'eliminate the professional donor entirely'.[2]

These risks are not confined to the American people. With the great expansion in recent years of plasmapheresis programs substantial quantities of plasma and blood products are being exported by pharmaceutical firms to many countries in the world.[3] The public health authorities in these countries have no means of testing the safety, purity and potency of these products in relation to the risk of hepatitis. They do not know and cannot investigate the characteristics and motives of the donors, nor are they informed of what medical safeguards, if any, have been adopted in the selection and screening of donors.

The hazards involved, both to the American people and internationally, were made more explicit in 1969 by reports on the activities of Southern Food and Drug Research, Inc., and its associated corporations. These corporations, operating in 3 states, acted as 'intermediate contractors' to some 37 major American pharmaceutical firms a number having large international markets. Their main role, as commercial enterprises, was to supply plasma, hyperimmune immunoglobulin and other products and to carry

[1] Wheeler, C. B., *op. cit.*, 1964, pp. 3–4.

[2] Allen, J. Garrott *et al.*, *J.A.M.A.*, 1962, p. 1085.

[3] See Chapter 6 and also *Hearings on S. 2560*, *op. cit.*, 1964 (referring to attempted shipments of plasma to Cuba, p. 158).

152

out clinical trials on human beings of proposed new pharmaceutical products. The supply of hyperimmune immunoglobulin (used for therapeutic purposes in connection with mumps, whooping cough, tetanus and smallpox) involved vaccinating donors to build up the antibodies in the plasma.[1] The technique mainly used was plasma-pheresis.

With the assistance of prison physicians (some of whom were remunerated by these corporations) extensive use was made of prisoners (who were paid for taking pills, vaccinations and supplying plasma) from 1962 to 1969. In all, these corporations are said to have conducted between 25 and 50 per cent of the initial drug tests (or first-phase tests usually carried out on healthy subjects) annually undertaken in the United States.

A series of investigations and inquiries into the activities of these corporations reported:

(1) Potentially fatal new compounds have been tested on prisoners with little or no direct medical observation of the results.

(2) Prisoners failed to swallow pills, failed to report serious reactions to those they did swallow, and failed to receive careful laboratory tests.

(3) Control records for validation purposes were totally inadequate, plasmapheresis rooms were 'sloppy' and gross contamination of the rooms containing donors' plasma was evident.

(4) One prisoner on plasmapheresis received back another man's red cells and was seriously damaged for life.

(5) Another prisoner, injected with a whooping cough vaccine, died.

(6) Large outbreaks of hepatitis occurred at various prisons, involving over 1000 prisoners of whom at least 6 died.

(7) It is alleged that several agencies of the Department of Health, Education and Welfare knew for years about the activities and standards of these corporations and did not curtail or stop them.

(8) Many internationally known pharmaceutical firms knew of the standards of medical supervision, laboratory and quality control being exercised by these corporations. No concerted or collective action was taken to stop using these intermediaries. Some firms remained the biggest customers of Southern Food and Drug Research, Inc., and its associated corporations. Those who were still using these facilities in 1969 are reported to have defended the validity of the data provided.

[1] It was estimated in 1964 that these corporations were responsible for about one-quarter of the entire national supply.

153

This is only a brief summary of an immense amount of documentation available in the United States.[1] We have not included here much material raising ethical and political issues similar to those made explicit in the Nuremberg Code.

This case—or series of cases—is relevant in a number of ways to the problems with which this chapter has been preoccupied—the issues of donor 'truthfulness'; theories of social costs in relation to blood and blood products; and questions of safety, purity and potency.

In private market terms, we see that 'untruthfulness' was maximized at many points in the system— from the prisoners themselves to officials employed by the pharmaceutical firms. The social costs involved extend far beyond the areas of cost-benefit analysis conventionally studied by economists and statisticians. They embrace the prisoners and their families (many of whom were Negroes); the prison system itself; the medical profession; the pharmaceutical industry in the United States; and the consumers of these products not only in the United States but in many countries of the world.

At least one conclusion can be drawn at this point. Governmental systems of licensing, inspection and quality validation appear to be helpless to control private markets in blood and blood products. Their ineffectiveness has contributed in recent years to the phenomenon in the United States of numerous legal suits based on negligence, implied warranty and various food and drug acts. What is involved, of course, is the question whether blood transfusion is a commercial transaction or a professional service. These matters are discussed in the next chapter.

III

There have been only a few studies of the risk of hepatitis following blood transfusion in Britain. In no case has the incidence been shown to be higher than 1 per cent and in the most recent study (from Birmingham) it was nil.[2] The risk of transmitting the disease

[1] A much fuller summary was published in *The New York Times*, July 29, 1969.

[2] Somayaji, B. N., 'Risk of Anicteric Hepatitis following Blood Transfusion', *Gut*, Vol. 8, No. 6, December 1967, p. 614. We exclude from this survey the particular problem of hepatitis outbreaks in dialysis units affecting staff and patients. This hazard appears to arise from the handling of infected blood, taking specimens and the use of infected instruments (Jones, P. O. *et al.*, 'Viral Hepatitis: A Staff Hazard in Dialysis Units', *Lancet*, i, 835, April 15, 1967). A study published in 1970 concluded that serum hepatitis is 'an uncommon disease' in Great Britain (Mathews, J. D. and Mackay, I. R., *Brit. Med. J.* i, 259, January 31, 1970).

through the use of large-pool plasma was recognized as long ago as 1945 and in that year national production in Britain of plasma prepared from small pools (less than 10 donors) was substituted. A study by the Medical Research Council in 1954 showed an incidence of 0·12 per cent after the use of small-pool plasma and 0·16 per cent after the transfusion of whole blood.[1] This report and an earlier one[2] suggest that the incidence of serum hepatitis in Britain is low compared with that reported from the United States.

Apart from the Birmingham study there are no data on recent trends in Britain. In the United States the number of reported cases of serum hepatitis is rising rapidly.[3] It is also clear that, when the data from these studies for whole blood transfusions are compared with the results of surveys undertaken in the United States in the late 1940s and early 1950s, the risks of morbidity and mortality are higher today among transfused patients. Though no causal relationship can (or could) be established it should be noted that over the past fifteen to twenty years the proportion of paid donors has very greatly increased.[4]

West Germany and Japan are two other countries in which studies of serum hepatitis have been reported. A German study in 1966 indicated an overall attack rate of post-transfusion hepatitis of 14 per cent.[5] In Japan, rates as high as 33·9 per cent have been recorded though it seems to be generally accepted that for the country as a whole the incidence ranges from 10 to 25 per cent.[6] One

[1] Ministry of Health, Medical Research Council and Dept. of Health for Scotland, 'Homologous Serum Jaundice', *Lancet*, **i**, 1328, June 26, 1954.

[2] Lehane, D. *et al*, 'Homologous Serum Jaundice', *Brit. Med. J.*, 1949, **ii**, 572.

[3] *Statistical Bulletin*, Metropolitan Life Insurance Company, summarizing trend reports from the U.S. Public Health Service, November 1968. In New York City there was a rise of approximately 50 per cent in the first five months of 1969 compared with the same period in 1968 in the number of reported cases of serum hepatitis (Hepatitis Surveillance Unit report, National Communicable Diseases Center, August 1969).

[4] See Chapter 6. Any precise interpretation of national or international trends is impossible in the present state of knowledge and partly because viral hepatitis includes two forms of the disease, infectious hepatitis and serum hepatitis. The two forms, while clinically indistinguishable, have important differences. Serum hepatitis (with which this study is concerned) is usually the result of medical procedures, most often the administration of blood and blood products.

[5] Creutzfeldt, W. *et al.*, *Germ. Med. Monthly*, *11*, 469, 1966.

[6] Shimizu, Y., and Kitamoto, O., 'The Incidence of Viral Hepatitis after Blood Transfusions', *Gastroenterology*, Vol. 44, No. 6, June 1963, and Shimada, N. *et al.*, 'Serum Hepatitis in Japan', *Proc. 10th Congr. int. Soc. Blood Transf.*, Stockholm, 1964, pp. 1066–70. Serum hepatitis has also been reported in Japan from the use of frozen blood (Sumida, S. *et al.*, *Lancet*, **ii**, 1255, December 9, 1967).

study, however, of the use of blood from paid donors at a central hospital in Tokyo showed that between 65 and 95 per cent of patients 'developed clear-cut evidence of serum hepatitis as evidenced by marked transaminase elevations occurring usually between six and twelve weeks after transfusion'.[1]

These disastrously high rates in Japan have been attributed almost entirely to the fact that approximately 98 per cent of all blood is bought and sold. The 'market' in blood is dominated by commercial blood banks who pay 'cut-rates' of around $1·40 per 200 c.c. of blood and obtain most of their supplies from slum dwellers.[2] These so-called 'professional blood sellers'—popularly known as 'tako' (octopus)—are said 'to visit two commercial banks a day, selling 200 c.c. at each bank. Before each visit they gulp a concoction of iron filings in salt water, and eat spinach and dried sardines, in the belief that this will thicken their blood'.[3] American Ambassador Reischauer contracted hepatitis in 1964 as a result of transfusions of contaminated blood in a Tokyo hospital.[4]

In the early days of blood transfusion in Japan it seems that donors were volunteers. The growth in materialism, the emphasis on productivity, and the decision to pay donors in order to supply blood to the Americans in Korea in 1951 were all factors contributing to the commercialization of blood and the rising trend of serum hepatitis. Today, it appears that the shortage of blood is even more acute in Japan than it is in the United States.[5]

With the steep rise in demand in many countries of the world for blood for transfusions and blood components there seems to have been as great—or even greater—rise in the national proportions

[1] Prince, A. M., and Gershon, R. K., *Transfusion*, Vol. 5, No. 2, March–April 1965.

[2] *Transfusion*, Vol. 4, 1964, p. 405. See also League of Red Cross Societies, Second Red Cross International Seminar on Blood Transfusion, Medico-Social Documentation No. 18, Geneva, 1960, pp. 20–1. Some commercial banks 'also buy so-called scrap blood—thin or impure blood—for use in a product to "rejuvenate the skin of middle-aged women" '. Still other private banks specialize in purchasing blood with a high percentage of white corpuscles. Donors of this latter type are paid an extra 300 yen (85 cents) per 200 c.c. (*Hearings on S. 2560*, *op. cit.*, 1964, p. 185.)

[3] *Transfusion*, 'Blood donors in Japan', Vol. 3, 1963, p. 213, and *Hearings on S. 2560*, *op. cit.*, 1964, p. 185.

[4] U.S. Senate, *Congressional Record*, June 15, 1967.

[5] See previous references to Japan and also Azuma, Y., 'Problem of Blood Donor Recruitment in Japan', *Proc. 8th Congr. int. Soc. Blood Transf.*, Tokyo, 1960, pp. 520–2.

of blood that are purchased.[1] In some countries—as in the United States and Japan—the commercialization of blood is discouraging and downgrading the voluntary principle. Both the sense of community and the expression of altruism are being silenced.

IV

Apart, however, from these moral and social issues which are further discussed in later chapters, three broad conclusions have emerged from the material so far presented.

The first is that a private market in blood entails much greater risks to the recipient of disease, chronic disability and death.

Second, a private market in blood is potentially more dangerous to the health of donors.

Third, a private market in blood produces, in the long run, greater shortages of blood.

These risks, in private market situations, are concealed from patients, potential patients and paid donors. Commercial blood banks and the pharmaceutical industry do not inform doctors and patients as to the source of blood for transfusion and its use in the preparation of blood products. Donors—particularly captive donors and those in plasmapheresis programs—are not made fully aware of the totality of the risks they may be running in donating too frequently, for too long periods of time, and in subnormal states of health. Blood is bought and sold in ignorance of safety, purity and potency.

These are some of the consequences and some of the social costs involved in applying the values of the marketplace to human blood. Others are discussed in the next chapter.

[1] Some estimates of the proportions of paid donors in a number of countries are given in Chapter 10.

Chapter 9

Blood and the Law of the Marketplace

I

This book, as Chapter 1 explained, is fundamentally about human values and their relationship to those institutions and services in society with which social policy is concerned. At this point, however, some readers may have begun to wonder whether it was turning into a technical exposition of blood transfusion services.

This is not so. It was, however, essential to examine in depth and on a comparative basis the issues of freedom of choice, uncertainty and unpredictability, quality, safety, efficiency and effectiveness and to relate such issues to the supply and distribution of human blood.

The choice of blood as an illustration and case study was no idle academic thought; it was deliberate. Short of examining humankind itself and the institution of slavery—of men and women as market commodities—blood as a living tissue may now constitute in Western societies one of the ultimate tests of where the 'social' begins and the 'economic' ends. If blood is considered in theory, in law, and is treated in practice as a trading commodity then ultimately human hearts, kidneys, eyes and other organs of the body may also come to be treated as commodities to be bought and sold in the marketplace.

Profitable competition for blood 'is a healthy thing', it is argued by some in the United States. It improves services, increases supplies of blood, and is the answer to a 'shiftless, socialistic approach'.[1] If competition for blood were eliminated, it is warned, it would 'be the entering wedge for the destruction of our entire anti-monopoly structure', and would threaten the interests of 'great pharmaceutical companies'.[2]

[1] Countless statements of such opinions have been made in the United States in recent years. See, as one example, Dice, R. E., 'Paid Donor Programs', *Proc. A.M.A. Conference on Blood and Blood Banking*, Chicago, 1964. Reference should also be made to *Hearings on S. 2560, op. cit.*, 1964, and *Hearings on S. 1945, op. cit.*, 1967.

[2] Carlinger, P., General Manager, Pioneer Blood Service, Inc., New York. Statement before the Senate Subcommittee on Antitrust and Monopoly, August 1, 1967 (*Hearings on S. 1945, op. cit.*, 1967, pp. 51–6).

158

The payment of donors and competition for blood should be introduced in Britain, urged two economists in a publication of the Institute of Economic Affairs in London in 1968.[1] Productivity would rise; supplies of blood would increase; 'a movement towards more efficiency in the blood market is a movement towards more efficiency in the economy as a whole'. The Editor, Mr Arthur Seldon, in a preface said that the authors 'have made an unanswerable case for a trial period in which the voluntary donor is supplemented by the fee-paid donor so that the results can be judged in practice, and not prejudged by doctrinaire obfuscation'.

In essence, these writers, American and British, are making an economic case *against* a monopoly of altruism in blood and other human tissues. They wish to set people free from the conscience of obligation. Although their arguments are couched in the language of price elasticity and profit maximization they have far-reaching implications for human values and all 'social service' institutions. They legitimate, for instance, the great increase since 1967 in the number of commercial hospitals in the United States.

The moral issues that are raised extend far beyond theories of pricing and the operations of the marketplace. Moreover, they involve the foundations of professional freedom in medical care and other service relationships with people, the concept of the hospital and the university as non-profit making institutions, and the legal doctrine in the United States of charitable immunity. Charity in that country would be subject under competitive conditions to the same laws of restraint and warranty and have the same freedoms as business men in the private market.

II

All these issues were crystallized and debated in the now famous Kansas City case of 1962. Before we pursue them it is instructive to review the causes and implications of this particular event. Briefly, the facts are these.[2]

In 1953 a meeting in the City of doctors, pathologists, hospital administrators and local citizens decided to form a non-profit

[1] Cooper, M. H. and Culyer, A. J., *The Price of Blood, op. cit.*, 1968.

[2] They are taken from: Federal Trade Commission, Washington, Final Order (8519), October 26, 1966; *Hearings on S. 2560, op. cit.*, 1964 and *Hearings on S. 1945, op. cit.*, 1967; Whyte, W. E., 'Federal Trade Commission Versus the Community Blood Bank of Kansas City *Et Al*', *Proc. A.M.A. Conference on Blood and Blood Banking*, Chicago, 1964; Jennings, J. B., *op. cit.*, and other quoted sources.

making community blood bank. There was a need for more blood which the local hospital blood banks were not fully supplying, and the local branch of the American Red Cross was at the time channelling the blood it collected to the Armed Forces in Korea. For the next two years there were endless disputes among the various interests involved (which need not concern us here) about power, institutional control and finance. Then, in May 1955, a commercial blood bank (calling itself the Midwest Blood Bank and Plasma Center) started operations.

The bank was owned and operated by a man and his wife. He had completed grade school, had no medical training, and had previously worked as a banjo teacher, secondhand car salesman and photographer. The blood bank procedures seem to have been actually directed by his wife. She called herself an R.N. but was not licensed as a nurse in either Kansas or Missouri, and did not show any evidence of experience or training in blood banking. Originally there had been a third partner but he had been chased out of the bank by the husband with a gun. A medical director was appointed to comply with public health regulations. He was aged 78, a general practitioner with no training in blood banking. The bank was inspected and licensed by the Federal authority, the National Institutes of Health.

It was situated in a slum area, displayed a sign reading 'Cash Paid for Blood', drew blood from donors described as 'Skid-Row derelicts', and was said by one witness to have 'worms all over the floor'. In 1958 another commercial bank, the World Blood Bank, Inc., was established in Kansas City and also began operations.

From 1955 onwards pressures of various kinds were brought to bear on relatives of hospital patients, members of associations and trade unions to provide blood on a replacement basis to these commercial banks. But local hospitals refused to accept blood from these sources to discharge patients' blood fees. These and other developments seem to have forced a solution to the disputes over the control of the non-profit community blood bank, and in April 1958 it commenced operations. Subsequently, it appears from the evidence that practically all the large local hospitals entered into blood supply contracts with the Community Bank and ceased operating their own banks. The Community Bank thus had a virtual monopoly.

The two commercial banks then complained to the Federal Trade Commission alleging restraint of trade. In July 1962, after an investigation lasting several years, the Commission issued a complaint against the Community Blood Bank and its officers, directors, administrative director and business manager; the Kansas City Area Hospital Association and its officers, directors, and executive director; three hospitals, individually and as representatives of the forty members of the Hospital Association; sixteen pathologists, and two hospital administrators.

The complaint charged the respondents with having entered into an agreement or planned course of action to hamper and restrain the sale and distribution of human blood in interstate commerce. They were charged with conspiring to boycott a commercial blood bank in the sale and distribution of blood in commerce, and that the conspiracy was to the injury of the public and unreasonably restricted and restrained interstate commerce in violation of Section 5 of the Federal Trade Commission Act of 1952. This Section of the Act declares that 'uniform methods of competition in commerce, and unfair or deceptive acts or practices in commerce, are declared unlawful'. Violation of a Commission 'cease and desist order', after it becomes final, subjects the violator to civil penalties up to $5,000 for each day that the violation continues.

The respondents appealed. After lengthy hearings before an Examiner for the Commission in 1963, a further appeal and more hearings before the full Trade Commission of five members, a ruling was issued in October 1966. By a majority of three to two the Commission decided that the Community Blood Bank and the hospitals, doctors and pathologists associated with it were illegally joined together in a conspiracy to restrain commerce in whole human blood.

The records, transcripts and exhibits in this marathon case ran to over 20,000 pages and cost the respondents and the taxpayers something approaching $500,000.

III

While the hearings were in progress Bills were introduced in both House and Senate to exempt non-profit blood banks from the antitrust laws. In particular, Senator Edward V. Long of Missouri waged a battle for over five years in the interests of non-profit blood banks and the principle that human blood should not be treated in law as an article of commerce. In 1964 and again in 1967 he introduced Bills in the Senate; they were considered by the Senate Subcommittee on Antitrust and Monopoly.[1] Both failed to make

[1] *Hearings on S. 2560, op. cit.*, 1964, and *Hearings on S. 1945, op. cit.*, 1967.

progress. Although they received a great deal of support (especially from members of the medical profession who felt themselves seriously threatened) progress was blocked owing to a number of complex factors and partly because of pressures exerted by various interests ranging for quite different reasons from commercial blood banks to the pharmaceutical industry.[1] It was also said that the Bills were opposed by the Justice Department on the ground that 'there was no good case for an exemption of blood banks from the anti-trust laws. The Justice Department has always taken this position; namely, that there must be a very over-riding reason, based on the public interest, for such an exemption to be effected through Congressional legislation'.[2]

For a society to apply the laws of the marketplace to medicine, declared Dr E. A. Dreskin (President in 1966 of the American Association of Blood Banks) 'is enforcing business practice over medical opinion'.[3]

Since 1865 (when the Constitution's Thirteenth Amendment took effect and made illegal in the United States the buying or selling of human beings and presumably of living human tissue as well), it is doubtful whether any analogous biological issue has caused so much concern among the medical profession and related interests.

Thousands of individuals and professional bodies expressed their opinion, from 1962 onwards, that the Commission's ruling represented a grave threat to the profession of medicine, to scientific standards in blood transfusion, to the survival of non-profit community blood banks, to the voluntary donor and, ultimately, to the patient. 'Consumerism' (as it has come to be called), supported by the State in the form of antitrust powers, would be made sovereign.[4]

---

[1] *Hearings on S. 2560, op. cit.*, 1964, and *Hearings on S. 1945, op. cit.*, 1967.

[2] Wheeler, C. B., *op. cit.*, 1964, p. 3. At the State level, some States, for example, California and Wisconsin, have specific laws declaring that blood transfusion is a service. Other States, for example, Florida, in a Supreme Court ruling in March 1967 decided that blood was a saleable commodity and, therefore, carried an implied warranty of fitness. The particular case in this ruling was brought against a blood bank by a patient who charged that the blood 'sold her' was 'impure and unfit for use', and as a result she contracted serum hepatitis following a transfusion (*A.M.A. News*, December 5, 1966, and Rouse, M. O., *Transfusion*, March–April 1968, Vol. 8, No. 2, p. 107).

[3] Dreskin, E. A., *Medical Tribune*, November 28, 1966.

[4] Some of the more important professional bodies who protested were: American Medical Association, American Hospital Association, American Association of Blood Banks, College of American Pathologists, and Community Blood Council of Greater New York (see *Hearings on S. 2560, op. cit.*, 1964 and *Hearings on S. 1945, op. cit.*, 1967).

'The significance of this hearing', said Dr Wheeler (chairman of the Legal Committee of the College of American Pathologists) 'is that it represents a direct threat to interprofessional communication. If physicians in any speciality meet to discuss the relative merits of any two services which they render and the scientific consensus of opinion results in a loss of profit to some third party (a third party not licensed to practice medicine and only concerned with his paramedical business) those physicians can be dragged through a half-a-million dollar legal proceeding brought by the Federal Government with its inexhaustible financial resources and legal manpower'.[1] One of the dissenting Commissioners pointed out (as many other authorities have done) that doctors would not be free to exercise their own professional medical judgment in accepting or rejecting blood from commercial blood banks.[2] Most doctors and surgeons would not, in fact, even know the source of the blood.[3] They would not be free to meet, discuss, and recommend the use or non-use of such blood. If they did so, they would be subject to a $5000 a day penalty for violation of the order; civil liability could also ensue.

Under the order, professional freedom was seriously restricted. It was illegal to take part in a collective decision (to 'conspire') not to buy commercial blood despite the general weight of evidence that such blood carried a much greater hepatitis risk. Altruism in the form of voluntary blood donations had to be made subservient to the values of the marketplace, even if the consequence of establishing the market was to disable and kill more people.[4]

The American Medical Association, in protesting, warned hospitals and doctors to change their 'billing' practices, and not to state the charge for blood as a separate charge.[5] They were caught in a dilemma, for this proposal struck at the basis of competition in private medical care and the Association's support of commercial

[1] Wheeler, C. B., op. cit., 1964, p. 3 and Hearings on S. 2560, op. cit., 1964, pp. 131–43.

[2] Federal Trade Commission, Final Order, op. cit., 1966.

[3] 'The laboratory director would not be able to rely on anyone else to screen his blood; he would have to do it himself' (Mainwaring, R. L., President elect, American Association of Blood Banks, Transfusion, Vol. 4, 1964, p. 68).

[4] If free choice of blood was not possible 'blood banking will no longer remain at the high level of scientific performance that exists today—and destruction or deterioration of these scientific principles will endanger the lives of patients' (Statement of the College of American Pathologists before the Subcommittee on Antitrust and Monopoly, United States Senate, August 1, 1967).

[5] Randall, C. H., Medicolegal Problems in Blood Transfusions, Committee on Blood, American Medical Association, 1963, p. 16.

blood banks in 1964.[1] Other interests found themselves confronted with similar dilemmas. Pathologists and physicians working in privately owned clinical laboratories, for example, found themselves arguing against the profit motive. This was not a small group for, in 1967, 95 per cent of all clinical laboratories in the United States certified for participation in the Medicare program were under commercial proprietary control. Most of them were approved for haematology tests.[2] Commercial blood insurance companies, however, strongly supported the Federal Trade Commission's ruling in the interests of competition and 'sound business practices'.[3] They were joined by sections of the pharmaceutical industry who did not wish to see commercial blood banking discouraged by 'restrictive practices'.[4]

Part of the Federal Commission's case that blood was an article of commerce was based on arguments for extending the doctrine of implied warranty (fitness for use) in the financial interests of consumers; in short, to make it easier for them to sue doctors, hospitals, blood banks, laboratories and so forth. A doctor should, for example, be found guilty of negligence if he obtained human blood from a bank that failed to meet adequate standards; he 'should have known' that the hepatitis virus was present in the blood. This doctrine could be extended to all other areas of medical practice as well as to other service relationships. Nonprofit hospitals would

[1] *Hearings on S. 2560, op. cit.*, 1964, p. 159.

[2] Standards in many laboratories appeared in 1967 to be very low. Another Senate Antitrust Subcommittee discussing what was described as a 'national laboratory crisis', received the following evidence in 1967: 'Serious deficiencies have been demonstrated to exist in the Nation's clinical laboratories. Studies by the National Communicable Disease Center and others indicate that unsatisfactory performance is demonstrated by 10 to 40 per cent of laboratories in bacteriological testing; by 30 to 50 per cent in various simple clinical chemistry tests; by 12 to 18 per cent in blood grouping and typing; by 20 to 30 per cent in haemoglobin measurements; by 40 to 80 per cent in differential characterization of blood cells; and by 20 to 30 per cent in measurement of serum electrolytes. There also exists considerable variation in results from laboratory to laboratory. This information indicates that erroneous results are obtained in more than 25 per cent of all tests analysed by these studies.' Only a few states have comprehensive legislation covering the licensing, inspection, and control of diagnostic medical laboratories. In evaluation studies related to blood transfusion it was reported that, for example, 4 out of every 10 laboratories tested in Illinois failed to determine the correct blood group and rhesus factor (*Congressional Record, Senate, S. 1731–6*, February 8, 1967, and *Social Security Bulletin*, U.S. Dept. of Health, Education, and Welfare, Vol. 31, No. 9, September 1968, pp. 19–24).

[3] *Hearings on S. 2560, op. cit.*, 1964, pp. 122–31.

[4] *Hearings on S. 1945, op. cit.*, 1967, pp. 51–6 and 114–15.

be regarded as engaged in trade or commerce for profit. Until 1964 hospitals, like churches, schools, colleges, universities, public libraries, and charitable institutions not operated for profit, were exempt from price discrimination provisions of the United States Code.

IV

Recent court decisions in the United States, argued Professor Randall 'have tended to shift more and more of what had previously been considered as "services" into the category of commodity transactions'.[1] This trend, and the activities of lawyers bent on legalizing more and more service relationships, have contributed to dramatic increases in the number and cost of malpractice and negligence suits in the whole field of medical care as well as in the case of blood transfusions.

The Lancet, looking at the American scene from the standpoint of different medico-legal relationships in Britain, attempted early in 1969 to describe the situation.

'The problem of malpractice liability is now acute. Premiums have risen in most States by from 50 to 100 per cent, and for a "high risk" physician practising in neurosurgery, plastic surgery, or obstetrics the premiums are becoming outrageous even if cover can be secured. Extremely adverse underwriting experiences are causing even the biggest insurance agencies to run for cover. It seems indeed that in California many have dropped right out of the market —and California has long been the pacemaker in this field. This has come about by a number of changes in medicine and in the laws. The position indeed is rapidly becoming nonsensical. The doctrine of *res ipsa loquitur* seems to have been extended to a dangerous point, almost to the extent that if a patient does not fully recover or dies there is a cause for suit. If miracle drugs don't produce miracles, it's the physician's fault. The doctrine of informed consent has similarly been pushed to extreme limits. It now seems that there is cause for suit if the patient before consenting to a procedure was not informed and did not comprehend every possible disaster that could befall. As a surgeon has very reasonably asked, where does this leave a young married lady with acute appendicitis whose prognosis worsens with every passing hour? Explanation alone, let alone comprehension, of every known disaster that can

---

[1] Randall, C. H., *Transfusion*, Vol. 4, 1964, p. 67.

occur with a simple appendicectomy would take hours and might seriously harm the patient.

'But, apart from this side of matters, the simple facts are that many more suits are being brought, legal costs are mounting, and awards are being monstrously inflated—several of over one million dollars have been made. Since cases may take years to settle, insurers have the impossible task of assessing what calls may be made on their resources seven or more years ahead. So they are getting out of the field, in some cases abruptly cancelling policies that have been extant for years. The affected physicians have to shop round quickly for fresh cover, almost always at the cost of heavily increased premiums'.[1]

It was estimated in 1969 that one in five of all physicians in the United States had been or was being sued for malpractice. Commercial insurance cover against malpractice cost physicians approximately $75,000,000 in 1968 but of this sum awards to patients totalled only about $18,000,000. The difference went on sales and promotion, administration, profits and legal fees.[2]

In the early 1950s malpractice claims were numbered in hundreds. By the late 1960s they were being filed at the rate of 7000–10,000 a year. In 1970 it was forecast on the basis of current trends that at least one physician in four could expect a claim to be filed against him before he retired from practice. Such claims could lead to bankruptcy if insurance cover were not obtained. In some parts of the country, for instance, in Southern California, physicians in practice for five years faced in 1969 a 50–50 likelihood of being hit with a claim and the attendant threat of a lawsuit.[3] It was reported in October 1969 that some younger physicians were emigrating from the State.[4]

Costs to the individual physician vary substantially according to risk classification and premium class laid down by insurance companies, extent of coverage effected (per suit and per year), geographical area, claims experience and other factors. A few examples must therefore suffice. For policies effected in the middle ranges of coverage ($300,000 for any one claim and $900,000 in any one year)

---

[1] *Lancet*, **i**, 98, January 11, 1969.

[2] These facts are taken from the results of a survey by the American Medical Association reported in *A.M.A. News*, April 14, 1969, p. 1.

[3] The information in this paragraph is taken from *Medical World News*, United States edition, October 24, 1969.

[4] Los Angeles County Medical Association reported in the *Los Angeles Times*, October 30, 1969.

a general surgeon in New York paid about $1165 a year, and for general practice (including minor surgery) the premium was around $350.[1] These premiums were ruling in the middle of 1968. In California the corresponding premiums were around $2130 and $1600. 'High-risk' surgeons (neurosurgery, orthopaedic surgery, obstetrics and gynaecology, plastic surgery, anesthesia, etc.) effecting reasonably adequate cover paid around $2812 a year in California and $1750 in New York. Even paediatricians (no surgery whatever) paid around $250 in New York and about double in California.[2] These, however, were 'standard' quotations and indicated minimum premiums. Much depends on past experience and individual circumstances; many physicians paid substantially more, some according to the American Medical Association as much as $12,000 to $15,000 a year.[3]

Standard premiums have been rising rapidly for a number of years. Towards the end of 1968 the Insurance Rating Board sanctioned further increases averaging across 28 States of approximately 50 per cent—varying from a rise of 6 per cent in Oregon to 150 per cent in Vermont.[4] By the end of 1969 even larger increases in premiums were sanctioned. Some surgeons in California were then charged $16,000 a year.[5] On the East Coast, one head of a department of radiology who had been paying $5000 a year to protect himself and as head of department faced a premium increase in 1969 to $35,000 for the same malpractice cover.[6]

Some of the causes for this trend were described in *The Lancet* article. Others that have been cited include: 'the breakdown in communications and rapport between physicians and their patients' and the fact that the practice of medicine in the United States has become more hurried;[7] the role of plaintiffs' attorneys whose fees (contingent fees) may vary from 30 to 50 per cent of any award;

[1] Additional premiums are payable to include X-ray therapy, electroshock therapy, etc.

[2] Information obtained from a number of insurance companies in different parts of the U.S.; Medical Society of the State of New York; Dr S. M. Rabson, Los Angeles and Professor J. N. P. Davies, Albany, New York.

[3] *A.M.A. News, op. cit.*, p. 13.

[4] *Medical World News*, Vol. 9, No. 43, October 25, 1968, p. 11.

[5] *Los Angeles Times*, October 30, 1969, and *Medical World News, op. cit.*, October 24, 1969.

[6] Reported in personal communication by Professor J. N. P. Davies, Department of Pathology, Albany Medical College of Union University, New York, November 6, 1969 (Professor Davies is not the radiologist referred to).

[7] Hudson, C. L., past president of the American Medical Association, *A.M.A. News*, November 18, 1968, p. 16.

the activities of some physicians 'who make a business out of testifying in malpractice cases' and a general tendency for courts to favour claimants when the evidence is conflicting.[1]

The consequences for some physicians can be serious both in terms of costs and in terms of career prospects and clinical freedom. They may find it difficult or impossible to obtain insurance cover ('The medical malpractice insurance market is sick'[2]); they may believe that if they support plaintiffs their own insurances may be cancelled or that their hospital rights to admit patients may be revoked.[3] In some areas, California for one, attempts are being made to reduce the costs of malpractice by developing arbitration procedures. Patients sign statements agreeing in the event of disputes about treatment to refer such disputes to arbitration. The advantages for the physician are that there is no jury, there are one or more arbitrators instead of a judge, and the law relating to arbitration (in some States) does not require a court reporter. Complete privacy is assured (the proceedings may be held in the physician's office), strict rules of evidence are abandoned, and the arbitrator's decision is not published. One disadvantage is—apart from the implications of persuading the patient when ill or suffering anxiety to sign away his right to sue the doctor—'to insist that the patient face the contingency of the doctor's possible malpractice at the very inception of the doctor-patient relationship'.[4] It is thought by some physicians that this may lead to more rather than fewer malpractice-minded patients.

A London medical journal, commenting on some of these developments, remarked: 'American justice appears to be speeding the final extinction of medicine as a profession'.[5] This may well be thought to be an exaggeration; much depends, of course, on the current definition of 'profession' in relation to medicine and the meaning, for doctors and patients alike, of professional freedom. What is clear, however, is that these processes of legalizing personal-service relationships in medicine generally as well as in the blood transfusion

[1] Hirsh, B. D., General Counsel of the American Medical Association, *A.M.A. News*, April 14, 1969, p. 1.

[2] The conclusion of the insurance trade journal *Best's Review* reported in *Medical World News*, *op. cit.*, October 24, 1969. In some States cover was unobtainable in 1969; in others competition had ceased while, in general, many insurance companies were refusing to carry malpractice insurance.

[3] Survey by the *Wall Street Journal*, 'Suing the Doctor', February 28, 1969.

[4] *Professional Liability Newsletter*, Legal Medicine Foundation, Berkeley, Vol. 1, No. 3, December 10, 1968, p. 2.

[5] *Pulse*, International News Bureau, April 1, 1967, p. 2.

system and other spheres are leading to 'legally defensive professional practice'. This is a matter to which we have already referred so we will content ourselves here with one quotation from a statement by one of the major liability insurance companies in California: '. . . physicians today are practising more legal medicine and probably relying less on their judgment. They order batteries of tests that might not be necessary. They order X-rays that might not be necessary; call for consultations, and only do this to protect themselves. It has had a tremendous impact on medicine . . . And I think the patient himself is going to suffer'.[1]

The extent to which patients were by 1970 suffering was vividly illustrated and documented in a 1060-page report of a Senate subcommittee, *Medical Malpractice: The Patient Versus the Physician* published at the end of 1969 as this book was going to press.[2] The subcommittee, under the chairmanship of Senator Ribicoff, collected a mass of evidence for two years on many aspects of medical malpractice in the United States: its phenomenal growth, causes and effects on 'the skyrocketing cost of health care'; the rising share of malpractice expenses attributable to the role played by the legal profession; the widespread development of defensive medical practice affecting more and more aspects of diagnosis and treatment; and the deterioration in physician-patient relationships as they increasingly become subject to legal and commercial values and practices. The American Medical Association told the subcommittee: 'Today the doctor is too busy to have many family friends and medical practice has unavoidably become impersonal. Instead of a family physician, the patient may have a string of specialists whom he calls on when needed. These are more apt to seem like impersonal businessmen to the patient than like a family friend'.[3]

The subcommittee, in summing up from its formidable array of evidence on medical malpractice, concluded that: 'The situation threatens to become a national crisis'.

Whatever the effects on the quality of medical care the costs are passed on to the public. These costs include two major elements (1) the costs of malpractice insurance (2) the costs of defensive medical practice. Both elements have contributed to the accelerating rise in the costs of medical care. By the middle of 1969 these costs were

---

[1] King, J. F., American Mutual Liability Insurance Co., San Francisco, reported in *A.M.A. News*, November 18, 1968.

[2] A Study submitted by the Subcommittee on Executive Reorganization to the Committee on Government Operations, United States Senate, 1969.

[3] *Op. cit.*, p. 3.

rising at more than double the increase in the cost of living. 'This Nation', reported the new Nixon Administration, 'is faced with a breakdown in the delivery of health care'.[1]

It is not, however, the purpose of this chapter to explore the causes or consequences of the 'breakdown'. We have been concerned to show the connections between the growth of commercial practices in certain sectors of medical care and the increasing application of the laws of the marketplace—of legalized and legitimated doctor-patient hostility. The second is a logical consequence of the first. A private market in blood or clinical laboratory services or hospital treatment or other sectors of medical care will, in the end, require to be supported and controlled by the same laws of restraint and warranty as those that obtain in the buying and selling of consumption goods.

The contrast with the role of the law—and litigious patients—in Britain can to some extent be expressed by comparing malpractice and insurance costs. Since 1965 the subscription rate for medical practitioners who have qualified in Britain to the Medical Defence Union and the Medical Protection Society has been £6 a year (newly qualified practitioners pay only £3 a year during the first three years of membership). As members, they have complete indemnity against malpractice claims, legal costs and all incidental or consequential losses, costs, charges and expenses. In 1967 the total membership of the two societies was approximately 105,000; in all, 264 cases of alleged professional negligence by medical practitioners were handled.[2]

It should not be assumed from these facts that all is well with disciplinary procedures and investigations of complaints by patients under the National Health Service. There are serious faults in the system as the Council on Tribunals has made clear in its annual reports. All too often the scales are weighted in favour of the doctor. There are, however, alternative remedies open to societies with systems of free medical care for situations wherein the interests of patients are neglected or overborne which would not involve treating the doctor as a businessman, providing a rich market for lawyers, the destruction of doctor-patient relationships, and the inflation of medical costs charged to the public for the same quantum of medical care.

[1] Press statement by Secretary of Health, Education and Welfare, 'Report on the Health of the Nation's Health Care System', Washington, July 10, 1969.

[2] Annual Reports, the Medical Defence Union and the Medical Protection Society, 1968.

These medico-legal differences between Britain and the United States are even more remarkable in the field of blood transfusion. In Britain, in recent years, the annual number of legal suits for negligence has either been nil or quite insignificant.[1] In the United States, there is an 'ever-increasing number of malpractice and negligence suits brought by recipients who have suffered harm from transfusions'.[2] Professor Randall, writing under the auspices of the A.M.A.'s Committee on Blood, pointed out in 1963 that 'Litigation involving blood transfusions seems to be increasing with geometrical progression'. 'More serious still', he noted, 'is the fact that a growing number of courts have been willing to overrule the doctrine of charitable immunity, and place hospitals in the same legal position as non-charitable institutions'.[3] 'The great majority of the Courts', he added, 'seem convinced that the doctrine of charitable immunity is unsound, and that none of the historical arguments on which it is based can stand analysis'.

In January 1969 the Federal Trade Commission's ruling of 1966 in the Kansas City case was eventually set aside by the Eighth U.S. Circuit Court of Appeals in St Louis.[4] Up to the end of 1969 no appeal had been made to the Supreme Court.

Though this may be the end of this particular case the fact that it happened is one illustration among many of the increasing commercialization of the blood banking system and of hospital and medical services in general. This trend must logically lead to more and more recourse to the laws and practices of the marketplace. There is no inconsistency in this development. If blood as a living human tissue is increasingly bought and sold as an article of commerce and profit accrues from such transactions then it follows that the laws of commerce must, in the end, prevail.[5] What this trend

[1] Generally, on the legal aspects of blood transfusion in Britain see Chapter IX in James, J. D., *Practical Blood Transfusion*, 1958.

[2] Diamond, L. K., 'History of Blood Banking in the United States', *op. cit.*, p. 5. Damages are also rising to unprecedented heights. In one case in California in 1965 damages of $700,000 were awarded because the blood of a child had not been properly checked (*Transfusion*, Vol. 5, No. 2, March/April 1965, p. 208). One blood insurance company in Arizona had suits amounting to $250,000 pending against it in 1964 (*Hearings on S. 2560, op. cit.*, 1964, p. 71).

[3] Randall, C. H., *Medicolegal Problems in Blood Transfusions*, *op. cit.*, 1963, pp. 1–2. See also *Cases on Blood Transfusions*, Law Department, A.M.A., 1967 and Wheeler, C. B., 'State Laws and Regulations', *op. cit.*, p. 6.

[4] *A.M.A. News*, January 27, 1969.

[5] Human blood was legally defined in the Kansas City case as: 'whole blood (human) is viable human tissue mixed with an anti-coagulant in a sterile container which must be stored and refrigerated and the admixture is a commodity

holds in store for the future of medicine in the United States, as legally it is increasingly treated as a trade and as the doctrine of charitable immunity disappears into the mists of history, is not a matter for this particular study. To consider all such legal ramifications would eventually lead us away from law and into the broader issues of medical ethics, the purpose of medicine and, ultimately, the value of human life.

and/or an article of commerce under the administrative practice of the National Institutes of Health' and 'whole blood (as so defined) is subject to "trade" and "commerce" within the meaning of those terms as used in the Federal Trade Commission Act' (*In the matter of Community Blood Bank of the Kansas City Area, Inc.*, FTC Docket 8519).

Chapter 10

Blood Donors in the Soviet Union and Other Countries

In Chapter 5 we set out an eight-fold typology of blood donors ranging from the paid donor at one extreme, primarily motivated to donate by the prospect of a cash payment, to the voluntary community donor at the other. This classification told us something about the reasons why people in the aggregate give or supply blood. Subsequently, we applied this typology to the donor populations in the United States and Britain and, in a limited way, Japan.

What has emerged from the discussion of this material is that looked at as a whole different social and political structures and value systems strongly determine the typology distributions. We found, for example, very great differences in the proportions of donors of varying types in the United States, Japan and Britain. These differences cannot be explained simply in terms of administrative and organizational structures of blood supply systems and patterns of medical care services. The causal factors are more fundamental than that; ultimately, explanations—and, admittedly, explanations that can never be more than partial—have to be sought in the history, the values and the political ideas of each society. Differences in the roles played by social gift-relationships cannot be accounted for in technical, organizational or purely economic terms.

Yet, in recent years, some political scientists and sociologists have been developing the thesis described as 'the end of ideology'. It has been argued that large-scale industrialized societies, increasingly ruled by technocracy and the demands of a mass consumption market, are tending to become more and more alike—to converge—in terms of their dominant value systems and political ideologies. This study throws doubt on such theories. There is no indication of convergence over the last twenty years in the pattern of blood donor gift-relationships when comparisons are made between the United States and Britain. It suggests that not for the

173

first time in the social sciences these theories have been formulated on the basis of indicators that can be measured and quantified— as in the acquisition, possession and distribution of material goods. Social indicators embodying transactions and relationships in non-economic categories are thus excluded. What counts is what is economically countable.

For these and other reasons it would have been instructive to have extended this study by examining blood supply systems and related social policy issues in various other countries. Regrettably, this was not possible; in the first place a vast amount of additional research would have been necessary and, in the second, very few data have been collected, analysed and published. In this chapter, therefore, all we do is to bring together a scattered amount of material for a number of countries—principally the Soviet Union. We begin by listing from a variety of sources estimates that have been made for 27 countries of the proportion of blood donors who are paid:

TABLE 17

Proportions of Paid Donors in Various Countries

Country	Year of approximate estimate	% paid	Source
Austria	1964	Some	(5)
Belgium	1960	Some	(6)
Bulgaria	1964	Some	(5)
Burma	1966	Substantial	(4)
Ceylon	1966	90	(4)
Czechoslovakia	1965	40	(5) and (8)
Denmark	1967	Some	(9)
France	1960	Small	(6)
German Democratic Republic	1964	85	(5)
German Federal Republic	1964	40–85	(5)
(West Berlin)	1962	100	(2)
Greece	1967	66	(5)
Hungary	1964	40	(5)
India	1960	83	(6)
Italy	1959	Substantial	(7)
Japan	1963	98	(4)
Korea (Republic of)	1960	90	(6)

174

Pakistan	1964	Some	(5)
Peru	1964	Most	(5)
Philippines	1966	98	(4)
Roumania	1964	75	(5)
Spain	1964	Substantial	(5)
Sweden	1965	100	(10)
Thailand	1964	80	(5)
United Arab Republic	1960	100	(6)
Uruguay	1964	Some	(5)
U.S.A.	1965–67	50	(Chapter 6)
U.S.S.R.	1965	50	(1)

Sources

(1) Vaughn, J., 'Blood Transfusion in the U.S.S.R.', *Transfusion*, No. 3, May–June 1967, p. 217.

(2) Council of Europe, *Problems of Blood Transfusion in Europe*, Strasbourg, 1962.

(3) Miller, G. W. 'International Aspects of Blood Banking', *Proc. A.M.A. Conf. on Blood and Blood Banking*, Chicago, 1964.

(4) League of Red Cross Societies, *Proc. IVth Red Cross International Seminar on Blood Transfusion*, Geneva, 1966.

(5) League of Red Cross Societies, *Proc. IIIrd Red Cross International Seminar on Blood Transfusion*, Geneva, 1964.

(6) League of Red Cross Societies, *Proc. IInd Red Cross International Seminar on Blood Transfusion*, Geneva, 1960.

(7) League of Red Cross Societies, *Proc. Ist Red Cross International Seminar on Blood Transfusion*, Geneva, 1959.

(8) Novák, J., and Dobrý, E., *The Transfusion Service in Czechoslovakia*, Prague, 1965.

(9) *Berlingske Tidende*, May 30, 1967.

(10) *Transfusion*, Vol. 5, No. 1, January–February 1967, p. 35.

In the countries listed in Table 18 donors are rewarded with fringe benefits of various kinds. These take the form of anything from one to ten days' paid leave from employment; free holidays for varying periods in rest homes, hotels and holiday centres; free meals and drink after donations; priority medical care treatment for the individual and his family; priority for housing; free transport for up to a month, and other benefits.

If a country is not listed in these two tables it must not be assumed that its transfusion services do not depend to some extent on paid and/or fringe benefit donors. The information is not available to provide a more comprehensive list. It should further be pointed out that many countries in Table 17 also reward other donors with fringe benefits of various kinds; this happens particularly, for example, in the U.S.S.R. and other East European countries.

TABLE 18

Donors Receiving Fringe Benefits in Various Countries

Country	Year of report	Source[1]
Yugoslavia (Defence Forces)	1964	(3)
Burma	1966	(4)
Portugal	1960	(6)
Bulgaria	1964	(5)
Ghana	1964	(5)

[1] For sources see Table 17.

Additionally, a number of countries appear to rely heavily for their blood supplies on captive donors, e.g. the Defence Forces in Switzerland and certain countries in the Soviet bloc.

Only in Britain, Eire and two or three other countries in the world can we state with certainty that the system is almost entirely voluntary; that there are no material rewards in money or kind; that all gifts are for strangers and are not 'tied' in any way to kinship, group or class; and that the proportion of captive donors is nil or minimal.

In the absence of data on the social and demographic characteristics of donors, the structure and organization of transfusion services, studies of demand and supply and other factors it is difficult to interpret the differences in these tables and particularly those for European countries. It is in Europe that the Red Cross has played an important role and it is, therefore, on the face of it surprising to find some European countries—e.g. Germany and Sweden—relying very heavily on paid donors, particularly as the League of Red Cross Societies emphasizes strongly the voluntary principle. 'One recognizes', wrote Dr Hantchef, Director of the Medico-Social Bureau of the League of Red Cross Societies, 'that blood, as a therapeutic product of human origin, should remain free from all commercial profit. It should form the object of an act of altruism and its gift should be free'.[1]

Even more striking is the extent to which the U.S.S.R. depends on material rewards for the recruitment of 'donors'. This emerged clearly in a comprehensive technical report on the Soviet Transfusion Services by an American hematologist, Dr J. Vaughn, who spent three months in the country in 1965 as part of the Soviet-American scientific exchange program.[2] Dr Vaughn visited the Central Insti-

---

[1] Hantchef, Z. S., *The Gift of Blood and some International Aspects of Blood Transfusion* (pamphlet), League of Red Cross Societies, Geneva, 1961, p. 6.

[2] Vaughn, J., *op. cit.*, 1967.

tutes of Hematology and Blood Transfusion, blood donor stations and hospitals in various cities and republics. He was impressed by some features—for example, the close co-operation between the transfusionist and the clinical hematologist—and critical of others. In summing up he commented 'the overall picture is rather reminiscent of blood transfusion practices in the United States and European countries just after the Second World War.' There was said to be little post-transfusion hepatitis—attributed to the careful screening of donors.

At the time of his visit use was being made in Moscow and Kiev of cadaver blood, exsanguination being carried out on those who had died suddenly. However, this source of blood represented only a very small proportion of the blood requirements of the Soviet Union and its use is reported to be declining, for technical reasons, throughout the Union.[1]

About half of all blood supplies in the Union are obtained from unpaid donors at factories, offices, colleges and palaces of culture (recreation clubs) and other institutions. They are recruited by the Union of Red Cross and Red Crescent Societies.[2] Donors are allowed a day off work to give their donation and a free meal afterwards; they are also given an extra day's holiday which, if they choose, they may add to their annual vacation. Other reports suggest that in some places donors may be rewarded with free public transport for a month, higher priority for housing and other 'fringe benefits'.[3]

The other half of all blood supplies comes from paid donors who attend blood-collecting stations. Although they get a day off work for donating they are not given a free meal or other benefits. In 1965 they were paid at the rate of 60 roubles ($66) per litre of blood (just over 2 English pints) and for the average donation received 15 to 25 roubles.[4] This remarkably high price for blood can best be appreciated when it is set against two other facts. The salary of a newly qualified physician in the Soviet Union was about 100 roubles

---

[1] *Hospital Services in the U.S.S.R.*, Report of the U.S. Delegation on Hospital Systems Planning, June–July 1965, U.S. Department of Health, Education and Welfare.

[2] Kisselev, A. E. and Lipats, A. A., 'The Union of the Red Cross and Red Crescent Societies of the U.S.S.R. and the Country's Blood Service', *Prob. Hemat. & Blood Trans.*, Moscow, 12: 3, June 1967 (in Russian).

[3] Sugrue, F., *op. cit.*, p. 83.

[4] The same figure of 60 roubles a litre was also reported by Wolstenholme, G. E. W., of the Ciba Foundation, London, in *Ethics in Medical Progress*, *op. cit.*, 1966, p. 32.

M

a month in 1965; the hospital specialist received about 300 roubles a month.[1] Minimum wages for all workers were raised to 60 roubles a month (from 40–45) in 1967.[2]

This is a far cry from the systems of mutual aid and gift relationships among the peasants of Russia in the nineteenth century described by Kropotkin.[3] To pay something like $20 a pint or approaching half-a-month's minimum wage could conceivably indicate a serious shortage of blood and blood donors. But without much more information about demand and supply and the characteristics of donors it would be wrong to speculate.[4] The stark fact remains, however, that in the Soviet Union—as in the United States —approximately half of all human blood is paid for. But whereas in the United States a profit is made in the blood market by commercial concerns there is apparently no profit on the transaction in the Soviet Union. However, the lavishness of the price paid may be producing a class of professional blood donors who depend to some extent for their income on the proceeds of selling their blood.

II

From time to time in this book certain basic questions have recurred; in some chapters they have been raised in terms of the individual donor, in others in terms of the social group, class or society as a whole. Why give blood voluntarily? Why give to strangers? What are the motives for selling blood? What are the characteristics of blood donors (or suppliers) of all types in regard to age, sex, marital status, income and social class and other factors, and in what respects—if at all—do they as a minority differ from the general population of medically eligible adults?

So far, our discussion has been limited in the main to considering a typology of donors, their chief characteristics, and to different institutions and systems developed in a number of countries for the recruitment of donors and the distribution and transfusion of blood and blood products. We have said that before we can begin to approach the question of individual motivation we have to understand better the ascertainable facts about donors and non-donors

[1] Vaughn, J., *op. cit.*, p. 226.

[2] Nove, A. and Katz, Z., reported in *New Society*, October 19, 1967.

[3] Kropotkin, P., 'Mutual Aid Amongst Modern Man', *The Nineteenth Century*, 1895 (L.S.E. pamphlet collection 11/95).

[4] The writer attempted in 1967 (after a visit to the U.S.S.R.) to obtain such information but without success from Dr M. A. Umnova, Director, Dept. of Isoserology and Rare Test Sera, Central Institute for Hematology and Blood Transfusion, Moscow.

and the fabric of values, social, economic and political, within which acts of giving, rewarding, compelling or selling take place.

Few motivation studies at the level of individual psychology have been undertaken in the world. Apart from the pilot survey carried out for this book, only a few studies of a limited nature have been conducted, chiefly in the United States, France, Australia, Sweden and South Africa. It is the purpose of this section of this chapter to review these studies and in Chapter 11 to describe in some detail the South African study because it raises certain fundamental questions about race relationships in blood donor systems. In a later chapter we summarize the findings of the donor survey in England.

It has been argued by some authorities that it is easier to understand the motives for selling one's blood in those countries where much of human life is brutal and cheap and where poverty and hunger dominate the lives of millions. There is no need to essay a Freudian or Jungian interpretation of the motives of slum or street dwellers in Calcutta who sell their blood for a little cash and organize themselves in blood sellers' trade unions.[1]

[1] The following extracts are from an article 'Voice of the National Blood Donation Movement in India' by Rakt Daan summarized in *Transfusion* (No. 3, 1963, p. 510).

'Blood donations help jawan and civilian alike. They are a symbol of human brotherhood, of man going to the rescue of suffering man.

'But then, in this country of poverty-stricken millions, donating blood is also a way of making a living. Many of those unable to earn their bread by the sweat of the brow try to earn it by the sale of blood. The maximum price a blood bank pays is a rupee an ounce, and 10 ounces can be usually sold at a time.

'It is estimated that 40,000 persons, mostly belonging to South India, maintain themselves by selling blood to the blood banks. About 300 of them are registered with the blood bank in the Rajenda Hospital, Patiala.

'During hospital hours the professional blood sellers squat outside the blood bank awaiting their turn—ill fed, half naked, unshaven. On an average two of them get the opportunity every day.

'According to the rules a person can donate blood once in three months. The blood sellers circumvent this by getting registered with different blood banks. Soon after selling their blood at one they go to another. The average seems to work out to three times a month. In one case a man sold his blood twice a day; in the morning at Ludhiana and in the evening at Patiala.

'A 23-year-old Punjabi youth, Prem Nath of Dalla village in Kapurthala district, perhaps holds the record—weighing just 126 lbs., he has already donated with 100 lbs. of his blood in the course of five years. To him it means livelihood. He has so far sold his blood 200 times at different hospitals in Punjab and outside. In Patiala alone he has sold it 150 times.

'According to a blood bank official, people who get used to this business of selling blood stick to it permanently. Almost all of them are honest, he added. Only a few of them are married and have children. The others spend the day

The proposition is then advanced that as standards of living rise and societies become richer (with effects on levels of education, the erosion of superstitious beliefs debarring blood donations, greater political and social stability and so forth) the commercialization of blood will decline. More people will come to see the moral, social and biological objections to the buying and selling of blood, and will also recognize the scientific dangers to themselves and their fellows in relying on an indigent, blood-providing proletariat. The voluntary giving of blood in affluent societies will symbolize a greater faith in life on earth and, as giving comes to embrace the stranger, will bring about a shift in values to more and wider acts of altruism in gift relations.

Such theories or beliefs are not borne out by the experience of the United States, Germany and Japan. These countries have registered in the last twenty years some of the largest and most rapid increases in economic growth, wealth accumulation and standards of living in the world. At the same time, it is these countries in particular which have also experienced more commercialization of blood, and have come increasingly to rely—as, perhaps, the Soviet Union has as well—on the buying of blood for money and other material rewards.

It was this concern generally about the growth of commercialization as it affects blood transfusion services as well as concern about the world shortage of blood that led the League of Red Cross Societies to choose for an international meeting in 1964 of delegates from 40 countries the subject of 'Blood Donor Motivation'.[1] Another factor causing some concern in recent years—particularly in Europe—was the problem created for blood transfusion services when people in countries which tend not to pay donors are attracted across frontiers by the offer of cash rewards in paid recruitment systems. For example, in 1968 certain German organizations in cities near the Dutch frontier were paying up to £4 a unit for blood to Dutch people in the province of Limburg (where an entirely voluntary system operated).[2]

in the hospital compound and the night on pavements. When hard-pressed they take to begging.

'Donors of this type have formed a sort of trade union. Their grouse is that the hospitals purchase blood at one rupee an ounce but sell it to patients at Rs. 2.50 nP per ounce. Their demand: No profiteering at our cost.'

[1] League of Red Cross Societies, *Proc. IIIrd Red Cross International Seminar*, *op. cit.*, 1964.

[2] *Pulse*, London, August 31, 1968, and personal communication Provinciaal Bestuur Van Limburg, Maastricht, Netherlands, March 26, 1969,

From the report of the Red Cross meeting in 1964 it is clear that most of the participants were interested in the psychology of motivation from the standpoint of improving their publicity and propaganda efforts to recruit more voluntary donors. Great emphasis was placed on the need to understand and recruit young donors as in a number of European countries the proportion of youthful volunteers was low (apart from captive Defence Forces' recruits) and the bulk of voluntary donors constituted an ageing population. In France, the average age for both sexes was reported to be 41–44 years, and in Brussels less than 6 per cent of male donors were aged under 25 (most voluntary donors in Belgium were said to be older working-class men).[1]

The main paper on motivation (which also reported on the replies to a League questionnaire from 47 countries) was presented by Dr J. P. Cagnard, Head of Service, National Blood Transfusion Centre, Paris. He pointed out that in answer to the question 'What, in the view of your Society, are the reasons for donors coming forward regularly or occasionally to offer their blood?' the almost unanimous reply was altruism or moral value.[2] He then discussed at a general level some of the psychological aspects of motivation and summarized reports from a number of countries ranging from France to Sierra Leone. Much of what he and other participants in the meeting had to say about attitudes, beliefs, taboos and religious doctrines in different cultural contexts has already been commented on in Chapters 2 and 5.

In reports from developing countries, the classification of reasons for the absence of voluntary blood donors was different from European reports and comprised a great many clusters of beliefs, superstitions and taboos. For example, it was believed that the drawing of blood:

1. rendered man impotent
2. made the human body subject to witchcraft
3. would result in the death of a man who gave blood for his wife before her death
4. would lead to sickness and inability to work
5. would prevent a woman from bearing children
6. would result in blindness
7. would be sacrilege and would violate the fundamental beliefs and ritual practices of the group

[1] *Op. cit.*, Introduction p. 3, Annex 1 and Part III, pp. 2–3.
[2] *Op. cit.*, Part 1, pp. 1–23.

8. represented an aggressive act and would contaminate or infect the individual with disease
9. is a way of ensuring the domination and mutiplication of the white man
10. violated certain religious conceptions (for example, Buddhism, particularly for the Chinese).

What emerged from these impressionistic reports from developed as well as developing countries concerning the difficulties of recruiting blood donors was the great importance of the factor of fear, specific and general. This led Dr Cagnard, in summarizing the results of a French study, to question 'whether motivation born of scientific study, political opinion and the study of commercial markets for "prospective" development, can be applied to such a human field, and whether it is possible to calculate, standardize, apportion and direct such elements as belong to the giving of part of one's self, i.e. the essence of human life, which raises moral, social, economical and even metaphysical problems'.[1]

III

The study, conducted in France by the Institute for the Study of Motivation and the Institute of Public Opinion in 1961, illustrated the strong symbolic significance of blood by showing that the reasons why individuals did not donate were fears of one kind or another.[2]

The study comprised, first, a questionnaire survey of 2024 people said to be a representative national sample of the adult French metropolitan population and, second, an open-ended interview with 148 people, 60 of whom had given blood and 88 who had never given blood. It was designed to collect data about French blood donors and, intensively, to elicit information concerning resistances to giving blood.

As regards the characteristics of donors, it is not possible to make detailed comparisons with our English survey partly because of differences in the methods used and partly because only a limited amount of data have been published. Moreover, the samples were too small to permit close examination. Only two broad comparisons

[1] Cagnard, J. P., *op. cit.*, p. 3.
[2] Simeray-Massé, M., and Riffault, H., 'La Signification Psychosociologique du Don du Sang en France', *Transfusion* (*Bulletin de la Société Nationale de Transfusion Sanguine et des Centres de Transfusion de France et de la Communaute*), 5 (i), 1962, p. 7.

can be made. First, the proportion of women donors is much lower in France than in England. Second, the total donor population is substantially older in France.

Of those who were not donors and who were asked about other people, 61 per cent thought that 'fear' was the main factor 'responsible for people hesitating to give blood', 22 per cent of the answers were classified under the headings of 'negligence, ignorance, and lack of opportunity'; 7 per cent 'occasional incapacity' and 10 per cent did not reply.

When people were asked about their own reasons for not giving blood the replies were very different. Only 9 per cent admitted to fear; 41 per cent said that they had not been asked; 10 per cent had not thought about it; 5 per cent had no time; 27 per cent reported physical incapacity (ill-health and age), and 8 per cent did not reply.

The authors of this study, in their conclusions and recommendations about publicity, stressed the significance of general and specific fears; fear of physical pain in donating; fear of weakening one's health; fear of seeing blood, and the fear (found mostly among women) of putting on weight after donating.

It is difficult to appraise the findings of this study because of its emphasis on the negative aspects and its concern to make recommendations which might aid propaganda techniques and recruit more and younger donors.

The survey of a sample of blood donors in 1964 by the American Red Cross (the findings on age and sex were reported in Chapter 6) also included questions about motives. A total of 12,097 people answered the question 'Why did you come to give blood today'? About 21 per cent of the answers showed clearly that the donations were 'tied' ('to build up credit for myself or family', designated donations, etc.) As to the remainder, the analysis was too vague and general to permit any interpretation (for example, answers which said 'I want to' and 'I give regularly on schedule' were aggregated with such answers as 'my duty' and 'civic duty'). Only 2 per cent were classified under the heading 'sense of gratitude'. When asked why other people did not give blood about 57 per cent stressed fears of one kind or another as the greatest deterrent.[1]

Two other American surveys in 1958 and 1964 of the characteristics of blood donors (also reported in Chapter 6) included questions

[1] A report on this survey was published in League of Red Cross Societies, *op. cit.*, 1966, Annex III.

on motives.[1] In both cases, however, the analyses were brief and general. Moreover, they drew on very different populations and the answers reflected much of the diversity in American blood banking systems. In one study 92 per cent were 'tied' credit donors, and in the other 76 per cent were paid. Little of value concerning the psychological processes of donating emerged from these studies.

Only four other detailed studies of blood donor characteristics and motives have been traced in the international literature though it must be admitted that, apart from the United States and Britain, the search has not been intensively conducted. Two of these were carried out in Australia, one in Sweden and one in South Africa.

Under the auspices of the Red Cross Blood Transfusion Service in Victoria, Miss E. Phillips attempted to investigate in 1960 the factors which encouraged and discouraged blood donors.[2] However, the response rate was low and the questionnaires analysed related to only 574 donors (14 per cent of whom were repaying blood debts to or investing blood credits in blood banks) and 226 non-donors who were selected through donors. One discouragement or 'resentment voiced frequently' by donors related to the charges made for transfusions. Apart from this point, most of the motive answers were couched in general terms about service to the community, individual and group pressures, repaying blood bank debts, fears of the unknown, fear of the needle, ignorance of the need for blood, and so forth. The second Australian study, also conducted for the Red Cross, was carried out in 1962–3 by Dr R. J. Walsh in Sydney.[3] It was in two parts: (1) a structured questionnaire completed by 260 new donors and (2) data on age and sex for 2881 new and old donors and the number of previous donations by those who were giving a second or subsequent donation. Again, the questions on motives yielded only general information similar to that obtained in the Victoria study. The age and sex characteristics study no doubt provided useful information for the Australian blood transfusion services but its value was limited as no attempt was made to compare the results with corresponding

[1] Irwin Memorial Blood Bank survey and Blood Services, Arizona, Study 1 (see Chapter 6). In a paper on community characteristics in Ohio, Rockwell, T. H. and Hanlon, R. F., came to the momentous conclusion that the rate at which a community consumes blood is related to the rate at which it donates blood (*Transfusion*, Vol. 3, 1963, p. 401).

[2] Phillips, E., 'A Study in Blood Donor Motivation', *Med. J. of Australia*, Vol. 11, November 4, 1961, p. 742.

[3] Walsh, R. J., 'Some Aspects of Voluntary Blood Donors in New South Wales', League of Red Cross Societies, *op. cit.*, 1966, Part II.

data for the population of Sydney. Only one broad comparison can be made with the results of the English survey; there was a substantially lower proportion of women blood donors in Sydney.

Finally, we refer to a survey of a quite different kind carried out in 1968 by Dr B. Gullbring, chief physician at the blood donor centre, Karolinska Hospital, Stockholm. This was a questionnaire survey of 2000 paid blood donors (of whom 1858 answered) at the Karolinska Hospital and a hospital in Uppsala. The main object of the survey was to ascertain whether these paid donors would give blood without payment.[1]

Since the start of organized blood donations in Sweden all donors have been paid. Under a 'free' health service today patients are not charged for blood received. Donors in Stockholm are paid 28 Sw. crowns a unit and in Uppsala 30 Sw. crowns a unit. These prices have remained unchanged since 1951 when a similar survey was undertaken. No specific studies have been made of the characteristics of these donors but it is reported that about 80 per cent in Stockholm are men (probably a higher proportion in towns where there are military establishments) and that the majority are aged 18–30.[2]

The demand for blood has increased greatly in Sweden over the past twenty years as it has in England, the United States and other countries. In relation to demand in Sweden there would seem to have developed a shortage of new paid donors (or suppliers). In 1968 the official regulations (there are no commercial blood banks in Sweden) stated that the interval between donations for each donor must be at least six weeks (a maximum of about eight donations a year compared with about two in Britain). If enough donors were available some authorities would wish on medical grounds to lengthen the interval to three months. Also, as another possible indication of shortage, it should be noted that a number of pharmaceutical and private firms were in 1969 importing plasma fractions, outdated blood and retroplacental blood from other countries. To lengthen the time interval to three months would, however, it has been estimated, mean increasing the number of donors by at least 50 per cent.

[1] This section on Sweden is mainly drawn from the following sources: Gullbring, B., 'Motiv för blodgivning', *Läkartidningen*, Vol. 66, No. 4, 1969, Sv. *Läkartidningen*, 49: 42–9, 1952, and personal communication September 1969; personal communication, Kabi Pharmaceuticals Ltd., London and Stockholm, July 1969, and personal communication, Swedish Institute for Cultural Relations, London, June 1969.

[2] Personal communication, Dr B. Gullbring, September 5, 1969.

In this situation the question was being asked in 1968 how donors would react if payment for blood was abandoned. It was not psychologically feasible to employ the personal inducement 'Give your blood free and you will get blood free if you need it' because patients are not charged for blood.

The survey was, therefore, undertaken by Dr Gullbring in 1968. Unselected, paid donors were asked to complete a simple check-list questionnaire.[1] Approximately 72 per cent of those answering said that they would give blood without a cash payment (but only 50 per cent as frequently as they do now); 24 per cent said they would not, and in 4 per cent of cases the question was not answered or the response was unclear. The replies of the 72 per cent as to the 'most important reason for your giving blood' are difficult to interpret partly because a high proportion of the group ticked more than one 'most important reason', and partly because no information was collected on number of previous donations, or on age, sex, marital status, occupation, income and other characteristics.

In these circumstances, and in a situation in which these donors may not regard themselves as 'sellers of blood' but as simply receiving a small recompense for their time and trouble, it is hard to guess what would happen if payments were abandoned. Inevitably, we again ask the question: who are these people? Are they students in need of extra cash, poor people, members of the Defence Forces, induced donors, or a cross-section of the eligible Swedish population?

Dr Gullbring also compared the results of this inquiry with a

1

Question 1
Which is the most important reason for your giving blood?

(a)	So that blood shall be available for treatment of the sick	Yes
		No
(b)	For the payment which is given for the donation	Yes
		No
(c)	Because I feel physically better after giving blood	Yes
		No
(d)	Do not know.	

Question 2
Would you give blood if you did not receive payment in cash (30 crowns)? Yes
No

If yes, as often as now?   Yes
No
If not, how often?

N.B. The answer is not to be signed, and is to be placed in the box specially provided for this purpose at the blood donor centre.

somewhat similar inquiry at the Karolinska Hospital in 1951 (748 respondents). In that year 34 per cent said they would give blood without a cash payment; 46 per cent said they would not; and in 20 per cent of cases the question was not answered, was 'don't know' or the response was unclear.

It is extremely hard to interpret these results and compare them with the 1968 results. There are many reasons which make comparison difficult. Dr Gullbring referred in his study to certain differences between the 1951 and 1968 questionnaires. The former did appeal more to idealism as this word was included in the check-list under 'main reason'. He also drew attention in his report to the fall in the relative value of 28 Sw. crowns between 1951 and 1968.[1] Moreover, no information was collected on the characteristics of donors in both years.

The dilemma is a very real one for the Swedish authorities. If payments for blood were abandoned and not enough voluntary donors came forward the consequences for patients could be disastrous. On the other hand, the alternative may be to increase substantially the value of the payment. This would, however, cause a rise in the costs of medical care; it could have other harmful social and medical consequences similar to those depicted in earlier chapters particularly the risk of serum hepatitis as there are substantial numbers of young drug addicts in Sweden; and, in a society of changing values, an increased emphasis on material rewards might not in the end produce adequate supplies of blood. Although the cultural contexts are different, it is clear that the 'commercialization of the blood market' in the United States and Japan has not solved the problem of shortages let alone the problems of 'safety, purity and potency'.

The Swedish dilemma suggests that it is easier for societies to abandon altruism as a motive for giving blood than it is to abandon the principles of economic man once they have been institutionalized and accepted. Perhaps only new generations of the eligible will be able to effect a change if they should come to see that socialism is also about giving.

[1] In 1968 28 Sw. crowns represented about 42s. in sterling. Average industrial and shop earnings in 1968 were approximately (converted into sterling) £35 per week. Thus, the payment for blood was equal to nearly 3 hours work (on the basis of an average working week of 48 hours). (Information provided by the Labour Attaché's Office, Swedish Embassy, London, July 1969.)

187

Chapter 11

A Study of Blood Donor Motivation in South Africa

I

Published in 1966 by The Institute of Social Research of the University of Natal, *Blood Donation: The Attitudes and Motivation of Urban Bantu in Durban* represents the most thorough and intensive study of its kind yet undertaken. It was commissioned by the Natal Blood Transfusion Service and carried out in Durban and its immediate environs by Mr H. L. Watts and Mr C. D. Shearing of the Institute. Much of the field work was done by six trained Bantu graduates which, no doubt, helps to explain the perceptive nature of some of the interview data elicited from poor and semi-literate Bantu workers.

The report runs to 210 pages and we can do no more than describe the research design and summarize some of the main findings.

The project comprised a group of inter-related studies. The main study (a sample of 250 adult Bantus) investigated attitudes and motivations by means of interviews and projective tests of two types —a story-type and a pictorial-type. A parallel study was made of a sample of 49 Bantu blood donors. Group discussions were conducted to obtain information on Bantu ideas and concepts of blood with Bantu medical students, domestic servants, high school girls, factory workers and labourers. Unstructured interviews were held with a variety of selected informants, e.g. school teachers (both White and Bantu), a medicine man (inyanga), a diviner (isangoma), factory officials and others. Essays on 'Blood—what it means to me' and 'Good and Bad Blood' were obtained from Bantu high school children. Team observations were made at a number of bleeding sessions. Finally, studies were made of responses to posters used by the Natal Blood Transfusion Service, and advertisements of patent medicines sold to the Bantu for 'blood complaints' were examined.

The main findings were:

1. The Bantu donor is statistically rare (a total of 1756 donors in an estimated population of about 167,400 Bantu adults aged 18–64).

188

2. They come mainly from institutional groups such as factories and schools and tend to be younger, better educated and with higher incomes than the average Bantu adult in Durban.

3. The concepts of blood held by the average manual worker Bantu closely link blood with health and are unfavourable to blood donation. Good blood—rich blood—is thought of as being a source of health. There are connections too with ancestor worship (our blood is their blood and we have no right to give it away). Bad blood—thin or weak blood—is associated with illness and disease. Blood is also seen by some as a possible carrier of witch-craft so there are resistances to the idea of receiving blood which might be used as a medium for bewitching. It seems to be widely held that blood is an irretrievable substance; once lost, it cannot be replaced. 'Blood is my life.' These concepts appear to reflect to a considerable extent the traditional views held by the Zulus, with some Xhosa and other less numerous language groups in Durban. It is not unimportant that the Zulu word used to denote 'giving' or 'volunteering' to give blood has connotations of 'sacrifice'.

4. The attitudes and beliefs of Bantu high-school children seem to be on the whole very similar to those held by the general adult population despite the influence of 'Western ideas' in the schools.

5. While beliefs in witchcraft are still widely held among Bantu adults these do not seem important in producing resistances to donation.

6. Fears and anxieties about pain are fairly widespread in the blood donor clinics. These are not relieved when there is ignorance about the processes and purposes of blood donation—as there is—and when the atmosphere in the clinics is impersonal, cold and authoritarian.

7. A marked characteristic of the Bantu blood donor is that he tends to give blood only once or twice. In 1965 the mean number of times that blood had been given by Bantu donors on the active list in the region served by Durban was 2·77 times. It was estimated that only one-eighth of those who had given blood were still active donors.

8. In the Bantu population at large there is widespread ignorance about, and fear of, blood donation. These beliefs and attitudes were not in general dispelled at the bleeding sessions. 'It is remarkable that again and again the observers noted that many donors did not seem to understand fully why they were donating'. Often there was little or no communication. In one clinic where the staff were White it was reported: 'In general the donors were very respectful and

subdued once they were inside the tent, although they talked quite a lot while they were standing outside the tent. They never asked the nurse anything, or initiated a conversation'. On the application of an 8-point knowledge score it was concluded that at least one-third of the donors had little or no knowledge about donation (this in part explains the high wastage rate).

9. The image held by some Bantu adults of the Blood Transfusion Service was a negative one in that it was seen as a governmental organization and 'White'. Suspicion and fear of the 'Government' and the White man were transferred to the Service. One of the observational reports said: 'There can be no running away from the fact that most of those donors' (that is, those at a particular session) 'are afraid of European nurses and doctors. They fear them in just the same way as they fear their bosses'. (Some donors were forced by their employers to donate—see below.) These attitudes appear to have been reinforced by the 'rather impersonal and cold atmosphere during donation'. Moreover, donors had to queue outside; no provision for seating was made at the bleeding sessions.

10. The knowledge among some of the Bantu that blood donors (or suppliers) were paid in the Southern Transvaal (on the gold mines) presented—said the report—a problem to the Natal Blood Transfusion Service. They felt they were being cheated; some thought that employers were being paid by the Service to recruit donors or were withholding the money from them. These beliefs may have been reinforced by the fact that hospital patients in Natal are charged for blood transfusions.[1]

These were some of the main findings of this study. They have been summarized briefly by the writer in his own words. If they do not faithfully express what the authors had to say in a much fuller and more comprehensive summary then no criticism or blame attaches to them.

The report went on to make a long series of recommendations for the benefit of the Natal Blood Transfusion Service which commissioned the study. They need not be described in detail here. They were mostly concerned with improving the image of the

[1] The recipient of the blood pays the Natal Blood Transfusion Service a fee of R7.50 (£3 15s. in 1967) for every unit of blood. This 'service fee' includes the crossmatching services provided by the Service to every hospital in Natal through the establishment of Natal Blood Transfusion Service staffed laboratories in all hospitals. If a recipient is not a private patient, as is the case with all non-Europeans and about 15 per cent of Europeans, he receives his treatment in the provincial hospitals as a provincial patient. He pays a nominal daily fee, in the case of the Bantu about 5s. a day (in 1967), which is all-inclusive.

Service among the Bantu; with making practical suggestions to aid recruitment; to reduce wastage (for example, it was proposed that a welcoming Bantu host or hostess should be present at all bleeding sessions); to increase motivation by making donors feel 'important' and 'wanted' and to see the Service as their Service. It was further suggested that the notion of 'giving' blood should be dropped and replaced by propaganda to 'lend' blood (as less sacrificial), and that throughout the Republic the practice of paying cash for blood should be eliminated.

The South African Institute for Medical Research at Johannesburg operates a Blood Transfusion Service specifically to meet the needs of hospitals on the Witwatersrand controlled by the gold mines, and obtains its supplies from employees of the mines. A recent development has been for the Service to extend the provision of blood to Bantu hospitals run by the Transvaal Provincial Administration. 'It is hoped that this trend will grow so that the Bantu races will become increasingly self-sufficient in supplying their needs for blood.'[1]

The gold mining industry could not operate without hospitals and medical services; blood supplies are also essential to deal with accidents, surgical cases and for therapeutic purposes. Suppliers are paid by the South African Institute for Medical Research. In 1967 the rates were: Bantus, Coloured and Asians R1·00 (10s.) for each pint of blood; White R4·00 (40s.) for each pint. At the official exchange rates ruling in 1967, the price per pint for blood from Whites was somewhat less than the current price paid to Negroes in New York. It is not known whether in order to maintain gold production in South Africa some recipients are charged, on private market principles, four times as much for 'White' blood as for 'Black' blood.

II

Two broad conclusions can be drawn from this study by the Institute of Social Research in Natal. The motivation analysis suggests that the underlying concepts of blood and attitudes to blood donation found among the Bantu are not dissimilar from those prevailing among more sophisticated societies in the West. Much the same pattern of fears and anxieties stemming from beliefs and myths

[1] *Annual Report of the South African Institute for Medical Research for 1964*, Johannesburg, p. 61.

about blood, its possession and loss, were depicted in the French study and also in some American work.[1] There appear to be common psychological processes operating which affect the problems of recruiting and retaining blood donors and suppliers.

Secondly, in considering the extent to which the typology of donors presented in Chapter 5 may be applicable, the evidence in the Natal study does not support a classification of the great majority of these Bantu donors as 'voluntary community donors'. Nearly all of them were recruited while they were members of an organization such as a factory, hospital, college or school, and about one-half of the sample were students. 'The striking feature is the insignificant number of donors who came forward to general clinics. The figures bear out the contention of the Natal Blood Transfusion Service that attempts in South Africa to secure donors from the general Bantu population (outside of institutional settings) have been largely unsuccessful.' Even then they only 'give' blood once or twice. They were fearful; many did not understand fully why they were donating; some 'only gave under pressure from their superiors'; some were forced by their employers to donate. At one bleeding session the observer noted about a group of donors: 'They informed me that they did not like the idea of being forced to give away their blood. They have always refused to donate in the past, but this year for reasons unknown to them they were forced to come. "Why did you come if you were not prepared to donate, despite being forced?" I asked. They were afraid of losing their jobs, so they had to come'.

We conclude, therefore, that the majority are more appropriately classified as 'captive donors' under Type F in the typology developed in Chapter 5. As such, and like many American Negroes, they are unlikely to internalize a wish to help the unseen stranger. The psychological processes of internalizing values in adult life can only be nourished in association with self-respect and personal freedom.

Under the Government's Blood Transfusion Regulations, 1962,[2] it is laid down (First Schedule, para. 10) that European and non-European blood donors shall be organized into separate European and non-European divisions so that:

[1] Simeray-Massé, M., and Riffault, H., *op. cit.*, 1962, and Dichter, E., 'A Brief Psychological Analysis of the Blood Donor Procurement Problem', Institute for Motivational Research Inc., Croton-on-Hudson, New York (typescript), 1952.

[2] Republic of South Africa, *Government Gazette Extraordinary*, Regulation Gazette 146, Vol. VI, No. 385, Pretoria, November 30, 1962.

(a) 'European and non-European blood donors are bled on separate premises or are bled on the same premises but are suitably separated; and

(b) the records of European and non-European donors and of their blood donations are kept separate'.

All containers of human blood and blood products have to be labelled by 'racial origin'[1] (Whites, Coloured, Indians or Asiatics, and Bantus).[2]

Apart from the blood procurement program of the South African Institute for Medical Research, there are five blood transfusion services in the Republic.[3] So far as the writer is aware no studies have been published (excluding the Natal study) which provide detailed information on the characteristics and motives of white donors and on systems of organizing and distributing blood supplies and blood products among the four 'racial origin' groups. Without such information it is not possible to attempt for the Republic as a whole any classification by donor type. In any event, racial segregation and policies of Apartheid introduce a whole set of complex factors which make much more difficult, if not impossible, any analysis of gift-relationships through such indicators as blood transfusion and medical care services.

Such questions as 'who is my stranger?' in terms of giving and receiving blood cannot be formulated without first understanding the meaning of Apartheid and, in particular, its application, effects and consequences over the whole field of medical care. Any explanations of gift-relationships or private market transactions in these areas make little sense unless they are set within the totality of values in a society. Myrdal made the same point in another context many years ago in *An American Dilemma*. After discussing the concept of 'unclean Negro Blood' he wrote: 'The Negro is segregated, and

---

[1] As they have to be by law in Louisiana and Arkansas in the United States. The American Public Health Association protested strongly in 1968 about the practice of segregating blood prior to transfusion according to the race of donor and recipient (*Medical Tribune* report, November 28, 1968).

[2] These 'definitions' or 'classifications' are in no sense scientific; their use in this chapter follows the racial statutes and case law developed by the Race Classification Board in Pretoria which even uses such mythical criteria as 'preponderance of blood'.

[3] South African Blood Transfusion Service, Natal Blood Transfusion Service, Eastern Province Blood Transfusion Service, Border Blood Transfusion Service and Western Province Blood Transfusion Service.

N

one deep idea behind segregation is that of quarantining what is evil, shameful, and feared in society'.[1]

As this book is not about the South African dilemma, we have therefore confined this chapter to presenting the main results of the Natal study.

[1] Myrdal, G., *The American Dilemma*, Harpers, New York, 1944, p. 100.

Chapter 12
Economic Man: Social Man

I

In an earlier chapter we referred to the study *The Price of Blood* by Mr M. H. Cooper and Mr A. J. Culyer commissioned by the Institute of Economic Affairs, a body whose research work is assisted by an advisory council of 17 well-known economists.

The authors, applying 'the simplest tools of economic analysis' to the problems of blood supply and demand, came to the following conclusions: (i) that human blood is an economic good; (ii) that it is possible to attach precise economic meaning to the idea of wastage; (iii) that paying donors for blood would increase supply by encouraging more donors to come forward and by providing an incentive to paid donors to attend sessions more frequently; (iv) that, despite the absence of cost statistics, a commercial market in blood would, if demand continues to rise in the future, provide supplies at a definite cost advantage. In Chapter 9 we quoted from the Preface by the Editor in which it was said 'The authors have made an unanswerable case for a trial period in which the voluntary donor is supplemented by the fee-paid donor so that the results can be judged in practice, and not pre-judged by doctrinaire obfuscation'.

In the Soviet Union, as we pointed out in Chapter 10, a similar crude utilitarianism prevails in the blood market although, unlike the United States, Japan and other countries, there are no 'banks' making a profit out of blood. Something like one-half of all blood supplies are bought and lavishly paid for in the Soviet Union. Those who have read and understood Marx's theory of commodity values and his justification of inequalities of reward (though not specifically in relation to human blood) should not be surprised. One of the fundamental omissions in his critique of capitalism was the absence of any formulation of a morality for a socialist society. The alternative to exploitation was as Professor MacIntyre has said 'simply a crude utilitarianism'.[1] Could we but change the prose

[1] MacIntyre, A., *A Short History of Ethics*, 1967, p. 214.

195

style, revise the illustrations and omit any reference to Marx such calculative—or 'consumerism'—notions would no doubt appeal to the economists in the United States who support a private market in blood.

Be that as it may, we do not propose to pursue these thoughts here or to comment in detail on the conclusions in *The Price of Blood*. To comment, conclusion by conclusion, would involve us in the boring task of repeating and summarizing all the evidence gathered together in earlier chapters about the operations and effects of commercial blood markets in the United States, Japan and other countries.

What we propose to do in this chapter is to discuss criteria of economic efficiency, administrative efficiency, costs per unit of blood and purity, potency and safety in relation to the blood distributive systems in the United States and Britain. We shall try for a few pages to behave like an economist and examine these systems by reference to economic criteria. We shall also have something to say, again in relation to blood, about the way in which ethical premises are avoided by economic writers on the supposition that the utilities of different persons are empirically comparable.

II

Looked at simply in economic terms, the 'cost' of any activity is the most valuable use to which the resources devoted to it might otherwise have been put—the social opportunity cost. Estimates made by the National Blood Resource Program and other authorities, cited in Chapter 4, indicate that in the American market, despite the shortages, something like 15–30 per cent of all blood collected is lost annually through out-dating involving 'a multi-million dollar annual loss'. Some part of this poured away waste, not prevented by the fact that blood is actually paid for, is due to physicians ordering much more blood than is actually transfused.[1]

Additional sources of waste arise from unnecessary surgical operations, for example, hysterectomy and appendectomy and unnecessary transfusions. That there is a great deal of clinically unnecessary surgery is an amply documented fact in American medical literature.[2] A further source of waste is attributable to the misuse or over-use of blood transfusions by physicians and surgeons

[1] Stengle, J. M., *op. cit.*, p. 3.

[2] On transfusion rates for various surgical operations and for maternity patients and trends in surgical procedures generally see all reports published under the Medical Audit Program and Professional Activity Study conducted

brought about in part by 'defensive professional practice'. This development was discussed in Chapter 9. Such is the widespread and growing fear of malpractice suits, in combination with the increasing difficulties encountered by 'high-risk' physicians and surgeons in obtaining commercial insurance cover against malpractice claims, that they order multitudes of tests, therapeutic procedures, X-rays and consultations to protect themselves. 'We have become', said Dr C. L. Hudson, past President of the American Medical Association, 'professionals of laboratory medicine.'[1]

In total, therefore, and including all forms of waste defined in Chapter 4, something between one million and one-and-a-half million units of blood were wasted in the United States in 1968. The weight of evidence suggests that total waste was substantially lower in the 1950s. The corresponding waste in an entirely voluntary system in England and Wales in the same year was infinitesimal.[2]

The American loss could conceivably have entailed wasted supplies of blood from half a million people (assuming an annual average of $2-2\frac{1}{2}$ units each). An economist, looking at these facts, would want to take into account at least two other tangible costs, the cost in terms of effort required and the cost in terms of time required; in the absence of precise data he would then attempt to impute such costs whether they were paid for (e.g. in time off work) or not.

We do not propose to embark on such a cost-benefit analysis.

by the Commission on Professional and Hospital Activities, Ann Arbor, Michigan, from 1961 to 1967. One study of blood use in five common operations concluded that for 2,000,000 patients in 1959–62 in the United States there was a 'waste' of 160,000 pints of blood. 'Or to be a bit melodramatic, more than 620 barrels' (Vol. 1, No. 13, August 15, 1963). In another study of 1035 common surgical cases in 21 general hospitals, reviewing physicians considered that 'either the use of blood was not justified or the clinical picture was questionable' (Report 16, *One- and Two-Pint Transfusions in Surgery*, February 28, 1961). For illustrations and references to studies of unnecessary surgery and transfusions see Tunley, R., *The American Health Scandal*, Harpers, New York, 1966 and Gross, M. L., *op. cit.*, 1966, pp. 176–7.

[1] *A.M.A. News*, Special Report on Malpractice Insurance, November 18, 1968, p. 14.

[2] See Appendix 2. An independent investigation into blood use in South London in 1960 reported that administrative waste was approximately 1 per cent (the national figure in 1961 was 2 per cent). This study also assessed the clinical need for transfusions. On seven criteria it was suggested that the medical use of blood was unnecessary in a proportion of cases accounting for 6·5 per cent of total blood use. This included single-pint transfusions, dying patients and other categories (Graham-Stewart, C. W., 'A Clinical Survey of Blood Transfusion', *Lancet*, ii, 421, 1960).

The data are not precise; for women donors the value of housewives' services cannot be measured (one element in the 'mass of contradictions' in the concept of the national income);[1] the exercise, in any event, would be futile in the context of the magnitude of total wastage; and, finally, these economic wastes, immense as they are, are completely dwarfed by the social costs—or externalities—of the market system and the social benefits of an alternative voluntary, gift-relationship system. Human welfare is an ethical concept. There is no such thing, as Mr Nath and others have remarked, as 'economic welfare'.[2]

Having said this we must point out that, although attempts have been made to value human life,[3] no money values can be attached to the presence or absence of a spirit of altruism in a society. Altruism in giving to a stranger does not begin and end with blood donations. It may touch every aspect of life and affect the whole fabric of values. Its role in satisfying the biological need to help—particularly in modern societies—is another unmeasureable element. In this book we have used human blood as an indicator; perhaps the most basic and sensitive indicator of social values and human relationships that could be found for a comparative study. If dollars or pounds exchange for blood then it may be morally acceptable for a myriad of other human activities and relationships also to exchange for dollars or pounds. Economists may fragment systems and values; other people do not.

We do not know and could never estimate in economic terms the social costs to American society of the decline in recent years in the voluntary giving of blood. The evidence in preceding chapters shows the extent to which commercialization and profit in blood has been driving out the voluntary donor. Moreover, it is likely that a decline in the spirit of altruism in one sphere of human activities will be accompanied by similar changes in attitudes, motives and relationships in other spheres. The ethical issues raised by the use of prisoners for blood product trials and plasmapheresis programs, reported in Chapter 8, is one example. The growth of profit-making hospitals, geared to short stays, high turnover and 'profitable' patients and which cannot foster a sense of community attachment is another example.

Once man begins to say, as he sees that dollars exchange for blood

[1] Robinson, J., *Economic Philosophy*, 1962, p. 130.

[2] Nath, S. K., *A Reappraisal of Welfare Economics*, 1968, p. 235.

[3] See for example Schultz, T. W., 'Investment in Human Capital', *Am. Econ. Rev.*, *51*, March 1, 1961.

supplies from Skid Row and a poor and often coloured population of sellers, 'I need no longer experience (or suffer from) a sense of responsibility (or sin) in not giving to my neighbour' then the consequences are likely to be socially pervasive. There is nothing permanent about the expression of reciprocity. If the bonds of community giving are broken the result is not a state of value neutralism. The vacuum is likely to be filled by hostility and social conflict, a consequence discussed in another context by Dr Mishan in his book *The Costs of Economic Growth*.[1] The myth of maximizing economic growth can supplant the growth of social relations.

We do not criticize economists for not measuring these social costs and benefits. Our complaint is directed to their intellectual naivety in failing to identify and describe them and to make explicit the spectrum of value choices in social as well as economic criteria. In saying this we recall that Keynes once expressed the hope that one day economists 'could manage to get themselves thought of as humble, competent people on a level with dentists'. This day has not yet dawned for some of the order who, after taking strong oaths of ethical neutrality, perform as missionaries in the social welfare field and often give the impression of possessively owning a hot line to God.

On quite a different level there are other types of social costs that are either ignored in economic cost-minimizing analyses of social policy or are not rigorously studied. We mention two by way of illustration. They are both examples of mixed externalities or, in other words, divergences between the costs borne by (or benefits accruing to) individual organizations or firms and the costs (or diswelfares) imposed upon (or benefits accruing to) the community as a whole.

The magnitude—in comparison with Britain—of the problem of serum hepatitis in the United States and Japan, attributable to the operation of commercial markets in blood, was depicted in Chapter 8.[2] Any adequate cost-benefit analysis would need to take into

[1] See especially Chapter 9, Mishan, E. J., 1967.

[2] Dr A. J. Zuckerman of the Department of Bacteriology and Immunology at the London School of Hygiene and Tropical Medicine criticized the Institute of Economic Affairs study *The Price of Blood* for completely ignoring 'the outstanding hazard of commercially supplied blood—namely, the risk of post-transfusion hepatitis' (*Brit. Med. J.*, **i**, 174, April 20, 1968). In 1966 he had pointed out: 'Even more significant is the fact that although infectious hepatitis cannot be considered a major cause of death it nevertheless ranked in 1959 in the U.S.A. second only to influenza among the deaths attributed to acute virus infections' (*Brit. Med. J.*, **ii**, 1136, November 5, 1966).

account (or at least identify) the costs of medical care to the individual and the community; the misuse of scarce resources (including human blood); the costs to the individual and the family in loss of earnings, perhaps for life; the costs of higher mortality rates in terms of implied money values placed on human life;[1] the costs of disease and death outside the American economy caused by the commercial export of contaminated plasma products[2]; and the costs, also arising in other countries, of importing from the United States methods and consequences of commercializing blood donor systems, and many other tangible and intangible externalities.[3] We may know something about the processes of maximizing economic growth but we have not even begun to identify the processes by which societies maximize diswelfares.

Secondly, no assessment of the costs and benefits of a commercial market in blood would be complete without some appreciation of the market effects on the roles, functions, standards of practice and behaviour of doctors and medical institutions, and the price of restricting professional freedom by legally subjecting medicine to the laws of the marketplace. Some of these issues were discussed in Chapter 9.

A substantial part of the measurable components of some of these costs, and particularly the waste of blood and the costs of administrative chaos,[4] are at present borne in the United States by the individual. The high costs of malpractice insurance and suits are also largely passed on to and borne by sick people in inflated medical bills. The costs of defensive medical practice in terms of the proliferation of tests, consultations, hospitalization and other unnecessary interventions are similarly passed on to and borne by the generality of patients. So are the profits in blood, blood products and blood processing made by commercial blood banks, commercial

---

[1] And the 'net annual dependency' of other members of the family (see Hayzelden, J. E., 'The Value of Human Life', *Public Administration*, Vol. 46, Winter 1968, p. 427).

[2] In 1961 there were two deaths in Israel caused by infected plasma processed and exported by a commercial blood firm in New York (Perlis, L., 'Blood Banks or Blood Business', address delivered at 16th Annual Meeting, American Association of Blood Banks, Detroit, November 1963, p. 6).

[3] For an enumeration of the main problems arising out of the general principles of cost-benefit analysis see Prest, A. R. and Turvey, R., *Surveys of Economic Theory: Vol. III—Resource Allocation*, Macmillan, London 1966, and Feldstein, M. S., 'Cost-Benefit Analysis and Investment in the Public Sector', *Public Administration*, Vol. 42, Winter 1964, p. 351.

[4] On administrative, clerical accounting and paperwork costs see Jennings, J. B., *op. cit.*, especially pp. 66–90.

laboratories and pharmaceutical companies. Those patients who need blood also have to bear the additional costs in some hospitals which aim to make a profit in their blood 'departments' to subsidize other departments of the hospital. Mostly, these costs and profit margins are allowed to lie where they fall—on patients and their families.

They bear most heavily on poor people, the sick and the handicapped in society. Viewed as a system of redistribution, they are heavily regressive. The poor who need blood thus add to the utility of those who have no such needs. Without, however, a great deal of research into the much wider area of medical costs and prices (to say nothing about insurance and legal costs and prices) it is impossible to estimate the additional costs attributable to commercial markets in blood in comparison with a voluntary, unpaid, 'free' system under the National Health Service in England. At a very practical level, though, we can say something about the comparative costs of delivering a unit of blood to the operating theatre, ready for use, in hospitals in England and Wales and the United States.

III

For the years ended March 31, 1964 and 1968, the National Blood Transfusion Service carried out a cost study of its operations, nationally and regionally, net of capital charges.[1] Costs were analysed under five main headings: (1) Blood Collection; (2) Blood Distribution; (3) Transport; (4) Laboratory; (5) Administration. No allowance was made for the unpaid services of voluntary workers (mainly married women and retired people in the community who assisted with general public sessions).

The costs covered salaries and wages, accommodation, repairs and maintenance, furniture and equipment, hire of halls, rent and rates, travelling and subsistence, mobile units (including new vehicles), drugs and other medical requisites and publicity. Also included were the costs of a substantial amount of Rh-antenatal testing (not generally covered in the U.S.A. cost estimates); the production of plasma and blood products; some research and development (again not generally included in U.S.A. costs) and 'Compensation to Donors'. This last item referred to compensation

---

[1] Copies of the reports were kindly provided by the Ministry of Health. Capital expenditure on new transfusion centres was estimated in 1969 to amount to approximately 10 per cent of the total running costs of the Service.

in cash for the cleaning or replacement of, or repairs to, clothing or personal possessions (e.g. stains from drops of blood, broken spectacles), reimbursement of wages for time lost by donors, and damages for negligence (the cost of damages paid to donors—a very substantial item in the United States—may or may not be included in American cost estimates depending on the incidence of bankruptcies among commercial blood banks). In 1967–8 the total amount of compensation paid to all donors in England and Wales was £808. In that year there were 1,446,551 blood donations. The costs of compensation thus amounted to one penny for every seven units of blood collected.

The result of this study showed that for the country as a whole in 1967–8 the average cost of a bottle of blood (excluding laboratory testing) delivered to the hospital was £1 6s. Including laboratory testing, the cost was approximately £2 a bottle. At the official rate of exchange ruling in 1969 the equivalent United States price was $4·80. No self-respecting Skid Row supplier exacted less than $5 for a potentially contaminated pint in 1969.

Only approximate figures for comparative purposes can be given for the United States partly because of differences in prices and costs, locally and regionally, and partly because of differences in charges, accounting procedures and profit margins by blood banks and hospitals. We can consider four sets of 'prices' for one unit of blood:[1]

1. The price paid to the supplier (the paid and professional donor). Most suppliers were paid $5–20 though some were paid as much as $25. For less common blood groups the price was substantially higher.[2] In 1956 in New York some Rh-negative type blood was bought for $41–50.[3] Payments made to plasmapheresis 'donors', sometimes on a quasi-salaried basis, were discussed in Chapter 6.

2. The blood replacement fee charged to patients who do not voluntarily replace blood used or find another donor. This fee was generally in the range $15–50.[4]

[1] The figures given mostly relate to 1966–8. Prices and costs were rising throughout the 1960s.

[2] *Hearings on S. 1945*, *op. cit.*, 1967, pp. 60 and 81–3, and Jennings, J. B., *op. cit.*, pp. 16 and 701.

[3] The New York Academy of Medicine, *Human Blood in New York City*, *op. cit.*, p. 27.

[4] *Hearings on S. 1945*, *op. cit.*, 1967, p. 97. In 1960 the national weighted mean fee charged by all members reporting in the AABB survey was $22.46 (American Association of Blood Banks, *op. cit.*, 1964, Table 3).

3. The price paid by hospitals to commercial blood banks.[1] This amounted to around $35 or more.[2]

4. The price charged to the hospital patient (no replacement of blood by the patient). Charges for the blood and processing ranged from $30 to $100.[3] Charges by hospitals who did not buy blood commercially were in the lower ranges; those that did were in the higher ranges.[4] The majority of hospitals and blood banks, however, operated a 2 for 1 replacement plan (and in some cases higher).[5] The patients' blood bill may thus have been increased.

It is impossible to say what these prices and costs actually include on average. Accounting procedures vary enormously; some of the data may or may not include blood typing and cross-matching costs, storage, technological education and research costs, infusion costs and so on. Moreover, standards of accounting and public information in the whole blood banking system are said to be low: 'The great discrepancies in charges and replacement policies which obtain in most areas,' wrote Dr R. F. Norris, 'make it most difficult for the patient and the layman to understand that he is not being exploited by the hospital'.[6]

These four sets of data do not, of course, represent 'costs' in economic terms. From the consumer's point of view what is material is the size of his blood bill from the hospital. As we have shown, this may vary from $30–100 a unit. If he does not or cannot replace the blood used he may have to pay up to $50 or more a unit. In addition, there may be charges for blood typing, cross-matching, infusion and other costs. These may add $10–20 to the bill.

Many patients, however, requiring blood or plasma need more

[1] Hospitals pay the American Red Cross a 'participation fee' per unit. It varies locally from about $6–13. This is not a true cost of collecting as the Red Cross is subsidized (*Blood Center Operations, op. cit.*, 1967).

[2] Report by the New York Council for Civic Affairs, *op. cit.*, 1967 and *Hearings on S. 2560, op. cit.*, 1964, p. 3.

[3] In 1960 the national weighted mean processing fee charged by all members reporting in the AABB survey was $9.17 (American Association of Blood Banks, *op. cit.*, 1964, Table 2). An American scholar, Mr F. Honigsbaum, living in London had to undergo surgery on a visit to the United States in 1968. He was charged over £150 for 11 pints (*Pulse*, London, May 17, 1969, p. 9).

[4] *Hearings on S. 2560, op. cit.*, 1964, pp. 43 and 159, Joint Blood Council, *op. cit.*, 1960, p. 37 and A.M.A. Guide for Medical Society Committees on Blood (pamphlet), 1967.

[5] *Hearings on S. 2560, op. cit.*, 1964, p. 162 and see Chapter 5.

[6] Norris, R. F., 'Hospital Programs of Blood Banking', *J.A.M.A.*, Vol. 193, No. 1, July 5, 1965, p. 46.

than one unit.[1] Elderly patients under the Medicare Program receiving an average 6½ pints would be charged $156. Private patients would probably pay more. In Britain, by contrast, private patients (non-resident or resident in National Health Service hospitals) are not charged for blood voluntarily given under the auspices of the Health Service Blood Transfusion system.[2]

For the many American patients requiring major surgery and large transfusions of blood the bills that confront them are crippling. In earlier chapters some illustrations were given of the large quantities of blood and blood products needed today by serious road accident cases, difficult obstetrical cases, 'artificial kidney' patients, those undergoing open-heart operations and other forms of cardio-vascular surgery and 'spare part' surgery. It is quite common in large numbers of these cases for 20 pints of blood to be needed for a single operation or for a single case. Judged by the prices charged in some of these cases for the blood itself plus the costs of laboratory work and the transfusion, patients receiving 20 pints had to meet a bill in 1968–9 of about $1200. At the official rate of exchange in 1969 the British equivalent would be £500. In one heart transplant case in California in 1968 the British equivalent price for the blood (300 units at $25 a unit), laboratory work and transfusion was £8361.[3]

In many cases like these the market incentive replacement fee becomes an irrelevant myth. Few patients with the help of their families and friends could hope to replace 20 or more pints of blood within two or three years. What often happens in such cases is that

[1] Among 333,156 elderly patients under the Medicare Program supplied with 1,028,273 pints of blood during the period July 1, 1966, to September 1, 1967, 27 per cent received 4 or more pints. They received in all more than half of all the blood (582,946 pints) or on average 6½ pints each. The bill for the blood alone for those patients receiving 6½ pints and who did not replace any of the blood was $156 (only about 25 per cent of all blood was replaced). The Medicare Program did not reimburse for the first 3 pints (see Chapter 5). Patients receiving only 3 pints and who were not reimbursed paid on average about $70. (Analysis supplied to the author by the Division of Policy and Standards, Bureau of Health Insurance, Social Security Administration, Baltimore, October 1968.)

[2] See Ministry of Health circular H.M. (69)28, March 1969. Private patients. whether undergoing surgery, abortions or other procedures, who often demand special tax deductibles for 'contracting-out' of the National Health Service seldom recognize the free benefits they receive as private patients from the blood transfusion service and other parts of the National Health Service.

[3] *The Times*, July 31, 1968. In another heart transplant case the blood bill sent to the patient's wife (the patient died fourteen days after the operation) was $7265 or one-quarter of the total hospital bill of $28,845.83 (*International Herald Tribune*, April 6, 1968).

the patient (and his or her family) becomes a 'blood indigent' as well as an 'income indigent'.

IV

In comparing commercialized blood market systems in the United States with a voluntary system functioning as an integral part of the National Health Service in Britain we have considered, in this chapter, four sets of criteria. These are basic criteria which economists would themselves apply in attempting to assess the relative advantages and disadvantages of different systems. They exclude, therefore, the much wider and unquantifiable social, ethical and philosophical aspects which, as this study has demonstrated, extend far beyond the narrower confines of blood distribution systems judged simply in economic and financial terms.

These four criteria which to some extent overlap are, briefly stated: (1) economic efficiency; (2) administrative efficiency; (3) price—the cost per unit to the patient; (4), purity, potency and safety—or quality per unit.

On all four criteria, the commercialized blood market fails. In terms of economic efficiency it is highly wasteful of blood; shortages, chronic and acute, characterize the demand and supply position and make illusory the concept of equilibrium; the market also involves heavy external costs. It is administratively inefficient; the so-called mixed pluralism of the American market results in more bureaucratization, avalanches of paper and bills, and much greater administrative, accounting and computer overheads. These wastes, disequilibria and inefficiencies are reflected in the price paid by the patient (or consumer); the cost per unit of blood varying in the United States between £10 and £20 (at the official rate of exchange in 1969) compared with £1 6s. (£2 if processing costs are included) in Britain—five to fifteen times higher. And, finally, in terms of quality, commercial markets are much more likely to distribute contaminated blood; in other words, the risks for the patient of disease and death in the form of serum hepatitis are substantially higher.

Paradoxically—or so it may seem to some—the more commercialized a blood distribution system becomes (and hence more wasteful, inefficient and dangerous) the more will the gross national product be inflated. In part, and quite simply, this is the consequence of statistically 'transferring' an unpaid service (voluntary blood donors, voluntary workers in the service, unpaid time) with much lower external costs to a monetary and measureable paid activity

205

involving costlier externalities. Similar effects on the gross national product would ensue if housewives were paid for housework or childless married couples were financially rewarded for adopting children or hospital patients cooperating for teaching purposes charged medical students. The gross national product is also inflated when commercial markets accelerate 'blood obsolescence'—or waste; the waste is counted because someone has paid for it.

What *The Economist* described in its 1969 survey of the American economy as the great 'efficiency gap' between that country and Britain[1] clearly does not apply in the field of human blood. On the economic and technical criteria employed in this study in relation to blood distribution systems such a conclusion needs to be reversed; the voluntary socialized system in Britain is economically, professionally, administratively and qualitatively more efficient than the mixed, commercialized and individualistic American system.

Another myth, the Paretian myth of consumer sovereignty, has also to be shattered. In commercial blood markets the consumer is not king. He has less freedom to live unharmed; little choice in determining price; is more subject to shortages in supply; is less free from bureaucratization; has fewer opportunities to express altruism; and exercises fewer checks and controls in relation to consumption, quality and external costs. Far from being sovereign, he is often exploited.

Those who suffer most and have the largest bills of all to pay are haemophiliacs. It is estimated that the incidence in the United States is 1 in 10,000 of the male population (lower estimates have been made for Britain). The fact that the disease is not only hereditary but may occur as a consequence of one of the most frequent mutations in medicine, means that the incidence may be expected to increase rather than decrease throughout the world.

Modern medical treatment now consists of human plasma and a variety of concentrated blood products. A ten-day course of treatment with these substances—say for a dental extraction—may require gifts from 60 blood donors each involving a potential risk of infecting the patient with hepatitis. In Britain, these products are prepared under the auspices of the National Blood Transfusion Service and are supplied at no cost to the patient under the National Health Service. They are not sold—or priced—commercially. The blood is given by voluntary donors.[2]

[1] *The Economist*, U.S.A. Report, May 10, 1969.
[2] Biggs, R., and Macfarlane, R. G., *Treatment of Haemophilia and other Coagulation Disorders*, Blackwell, Oxford, 1966.

In the United States where clinically some of the products are considered to be less satisfactory they are produced and marketed commercially. At retail prices ruling in 1966, the cost to an average adult of a ten-day course of treatment with human plasma products was about $2250. In 1969 it was reported: 'Many patients require plasma or plasma concentrate therapy three times a month or more. By the end of the year, this patient has a staggering plasma bill. In families of two or more haemophiliac youngsters, the financial burden is even more acute. The financial aspects alone can cause family problems and disruption. Patients often relate guilt feelings because of the financial burden they cause their families'.[1] They are also continually reminded by these market forces that for their survival from one bleeding episode to the next they are dependent on blood supplies from strangers. They are 'bad risks'; non-insurable by the private market in the United States; not acceptable by profit-making hospitals.

It has been estimated that if all the needs of haemophiliac patients in the United States were fully met they would require about one-eighth of all the blood collected each year in the country—or about 1,000,000 pints.[2]

In England, where it is estimated that there are more than 2000 patients with severe haemorrhagic disorders,[3] the problems they face are in no way comparable to those confronting similar patients in the United States. They would not wish to emigrate. While there are serious difficulties in the technical production of adequate quantities of the appropriate blood products (which use only certain of the valuable constituents of plasma) there is no shortage of blood, and no problems for the patient in paying for the blood and medical treatment.

One of the most perceptive and fascinating historical studies of the last of the Romanovs and the fall of Imperial Russia, *Nicholas and Alexandra*, written by Robert K. Massie, centres on the most famous haemophiliac of all, the Tsarevich Alexis, the only son and

---

[1] Taylor, C., 'Haemophilic Center at Work', *Rehabilitation Record*, Rehabilitation Services Administration, Dept. of Health, Education and Welfare, Washington, Vol. 10, No. 2, March–April 1969, pp. 1–6. A study of 177 haemophiliac patients by the University Department of Psychiatry in Sheffield in 1968 failed to confirm American findings that haemophilia is liable to cause marked psychiatric symptoms. There was also no evidence of acute financial and occupational difficulties (Bronks, I. G., and Blackburn, E. K., 'A Socio-Medical Study of Haemophilia and Related States', *Brit. J. prev. soc. Med.*, 1968, *22*, 68–72).

[2] Personal communication, Dr J. M. Stengle, *op. cit.*, October 16, 1968.

[3] Biggs, R. and Macfarlane, R. G., *op. cit.*, 1966, p. 325.

heir of Nicholas II, last Tsar of all the Russias.[1] Mr Massie was moved to embark on this study after his discovery that his own son was a haemophiliac. He wanted to understand how other families dealt with the problems raised by this blood disease; he also wanted to help American families who were dependent on gifts from strangers. In the course of his work he showed how haemophilia—before science made blood transfusions possible—helped to change the course of history.

From Imperial Russia we move to Communist Russia and quote from Alexander Solzhenitsyn's great work *Cancer Ward*,[2] banned in the Soviet Union, as a fitting conclusion to this chapter.

Shulubin, a cancer patient in a hospital in Central Asia is talking to Kostoglotov, a former prisoner in a labour camp now in exile as a patient in the same hospital. 'He (Shulubin) spoke very distinctly, like a master giving a lesson.

' "We have to show the world a society in which all relationships, fundamental principles and laws flow directly from moral ethics, and from them *alone*. Ethical demands would determine all calculations: how to bring up children, what to prepare them for, to what purpose the work of grown-ups should be directed, and how their leisure should be occupied. As for scientific research, it should only be conducted where it doesn't damage ethical morality, in the first instance where it doesn't damage the researchers themselves".'

Kostoglotov then raises questions. ' "There has to be an economy, after all, doesn't there? That comes before everything else." "Does it?" said Shulubin. "That depends. For example, Vladimir Solovyov argues rather convincingly that an economy could and should be built on an ethical basis." '

' "What's that? Ethics first and economics afterwards?" Kostoglotov looked bewildered.'

[1] Atheneum, New York, 1967.
[2] Vol. 2, translated Bethell, N., and Burg, D., Bodley Head, London, 1969.

Chapter 13
Who is my Stranger?

I

In this chapter we return to the theme of 'the gift'. In an earlier one (Chapter 5), setting out a typology of donors, we drew attention to the similarities and dissimilarities between the blood gift in modern societies and forms and manifestations of giving and gift-exchange in primitive societies. The social and economic aspects of gift-exchange as a universal phenomenon offer material, as Lévi-Strauss has said, for 'inexhaustible sociological reflection'. No one has done more to provoke such reflection than Lévi-Strauss himself, especially in his book *The Elementary Structures of Kinship*.[1]

Both Lévi-Strauss and Mauss, in analysing materials from an immense range of culturally diverse societies, are tempted from time to time to speculate about the relevance of the rules and functions of giving in such societies to present-day institutions in the West. Mauss was eventually led to see modern forms of social security, expressing 'solicitude or co-operation', as a renaissance of 'the theme of the gift'. Had he been born later he might well have explored comparatively the concept of socialized medical care as exemplified by Britain's National Health Service or the principles underlying systems of voluntary blood donorship. When he was in his seventies, blood transfusion services were in their infancy; today, they are practically universal and world demand for blood is estimated to be growing at a much faster rate than adult population growth, economic growth and other physical indicators.[2] What seemingly lags far behind this imperative demand from medical science in most countries—and especially in the United States and Japan—is the rate of 'social growth' in the form of adequate numbers of voluntary donors. This refusal to give without immediate reward could be interpreted—if translated into the context of the primitive societies studied by Mauss—as a 'refusal of friendship and inter-course'.

[1] Revised edition (ed. R. Needham), Eyre & Spottiswoode, 1969.
[2] *Proc. Conf. American Association of Blood Banks*, Los Angeles, 1966.

O

Lévi-Strauss had comparative pictures also in mind in deploying examples of gift transactions in the West. 'In North American society, which often seems to seek the reintegration into modern society of the very general attitudes and procedures of primitive cultures, these occasions (festivals) assume quite exceptional proportions. The exchange of gifts at Christmas, for a month each year, practised by all social classes with a sort of sacred ardour, is nothing other than a gigantic *potlatch*, implicating millions of individuals, and at the end of which many family budgets are faced with lasting disequilibrium . . . even in our own society the destruction of wealth is a way to gain prestige.'[1]

These and other examples drawn from both complex and traditional societies indicate that the personal gift and counter-gift, in which givers and receivers are known to each other, and personally communicate with each other, is characterized by a great variety of sentiments and purposes. At one end of the spectrum, economic purposes may be dominant as in some forms of first-gifts which aim to achieve a material gain or to enhance prestige or to bring about material gain in the future. At the other end are those gifts whose purposes are predominantly social and moral in that as 'total social facts' they aim to serve friendly relationships, affection and harmony between known individuals and social groups.

Within all such gift transactions of a personal face-to-face nature lie embedded some elements of moral enforcement or bond. To give is to receive—to compel some return or create some obligation— either in the form of a similar or different material gift or in the overt expression of sentiment, pleasure or pain, manifested in physical acts of behaviour on the part of the recipient. No such gift is or can be utterly detached, disinterested or impersonal. Each carries messages and motives in its own language.

Both Lévi-Strauss and Mauss—and other anthropologists— have sought to show that exchange in primitive societies consists not so much in economic transactions as in reciprocal gifts, that these reciprocal gifts have a far more important function in these societies than in our own, and that this primitive form of exchange is not merely nor essentially of an economic nature but is what Mauss called 'a total social fact', that is, an event which has significance that is at once social and religious, magic and economic, utilitarian and sentimental, jural and moral. Dalton concluded from a survey of the literature that economic theory, developed to analyse

[1] Lévi-Strauss, C., *op. cit.*, p. 56.

the structures, processes and problems of market-organized industrialism, was not relevant to primitive economies.[1]

Tönnies in his classic study of European societies, *Gemeinschaft und Gesellschaft* (strangely neglected by the French anthropologists) developed what he called the 'Fellowship Type' in Gemeinschaft-like relationships. Gift-exchanges in such community oriented societies were, he argued, essentially mutual depending on equality of knowledge or volition in performance. By contrast, Gesellschaft-like relationships (in which economic man was dominant) were governed by the principle, *Do, ut des* (I give, so that you will give). 'What I do for you, I do only as a means to effect your simultaneous, previous or later service for me. Actually and really I want and desire only this. To get something from you is my end; my service is the means thereto, which I naturally contribute unwillingly.'[2] Strong elements of compulsion dominated this type of gift relationship which, according to Tönnies, often had as its purpose a desire for status, power or material gain.

But in our societies, argued Lévi-Strauss, the proportion of goods transferred according to the gift-exchange modalities of primitive societies is 'very small in comparison with those involved in commerce and merchandising. Reciprocal gifts are diverting survivals which engage the curiosity of the antiquarian . . .'.[3] The examples he gives—whether they are regarded as 'survivals' or not—relate to physical objects all of which have utility; they are bought and sold in the market. They involve the use of money which could have been put to other purposes and which might have been more (or less) profitable to the giver. Other writers, like Schwartz and Veblen, discuss the psychology of the gift in the context of economic commodities being used as vehicles and instruments for realities of another order. Thus, such gifts presuppose some element of calculating 'economizing' behaviour. In so far as these forms of gift-exchange in modern societies are partly or mainly economic in form or intent then it could follow that certain kinds of action or behaviour often regarded as primarily social might be considered to be primarily economic in intent. Like Blau, this would lead us to apply the principles of marginal utility analysis from economics to exchange in social life.[4]

[1] Dalton, G., 'Economic Theory and Primitive Society', *American Anthropologist*, Vol. 63, February 1961.

[2] Tönnies, F., *Community and Association (Gemeinschaft und Gesellschaft)*, translated and supplemented Loomis, C. P., London, 1955, pp. 20–1.

[3] Lévi-Strauss, C., *op. cit.*, p. 61.

[4] Blau, P. M., *Exchange and Power in Social Life*, Wiley, New York, 1964.

Whatever the general validity of these theories concerning gift-exchange relationships of a Gesellschaft-like type they entirely neglect large areas of gift actions and behaviour in both personal and impersonal contexts which do not involve physical objects, which are difficult or impossible to price and quantify in economic terms, and which, while involving an act of giving, carry no explicit right, expectation or moral enforcement of a return gift. If it were possible to apply to such actions the metaphysical concept of utility it would be found that they are not processes, relationships or things which generally people want to acquire, possess or buy. They have no exchange value.

Yet, as we have argued in this study, social gifts and actions carrying no explicit or implicit individual right to a return gift or action are forms of 'creative altruism' (in Sorokin's words).[1] They are creative in the sense that the self is realized with the help of anonymous others; they allow the biological need to help to express itself. Manifestations of altruism in this sense may of course be thought of as self-love. But they may also be thought of as giving life, or prolonging life or enriching life for anonymous others. That they may, incidentally, create economic wealth by sustaining life is subsidiary in conception, conduct and objective.

We speak here, of course, of those areas of personal behaviour and relationships which lie outside the reciprocal rights and obligations of family and kinship in modern society. We are thus chiefly concerned—as much of social policy is—with 'stranger' relationships, with processes, institutions and structures which encourage or discourage the intensity and extensiveness of anonymous helpfulness in society; with 'ultra obligations' which derive from our own characters and are not contractual in nature.[2] In the ultimate analysis it is these concerns and their expression which distinguish social policy from economic policy or, as Kenneth Boulding put it, '. . . social policy is that which is centred in those institutions that create integration and discourage alienation'.[3]

II

In an earlier chapter we pointed out that the gift of blood had certain attributes which distinguished it from many other forms of

[1] Sorokin, P. A., *The Ways and Power of Love*, Beacon Press, Boston, 1954.

[2] For a philosophical discussion of 'ultra obligations' see Grice, G. R., *The Grounds of Moral Judgement*, C.U.P., 1967.

[3] Boulding, K. E., 'The Boundaries of Social Policy', *Social Work*, Vol. 12, No. 1, January 1967, p. 7.

gift and in a series of propositions we described these attributes. Most if not all of them are not to be found in any total sense in the forms of gift-exchange analysed by Lévi-Strauss, Schwartz, Blau and others which, interpreted structurally, lead to the elaboration of marginal utility models. Such models or theories of market exchange are, we suggest, irrelevant to an understanding of the place of blood in modern systems of medical care.

＼ As we have explained earlier, in reflecting on the nature of medical care and its associated social and psychological elements we were eventually forced, by a process of logical inevitability, to more concrete generalizations and to ask whether the blood transfusion services and the use and distribution of human blood should be treated as a market consumption good. From an affirmative answer much could flow; the implications could extend to affect our thinking over wide areas of social policy and what are conventionally called 'the social services'. Hospitals, nursing homes, clinical laboratories, schools, universities and even, perhaps, churches would no longer be protected by laws or common conventions of 'charitable' immunity; they would be exposed to the forces of economic calculation and to the laws of the marketplace.

Blood transfusion services were selected as material for a case study on a comparative basis to illumine the problems of social policy in general and medical care in particular. The reasons for this selection were explained in Chapter 1. But other areas of gift relationships in modern society might have been chosen for detailed examination from a large and expanding social policy territory of stranger relationships and transactions of a non-economic character. Some indications of this territory, actual and potential, of a 'caring community' in Britain were given in the Seebohm Report: 'This new department (of social service) will, we believe, . . . enable the greatest possible number of individuals to act reciprocally, giving and receiving service for the well-being of the whole community'.[1]

We could, for example, have taken for study the giving role of the patient as 'teaching material', and as research material for experimentation and the testing of new drugs and other diagnostic and therapeutic measures. Millions of people in Western societies every year are expected to give themselves, without price or a contractural reward, in these situations. Moreover, measured in terms of time and numbers, the demand is increasing. To qualify as a doctor in Britain, it is probable that the average medical student

[1] *Report of the Committee on Local Authority and Allied Personal Social Services*, Cmnd. 3703, 1968, p. 11.

213

now needs access to or contact with in one form or another some 300 different patients. This contribution from patients to the training of a professional élite will be substantially higher when the recommendations of the Royal Commission are fully implemented.[1] They are no longer 'charity' patients and could not in the 1970s, whatever the future of the National Health Service, be treated as such. Should their contribution to medical education, therefore, be paid on market criteria?

At present, patients as strangers are asked or expected to behave as givers on the unspoken assumption that they may benefit; sometimes their consent is sought; sometimes they are simply informed; often nothing is said.[2] Their willingness to be 'taught on' and to give of themselves, physically and psychologically, is presumed. It is taken for granted in the name of research, the advancement of medical science, society's need for doctors, the better training and more rapid progression of doctors professionally and financially and, ultimately, for the good of all patients irrespective of race, religion, colour or territory.

Gift transactions of this type between strangers—at present unpriced in non-market situations—are by no means unilateral transfers. Patients may benefit immediately more from contact with medical students than with consultants. Doctors in teaching roles give more to patients than a strict definition of their duties may warrant. But the benefits of teaching, experimentation and research —often inextricably mixed up—mostly accrue in the long run. They are not immediately a 'return gift' to the individual patient. While there may be 'fall-out' benefits they are not at once obvious to the patient. Among medical students, doctors ascending career ladders, research workers and scientists, however, the connections are more obvious and more personal. As individuals they expect to benefit in the short run from these gift transactions. The benefits to patients mostly accrue in the long-run; they further the well-being of some future collectivity of patients. If old age pensioners with chronic bronchitis put to themselves the Hobbesian question—why should men do other than act to their own immediate advantage?—they might start charging for the gifts they make which are more likely to benefit future cohorts of chronic bronchitics.

---

[1] *Report of the Royal Commission on Medical Education 1965–8*, Cmnd. 3569, H.M.S.O., London, 1968.

[2] For an explanation of the problems of defining 'true' or 'informed' consent see *Medical Research Council, Annual Report 1962–3*, Cmnd. 2382, H.M.S.O., London, 1964 and Pappworth, M. H., *Human Guinea Pigs*, London, 1967.

All personal service professions in an increasingly professionalized world are becoming—like medicine—more dependent on other people to further their professional aspirations. Sociologists need co-operative field and control material; psychologists need laboratory volunteers; psychiatric students need the mentally ill; social workers-to-be need clients; various professional groups within and without the pharmaceutical industry need healthy volunteers as well as diseased patients for drug trials; student teachers need pupils, and so on.

Considered individually as examples of stranger relationships, more people are expected to contribute—to give—to serve the interests of other people. There is in all these transactions an unspoken assumption of some form of gift-reciprocity; that those who give as members of a society to strangers will themselves (or their families) eventually benefit as members of that society. More often than not, however, such donors are in captive situations; the transaction cannot, therefore, be considered to be spontaneously altruistic in its most attainable form. There is, nevertheless, a vague and general presumption of a return gift at some future date, but a gift that may not be deliberately sought or desired by the individual concerned—as with voluntary blood donors. Few people when well wish to be ill; few people desire operations, blood transfusions, inpatient treatment or social care from social workers. More and more instruments of social policy are in action requiring, as scientific knowledge advances *pari passu* with professionalization, these acts of 'voluntaryism' which carry with them no wish for return acts or return gifts.

This is but one brief illustration of a number of social policy areas in which gift transactions take place and which might have been developed at length as case studies in this book. Another unexplored area of a different type—though also containing elements of altruism and self-interest—relates to the institution of foster care. At present we know little about the attitudes and motivations of foster parents and about who gives and who receives in systems of child care outside the family. It would seem that foster care is in Britain an essentially working-class institution.[1] Why do not the middle classes participate to the same extent? Is this another area of unquantified redistribution because foster parents though receiving payment are not rewarded on market criteria? Or because—as Sir Denis Robertson once said—love is a 'scarce

[1] See Parker, R., *Decision in Child Care*, 1966, especially pp. 68–9, and Dinnage, R, and Kellmer Pringle, M. L., *Foster Home Care—Facts and Fallacies*, 1967.

resource'?[1] In the interests of society as a whole this resource is needed if the children concerned (as well as society) are not to suffer harm immediately and in the future. In this area also we might have raised questions about foster parents and the gift of foster care of a similar nature to the questions asked about the characteristics and motives of blood donors.

Or, to take one other example, we might have explored the gift transactions of Regional Eye Banks under the National Health Service in the prevention and reduction of blindness. At one such bank, the South Eastern Regional Eye Bank, 448 eyes were donated in 1965—a number that had been steadily rising.[2] Because the supply of donated eyes is much less in other countries without a National Health Service than it is in Britain, 73 of these 448 corneas were exported as free gifts to India, Jamaica, South Africa, Singapore, Turkey, Hong Kong and other countries.[3] Should human eyes, bequeathed by donors or given by relatives to unknown strangers, be treated as a consumption good and sold to the highest bidders? These are not just idle theoretical questions as experience in the United States and other countries has shown in recent years in the expanding area of organ transplantation.[4]

III

'Modern social welfare' wrote Wilensky and Lebeaux, 'has really to be thought of as help given to the stranger not to the person who by reason of personal bond commands it without asking. It assumes a degree of social distance between helped and helper'.[5] The degree will vary from the social distance separating the patient from medical students engaged in examining, feeling and questioning to that of blood donors who do not know and can never see the recipient of the gift.

The givers in these relationships—whether captive or altruistically

[1] Robertson, D., *Economic Commentaries*, 1956, p. 154.

[2] Personal communication, Sir Benjamin Rycroft and P. V. Rycroft, December 1966 and see also Wolstenholme, G. E. W., and O'Connor, M., *ibid.* pp. 43–50.

[3] New eye donors in Britain were being registered at a rate of about 1000 a month in 1965 (*Report of the Central Health Services Council for 1965*, H.M.S.O., 1966).

[4] For an informative discussion of the ethical and legal problems of organ transplantation see Wolstenholme, G. E. W., and O'Connor, M., *ibid.*

[5] Wilensky, H. L. and Lebeaux, C. N., *Industrial Society and Social Welfare*, Russell Sage, New York, 1958, p. 141.

voluntary—may themselves be harmed by the act of giving. Blood donors can be harmed—in rare cases mortally—by giving. Patients can be harmed, physically and psychologically, by giving themselves, willingly or unwillingly, knowingly or unknowingly, as teaching material. So can pupils, clients, foster parents and many other categories of people in a variety of 'giving' social policy situations. There are risks to the giver as well as to the receiver in these social gift transactions.

Welfare propositions in economic theory rest to a large extent on an often unexpressed ethical proposition—the 'Paretian optimum'. Any change is for the better as long as nobody is worse off and at least one person is better off, each in his own estimation. But in the whole area of social gift-relationships this proposition is inapplicable. Givers are in no position themselves to evaluate gains and losses to themselves or to others. Professional arbiters decide but they, in turn, can seldom estimate as individuals the gains and losses for either the givers or the recipients. Their interventions are transitory and episodic; they seldom know the ultimate outcome. Those economic theorists who in assuming God-like mantles apply the Paretian optimum to increasing areas of social transactions have been blinded by their own calculus. In their blinkered pursuit of economic arithmetic they and those who follow them endanger society's unmethodical knowledge of the living man.

While physicists have increasingly been yielding theoretical territory many economists have been claiming more. In a remarkable book *The World View of Physics*, first published in English in 1952 Von Weizsäcker had this to say: 'Yielding step by step to the pressure of new data, scientists have given up more and more completely the presupposition that classical mechanics or a theory modelled on it is valid for the whole of nature. Instead the attempt is made to develop an independent theory of the phenomena not apprehended by classical mechanics and, conversely, to understand classical mechanics as a "limiting case" of the new theory, i.e. as the result of its application to a definite, restricted field of inquiry'.[1]

Ethical considerations are, as we said earlier, also endangered when scientific, technological and economic considerations are uppermost. Concrete illustrations of this danger—particularly to captive donors—are increasingly being provided by those engaged

[1] Weizsäcker, C. F. von, *The World View of Physics*, Routledge & Kegan Paul, London, 1952, p. 69.

217

in the world of medical science.[1] One example was given in earlier chapters of the use of plasmapheresis techniques by the pharmaceutical industry in the United States. Many others could be drawn—if this were a full-length survey—from what the *British Medical Journal* described in 1963 as the 'alarming rate of increase in experiments on human beings'.[2] But two examples—relevant to this case study of human blood—must suffice.[3]

The first relates to a study of hepatitis infection undertaken at a University College of Physicians and Surgeons in the United States and reported in August 1969.[4] Earlier studies by other investigators had shown that a serum factor, hepatitis antigen, was specifically associated with viral hepatitis. The university investigators tested 2211 units of blood of which 16 were found to contain the antigen. These 16 units of blood were transfused into 16 different patients. A control group of patients received blood which did not contain the antigen. Of 12 surviving recipients of blood containing the antigen 9 (75 per cent) developed hepatitis. The incidence of hepatitis in recipients of antigen-negative blood was 5·8 per cent (4 of 69). 'Our observations', said the authors, 'indicate . . . an impressive correlation between the presence of hepatitis antigen in donor blood and the development of hepatitis following transfusion'. The question raised by this investigation is whether in the light of the findings of earlier studies blood containing the hepatitis antigen should have been transfused to patients. It is assumed that these patients and/or their relatives were informed of the possible risks involved.

[1] Western scientific medicine appears to be making increasing use of two 'captive volunteer' groups for research and experimental purposes (1) primitive peoples in Africa and South America (2) prisoners in the United States and South Africa. The main area of research interest in relation to the first group is coronary heart disease and its reported connection with diet (one of the major health preoccupations of Western man). Many studies involve the provision for a short period of comprehensive medical care. When the research facts have been collected medical care is withdrawn (see, for example, Shaper, A. G. and Jones, K. W., 'Serum-Cholestrol in Camel-Herding Nomads', *Lancet*, ii, 1305, 1962). As regards the use of prisoners, see references in this book to plasmapheresis; Davis, A. J., *Trans-Action*, December 1968 (describing extensive laboratory experiments in Philadelphia gaols) and Wolstenholme, G. E. W. and O'Connor, M., *Ethics in Medical Progress, op. cit.*

[2] *Brit. Med. J.*, editorial 'Ethics of Human Experimentation', July 6, 1963, p. 1.

[3] For more documentation and references to some 200 papers see Pappworth, M. H., *Human Guinea Pigs, op. cit.*, and letter to *Brit. Med. J.*, on the ethics of liver transplants, June 7, 1969, p. 631.

[4] Gocke, D. J., Greenberg, H. B. and Kavey, N. B., 'Hepatitis Antigen', *Lancet*, ii, 248, 1969.

The second example concerns an experimental study, reported in 1967, which took place at Willowbrook State School, Staten Island, New York, an over-crowded institution containing some 6000 mentally retarded patients predominantly children. Those in the experiment were children aged 3 to 10 years of age 'whose parents gave written consent after being informed of the details, potential risks, and potential benefits of the investigation'.[1] No information was published about the actual methods of the consent procedure and how it was carried out.

The purpose of the experiment was an attempt to elucidate the origins of serum hepatitis and to evaluate the possibility that there are several immunologically distinct types of the disease. The institution had a history of endemic infections. This in part was said to be a justification for the experiment. Groups of these children were in a series of trials exposed to hepatitis.

Scientific lessons were, of course, learnt for the benefit of society from these studies of mentally retarded children who participated as givers. As the *Journal of the American Medical Association* commented: 'these recent studies . . . represented an important contribution to our knowledge of hepatitis that would have been impossible without the judicious use of human beings in carefully controlled experimental studies'.[2]

Judicious means justify the ends; a plea made more urgent by the increasing commercialization of blood in the United States and the increasing use of 'derelict' and Skid-Row populations as a source of blood. It is doubtful whether this experiment would have taken place had social policy considerations dominated the supply and distribution of blood rather than the economics of the market.[3]

In these expanding fields of human experimentation—as with plasmapheresis programs—virtually all the strangers who give, by inducement, for money or in captive situations, are poor people; the indigent, the deprived, the educationally handicapped, the socially

[1] Krugman, S., Giles, G. P., and Hammond, J., 'Infectious Hepatitis', *J.A.M.A.*, Vol. 200, No. 5, May 1, 1967, p. 365.

[2] *J.A.M.A.*, Editorial, Vol. 200, No. 5, May 1, 1967, p. 407.

[3] 'In initial trials of any new agents, the investigator must be genuinely open-minded concerning the possibility that the drug is worth a trial and that it may be as good as, or perhaps better than, one or more of those already available. Strong convictions for or against its value in the treatment of a disease can render it unethical for him to use or withhold the agent under trial or to use a placebo; in this case he should not undertake the investigation' (*Principles for the Clinical Evaluation of Drugs, Report of a W.H.O. Scientific Study Group*, World Health Organization, Tech. Rep. Ser., 1968, No. 403, p. 6).

219

inadequate (in and out of prisons and other institutions), and all those described by an American sociologist as 'inept' in advancing a hypothesis that modern economic systems 'utilize the inept more efficiently'.[1]

How some of the 'inept' in captive prison situations have been utilized for the presumed benefit of society in clinical trials undertaken for profit by an American drug corporation was described in Chapter 8. Among those who were utilized, some died and some were disabled. These are the human cost facts that can be and were counted but what cannot be assessed are the moral effects on all those who were involved, in one form or another, in this and similar experiments which 'utilize' the poor and the inept; physicians, prison staff, prisoners, technicians, administrators and officials of the pharmaceutical companies involved, and many others. What effects do such experiences have on their values and on their attitudes and behaviour towards the 'inept' in society? The ethical consequences—or disvalues—of market experiments of this kind extend far beyond the biological damage actually done to those who are utilized.

What is also a fact that could be counted—if anyone thought of counting—is that in the United States and certain other Western societies poor people and those classed as 'indigents' are the providers of most of the teaching and research material needed to sustain the fabric of medical systems. Many American teaching hospitals are facing a crisis in the 1970s as the relative proportions of indigents in the locality decline. The rapid growth of profit-making hospitals (referred to in Chapter 8) is likely to accentuate the shortage of 'clinical material' for teaching and research—with consequential effects on the American output of doctors. The corporations who operate these hospitals have decided not to treat 'indigent' or 'charity' patients and not to provide emergency, obstetrics or paediatric departments 'which, traditionally, are money-losers in hospitals'.[2]

With rising standards of living the availability and number of poor charity patients would also have presented problems in Britain but the advent of the National Health Service saved the situation as it brought in after 1948 millions of Health Service potential 'teaching cases'. Even so, some element of discrimination is still practised in favour of some private patients. They are not required

[1] Goode, W. J., 'The Protection of the Inept', *Amer. Soc. Review*, Vol. 32, No. 1, February 1967, pp. 5–19.

[2] *Wall Street Journal*, October 13, 1969.

or expected to the same extent to make stranger gifts for the eventual benefit of society at large—just as the rich of New York and Chicago write cheques for blood bills without thought of tomorrow or the social direction of their society.

IV

We have continually in these discussions of gift relationships asked the question: who gives and why? In this chapter we have placed these same questions in a much broader social service context. An essential corollary is the further question: who in fact benefits from all these unpaid social transactions? Do the poor benefit proportionately as much or more in relation to their social and medical needs as the rich for the gifts they make in the interests of science, of medicine, of the medical and other professions and of society? What return gifts does society make?

In the preceding chapter we discussed certain social costs arising from the wastes, shortages, inefficiencies, unethical practices and hazards involved in the American commercial blood market. We concluded that despite the difficulties of measuring such costs in money terms a disproportionate part was borne by poor people, the sick and the handicapped.

In this chapter we have extended the discussion of costs and benefits to encompass a far wider area of social policy. An economic statistician, specializing in cost-benefit analysis, and looking at the scene with the aid of quantifying spectacles might see this whole area of social gift transactions as a great and growing redistributive process favouring—in some societies—the rich and the privileged; a process, moreover, stimulated by advances in science and technology, by the growth of professionalism and the personal service occupations, and by systems of buying and selling medical care and other social services through which gifts are received but are not returned in kind or money.[1]

Could our statistician then, pursuing further and on a comparative basis this statistical fantasy, bring together and merge, in an immense series of tables, all his social redistribution data with the conventional income and wealth data available for Britain, the United States and other countries? Is it not possible that the results would show for some economic and social systems large flows of total redistribution from the poor to the rich? In other words, would

[1] In Britain, private patients who find the National Health Service uncongenial are not charged for blood received from the National Health Service.

not the social gifts from the economically poor more than outweigh the combined effects of progressive taxation and the cash transfers of social welfare programs?

However many computers were provided for our statistician, and whatever advances were made on 'theories of public goods' developed by Samuelson[1] and others he would, in the end, have to confess to failure. The task would be beyond him because, in the first place, most of the hard facts about the beneficiaries of services in kind are missing. To take the case of blood transfusions again, no national data exist for any country in the world which show the distribution of blood recipients by sex, age, social class, income group and other characteristics. There are certain indications—particularly in the United States—of a positive relationship between the incidence of blood transfusions and the utilization by higher income groups of certain sectors of medical care services.[2] But none of the studies that have been made in the United States and Britain are comprehensive in scope and analysis.

The sample survey in 1967 of some 3800 blood donors, reported in Chapter 7, suggested that the families of higher income/social class groups received proportionately more blood than the families of lower income/social class groups. This survey was, however, from the viewpoint of estimating the beneficiaries and benefits of blood transfusions on a limited scale. We have to conclude, therefore, that even in this relatively small area of social policy our statistician would not be able to answer on a national basis the question: who receives blood?

Nor could he even begin to answer some of the more metaphysical and distributive questions that have recurred again and again in this book. He would not, for example, be able to identify and evaluate all the 'externalities' or 'disvalues' in the total redistributive process. What implied money values would he place on the human lives saved and lost, on sickness induced and prevented, even if he

[1] See, for example, Samuelson, P. A., 'The Pure Theory of Public Expenditure', *Review of Economics and Statistics*, XXXVI, 1954, 'Diagrammatic Exposition of Theory of Public Expenditure', *op. cit.*, XXXVII, 1955, and 'Aspects of Public Expenditure Theories', *op. cit.*, XL, 1958.

[2] Two of the main American sources of medical care utilization data are: (1) *Vital and Health Statistics Data from the National Health Survey*, National Center for Health Statistics, Public Health Service, U.S. Department of Health, Education and Welfare, 1960–9 and (2) Commission on Professional and Hospital Activities, *Medical Audit Program Reports*, Ann Arbor, Michigan, 1963–9. Sources of data for England and Wales are the *Report on Hospital In-patient Inquiry* for 1961 and 1966 and *Annual Report of the Ministry of Health*, Department of Health and Social Security and General Register Office. See also Morris, J. N., *Uses of Epidemiology* (2nd edn), Livingstone, 1964.

had all the demographic data? What prices would he expect medical students, doctors and many other professional aspirants and groups to pay for the right to treat people as teaching, learning, research and scientific experimental material? What allowances would he make for the external costs of malpractice and counter-malpractice claims as more areas of stranger-relationships became subject to the laws of the marketplace? What profitability value would he accord to a spirit of altruism in society today and in the future, its absence or its presence as an element of free choice for individuals? How would he cost the consequences to a society in which people, by simply writing cheques for blood, say 'I need no longer suffer from or experience a sense of duty, of obligation, of responsibility for strangers'? How then would he quantify the costs of violence?

All this is not pure speculation. There is growing disquiet in the United States, Japan and other countries with expanding commercial blood programs that such programs are driving out the voluntary system. Insurance companies are said to be stifling the spirit of giving and thereby harming society by selling policies which provide for cash reimbursement of the cost of blood transfused. The pharmaceutical industry, in developing commercial plasmapheresis programs, is similarly under criticism for encouraging among the public at large the notion that dollars can substitute for blood. Even the President of the American Medical Association was led to say in 1968 '. . . money payments for blood can destroy the motivation of the family and friends to replace the blood and could result in the creation of many "semi-professional" donors who would contribute too frequently, to the detriment of their own health. It also would increase premiums and rates for this portion of insurance plans; would tend to commercialize what have been community-spirited voluntary contributions; and could affect the amount of blood available in time of national catastrophe'.[1]

Such externalities cannot be measured in statistical or monetary terms. As Edgeworth once said in another context: 'We cannot *count* the golden sands of life; we cannot *number* the "innumerable smiles" of seas of love'.[2]

It is here that we can discern some of the fundamental distinguishing marks of social policy which differentiate it from economic policy. Because it has continually to ask the question 'who is my

[1] Rouse, M. O., 'Blood Banking and Blood Use', *Transfusion*, Vol. 8, No. 2, March–April 1968, p. 106.
[2] Edgeworth, F. Y. (original italics), *Mathematical Psychics*, Kegan Paul, London, 1881, p. 8.

stranger' it must inevitably be concerned with the unquantifiable and unmethodical aspects of man as well as with those aspects which can be identified and counted. Thus, in terms of policies, what unites it with ethical considerations is its focus on integrative systems: on processes, transactions and institutions which promote an individual's sense of identity, participation and community and allow him more freedom of choice for the expression of altruism and which, simultaneously, discourage a sense of individual alienation.

This book, centring on gift relationships, is an attempt at measurement in respect of one such institution. It has also advanced three inter-related theses. First, that gift-exchange of a non-quantifiable nature has more important functions in complex, large-scale societies than the writings of Lévi-Strauss and others would suggest. Second, the application of scientific and technological developments in such societies, in further accelerating the spread of complexity, has increased rather than diminished the scientific as well as the social need for gift relationships. Third, for these and many other reasons, modern societies now require more rather than less freedom of choice for the expression of altruism in the daily life of all social groups. While this requirement has been argued primarily on social, ethical and biological grounds it is also justified on scientific and economic criteria.

v

To end this chapter we move from abstract generalizations about gift relationships and unanswered questions about social redistribution to report concretely on some blood donor responses in England. We end, therefore, on an individual note by quoting what some donors had to say about their motives for giving when they took part in the questionnaire survey in 1967.

First, however, we have to repeat a few warnings scattered throughout this book and offer some general observations.

The assumption should not be drawn from the comparative material presented in this study that, in terms of moral values, there is anything particularly unique or meritorious about the British people in their commitment to and support of a voluntary blood donor program. In many other countries beside Britain and the United States there are countless numbers of voluntary community donors. If asked, there is no reason to doubt that many would respond by expressing similar sentiments of altruism and reciprocity. What we cannot write about (apart from a few countries) are their numbers, proportions, characteristics, representativeness, and so forth. But just because we have presented a mass of facts about voluntary donors in Britain and few facts about voluntary donors in many other countries there must not, we repeat, be thoughts about chosen people. In any event the blood donor, however he is classified by type (see Chapter 5), represents only a minority in a total eligible population.

Nor must it be concluded from what we have written that all is well with all British social institutions and distributive welfare systems; with, in short, the 'social condition of Britain'. As a corrective, perhaps for some who may err in interpretation, it needs to be said that the themes pursued in this book are linked to the issues of social justice raised in the author's *Commitment to Welfare* and *Income Distribution and Social Change*.

What is unique as an instrument of social policy among the countries we have surveyed is the National Health Service and the values that it embodies. Attitudes to and relationships with the National Blood Transfusion Service among the general public since 1948 can only be understood within the context of the Health Service. The most unsordid act of British social policy in the twentieth century has allowed and encouraged sentiments of altruism, reciprocity and social duty to express themselves; to be made explicit and identifiable in measurable patterns of behaviour by all social groups and classes. In part, this is attributable to the fact that, structurally and functionally, the Health Service is not socially divisive; its universal and free access basis has contributed much, we believe, to the social liberties of the subject in allowing people the choice to give or not to give blood for unseen strangers.

Of course, in probing the deeper human motives for giving and return-giving, for altruism and self-love, it would be facile to suggest that socialized medicine was wholly responsible. We have not said that at all. What we do suggest, however, is that the ways in which society organizes and structures its social institutions—and particularly its health and welfare systems—can encourage or discourage the altruistic in man; such systems can foster integration or alienation; they can allow the 'theme of the gift' (to recall Mauss's words)—of generosity towards strangers—to spread among and between social groups and generations. This, we further suggest, is an aspect of freedom in the twentieth century which, compared with the emphasis on consumer choice in material acquisitiveness, is insufficiently recognized. It is indeed little understood how modern society, technical, professional, large-scale organized society, allows

P

few opportunities for ordinary people to articulate giving in morally practical terms outside their own network of family and personal relationships.

We have from time to time in asking questions about gift relationships employed the words 'motives' and 'motivation'. Their use may have promised too much. We did, however, a long while ago—in Chapter 2—draw attention to the association of blood, its possession, inheritance, loss and transfusion, with religious beliefs, theories and concepts of race, kinship, ancestor-worship and so forth and its many symbolical properties. The very thought of blood touches the deepest feelings in man about life and death. Consequently, we said, any attempt to study individual motives for giving or not giving blood would face some extremely demanding conceptual and analytical problems. In any event, we concluded, these could not even be formulated until we had the basic facts about the social and demographic characteristics of a sample of blood donors.

In Chapter 7 and Appendix 4 we presented an analysis of the facts derived from the pilot study in certain areas of England for some 3800 donors. We shall not attempt to repeat the findings here. As regards that part of the questionnaire which asked about reasons for giving blood, we expressed our hesitations about the value of such questions and the difficulties of interpreting the responses. Hence, the analysis of the results in Appendix 6 was undertaken in a relatively straightforward manner; no attempt is made to speculate widely and deeply, and no statistical tests of significance adorn the tables. The analysis is chiefly confined to a classification of the answers to question 5 under fourteen main heads. The generally uncomplicated way in which this question was answered does not justify a complicated motivational analysis.

These fourteen heads are set out in Table 38 along with the proportions of donor replies judged to fall in one or other category. We now provide below some examples of individual replies to illustrate each category of answer to Question 5 ('Could you say why you *first* decided to become a blood donor?'). They were selected because they seemed to express more vividly different categories of replies than many stereotyped answers like 'Because I want to help to save lives in hospital'. A purely random selection would have been less interesting.

1. *Altruism (26·4 per cent of answers)*

The great majority of answers in this category expressed in general terms a desire to help:

'Knowing I mite be saving somebody life' (single woman, aged 40, power press operator, £10–15 a week, 10 donations).

'Anonymously, without financial reward to help others' (married man, aged 34, no children, insurance claims official, £20–30 a week, 23 donations).

'You cant get blood from supermarkets and chaine stores. People them selves must come forword, sick people cant get out of bed to ask you for a pint to save thier life so I came forword in hope to help somebody who needs blood' (married woman, aged 23, no children, machine operator, £15–20 a week [chief earner, electrician] 4 donations).

'No man is an island' (married man, aged 36, two children, foreman maintenance fitter, £30–50 a week, 21 donations).

'I thought it just a small way to help people—as a blind person other opportunities are limited' (married man, aged 49, no children, piano tuner, £15–20 a week, 26 donations).

'I felt it was a small contribution that I could make to the welfare of humanity' (married man, aged 45, four children, bank manager, £30–50 a week, 26 donations).

'A desire to help other people in need' (single man, aged 51, road labourer, £10–15 a week, 11 donations).

Some donors singled out for help the Health Service in its various manifestations:

'Just to help the Hospitals' (married woman, aged 61, two children, husband retired, £10–15 a week, 45 donations).

'At the age of 18 I decided that it was a good thing for anyone capable and healthy to donate blood for the good of other people and the advancement of medical science' (married woman, aged 28, three children, husband carriage serviceman [railways], £10–15 a week, 12 donations).

'I get my surgical shoes thro' the N.H.S. This is some slight return and I want to help people' (married man, aged 53, one child, insurance agent, £15–20 a week, 20 donations).

A small proportion of donors specified those who should be helped:

'To help babies that are borne with bad blood' (married man, aged 23, one child, skilled boot polish worker, £15–20 a week, 12 donations).

227

2. *Gratitude for good health (1·4 per cent of answers)*

'Because I am fortunate in having good health myself and like to think my blood can help some-one else back to health, and I felt this was a wonderful service I wanted to be part of' (widow, aged 63, four children, widows' pension, less than £10 a week, 25 donations).

'Briefly because I have enjoyed good health all my life and in a small way it is a way of saying "Thank you" and a small donation to the less fortunate' (married man, aged 53, two children, retired police officer now welfare officer, £20–30 a week, 11 donations).

'To me it is a form of thanking God for my own good health' (married woman, aged 64, two children, clerk, £20–30 a week [husband also a clerk], 47 donations).

3. *Reciprocity (9·8 per cent of answers)*

In Chapter 7 we showed the proportions of donors who had themselves received transfusions. Many of them gave this as the reason in filling in the questionnaire:

'After being told that my own life had been saved by transfusions—childbirth. Determined to repay' (married woman, aged 46, five children, husband toolmaker, £20–30 a week, 6 donations).

'To try and repay in some small way some unknown person whose blood helped me recover from two operations and enable me to be with my family, thats why I bring them along also as they become old enough' (married woman, aged 44, three children, farmer's wife, more than £50 a week, 8 donations).

Over 40 per cent of those whose answers were classified under 'reciprocity' referred to transfusions received by relatives or friends:

'Some unknown person gave blood to save my wifes life' (married man, aged 43, two children, self-employed window cleaner, £15–20 a week, 56 donations).

'A young niece died from Luekemia after having several transfusions which prolonged her life a little. After discussing this with a friend who was already a donor, I went along with her to the next session' (married woman, aged 59, one child, husband sheet metal worker, £20–30 a week, 12 donations).

'My husband aged 41, collapsed and died, without whom life is very lonely—so I thought my blood may help to save some-one the heart ache I've had' (transfusion received by husband before he died) (widow, aged 47, one child, school meals service cook, less than £10 a week, 16 donations).

Another substantial group of donors gave blood because they thought that in the future they or a member of their family might need it:

'Someone in my family may one day need blood. I would like to think that someone will be there then, so I give mine knowing that some unknown person will be eternally grateful' (married woman, aged 28, no children, industrial chemist [husband motor mechanic], £20–30 a week, 13 donations).

'I have a motor Bike and someday I may need blood to help me, so why shouldnt I give mine to help someone who may have had an accident' (married man, aged 50, two children, waterman textiles, £15–20 a week, 4 donations).

4. *Replacement (0·8 per cent of answers)*

These were donors who thought that someone in the family should give blood and who said that they were replacing a member who could not—or could no longer—donate:

'My mother was a donor for a number of years and when she died in 1958 I decided to carry on in her place' (married man, aged 49, five children, bricklayer, £20–30 a week, 16 donations).

'When my wife was refused as donor due to anaemia I stepped in' (married man, aged 63, one child, bus driver, £15–20 a week, 23 donations).

'My son was killed on the road, he was a Blood Donor and I knew they did their best to save him and because I know he would be pleased I am carrying on as long as I can to help someone I hope' (married woman, aged 63, four children, husband timber sawyer, £10–15 a week, 19 donations).

5. *Awareness of need for blood (6·4 per cent of answers)*

All donors in this category said that they gave blood because they had become aware of the need for it. The circumstances in which they recognized need varied considerably:

'Being in the construction side of building you see many people hurt and it makes you feel as though you have done a little bit to help' (married man, aged 25, no children, scaffolder, £30–50 a a week, 3 donations).

'Owing to the nature of my work I feel the need to give to the unfortunate people who require blood after an accident. Having seen so much lost in the course of my work I thought my health could stand helping others' (married man, aged 49, three children, ambulance driver, £20–30 a week, 23 donations).

'A sister had to receive five pints after an illness and I realized how much benefit could be had by receiving blood from a donor' (married woman, aged 62, three children, husband company director, £30–50 a week, 17 donations).

'After seeing a bad accedent I thought it was the best way I could help' (single woman, aged 22, upholstress, father rubber tyre beader £20–30 a week, 5 donations).

'In order to help maintain the supply of blood so urgently needed at all times' (married man, aged 59, three children, postman, £10–15 a week, 10 donations).

6. *Duty (3·5 per cent of answers)*

The distinction between 'Altruism' (Category 1) and 'Duty' was extremely difficult to draw. There were the donors who said quite simply that they *wanted* to help other people; there were donors who said or implied that as a matter of conscience, or duty or feelings of guilt they *ought* to help other people. The difference in these responses—if there really is or could be a difference—may well lie in the accidental choice of words by individual donors. But, as we said earlier, there is no justification for reading more into these responses about motives than appears on the surface of language. Hence, the classification into categories was undertaken on the basis of what people actually wrote on the questionnaire. Some examples of 'duty' answers are:

'Sense of duty to the community and nation as a whole' (married man, aged 31, three children, chargehand fitter, £15–20 a week, 7 donations).

'My conscience—having served 5 years on active service in the war (1939–45) helping to destroy life, and during this period my wife was receiving blood to save her life, it occurred to me, after demobilization, that I could at least ease my conscience' (married man, aged 52, 1 child, clerical officer civil service, £20–30 a week, 58 donations).

'Feeling of guilt at receiving so much in life and giving so little' (single woman, aged 60, school teacher, £20–30 a week, 20 donations).

'Primarily to "conform" with teenage contemporaries—desire "to be of service" to others was a secondary reason' (married man, aged 37, two children, contracts engineer, £20–30 a week, 26 donations).

'During the war I was afraid I would be considered too old to help my country. Giving blood, as I started to do then, was just a balm to my pride. I was called up late for service, which restored my pride. Afterwards I just carried on donating. With other voluntary jobs I have undertaken, I have just felt the job was there, and I was available. Other jobs were in trade unions or political parties. I have never thought "Why should I do it? I'll leave it to someone else". I have thought "Why should not I do this?" I am not a do-gooder, at least, I don't feel like one nor think like one' (married man, aged 62, three children, compositor, £15–20 a week, 28 donations).

'I am a father of two, and feel that if I, or any of mine ever need blood, they have a moral right to it. It is an obligation of a father' (married man, aged 55, two children, motor mechanic, £15–20 a week, 33 donations).

'I have been a mental patient (PSYCOPATH) and I have always tried to help people. Also I tried to commit suicide by stabbing myself and a transfusion saved me' (single man, aged 19, labourer, £10–15 a week, 2 donations).

7. *War effort (6·7 per cent of answers)*

In comparison with the preceding category, most of the answers classified here were fairly straightforward. Naturally, they all came from donors over the age of 40:

'During war service in the W.A.A.F. I was made aware of the need to give blood to help injured servicemen and civilians and afterwards I realized that it was also necessary in peace time' (single woman, aged 45, bank clerk, £20–30 a week, 40 donations).

'Came unscathed through 1939–45 war; felt "owed" something' (married man, aged 43, three children, chief establishment assistant local government, £30–50 a week, 30 donations).

'1941. War. Blood needed. I had some. Why not?' (married man, aged 47, three children, sales representative, £20–30 a week, 10 donations).

'I first gave blood during the last war to try and help save people from the results of war to which I am very strongly opposed— prefer to preserve life as against destroying it' (married woman,

231

aged 53, 1 child, part-time actress and housewife, £30–50 a week, [husband television producer], 20 donations).

8. The Defence Services since 1945 (5·0 per cent of answers)

This category, partly associated with the preceding one, comprises donors who said that they first gave blood as members of the Services. Some of the answers indicate that the respondents became donors at least partly because of certain benefits, e.g. 48-hour passes, being excused drill, etc. Other answers suggest that the act of donating was not entirely voluntary; that there were, as we discussed in our typology of donors, external pressures 'to volunteer'. However, the majority of donors placed in this category did not specify either benefits or pressures; the most usual wording employed took the form 'I answered an appeal for blood while in the Army.' Some illustrations of the responses of donors in this category who whatever the reasons given for the first donation had continued to donate are:

'Gave blood when in the services (seemed a good way to get out of an afternoons duties!). Later there was a general appeal for blood where I live' (married man, aged 37, two children, sales office manager, £30–50 a week, 9 donations).

'It was a good excuse for a good cup of tea and the afternoon off duty whilst serving in the Navy' (married man, aged 42, three children, maintenance engineer printing, £30–50 a week, 49 donations).

'Request for voluntary donors whilst serving in Forces' (married man, aged 41, no children, sales representative, £20–30 a week, 6 donations).

'Told to volunteer in R.A.F.! Subsequently as a civilian happened to pass a blood donor session (not well advertised) and called in on spur of moment' (married man, aged 41, two children, local government clerk, £30–50 a week, 36 donations).

9. Rare blood group (1·1 per cent of answers)

The general idea expressed in this type of answer was that the discovery that they were in a rare blood group was instrumental in the donor deciding to give blood. Such answers further imply that because one's blood is rare or unique there is a particular responsibility to make it available to others who may need it. To learn also that one has in one's make-up some element of 'uniqueness' may contribute to feelings of self-respect as well as to acts of giving.

'My blood is fairly rare—this I did not discover until I had had my twins (4th pregnancy). I now have six children which is most unusual because of my group. Maybe my blood may help some other mother. I give blood in gratitude for my good fortune' (married woman, aged 42, six children, school teacher [husband also school teacher, £30–50 a week], 20 donations).

'Curiosity first. Then continued when I discovered I had a rare blood group. I like to think that a life may be saved by my blood' (married man, aged 53, two children, engineering toolmaker, £15–20 a week, 25 donations).

'My mother is of a rare blood group and I thought perhaps I would be. I was not, but felt my blood would still be needed' (married woman, aged 23, no children, hairdresser [husband advertising art director £30–50 a week], 10 donations).

10. *To obtain some benefit (1·8 per cent of answers)*

These were fairly straightforward answers the great majority of which were concerned with benefits to the donor's physical health; nose bleeding, regular health checks, learning one's blood group, etc. A few donors, however, introduced more complex reasons:

'From being a boy I had suffered from constant nose bleeding and since I became a donor I have not had a single nose bleed' (married man, aged 43, two children, newsagent, £30–50 a week, 17 donations).

'I wanted to do something to convince myself I was 18 and I always wanted to be a blood donor—snob appeal' (married woman, aged 20, no children, donor attendant blood transfusion service [husband car fitter £15–20 a week] 6 donations).

11. *Personal appeal (13·2 per cent of answers)*

In this category were placed the answers of donors who said that they had been influenced to give blood by encouragement, requests and appeals on a personal basis:

'A workmate convinced me of the need for more donors' (married man, aged 35, one child, form grinder/miller [machine tools], £20–30 a week, 20 donations).

'A pretty young nurse walked round the factory I was working in' (married man, aged 41, three adopted children, development

233

engineer [pressure diecasting non-ferrous], £30–50 a week, 17 donations).

'Coerced by my husband as I was rather apprehensive' (married woman, aged 35, two adopted children, husband teacher technical education, £30–50 a week, 16 donations).

12. *General appeal (18·0 per cent of answers)*

These were mainly short answers by donors who said that they had been influenced by a general appeal:

'I heard the appeal on the B.B.C.' (married woman, aged 61, three children, husband old age pensioner, less than £10 a week, 16 donations).

'On seeing T.V. Advert I thought what great help to patients it could be, with so little effort by giving' (married man, aged 45, 1 child, builder's manager, £20–30 a week, 7 donations).

'I became a donor when the Unit came to the firm at which I worked, and ask for donors because of a shortage of blood' (married man, aged 42, six children, glass furnace operator, £15–20 a week, 19 donations).

'I read the notice the appeal for donors in the Putney Hospital waiting room' (widower, aged 56, five children, manager [cleaning], £20–30 a week, 7 donations).

13. *Miscellaneous (5 per cent of answers)*

All types of answers occurring less than twenty times in the whole of the sample were put in this category. They varied greatly, ranging from the obviously frivolous to serious essays of a personal nature:

'To get a good cup of tea' (married man, aged 24, one child, store-keeper [lock and door closers], £15–20 a week, 4 donations).

'I went along to hold my husbands hand' (married woman, aged 39, two children, husband shop manager [grocery], £15–20 a week, 32 donations).

'No money to spare. Plenty of blood to spare' (married man, aged 35, two children, painter and decorator, £15–20 a week, 19 donations).

'After seeing fellow hitch hikers in Greece selling their blood for a few pounds a pint to raise some money for food. It made me realize what a good system the voluntary system is' (single man, aged 23, industrial chemist [abrasive wheel industry], £15–20 a week, 2 donations).

14. *More than one type of answer (0·9 per cent of answers)*

Some donors gave answers which included more than one of the categories we have employed in the analysis in Appendix 6. Most of them seemed to recognize that the decision to give blood is often a complex process and that, consequently, they could not distinguish a single or predominant motive:

'I feel that with blood it would have to be used for the purposes it was given, no deductions for administrative purposes like so many Charity Organizations. Blood is something which could not come out of the rates. I have also now become a car driver and know that I use a dangerous weapon. And as a hypochondriac who has not visited a doctor for illness for some 7 years I felt that I would like to have some sort of blood test and felt sure, rightly or wrongly, that if I became a donor my blood would go through a test of some kind—at least I would know I had blood' (married man, aged 33, no children, company secretary, £30–50 a week, 2 donations).

'My group is rather rare. I drive everyday. I see blood on the road every week. One day it may be mine. With that cheerful thought one may regard donating as an investment' (single man, aged 25, advertising copywriter, £20–30 a week, 4 donations).

'It is in my estimation, a good way to keep a half yearly check on my own health. The thoughts of my own children at some time needing a donor's blood' (married man, aged 40, two children, foreman building maintenance, £20–30 a week, 4 donations).

This is what some of the donors had to say in their own words about their reasons for giving. The vividness, individuality and diversity of these responses add life and a sense of community to the statistical generalities in Appendix 6. To speculate further about the psychology of these relationships would require not only depth interviews and a larger sample but, maybe, the insights of a Freud, a Jung and a Lévi-Strauss.

All we can do is to call attention to the facts and the donors' own statements. Over two-fifths of all the answers in the whole sample fell into the categories 'Altruism', 'Reciprocity', 'Replacement' and 'Duty'. Nearly a third represented voluntary responses to personal and general appeals for blood. A further 6 per cent responded to an 'Awareness of Need.' These seven categories accounted for nearly 80 per cent of the answers suggesting a high sense of social responsibility towards the needs of other members of society. Perhaps this is one of the outstanding impressions which emerges from the survey.

Chapter 14
The Right to Give

I

We need not wait for the Moralist's verdict before calling one kind of action good and another bad.

LAN FREED

In this final chapter we make no attempt to summarize the many issues of social, economic, medical and political interest raised in this book ranging from the definition of 'the gift' in an Apartheid society to the redistributive role of the seller of blood in the United States, the Soviet Union and Japan. Much that we have written is fundamentally about a conflict of ideas; of different political concepts of society and the role of the private market in the area of social policy; of (in Isaiah Berlin's words) 'the central question of politics—the question of obedience and coercion. "Why should I (or anyone) obey anyone else?" "Why should I not live as I like?" '[1] Why should I not 'contract out' of 'giving relationships'? Such themes are clearly not amenable to condensation.

Instead, we aim to provide some interpretative comment on the responses of the voluntary donors recorded in the preceding chapter, and to relate certain issues of principle and practice raised in this study to the potential role that governmental social policies can play in preserving and extending the freedom of the individual.

II

Practically all the voluntary donors whose answers we set down in their own words employed a moral vocabulary to explain their reasons for giving blood. Their view of the external world and their conception of man's biological need for social relations could not be expressed in morally neutral terms. They acknowledged that they could not and should not live entirely as they may have liked if they

[1] Berlin, I., *Four Essays on Liberty*, 1969, p. 121.

237

had paid regard solely to their own immediate gratifications. To the philosopher's question 'what kind of actions ought we to perform?' they replied, in effect, 'those which will cause more good to exist in the universe than there would otherwise be if we did not so act'.

For most of them the universe was not limited and confined to the family, the kinship, or to a defined social, ethnic or occupational group or class; it was the universal stranger. Unlike some of the 'tied', 'credit' and 'deposit' systems depicted in earlier chapters there was no prescribed and specified discrimination in the destination of the gift. One of the principles of the National Blood Transfusion Service and the National Health Service is to provide services on the basis of common human needs; there must be no allocation of resources which could create a sense of separateness between people. It is the explicit or implicit institutionalization of separateness, whether categorized in terms of income, class, race, colour or religion, rather than the recognition of the similarities between people and their needs which causes much of the world's suffering. By not doing something—by not giving donors a 'right' to prescribe the group characteristics of recipients—the Service thus presumes an unspoken shared belief in the universality of need. This case study of blood donor systems demonstrates the extent to which the policy values of the Service are held in common by the individual voluntary donor in Britain.

It also shows that detailed, concrete programs of political change —undramatic and untheatrical as they may often appear to be— can facilitate the expression of man's moral sense. Thus, it serves as an illustration of how social policy, in one of its potential roles, can help to actualize the social and moral potentialities of all citizens.

None of the donors' answers was purely altruistic. They could not be for, as we concluded in Chapter 5, no donor type can be depicted in terms of complete, disinterested, spontaneous altruism. There must be some sense of obligation, approval and interest; some feeling of 'inclusion' in society; some awareness of need and the purposes of the gift. What was seen by these donors as a good for strangers in the here-and-now could be (they said or implied) a good for themselves—indeterminately one day. But it was not a good which they positively desired for themselves either immediately or ultimately.

In certain undesired circumstances in the future—situations in which death or disability might be postponable—then the performance by a stranger of a similar action would constitute for them or their families a desired good. But they had no assurance of such action nor any guarantee of the continued existence of the National Health Service. Unlike gift-exchange in traditional societies, there is in the free gift of blood to unnamed strangers no contract of custom, no legal bond, no functional determinism, no situations of discriminatory power, domination, constraint or compulsion, no sense of shame or guilt, no gratitude imperative and no need for the penitence of a Chrysostom.

In not asking for or expecting any payment of money these donors signified their belief in the willingness of other men to act altruistically in the future, and to combine together to make a gift freely available should they have a need for it. By expressing confidence in the behaviour of future unknown strangers they were thus denying the Hobbesian thesis that men are devoid of any distinctively moral sense.

As individuals they were, it may be said, taking part in the creation of a greater good transcending the good of self-love. To 'love' themselves they recognized the need to 'love' strangers. By contrast, one of the functions of atomistic private market systems is to 'free' men from any sense of obligation to or for other men regardless of the consequences to others who cannot reciprocate, and to release some men (who are eligible to give) from a sense of inclusion in society at the cost of excluding other men (who are not eligible to give).

These donors to the National Service we have described in much detail were free not to give. They could have behaved differently; that is to say, they need not have acted as they did. Their decisions were not determined by structure or by function or controlled by ineluctable historical forces. They were not compelled, coerced, bribed or paid to give. To coerce a man is to deprive him of freedom. Yet, as this study has shown comparatively, private market systems in the United States and other countries not only deprive men of their freedom to choose to give or not to give but by so doing escalate other coercive forces in the social system which lead to the denial of other freedoms (and maybe life itself) to other men who biologically are in no position to choose—the young and the old, the sick, the excluded and the inept as well as the sellers of blood.

Nor does the denial of freedom end there. As Chapter 9 has shown, clinical and professional freedoms are eroded among doctors and other health workers; the rights of patients are endangered by the associated growth of profit-maximizing hospitals and laboratories,

239

and the medical ignorance of patients is exploited by the development of legally defensive medical practice.[1]

III

As freedoms are lost in the blood marketplace truth is an accompanying victim. In studying different blood donation, clinical laboratory and medical care systems we were led to ask, in earlier chapters, what particular conditions and arrangements permit and encourage maximum truthfulness on the part of donors—the maximum now demanded by medical science? To what extent can honesty be maximized? Is a society's need for honesty in one critical area of life compatible with incentives towards dishonesty in others? We were led to these questions not simply because of a belief in the will to know what is true as a value in itself but because of its crucial role today in the application of scientific medicine.

The paid seller of blood is confronted and, moreover, usually knows that he is confronted with a personal conflict of interests. To tell the truth about himself, his way of life and his relationships may limit his freedom to sell his blood in the market. Because he desires money and is not seeking in this particular act to affirm a sense of belonging he thinks primarily of his own freedom; he separates his freedom from other people's freedoms. It may be of course that he will not be placed or may not fully realize that he has been placed (as we have suggested in Chapter 8) in such situations of conflicting interests. If so, it can only be because medicine in the person of the doctor has failed to fulfil its scientific basis; it is not seeking to know what is true. In this as in increasingly large areas of medical care today the rationality of applying scientific knowledge now imposes on medicine new obligations to make explicit (where they are concealed) and to eliminate situations of conflicting interests. These obligations are logical consequences of the transformation of folk medicine into scientific medicine. They raise in scientific forms the question of 'truth maximization'. The social costs of untruthfulness are now clear and, as we showed in Chapter 8, they fall randomly on rich and poor alike. The dishonesty of donors can result in the death of strangers.

The unethical consequences of not seeking to know what is true in one sector of medical care spreads corrosively into other sectors

---

[1] The loss of these freedoms is not recognized in Professor Milton Friedman's *Capitalism and Freedom*, University of Chicago Press, 1962.

and begins to envelop broader areas of social life and non-market institutions; some evidence of the growth of unethical practices affecting prisons, homes for retarded children, hospitals and clinical laboratories was provided in earlier chapters. It seems that more people have less protection against new forms of exploitation as market considerations and the conformities of market behaviour invade the territory of social policy.

In the nineteenth century the unethical consequences of the market in exploiting the poor and inept (as we may judge these consequences today) were often justified in the name of political science or the new economic science. Today, there is no scientific justification for the application of the values of the marketplace to the areas of social policy we have surveyed in this book. Science, in this context, is not the untested theoretical 'social science' of the nineteenth century, non-Marxist and Marxist. We speak here of a universal body of tested and repeatable biological truths.

The role of social policy (embracing, *inter alia*, medical care and associated welfare systems) has thus to be redefined in a broader perspective. In the past, in Britain and other large-scale industrial societies, social policy provisions were economically and politically justified (or so it was argued) as functional necessities. There was really little choice for society. The functional necessities of public health, factory and labour legislation, primary education and so forth made, in a sense, social policy virtually inevitable. According to this interpretation of history, such limited or residual interventions by the state were needed to prevent the collapse of a particular kind of society, and to operate as instruments of social control in relation to those elements in the population who threatened or were thought to threaten the established order.

This at any rate is one *post hoc* definition of the role of social policy. It has given rise to deterministic welfare theories and has contributed to the belief that moral problems of choice can be resolved or avoided by technological means and by 'social engineering' answers like negative income taxation. No better example of crude determinism could be found today than the pathetic belief, held in some quarters in the United States, that the computer in alliance with plasmapheresis technology will solve the moral dilemmas of the market in blood. The ancient faith, as Berlin has expressed it, in a 'final solution'[1] reappears, with affluence, dressed in technological garments.

It is because we reject both the notion of historical inevitability

[1] Berlin, I., *op. cit.*, p. 167.

in the making of social policy and the fetish of the final solution that we have ended this study with some discussion of the individual's right and freedom to give. We have tried to argue in relation to this particular area of human conduct that certain instruments and institutions of policy have a potential role to play in sustaining and extending personal freedoms. These have positive and negative aspects; both have to be exercised politically and have to be continually facilitated if they are to survive.

In a positive sense we believe that policy and processes should enable men to be free to choose to give to unnamed strangers. They should not be coerced or constrained by the market. In the interests of the freedom of all men they should not, however, be free to sell their blood or decide on the specific destination of the gift. The choice between these claims—between different kinds of freedom—has to be a social policy decision; in other words, it is a moral and political decision for society as a whole.

There are other aspects of freedom raised in this study which are or can be the concern of social policy. Viewed negatively or positively they relate to the freedom of men not to be exploited in situations of ignorance, uncertainty, unpredictability and captivity; not to be excluded by market forces from society and from giving relationships, and not to be forced in all circumstances—and particularly the circumstances described in this study—to choose always their own freedom at the expense of other people's freedom.

There is more than one answer and there should be more than one choice in responding to the cry 'Why should I not live as I like?' The private market in blood, in profit-making hospitals, operating theatres, laboratories and in other sectors of social life limits the answers and narrows the choices for all men—whatever freedoms it may bestow, for a time, on some men to live as they like. It is the responsibility of the state, acting sometimes through the processes we have called 'social policy', to reduce or eliminate or control the forces of market coercions which place men in situations in which they have less freedom or little freedom to make moral choices and to behave altruistically if they so will.

The notion of social rights—a product of the twentieth century—should thus embrace the 'Right to Give' in non-material as well as material ways. 'Gift relationships', as we have described them, have to be seen in their totality and not just as moral elements in blood distribution systems; in modern societies they signify the notion of 'fellowship' which Tawney, in much that he wrote, conceived of as a matter of right relationships which are institutionally based. Voluntary blood donor systems, analysed in this book, represent one practical and concrete demonstration of fellowship relationships institutionally based in Britain in the National Health Service and the National Blood Transfusion Service. It is one example of how such relationships between free and equal individuals may be facilitated and encouraged by certain instruments of social policy. If it is accepted that man has a social and a biological need to help then to deny him opportunities to express this need is to deny him the freedom to enter into gift relationships.

IV

These issues of freedom and the role of social policy instruments in extending and safeguarding freedoms, have been specifically addressed in this study to particular groups in the population: to those who may give or receive blood; to those who are eligible and not eligible to give; and to doctors, pathologists, administrators and many categories of workers in the health field concerned to serve patients and to remain true to their ethical standards. They are all involved in one way or another, as citizens, as health workers or patients, in these issues which today, as this study has shown, have international as well as national implications. Ultimately, it is they who have to decide in their different capacities whether their freedom and other men's freedom is to be curtailed by the forces of the market or safeguarded and extended by the intervention of the state acting through the instrument of non-discriminatory social institutions.

They should be clear about the nature of the choices that confront them and of the consequences for them and for society as a whole that may flow from the choices made. Part of the argument of this book is that the true nature of the choices in the social policy field— as demonstrated in this particular case study of blood donor systems —is not made apparent by those who advocate the extension of market behaviour to medical care, blood transfusion services, education and other instruments of the 'social'. Choice cannot be abstracted from its social context, its values and disvalues, and measured in 'value free' forms. Blood distribution systems cannot be treated as autonomous independent processes.

Theoretical welfare economics proceeds from a number of definite assumptions, factual and ethical, which as de Graaff has said, 'are seldom stated explicitly'.[1] 'The greatest contribution', he concluded

[1] Graaff, J. de V., *Theoretical Welfare Economics*, 1967, C.U.P., p. 1.

at the end of his analysis, that 'economics is likely to make to human welfare, broadly conceived, is through *positive* (original italics) studies—through contributing to our understanding of how the economic system actually works in practice—rather than through normative welfare theory itself.'[1]

In a small way this is what this book has attempted by studying blood donor systems over a large part of the real world and by analysing their effects in social, ethical and political terms as well as through the employment of economic criteria. What has emerged as a major consequence is the significance of the externalities (the values and disvalues external to but created by blood distribution systems treated as entities) and the multiplier effects of such externalities on what we can only call 'the quality of life'. At one end of the spectrum of externalities is the individual contaminated with hepatitis; at the other, the market behaviour of economically rich societies seeking to import blood from other societies who are thought to be too poor and economically decadent to pay their own blood donors.

'External effects' which result from the commercialization of medical care and blood donor systems in one country now have to be redefined and evaluated in international terms. They extend beyond the quantifiable and non-quantifiable consequences of importing blood and plasma; they include the immeasurable effects of exporting as models to economically poorer countries the values and methods of commercialized blood markets; the cumulative effects of maximizing profits in hospitals in one country on the international distribution of doctors and nurses (there are no short-term profits to be made on the training of medical manpower as American experience has shown); and the effects of extending on an international scale the operations of profit-making hospital corporations. In January 1970, American Medical Enterprises Corporation, through its subsidiary, American Medical International N.V., a Netherlands Antilles corporation, completed the sale of a large eurodollar bond issue (underwritten by a London merchant bank) and announced plans to develop profit-making hospitals and medical facilities in Britain and other countries.[2] Dollar millionaires have emerged 'almost overnight' from the growth of profit-making hospitals in the United States.[3]

The question of choice and the issues of freedom and the role

---

[1] Graaff, J. de V., *op. cit.*, p. 170.
[2] *Times Business Review* and *Guardian*, January 12, 1970.
[3] *Wall Street Journal*, October 13, 1969.

of social policy have thus to be seen in this wider context of externalities. It is not enough to present the case for 'consumer choice' simply in terms of the individual's 'sovereign right' to buy medical care or be paid for supplying blood. This is only the first stage in the processes of political choice. A later one in the escalation of externalities may be the creation of a blood proletariat servicing larger areas of the world and not just the American and Japanese peoples.

To what extent were the citizens of these and other countries made aware of the true nature and consequences of these choices? Who made these choices about harmfulness, beneficence, justice and freedom?

We cannot answer these questions. But we can now say at the end of this study that the rejection of altruism and the choice of the private market in blood donor systems had consequences which may be evaluated in non-ethical and ethical terms. The distinction between these two systems of evaluation, as developed by Loring[1] and others, has often been blurred in the case of this particular study. We make no attempt to disentangle them here. Generally, however, statements of a non-ethical value type make attributions of goodness and badness, beneficence and harmfulness, without implying to persons or things ethical values. Such attributions (to use Karl Popper's words) 'are based on a broad common fund of experience, and on universal assumptions about certain basic kinds of experiences which anyone wants to have or wants to avoid. Thus these attributions contain useful information; they are capable of being rationally discussed; and—in their appropriate contexts—they are up to a point empirically testable'.[2] Ethical evaluations, as applied to conduct, may be based on the idea of *duty*, in the Kantian sense, and on the closely associated ideas of absolute 'rightness' and 'wrongness' and the categorical 'ought'. Which system of evaluation is applicable—or should be applicable—to those who buy, sell and make a profit in human blood or are both applicable?

From our study of the private market in blood in the United States we have concluded that the commercialization of blood and donor relationships represses the expression of altruism, erodes the sense of community, lowers scientific standards, limits both personal and professional freedoms, sanctions the making of profits in hospitals and clinical laboratories, legalizes hostility between doctor and patient, subjects critical areas of medicine to the laws of the marketplace, places immense social costs on those least able to

[1] Loring, L. M., *Two Kinds of Value*, Routledge, 1966.
[2] Popper, K., Foreword to Loring, L. M., *op. cit.*, p. viii.

245

bear them—the poor, the sick and the inept—increases the danger of unethical behaviour in various sectors of medical science and practice, and results in situations in which proportionately more and more blood is supplied by the poor, the unskilled, the unemployed, Negroes and other low income groups and categories of exploited human populations of high blood yielders. Redistribution in terms of blood and blood products from the poor to the rich appears to be one of the dominant effects of the American blood banking systems.

Moreover, on four testable non-ethical criteria the commercialized blood market is bad. In terms of economic efficiency it is highly wasteful of blood; shortages, chronic and acute, characterize the demand and supply position and make illusory the concept of equilibrium. It is administratively inefficient and results in more bureaucratization and much greater administrative, accounting and computer overheads. In terms of price per unit of blood to the patient (or consumer) it is a system which is five to fifteen times more costly than the voluntary system in Britain. And, finally, in terms of quality, commercial markets are much more likely to distribute contaminated blood; the risks for the patient of disease and death are substantially greater. Freedom from disability is inseparable from altruism.

Appendix 1

Notes on Blood and Blood Transfusion Services in England and Wales[1]

THE COMPOSITION OF BLOOD

Blood is made up of minute elements or cells suspended in a pale yellow fluid, the plasma. The cells are so small that a drop of blood contains about 250,000,000 red corpuscles, 400,000 white corpuscles and 15,000,000 platelets.

Red corpuscles carry oxygen from the lungs to every part of the body so that the tissues may breathe. They are manufactured in red bone marrow.

White corpuscles form part of the body's defence system and will normally increase in number to attack and destroy any germs which invade the body.

Platelets take part in the clotting of blood and so help to stop bleeding when blood vessels are cut or damaged.

Plasma acts mainly as a carrier, transporting the corpuscles and platelets to all parts of the body, as well as foodstuffs and waste products. It is a valuable transfusion fluid and has the advantage that it can be stored without refrigeration for several months without deterioration. If suitably prepared, plasma can be given safely to patients of any of the four blood groups. It is the fluid portion of blood which has been rendered incoaguable and from which corpuscles have been removed.

Serum, the fluid separated from blood which has been allowed to clot, can be used in the same way as plasma. It is more easily filtered than plasma and has similar keeping properties.

Plasma and serum are usually dried and in this form they keep for very long periods of time. They are prepared for use by adding sterile distilled water or salt and glucose solution.

[1] Extracted and adapted from *Blood Transfusion and the National Blood Transfusion Service*, Department of Health and Social Security, H.M.S.O., 1968. For more information see *Notes on Transfusion*, H.M.S.O., 1963, and *The Practitioner*, Special Number on Blood Transfusion, Vol. 195, No. 1166, August 1965.

The ABO Blood Groups[1]

The four main blood groups became known as a result of Landsteiner's research in the early part of the twentieth century and can briefly be described as follows:

'Anyone belonging to blood group A has, on his red blood corpuscles, a chemical substance (or group-substance) called A; a group B person has the B substance: AB has both A and B substances; while group O has neither of them'.

These group-substances (A and B) can be identified by their reactions with the two antibodies (anti-A and anti-B) which exist in the liquid part (plasma) of the blood. The chief characteristic of these blood-group antibodies is that they will cause the red corpuscles containing the appropriate group-substance to come together in clumps and, if strong enough, may destroy the corpuscles completely. It thus follows that an individual's plasma cannot normally contain an antibody which reacts with his own red corpuscles. Thus the plasma of group AB blood contains neither anti-A nor anti-B, that of group A blood contains anti-B, but not anti-A, that of group B blood contains anti-A but not anti-B and that of group O blood contains both anti-A and anti-B.

When blood for transfusion is needed, it must therefore be of a type which will not be affected by any antibody in the patient's plasma. It is preferable for a patient to receive blood of his own group and most careful tests and cross checks have to be done to ensure this, although in an emergency group O blood may be given to patients of any ABO blood group.

In practice it is found that the antibody present in the donor's plasma is so diluted after transfusion that only exceptionally does it affect the recipient's red cells.

The Rhesus Factor and Ante-Natal Tests

One factor besides the ABO groups is of the utmost importance in transfusion work—the rhesus (Rh) factor. This factor or substance is carried, like the A and B substances, on the red cells of the blood. The Rh substance is so called because in certain respects it resembles a substance occurring in the red cells of the rhesus monkey.

Some 5 out of 6 people (or about 82–3 per cent) are Rh-positive,

[1] See also Mourant, A. E., *Blood Groups and the Study of Mankind*, a short and popular explanatory brochure for blood donors in Britain (Department of Health and Social Security, H.M.S.O., 1965). *Blood Groups in Man* by Race, R. R., and Sanger, R., is one of the standard textbooks (Blackwells, Oxford, 5th edn, 1968).

that is, they have the Rh factor in their blood. Those who have not are known as Rh-negative and comprise about 17–18 per cent of the population.

If a person who is Rh-negative is transfused with Rh-positive blood, his body may begin to make antibodies which attack and destroy the transfused blood. The process of making antibodies is known as sensitization and a very small transfusion of Rh-positive blood may be sufficient to start the process. While no immediate ill-effects are seen the first time an Rh-negative person receives Rh-positive blood, the sensitization that usually results may cause a serious reaction if a second such transfusion is given later.

Likewise the Rh-negative wife of an Rh-positive husband may bear an Rh-positive child. The mother may be sensitized by the Rh factor present in her unborn child; she may produce antibodies which pass into the child and, by destroying its red blood cells which contain the Rh factor, cause a serious form of anaemia, accompanied by jaundice (haemolytic disease of the newborn).

It should be emphasized that only a small proportion of the offspring of Rh-negative mothers and Rh-positive fathers suffer from this disease (about 1 in 250 births) and that the disease usually appears only after one or more healthy Rh-positive children have been born. It does not follow that, because the Rh groups of the mother and father differ in the way described, their children will be affected.

The discovery of the Rh factor has made transfusion safer and, by explaining the cause of this obscure form of anaemia in infants, has enabled appropriate treatment to be given. The Rh antibodies derived from the mother, which are present in the infant's circulation, lose their effect within a few weeks of birth, and transfusion of Rh-negative blood will usually save the lives of seriously affected infants by helping them over this critical period. Moreover, by ensuring that women, if they have to be transfused, are given blood of the right Rh group, it is possible to avoid many cases of sensitization to the Rh factor; should sensitization occur as a result of transfusion, however, it may cause anaemia and jaundice to appear in their earlier offspring, who would have been healthy had the mother not become sensitized.

Simple laboratory tests can determine which women are Rh-negative and whether these Rh-negative women are forming Rh antibodies during pregnancy, and it is possible to predict with some certainty during the ante-natal period whether haemolytic disease of the newborn is likely to occur. It is now known that sensitization of an Rh-negative mother to the Rh factor is brought about by leakage into her circulation of Rh-positive red blood cells from the infant at the time of delivery. Sensitization can be prevented by rapidly removing the child's cells from the circulation. A substance, extracted from the blood of individuals who have been sensitized to the Rh factor, will bring about the removal and so will prevent sensitization. The National Blood Transfusion Service has organized and encouraged the Rh testing of patients at ante-natal clinics since 1946. Preparations can thus be made for such women to have their babies in hospital without charge where the right blood will be freely available for any who are born suffering from haemolytic disease.

Rare Blood Groups

Apart from the main ABO groups and Rhesus blood groups, fourteen other blood group systems are now known.[1] Occasionally it is necessary to find a donor or donors whose blood is of a very rare group or combination of groups. Such donors may be needed in a special case where a patient who has received many transfusions has formed antibodies against a great many of the common groups, so that he can receive blood only if it is of the same rare group or combination of groups as his own. In such cases, because the type of blood required is very rare, only a few donors in Britain would be suitable and, without special measures, finding them would be difficult and would take much time. To facilitate the finding of the right donors quickly on such an occasion, about 2000 donors in Britain had volunteered by 1968 to have their blood very fully tested, and to give donations at very short notice if required. Their names and full groupings have been compiled into a special national register maintained by the Blood Group Reference Laboratory, a copy of which is kept in each Regional Transfusion Centre. This makes it possible to select and trace the appropriate donors in the same or other regions without delay and to make special arrangements for them to give blood and for the blood to be rushed, if necessary, from a donor living, say, in Newcastle to a patient in the south-west of England.

The Laboratory also acts as the World Health Organization International Blood Group Reference Laboratory.

---

[1] And over 100 identified blood factors (see Wiener, A. S., 'Blood Groups in Man and Lower Primates: A Review', *Transfusion*, Vol. 3, No. 3, May–June 1963, p. 173).

Blood Products

A number of special products are prepared from blood; some of the more important ones are briefly described below. In Britain, the preparation of these products is the responsibility of the Blood Products Laboratory of the National Blood Transfusion Service.

Fibrin Foam is a dry artificial sponge of human fibrin. It is made by clotting with thrombin a foam of a solution of fibrinogen. It can be used in conjunction with thrombin to control bleeding in operations where the tying of blood vessels is not advisable or possible. It is also of great value in brain and spinal surgery where nerve cells, which might be destroyed by other methods of stopping bleeding, would not grow again.

Thrombin is the enzyme which converts fibrinogen into fibrin. It is prepared from prothrombin which is extracted from blood plasma, and is a valuable agent for clotting blood and can be used either alone or in conjunction with fibrin foam or fibrinogen.

Fibrinogen is a protein, extracted from plasma, which clots when mixed with thrombin. In this form it is used as an adhesive to keep skin grafts in position. Solutions of fibrinogen are used as a transfusion fluid for the treatment of certain conditions in which the fibrinogen usually present in the plasma has disappeared or fallen to a low level.

Immunoglobulin, another part of plasma, carries the various antibodies present in normal adults. Immunoglobulin has proved of value in the prevention and attenuation of measles, in the prevention of rubella, of poliomyelitis in certain defined circumstances, and possibly of infectious hepatitis. It is also used for treating individuals who have very little or no immunoglobulin in their blood; this condition may be congenital, and therefore becomes apparent early in life, or may be acquired later in life. A specific immunoglobulin, anti-D immunoglobulin, is separated from plasma collected from individuals sensitized to the Rh factor. It is used for the prevention of haemolytic disease of the newborn.[1]

Anti-haemophilic Factor, the substance missing from the blood of persons with haemophilia, can be prepared from the plasma of healthy individuals and will control bleeding in haemophiliacs. It is an unstable substance and its separation and concentration is not yet carried out on a large scale. Anti-haemophilic factor can be separated in a less refined form by freezing and thawing plasma. The anti-haemophilic factor is contained in a cold insoluble precipi-

---

[1] See also references in Chapters 2 and 3.

tate—or cryoprecipitate. Anti-haemophilic factor is prepared in this way in Regional Transfusion Centres in Britain.[1]

Plasma Substitutes

There is no substitute for whole blood but certain solutions have been made which have some of the properties of plasma and can be used as temporary blood-volume expanders to make good loss of blood. Gum saline solution, little used now, was introduced in the First World War. Since the last war, solutions of dextran (a sugar derivative), polyvinylpyrrolidone (a plastic), and gelatin (derived from animal hides and bones) have been tested. All of them have the ability to replace temporarily plasma which has been lost from the circulation. Plasma substitutes are useful supplements to supplies of blood and plasma for the treatment of certain conditions; particularly is this so in countries where there are no plants for the preparation of dried plasma and where transfusion services are not highly developed or cannot be organized. But, as the National Blood Transfusion Service has emphasized, 'the development of plasma substitutes in no way reduces the need for blood donors in this country, where the use of whole blood and its derivatives continues to demand an ever-increasing number of human volunteers'.[2]

THE NATIONAL BLOOD TRANSFUSION SERVICE: MEDICAL EXAMINATION AND CARE OF DONORS[3]

Medical History

The decision whether a person is fit to act as a blood donor rests solely with the doctor who is to collect the blood.

The examination to which a donor is subjected must determine whether the donor is in normal health. Of this the donor is the best judge, and if he will truthfully answer simple questions concerning his medical history and general health, the main part of the examination has been done. The donor should thus be subjected to a short series of questions about his present health and medical history.

(a) *Each time* a donor presents himself he should be questioned to satisfy the doctor:

[1] See Chapter 12 for some discussion of the problems of haemophiliacs.
[2] *Blood Transfusion and the National Blood Transfusion Service, op. cit.*, p. 11.
[3] Extracts from N.B.T.S. Memorandum on the Selection, Medical Examination and Care of Blood Donors (unpublished), December 1963.

(i)   that he is in normal health

(ii)   that he is not suffering and has not recently suffered from,

      (*a*) any serious illness

      (*b*) intercurrent infection (e.g. tonsillitis, laryngitis, boils), and

      (*c*) an infectious disease in the past 2 years nor, as far as he knows, been in contact with any case of infectious disease during the past 6 months.

Note: An individual who has had *undulant fever* or *glandular fever* within the past 2 years, or *leptospirosis* within the past year, should not be accepted as a donor.

(iii) that he has not received transfusions of blood or plasma within the past 6 months.

(iv) that he has not received smallpox vaccine or yellow fever vaccine within the past 3 weeks or poliomyelitis vaccine within the past 2 weeks.

(b) *At enrolment* all donors should be specifically questioned about the following conditions:

*Allergy (hay fever, food sensitivity, hives, asthma, etc.)	Heart disease
Anaemia	*Hypertension
Cancer	*Jaundice or hepatitis
Diabetes	Kidney disease
Epilepsy	Stroke
Goitre	Tuberculosis
	*Tropical diseases

Existence of any of these conditions usually disqualifies but persons with a history or evidence of them may be accepted, deferred or rejected after consideration (see NOTE A on conditions marked*).

Records: A written record is desirable of the answers given at the time of enrolment regarding these diseases. It should be initialled or signed by the donor, or by the clinic clerk taking the medical history if the donor's signature is not for some reason obtained. In practice, a simple method of recording the answers has been found to be the completion of the 'medical history box' on the donor registration card (N.B.T.S. 101) at the time of enrolment of the donor, or when he presents himself to give blood for the first time, the entry in the 'box' being initialled by the donor (or clerk).

On subsequent occasions, the donor should be shown a list of the above conditions, e.g. N.B.T.S. 110, and asked to sign either this form, which is attached to the donor session work sheets, or the N.B.T.S. 101, to show that he has read the list.

(c) *Venereal diseases:* It is not customary to question donors about venereal disease. Information may, however, be volunteered. A person who is known to have, or to have had, syphilis is unacceptable as a donor.[1]

An accepted syphilis test shall be performed each time a donor is bled; donors whose blood reacts positively shall be excluded permanently from the donor panel.

(d) *Toxoplasmosis:* It is not practicable to test for the presence of toxoplasma as a routine and it is not known whether the blood of persons recently ill from toxoplasmosis is infective. It would seem wise not to accept blood from volunteers with a known history of toxoplasmosis until a year has elapsed from the complement fixation test becoming negative.

(e) *Oral contraceptives:* Volunteers who are taking oral contraceptives are not debarred from giving blood. The progestogens are short-lived so that any amount that might be contained in blood from such donors could not have an effect lasting for more than a few hours at the most in the recipient.

(f) *Pregnancy:* Mothers should not act as donors during pregnancy or until a period of one year has elapsed since the last confinement. In certain circumstances, e.g. to collect serum containing antibodies, mothers may be bled before the lapse of this time, if shown by medical examination to be fit to give blood.

Examination of Donor

(a) The medical history should be coupled with a careful assessment of the donor's appearance. The experienced doctor can detect at a glance the potentially unsuitable donor. Those of poor physique, the debilitated, the undernourished, the mentally unstable, and those bearing the obvious stigmata of disease should not be bled.

(b) The superficial medical examination (auscultation and percussion of the chest, pulse, and blood pressure) is, in general, so incomplete and unrevealing that it is in most cases not of great value.

In some cases, particularly in middle-aged and older donors, examination of the pulse may reveal unsuspected defects of the cardiovascular system, which may be confirmed by measurement of the blood pressure. While it is usually sufficient to rely on a normal

[1] See Therapeutic Substances Regulations, 1963, Statutory Instrument, No. 1456, Pt II, para. 4, and British Pharmacopoeia, 1963.

medical history, general appearance, and haemoglobin level, it is advisable to examine the pulse and, if considered necessary, the blood pressure in these older donors.

(c) *Haemoglobin:* The haemoglobin should be determined each time the donor presents himself. Female donors with less than 12·5 g haemoglobin per 100 ml (85 per cent Haldane) or male donors with less than 13·3 g haemoglobin per 100 ml (90 per cent Haldane) should not be bled. The type of test is left to the discretion of the Regional Transfusion Directors, but the Phillips–Van-Slyke copper sulphate method[1] using a sample of blood obtained from the finger, is recommended for use as a screen test.

Donors whose haemoglobin is below the appropriate level should be informed that they are not fit to be bled at present. In these cases, it may be advisable and helpful, if a screen test has been used to take a sample of blood (and preferably also at the same time a blood film) for an exact determination of the haemoglobin level and, if possible, a red blood cell count, etc., the result of which may, at the Regional Transfusion Director's discretion, be communicated to the donor, with the advice that he should consult his own doctor.

These procedures should be carried out meticulously. They are the most wearing parts of the routine collection of blood, but, if skilfully used, will lead to the rejection or deferment of donors unfit to be bled. When in doubt, it is better to reject or defer. The medical officer should see that an appropriate entry is made upon the donor's record card.

In general, only persons in normal health with a good medical history should be accepted as donors.

Medical Care of Donors

Apart from courteous and considerate treatment by all members of the blood-collecting team, the donor's medical well-being should be assiduously watched by the medical officer and the members of the team while he is at a blood donor session. The donor's medical well-being depends upon:

1. The use of carefully prepared sterile apparatus.

2. An immaculate technique of venepuncture. Sterilization of the skin should be carried out by a well-tried method, such as that described in Medical Research Council Memorandum No. 34 (1957, H.M.S.O.).

3. Skilfully performed venepuncture preceded by injection of a

[1] *J. Biol. Chem.* (1950), **183**, 305.

local anaesthetic. Normally, not more than 420–440 c.cm of blood should be withdrawn. No matter how skilled the doctor he will occasionally 'miss' a vein. Further attempts should not be made without the donor's permission. It is usually not advisable to use the other arm, unless there is some special reason for making another attempt. In factories, it is good policy never to use the other arm.

4. The enforcement of a definite routine upon the donor during the resting period after withdrawal of blood. The resting period is of special significance in regard to the prevention of the 'delayed faint' (see (5) below).

(a) A donor attendant should assist the donor to the rest room, where he should lie recumbent for at least 15 minutes by the clock, after which he should sit up for at least 5 minutes.

(b) During the resting period of 20 minutes, the donor should consume at least one cup of fluid and a few biscuits.

(c) Before the donor leaves, the site of venepuncture should be inspected, preferably by the doctor, who will on occasion be able to forestall complaints from a donor by warning him that his arm will become bruised from a haematoma, etc. A form of dressing should be placed over the venepuncture. The donor may be given tabs. ferrous sulphate gr iii, sufficient for 7 days, if the medical officer considers this desirable. It is not intended that the practice of issuing iron tablets to all donors, which is customary in some regions, should cease.

(d) Small cards giving advice to donors should be displayed in the rest room.

5. The immediate and considerate treatment of those who faint. A proportion of donors, variously estimated at 2–5 per cent faint. This is usually only a transient matter, quickly recovered from, but in a few instances prolonged and troublesome. The 'delayed faint' is the potentially dangerous type, since the donor may be in the street or at work. Fainting is probably psychological in origin and cannot be forecast by the most elaborate medical examination.

The importance of these measures and the reasons for them must be carefully impressed upon the lay members of the bleeding team. The reputation of the National Blood Transfusion Service and the readiness with which donors will volunteer depends largely upon the standard of medical care given to the donor.

Donors: Complaints and Accidents

The need for sympathetic, prompt and thorough investigation of all complaints made by the donors, no matter how trivial, is obvious.

Complaints of a medical nature should invariably be investigated by a doctor. The following routine, which has proved of value in practice, is recommended:

1. Minor accidents and any untoward incidents occuring during a blood collecting session, e.g., haematoma, fainting, damage to, or loss of, a donor's property, should be noted at the time upon the donor's record card or donor session work sheet. The recording of apparently trivial incidents has, in practice, proved of value as long as two years later.

2. Serious incidents or accidents occurring during blood collecting sessions, or complaints made direct to the regional transfusion centre, should be fully recorded in a book kept for the purpose, together with full notes of the investigation made.

An analysis of complaints and accidents thus recorded should be made annually, using the following headings: haematoma, cellulitis, thrombosis, accidents due to fainting, dermatitis, unclassified, total; ratio to total number of donors bled; number of accidents serious enough to merit financial compensation, together with, if available, the amount of compensation paid.

NOTE A ON CERTAIN CONDITIONS
CAUSING REJECTION OR DEFERMENT

1. *Allergy.* Persons who give a history of frequent severe allergic manifestations should not be accepted as donors. Otherwise donors need only be rejected if they are suffering from an allergic attack when they present themselves.

2. *Hypertension.* The hypertensive should be treated on his merits. In general, the practice of accepting hypertensives as donors is not recommended, because of the possible complications which may follow a sudden lowering of arterial tension caused by the withdrawal of blood. Such persons should not be bled without their own doctor's recommendation in writing, and then only if the medical officer concerned is himself satisfied that they are fit to be bled. It is felt that if hypertensives are to be bled for the relief of symptoms, they should be bled by the family doctor, or in a hospital, where complications, should they occur, can be dealt with more satisfactorily than at a donor session.

3. *Jaundice or hepatitis.* A person, giving a history of jaundice or hepatitis (other than a history of neonatal jaundice or an incontro-

R

vertible history of obstructive jaundice in which the occurrence of viral hepatitis can be excluded) or who has been in contact with a case of hepatitis in the past 6 months, should not be accepted as a donor.

4. *Tropical diseases.* Donors should be asked if they have visited places abroad (other than in Europe or North America) or recently lived in such places. The most important disease to bear in mind when considering the fitness of such donors is malaria because of its world-wide incidence, but certain other tropical diseases must also be considered before accepting, deferring or rejecting such donors (see NOTE B).

NOTE B ON TROPICAL DISEASES

The following notes give general guidance regarding the fitness of persons as donors who have had certain tropical diseases, or who have returned to the U.K. from certain tropical countries:

1. *Malaria.* (a) The blood of those who have had malaria or who are natives of or who have lived until recently in endemic malarious areas may be used only for preparing plasma. (b) The blood of U.K. residents, born in U.K. and normally resident there, who have visited or passed through endemic malarious areas may be used as whole blood providing they have been back in the U.K. for at least 8 weeks, have had no feverish illness since returning, and have taken anti-malarial drugs for one month after return. If there is any doubt, blood from such donors should be used only for preparing plasma.

2. *Amoebic dysentery.* Does not debar.

3. *Schistosomiasis.* Does not debar.

4. *Filariasis.* Does not debar.

5. *Kala-azar.* Persons giving a history of kala-azar should not be enrolled as donors.

6. *Relapsing fever.* Persons may be accepted as donors 2 years after recovery from the disease.

7. *Trypanosomiasis.* The blood of persons who have resided in endemic areas should be used only for preparing plasma.

8. *Yaws.* As for syphilis.

9. *Yellow fever.* The virus is said to be present in the blood stream only during the disease. A history of yellow fever therefore does not debar.

258

10. *Dengue fever*
    Rift Valley fever
    Sandfly fever } A history of any of these diseases
    West Nile virus fever } does not debar.
    Arthropod-borne
      encephalitides

11. *General.* Persons returned from Africa should not be used as donors until 8 clear weeks after arriving in the U.K. The diseases in (10) above, for example, may take the form of a short-lived viraemia, without specific clinical symptoms. Persons harbouring any of these viruses will automatically be excluded during the potentially dangerous period by adopting this 8-week period of 'quarantine'.

Appendix 2

Notes on the Use of Blood in the United States and England and Wales in 1956

In an attempt to account for the discrepancies between whole blood collected and transfused in the U.S. in 1956 the Joint Blood Council made an analysis of units collected and units transfused by regional breakdowns and per 1000 population. The Report came to the conclusion that, in total, of the 4,470,000 whole blood units collected 2,517,000 (or 56 per cent) were used for purposes of transfusion (p. 17).[1] This left 44 per cent of whole blood to be accounted for. Of this proportion, less than 1 per cent of fresh blood was converted into plasma (p. 30).

The balance of 43 per cent could be accounted for in the following ways:

(i) Outdated blood converted into plasma
(ii) Blood used for research and testing control purposes
(iii) Blood wasted for:
    (a) technical reasons (contaminated, haemolysed, 'short' bottles)
    (b) administrative reasons (see Chapter 4).
(iv) Errors in response for collections and use.

The Report made estimates under (i) and arrived at the following proportions (p. 34): American Red Cross 8·2 per cent; Community Blood Banks 4·4 per cent; short-term hospitals 3·6 per cent; long-term hospitals 3·0 per cent. The total of units of outdated blood converted into plasma was 264,000 or 5·9 per cent.

No precise estimates were made for (ii) and (iii).

To compare these proportions and to obtain estimates for (ii) and (iii) a statistical study was made of the 1956 monthly regional reports for the National Blood Transfusion Service in England and Wales. The region selected for study was the largest, the Sutton (the South-East and South-West region). To summarize the results:

[1] These figures relate to the total of collections and transfusions actually reported in the survey. They were grossed up by a combination of guesses and estimates to 5,100,000 units collected and 4,500,000 units transfused.

A. Units (bottles) of whole blood collected
   and issued to hospitals for transfusion
   less bottles returned to the regional
   centre   123,610
B. Bottles returned   6,969   5·6%
C. Converted into plasma   13,418   10·8%
D. Research and testing control purposes   2,836   2·3%
E. Wasted blood (technical and
   administrative)   1,116   ·9%

As a check on the plasma figure, it should be noted that, for England and Wales as a whole, the ratio in 1956 of blood issued to dried plasma issued was 18·8:1. Allowing for the fact that each plasma bottle contained the plasma from slightly more than two bottles of whole blood the proportion works out at 9·4 per cent— about 1 per cent lower than the proportion for the Sutton Regional Centre.

For purposes of illustration we may now apply these proportions to the 1956 J.B.C. survey results:

	U.S. estimates		E/W proportions applied to U.S. estimates	
Units of whole blood collected	4,470,000		4,470,000	
Units of whole blood transfused	2,517,000	56%	2,517,000	56%
	1,953,000		1,953,000	
Units of fresh blood converted to plasma	19,500	1%	483,000	10·8%
	1,933,500			
Outdated blood converted to plasma	264,000	5·9%		
	1,669,500		1,470,000	
Research and testing control purposes (say)	103,000		103,000	2·3%
	1,566,500		1,367,000	

261

Wasted blood (technical
and administrative)   ?   40,000   0·9%

               1,327,000

It seems unlikely from what is known about the use of dried plasma in the United States in the middle 1950s that a substantially smaller proportion of whole blood was used as dried plasma than in England and Wales at the same time. To allow for discrepancies in reporting it thus seems reasonable to apply the proportion of 10·8. Nor is it reasonable to allow for a smaller proportion to be devoted to research and for testing purposes.

If we then assume the same proportion of wasted blood we are left with 1,327,000 units unaccounted for—or 30 per cent of the total number of units collected. Some proportion of these units must be attributed to 'administrative waste'; some part to errors and non-reporting in the J.B.C. Survey.

As a footnote to this appendix, we give below the results of a similar analysis of the 1961 statistics for the Sutton Regional Centre:

A	147,817	
B	5,333	3·6%
C	15,025	10·2%
D	2,828	1·9%
E	3,302	2·2%

For England and Wales as a whole in 1965 the proportion of dried plasma issued (calculated on the same basis as for 1956) was 8·3 per cent, in 1966 12·4 per cent and in 1967 12·4 per cent.

Appendix 3
Regional Statistics for England and Wales, 1951–65

In Chapter 4, national statistics were provided showing the number of blood donors, donations and issues of blood for the years 1946–68. In this appendix we give more detailed information derived from a special regional analysis of the monthly returns reported by each Regional Transfusion Centre to the headquarters of the National Blood Transfusion Service at the Department of Health and Social Security. The returns were kindly provided for analysis by the Department.

The areas served by these Centres correspond to the areas of the Regional Hospital Boards except for the fact that two Centres serve the four Metropolitan Board areas and, since April 1, 1959, the area of the Wessex Hospital Board formerly included in the area of the S.W. Metropolitan Board.[1] The Centres, controlled by Medical Directors, are administered on behalf of the Department by the Regional Hospital Boards. The Medical Research Council

[1] *Regional Transfusion Centre*

		Regional Hospital Board
Newcastle	(1)	Newcastle
Leeds	(2)	Leeds
Sheffield	(3)	Sheffield
Cambridge	(4)	East Anglia
North London (Edgware)[a]	(5)	N.E. Metropolitan
	(6)	N.W. Metropolitan
South London (Sutton)[b]	(7)	S.E. Metropolitan
	(8)	S.W. Metropolitan
Oxford	(9)	Oxford
Bristol	(10)	South West
Cardiff	(11)	Welsh
Birmingham	(12)	Birmingham
Manchester	(13)	Manchester
Liverpool	(14)	Liverpool

[a] In 1955 a new Regional Centre was opened at Brentwood, Essex, to serve the N.E. Metropolitan area but administration continued for the whole of North London at Edgware. In 1958 Brentwood became an independent Centre.

[b] From April 1, 1959, the South London Centre served the Wessex Board area.

Blood Group Reference Laboratory and Blood Products Laboratory are administered for the Department by the Medical Research Council, and in the case of the latter administration is delegated by the Medical Research Council to the Lister Institute of Preventive Medicine. The function of the first is the holding of stocks of rare sera, the examination of blood samples sent from regional laboratories for the identification of irregular agglutinens and agglutinogens, the distribution to regional centres of grouping sera and the maintenance of a panel of special donors of very rare blood groups. The second is responsible for the preparation of blood products (such as fibrin foam, thrombin, fibrinogen, immunoglobulin and the anti-haemophilic factor), for research into the production and uses of plasma fractions and plasma substitutes and for the operation of the plasma-drying plant.

The Department of Health and Social Security co-ordinates the activities of these Centres and Laboratories and, with the help of two advisory committees, formulates the general policy of the Service. One advisory committee is composed of the medical directors of the fifteen units and the other of the regional donor organizers. Their functions are to help formulate professional, technical and publicity policy, to obtain over-all uniformity of procedures, methods and equipment and to establish minimum standards: e.g. for the medical examination of blood donors and certain serological procedures.

The total number of paid staff employed in the 15 units in 1967 was 2313 (counting two part-time members as equivalent to one whole-time member), of whom 70 were doctors. Substantial numbers of voluntary workers (many aged over 65 and ex-donors) also undertook various tasks at the blood collection sessions with the mobile teams.

Each Centre is responsible for meeting the transfusion needs of its region and certain national commitments. This responsibility entails the following activities.

(a) *The recruitment and organization of panels of voluntary donors.* Each Centre works closely with voluntary organizations, the management of firms and the trades unions and many other organizations. These functions are the responsibility of Regional Donor Organizers[1] whose task is to ensure that sufficient blood is

[1] For more information about donor organization, see James, J. D., 'Donors and the Collection of Blood', *The Practitioner*, No. 1166, Vol. 195, August 1965, pp. 152–8, and James, J. D., *Practical Blood Transfusion*, Blackwell, Oxford, 1958.

collected to meet the needs of all the hospitals in the region and certain quotas of blood required by the two Central Laboratories. All the usual methods of publicity are used.[1] Men and women between the ages of 18 and 65 are accepted as donors.

(b) *The collection and distribution of blood.* The majority of donations are collected by self-contained mobile teams, which carry the equipment necessary to convert, for example, a village or church hall into a temporary blood-collecting centre. The fitness of donors is judged by their appearance and medical history and a haemoglobin screening test (see Appendix 1). In 1963, the rejection rate from all causes was 8·6 per cent of donors attending, and the rejection rate, due to anaemia, of newly enrolled women donors was 6·43 per cent.

On each donation the ABO and Rh groups are determined and a syphilis test is done. When the cells do not contain the D, C and E antigens, the blood is issued as Rh-negative; all other is issued as Rh-positive. The blood is stored at 4°C to await distribution to hospitals. Its life is usually considered to be twenty-one days. The regional transfusion centre distributes the blood in insulated boxes or refrigerator vehicles to hospital blood banks which are usually in the care of the hospital pathologist or haematologist. Blood not used by the expiry date is returned to the regional transfusion centre, where the plasma is separated from the red cells and sent to the Blood Products Laboratory. By far the greater part of the blood provided is citrated whole blood, but each Centre also provides other preparations, such as concentrated red cells, washed red cells, whole blood specifically collected for operations upon the heart, and frozen fresh plasma.

(c) *Blood grouping.* Each Centre is responsible for blood grouping, testing and cross-matching and maintains a regional blood bank and area blood banks and banks at hospitals with pathological laboratories.

(d) *The distribution to hospitals of transfusion-giving sets, grouping sera, dried 10-donor pool plasma and plasma fractions* such as fibrinogen and albumin with distilled water for their reconstitution. Arrangements, differing in detail from region to region, exist for general practitioner obstetricians to obtain dried plasma, distilled water and giving sets.

(e) *Investigation of transfusion problems.* The Regional transfusion centre acts as a reference centre for transfusion problems arising in the regional hospitals.

---

[1] For details see *Annual Report of the Ministry of Health for 1958*, Pt 1, pp. 37–40.

265

(f) *Blood grouping of antenatal patients.* The National Blood Transfusion Service was the most appropriate organization on which to base the diagnosis and treatment of haemolytic disease of the newborn. In 1946, the Service began to make the necessary blood-grouping tests and, in many instances, to undertake the treatment of affected infants; and also to stimulate and help the organization of this work in the regions. Today there are facilities for testing every expectant mother and, when necessary, for treating her infant. In 1968, the regional transfusion centres tested 595,528 specimens related to pregnancy, compared with some 26,000 in 1946.

(g) *Teaching and research.* Teaching is a most important activity of the Service, and courses of instruction for doctors, nurses and laboratory technicians are given at regional transfusion centres. These courses have contributed to a wider appreciation of the hazards of transfusion and to raising the general standard of blood grouping and compatibility testing. The Ministry's policy is to site regional transfusion centres close to medical schools or teaching hospitals whenever possible, because it is considered that such an association will tend to stimulate research and investigation in the centres and to maintain the high technical standards of the Service, which must continue to be much more than a blood supply organization. This policy is being implemented, so far as possible, as re-accommodation of centres becomes necessary. Several regional transfusion directors hold honorary appointments in medical schools and in some of these give instruction in transfusion.[1]

For the purposes of this study, carried out in 1967, it was decided to select for statistical examination the regional data for the years 1951, 1956, 1961 and 1965. Unfortunately, the monthly returns for some of the Centres either could not be traced or had been destroyed for the years 1951 and 1956. Separate figures for (1) General Public donors; (2) Services donors (army, navy and air force); (3) Institutional donors (at factories, offices, universities, etc.) cannot, therefore, be inserted for these years.

The first two tables relate to General Public civilian donors; that is, members of the public who volunteer to donate blood and are enrolled on panel registers. They signify their willingness to be called about once every six months. The Service recognizes, however, that these calls (generally 14 day's notice) may be inopportune or

---

[1] This information on organization and functions is taken from Maycock, W. D'A., 'The National Blood Transfusion Service', *The Practitioner, op. cit.,* 1965, pp. 147–51.

inconvenient due to a variety of factors (domestic factors, holidays, changes in residence, employment, working hours, etc. etc.). Allowances are, therefore, made in estimating and varying the 'call-up' rate according to local experience and other variables so as to maintain an even balance between the demand for blood of different groups in each region and the supply, and thus avoid any wastage of out-dated blood. The whole exercise calls for considerable skill in estimating demand (which varies locally, seasonally, by blood group and is constantly rising) and supply (which also varies seasonally and locally in terms of the reporting rate of donors called).

One indication that there has not been any shortage of blood or blood donors since 1948 is the fact that the Service has not felt any necessity to study the phenomena of donor enrolment rates and reporting rates by blood group, locality, age, sex, occupation and other characteristics. Supply has apparently been inexhaustible. The real problem has been to 'manage' it efficiently. This explains, probably more than any other factor, the varying use of Institutional donors. The use of such donors greatly reduces the element of non-reporting and, in terms of the administrative costs involved, a bottle of blood can be obtained more cheaply from an Institutional donor than from a General Public donor. The same considerations of speed, high reporting rates and administrative costs apply also to Service donors.

Table 19 shows the estimated effective civilian donor panel on a regional basis for each of the four years.

For the country as a whole, the size of the panel more than doubled over the 14 years. Apart from Birmingham, most other regions practically doubled (and in one case nearly trebled) their effective donor panels.

The general trend is remarkably consistent, and shows that all parts of the country contributed to meeting the rising demand for blood from the National Health Service.

The composition of each panel is constantly changing due to population movements, donors reaching the retirement age for donations, and many other factors. It becomes necessary, therefore, for Donor Organizers to recruit an appropriate number of new donors each year to allow for 'natural wastage', and also to increase their effective strengths to meet the estimated (and increasing) demand for blood. Again, these regional estimates call for much expertise and experience; it is psychologically important, for example, to see that donor panels are *effective* donor panels; in other words, actually to call for donations from those who have volunteered to give. Not to do so could invite disappointment and a sense that a proffered 'gift' was not wanted.

Table 20 shows the results of a multitude of regional decisions in estimating and forecasting. Nationally, the number of new donors enrolled per 1000 of the population (column A) virtually doubled between 1951 and 1965. The number of new donors giving their first donation also nearly doubled (column B). All regions

TABLE 19

Estimated Total Effective Civilian Donor Panel at June 30, per 1000 Population at that Date

Region	1951	1956	1961	1965
1. Newcastle	13·1	14·2	24·1	28·2
2. Leeds	14·5	20·1	28·6	26·2
3. Sheffield	9·6*	13·9*	15·9*	18·7
4. Cambridge	8·3*	13·5*	12·9	24·1
5. N.E. Metropolitan ⎫	10·9*	13·5*	23·4*	26·8
6. N.W. Metropolitan ⎭			24·3*	31·1
7, 8. South London	12·0	10·8	16·1	20·3
9. Oxford	16·8	18·6	25·6	24·3
10. Bristol	9·8*	14·3*	15·7	19·3
11. Cardiff	7·1*	11·3	16·7	19·9
12. Birmingham	9·0	9·1	12·0	11·4
13. Manchester	9·1	13·9	20·0	23·4
14. Liverpool	16·8	18·8	22·0	26·9
England and Wales	10·6*	14·3*	20·1*	22·8*

*Effective civilian donor panel as at December 31.

contributed, the differences between them in respect to both categories being somewhat less in 1965 than in 1951.

So far as General Public donors are concerned, Table 20 shows—as one would expect—that the call rate per 1000 of the population increased in nearly all the regions between 1951 and 1965. The largest increases took place in the Northern regions; Leeds 25 to 60; Liverpool 26 to 58; Manchester 13 to 42 and Newcastle 22 to 40. By contrast, Oxford rose only from 30 to 34 and South London actually fell from 30 to 29.

The interpretation of these trends is complex and, in the absence of regional data on differences in the demand for blood, not worth attempting. In any event, apart from the unknown demand factors, the supply variables are many including, for example, regional differences in the characteristics of effective civilian donor panels, regional differences in the use made at different times of Services donors and Institutional donors, and regional differences in reporting rates.

TABLE 20

Number of Civilian Donors Enrolled and Bled per 1000 of the Population

		1951		1956		1961		1965	
	Region	A	B	A	B	A	B	A	B
1.	Newcastle	2·7	2·7	4·9	3·4	4·9	4·1	6·4	5·1
2.	Leeds	4·0	3·1	4·6	2·6	4·6	4·0	8·0	6·1
3.	Sheffield	1·5	1·2	1·9	2·3	2·7	2·6	2·6	2·6
4.	Cambridge	2·4	2·1	2·6	2·0	4·6	3·8	5·4	4·1
5.	N.E. Metropolitan	1·6	3·7	1·1	2·7	6·2	4·9	5·7	4·6
6.	N.W. Metropolitan					6·6	5·0	5·0	7·1
7, 8.	South London	2·7	2·1	1·2	1·8	3·7	2·8	4·1	3·2
9.	Oxford	4·9	3·6	5·0	3·6	3·6	4·5	4·8	4·8
10.	Bristol	2·3	2·3	1·9	1·9	3·0	3·0	4·1	4·1
11.	Cardiff	2·0	2·0	2·2	2·2	2·7	2·7	3·4	3·4
12.	Birmingham	1·7	1·6	2·1	2·0	2·9	2·8	3·2	3·1
13.	Manchester	3·8	1·8	7·4	3·8	8·0	4·4	8·0	6·1
14.	Liverpool	8·4	6·5	8·6	6·9	10·0	9·7	8·5	8·5
	England and Wales	2·6	2·4	3·1	2·7	4·7	3·9	5·1	4·6

A: Number of new civilian donors enrolled per 1000 of the population.

B: Number of new civilian donors bled per 1000 of the population. These proportions are based on:

> The total number of civilian donors enrolled from January to December each year.
>
> The total number of new civilian donors bled (for the first time) for January–December each year.
>
> The mid-year (June 30) estimates of population.

The reporting rates are interesting from a number of angles; the rates for General Public donors, extracted from Table 21, are set out in Table 22.

269

TABLE 21
Donor Call Rates and Reporting Rates by Regions, 1951–65

Region		1951 1	1951 2	1951 3	1956 1	1956 2	1956 3	1961 1	1961 2	1961 3	1965 1	1965 2	1965 3
1. Newcastle	A	21.5	3.2	1.2	30.6	3.3	4.1	36.9	1.1	12 6	40.0	0.8	20.0
	B	46.7	89.2	73.0	52.5	94.1	75.6	53.7	83.2	74.5	52.2	86.0	66.5
2. Leeds	A	125.1	[3]	10.2	35.7	[3]	0.07	47.0	[3]	[3]	60.1	[3]	[3]
	B	149.3	[1]	245.0	47.4	[5]	6	50.0	[7]	8	51.5	[9]	10
3. Sheffield	A	24.0	0.3	0.6	31.3	0.06	2.1	26.3	0.8	3.7	30.3	0.3	3.8
	B	45.0	100.0	100.0	44.2	100.0	99.8	55.2	100.0	96.1	54.1	100.0	98.7
4. Cambridge	A	15.4 (totals of 1, 2, 3 estimated only)			27.5 (totals of 1, 2, 3)			27.9	7.1	4.6	35.5	2.9	9.2
	B	100.0			74.2			75.0	100.0	100.0	69.9	81.1	91.7
5. N.E. Metrop.	A	29.0 (totals of 1, 2, 3)			A 34.2 (totals of 1, 2, 3)			35.2	0.8	16.6	43.6	0.4	19.6
	B	55.6			B 61.4			48.8	80.0	80.0	48.4	80.0	79.2
6. N.W. Metrop.	A							26.6	1.1	18.8	26.7	1.0	23.7
	B							51.0	90.1	94.4	55.7	94.7	86.9
7, 8 South London	A	30.1	3.8	1.5	22.0	2.8	2.5	24.9	0.6	4.9	28.6	0.7	5.4
	B	53.4	101.0	100.0	56.2	100.0	96.8	59.6	100.0	93.3	61.2	94.4	93.6
9. Oxford	A	30.1	5.2	3.0	31.2	6.4	6.2	30.7	6.6	14.0	34.0	2.8	13.9
	B	49.0	98.4	80.0	55.2	100.0	65.6	61.0	100.0	70.0	63.7	100.0	71.6
10. Bristol	A	15.8 (totals of 1, 2, 3)			19.2 (totals of 1, 2, 3)			12.9	4.2	6.2	32.8	3.2	8.9
	B	103.0			107.0			106.0	107.0	111.0	60.5	98.2	94.0
11. Cardiff	A	16.8 (totals of 1, 2, 3)			13.6 (totals of 1, 2, 3)			15.0	[3]	13.2	21.9	[3]	15.5
	B	47.2			43.5			52.4	[12]	65.7	47.7	[13]	68.2
12. Birmingham	A	13.8	1.6	1.8	17.1	3.9	4.5	21.4	1.2	7.0	23.8	0.4	7.2
	B	63.2	100.0	100.0	60.4	100.0	92.4	62.8	100.0	100.0	65.1	100.0	100.0
13. Manchester	A	12.5	1.3	2.0	22.8	1.6	3.0	30.7	0.01	5.4	42.3	[2]	7.9
	B	52.4	100.0	97.8	52.0	94.8	95.8	54.6	100.0	96.2	47.6	[2]	98.2

14.														
Liverpool	A	25.7	6.2	8.5		30.0	8.1	9.4	50.6	1.4	18.9	58.4	0.9	19.4
	B	47.5	100.0	100.0		47.0	100.0	99.5	44.2	100.0	100.0	39.5	100.0	100.0
England and Wales	A	24.1 } (totals of 1, 2, 3)				30.9 } (totals of 1, 2, 3)			28.6	1.2	8.8	35.0	0.8	10.8
	B	60.1 }				62.8 }			56.1	108.0	90.6	54.3	105.0	88.1

A: Number of donors called per 1000 of the population.
B: Percentage of donors called reporting.

Col. 1: General Public.
Col. 2: Services.
Col. 3: Institutional.

A percentage in excess of 100 means that the number reporting exceeded the number called.

1 Ten months only.
2 No donors called or reporting.
3 No donors called.
4 2605 donors reported.
5 2433 donors reported.
6 200 donors called, 2236 reported.
7 3436 donors reported.
8 7459 donors reported.
9 2251 donors reported.
10 9354 donors reported.
11 4355 donors reported.
12 1903 donors reported.
13 1925 donors reported.

With the exception of Manchester and Liverpool, all the regions with records for 1951 reported increases during the 14 years. In general, the chief impression given by this table is the high degree of consistency in reporting rates over the period. The differences between the regions could be accounted for by differences in administrative methods, the characteristics and responses of donors, changes in the composition of donor panels, and other factors as well as seasonal differences in demand and supply (reporting rates decline, for example, during summer holiday periods, whereas the demand for blood may increase). Whatever the reasons it can be concluded that there is no evidence that members of the general public are less likely in a more affluent society to enrol as donors and to respond to a call to give. On the contrary, the general movement of these statistics suggest that they are more likely to enrol and to respond.

For General Public donors only, the aggregate figures for England and Wales are:

	%		%
1948	45	1961	54
1953	49	1962	55
1955	52	1963	54
1956	51	1964	54
1957	52	1965	54
1958	53	1966	54
1959	55	1967	53
1960	55	1968	52

A word of explanation needs to be added concerning the high reporting rates (up to 100 per cent and over) for Institutional and Services donors. The arrangement generally takes the form of the institution or unit itself making an appeal for voluntary donors on a specified day, and undertaking to provide for the collecting team an agreed number of donors who can be handled in a session. It is not possible, therefore, in such circumstances to estimate non-response.

In Table 23 (p. 274) we show for the four years and by region the respective contributions made by donors in the three categories. We list below some general comments on this table:

1. For the country as a whole in 1961 and 1965 approximately two-thirds of all the blood donated came from members of the General Public and one-third from Institutional donors. While the proportions were about the same in both years the actual

272

TABLE 22

Regional Trends in General Public Donor Reporting Rates 1951–65[1]

	1951	1956	1961	1965	% change 1951–65
Newcastle	47	53	54	52	+11
Leeds	49	47	50	52	+6
Sheffield	45	44	55	54	+20
Cambridge	—	—	75	70	
N.E. Metropolitan	—	—	49	48	
N.W. Metropolitan	—	—	51	56	
South London	53	56	60	61	+15
Oxford	49	55	61	64	+31
Bristol	—	—	—	61	
Cardiff	—	44	52	48	
Birmingham	63	60	63	65	+3
Manchester	52	52	55	48	−8
Liverpool	48	47	44	40	−17

[1] Percentage of donors called reporting.

number of full bottles obtained rose by 153,000 (General Public) and 85,000 (Institutional). Donations from members of the Services fell by 18,000 from 55,000 to 37,000, a consequence, no doubt, of reductions in Services manpower.

2. The totals for the 8 regions showed for 1961 and 1965 a somewhat higher proportion of General Public donors than for all regions. Over the fourteen years there was little change in the proportionate contribution from the General Public. The main change that occurred was the switch from Services donors in 1951 and 1956 to Institutional donors in 1961 and 1965. The relatively high proportion (in relation to the manpower universe) of Services donors in the 1950s can be attributed, as a legacy of tradition and practice, to the Second World War. During the war the appeal to members of the Services to give blood was significant both in terms of their own comrades and of the needs of civilians injured in air raids.

3. In all four years there were substantial regional differences in the proportionate contributions from the General Public. Leeds, Sheffield, South London and Manchester show consistently high proportions; Liverpool, Cardiff and N.W. Metropolitan consistently low ones. Consequently, there are also large differences in the use made by regions of Institutional donors.

TABLE 23

Percentage Distribution of Donations by Category and Region 1951–65

(based on number of full bottles of blood obtained)

	1951			1956			1961			1965		
	1	2	3	1	2	3	1	2	3	1	2	3
1. Newcastle	72	21	7	70	15	15	66	3	31	59	2	39
2. Leeds	91*	6*	3*	92	4	4	88	4	8	89	2	9
3. Sheffield	93	2	5	83	4	13	77	4	19	80	1	19
4. Cambridge					—		64	22	14	70	7	23
5. N.E. Metropolitan					—		55	2	43	56	1	43
6. N.W. Metropolitan					—		43	3	54	41*	2*	57*
7, 8. South London	75	16	9	70	16	14	74	3	23	75	3	22
9. Oxford	66*	23*	11*	62	23	15	60	8	32	62	8	30
10. Bristol					—		56	17	27	63	10	27
11. Cardiff				50	14	36	46	4	50	48	3	49
12. Birmingham	72	13	15	56	20	24	62	5	33	67	2	31
13. Manchester	67	13	20	72	10	18	76	0	24	72	0	28
14. Liverpool	46	23	31	45	27	28	53	3	44	51	2	47
England and Wales					—		64	5	31	64	3	33
Eight Regions with 1951–65 records	73	15	12	69	15	16	70	4	26	71	2	27

Col 1: General Public. 2: Services. 3: Institutional.

*Estimated on basis of the number of donors reporting in each category.

No obvious explanations for these regional differences emerge from the statistics presented in this appendix. When the regions are ranked for various indicators (size of civilian donor panels, donors called and bled, call rates and reporting rates) no clear pattern results. Rank orders fall into no coherent arrangement or trend. It would thus seem that the differences are explicable only in terms of different and varying regional policies and practices in relation to donor recruitment,[1] donor organization and, possibly, local differences in the characteristics and motivations of donors. Other factors, which cannot be measured in this context, relating to varying employment situations, shift working and the increasing employment of married women, may also have led some regional donor organizers to make more use of Institutional donors.[2] Administrative cost criteria as well as the growing problem of transport difficulties for donors in certain areas may well have constituted additional arguments for taking blood transfusion teams to donors instead of expecting donors to make their own way to transfusion centres.

[1] For some information on area recruitment campaigns see *Abstracts of Efficiency Studies in the Hospital Service*, No. 105, *Blood Transfusion Service*, H.M.S.O., 1967.

[2] Conversely, in some areas difficulties with private employers, unwilling to allow employees an hour off work to give blood, may have influenced Regional Directors to rely more strongly on General Public donors (see, for example *Daily Telegraph*, May 20, 1967).

Appendix 4
The Donor Survey: The Characteristics of Donors

Table 24, which is discussed in Chapter 7, relates to a total of 3810 donors (M. 2298, F. 1512).

TABLE 24
Percentage Distribution of the Marital Status of All Donors by Sex, Age and Session Type

Age	Sex	Marital status	G.P.	I.	D.S.	Total		E.W. (ages 20–64 only)
			%	%	%	%		%
18–24	M	M.	23	34	10	23	(31)[1]	33
		S.	77	66	90	77	(69)[1]	67
		W/D/S	0	0	0	0	(0)[1]	0
		N.	(237)	(135)	(126)	(498)		
18–24	F	M.	36	22	0	31	(37)[1]	59
		S.	64	78	0	69	(63)[1]	41
		W/D/S	0	0	0	0	(0)[1]	0
		N.	(245)	(102)		(347)		
25–29	M	M.	79	83	100[2]	81		73
		S.	20	16	0	18		26
		W/D/S	1	1	0	1		1
		N.	(185)	(141)	(5)	(331)		
25–29	F	M.	69	56	0	66		85
		S.	27	36	0	29		14
		W/D/S	4	8	0	5		1
		N.	(146)	(36)		(182)		
30–34	M	M.	85	92	0	87		84
		S.	14	7	100[3]	12		15
		W/D/S	1	1	0	1		1
		N.	(173)	(116)	(2)	(291)		
30–34	F	M.	80	47	0	76		89
		S.	15	40	0	18		9
		W/D/S	5	13	0	6		2
		N.	(121)	(15)		(136)		

35–39	M	M.	90	91	100[4]	90	86
		S.	8	5	0	7	12
		W/D/S	2	4	0	3	2
		N.	(196)	(105)	(1)	(302)	
35–39	F	M.	85	65	0	82	89
		S.	10	30	0	13	8
		W/D/S	5	5	0	5	3
		N.	(144)	(20)		(164)	
40–44	M	M.	92	93	0	92	88
		S.	6	5	0	6	10
		W/D/S/	2	2	0	2	2
		N.	(178)	(93)		(271)	
40–44	F	M.	86	56	0	82	88
		S.	11	32	0	14	8
		W/D/S	3	12	0	4	4
		N.	(140)	(25)		(165)	
45–49	M	M.	90	95	0	92	88
		S.	8	2	0	6	9
		W/D/S	2	3	0	2	3
		N.	(174)	(67)		(241)	
45–49	F	M.	84	73	0	82	85
		S.	11	10	0	11	9
		W/D/S	5	17	0	7	6
		N.	(152)	(30)		(182)	
50–54	M	M.	90	88	0	89	88
		S.	8	10	0	9	9
		W/D/S	2	2	0	2	3
		N.	(124)	(50)		(174)	
50–54	F	M.	77	62	0	74	80
		S.	10	24	0	13	10
		W/D/S	13	14	0	13	10
		N.	(112)	(29)		(141)	
55–59	M	M.	88	91	0	89	87
		S.	7	3	0	7	8
		W/D/S	5	6	0	4	5
		N.	(99)	(34)		(133)	
55–59	F	M.	65	82	0	67	73
		S.	17	18	0	17	12
		W/D/S	18	0	0	16	15
		N.	(115)	(11)		(126)	

TABLE 24 (*cont.*)

Percentage Distribution of the Marital Status of All Donors by Sex, Age and Session Type

Age	Sex	Marital status	G.P.	I.	D.S.	Total	E.W. (ages 20–64 only)
			%	%	%	%	%
60–64	M	M.	91[5]	100[8]	0	93[5]	85
		S.	7	0	0	5	8
		W/D/S	2	0	0	2	7
		N.	(46)	(11)		(57)	
60–64	F	M.	54	50[9]	0	53	63
		S.	21[6]	50	0	22[6]	13
		W/D/S	25[7]	0	0	25[7]	24
		N.	(67)	(2)		(69)	

[1] Total of all donors aged 20–24 only.   [2] Only 5 donors.
[3] Only 2 donors.   [4] Only 1 donor.
[5] Including 1 donor 65+.   [6] Including 1 donor 65+.
[7] Including 2 donors 65+.   [8] 11 donors.
[9] 1 married donor, 1 single donor.

The following tables analyse the characteristics of social class and income group in combination with sex, age, marital status, session type and number of donations and compare the results with certain universe data for England and Wales for 1966 (Census reports).

For this analysis tables were prepared covering almost every conceivable kind of breakdown. Only the main ones are reproduced here: to publish them all would be crazy and costly. The whole collection, however, is in the author's undestroyed files and may be seen on request.

First, a few notes of explanation.

Social Class Key
  0. Not answered
  I. Professional, etc., occupations
  II. Intermediate occupations
  III. Skilled occupations
  IV. Partly skilled occupations

V. Unskilled occupations
6. Economically inactive (including students, inmates of institutions, and those living on private means or Supplementary Benefits).
7. Retired.
8. Members of Defence Services
9. Not enough information for classification

Housewives and married women (whether economically active or not) were assigned to social class of husband (if widowed, divorced or separated to social class of chief earner in household).

Where single male and female donors completed both Questions 12 and 13 he or she was assigned to the social class of the chief earner in the household. In other cases they took their own social class. Donors in the Defence Services (134 males) are generally excluded from this social class analysis. Most of them in fact might appropriately be assigned to classes III–V (in certain tables this adjustment is made).[1] On January 1, 1967, the number of males in the Services totalled 349,017 (source: Ministry of Defence). These donors in the 'sample' therefore represented 38 per 100,000 males in the Defence Services male population compared with 2280 males and females per 100,000 males and females in the general population of England and Wales (based on effective civilian donor panel as at December 31, 1965).

Income Group of Chief Earner (see Questionnaire)

Sources of universe data. Distribution of normal weekly earnings of employees: see *Family Expenditure Survey Report for 1966*, Ministry of Labour and Thatcher, A. R., 'The Distribution of Earnings of Employees in Great Britain', *Journal of the Royal Statistical Society*, especially Table 5, Vol. 131, Pt 2, 1968. See also *Abstract of Regional Statistics*, No. 3, 1967, H.M.S.O., Table 44.

In the next Table (25) we take the social class of all chief earners in the donor's family and present the raw data for sex, marital status, number of donations and session type. This table includes 3681 donors.

[1] The factor of donor session is important here as non-commissioned ranks and below attend at different times from officers.

TABLE 25

*Social Class of Chief Earner in Donor's Family by Sex,
Marital Status, Number of Donations and Session-Type*

Type of session	No. of dona- tions	Marital status	0	I	II	III	IV	V	6	7	8	9	Total
							Social class—Male						
GENERAL PUBLIC	1	M	0	3	6	15	3	0	0	0	0	0	27
		S	0	4	8	24	5	1	0	0	0	1	43
		W/D/S	0	0	0	0	1	0	0	0	0	0	1
		Total	0	7	14	39	9	1	0	0	0	1	71
	2	M	0	6	8	31	4	1	0	0	0	0	50
		S	0	1	11	22	6	2	0	0	0	0	42
		W/D/S	0	0	0	1	0	0	0	0	0	0	1
		Total	0	7	19	54	10	3	0	0	0	0	93
	3	M	0	6	8	24	4	1	0	0	0	0	43
		S	0	3	16	24	4	1	0	0	0	0	48
		W/D/S	0	0	0	3	0	0	0	0	0	0	3
		Total	0	9	24	51	8	2	0	0	0	0	94
	4	M	0	3	12	34	4	0	0	0	1	0	54
		S	0	1	6	13	3	0	0	0	0	2	25
		W/D/S	0	0	0	4	1	0	0	0	0	0	5
		Total	0	4	18	51	8	0	0	0	1	2	84
	5–9	M	0	34	55	134	18	1	0	0	0	5	247
		S	0	8	11	27	12	2	0	0	0	1	61
		W/D/S	0	0	1	2	0	0	0	0	0	1	4
		Total	0	42	67	163	30	3	0	0	0	7	312
	10–14	M	0	30	43	108	17	2	0	1	0	2	203
		S	0	1	6	18	5	2	1	0	0	2	35
		W/D/S	0	0	1	4	1	0	0	0	0	0	6
		Total	0	31	50	130	23	4	1	1	0	4	244
	15–29	M	1	34	71	176	29	5	0	1	1	3	321
		S	0	3	9	13	3	0	0	0	0	0	28
		W/D/S	0	0	0	2	2	0	0	0	0	0	4
		Total	1	37	80	191	34	5	0	1	1	3	353
	30–50	M	0	4	31	50	9	1	0	0	0	2	97
		S	0	2	2	7	0	2	0	1	0	0	14
		W/D/S	0	0	0	0	0	0	0	0	0	0	0
		Total	0	6	33	57	9	3	0	1	0	2	111

Type of session	No. of dona-tions	Marital status	0	I	II	III	IV	V	6	7	8	9	Total
						Social class—Male							
GENERAL PUBLIC	50+	M	0	4	7	9	1	1	1	0	0	0	23
		S	0	0	0	0	0	0	0	0	0	0	0
		W/D/S	0	0	0	0	0	0	0	0	0	0	0
		Total	0	4	7	9	1	1	1	0	0	0	23
	Not answered	M	0	2	3	9	0	0	0	1	0	1	16
		S	0	0	2	4	0	0	0	1	0	0	7
		W/D/S	0	0	0	0	0	0	0	0	0	0	0
		Total	0	2	5	13	0	0	0	2	0	1	23
INSTITUTIONS	1	M	0	1	1	34	8	0	0	0	0	0	44
		S	0	2	2	11	4	1	0	0	0	0	20
		W/D/S	0	0	0	0	1	0	0	0	0	0	1
		Total	0	3	3	45	13	1	0	0	0	0	65
	2	M	1	5	4	38	14	1	0	0	0	1	64
		S	0	3	7	13	0	1	1	0	0	2	27
		W/D/S	0	0	0	0	0	0	0	0	0	0	0
		Total	1	8	11	51	14	2	1	0	0	3	91
	3	M	0	6	12	24	13	1	0	0	0	2	58
		S	0	1	5	10	1	0	0	0	0	1	18
		W/D/S	0	0	0	2	0	0	0	0	0	0	2
		Total	0	7	17	36	14	1	0	0	0	3	78
	4	M	0	4	4	22	2	0	0	0	0	1	33
		S	0	0	5	10	3	0	0	0	0	0	18
		W/D/S	0	0	0	0	0	0	0	0	0	0	0
		Total	0	4	9	32	5	0	0	0	0	1	51
	5–9	M	1	22	30	102	20	2	0	0	0	2	179
		S	0	5	5	14	4	2	0	0	0	1	31
		W/D/S	0	1	0	1	0	0	0	0	0	0	2
		Total	1	28	35	117	24	4	0	0	0	3	212
	10–14	M	0	10	14	51	7	0	0	0	0	1	83
		S	0	0	1	3	1	1	0	0	0	0	6
		W/D/S	0	0	1	2	0	0	0	0	0	0	3
		Total	0	10	16	56	8	1	0	0	0	1	92
	15–29	M	0	15	11	41	11	1	0	0	0	2	81
		S	0	0	0	0	0	1	0	0	0	0	1
		W/D/S	0	0	1	2	0	0	0	0	0	0	3
		Total	0	15	12	43	11	2	0	0	0	2	85

TABLE 25 (*cont.*)

Social Class of Chief Earner in Donor's Family by Sex,
Marital Status, Number of Donations and Session-Type

Type of session	No. of donations	Marital status	0	I	II	III	IV	V	6	7	8	9	Total
INSTITUTIONS	30–50	M	0	2	5	6	0	1	0	0	0	0	14
		S	0	0	0	0	0	0	0	0	0	0	0
		W/D/S	0	0	0	0	0	0	0	0	0	0	0
		Total	0	2	5	6	0	1	0	0	0	0	14
	50+	M	0	0	0	2	0	0	0	0	0	0	2
		S	0	0	0	0	0	0	0	0	0	0	0
		W/D/S	0	0	0	0	0	0	0	0	0	0	0
		Total	0	0	0	2	0	0	0	0	0	0	2
	Not answered	M	0	2	3	32	3	2	0	0	0	4	46
		S	0	1	1	11	1	1	0	0	0	2	17
		W/D/S	0	0	0	0	0	1	0	0	0	0	1
		Total	0	3	4	43	4	4	0	0	0	6	64
GENERAL PUBLIC AND INSTITUTIONS COMBINED	1	M	0	4	7	49	11	0	0	0	0	0	71
		S	0	6	10	35	9	2	0	0	0	1	63
		W/D/S	0	0	0	0	2	0	0	0	0	0	2
		Total	0	10	17	84	22	2	0	0	0	1	136
	2	M	1	11	12	69	18	2	0	0	0	1	114
		S	0	4	18	35	6	3	1	0	0	2	69
		W/D/S	0	0	0	1	0	0	0	0	0	0	1
		Total	1	15	30	105	24	5	1	0	0	3	184
	3	M	0	12	20	48	17	2	0	0	0	2	101
		S	0	4	21	34	5	1	0	0	0	1	66
		W/D/S	0	0	0	5	0	0	0	0	0	0	5
		Total	0	16	41	87	22	3	0	0	0	3	172
	4	M	0	7	16	56	6	0	0	0	1	1	87
		S	0	1	11	23	6	0	0	0	0	2	43
		W/D/S	0	0	0	4	1	0	0	0	0	0	5
		Total	0	8	27	83	13	0	0	0	1	3	135
	5–9	M	1	56	85	236	38	3	0	0	0	7	426
		S	0	13	16	41	16	4	0	0	0	2	92
		W/D/S	0	1	1	3	0	0	0	0	0	1	6
		Total	1	70	102	280	54	7	0	0	0	10	524

Social class—Male (column headings 0, I, II, III, IV, V, 6, 7, 8, 9)

Type of session	No. of dona- tions	Marital status	Social class—Male										
			0	I	II	III	IV	V	6	7	8	9	Total
GENERAL PUBLIC AND INSTITUTIONS COMBINED	10–14	M	0	40	57	159	24	2	0	1	0	3	286
		S	0	1	7	21	6	3	1	0	0	2	41
		W/D/S	0	0	2	6	1	0	0	0	0	0	9
		Total	0	41	66	186	31	5	1	1	0	5	336
	15–29	M	1	49	82	217	40	6	0	1	1	5	402
		S	0	3	9	13	3	1	0	0	0	0	29
		W/D/S	0	0	1	4	2	0	0	0	0	0	7
		Total	1	52	92	234	45	7	0	1	1	5	438
	30–50	M	0	6	36	56	9	2	0	0	0	2	111
		S	0	2	2	7	0	2	0	1	0	0	14
		W/D/S	0	0	0	0	0	0	0	0	0	0	0
		Total	0	8	38	63	9	4	0	1	0	2	125
	50+	M	0	4	7	11	1	1	1	0	0	0	25
		S	0	0	0	0	0	0	0	0	0	0	0
		W/D/S	0	0	0	0	0	0	0	0	0	0	0
		Total	0	4	7	11	1	1	1	0	0	0	25
	Not answered	M	0	4	6	41	3	2	0	1	0	5	62
		S	0	1	3	15	1	1	0	1	0	2	24
		W/D/S	0	0	0	0	0	1	0	0	0	0	1
		Total	0	5	9	56	4	4	0	2	0	7	87
			Social class—Female										
GENERAL PUBLIC	1	M	0	6	5	26	4	4	0	1	0	2	48
		S	0	1	11	20	5	0	0	1	1	2	41
		W/D/S	0	0	1	0	1	0	3	0	0	0	5
		Total	0	7	17	46	10	4	3	2	1	4	94
	2	M	0	7	17	25	4	0	0	0	0	0	53
		S	0	2	11	18	4	1	0	0	2	3	41
		W/D/S	0	0	1	0	1	0	0	0	0	0	2
		Total	0	9	29	43	9	1	0	0	2	3	96
	3	M	0	7	15	22	7	1	0	0	1	2	55
		S	0	2	8	14	4	2	0	0	0	0	30
		W/D/S	0	0	1	3	0	1	0	0	0	0	5
		Total	0	9	24	39	11	4	0	0	1	2	90
	4	M	0	6	27	36	6	0	0	1	0	0	76
		S	0	3	8	12	5	0	0	0	0	0	28
		W/D/S	0	0	1	6	1	1	1	0	0	0	10
		Total	0	9	36	54	12	1	1	1	0	0	114

TABLE 25 (*cont.*)

Social Class of Chief Earner in Donor's Family by Sex, Marital Status, Number of Donations and Session-Type

Type of session	No. of donations	Marital status	0	I	II	III	IV	V	6	7	8	9	Total
						Social class—Female							
GENERAL PUBLIC	5–9	M	0	35	66	99	15	3	2	1	2	4	227
		S	0	7	23	35	5	4	2	1	0	2	79
		W/D/S	0	1	3	6	4	0	1	0	1	0	16
		Total	0	43	92	140	24	7	5	2	3	6	322
	10–14	M	0	25	31	64	16	2	1	4	1	6	150
		S	0	3	5	14	3	0	0	0	1	0	26
		W/D/S	0	0	1	9	3	0	1	0	0	0	14
		Total	0	28	37	87	22	2	2	4	2	6	190
	15–29	M	1	25	47	55	18	1	4	2	6	6	165
		S	0	1	10	17	1	0	1	1	1	0	32
		W/D/S	1	0	2	8	1	1	4	2	1	0	20
		Total	2	26	59	80	20	2	9	5	8	6	217
	30–50	M	0	6	15	19	5	0	1	4	0	0	50
		S	0	0	5	6	2	0	2	3	0	0	18
		W/D/S	1	0	1	5	0	0	3	0	0	0	10
		Total	1	6	21	30	7	0	6	7	0	0	78
	50+	M	0	1	2	1	2	0	0	1	0	1	8
		S	0	0	0	1	1	0	0	0	0	0	2
		W/D/S	0	0	0	0	0	0	1	0	1	0	2
		Total	0	1	2	2	3	0	1	1	1	1	12
	Not answered	M	0	6	1	10	3	0	0	0	0	1	21
		S	0	2	2	4	1	0	0	0	0	0	9
		W/D/S	0	0	0	0	0	0	1	0	0	0	1
		Total	0	8	3	14	4	0	1	0	0	1	31
INSTITUTIONS	1	M	0	0	4	8	2	0	0	0	0	0	14
		S	0	1	2	10	2	0	0	0	0	0	15
		W/D/S	0	0	0	0	0	0	0	0	0	0	0
		Total	0	1	6	18	4	0	0	0	0	0	29
	2	M	1	2	2	13	3	0	0	0	0	2	23
		S	0	1	5	9	6	1	0	0	0	3	25
		W/D/S	0	0	0	2	1	0	0	0	0	0	3
		Total	1	3	7	24	10	1	0	0	0	5	51

Type of session	No. of dona-tions	Marital status	0	I	II	III	IV	V	6	7	8	9	Total
INSTITUTIONS	3	M	0	0	0	5	2	0	0	0	0	0	7
		S	0	0	6	18	2	0	0	0	0	1	27
		W/D/S	0	0	0	1	0	0	0	0	0	0	1
		Total	0	0	6	24	4	0	0	0	0	1	35
	4	M	0	4	4	10	2	0	0	0	0	0	20
		S	0	1	2	5	3	0	0	0	0	0	11
		W/D/S	0	1	0	0	0	0	0	0	0	0	1
		Total	0	6	6	15	5	0	0	0	0	0	32
	5–9	M	0	3	6	21	2	1	0	1	0	1	35
		S	0	0	2	12	3	0	0	0	0	1	18
		W/D/S	0	0	0	6	4	0	0	0	0	0	10
		Total	0	3	8	39	9	1	0	1	0	2	63
	10–14	M	0	0	0	6	0	0	0	0	0	2	8
		S	0	0	1	3	0	0	0	0	0	0	4
		W/D/S	0	0	0	0	0	0	0	0	0	0	0
		Total	0	0	1	9	0	0	0	0	0	2	12
	15–29	M	0	0	1	4	0	0	0	0	0	0	5
		S	0	0	0	5	0	0	0	0	0	0	5
		W/D/S	0	0	0	1	0	0	0	0	0	0	1
		Total	0	0	1	10	0	0	0	0	0	0	11
	30–50	M	0	0	1	0	0	0	0	0	0	0	1
		S	0	0	1	0	0	0	0	0	0	0	1
		W/D/S	0	0	0	0	0	0	0	0	0	0	0
		Total	0	0	2	0	0	0	0	0	0	0	2
	50+	M	0	0	0	0	0	0	0	0	0	0	0
		S	0	0	0	1	0	0	0	0	0	0	1
		W/D/S	0	0	0	0	0	0	0	0	0	0	0
		Total	0	0	0	1	0	0	0	0	0	0	1
	Not answered	M	0	2	2	4	4	0	0	0	0	3	15
		S	0	1	2	7	5	0	0	0	0	4	19
		W/D/S	0	0	0	4	1	0	0	0	0	0	5
		Total	0	3	4	15	10	0	0	0	0	7	39
GENERAL PUBLIC (see over)	1	M	0	6	9	34	6	4	0	1	0	2	62
		S	0	2	13	30	7	0	0	1	1	2	56
		W/D/S	0	0	1	0	1	0	3	0	0	0	5
		Total	0	8	23	64	14	4	3	2	1	4	123

285

TABLE 25 (*cont.*)

Social Class of Chief Earner in Donor's Family by Sex,
Marital Status, Number of Donations and Session-Type

Type of session	No. of dona-tions	Marital status	0	I	II	III	IV	V	6	7	8	9	Total
						Social class—Female							
GENERAL PUBLIC AND INSTITUTIONS COMBINED		M	1	9	19	38	7	0	0	0	0	2	76
	2	S	0	3	16	27	10	2	0	0	2	6	66
		W/D/S	0	0	1	2	2	0	0	0	0	0	5
		Total	1	12	36	67	19	2	0	0	2	8	147
		M	0	7	15	27	9	1	0	0	1	2	62
	3	S	0	2	14	32	6	2	0	0	0	1	57
		W/D/S	0	0	1	4	0	1	0	0	0	0	6
		Total	0	9	30	63	15	4	0	0	1	3	125
		M	0	10	31	46	8	0	0	1	0	0	96
	4	S	0	4	10	17	8	0	0	0	0	0	39
		W/D/S	0	1	1	6	1	1	1	0	0	0	11
		Total	0	15	42	69	17	1	1	1	0	0	146
		M	0	38	72	120	17	4	2	2	2	5	262
	5–9	S	0	7	25	47	8	4	2	1	0	3	97
		W/D/S	0	1	3	12	8	0	1	0	1	0	26
		Total	0	46	100	179	33	8	5	3	3	8	385
		M	0	25	31	70	16	2	1	4	1	8	158
	10–14	S	0	3	6	17	3	0	0	0	1	0	30
		W/D/S	0	0	1	9	3	0	1	0	0	0	14
		Total	0	28	38	96	22	2	2	4	2	8	202
		M	1	25	48	59	18	1	4	2	6	6	170
	15–29	S	0	1	10	22	1	0	1	1	1	0	37
		W/D/S	1	0	2	9	1	1	4	2	1	0	21
		Total	2	26	60	90	20	2	9	5	8	6	228
		M	0	6	16	19	5	0	1	4	0	0	51
	30–50	S	0	0	6	6	2	0	2	3	0	0	19
		W/D/S	1	0	1	5	0	0	3	0	0	0	10
		Total	1	6	23	30	7	0	6	7	0	0	80
		M	0	1	2	1	2	0	0	1	0	1	8
	50+	S	0	0	0	2	1	0	0	0	0	0	3
		W/D/S	0	0	0	0	0	0	1	0	1	0	2
		Total	0	1	2	3	3	0	1	1	1	1	13
		M	0	8	3	14	7	0	0	0	0	4	36
	Not	S	0	3	4	11	5	0	0	0	0	4	27
	answered	W/D/S	0	0	0	4	1	0	1	0	0	0	6
		Total	0	11	7	29	13	0	1	0	0	8	69

There were 52 males in classes 0 and 6–9 leaving a total of 2112 male donors, and 119 females in these classes leaving a total of 1398 female donors.

The percentage distribution of social class by sex is shown in Table 26 alongside the 1966 distributions for England and Wales for ages 20–64:

TABLE 26

Percentage Distribution of Social Class by Sex

(ages 18–64)

	Male Social class						Female Social class				
	I	II	III	IV	V		I	II	III	IV	V
	%	%	%	%	%		%	%	%	%	%
Donor sample (2070) (Unadjusted)	11	19	57	11	2	(1390)	12	25	50	11	2
Donor sample (2245) (Adjusted)	10	17	58	12	3	(1454)	11	24	50	13	2
England and Wales (1966 sample census)	5	15	52	20	8		1	16	45	30	8

The adjustments were made to include donors in category 8 (members of the Defence Services) and 9 (insufficient information). The numbers were: category 8, 2 males and 18 females; category 9, 39 males and 46 females. The 134 male members of the Defence Services were also included in the adjustment.

The adjustment for categories 8 and 9 took the form of distributing these donors to social classes III, IV and V in proportion to the M/F distributions for England and Wales at all ages 20–64.[1] A similar adjustment was made for the 134 Defence Services donors but the redistribution to classes III, IV and V was based on the England and Wales distribution for ages 20–24.

An inspection of the questionnaires for category 9 showed that practically all these 85 donors could be classified under the heading

[1] Male ratios: category 8, 66:22:12, category 9, 64:25:11. Female ratio: categories 8 and 9, 59:33:8.

TABLE 27
Percentage Distribution of Income per Week before Tax of Chief Earner in Donor's Family by Sex and Social Class

Males (G.P. and I. combined)

Social class	Number	No response	Less than £10	£10–15	£15–20	£20–30	£30–50	£50 plus	Total
I	226	5	0	1	4	31	44	20	100
II	425	4	0	3	8	41	36	12	100
III	1172	17	0	6	33	51	9	1	100
IV	221	4	0	22	44	30	4	0	100
V	36	2	0	50	39	11	0	0	100
Defence Services[1]	3	0	0	0	33	0	33	33	100
All Classes	2083	32	0	7	26	44	18	5	100
Females (G.P. and I. combined)									
I	154	8	1	1	7	25	39	27	100
II	339	24	3	4	13	35	31	14	100
III	648	41	5	18	36	36	5	0	100
IV	152	12	10	47	32	10	1	0	100
V	24	0	13	58	25	4	0	0	100
Defence Services[1]	13	5	38	23	8	23	8	0	100
All Classes	1330	90	5	16	26	31	15	7	100

[1] Chief earner in donor's family.

of 'manual work' but insufficient information was given to allot them to class III, IV or V. As regards donors in the Defence Services, it is known that the great majority come from manual worker households.

Overall, however, the adjustments make only a small difference to the percentage distributions. A similar analysis was made of the percentage distribution of the social class of all donors by sex and marital status. Again, only marginal differences were found.

Considering the way in which the 'sample' was picked and responded it is perhaps remarkable that the similarities with national data on social class are as good as they are. Social classes I, II and III are over-represented and IV and V under-represented—particularly for females. There are a number of factors which may account for this but we defer comment until we have examined further breakdowns.

In the questionnaire donors were asked the approximate weekly income before tax of the chief earner in the family; six ranges of income were provided for ticking. Of the total sample, and excluding the 134 members of the Defence Services (to whom the question was not relevant) 32 males and 90 females did not respond. The following tables relate, therefore, to 2083 males and 1330 females.

TABLE 28
Percentage Distribution of the Social Class of Donors by Sex and Income Group

Males (G.P. and I. combined)

Social class	Less than £10	£10–15	£15–20	£20–30	£30–50	£50 plus	Total All income groups
I	0	1	2	8	27	43	11
II	25	7	7	19	41	49	20
III	75	47	71	65	30	6	56
IV	0	33	18	7	2	1	11
V	0	12	2	1	0	0	2
D.S.[1]	0	0	0	0	0	1	0
Total	100	100	100	100	100	100	100
Number	4	151	547	905	369	107	2083

T

TABLE 28 (*cont.*)
Percentage Distribution of the Social Class of Donors by Sex and Income Group

Females (G.P. and I. combined)

							All income groups
I	1	1	3	9	29	45	12
II	14	7	13	29	52	53	25
III	49	52	68	57	17	2	49
IV	23	33	14	4	1	0	11
V	5	6	2	0	0	0	2
D.S.[1]	8	1	0	1	1	0	1
Total	100	100	100	100	100	100	100
Number	65	220	341	407	204	93	1330

[1] Chief earner in donor's family.

Obviously, these tables must be interpreted with caution; the question was only an approximate one. It may have been understood and answered differently by some donors, and there are also, as we have already said, factors of selection involved. Although a general pattern of agreement between social class and income can be discerned the following points should be noted:

Social class I	Males	36 per cent earned less than £30 p.w.
	Females	34 per cent earned less than £30 p.w.
Social class II	Males	52 per cent earned less than £30 p.w.
	Females	55 per cent earned less than £30 p.w.
Social class III	Males	6 per cent earned less than £15 and 10 per cent more than £30 p.w.
	Females	23 per cent earned less than £15 and 5 per cent more than £30 p.w.
Social class IV	Males	4 per cent earned more than £30 p.w.
	Females	1 per cent earned more than £30 p.w.
Social class V	Males	50 per cent earned less than £15 p.w.
	Females	71 per cent earned less than £15 p.w.
All classes	Males	7 per cent earned less than £15 and 5 per cent more than £50 p.w.
	Females	21 per cent earned less than £15 and 7 per cent more than £50 p.w.

Some explanations for these apparent discordances—and the over-representation of classes I and II in the sample—could be found among the following reasons: over-statement of occupation, especially by wives reporting on their husbands (a well-known phenomenon); younger donors with low beginning salaries in class I and II occupations; and under-reporting of earnings, again especially among wives. There was evidence of a tendency to upgrade 'status'; for example, there were quite a number of 'directors' who reported surprisingly low weekly earnings and some of them, in answering other questions, did so in ungrammatical style and with poor spelling. In coding for social class, however, we had no option but to accept the respondents' statements. This factor alone could account for a substantial part of the over-representation of classes I and II in the sample.[1]

[1] After the analysis of social class had been completed and the tables in this Appendix prepared we submitted 171 questionnaires for a second opinion on the coded classification of the occupations stated by donors. We would like to acknowledge here the help we received in this matter from Professor J. N. Morris and Mrs Greystoke of the Social Medicine Research Unit at the London School of Hygiene.

These 171 questionnaires were selected by the writer out of the total of 3810 because of some doubt whether the Registrar General's classification instructions had been correctly followed. In 104 cases the original classifications were confirmed. Of those that were changed, 48 were male and 19 female.

Among the males, 38 were downgraded from S.C.I to S.C.II and III and 5 were upgraded from S.C.II and III to S.C.I. Also, 3 were downgraded from S.C.II to S.C.III and 2 from S.C.III to S.C.IV. Among the females, 14 were downgraded from S.C.I to S.C.II and III, 4 from S.C.II to S.C.III and IV and 1 from S.C.III to S.C.V.

We concluded, therefore, that there was some tendency in a proportion of doubtful cases in the original classifications to ascribe a higher social class than was warranted on the information provided by donors. Incorporating these 67 changes in Table 26 led to the following results:

	Male Social class					Female Social class				
	I %	II %	III %	IV %	V %	I %	II %	III %	IV %	V %
Donor sample (adjusted)	10	17	58	12	3	11	24	50	13	2
Donor sample (adjusted and incorporating second opinion revisions)	9	17	59	12	3	10	24	51	13	2

In view of the relatively small effect on the social class distributions of the second opinion changes following an inspection of 171 selected questionnaires it was decided not to review the balance of 3639 questionnaires. It was not thought worthwhile in terms of the labour and costs involved to re-work all the statistical data.

In Table 29 we compare the percentages for 'All Classes' with data from the 1966 Family Expenditure Survey:

TABLE 29

Percentage Distribution of Income per Week before Tax of Chief Earner in All Donor Families by Sex and for Employees in F.E.S. 1966

	Number in sample	Less than £10	£10–15	£15–20	£20–30	£30–50	£50 plus	Total
Male donors	2083	0	7	26	44	18	5	100
Female donors	1330	5	16	26	31	15	7	100
Employees (males only)[1]	2143	1	16	32	38	11	2	100

[1] 'Normal weekly earnings' (gross earnings) of full-time men employees (excluding 'youths'). The sample included manual, shop assistants, clerical workers, managerial, administrative, professional and technical but excluded the Defence Services and persons who worked for less than 10 hours per week. (For source see earlier note.) Approximately 48 per cent of full-time women workers in this F.E.S. sample earned less than £10 per week.

Subject to the reservations we have already expressed about the donor sample and other reservations about the Family Expenditure Survey data it would seem, on the face of it, not unreasonable to claim that in terms of income and social class the blood donor population is broadly representative of the general 'eligible' population. Between one-half to two-thirds of all blood donors of both sexes are in social class III and earn £15–30 p.w. before tax. There is some over-representation of classes I and II and donors (or chief earners) earning more than £30 p.w. and, conversely, some under-representation of classes IV and V and donors (or chief earners) earning less than £15 p.w.[1]

These differences could also in part be accounted for by the selection of the three Regional Centres as nearly 75 per cent of all donors came from the relatively more prosperous Birmingham

[1] Nevertheless, we should note that about 13 per cent of all chief earners in donor households might be classified (if all the facts were known) as 'in need' by Supplementary Benefit standards.

and South East Metropolitan areas.[1] Another selective factor involved can be found in the practices of blood donor teams preferring to hold sessions at the larger factories, shops and offices (for administrative and financial reasons). This means that in proportion to their numbers in the general population unskilled and semi-skilled workers in the building and agricultural industries, for example, as well as those employed in small work units, are not offered the opportunity of donating blood at their workplace. In a national situation in which there is no shortage of voluntary blood donors this policy is understandable. An analysis of Tables 27 and 28 by Type of Donor Session showed that 15 per cent of all chief earners in General Public donor households earned less than £15 p.w. The corresponding figure for Institutional donor households was 10 per cent. In other words, there were proportionately fewer poor people among Institutional donors. We comment further on this question of representativeness in Chapter 7.

All this material on social class and income was further analysed by marital status, age, the employment status of married women and other variables. At this stage, however, the numbers in many of the cells become so small and the tables so inordinately lengthy that it was decided not to reproduce them here. However, certain facts of nterest and general patterns emerged which are noted below.

1. Single M/F donors providing information on incomes reported on average lower incomes of chief earners than married M/F donors.

2. Among the widowed, divorced and separated donors, 14 per cent of males reported earnings of less than £15 p.w., and 71 per cent of females did so. Among those answering the relevant questions, there were 36 males and 102 females the great majority of whom were widowed.

3. Approximately 84 per cent of widowed, divorced and separated wives (most of whom were aged over 40) were in S.C. III–V (24 per cent in S.C. IV–V).

4. Young single male donors (ages 20–29) reported proportionately more S.C. I–II chief earners than married male donors of the same ages.

5. Among married male donors, those aged 20–24 had proportionately fewer S.C. I–II classifications than at higher ages.

[1] Analyses by social class, sex and marital status for each region separately showed higher social class I–II proportions in Birmingham and the South East than in Manchester among chief earners in all donor households, married men chief earners, and chief earners in households of married women donors and single men donors.

6. Among married male donors, those aged 50–64 contained to a substantial (and statistically significant) extent a higher proportion of S.C. IV–V donors than at ages 18–49.

7. Among both married and single female donors, those aged 20–29 had proportionately more S.C. III chief earners than at older ages.

8. Proportionately more married female donors aged 50–64 reported chief earners in S.C. IV–V than younger married female donors.

9. Included in the sample were 978 married women donors. The proportions by social class of husbands who were in full-time employment were: S.C. I—48 per cent, S.C.II—54 per cent, S.C.III—65 per cent, S.C. IV—67 per cent and S.C. V—67 per cent. These proportions are substantially higher than for the general population.[1] Combining the role of housewife with a full-time paid occupation does not appear to have deterred them from voluntarily giving blood. Analysed by age, 24 per cent were aged 18–29, 39 per cent 30–44, 25 per cent 45–54 and 12 per cent 55–64. Of the total, 88 per cent were General Public donors; only 12 per cent gave blood at their workplace.

10. The percentage distribution of housewives by social class of husbands who were not in full or part-time employment was: S.C. I—52 per cent, S.C. II—46 per cent, S.C. III—34 per cent, S.C. IV—31 per cent and S.C. V—33 per cent.[2] In all, there were 436 of these donors distributed fairly evenly over the age groups 25–59.

11. Of the total sample of donors, 103 or 3 per cent were born outside the United Kingdom. No questions were asked about ethnic group.

In addition to these social and demographic questions, respondents were also asked 'How many children have you?' To keep the questionnaire as short as possible no details were sought concerning the age and sex of the children, whether they were still living and so forth. It was recognized that the wording of the question was very general, liable to be interpreted in different ways, and that it was unlikely to yield any data which could be intensively cultivated. It was hoped, however, that the answers would enable us to divide

[1] See Table 20, Registrar General's Report on the 1966 Census and Hunt, A., *A Survey of Women's Employment*, Government Social Survey, Vol. 1, March 1968, H.M.S.O.

[2] These percentages do not in all cases add up with those under 9. The reason is that a few donors were unclassifiable.

TABLE 30

Percentage Distribution of Number of Children of Married Donors by Age, Sex and Social Class[1]

MALE

Social classes	I–II				III				IV–V				All classes			
No. of children	18–29	30–44	45–64	Total	18–29	30–44	45–64	Total	18–29	30–44	45–64	Total	18–29	30–44	45–64	Total
	%	%	%	%	%	%	%	%	%	%	%	%	%	%	%	%
0	46	12	10	17	39	13	14	20	43	10	15	17	41	12	13	18
1–3	53	81	82	77	58	77	76	72	57	76	77	74	57	79	78	74
4+	1	7	8	6	3	10	10	8	0	14	8	9	2	9	9	8
	100	100	100	100	100	100	100	100	100	100	100	100	100	100	100	100
Number	93	263	167	523	237	426	277	940	28	72	87	187	358	761	531	1650

FEMALE

Social classes	I–II				III				IV–V				All classes			
No. of children	18–29	30–44	45–64	Total	18–29	30–44	45–64	Total	18–29	30–44	45–64	Total	18–29	30–44	45–64	Total
	%	%	%	%	%	%	%	%	%	%	%	%	%	%	%	%
0	59	14	12	21	64	12	9	27	25	10	17	17	58	13	11	23
1–3	41	77	78	71	35	78	79	65	75	80	75	77	41	77	78	69
4+	0	9	10	8	1	10	12	8	0	10	8	6	1	10	11	8
	100	100	100	100	100	100	100	100	100	100	100	100	100	100	100	100
Number	69	166	145	380	129	161	137	427	24	35	48	107	222	362	330	914

[1] Some married donors did not state the number of children they had. They are excluded from this table. This mainly accounts for the differences between the totals of donors in this table and the totals of married donors in the sample.

the sample of married donors into those with and those without children.

In the event, the data turned out to be more interesting than expected and, internally at any rate, surprisingly consistent when analysed by age and social class.

Table 30 (p. 295) presents some of the results.

These distributions—particularly for males—are in accord generally with what is known on the national plane about family size distributions and social class. It is of interest to note in addition to the regularities from class to class:

(a) Males. The proportions childless do not differ markedly by social class.

(b) Males. There is a slight tendency for the proportions of donors with 4+ children to be inversely related to social class (which is what one might have expected).

(c) Females. The distributions at the younger ages are, of course, affected by the fact that expectant and nursing mothers are ineligible as blood donors.

(d) Females. With the exception of S.C. IV–V (where the numbers are small) there are no markedly discrepant differences in the distributions.

Overall we conclude that donors in all social classes with larger families (or whose larger families had grown up) made their contribution to the National Blood Transfusion Service along with the childless and those with 1–3 children. Looked at from the perspective of motivation, it may be significant that of all married donors of all classes aged 30–44 9 per cent had 4+ children. In S.C. IV–V the proportion is as high as 12 per cent. The thought may have been present among these donors that their children might need blood transfusions in the future.

For Table 31 we have extracted the data from the 1961 Census Fertility Tables.[1]

In comparing these distributions with those for All Classes (Female) in Table 30 the effects of childbearing at ages 18–29 are apparent. At ages 30–44 there is remarkably little difference especially when we remember, once again, how the 'sample' of 914 married women was 'selected' in contrast to the census collection of data for over 10,000,000 married women. At ages 45–64, proportionately

---

[1] Registrar General, Fertility Tables Nos. 1 and 32, 1961 Census (the 1966 sample census data were not available when this study went to press).

TABLE 31
Percentage Distribution of Number of Children of Married Women in England and Wales by Age (1961)

No. of children	Age 18–29	30–44	45–64	Total
	%	%	%	%
0	33	14	20	20
1–3	64	73	65	68
4+	3	13	15	12
	100	100	100	100
Number	2,006,385	3,945,850	4,377,604	10,329,839

fewer childless married women are donors whilst those with 1–3 children report a higher proportion and those with 4+ children a somewhat lower proportion than the national distributions.

To complete this analysis of family size we include one more table because of the bearing of this information on the question of family blood donor motivation:

TABLE 32
Percentage by Age of Married Women Donors with no Children and their Mean Family Sizes compared with 1961 Census Data for England and Wales

Age	Percentage of married women donors with no children	Percentage of all women, England and Wales, with no children	Mean family size of married women donors	Mean family size of all women, England and Wales
	%	%		
20–4	84	44	0·25	0·83
25–9	36	24	0·90	1·45
30–4	13	15	1·70	1·90
35–9	10	13	1·99	2·06
40–4	15	13	1·93	2·10
45–9	10	15	2·05	2·02
50–4	13	20	1·83	1·92
55–9	12	23	1·80	1·90
60–4	24	24	1·54	2·00
All ages 18–64			1·61	1·83

297

After age 29, the percentages of married women donors without children in this survey are lower than the national averages for all women. If these figures are accepted as broadly typical and comparable, it follows that married women with children are more likely to be blood donors than childless married women. The differences in mean family size after age 35 are small though it has to be remembered (i) that the donor averages exclude 'ineligibles' for reproductive and health reasons and (ii) that the national averages include spinsters, widows and the divorced as well as the 'non-healthy'.

So far in this appendix all the data we have analysed relate to a population of donors; not to the number of donations given by each donor. Apart from a small number of first-time donors (15 male and 2 female) and 24 first-time Defence Services donors, all other donors had given at least one previous donation.

With the information provided on the questionnaire about the number of previous donations (checked by reference to donor records) we could, in fact, repeat the whole of this analysis by age, sex, marital status, social class, session type and so forth in terms of the total number of donations contributed by the sample population.

We do not, however, propose to do so. The results do not add materially to the general conclusions we have already reached. For those who may be interested we presented some raw data in Table 25 and other tables may be obtained on request from the writer.

There is, however, one aspect of this mine of information on numbers that has a bearing on the general theme developed in Chapter 7 and elsewhere; it relates to the consistency, regularity and attachment of these donors to the voluntary activity of giving blood—for this is no transient population of donors motivated by sudden crises or urgent television appeals for blood. We present below, therefore, a limited set of statistics.

Excluding the first-timers, we were left with a total of 3616 (male 2167, female 1449) for which we had data about the number of donations and other characteristics.[1] In all, this population had contributed 43,391 pints of blood.

Of the total, 62 per cent was contributed by males and 38 per cent by females. These percentages are not very different from those in Table 8 in which it was shown that, in terms of the *number* of donors, 60 per cent were males and 40 per cent females.

[1] In the social class analysis, a small number were excluded because they were either economically inactive, retired, members of the Defence Services or unclassifiable.

TABLE 33

Percentage Distribution of Total Blood Donated by Numbers and Sex[1]

Sex	Number of donations (the figures in brackets refer, first, to the total of pints of blood donated and, second, to the number of donors)				Totals
	1–4	5–14	15–29	30+	
	%	%	%	%	%
M.	7	32	36	25	100
	(1798:719)	(8690:869)	(9698:431)	(6660:148)	(26,846:2167)
F.	8	36	31	25	100
	(1350:540)	(5880:588)	(5130:228)	(4185:93)	(16,545:1449)

[1] This table excludes the current donation. The multipliers used in each donation group were: 1–4 2·5; 5–14 10; 15–29 22·5; 30+ 45.

One of the striking facts about Table 33 is that despite the intervention of periods of ineligibility for reproduction and child-rearing the percentage distributions for women are very close to those for men. Those who gave most—the long-service donors—contributed, both sexes alike, 25 per cent of all the blood donated by the sample. Of the men among the long-service donors, 91 per cent were married and 9 per cent were single—somewhat higher proportions of the married than in Table 24 for the donor population and the general population of England and Wales. Among the women the percentages were: married 62 per cent, single 25 per cent and widowed/divorced/separated 13 per cent. The marital status pattern is thus very different for women. Again we find a substantial contribution being made by widows (in the W/D/S category they were, in fact, nearly all widows) the majority of whom were in S.C. III–IV.

To assess the respective contributions of the five social classes it is necessary to analyse the data by age. Unless this is done allowance is not made for the different class and age structures in the donor population. In Table 34 (p. 300) we use three broad age groups.

In general, the number of donations increases with age in all social classes and for both sexes. It is interesting to note, however, that the contribution of relatively new donors (those in the group 1–4) at ages 45–64 still constitutes a sizeable proportion of all the blood donated by that age group: this is particularly true of men

299

TABLE 34
Percentage Distribution of the Number of Donations by Sex, Age and Social Class[1]

MALE — Age 18-29

S.C.	Number of donations 1-4 %	5-14 %	15-29 %	30+ %	Total %	No. of donors	Total blood (in pints)
I	40	60	0	0	100	62	432
II	54	43	3	0	100	124	787
III	56	39	4	1	100	382	2443
IV	50	44	6	0	100	64	450
V	60	30	10	0	100	10	68
D.S. (S.C. III-V)	86	14	0	0	100	104	365

FEMALE

S.C.	Number of donations 1-4 %	5-14 %	15-29 %	30+ %	Total %	No. of donors	Total blood (in pints)
I	65	35	5	0	100	40	230
II	79	19	1	1	100	88	410
III	74	25	1	0	100	219	993
IV	87	10	3	0	100	40	148
V	87	13	0	0	100	8	28
D.S. (S.C. III-V)	75	25	0	0	100	4	18

							Age 30–44							
I	12	52	31	5	100	104	1517	20	59	17	4	100	59	695
II	19	46	26	9	100	175	2637	34	48	15	3	100	117	1222
III	22	46	27	5	100	461	6163	28	50	19	3	100	202	2291
IV	37	38	24	1	100	74	798	30	52	10	8	100	50	591
V	11	56	22	11	100	9	143	33	67	0	0	100	6	45
D.S.	25	75	0	0	100	4	33	33	33	33	0	100	3	35
							Age 45–64							
I	20	36	35	9	100	56	902	13	45	31	11	100	45	755
II	12	32	33	23	100	126	2687	17	36	33	14	100	127	2267
III	15	35	32	18	100	288	5563	19	42	25	14	100	199	3291
IV	27	35	28	10	100	79	1188	30	36	23	11	100	53	770
V	21	21	29	29	100	14	308	25	37	25	13	100	8	125
D.S.	50	0	50	0	100	2	25	0	27	64	9	100	11	233

¹ This table excludes the current donation.

and women in social classes IV–V. Other points which emerge
from this table include:
  (i) The contribution of male donors at age 18–29 giving 15–29
      donations—particularly among manual workers.
 (ii) The contribution of long-service donors (those giving 30+
      donations) among both sexes at age 30–44.
(iii) The sex differences in the total of blood donations by age, thus:

	Total Pints of Blood	
	Male	Female
Age 18–29	4,545	1,827
Age 30–44	11,291	4,879
Age 45–64	10,673	7,441

It has to be remembered, of course, that these contributions were
not all made during the specified years; they may have been spread
over a long period of life.

Lastly, we summarize in Table 35 the social class proportions:

TABLE 35
*Percentage Distribution of Total Blood Donated by Age, Sex and
Social Class*[1]

	MALE	FEMALE
	Age 18–29	
	%	%
Social class I	10	13
II	17	22
III	60	55
IV	11	8
V	2	2
	100	100
	Age 30–44	
Social class I	14	14
II	23	25
III	55	48
IV	7	12
V	1	1
	100	100

[1] The small amounts of blood donated by members of the Defence Services
have been proportionately distributed in this table among S.C. III, IV and V.
This table also excludes current donations.

Age 45–64

Social class	I	9	10
	II	25	30
	III	52	47
	IV	11	11
	V	3	2
		100	100

A comparison of these social class percentages with those given in Table 26 for the donor population shows only small differences. There is some tendency in Table 35 for S.C. I–II (both sexes) to exhibit higher percentages and, conversely, for S.C. IV–V to exhibit lower ones. The reasons given earlier in this appendix to account for at least part of the over-representation of S.C. I–II and under-representation of S.C. IV–V are equally applicable to Table 35.

In Chapter 7 we attempt to summarize this analysis of the characteristics of donors.

Appendix 5
Donor Survey Questionnaire

CONFIDENTIAL   *Please bring this form*
                                        to your session

LONDON UNIVERSITY STUDY OF
VOLUNTARY BLOOD DONORS

(If you have any difficulty in completing this form, Miss West, State Registered Nurse, will be at your session to help you and to collect your form.)

1. How many blood donations have you given?............ What is your blood group?............
2. Have you ever received a blood transfusion? Yes............ No............
    (Please tick correct answer)
3. Have any of the following persons (*not including yourself*) ever given or received blood? Please write 'yes' or 'no' in the appropriate space. Cross out those parts which do not apply.

	Parent	*Husband/Wife*	*Children*	*Other relative or friend*
Given	....	....	....	....
Received	....	....	....	....

4. Please tick on the list below the *main* reason why you give blood?
    .... a. General desire to help people
    .... b. To repay in some way a transfusion given to someone I know
    .... c. In response to an appeal for blood
    .... d. Some of my friends/colleagues give blood and encouraged me to join them
    .... e. Another reason (please state)
5. Could you say *why* you *first* decided to become a blood donor? Please write in the space below.

6. What more do you think the service could do to persuade people to be blood donors? Any suggestions you may have which might make the need for donors better known would be appreciated.

Please write in the space below.

In order to sort out the information we obtain into various groups of voluntary blood donors, we would like to know a little about your family background. We would be grateful, therefore, if you would answer the following questions. We would remind you that we *DO NOT* ask for your name or address and it is *NOT* entered on this form.

7. Age .... 8. Sex—Male .... 9. Married ....
   Female .... Single ....
   (Please tick correct answer) Widowed or ....
   Divorced ....

10. How many children have you? ....

11. In which country were you born?

12. What is the occupation of the *chief earner* in your family and in what industry or type of business does he or she work?
    Occupation
    Industry

13. If you are not the chief earner in the family what is your occupation and industry?
    Occupation
    Industry

14. Is the chief earner at present employed? ....
    or unemployed? ....
    (Please tick correct answer)

15. Into which of the following income groups does the chief earner in your family come?
    Approximate weekly income before Tax: (please tick one of the following)

    Less than £10 ....
    £10 but less than £15 ....
    £15 but less than £20 ....
    £20 but less than £30 ....
    £30 but less than £50 ....
    More than £50 ....

16. If you are a *married woman* are you in paid employment?
    Please tick Yes ....
    No ....

Appendix 6
Analysis of Blood Donor Motives

(Survey 1967)

JOHN BEDDINGTON

Rate of Response

The rate of response of donors to the non-factual questions and particularly questions 4–5 was influenced mainly by the time available for donors to complete the questionnaire. This effect was more noticeable in the response to question 5, where answers of necessity had to be first considered and then put into words than in question 4 where the check-list provided afforded an easy solution for those with limited time.

The differences in the conduct of the survey between the General Public sessions and the Institutional and Defence Services sessions which resulted in I. and D.S. donors being left with a limited amount of time has already been noted.[1] The effect of these differences is indicated below:

TABLE 36
Response Rate of Donors to Question 5

Type of donor	% Not answering	Total number of donors
All Donors	12·2	3821
General Public	9·7	2658
Institutions	17·2	1029
Defence Services	24·9	134

An analysis of the response rates of other sub-sets of the sample did not indicate that there was any appreciable difference in the response rates of donors with different demographic and social characteristics.

[1] See Chapter 7.

The Questions

Two questions in the questionnaire were aimed at eliciting answers concerning the reasons blood donors have for giving blood:

Q. 4.   Please tick on the list below the *main* reason why you give blood?
  (a) General desire to help people
  (b) To repay in some way a transfusion given to someone I know
  (c) In response to an appeal for blood
  (d) Some of my friends/colleagues give blood and encouraged me to join them
  (e) Another reason (please state)

Q. 5.   Could you say why you *first* decided to become a blood donor?

The choice of questions, in retrospect, was unfortunate, in that many donors were confused by the wording and clearly did not understand what sort of answers were expected.[1] The general idea behind the choice of questions was to elicit, in response to question 4, the main motives blood donors have for giving and continuing to give blood; and in response to question 5 to discover what factors had been instrumental in influencing the donors' original decision to give blood. The wording of the questions was chosen accordingly and the check-list for question 4 was taken from an American Red Cross survey in the hope that some comparative data would be obtained. This check-list was the source of confusion for it contained answers of just the type that were appropriate in answer to question 5, namely, items (c) and (d) described the sort of factors influential in a donor's original decision to give blood, but were not indicative of his reasons for continuing to do so. Not surprisingly, this confusion was reflected in the answers given to the questions.

The response to question 4 was, therefore, largely uninterpretable. Many donors ticked more than one item on the check-list, others ticked items and wrote replies to the open-ended section and some ticked all four categories. The result was that it was impossible to determine whether these reflected a combination of main motives, a main motive and the factor(s) originally influencing the decision to give blood or perhaps more likely general confusion. The relative frequency of the types of response to question 4 is given in Table 37.

[1] This became apparent as the survey progressed. Unfortunately little could be done at this late stage especially as the surveyors were committed to being as inconspicuous as possible.

TABLE 37

Percentage Distribution of the Answers Ticked[1] in Answer to Question 4

	a	b	c	d	Total
No. of answers	2051	297	1287	461	4096[2]
%	50·1	7·2	31·4	11·2	100

[1] There were 350 donors who answered by writing in a further reason in Section *e* of question 4. (This figure includes donors who only answered Section 4*e* and donors who in addition ticked one or more of *a*, *b*, *c*, *d*.)

[2] Includes multiple answers.

The confusion manifesting itself in the answers given to question 4 not unnaturally had some effect on the replies to question 5; in this case, however, the result was by no means so confusing. Answers to question 5 fell broadly into two groups; first, those which mentioned factors involved in the initial decision to give blood and were in fact the sort of answer that had been originally hoped for and, second, those which described the reasons why donors give and continue to give blood.

To attempt to distinguish between these two types of answer in individual cases would have often involved a degree of interpretation of the donor's answer that was not warranted by the information provided. However, it will be seen that the answers as categorized below can in many cases (though not all) be characterized in this way.

The analysis of the answers given to question 5 set out in Tables 38 to 42 must, therefore, be treated with caution as it indicates neither the relative frequency of the main motives of blood donors nor does it indicate the relative frequency of the type of factors influencing the blood donor's original decision to give blood. It simply sets out the relative frequency of the types of answers donors gave to question 5 and how this relative frequency varied in relation to certain donor characteristics.

The results are, we believe, of value if they are viewed in a broad sense; they indicate the main areas of sentiment and motive expressed and written down in the donor's own words. We claim no more than that; this is what 3325 donors, given an opportunity to consider the question and to write an answer, had to say. The difficult task then was to summarize and categorize these written responses into some sort of conceptual order. After much trial and discussion we finally settled on 14 categories and each answer to question 5 was allocated to one of them. Inevitably, in this process, the vivid and individual quality of many of the answers disappeared into neutral percentages. However, in Chapter 13, where we attempt to draw out from this analysis some of the central conceptions expressed, we also use as thematic illustrations the actual words of some of the donors themselves.

In addition to the value of analysing the answers in this way, we think it was useful to ask questions about motives for there are certain lessons to be drawn which should be helpful in any future survey of a similar kind. For one thing we learnt that we should not have imported the American check-list; this was the major cause of confusion. The decision to include it was taken at a late stage in the vain hope (as we now see) of obtaining comparative data; hence, it was not unfortunately included in the questionnaire which was first piloted. This is not to say, however, that we would eliminate all check-list questions from future surveys; we are, however, as a result of our experience, extremely sceptical of the applicability of this particular method to the complex problem of understanding and analysing the motives of blood donors.

The Answers to Question 5

In categorizing the answers given to this question the attempt was made to bring together, into one category, answers which expressed a very similar general sentiment concerning blood donation and answers which described similar experiences involved in the original decision to give blood. Of necessity this process involved varying degrees of interpretation of the donor's answer. In most cases, however, not only the general sense but also the wording of the answers were very similar. In other cases where manifestly the categories employed were not homogeneous the percentage composition of the category by type of answer is noted.[1] In Tables 38 to 42 the relative frequency of the categories is given for various sub-sets of the sample, these being determined by the sex, age, marital status and social class of the donors concerned.

1. *Altruism general and particular (26·4 per cent of answers)*

The general sentiment expressed by donors in this category of answer was a desire to help. The category was not homogeneous and answers fell into four distinct types:

---

[1] Due to a necessary limitation on the length of this appendix the variation of this composition within categories for various sub-sections of the sample has not been given.

(A)   By far the most numerous was a very general answer in which the wording employed was often that of question 4 (a) 'A general desire to help people'. Some donors even employed ditto marks.

The three other types of answer all singled out for help particular groups; these groups were of varying degrees of abstraction:

(B)   This type of answer consisted of donors who stated that they gave blood to help society or the state.

(C)   Donor answers of this type singled out for help the National Health Service in its various manifestations from 'Doctors and Nurses' to 'Medical Research' and, more generally, 'the Health Service'.

(D)   The intended recipients of aid in this type of answer were 'Babies'.

It seems likely that category 1 was inflated by the influence of item (a) on the check-list in question 4 and that some donors gave type (A) answers of this category and specifically added 'Babies'. This is partially corroborated by the information set out in Table 38. It was noted further that the variation of the frequency of this category from General Public donors to Institutional and Defence Service donors was brought about by an increase in answers of type (A), not in an increase in answers of types (B)–(D).

The overall composition of answers in this category (Altruism General and Particular) was:

	%
Type (A)	89·6
Type (B)	5·6
Type (C)	3·5
Type (D)	1·3
	100

2.   *Gratitude for Good Health (1·4 per cent of answers)*

This category consisted of answers in which donors stated that they had been healthy all their lives and gave blood because they were grateful for this. The relative frequency of this category as would be expected increased with increasing age,[1] but less easily explicable is the finding that it was more frequent among women donors than men.[2] It may be that in any explanation of this differ-ence 'good health' might need to be interpreted broadly to include

---

[1] See Table 41.   [2] See Table 42.

the social and psychological as well as the physical aspects of health.

3. *Reciprocity (9·8 per cent of answers)*

The central idea in this category of answers was that the process of blood donation and transfusion is essentially, or should essentially be, a reciprocal one. There were three broad types of answer:

(E) Donors who stated that they were giving blood to repay a transfusion that they themselves had once received.

(F) Donors who stated that they were giving blood to repay a transfusion given to a relative or close friend.

(G) Donors who stated that they were giving blood because in the future they or a member of their family might need it.

The relative frequency of this category did not vary much within sub-sets of the sample except for the fact that it figured less prominently among donors over the age of 60.[1] Type (G) answers were, as would be expected, most frequent among married men.

The percentage composition of this category (Reciprocity) was:

	%
Type (E)	17·4
Type (F)	43·0
Type (G)	39·6
	100

4. *Replacement (0·8 per cent of answers)*

The general notion here was a conviction among donors that at least one member of a family should give blood. Various reasons were advanced by donors to explain why certain members of their family could no longer give blood; the respondents then went on to state that they had taken their place.

The numbers involved in this category were few and thus any interpretation must be questionable; however, its non-occurrence among widowed, divorced and separated donors is rather what one would expect.[2]

5. *Awareness of need for blood (6·4 per cent of answers)*

In this category we have brought together a combination of types of answer in which the main idea was that donors gave blood because they had become aware of the need for blood. The different

---

[1] See Table 41.   [2] See Table 40.

types of answer all involved different descriptions of the circumstances in which donors had come to be aware of the need.

(H)   Donors of this type had become aware of the need for blood through their job or, in a few cases, voluntary work. The jobs mentioned were hospital work of all sorts, the police and firemen; voluntary work was generally associated with medical activities such as the Red Cross and St John's Ambulance Brigade.

(I)   These donors had become aware of the need for blood whilst experiencing a spell of hospital inpatient care (but not involving a transfusion).

(J)   This category consisted of donors who had become aware of the need for blood while visiting relatives or friends in hospital.

(K)   More dramatic were donors who came to realise the need for blood after witnessing accidents of some kind. Motoring accidents were usually the ones mentioned; however, several donors had been made aware by television coverage of accidents and, in particular, the Aberfan disaster was mentioned.

(L)   In this category were donors who stated that because *they* were motorists they recognized the need for blood. Presumably the Road Safety campaigns and the reporting of road accident statistics had some influence here.

All the answers under this heading suggest that these donors, having become aware of the need, accepted an individual responsibility for making a personal contribution. They made the connection; the responsibility was not left to someone else or the state.

The relative frequency of this category did not vary much in sub-sets of the sample, although it was much more prominent among General Public donors.[1]

The percentage composition of this category was:

	%
Type (H)	48·2
Type (I)	21·4
Type (J)	5·4
Type (K)	14·3
Type (L)	10·7
	100

[1] See Table 38.

6.   Duty (3·5 per cent of answers)

The general idea expressed in this category was that donors gave blood because they felt that they had a duty to do so. The answers were broadly of two types:

(M)   Donors who indicated that they believed they had a religious duty to give blood.[1]

(N)   Donors who felt that they had a duty to society to give blood.

There is, of course, some overlap here between answers allocated to this category and to categories 1 and 5. Those indicating or stressing the giving of blood as a 'duty', secular or religious, were placed in this category.

There appeared to be no marked fluctuations in the frequency within sub-sets of the sample.

The percentage composition of this category was:

	%
Type (M)	16·1
Type (N)	83·9
	100

7.   War Effort (6·7 per cent of answers)

A substantial number of donors first gave blood during the Second World War. This category consists, therefore, of donors who mentioned this as the reason for deciding to become a donor.

Naturally, answers of this kind only occurred among donors over the age of 40[2] and, surprisingly, were more frequent among women than men.[3] It was also more frequent in social classes I–II.[4]

8.   The Defence Services since 1945 (5·0 per cent of answers)

This category, partly associated with the preceding one, comprises donors who said that they first gave blood as members of the Services. Most of them were married men aged 25–39 in social class III.[5]

Some of the answers indicate that the men became donors at least partly because of certain benefits, e.g. 48-hour passes, being excused drill, etc. Other answers suggest that the act of donating was not entirely voluntary; that there were, as we have suggested

---

[1] Donors were not asked to state their religion. Some did so; a number of faiths were mentioned including one Buddhist.
[2] See Table 41.   [3] See Table 39.
[4] See Table 42.   [5] See Tables 39 to 42.

in our typology of donors (see Chapter 5) external pressures 'to volunteer'. However, the majority of donors placed in this category did not specify either benefits or pressures; the most usual wording employed took the form 'I answered an appeal for blood while in the Army'. The fact that after leaving the Defence Services they continued to donate does not suggest that material considerations were of great importance.

9. *Rare Blood Group (1·1 per cent of answers)*

The general idea expressed in this type of answer was that the discovery that they were in a rare blood group was instrumental in the donor deciding to give blood. Such answers further imply that because one's blood is rare or unique there is a particular responsibility to make it available to others who may need it.

This category of answer was more frequent among women.[1] The explanation may lie in the practice of giving Rh-negative women undergoing hospital care a card informing them that they may have Rh-negative blood.

10. *To obtain some benefit (1·8 per cent of answers)*

Donors in this category stated that they either originally gave, or continued to give, blood to obtain some benefit. Answers fell into three distinct types:

(O) Donors who originally gave in order to discover their blood group.
(P) Donors who gave blood in order that they should have a regular health check by the Blood Transfusion Service.
(Q) Donors who believed that the process of blood donation was a benefit to their health. Particular benefits cited were that it cured nose bleeding, reduced the incidence of migraine attacks or generally made the donor feel fitter.

The higher incidence of this category among Defence Service donors[2] was largely due to donors who gave type (O) answers.

The percentage composition of this category was:

	%
Type (O)	37·5
Type (P)	25·0
Type (Q)	37·5
	100

---

[1] See Table 39.

[2] See Table 38.

11. *Personal Appeal (13·2 per cent of answers)*

This category consisted of donors who stated that they had been originally influenced to give blood by encouragement, requests or appeals made by individuals well known to them; either relatives, friends or colleagues at work. Such answers occurred more frequently among younger donors, single donors and general public donors.[1]

12. *General Appeal for Donors (18·0 per cent of answers)*

In this category were included all donors who stated that they had originally been influenced by an organized appeal made by the Blood Transfusion Service. The predominant form of communication cited was a personal appeal to the donor by a member of the Service, although all forms of the mass media were mentioned by different donors. These answers of a somewhat general nature occurred most frequently in the higher social classes among donors attending general public sessions.[2]

13. *Miscellaneous (5 per cent of answers)*

All types of answer occurring less than 20 times in the whole of the sample were put in this category. They varied greatly, ranging from the obviously frivolous to long and serious essays of a personal nature. Most of them were written by younger donors.[3]

14. *More than one type of answer (0·9 per cent of answers)*

Some donors gave answers which included more than one of the categories we have employed in this analysis.

Most of these donors seemed to recognize that the decision to give blood is often a complex process and that, consequently, they could not distinguish a single or predominant motive.

Summary

The temptation to speculate in detail about this material and the accompanying Tables 38 to 42 is strong, particularly as we are reporting on the first detailed survey of its kind in the world about blood donors and their characteristics and motives. Many of the answers and their frequency distributions among different groups of donors raise intriguing questions about motives for first giving blood and, equally important, for continuing to give blood. Inevitably, they also raise questions about the nature of the society and

[1] See Tables 38, 40, 41.   [2] See Tables 38 and 42.   [3] See Table 41.

TABLE 38

Percentage Distribution of Categories of Donor Answers to Question 5 for All Donors and by Session Type

Session type	1 Altruism %	2 Gratitude for good health %	3 Reciprocity %	4 Replacement %	5 Awareness of need %	6 Duty %	7 War effort %	8 Defence services %	9 Rare blood group %	10 Benefit %	11 Personal appeal %	12 General appeal %	13 Miscellaneous %	14 More than one answer %	Total %
General Public	23·7	1·9	9·4	1·0	7·5	3·5	8·0	4·9	1·3	1·7	15·4	18·5	2·4	0·8	100 (2400)
Institutions	32·8	0·6	10·5	0·2	3·9	3·5	4·1	6·0	0·7	1·7	7·4	16·9	10·6	1·1	100 (824)
Defence Services	35·8	0·0	11·0	0·0	2·9	2·9	0·0	0·0	0·0	4·9	10·0	13·8	17·8	0·9	100 (101)
All	26·4	1·4	9·8	0·8	6·4	3·5	6·7	5·0	1·1	1·8	13·2	18·0	5·0	0·9	100 (3325)

TABLE 39

Percentage Distribution of Categories of Donor Answers to Question 5 by Sex

Sex	1 Altruism %	2 Gratitude for good health %	3 Reciprocity %	4 Replacement %	5 Awareness of need %	6 Duty %	7 War effort %	8 Defence services %	9 Rare blood group %	10 Benefit %	11 Personal appeal %	12 General appeal %	13 Miscellaneous %	14 More than one answer %	Total %
Male	25·3	0·6	9·4	0·8	5·3	3·7	5·1	8·2	0·7	1·8	13·3	18·9	6·0	0·9	100 (1976)
Female	27·8	2·7	10·4	0·6	8·2	3·4	9·2	0·3	1·8	1·6	13·0	16·6	3·5	0·9	100 (1349)

TABLE 40
Percentage Distribution of Categories of Donor Answers to Question 5 by Marital Status

Marital status	1 Altruism	2 Gratitude for good health	3 Recipro-city	4 Replace-ment	5 Aware-ness of need	6 Duty	7 War effort	8 Defence services	9 Rare blood group	10 Benefit	11 Personal appeal	12 General appeal	13 Miscel-laneous	14 More than one answer	Total
	%	%	%	%	%	%	%	%	%	%	%	%	%	%	%
Married	24·5	1·3	10·5	0·8	6·5	3·8	7·7	6·3	1·4	1·6	11·6	18·9	4·1	0·8	100 (2373)
Single	31·6	1·0	7·9	0·7	6·7	3·0	3·7	1·4	0·7	2·0	15·8	16·8	7·5	1·2	100 (826)
W/D/S	31·3	3·9	13·3	0·0	6·2	1·5	8·6	2·3	0·0	2·3	11·8	12·5	5·5	0·8	100 (126)

TABLE 41
Percentage Distribution of Categories of Donor Answers to Question 5 by Age

Age (both sexes)	1 Altruism	2 Gratitude for good health	3 Recipro-city	4 Replace-ment	5 Aware-ness of need	6 Duty	7 War effort	8 Defence services	9 Rare blood group	10 Benefit	11 Personal appeal	12 General appeal	13 Miscel-laneous	14 More than one answer	Total
	%	%	%	%	%	%	%	%	%	%	%	%	%	%	%
18–19	33·5	0·0	12·0	0·6	4·5	3·9	0·0	0·0	0·6	1·9	19·0	12·0	11·4	0·6	100 (156)
20–24	33·5	1·4	9·1	0·1	5·3	3·2	0·0	0·0	0·9	2·5	17·8	16·6	8·5	1·1	100 (560)
25–29	29·7	1·4	10·1	1·2	7·1	2·9	0·0	5·2	1·2	2·3	15·3	18·3	4·4	0·9	100 (442)
30–34	23·2	0·8	8·7	0·0	6·4	3·2	0·0	16·9	0·2	2·1	13·4	19·5	4·8	0·8	100 (373)
35–39	23·4	0·2	10·9	0·7	7·0	6·2	0·0	10·5	1·2	2·0	14·3	18·3	4·6	0·7	100 (414)
40–44	23·1	2·0	10·4	1·6	6·0	2·0	11·4	3·4	1·6	1·2	13·5	20·2	3·4	0·2	100 (386)
45–49	22·9	1·8	10·9	1·5	6·2	4·4	17·8	3·4	0·6	0·4	7·5	18·6	2·7	1·3	100 (382)
50–54	21·3	2·2	12·7	0·3	8·7	3·7	14·2	1·8	2·2	1·4	8·7	18·9	2·9	1·0	100 (275)
55–59	23·0	3·1	9·3	0·0	6·6	2·6	19·9	2·2	1·7	1·7	8·8	16·3	3·1	1·7	100 (226)
60–64[1]	27·1	0·8	1·8	1·8	7·2	3·6	24·3	1·8	1·8	0·0	7·2	20·8	1·8	0·0	100 (110)

[1] Excluding 1 male aged 65.

317

TABLE 42

*Percentage Distribution of Categories of Donor Answers
to Question 5 by Social Class[1]*

Social class	1 Altruism	2 Gratitude for good health	3 Reciprocity	4 Replacement	5 Awareness of need	6 Duty	7 War effort	8 Defence services	9 Rare blood group	10 Benefit	11 Personal appeal	12 General appeal	13 Miscellaneous	14 More than one answer	Total
	%	%	%	%	%	%	%	%	%	%	%	%	%	%	%
I	18·3	0·5	9·1	1·4	4·3	3·9	7·7	5·0	1·1	1·1	17·6	23·4	5·7	0·9	100 (364)
II	24·7	2·1	7·2	0·9	6·3	5·3	7·4	3·8	1·2	1·1	14·6	20·0	4·3	1·1	100 (726)
III	26·8	1·3	11·0	0·7	7·5	3·1	6·0	6·4	1·1	1·7	12·6	16·4	4·7	0·7	100 (1627)
IV	33·9	1·0	11·1	0·6	5·5	2·1	5·3	3·7	1·8	2·4	8·3	18·8	4·3	1·2	100 (325)
V	33·6	1·7	10·5	0·0	5·2	1·7	3·5	1·7	1·7	1·7	22·9	10·6	5·2	0·0	100 (57)
Defence Services	33·6	0·8	10·1	0·0	5·0	2·5	2·5	1·7	0·0	4·2	9·3	14·4	15·1	0·8	100 (119)

[1] The total number of donors in this table differs from the totals in preceding tables because some donors could not be classified. The total for the Defence Services also differs from that given in Table 39 because some donor wives had husbands in the Services.

the texture of human relationships within that society which permits or encourages the kind of responses depicted in this analysis. These broader themes are pursued elsewhere; in this appendix we resist firmly the desire to speculate in detail.

Considering the ways in which these data were obtained, the subjective processes involved in categorizing and coding the answers and other factors, we are struck by the regularities and consistencies depicted in these tables. There are no large inexplicable differences. When the answers are analysed by sex, age, marital status and social class there is a substantial measure of uniformity and homogeneity.

Over two-fifths of all the answers fell into the categories of 'Altruism', 'Reciprocity', 'Replacement' and 'Duty'. Nearly a third represented voluntary responses to personal and general appeals for blood. A further 6 per cent responded to an 'Awareness of Need'. These seven categories accounted for nearly 80 per cent of the answers suggesting a high sense of social responsibility towards the needs of other members of the society. Perhaps this is one of the outstanding impressions which emerges from the analysis.

Appendix 7
Acknowledgements

The author wishes gratefully to acknowledge the assistance he has received from the following individuals and agencies over the period 1964–70 in the form of advice and information of a technical and statistical nature. Some of these sources are cited in the text; others have not been specifically named. All those who have helped the author cannot, of course, be held responsible for any errors of fact or interpretation in this book.

Professor J. Garrott Allen, Stanford University School of Medicine, California.

Dr J. B. Alsever, Blood Services, Scottsdale, Arizona.

American Blood Bank Service, Inc., Miami, Florida.

American Medical Association, Chicago.

Senator K. Anderson, Minister of State for Customs and Excise, Sydney, New South Wales.

Armour Pharmaceutical International, Chicago.

Aurora Area Blood Bank, Aurora, Illinois.

Banco de Sangre Metropolitano, Inc., Santurce, Puerto Rico.

Blood Bank of Hawaii, Honolulu, Hawaii.

Mr P. Carlinger, Pioneer Blood Service, Inc., New York.

Central Blood Bank of Pittsburgh, Pittsburgh.

Dr A. S. Chrisman, American National Red Cross, Washington.

Commonwealth of Massachusetts, Department of Public Health, Boston.

Community Blood Bank of the Kansas City Area, Inc., Missouri.

Community Blood Bank of Marion County, Inc., Indianapolis.

Greater New York Blood Program, New York.

Dr T. J. Greenwalt, Medical Director, American Red Cross, Washington.

Mrs D. Greystoke, Social Medicine Research Unit, London School of Hygiene and Tropical Medicine, London.

Dr B. G. Grobbelaar, Natal Blood Transfusion Service, Durban, South Africa.

Dr B. Gullbring, Karolinska Hospital, Stockholm, Sweden.

Mr J. B. Jennings, Operations Research Center, Massachusetts Institute of Technology, Cambridge, Massachusetts.

John Elliott Blood Bank, Inc., Miami, Florida.

Kabi Pharmaceuticals Ltd., London and Stockholm.
Professor T. Kamegai, Toho University School of Medicine, Tokyo, Japan.
Dr A. Kellner, New York Blood Center, New York.
Dr S. V. Kevy, Children's Hospital Medical Center, Boston.
Dr R. S. Koff, Massachusetts General Hospital, Boston.
Dr L. Lasagna, Johns Hopkins University, Baltimore.
Lilly Research Laboratories, Indianapolis.
Senator Edward V. Long, United States Senate, Washington.
Dr R. L. Mainwaring, Oakwood Hospital, Dearborn, Michigan.
Dr I. Malootian, Boston University Medical Center, Boston.
Dr C. C. Mason, Chicago Blood Donor Service, Inc., Chicago.
Merck Sharp and Dohme International, New York.
Dr I. Merriam, Social Security Administration, Department of Health, Education, and Welfare, Washington.
Milwaukee Blood Center, Inc., Milwaukee, Wisconsin.
Mount Sinai Medical Research Foundation, Chicago.
Dr R. Naito, The Green Cross Corporation, Osaka, Japan.
New York Academy of Medicine, New York.
Dr H. A. Oberman, University of Michigan, Ann Arbor, Michigan.
Dr J. P. O'Riordan, Blood Transfusion Service Board, Dublin, Eire.
Ortho Research Foundation, Raritan, New Jersey.
Österreichisches Institut Für Haemoderivate, Vienna.
Parke-Davis & Co., Detroit Michigan.
Peninsula Memorial Blood Bank, Burlingame, California.
Dr R. B. Pennell, Blood Research Institute, Inc., Jamaica Plain, Massachusetts.
Mr. L. Perlis, American Federation of Labour and Congress of Industrial Organizations, Washington.
Pfizer Diagnostics, New York.
Pharmaceutical Manufacturers Association, Washington.
Pitman-Moore, Division of the Dow Chemical Co., Indianapolis.
Professor and Mrs Garth Plowman, London School of Economics, London.
Dr S. M. Rabson, Los Angeles, California.
Sir Benjamin Rycroft, London.
Mr P. V. Rycroft, South Eastern Regional Eye Bank, Sussex.
Sacramento Medical Foundation Blood Bank, Sacramento, California.
San Diego Blood Bank, San Diego, California.
Dr P. J. Schmidt, Blood Bank Department, National Institutes of Health, Bethesda, Maryland.
Professor Alvin Schorr, Brandeis University, Waltham, Massachusetts.
Dr M. Shapiro, South African Blood Transfusion Service, Johannesburg, South Africa.
Dr G. Silver, Department of Health, Education, and Welfare, Washington.
Dr V. N. Slee, Commission on Professional Hospital Activities, Ann Arbor, Michigan.

South African Embassy, London.
Spokane and Inland Blood Bank, Spokane, Washington.
Community Blood Bank and Service, Inc., Hoboken, New Jersey.
Community Blood Center, Dayton, Ohio.
Dr J. P. Conrad, Department of Corrections, Sacramento, California.
Courtland Laboratories, Los Angeles.
Cutter Laboratories, Berkeley, California.
Dr R. Czajkowski, late of King County Central Blood Bank, Seattle.
Dade Reagents Inc., Miami, Florida.
Professor J. N. P. Davies, Albany Medical College of Union University, Albany, New York.
Dr W. E. Dismukes, National Communicable Disease Center, Atlanta, Georgia.
Dr I. Douglas-Wilson, *The Lancet*, London.
Professor H. F. Dowling, University of Illinois, Chicago.
Dr H. Bruce Dull, National Communicable Disease Center, Public Health Service, Atlanta, Georgia.
Dr E. A. Dreskin, American Association of Blood Banks, Greenville, South Carolina.
Essex County Blood Bank, East Orange, New Jersey.
Dr L. A. Falk, University of Pittsburgh, Pittsburgh.
Food and Drug Administration, Department of Health, Education, and Welfare, Washington.
Mr K. W. Forbes, Travenol International Laboratories, Illinois.
Dr E. A. Friedman, State University of New York, New York.
Dr Z. S. Hantchef, International Red Cross, Geheva.
Mrs B. M. Hemphill, American Association of Blood Banks, San Francisco.
Dr I. Gladston, Department of Mental Health, Connecticut.
Garden State Blood Bank Inc., Newark, New Jersey.
Dr J. H. S. Gear, South African Institute for Medical Research, Johannesburg, South Africa.
Mr C. J. Stetler, President, Pharmaceutical Manufacturers Association, Washington.
Professor and Dr R. Stevens, Yale University, New Haven, Connecticut.
Mr F. Sugrue, United Community Funds and Councils of America, Inc., New York.
Swedish Embassy (Labour Attaché), London.
Swedish Institute for Cultural Relationships, London.
Tacoma-Pierce County Blood Bank, Inc., Tacoma, Washington.
Travenol Laboratories, Inc., Illinois.
Tri-Counties Blood Bank, Inc., Santa Barbara, California.
Dr J. T. Tripp, Division of Biologics Standards, National Institutes of Health, Bethesda, Maryland.
U.S. Department of Commerce, Bureau of International Commerce and Foreign Trade Division, Washington.

ACKNOWLEDGEMENTS

Mr Van Limburg, Provinciaal Bestuur, Maastrucht, Netherlands.

Wadley Institutes of Molecular Medicine, Dallas, Texas.

Dr E. L. Wallace, School of Business Administration, State University of New York at Buffalo, New York.

Wall Street Journal Inquiry Department, New York.

Professor Dr R. Zenker, University of Munich, Western Germany

N*

Index